This Must Be the Place

Edited by Tie Jojima and Karen Marta

Aimé Iglesias Lukin

This Must Be the Place

An Oral History of Latin American Artists in New York, 1965–1975

Americas Society / ISLAA

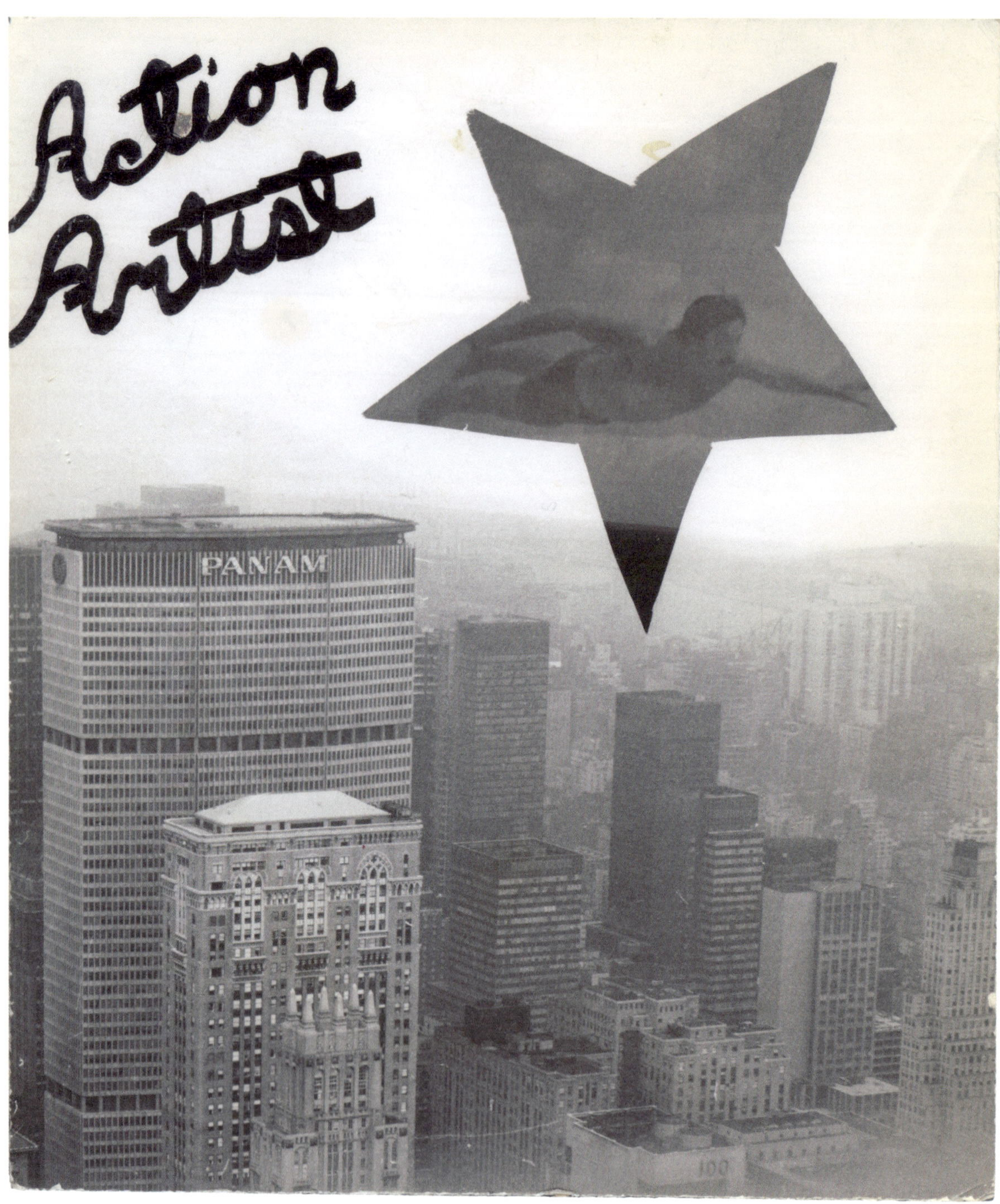

Collage with photograph of Juan Downey flying over New York by Bill Gerstein, ca. 1973. The Juan Downey Foundation, New York

Home is where I want to be
But I guess I'm already there
I come home, she lifted up her wings
I guess that this must be the place

—Talking Heads, "This Must Be the Place (Naive Melody)," 1983

Aimé Iglesias Lukin

Introduction

Published on the occasion of the exhibition *This Must Be the Place: Latin American Artists in New York, 1965–1975*, held between September 2021 and May 2022 at Americas Society, this book is dedicated to the Latin American artists who made New York City their home in the 1960s and 1970s and to their ongoing legacy, which still has many shadows to cast. In particular, this publication honors the memory of Jaime Davidovich, who was a strong supporter of this research project since day one.

Our co-publisher, the Institute for Studies on Latin American Art (ISLAA), was our editorial partner as well as a key source of documents and materials thanks to its important archive. Born out of the ten years of work for my master's degree and doctoral dissertation, *This Must Be the Place: Latin American Artists in New York, 1965–1975* substantially expands that research and, crucially, was fed by the collaborative spirit and input of numerous colleagues and the generosity of the artists themselves. The many conversations with artists, in which they recommended the works of yet other artists—often friends—correspond to the mutually supportive spirit of the artistic communities portrayed in this book.

While some of these artists have achieved recognition, with important retrospectives and monographs, many others have been overlooked by the art historical canon. To foreground their voices, we decided to make them the protagonists of their stories, allowing them to relate their experiences in their own words. As a result, the format of this book is an oral history rather than an exhibition catalogue (a catalogue was published in Americas Society's pocketbook series). Prioritizing visual documentation over artworks, we have chosen to tell, with informal intimacy, the rich personal narratives of more than forty Latin American artists, and to show the collaborative networks that made their art possible. In the pages that follow, we take a fresh and in-depth look at this influential generation of cultural workers and the communities they forged in an era of political and social upheaval.

The oral history is organized into three thematic chapters with introductory essays by Tie Jojima that provide a connective thread for the artists' own testimonies. The sources of each testimony are listed in order of page number at the end of the book. Chapter 1, "The City," investigates the impact of the physical and social atmosphere of New York City, highlighting the artists' initial impressions, the connections they established, and their desire to transform their new home through urban interventions. Chapter 2, "Community and Institutions," focuses on their disaffiliation with the city's existing art institutions, as they challenged curatorial norms, put pressure on exclusionary practices, and founded more inclusive alternatives. Chapter 3, "Politics, Identity, and the Body," explores the artists' engagement with politics and activism. In line with the many political movements of the time, including the civil rights and anti-Vietnam War movements, Latin American artists' activism stood in solidarity with resistance movements against dictatorial regimes in Latin America, and against the marginalized status of their communities in New York. This chapter also presents the artists' widespread practice of centering their own bodies in performance and video works, which became influential to the era's emerging politics of representation. We are aware that this material could have been organized in a multitude of different ways, and, although we have included as much archival material as possible based on the networks we traced in our research process, we must, at this historical remove, acknowledge the inevitability of absences and omissions.

My introductory essay offers historical context for the period, and highlights some of the most important contributions these artists and artist collectives have made to art history. Three accompanying essays present case studies on specific artists and groups, whose stories exemplify important social issues this generation of artists faced. Abigail Lapin Dardashti focuses on Abdias do Nascimento and his engagement with African American art and activism, his connections with Nuyorican artists Marcos Dimas and Jorge Soto Sánchez, and the transnational and transdisciplinary spirit of his activities in New York. Harper Montgomery's essay focuses on Cildo Meireles, emphasizing the transgressive nature of this generation's art practice, and framing Meireles's *Insertions* series as a subversive act of resistance to US imperialism and the global art market, and its role in making New York the center of the international art world. Yasmin Ramirez's essay presents the year 1969 as a turning point in art and activism, a critical moment that solidified the self-consciousness of Nuyorican communities as a group.

In mapping these relationships and their overlapping milieus, this book enacts a double recuperation: it gives visibility to the many names that have yet to enter existing narratives, and it considers the artworks of more established artists not as individual exceptions, but as part of a generational shift that was only possible through the dialogue *all* of these artists had with one another and with their US counterparts. Our hope is that this exhibition and publication are the first of many to study the networks and initiatives these artists created, and that they serve as inspiration for future research into the many interconnections between artworks, communities, and lives that have yet to be celebrated.

Aimé Iglesias Lukin

This Must Be the Place

This is a book about a love story, one between a group of artists and the city in which they lived and worked. Migrating from different parts of Latin America during the 1960s and 1970s, in search of professional opportunities or evading difficult political circumstances, they arrived in New York City with the hope of integrating into and impacting the experimental art center the city had become during those years. But, as in any love story, the romance was hardly easy, bringing up questions about the uncertainty of belonging.[1] This is reflected in the opening line of the 1983 Talking Heads song "This Must Be the Place (Naive Melody)," which inspired the title of this book: "Home is where I want to be."[2] Written and composed by David Byrne, the song's existential wager about belonging—described in the chorus, in which "This must be the place" becomes "I guess that this must be the place"—is a fitting reflection on a post-'60s and '70s New York City and an echo of how these artists' experiences were defined by alienation as well as a sense of kinship with fellow émigrés. Located not only in a temporal and ideological liminality, but also in a very specific geographical in-between created by migration, these communities of artists from Latin America and the Spanish-speaking Caribbean did not constitute a single front, but functioned as interconnected circles often isolated from one another through differences of national origin, race, and class.[3]

Caribbean and Nuyorican artists created artistic associations to help their diasporic communities—particularly in East Harlem, Lower East Side, and the Bronx, which, while well established, were subject to social segregation.[4] The recent émigrés from South America tended to associate in solidarity initiatives denouncing the United States–supported dictatorships in the region.[5] While most came to the city in search of opportunities, many became exiles while in the United States, unable to return to their home countries due to the political upheaval. Settling in the city permanently or for just a few years, their aesthetic and cultural contributions

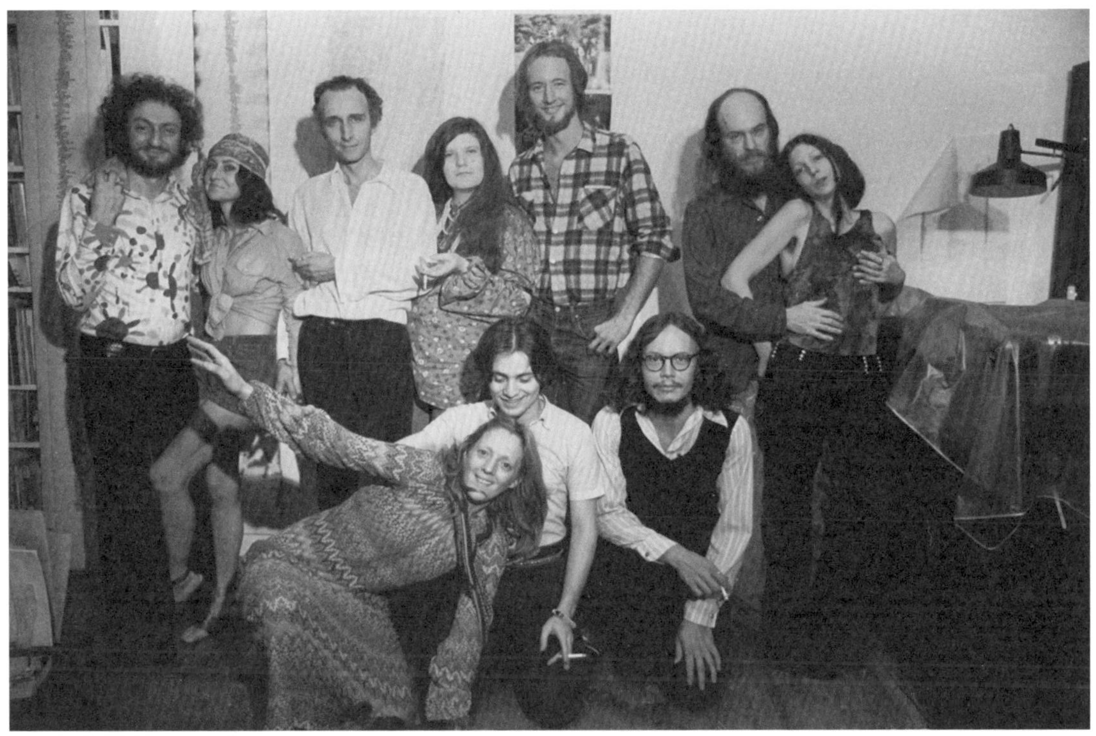

diversified postwar American art and helped shape the city into a unique cultural contact zone in a politically tumultuous era. Contributing styles and ideas, they enriched the local art scenes in which they interacted while also creating their own circles—and, in the process, redefining the idea of Latin American identity.

The testimonies compiled in this book describe these artists' impressions of the city upon their arrival, the new artistic possibilities they encountered, the connections they were able to establish (and the exclusion they endured from existing art institutions), and the communities they formed in an effort to gain visibility and collectively reimagine their sense of identity and place. In the midst of the Cold War, a time when the Iron Curtain cast long shadows and created substantial divisions between communities across the world, the political and cultural identities of these artists as Latin Americans became a framework for understanding their place in the capital of the Western world.

Many came from metropolitan contexts and had worked for decades within their own experimental avant-gardes, arriving with radical ideas. In New York, they participated in the expansion of media and the integration of art and life typical of the era while distinguishing themselves from their North American counterparts through their explicit treatment of issues of identity, migration, and a sociopolitical critique of the relationship between the United States and their home countries. In our contemporary world, in which migration is a key political discussion, to demonstrate the contributing role of immigrants to an

Fig. 1 Leandro Katz, Zulema "Beba" Damianovich, Claudio Badal, Gwen Harris and friend, David Lee and friend, Marta Minujín, Marcial Berro, and Ted Castle, New York, 1972 (self-shot). Leandro Katz Archive

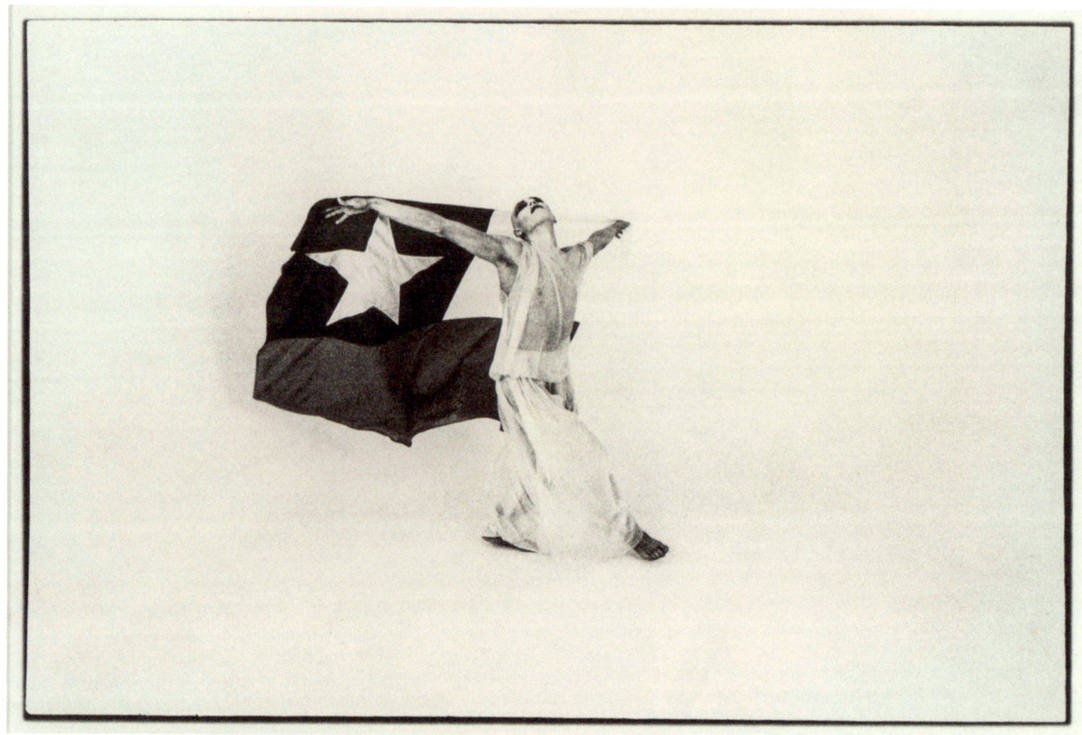

international art center becomes not only a task of historical recuperation, but also a political strategy that challenges the idea that identity is ever fixed.

As national, regional, political, social, and artistic identities were being examined collectively at their intersections, many migrant artists sought to redefine how they positioned their identities, both at home and in the United States. A series of solidarity initiatives denouncing the political violence and dictatorships springing up all over the Southern continent precipitated a new level of awareness about being Latin American. These artists had to contend with their relationship with the United States, the nation that was in part responsible, via its foreign policy decisions, for many of the atrocities committed in Latin and Central America during the second half of the twentieth century.[6] As Argentine artist Luis Felipe Noé wrote in 1966 while living in New York under the patronage of a Guggenheim Fellowship:

> The question is not to be or not in the country of origin, but not to be uprooted, acting with cultural independence, trying to favor our creative mechanism. Creating roots does not mean for Latin Americans to remain in their countries, but much more: to begin to elaborate, as far as possible, within the continent that is yours, the same cultural adventure.[7]

The very notion of Latin America as a single geographic or political category is unstable and often deemed problematic, since the use of the term overlooks the

Fig. 2 Francisco Copello, *El mimo y la bandera* (The mime and the flag), 1975. Juan Yarur Torres Collection, Fundación AMA diverse languages, ethnicities, and national experiences of those it describes.[8] This categorization was useful for these émigrés, less as a definition but more as an identification that these artists claimed in much of their work and in collective statements. Race enforced another layer of exclusion for some of these artists.[9] Freddy Rodríguez's embrace of the sixteenth-century figure of the *cimarrón*—a runaway African slave living in a maroon community—exemplified the many different strategies these artists used to carve out a space for themselves in a system that excluded them because of racism. As Rodríguez said:

> In an alter ego, there is an identification with this character because he chases freedom constantly. I've used painting to search for that freedom. . . . [T]he *cimarrón* breaks with everything that is conventional in painting and at the same time opens the door to any type of pictorial expression.[10]

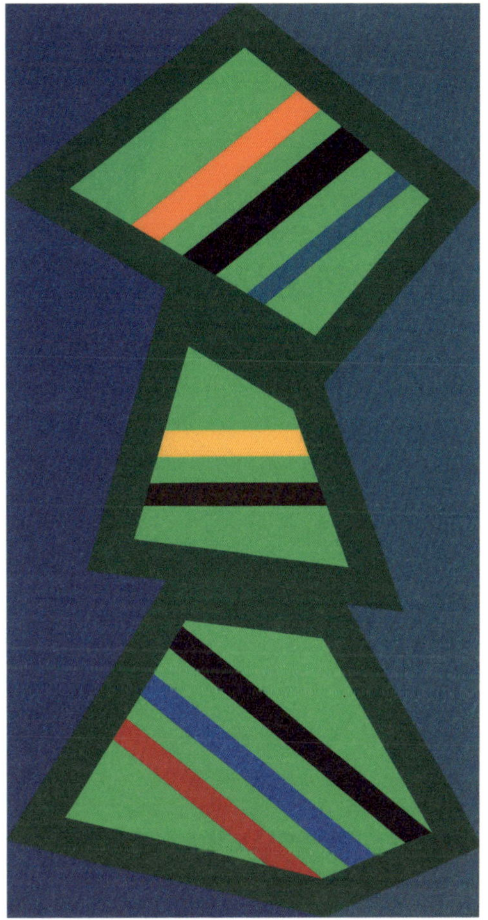

In 1970, the United States census included the term "Hispanic" as an identifier to collect data, arbitrarily organizing people around the Spanish language. For Portuguese-speaking Brazilian artists, this designation felt derivative of the colonial divisions imposed early on in the history of the conquest of the Americas by the Europeans, as when the 1494 Treaty of Tordesillas linguistically and culturally separated Brazil from the rest of the continent.[11] Challenging that divide in search of regional unity, artists like Cildo Meireles proposed belonging to a region called the Southern Cross, while Rubens Gerchman proposed using *portuñol* or *espanholês* as a language in order to rethink the idea of Latin America in New York.[12] For these artists, the city acted as a neutral ground where national origin was less operative, in part through the imposition of reductive labels but also through their efforts for a regional coalition. Many found that "it was not until I came to New York that I realized I was Latin American."[13] Their chosen status as "Latin Americans" allowed these artists to engage in political solidarity, reclaiming the reductive categorization enforced upon them by American society.

This great influx of artists from Latin America in the '60s and '70s was propelled by US international diplomacy. During the

Fig. 3 Freddy Rodríguez, *Y me quedé sin nombre* (And I was left without a name), 1974. Whitney Museum of American Art, New York; purchase, with funds from the Painting and Sculpture Committee 2021.20

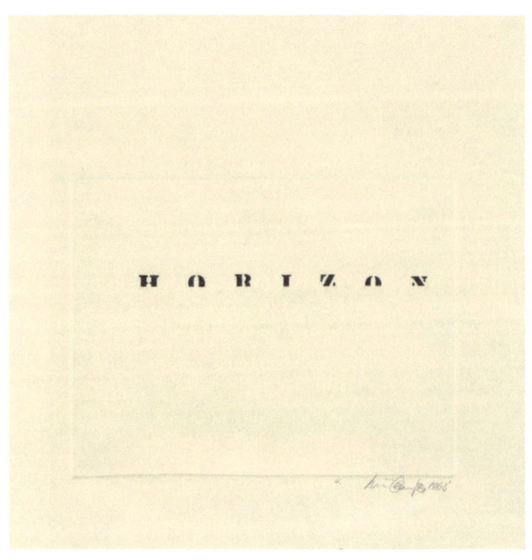

first half of the twentieth century, when Paris was considered by many to be the cultural epicenter of modern art, artists from all over the Americas traveled to Europe to study, a rite of passage that exposed them to the newest trends, which they brought back to their home countries and into the local art scenes.[14] But with the world powers' reordering after War World II and through a series of governmental and private sector efforts to bring modern art to the United States, by the 1960s New York had become a new international center for art experimentation.[15] During this period, the United States also became more invested in its relations with Latin America, following the principles of the Good Neighbor Policy and guided by international developmentalist policies taking strength in the hemisphere. US cultural diplomacy in Latin America was channeled through two key institutions: the Pan-American Union located in Washington, DC, the capital of foreign policy; and the Center for Inter-American Relations (CIAR, today's Americas Society) in New York, the capital of finance. These institutions took a particular interest in visual art, creating the first organizations dedicated to Latin American art in the United States.[16] Since its founding in 1965, CIAR supported the travel of curators and artists to Latin America; financed traveling exhibitions of American art to cities like Caracas, São Paulo, Mexico City, and Buenos Aires; and at the same time organized touring exhibitions of Latin American art in the United States.

Key institutions like the Museum of Modern Art and the Guggenheim Museum took a new interest in Latin American art and began hosting exhibitions dedicated to it. *The Emergent Decade*, for example, curated by Thomas M. Messer in 1967, presented new trends in abstraction on the continent.[17] Through its fellowship program, the Guggenheim Foundation began to support one-year stays in New York for dozens of Latin American artists, including Luis Camnitzer, Hélio Oiticica, Marta Minujín, Leandro Katz, César Paternosto, and Alejandro Puente. However, some of these artists were aware of the risks of internationalism.

As Hélio Oiticica wrote in the catalogue for *Information*, the iconic exhibition of global Conceptual art, "i am not here representing Brazil; or representing anythingelse : the ideas of representing-representation-etc. are over," warning the reader—and the curator—of any possible tokenism in his inclusion in the exhibition (fig. 5).[18] This would be the first—and only—presentation of his work in an institution. Oiticica always had a complicated relationship with *Barnbilônia*, as he dubbed Manhattan (fig. 6).[19] In the beginning, he dreamed of using New York as a platform to export

Fig. 4 Luis Camnitzer, *Horizon*, 1968. Inter-American Fund, The Museum of Modern Art, New York

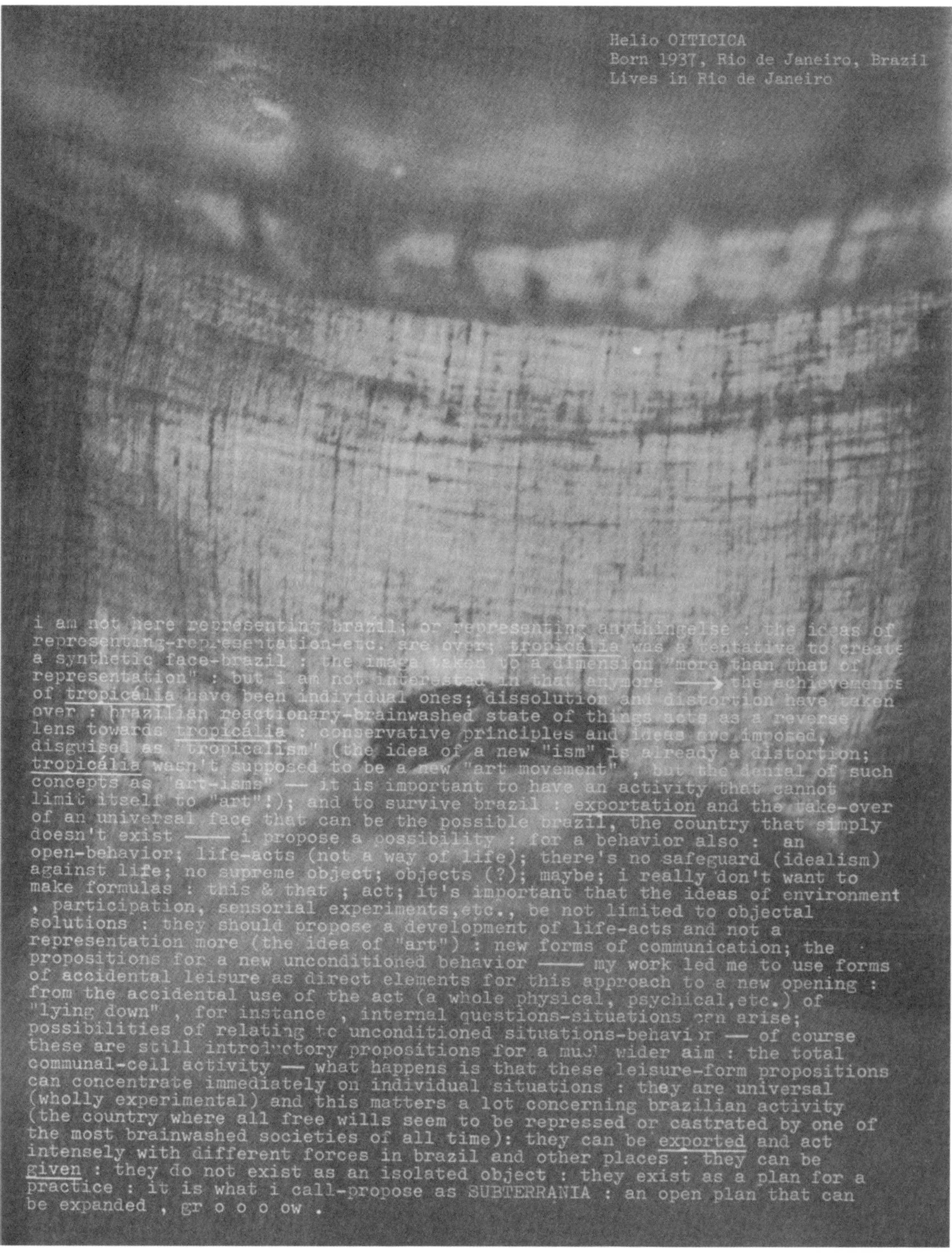

Helio OITICICA
Born 1937, Rio de Janeiro, Brazil
Lives in Rio de Janeiro

i am not here representing brazil; or representing anythingelse : the ideas of representing-representation-etc. are over; <u>tropicália</u> was a tentative to create a synthetic face-brazil : the image taken to a dimension "more than that of representation" : but i am not interested in that anymore ⟶ the achievements of <u>tropicália</u> have been individual ones; dissolution and distortion have taken over : brazilian reactionary-brainwashed state of things acts as a reverse lens towards <u>tropicália</u> : conservative principles and ideas are imposed, disguised as "tropicalism" (the idea of a new "ism" is already a distortion; <u>tropicália</u> wasn't supposed to be a new "art movement" , but the denial of such concepts as "art-isms" — it is important to have an activity that cannot limit itself to "art"!); and to survive brazil : <u>exportation</u> and the take-over of an universal face that can be the possible brazil, the country that simply doesn't exist —— i propose a possibility : for a behavior also : an open-behavior; life-acts (not a way of life); there's no safeguard (idealism) against life; no supreme object; objects (?); maybe; i really don't want to make formulas : this & that ; act; it's important that the ideas of environment , participation, sensorial experiments,etc., be not limited to objectal solutions : they should propose a development of life-acts and not a representation more (the idea of "art") : new forms of communication; the propositions for a new unconditioned behavior —— my work led me to use forms of accidental leisure as direct elements for this approach to a new opening : from the accidental use of the act (a whole physical, psychical,etc.) of "lying down" , for instance , internal questions-situations can arise; possibilities of relating to unconditioned situations-behavior — of course these are still introductory propositions for a much wider aim : the total communal-cell activity — what happens is that these leisure-form propositions can concentrate immediately on individual situations : they are universal (wholly experimental) and this matters a lot concerning brazilian activity (the country where all free wills seem to be repressed or castrated by one of the most brainwashed societies of all time): they can be <u>exported</u> and act intensely with different forces in brazil and other places : they can be <u>given</u> : they do not exist as an isolated object : they exist as a plan for a practice : it is what i call-propose as SUBTERRANIA : an open plan that can be expanded , gr o o o ow .

Fig. 5 Hélio Oiticica, artist statement, *Information*, ed. Kynaston L. McShine (New York: Museum of Modern Art, 1970), 103

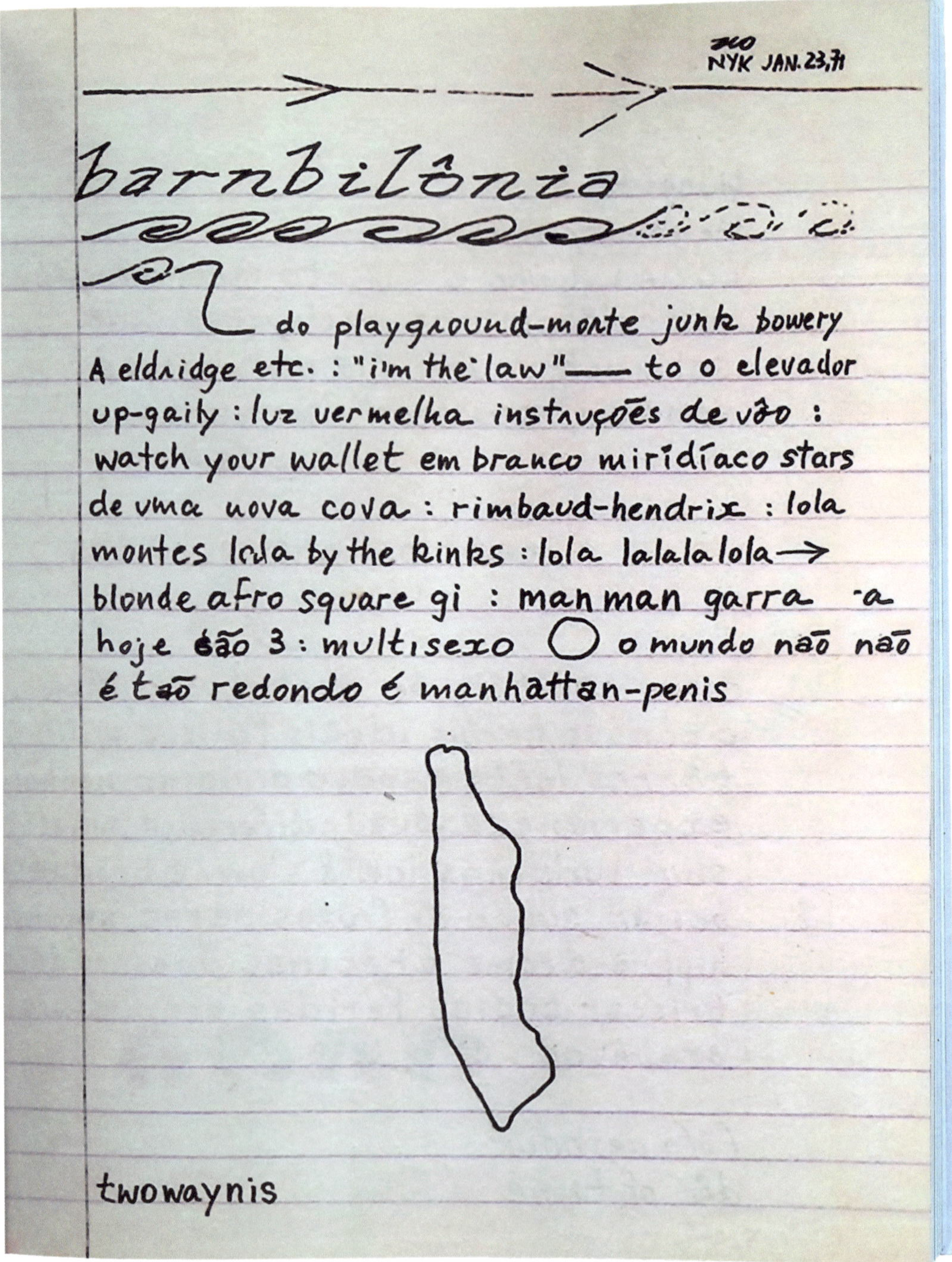

NYK JAN. 23, 71

barnbilônia

do playground-monte junk bowery
A eldridge etc. : "i'm the law" —— to o elevador
up-gaily : luz vermelha instruções de vôo :
watch your wallet em branco miridíaco stars
de uma nova cova : rimbaud-hendrix : lola
montes lola by the kinks : lola lalalalola →
blonde afro square gi : manman garra -a
hoje são 3 : multisexo ◯ o mundo não não
é tão redondo é manhattan-penis

twowaynis

Fig. 6 Hélio Oiticica, *Barnbilônia*, 1971. AHO/PHO, 1738/70, p.38, Projeto Hélio Oiticica elements of his Brazilian culture globally, but he quickly grew disenchanted with the city's mainstream art scene, seeking refuge in underground countercultures.

Immigrant artists who came to New York under the auspices of organizations like CIAR chose to both embrace and resist their political agendas, complicating the narratives these institutions advanced. Many artists felt conflicted about representing Latin America in a country that had interfered in conflicts in the region, especially knowing that they were being tokenized as Latin American artists. Liliana Porter expressed ambivalence toward showing her work at MoMA's in 1973:

> One felt guilty not just for being so far away but also for being in a territory that clearly was associated with the dictatorships. Every act became symbolic. So, on one hand, I felt happy to receive an invitation from MoMA, and on the other hand I questioned the institution, given that many of their board members were implicated in the United States' policies in Latin America. For that reason, when I finally decided to exhibit there, I did it with an announcement that recognized the conflict. At the same time, in New York there was a struggle to integrate minorities and recognize their equal rights, and this had a way of forcing institutions to offer a quota for minorities in order to demonstrate their political correctness. . . . The purpose of my declaration was to make that benefit a little more complicated.[20]

CIAR's inaugural 1967 exhibition, *Artists of the Western Hemisphere: Precursors of Modernism, 1860–1930*, curated by Stanton L. Catlin, prompted a group of artists to write in a letter to the editor of the *New York Times* that it was "a show that exhibits an aspect of colonial culture," insinuating that Latin American art was still dependent on European influence.[21] This was the first in a series of protests against CIAR's representation of the region.[22] Protests like these catalyzed the creation of new spaces and associations such as El Museo Latinoamericano, MICLA, *Cha/Cha/Cha*, the New York Graphic Workshop, Taller Boricua, and El Museo del Barrio, where artists could propose new, less folkloristic representations of Latin American art. Bolstered by the creation of these new institutions, these artists played a key role in the late-sixties avant-gardes, contesting the formalist legacy of Abstract Expressionism, catalyzing a renegotiation of what Latin American art was, and challenging the traditionalist and colonialist views dominant in US institutions at the time.

Studying these artists' work through the lens of migration and political solidarity demonstrates how their work advanced issues of identity politics, affect, and community, something that would not be popularized in critical theory until the eighties with multiculturalism. This book also challenges the common reading of these artists as conceptualists, a term that, while useful, is incomplete or too broad in itself.[23] Latin American Conceptualism has been traditionally historicized as distinct from the formalist approach in the North due to its political content, unavoidable in the context in which these artists worked.[24] More recently, studies have challenged this canon, showing the *political* character of much US Conceptual art, but also expanding what political can mean through other types of strategies, such as affect.[25] These artists, from their unique positioning inside and outside

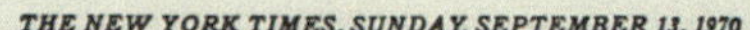

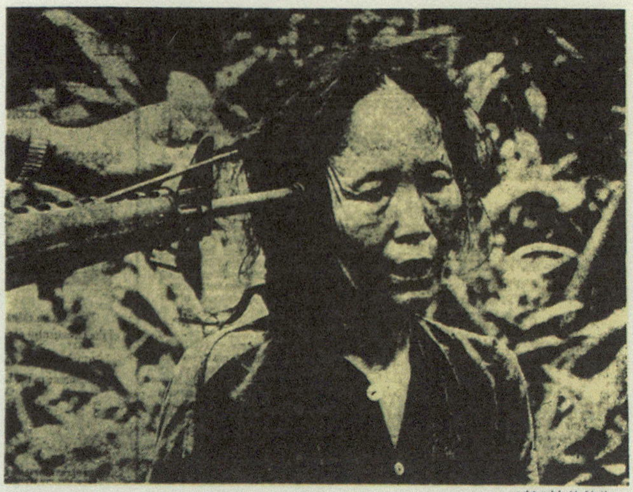

This woman is
northvietnamese
southafrican,
puertorrican,
colombian,
black,
argentinian,
my mother,
my sister,
you, I.

Fig. 7 Liliana Porter, *Untitled (The New York Times, Sunday, September 13, 1970)*, 1970.
Courtesy of the artist and Krakow Witkin Gallery, Boston

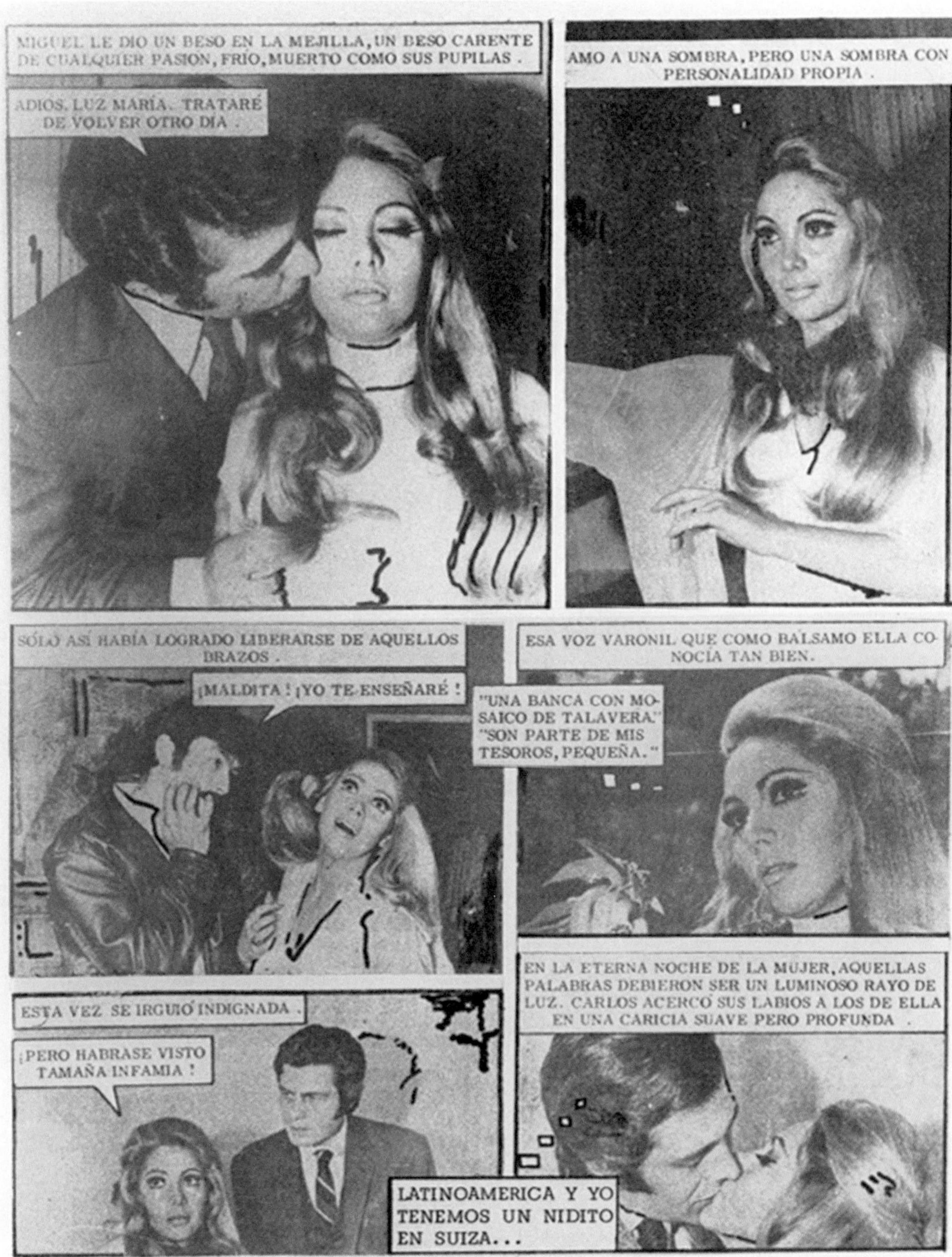

Fig. 8 Leandro Katz, cover illustration for *Latinoamérica y yo tenemos un nidito en Suiza* (Latin America and I have a little nest in Switzerland) (New York: TVRT Press, 1970). Leandro Katz Archive

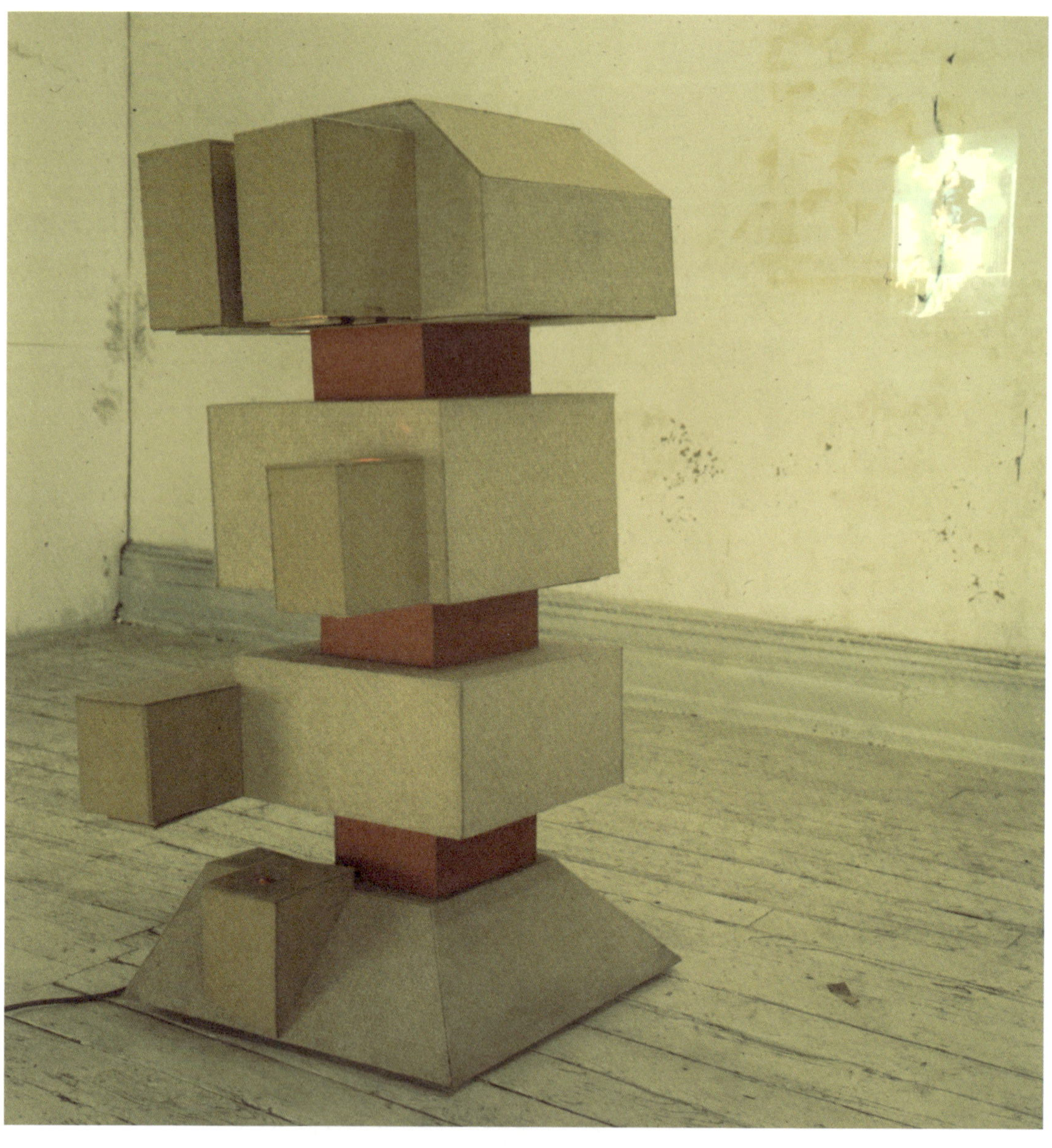

Fig. 9 Juan Downey, *Nostalgic Item*, 1967. Installation view, Murray Hill Studio, Washington, DC. The Juan Downey Foundation, New York

advanced complex understandings of place and identity, not only denounced the political realities in their home countries but also read and critiqued American culture through the eyes that only an outsider can have. Juan Downey and Jaime Davidovich, for example, used mixed media that integrated cybernetics, video, and TV–technologies of the future–to investigate the past.[26] They produced works such as *Nostalgic Item* (1967; fig. 9) and *La patria vacía* (1975; fig. 10) that discussed nostalgia and attested to the unique position they were in, situated at a greater geographical distance, to interpret the volatile political realities of their home countries, while also offering an affect-infused alternative for the revision of experimental media and technological discourse that was taking hold in the neo-avant-garde movements of New York at the time.

This book foregrounds the voices of these Latin American artists with the intention of inspiring many more studies that highlight the contributions of migrant artists to the arts of America–both the country and the continent. In undertaking the work of unmaking and remaking their collective identities, these artists tell the history of cultural pluralism and its contradictions. Declaring New York, even if only temporally, as "the place," these artists' testimonies and artworks serve as documents of place-making, a form of geographical and social localization that revolutionized the New York art world and created a legacy for immigrant artists in the generations to come.

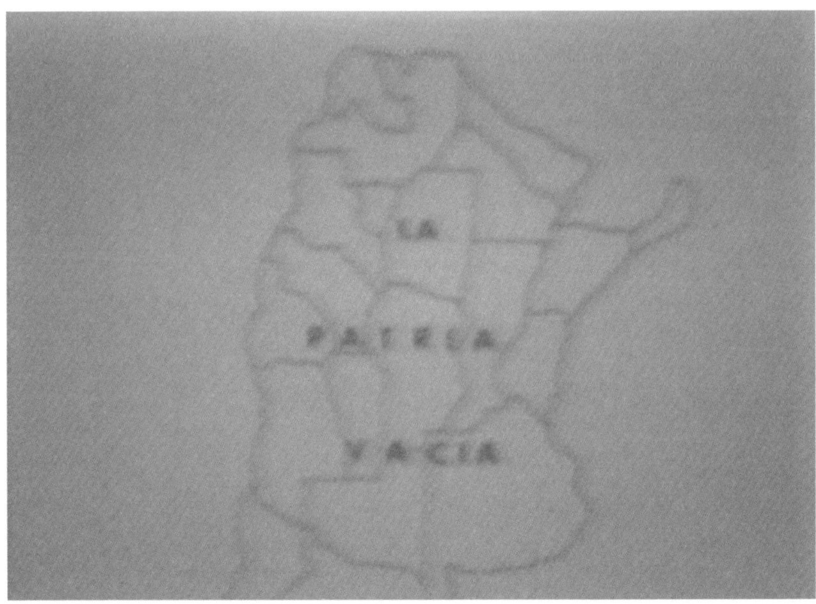

Fig. 10 Jaime Davidovich, still from *La patria vacía* (The empty homeland), 1975. Jaime Davidovich Foundation

NOTES

[1] This essay, the research for this book, and the 2021–22 exhibition at Americas Society are partially based on my doctoral dissertation, "This Must Be the Place (Latin American Artists in New York, 1965-1975)," (PhD diss., Rutgers University, 2021).

[2] "This Must Be the Place (Naive Melody)," track 9 on Talking Heads, *Speaking in Tongues*, Sire 23883, 1983, 33⅓ rpm.

[3] As described by Homi K. Bhabha, nationhood and community are negotiated in "interspaces" in late modernity. Homi K. Bhabha, *The Location of Culture* (New York: Routledge, 1994), 5.

[4] See Yasmin Ramirez's essay in this volume, 395–403. Important studies of these diasporic communities are: E. Carmen Ramos, *Our America: The Latino Presence in American Art* (Washington, DC: Smithsonian American Art Museum; London: D. Giles Limited, 2014); Taina B. Caragol Barreto, "Boom and Dust: The Rise of Latin American and Latino Art in New York Exhibition Spaces and the Auction House Market, 1970s–1980s" (PhD diss., City University of New York, 2013); and Johanna Fernández and Yasmin Ramirez, eds., *¡Presente! The Young Lords in New York* (New York: Bronx Museum of the Arts, 2015).

[5] The interconnections between these groups need further study. Marcos Dimas has stated Taller Boricua's connection with the New York Graphic Workshop, in an interview with the author, September 15, 2021. Nitza Tufiño remembered many solidarity initiatives of Taller Boricua in regard to the Chilean coup d'état, including a protest against the assassination of former ambassador Orlando Letelier, in an interview with the author, September 23, 2021; see chapter 3, 260–61. The founding of Cayman Gallery in SoHo in 1973 provided a much-needed space that showcased and connected both communities; see chapter 2, 170–71.

[6] See examples of these solidarity initiatives to denounce the political situation in South America in chapter 3, 251-67.

[7] Luis Felipe Noé, "La responsabilidad del artista que se va de América Latina y la del que se queda," *Mirador : una publicación de la Fundación Interamericana para las Artes* 1, no. 7 (July 1966): 2, 4 (my translation).

[8] As detailed by Walter Mignolo, "Latin America" is a complex and relatively new category, first used in 1836 by French liberal economist and intellectual Michel Chevalier, who traveled to Central America and coined the term to associate Mexico, Central and South America with Latin Europe. Mignolo argues, "The idea of 'Latin' America that came into view in the second half of the nineteenth century depended in varying degrees on an idea of 'Latinidad'—'Latinity,' 'Latinitée'—in use in France at the time. 'Latinidad' was precisely the ideology under which the identity of the ex-Spanish and ex-Portuguese colonies was located . . . in the new global, modern/colonial world order." The creole-Mestizo elites later adopted the term to differentiate from Spanish and Portuguese culture. See Walter Mignolo, *The Idea of Latin America* (Oxford: Blackwell, 2005), 58.

[9] See Abigail Lapin Dardashti's essay in this volume, about Brazilian Black artist Abdias do Nascimento's art and activism and his engagement with other artists in New York, 405–9.

[10] Freddy Rodríguez, interviewed in Manuel Núñez, "Las ideas de Freddy Rodríguez," *Hoy*, Isla Abierta section, April 30, 1988, 4.

[11] The Treaty of Tordesillas, signed on June 7, 1494, was the agreement between the Portuguese and the Castilian monarchies that divided the areas of navigation and conquest in the Atlantic Ocean and the lands (and peoples) in America by establishing an imperial border on the meridian located 370 leagues west of the Cape Verde Islands.

[12] "I am here in this exhibition, to defend neither a career nor any nationality." Instead, Meireles stated he would rather "speak about a region which does not appear on official maps, a region called the Southern Cross." See Kynaston L. McShine, ed., *Information* (New York: Museum of Modern Art, 1970), 85. See also this volume, 169. "My proposal attempts to develop a consciousness that opposes that of the White European-North-American Men that we are heirs by extension. I would propose a thinking that was Brazilian/Latin-American, something like portuñol or espanhôles in an artistic sense, because paradoxically I have never experienced Brazil and Latin America as much as now, far away from there, from my culture, from my friends." Rubens Gerchman, "Uma arte Brasileiro/Latino-Americana," in Ferreira Gullar, ed., *Arte Brasileira hoje: situação e perspectivas* (Rio de Janeiro: Paz e terra, 1973), 163. Also cited in Dária Jaremtchuk, "Experiências em Nova Iorque na década de 1970," *ARS* (São Paulo) 6, no. 12 (2008): 108.

[13] César Paternosto, interview with the author, November 1, 2013. Liliana Porter also stated, "I was not so conscious of being Latin American . . . You had an accent and you were aware that you were from another place. But I think that the stronger differentiation appeared later with the category 'Hispanic.'" Andrea Giunta, "A Conversation with Liliana Porter and Luis Camnitzer," in *The New York Graphic Workshop, 1964–1970*, ed. Gabriel Pérez-Barreiro (Austin: Blanton Museum of Art, the University of Texas at Austin, 2009), 45. See also chapter 3, 329–45.

[14] See Harper Montgomery, *The Mobility of Modernism: Art and Criticism in 1920s Latin America* (Austin: University of Texas Press, 2017); Tatiana Flores, "Beyond Centre-Periphery: Modernism in Latin American Art," in *The Modernist World*, ed. Allana Lindgren and Stephen Ross (London: Routledge, 2017); and Michele Greet, *Transatlantic Encounters: Latin American Artists in Paris Between the Wars* (New Haven, CT: Yale University Press, 2018).

[15] See Serge Guilbaut, *How New York Stole the Idea of Modern Art: Abstract Expressionism, Freedom, and the Cold War* (Chicago: University of Chicago Press, 1995); and Francis Frascina, ed., *Pollock and After: The Critical Debate*, 2nd ed. (London: Routledge, 2000).

[16] The Pan American Union (PAU) was established in 1890 as part of the International Union of American Republics, precursor to the Organization of American States (OAS), which was founded in 1948. The first OAS secretary-general, the Colombian politician Alberto Lleras Camargo, was a strong supporter of cultural programs at PAU as a means for facilitating soft diplomacy. Art exhibitions, concerts, and publications were promoted and organized by José Gómez Sicre, director of the visual arts section of the PAU. This understanding of cultural exchange derived from the Good Neighbor Policy (ca. 1933–45), by which the United States sought to prevent influence from the Axis countries and guarantee fluid trade exchange within the hemisphere. See Claire Fox, *Making Art Panamerican: Cultural Policy and the Cold War* (Minneapolis: University of Minnesota Press, 2013); Michael Gordon Wellen, "Pan-American Dreams: Art, Politics, and Museum-Making at the OAS, 1948–1976" (PhD diss., University of Texas at Austin, 2012). For a history of the CIAR, see John A. Farmer and Ilona Katzew, eds., *A Hemispheric Venture: Thirty-Five Years of Culture at the Americas Society, 1965–2000* (New York: Americas Society, 2000); and José Luis Falconi and Gabriela Rangel, eds., *A Principality of Its Own: 40 Years of Visual Arts at the Americas Society* (New York: Americas Society, 2006).

[17] Thomas M. Messer, *The Emergent Decade: Latin American Painters and Painting in the 1960's* (New York: Solomon R.

Guggenheim Museum, 1967). For a discussion of this and related exhibitions, see Delia Solomons, "Staging the Global: Latin American Art in the Guggenheim and Carnegie Internationals of the 1960s," *Journal of Curatorial Studies* 3, nos. 2–3 (June 2014): 290–319.

[18] Hélio Oiticica, artist statement, in Kynaston L. McShine, ed., *Information* (New York: Museum of Modern Art, 1970), 103. (The idiosyncratic punctuation and spacing Oiticia favored in his texts are retained ithroughout this book.) Curated by Kynaston McShine at The Museum of Modern Art, *Information* opened to the public on July 2, 1970, with the work of a hundred and fifty artists from fifteen countries presenting the "strongest 'style' of international movement of the last three years," and who came "from a culture that has been considerably altered by communications systems such as television and film, and by increased mobility." Nineteen of these artists came from Latin America, including Rafael Ferrer, Cildo Meireles, Marta Minujín (in the catalogue only), the New York Graphic Workshop, Hélio Oiticica, and Alejandro Puente. In addition to the exhibition catalogue, see Anna Katherine Brodbeck, "'A Third Way': Information (1970) and the International Exhibition of Contemporary Art from Latin America," in *Transnational Latin American Art from 1950 to the Present Day* (1st International Research Forum for Graduate Students and Emerging Scholars, The University of Texas at Austin, November 6–8, 2009).

[19] Frederico Oliveira Coelho and César Oiticica Filho, eds., *Hélio Oiticica: conglomerado newyorkaises* (Rio de Janeiro: Azougue Editorial, 2013), 83.

[20] Liliana Porter, Inés Katzenstein, and Gregory Volk, *Liliana Porter: in conversation with/en conversación con Inés Katzenstein* (New York: Fundación Cisneros/Colección Patricia Phelps de Cisneros, 2013), 53–54.

[21] Rodolfo Abularach et al., letter to the editor, *New York Times*, October 8, 1967, 25. (Signed by Rodolfo Abularach, Amado Aldaraca, Pedro Briceno, Luis Molinari Flores, Enrique Castro-Cid, Luis Canmitzer [*sic*], Liliana Porter, Julio Alpuy, Pablo Agudelo, Marta Menujin [*sic*], Gabriel Morera, Honorio Morales, Hilario Madrazo, Luis Lopez Losa, Juan Gomez Quiroz, Luis Felipe Noé, and Omar Rayo.)

[22] See chapter 2, pp. 300–303. The best account of these events is given by Luis Camnitzer in "The Museo Latinoamericano and MICLA," in *A Principality of Its Own*, ed. Falconi and Rangel, 216–29. I have researched this topic for my master's and as part of my doctoral dissertation, and my ideas were published in a series of texts, the most recent of which is "A Publication of One's Own: Identity and Community among Migrant Latin American Artists in New York c. 1970," in *Art and Migration: Revisioning the Borders of Community*, ed. Bénédicte Miyamoto and Marie Ruiz (Manchester: Manchester University Press, 2021), 186–210.

[23] Benjamin H. D. Buchloh's Conceptualism could be considered a parachute category: "From its very beginning, the historic phase in which Conceptual Art was developed comprises such a complex range of mutually opposed approaches that any attempt at a retrospective survey . . . resist[s] a construction of its history in terms of a stylistic homogenization." Benjamin H. D. Buchloh, "From the Aesthetic of Administration to Institutional Critique (Some Aspects of Conceptual Art, 1962–1969)," in *L'art conceptuel, une perspective*, ed. Claude Gintz (Paris: Musée d'Art Moderne de la Ville de Paris, 1989), 41.

[24] The canonization of Latin American Conceptual art was established by Mari Carmen Ramírez in her essay for MoMA's 1993 survey of Latin American Art. See Mari Carmen Ramírez, "Blueprint Circuits: Conceptual Art and Politics in Latin America," in *Latin American Artists of the Twentieth Century*, ed. Waldo Rasmussen (New York: Museum of Modern Art, 1993), 156–67. Ramírez's counterpart in the nascent project to promote Latin American Conceptual art was Luis Camnitzer, particularly through his curatorial work for *Global Conceptualism: Points of Origin, 1950s–1980s* (New York: Queens Museum of Art, 1999) but also in his book *Conceptualism in Latin American Art: Didactics of Liberation* (Austin: University of Texas Press, 2007). See also Mari Carmen Ramírez and Héctor Olea, *Inverted Utopias: Avant-Garde Art in Latin America* (New Haven, CT: Yale University Press, 2004).

[25] See Julia Bryan-Wilson, *Art Workers: Radical Practice in the Vietnam War Era* (Berkeley: University of California Press, 2010); and Eve Meltzer, *Systems We Have Loved: Conceptual Art, Affect, and the Antihumanist Turn* (Chicago: University of Chicago Press, 2013).

[26] Downey and Davidovich collaborated with Gordon Matta-Clark on projects such as *Fresh Air* (1972) and *Reality Properties: Fake Estates (Queens Project)* (1975). Downey was close to Nam June Paik and, like him, used television and media as key tools to interrogate American culture, in projects such as *The Live Show!* (1979–84).

1. The City

NEW YORK is already on itself a spectacle-effect with no space for experimental activities.

—Hélio Oiticica

Brazilian artist Hélio Oiticica wrote the above to his brother in 1973, reflecting both on the perceived grandiosity and sense of awe the city instills in its visitors, and on the constraints he encountered while navigating art institutions.

In the early 1970s, New York City reached a low-point in the perceived degradation of its streets, parks, subway system, and public institutions. At this point, a contentious process of urban renovation began to slowly transform the city into the global capital of finance, culture, and tourism it is today.[1] The civil rights movement, anti-war protests, and other forms of activism (including arts activism, see chapter 3) sought to reshape the social and political dimensions of the city. Reflecting on the complex realities of New York's urban and social landscape during that period, Latin American artists engaged in Conceptual practices to depict their lived experiences, intervene in the public sphere, and imagine a new city for themselves.

This chapter looks at the city itself, including its built environment, people, and media landscape, as a structuring framework for artistic practices, defining possibilities and constraints for the creation of art. Situating the heterogeneous practices of the artists covered in this chapter in relation to the city helps us to understand their work in regard to the artists' distinct positionalities as migrants. Not only were they moved by a sense of amazement by the city, they were also responding to its constant process of transformation. In collecting the documents, photographs, and testimonies presented here, our focus on the city of New York allowed us to shift one of the obvious questions guiding this project—"What did Latin American artists do in New York?"—to, "What did New York do to these artists?"

Working outside major art institutions and with little to no possibility of selling works on the art market, most of these artists survived with limited financial resources. Many came to New York on fellowships, while others had to work multiple jobs to make ends meet.[2] Most of these artists ended up renting lofts in Lower Manhattan, an area perceived as unsafe and steeped in poverty and violence. The history of artists living in lofts is widely documented and integral to narratives of American art in the 1960s and 1970s.[3] Entire buildings with loft apartments were inhabited by artists from all over the world who created works and organized exhibitions and performances in spacious storefronts. While artists living in these precarious situations shared an attitude of experimentation and adventure—they had nowhere to go but forward—the reality of loft living was difficult. Many apartments did not have proper infrastructure, and artists often did not sign formal leases with landlords. Some of the testimonies collected in this chapter demonstrate the hardship of loft living (moving away from the romanticization of artistic resilience against all sorts of odds), while others present the loft as a space for parties, dance and performance, community, and creative exchange.

The structural issues underpinning the precarity of housing in New York were also reflected in the transit system. The New York subway was in a deplorable state as a result of fiscal crisis and mismanagement since the early 1960s.[4] Widely documented in photographs and testimonies from the 1970s, the subway was a space synonymous with violence, graffiti, and closures due to lack of maintenance. Embracing the double meaning of "underground" as the physical level underneath the surface and as a metaphor for people existing and working outside of mainstream spaces, Latin American artists took on the subway as an alternative space for art-making. Anna Bella Geiger, for instance, created a series of works in the New York subway around the concept of a "limit situation," a term that designates the threshold between one state and another, reflecting on both the threat of violence in the subway and the military violence in her home country of Brazil. Hélio Oiticica also went to the subway for his performances with the *Parangolé* cape, in which he asked people on the train to wear the cape and perform for the camera.[5]

Engaging with the social landscape of the city, which underwent radical transformations on many fronts, artists created works with the goal of transforming the public sphere—here understood to encompass not only physical space but also the media landscape.[6] The group CHARAS, for instance, built geodesic domes in vacant lots on the Lower East Side to activate those spaces and challenge the process of real estate speculation and gentrification in the area. Other artists became involved in the creation of interventions that literally changed street infrastructure, such as street signs and telephone booths (Eduardo Costa and Marta Minujín, respectively).

Many artists from Latin America, especially Argentina and Brazil, had been experimenting with television and video back in their home countries.[7] In New York, they created video art to highlight social issues and fostered networks based on video production, an indication of their desire to become part of the city's public sphere.

NOTES

[1] This process was largely pushed by government, corporations, banks, and real estate developers, and resulted in the displacement of communities as well as an oppositional activism. For more on this process, see Samuel Zipp, *Manhattan Projects: The Rise and Fall of Urban Renewal in Cold War New York* (New York: Oxford University Press, 2010).

[2] Among the artists who received Guggenheim Fellowships are Luis Camnitzer, Antonio Dias, Rubens Gerchman, Leandro Katz, Marta Minujín, Hélio Oiticica, and Regina Vater.

[3] See Melissa Rachleff, *Inventing Downtown: Artist-Run Galleries in New York City, 1952–1965* (New York: Grey Art Gallery, 2017).

[4] For more on the impact of the subway on the cultural imaginary, see Sunny Stalter-Pace, *Underground Movements: Modern Culture on the New York City Subway* (Amherst: University of Massachusetts Press, 2013).

[5] For more on Oiticica's concept of *subterrânea*, see his submission for the exhibition catalogue of *Information*, fig. 5, 15.

[6] For more on the late 1960s as a pivotal moment for the city, see Yasmin Ramirez's essay in this volume, 395–403.

[7] Early examples include Flávio de Carvalho's *Experiência n. 3* (1956), Marta Minujín's *Simultaneity in Simultaneity* (1066), and Hélio Oiticica's *Tropicália* (1967).

For artists who moved from Latin American countries to New York City, initial impressions were revealing. Sometimes translating their lived experiences of the metropolis into visual forms, such as street photography or Conceptual works engaging the city, they recorded their early responses as they found their places in the local cultural milieu. Moving through the social circles of other immigrant artists, as well as those of more established figures such as Andy Warhol and George Maciunas, Latin American artists formed an integral part of the neo-avant-garde scene developing in the period.

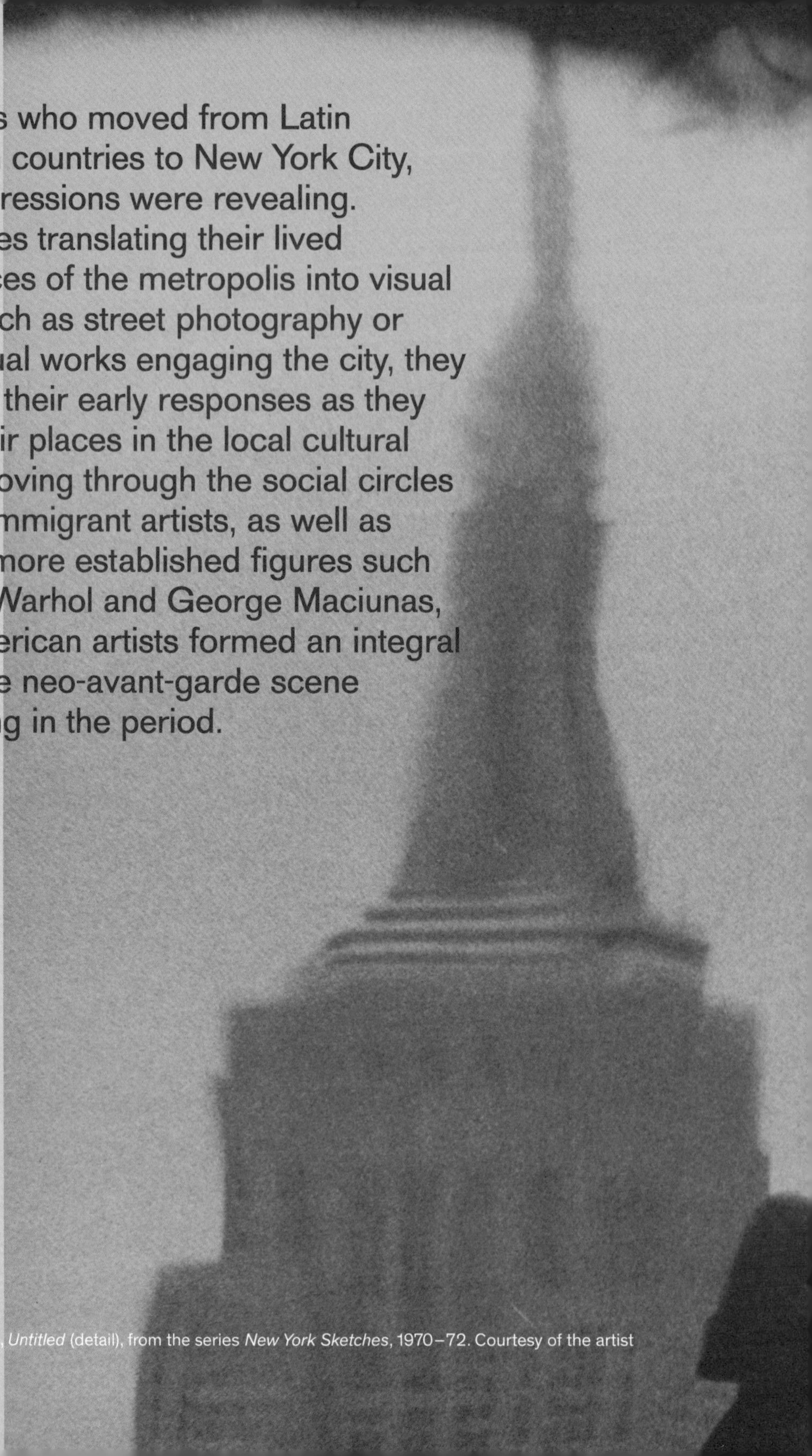

Miguel Rio Branco, *Untitled* (detail), from the series *New York Sketches*, 1970–72. Courtesy of the artist

Initial Impressions of the City

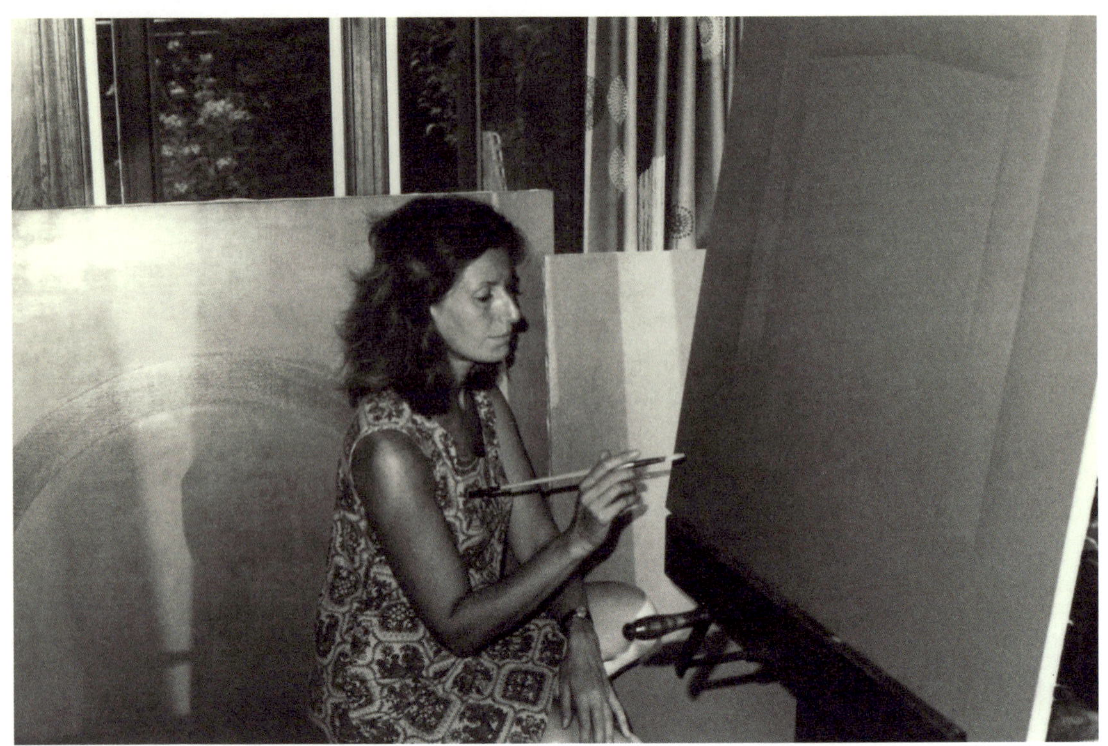

Some of the joys [of living in New York] were the extraordinary art I saw in the museums and galleries, the great sense of freedom to create, the highly stimulating feeling of being surrounded by all of the arts coming together, and by so many artists both American and from all over the world.

— Raquel Rabinovich

Raquel Rabinovich in her studio, Huntington, New York, 1972. Raquel Rabinovich Archive

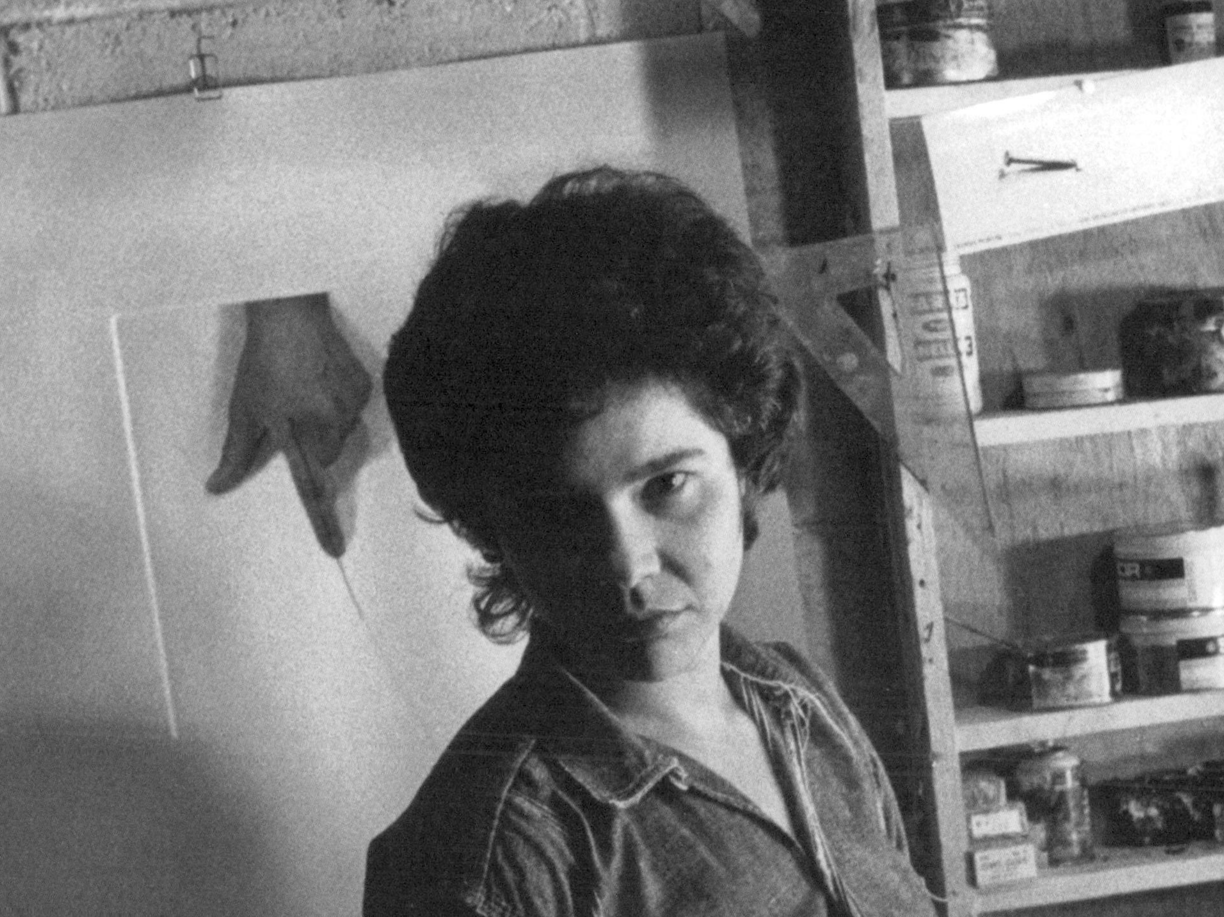

What struck me most was the feeling that one sometimes gets in New York that "everything is possible," and that if there were any obstacles to making something happen, they had more to do with me than the environment. In other words, it was the feeling of being in a place that was overloaded with stimuli–things to see, study, experiment with, and learn. It was also the sensation of being in the twentieth century, of living in the present moment.

I still remember the impact that the graphic force of the billboards and other advertising media had on me when I first arrived in New York in 1964. The food packaging in the supermarkets had the same effect. Pop art appropriated that language, almost literally, and simply placed it within the context of fine arts.

– Liliana Porter

Liliana Porter in her studio, New York, 1973. Liliana Porter Archive

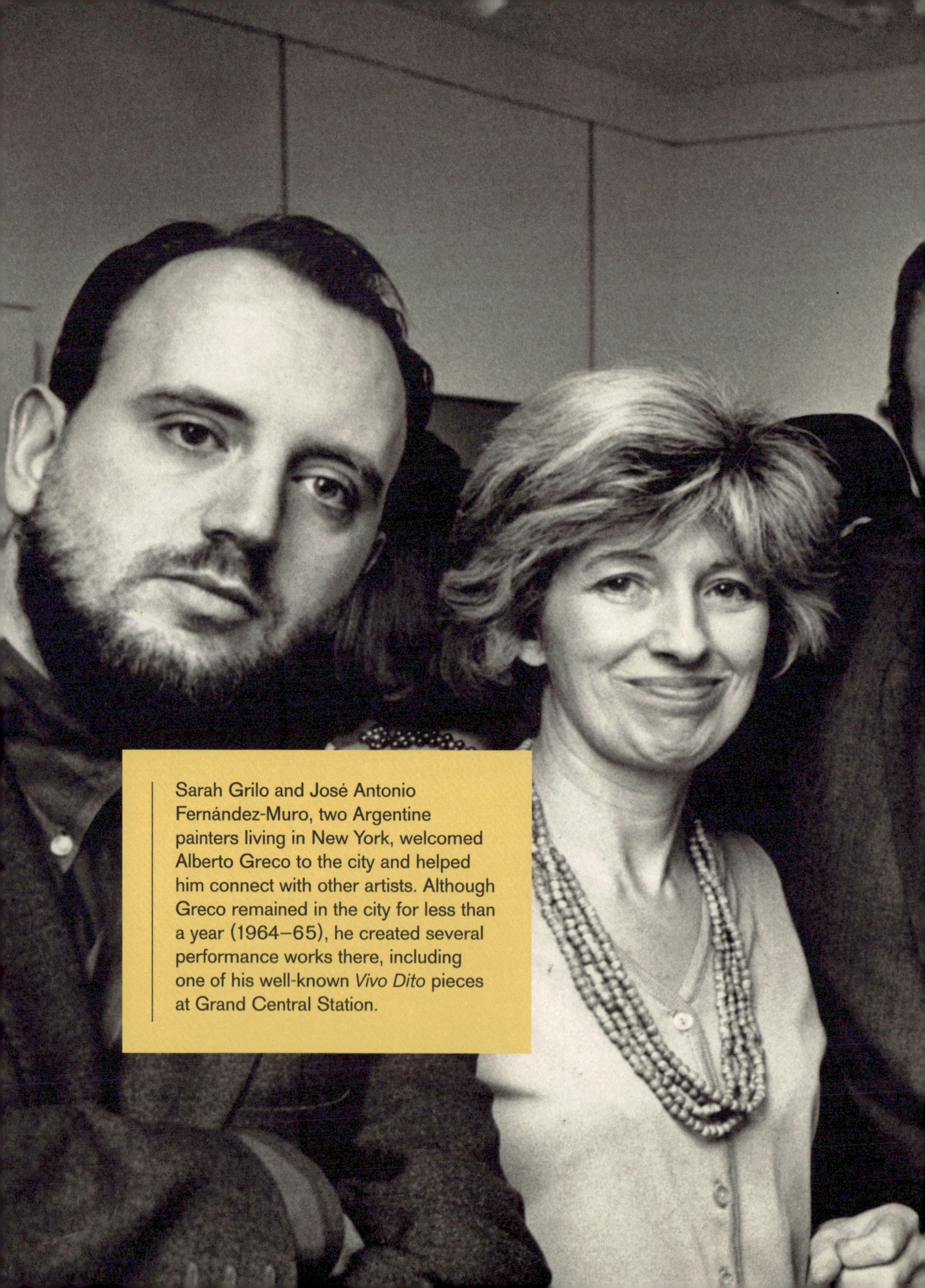

Sarah Grilo and José Antonio Fernández-Muro, two Argentine painters living in New York, welcomed Alberto Greco to the city and helped him connect with other artists. Although Greco remained in the city for less than a year (1964–65), he created several performance works there, including one of his well-known *Vivo Dito* pieces at Grand Central Station.

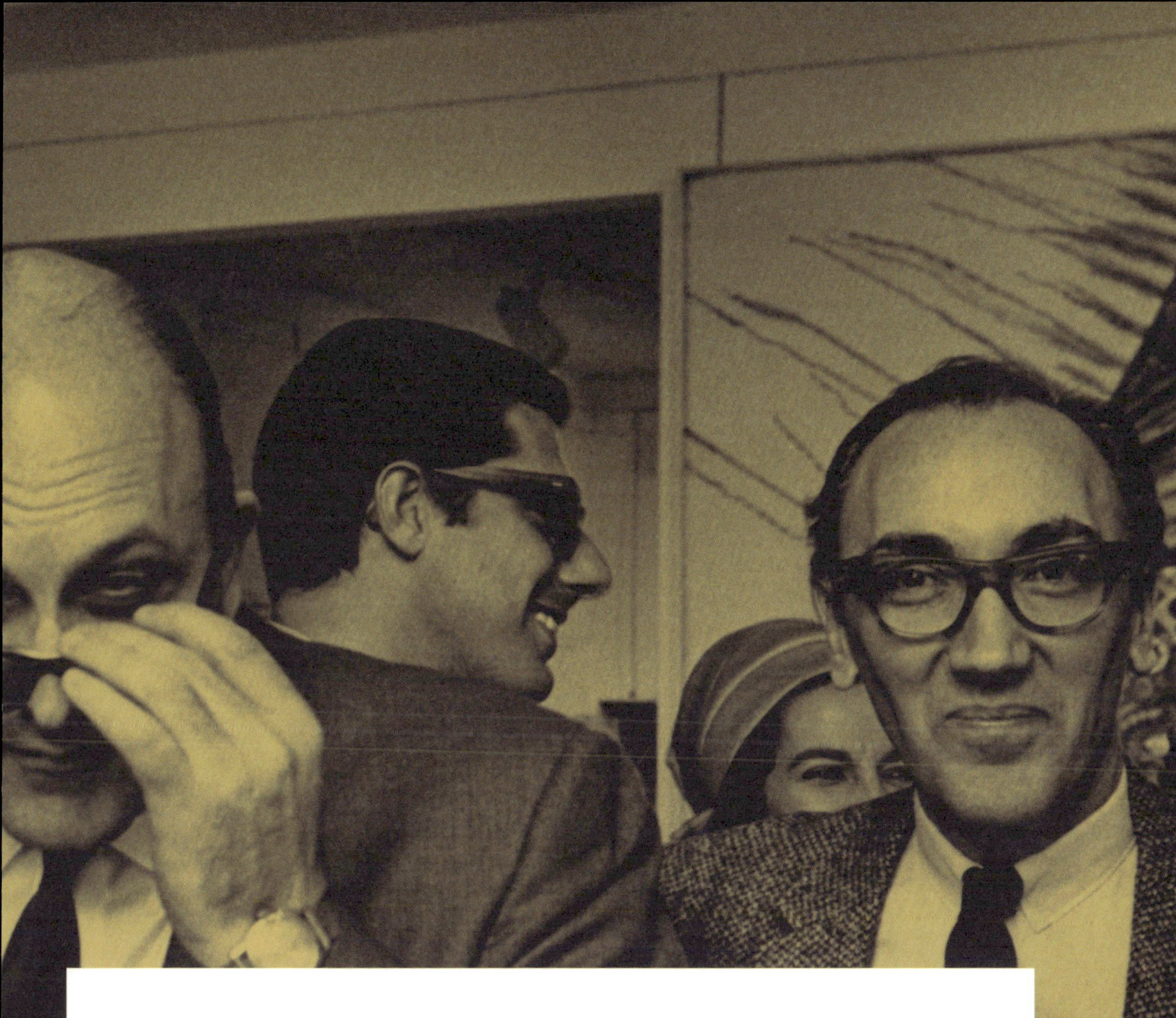

When he [Alberto Greco] saw New York he was frankly dazzled and said: this city is how I imagined a city has to be! I will stay here, I will die here and I will never leave here again!

— Sarah Grilo and José Antonio Fernández-Muro

Alberto Greco, Sarah Grilo, Leopoldo Torre Nilsson, and Jose Antonio Fernández-Muro, New York, 1964. Institute for Studies on Latin American Art (ISLAA) Library and Archives

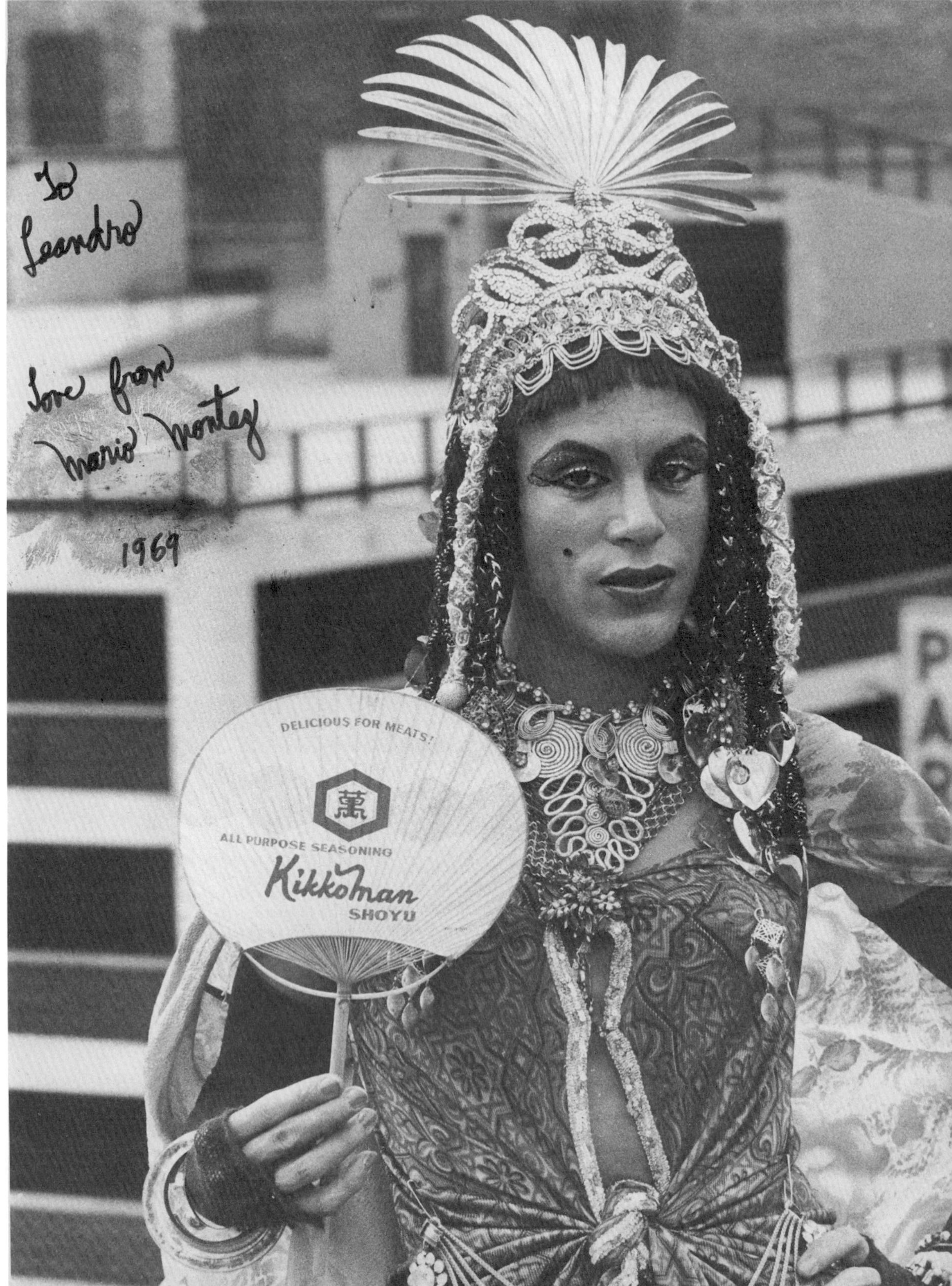
To
Leandro
Love from
Mario Montez
1969
DELICIOUS FOR MEATS!
ALL PURPOSE SEASONING
Kikkoman
SHOYU

Within two or three blocks, if you went out on a walk you'd meet everybody, and so encounters would take place on the street, from which you'd organize going somewhere or doing something. We might run into Jack Smith–who'd just be emerging at his favorite twilight hour to eat–or Charles Ludlam, Hélio Oiticica, Warhol's drag stars, such as Candy Darling, Jackie Curtis . . . We were neighbors, we were living in the East Village, on the Lower East Side, because that was where we could make the rent.

– Leandro Katz

Mario Montez Kiss, 1969. Leandro Katz Archive

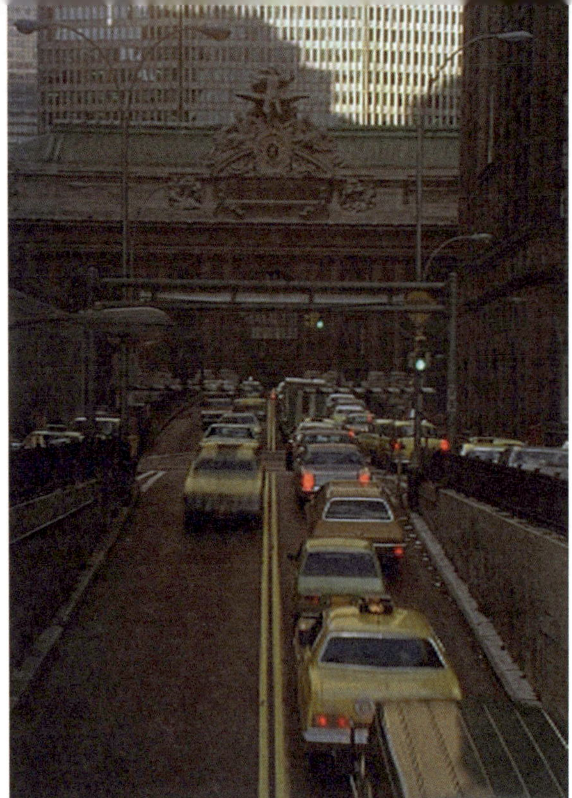

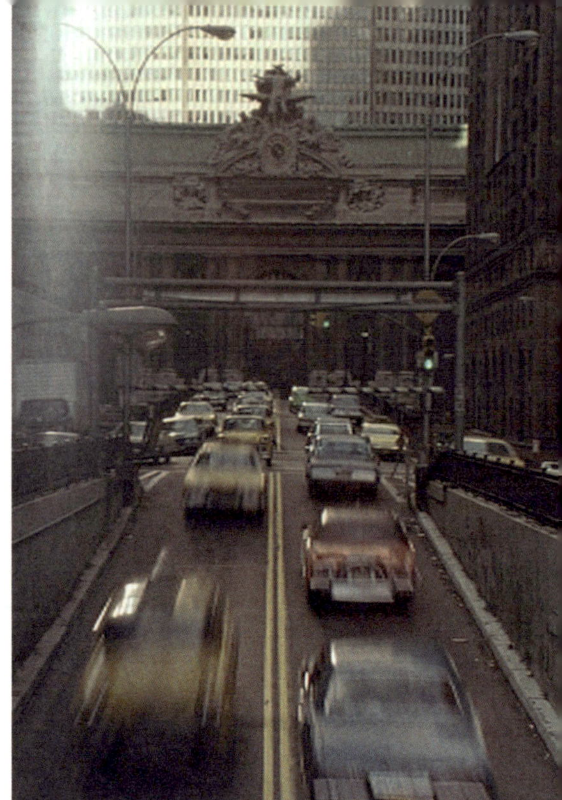

It was dreadful for me to arrive in New York, because everybody was saying, oh, it is a dangerous place, you know? Everything that people could say bad about New York they said to me, but I was–anyway, I loved challenges, but when I arrived in New York I remember–the first day, the first week I just walked one block–I only knew one block. I went one block at a time, and then in the end I loved New York and I really–actually, I went to France and I–because I really want to know Europe, and I went to Paris, and I hated Paris. When I came back to New York I was like I was coming back home, you know, because I felt much–I feel much more–there is an energy that we Brazilians have that is much more in contact with the American energy, more than with the French culture, you know.

Leandro Katz, stills from *Paris Has Changed a Lot*, 1976/2012.
Leandro Katz and Henrique Faria, New York

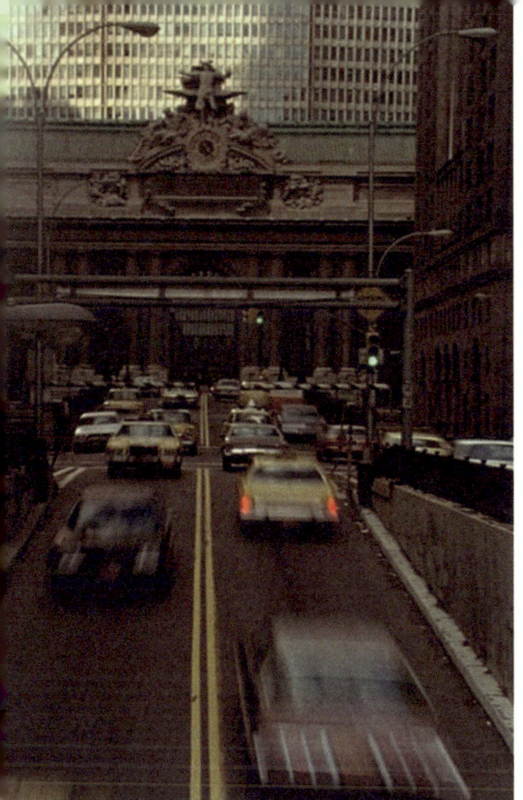

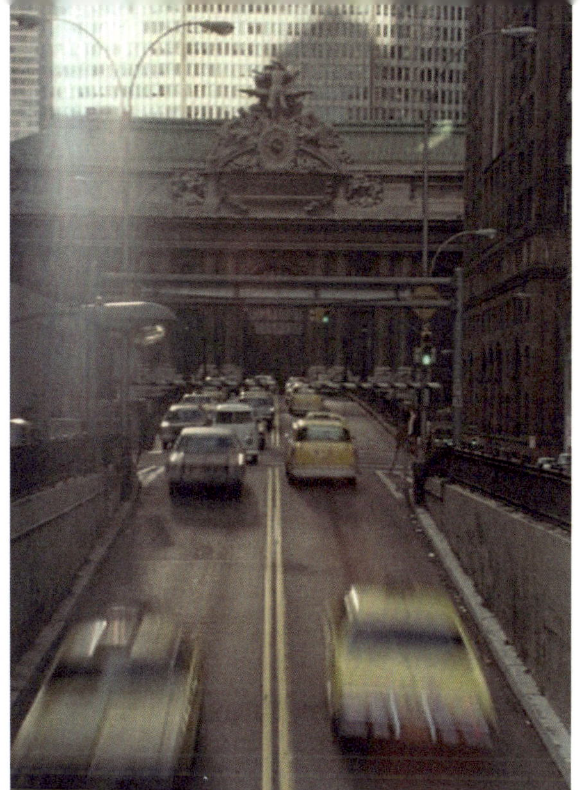

I lived for my work and I lived to know better the city. I knew very few Brazilians. New York has so much to offer . . . I felt isolated but the energy of New York at that time was so incredible that I was very excited to be there, and also to have the company of Hélio [Oiticica] all the time telling me about all these things, not only telling me about New York but about the universal culture, that could, through New York, become available to me.

But everything in New York is black and white, is very sharp and very defined. New York is all orthogonal. There are no curves, you know, because Latin America is full of curves. New York is not. But this is a fantastic training camp.

– Regina Vater

Leandro Katz, *Manhattan Gandhi, Second Avenue and 2nd Street*, 1970. Leandro Katz Archive

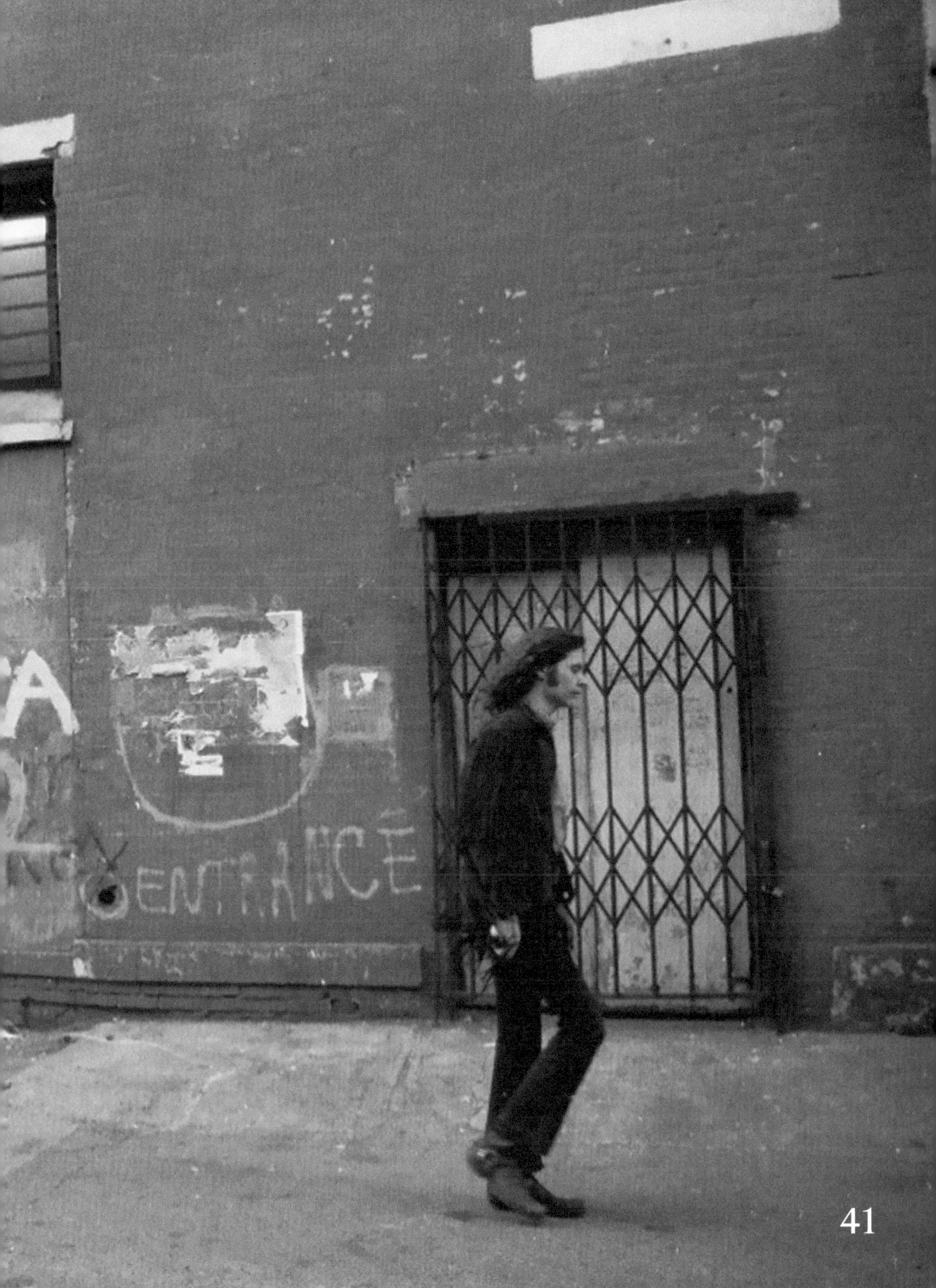
ENTRANCE

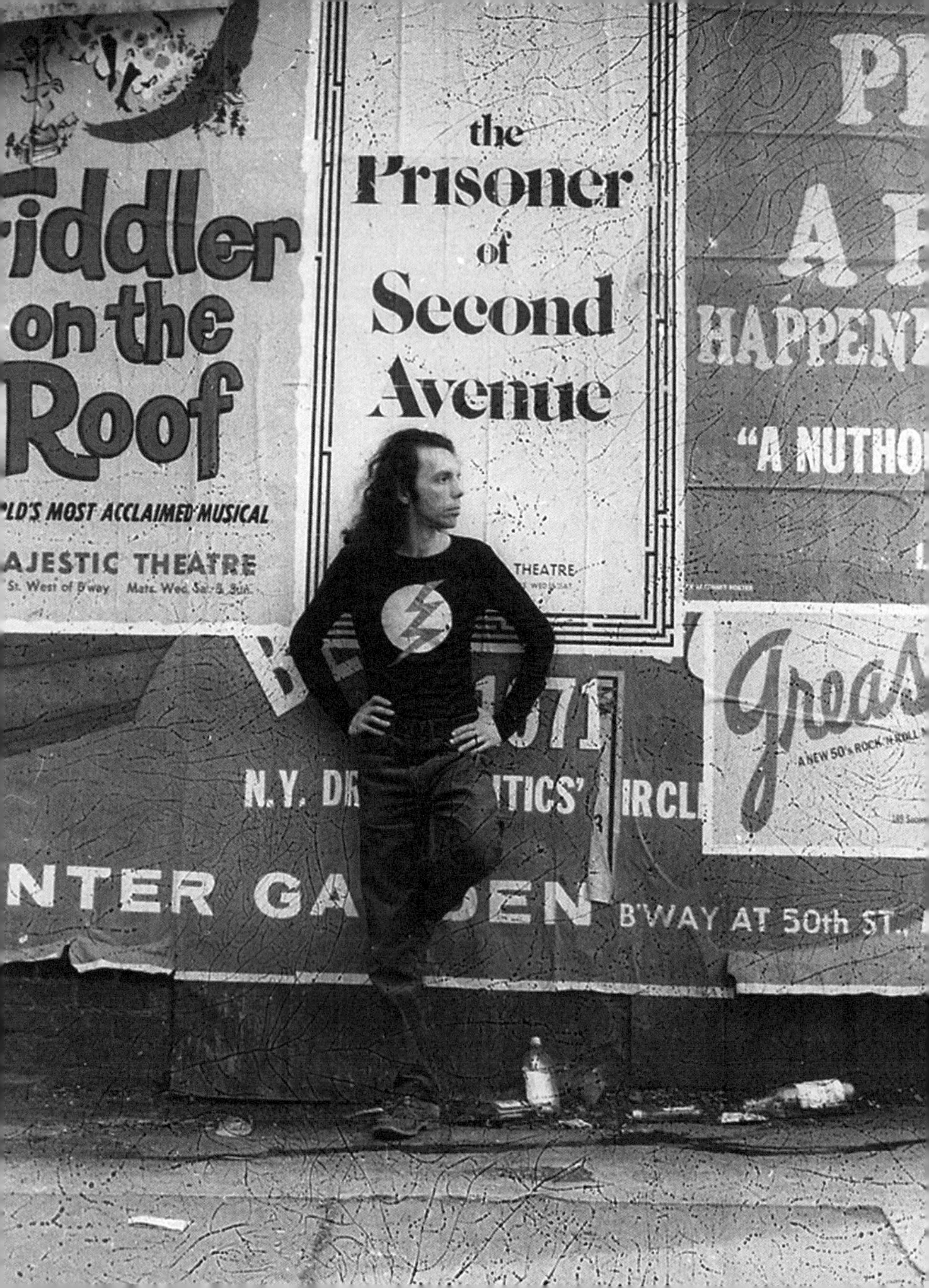

iddler
on the
Roof
LD'S MOST ACCLAIMED MUSICAL
AJESTIC THEATRE
the
Prisoner
of
Second
Avenue
THEATRE
HAPPEN
"A NUTHO
N.Y. DR
ITICS'
IRCL
NTER GA
DEN
B'WAY AT 50th ST.,

[I will] go to New York for a while, as it is the only place, outside Rio, where I can breathe; I love the violence of New York; everyone is crazy, you can go to the cinema in the middle of the night, or to Harlem, etc.

— Hélio Oiticica

> In a letter to his close friend and fellow Brazilian artist Lygia Clark, Oiticica describes his plans to move to New York. While he romanticized the violence of the city, he was optimistic that its vibrancy would equal that of his hometown of Rio de Janeiro. The letters the two artists exchanged between 1964 and 1974 are important registers of their aesthetic thinking, creativity, and admiration for one another.

No one knew Oiticica's previous work and he became a friend and supporter not only of my photographic work but also of the Super 8 films I made with his camera. Oiticica was an antagonist and went against the art market and its speculative side. He was an extremely generous person and a supporter of the creative processes of young artists.

— Miguel Rio Branco

Hélio Oiticica in front of a poster for Neil Simon's play *Prisoner of Second Avenue* in Midtown Manhattan, 1972. Projeto Hélio Oiticica

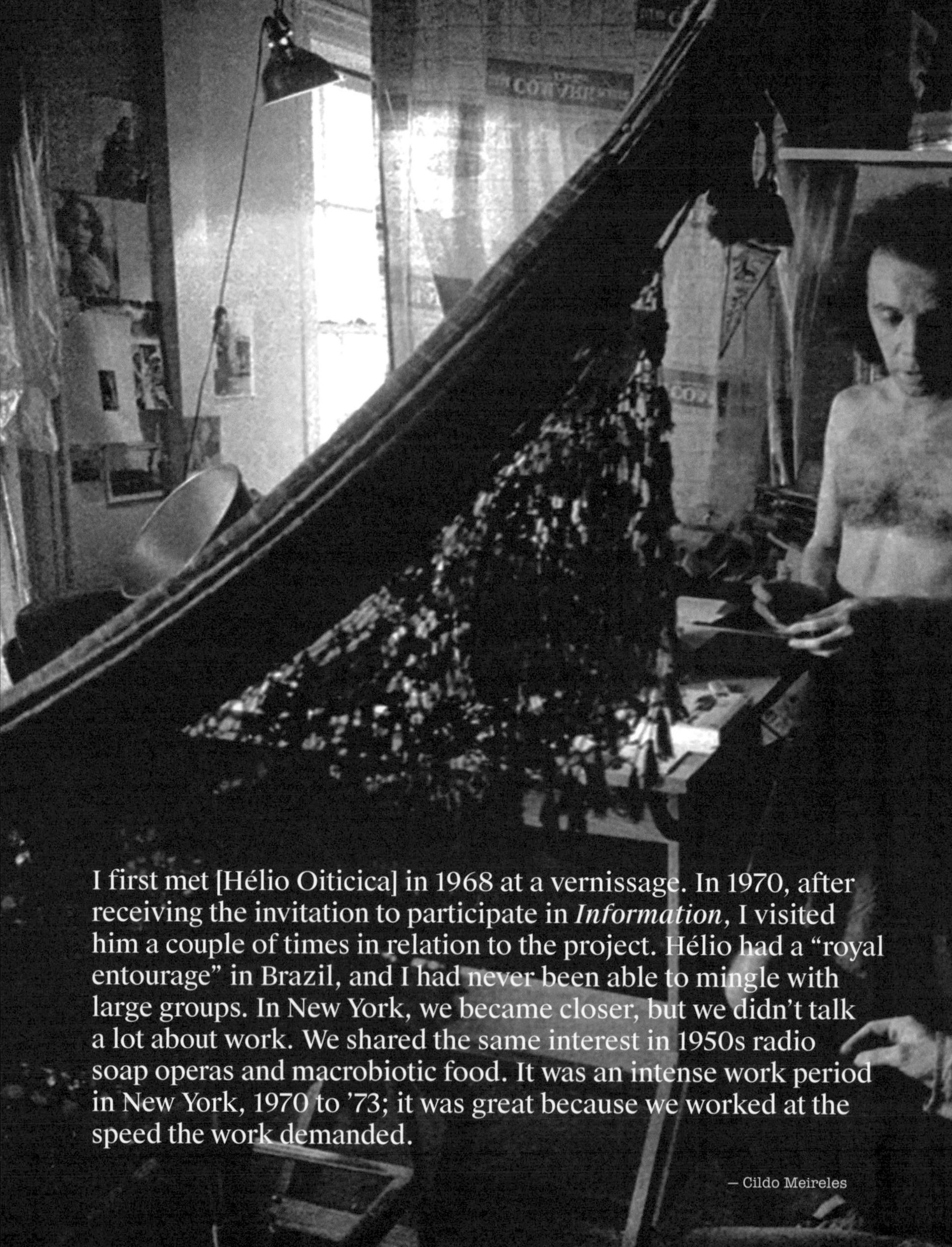

I first met [Hélio Oiticica] in 1968 at a vernissage. In 1970, after receiving the invitation to participate in *Information*, I visited him a couple of times in relation to the project. Hélio had a "royal entourage" in Brazil, and I had never been able to mingle with large groups. In New York, we became closer, but we didn't talk a lot about work. We shared the same interest in 1950s radio soap operas and macrobiotic food. It was an intense work period in New York, 1970 to '73; it was great because we worked at the speed the work demanded.

— Cildo Meireles

I grew up and started to assiduously attend Loft 4. In New York, Hélio said I should quit school and live there, where I would "learn so much more"! When I was not able to go to New York [from Swarthmore College, close to Philadelphia], we spoke on the phone—an important means of communication back then and which Hélio used a lot. I met many people there—he loved to welcome artists, friends, companions. It was at this time that I started to photograph and to shoot Super 8 and 16 mm films.

Hélio was always working. Everything was an artwork, in constant and permanent creation/invention/ experimentation, in progress. His period in New York was marked, mainly, by writing. Dozens of notebooks, several thousand handwritten and/or typewritten sheets, besides drawings and work projects form the repertoire of his bigger goal: to publish a book that would be called Newyorkaises or Conglomerado, which, however, never happened.

— Andreas Valentin

Thomas Valentin, *Hélio Oiticica and Andreas Valentin at Loft 4*, 1973. Courtesy of Andreas Valentin

I lived in Little Italy, close to Canal Street, where you could find any type of material at very low cost. I was not directly inspired by the city, which I always found uncomfortable to live in. I drew a lot, I came up with many projects, including films and wall objects: a series called *The Art of Transference*, for instance, several works in which squares of canvas, glass, mirror, and cardboard made up the mail materials . . . fragile things that reflected the way I felt. I was still recovering from a facial paralysis and could not yet speak clearly. I wasn't feeling too sociable.

[New York] didn't change my way of working, which is always motivated by lived experience; maybe the American way of life just didn't resonate for me. As a result, my work became even more radical, almost devoid of flesh. My time in New York–from 1972 to roughly mid-1973–did away with any inclination to live there. . . . I was already very involved with my Super 8 films, and I organized a few screenings in my New York studio, which was a big loft. We lived unpretentiously, hippie style, on very little money and plenty of conversation.

— Antonio Dias

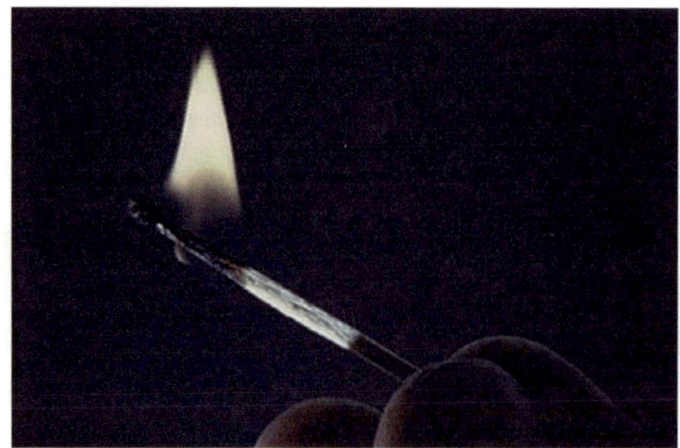

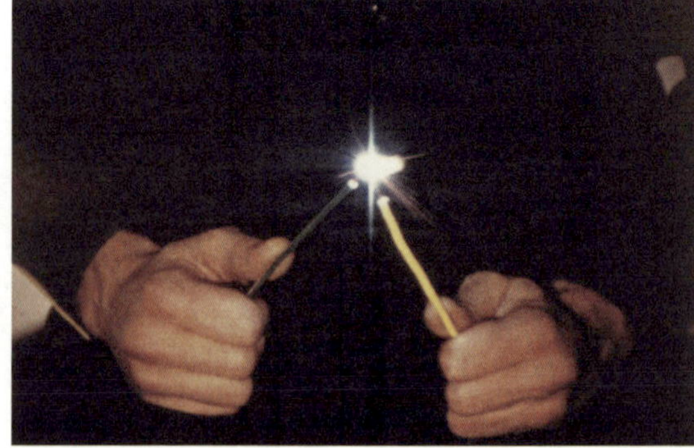

Antonio Dias, stills from *The Illustration of Art II*, 1971 (left), and *The Illustration of Art III*, 1971 (right).
Antonio Dias Estate and Nara Roesler

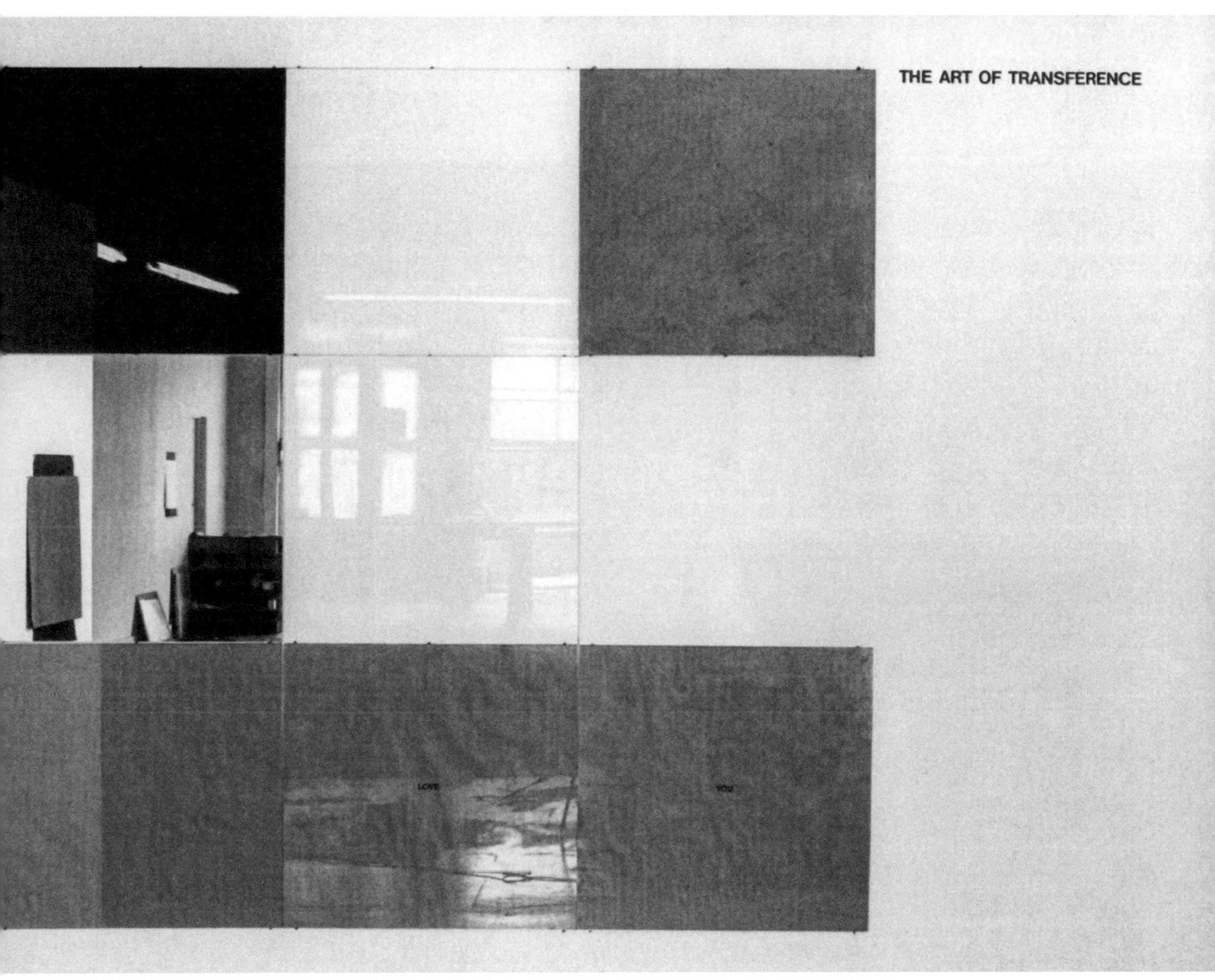

Antonio Dias, *The Art of Transference, Artist's Studio in New York*, 1972.
Antonio Dias Estate and Nara Roesler

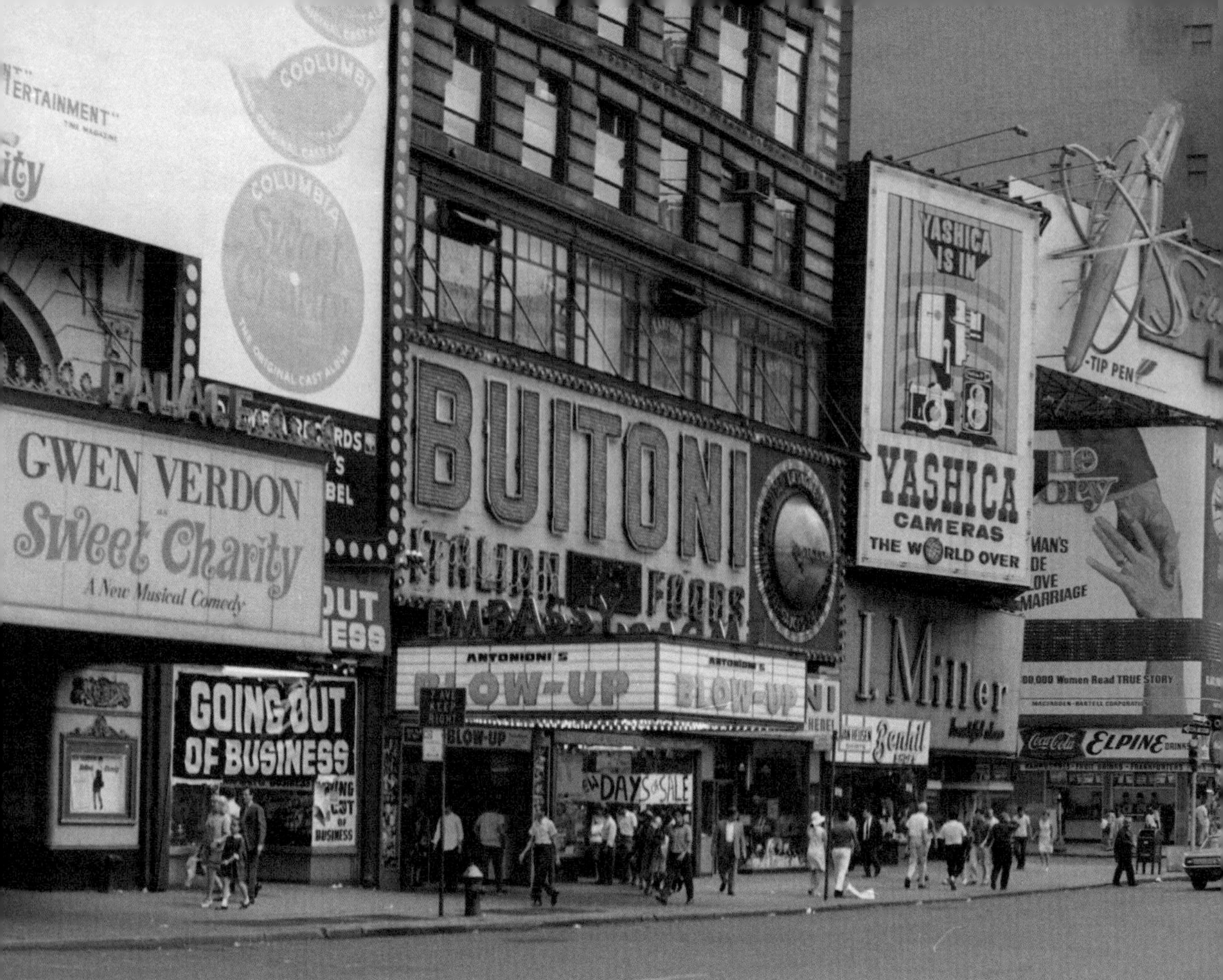

[The first photos of Manhattan that I took were of] the streets, and then there is something very important, which is my reaction to New York. Because New York–for a person coming from Santiago to New York–you have no way of being able to compare it in any way: the experience of going to a city like this, the personal experience at street level. Your feet are planted on the ground, you are looking at things through your eyes in a fabulous, a great panorama, right? A photo worked [on] the laboratory, who knows for whom, no, it's your own experience, your eyes, your ears, do you understand? Then you react and obviously if a musician comes, they react in a totally different way from that of a photographer, or what it would be for a filmmaker like Jaime Barrios.

— Marcelo Montealegre

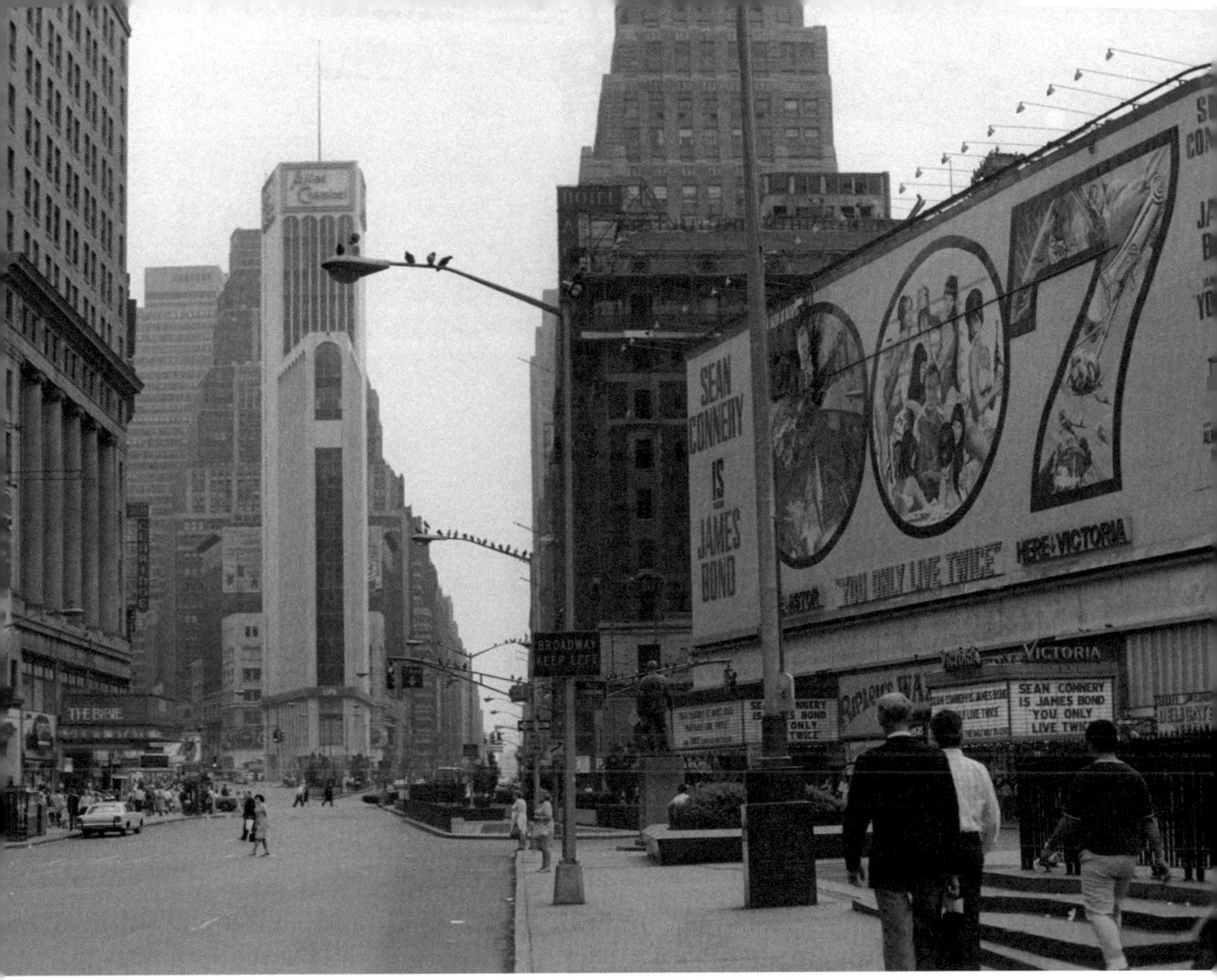

Marcelo Montealegre, *Panoramic View of New York*, 1967.
Marcelo Montealegre Archive

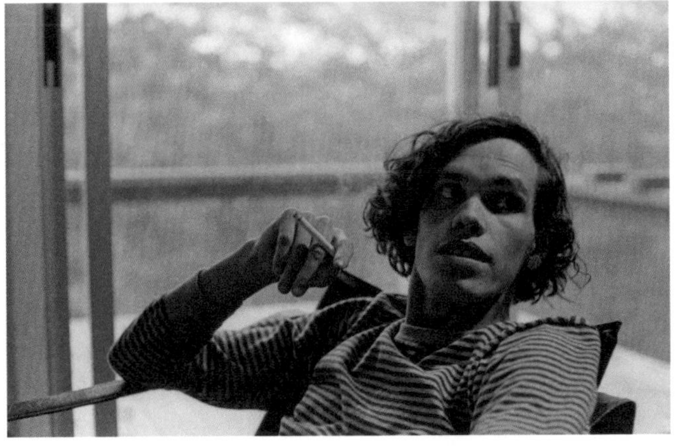

Marcelo Montealegre, *Jaime Barrios in East Hampton*, 1967.
Marcelo Montealegre Archive

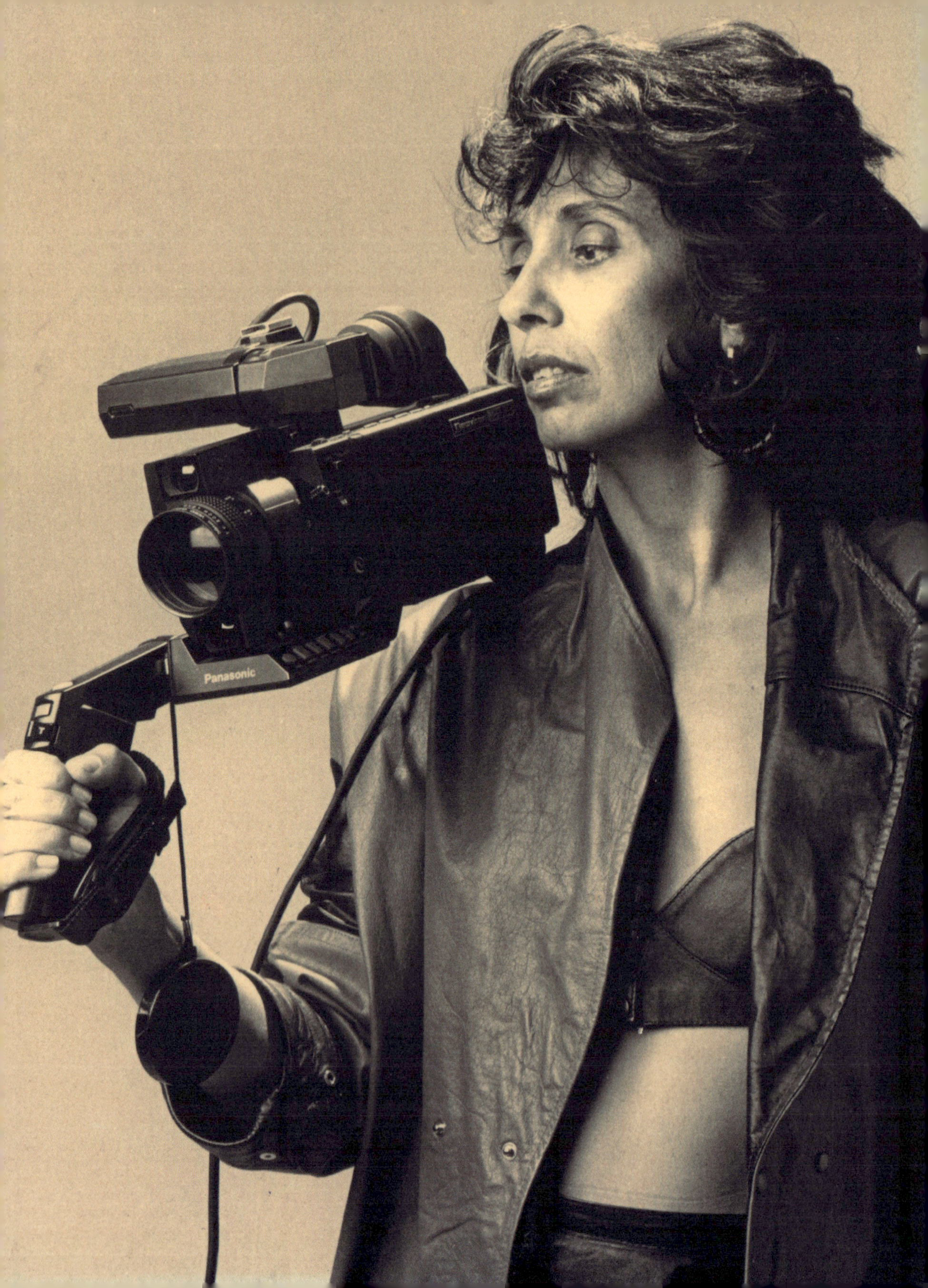
Panasonic

I arrived here in 1973 [and was] then living with José Roberto Aguilar. In Brazil, the military dictatorship was censoring the arts in general. Aguilar was a painter and I was working mainly in photographs and Super 8 films. We lived in the West Village in a building just for artists, where all of them belonged to the underground scene in New York. This was the building where my video guru Nam June Paik lived, and where Merce Cunningham had a dance studio on the top floor. I would also hang out with Hélio Oiticica, who also lived in the Village. I used to go to the CBGB punk club a lot to see punk bands play. We didn't have a lot of money but we had a very intense cultural life with artists at the time who performed at galleries in lofts, like John Cage and Yoko Ono, who also did video art. I bought a 1974 Sony black/ white camera and that's how I started making videos, with a camera in my hand and an idea in my head.

— Sonia Miranda

Sonia Miranda, *New York 1978*, 1978. Courtesy of the artist

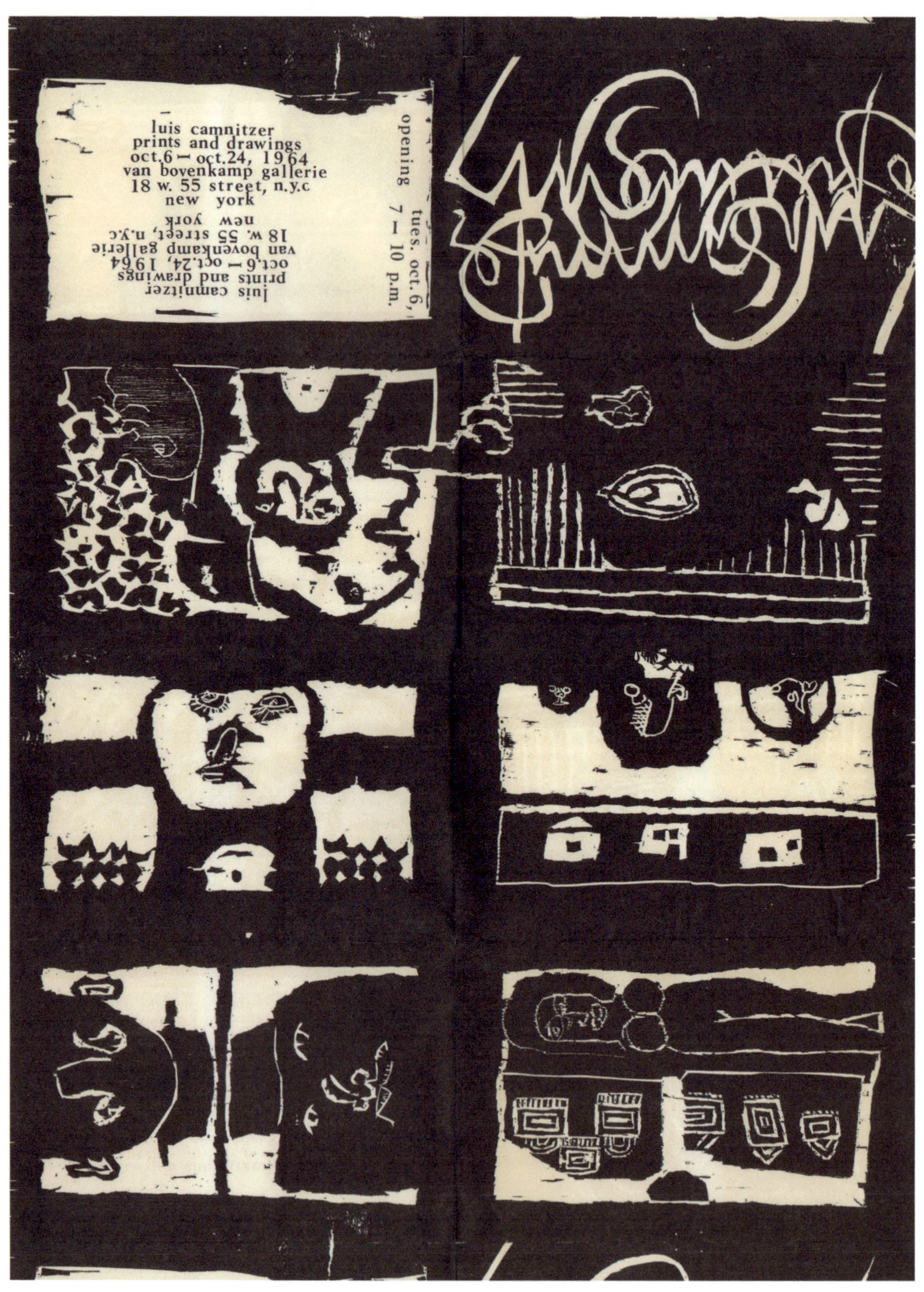

Exhibition poster, *Luis Camnitzer: Prints and Drawings*, Van Bovenkamp Gallerie, New York, October 6–24, 1964. Institute for Studies on Latin American Art (ISLAA) Library and Archives

Old friends of my parents who had settled in New York came to pick me up from the airport. On that ride I was struck by the bigness. Oddly, the first thing the friends told me on the way into the city was that if I was ever hit by a car in New York, I should stay on the ground and not move because a lawyer would appear very soon and handle matters.

— Luis Camnitzer

I was sharing an apartment with [Luis Felipe] Noé. We had endless discussions about everything. He is definitely an original mind, and kept challenging my attachment to printmaking. It was a great pedagogical experience for me.

— Luis Camnitzer

Luis Felipe Noé, *Autorretrato* (Self-portrait), 1966. Printed at the New York Graphic Workshop. Liliana Porter Archive

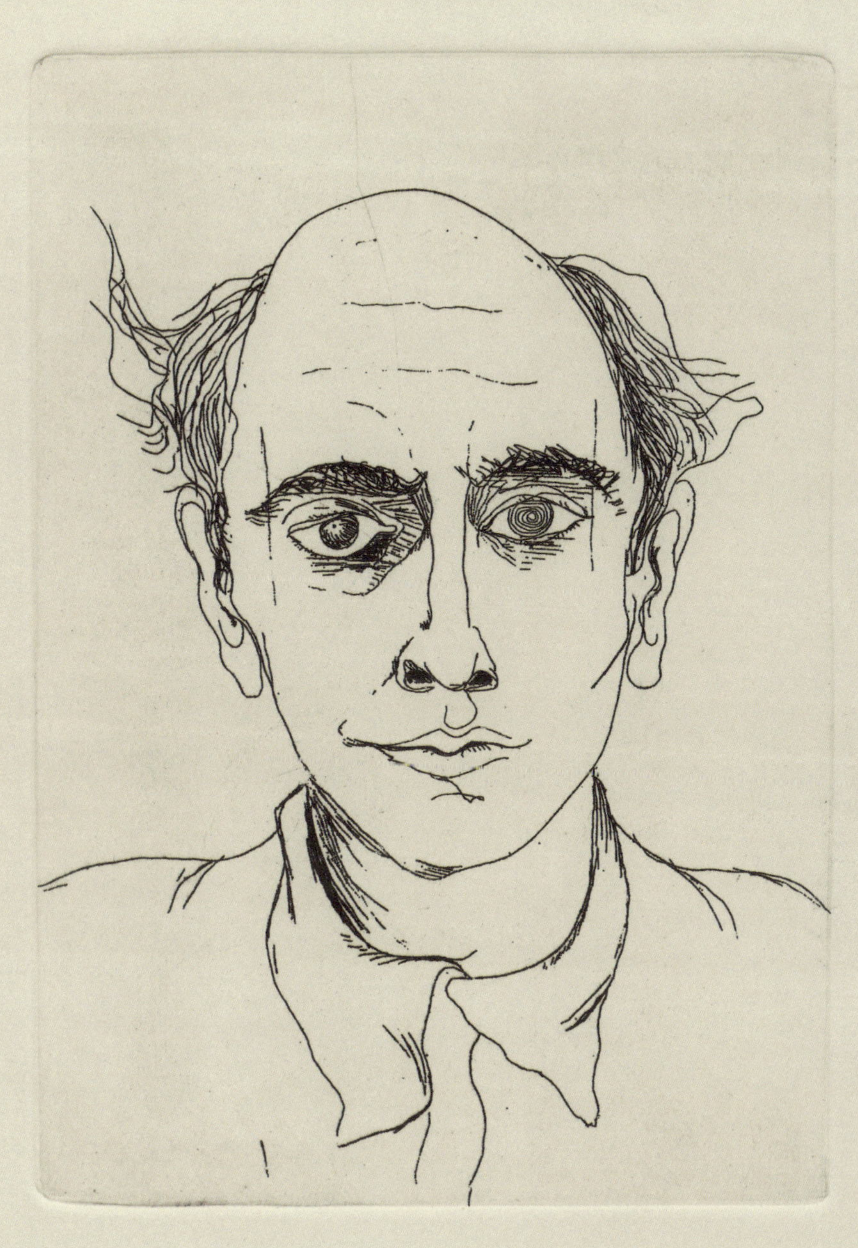

NOÉ. AUTORRETRATO PRUEBA DE TALLER (1966)

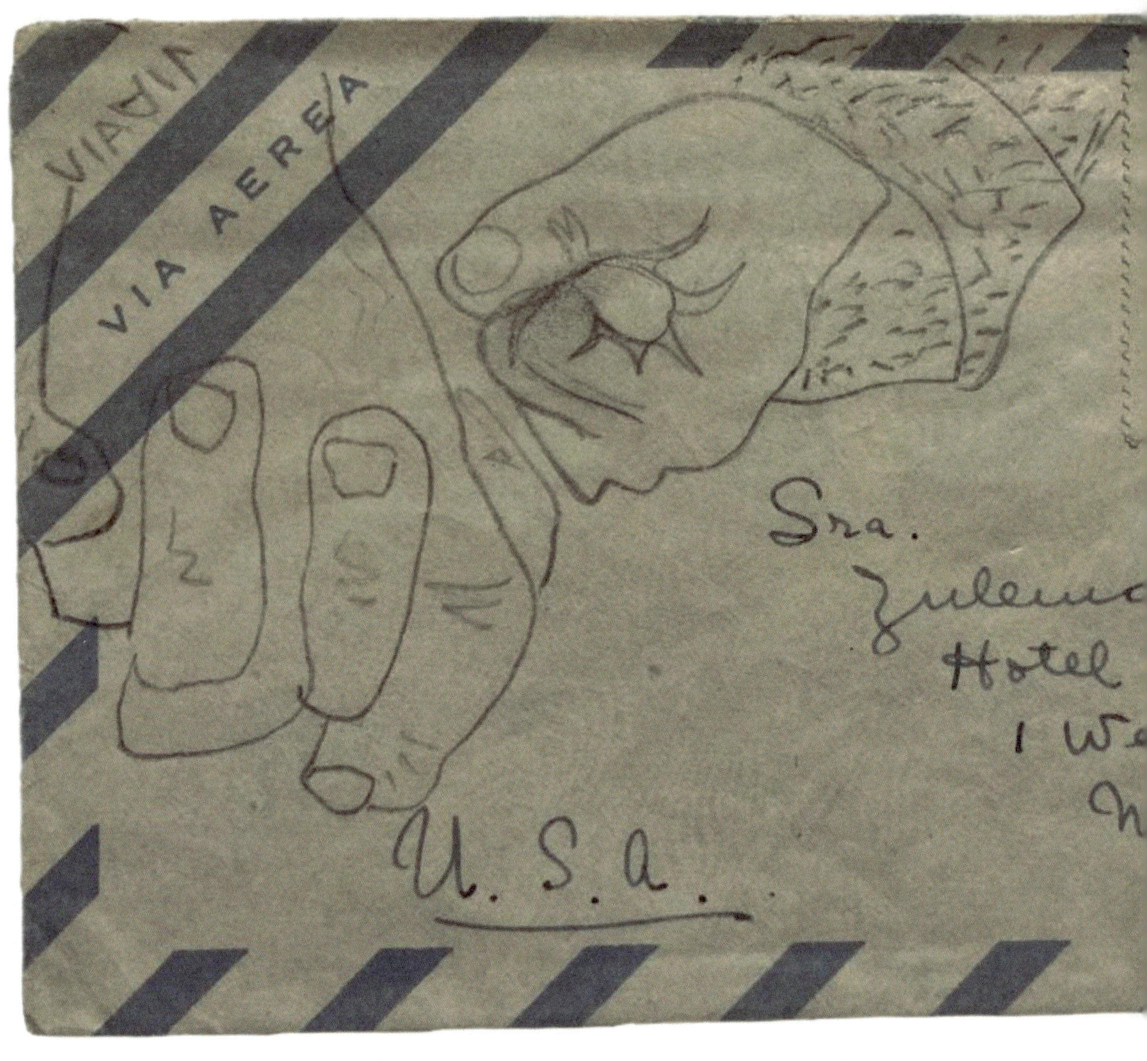

Zulema “Beba” Damianovich, envelope with drawing, 1956. Courtesy of the estate of the artist

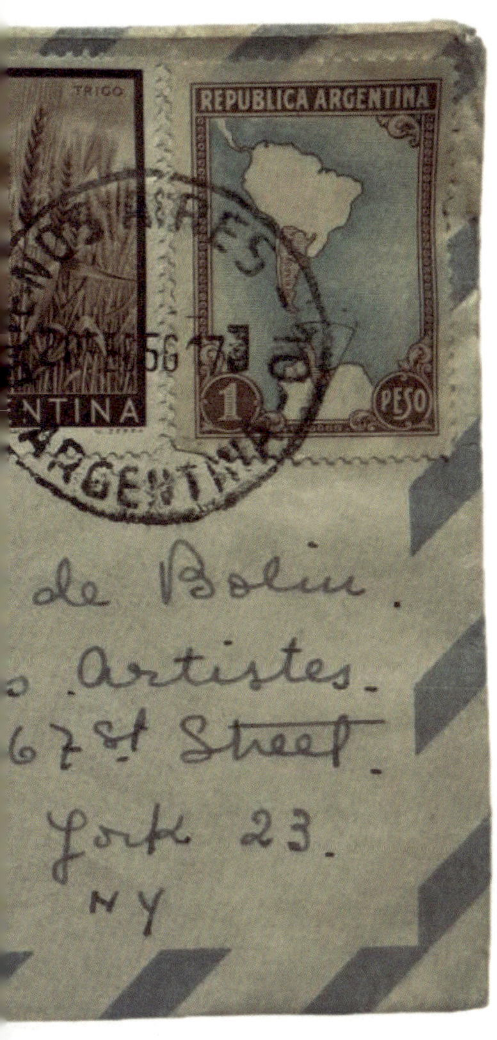

[Zulema "Beba" Damianovich] was a reference for artists when they arrived. She was [later] close with Hélio Oiticica. When Leandro Katz came to the United States, she became friends with him. She was twenty years older than most of us.

— Jaime Davidovich

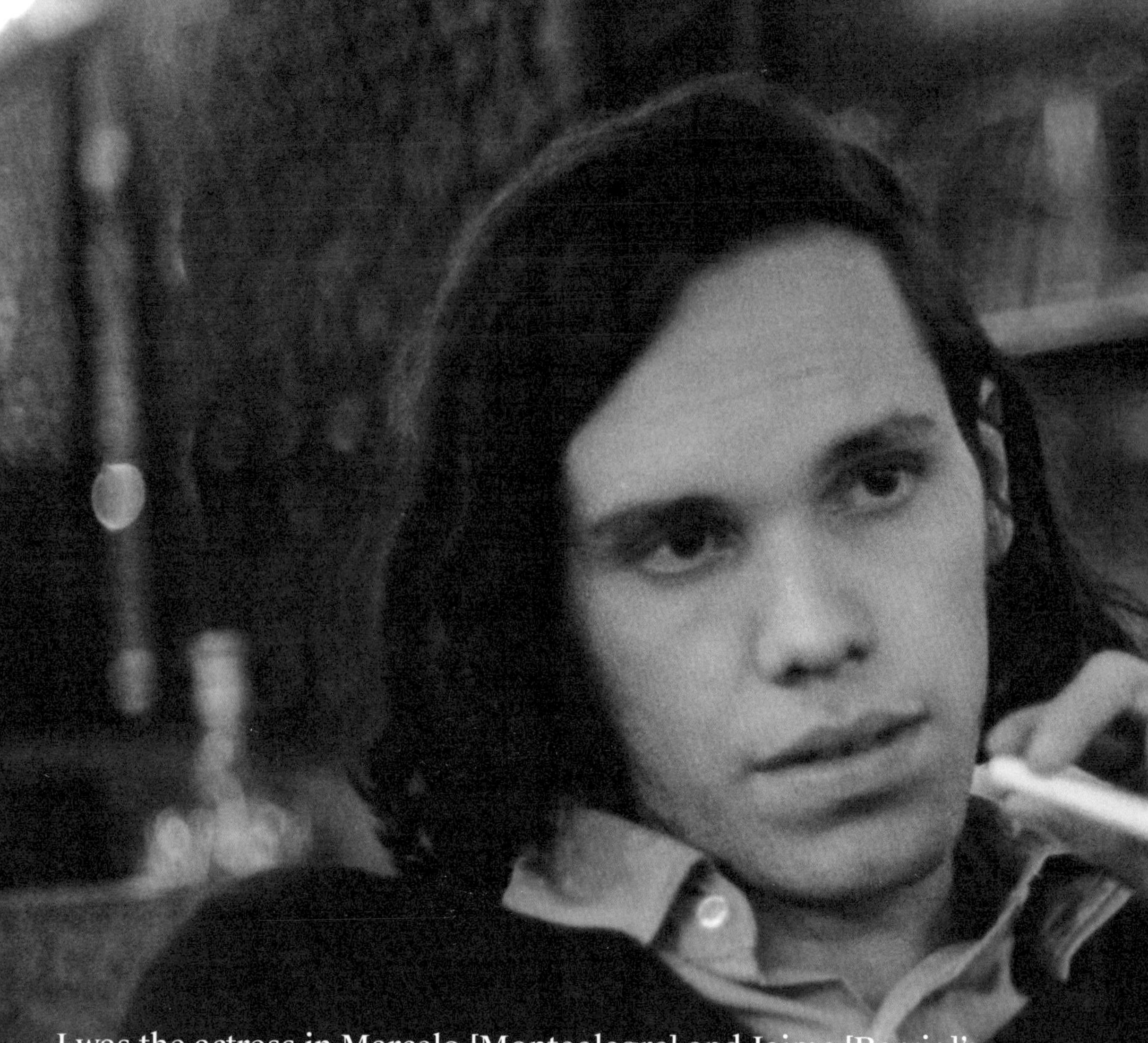

I was the actress in Marcelo [Montealegre] and Jaime [Barrio]'s *Virginia Cows* (1969). They introduced me to cinema, and I was opened to the possibilities of multimedia. Before that I was not so interested in it. This experience helped me when I went back to Chile to teach dance at La Escuela ARCIS. Marcelo has the making of the film documented in photos and a big collection of photos he took of my life in New York. My friendship with him was very important for me in New York.

— Carmen Beuchat

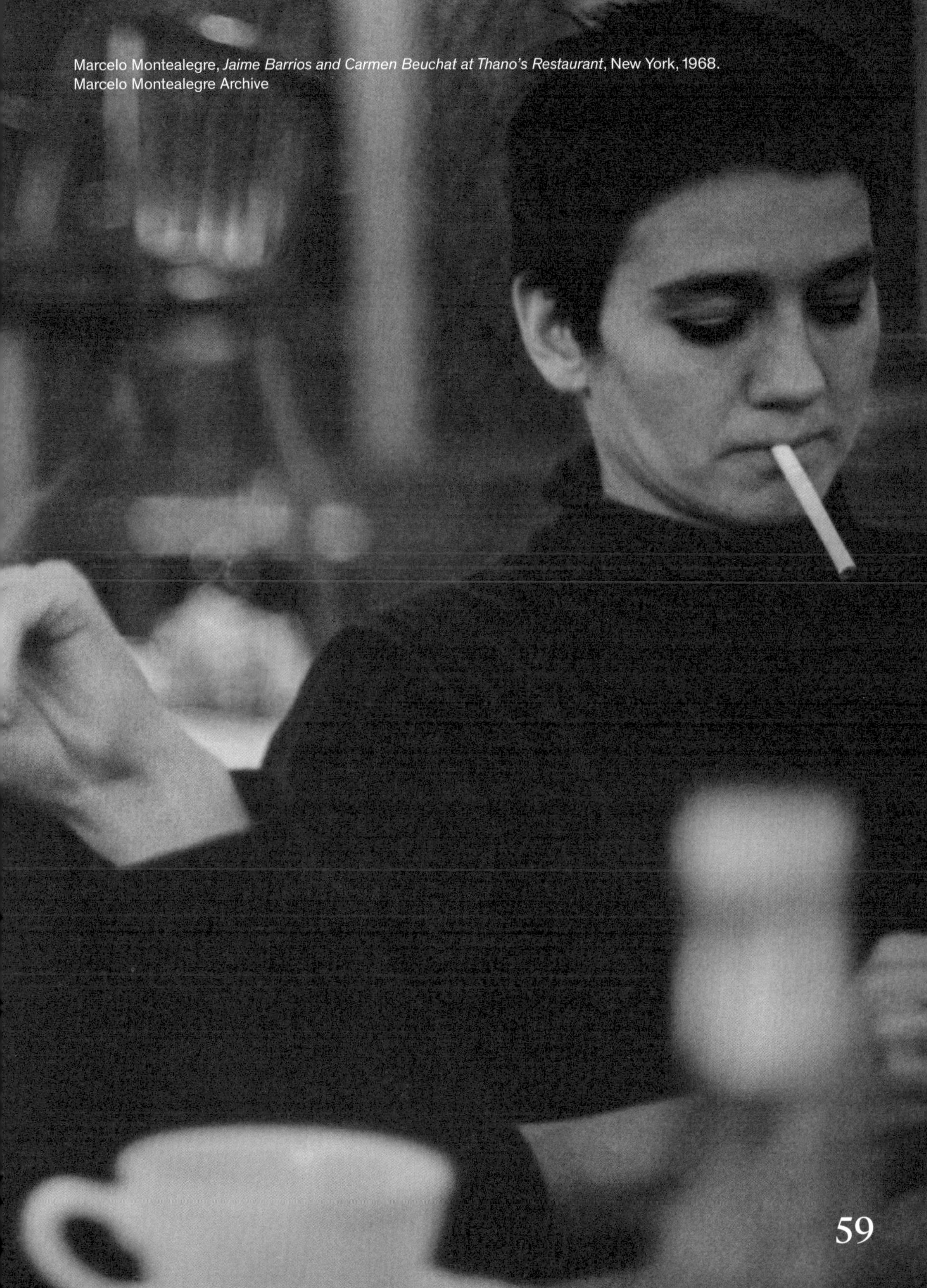

Marcelo Montealegre, *Jaime Barrios and Carmen Beuchat at Thano's Restaurant*, New York, 1968.
Marcelo Montealegre Archive

[When I arrived in New York] it was gloomy, and it scared me because it was all empty and there were cars with gangsters on the road and prostitutes. And on top of that, I went first to a horrible hotel where you picked up the bedsheets and there were cockroaches. So I went to the Chelsea [Hotel], and everyone was crazy. I met a lot of people there. I stayed at the Chelsea until I moved into an apartment with the money from the Torcuato Di Tella Prize, because I could only afford to live. It was an empty apartment on University Place and 13th Street . . . I met everyone there, like de Kooning, Carolee Schneemann, Allan Kaprow. They all went to that bar, Max's [Kansas City]. I started going there every night and eating for free, because at seven in the evening they gave free fried chicken, salad, everything. So all the artists went and there I met thousands of people.

— Marta Minujín

Marta Minujín at the opening of *Minucode*, Center for Inter-American Relations, New York, May 27, 1968. Marta Minujín Archive

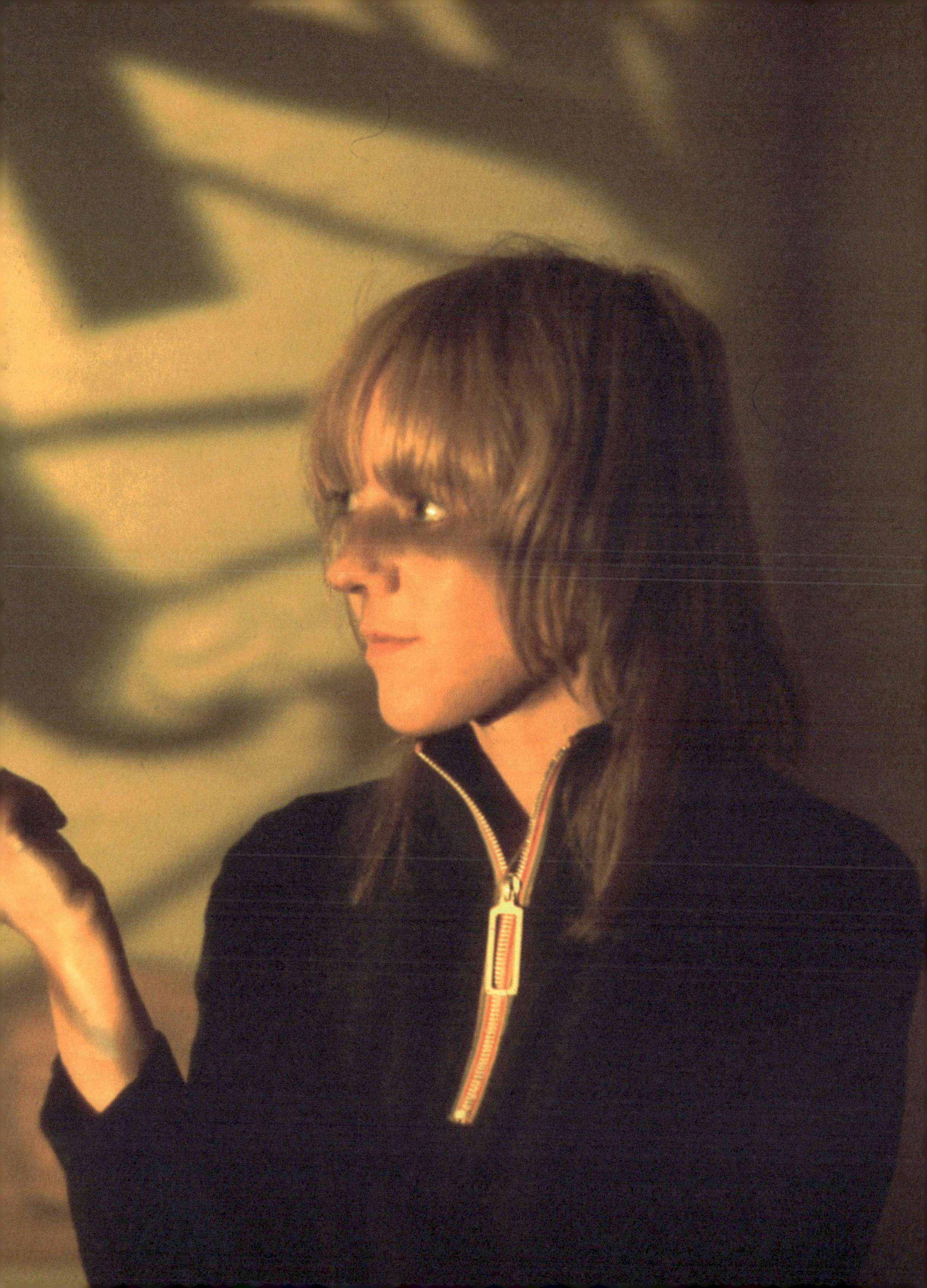

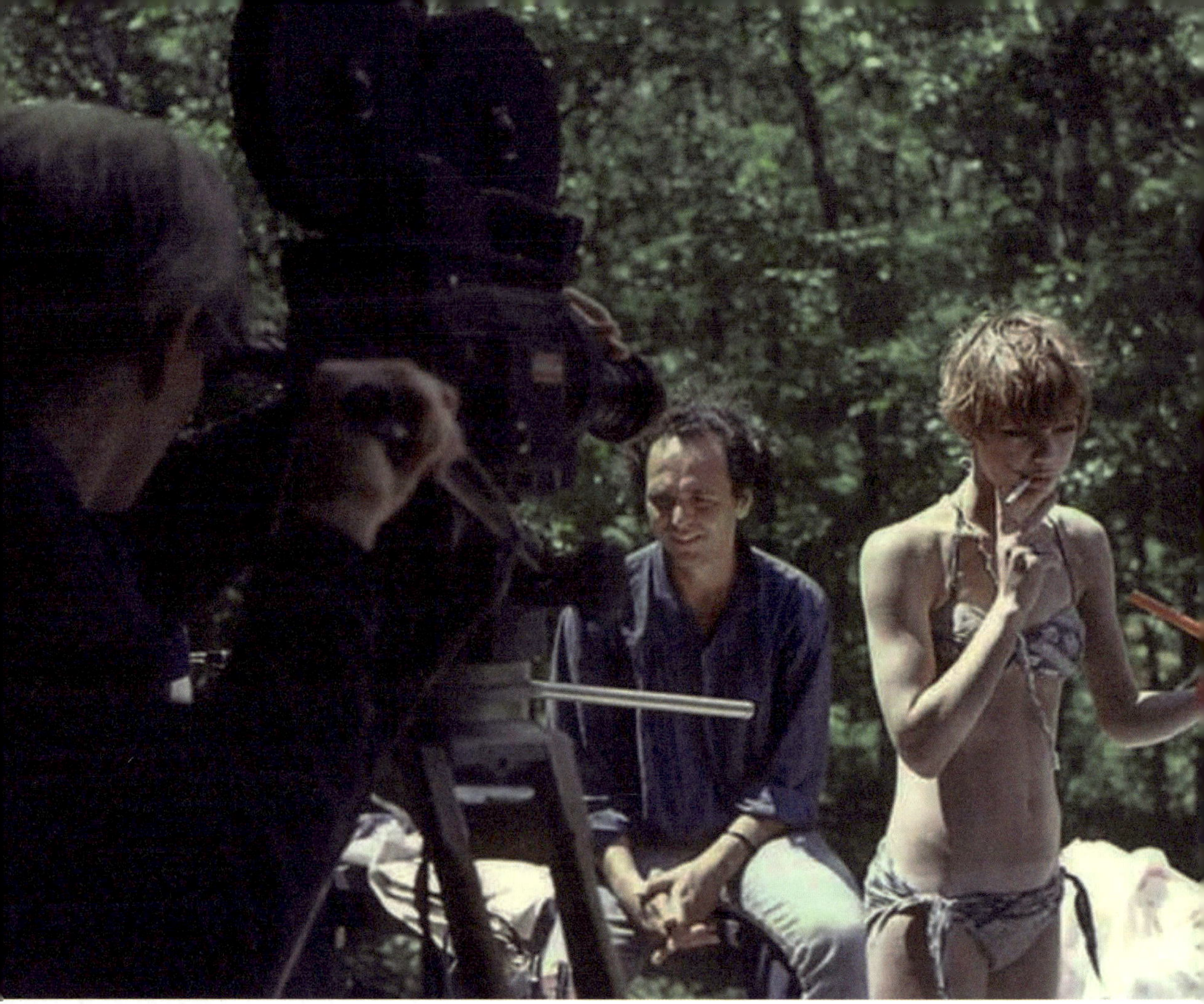

[I have painted] professionally since I came to New York [in 1959]. I believe that New York gave me the sense of freedom, the American idea of freedom: do what you want to do, develop yourself to where you want. Here I found what I couldn't find in the last years that preceded the nightmare of Castro's Cuba: new thoughts, opportunities and the approach of what to do with myself.

— Waldo Balart

Marcelo Montealegre, *Andy Warhol, Waldo Balart, Edie Sedgwick, and Simone Swanson during the shooting of **** (Four Stars)*, East Hampton, New York, 1967. Marcelo Montealegre Archive

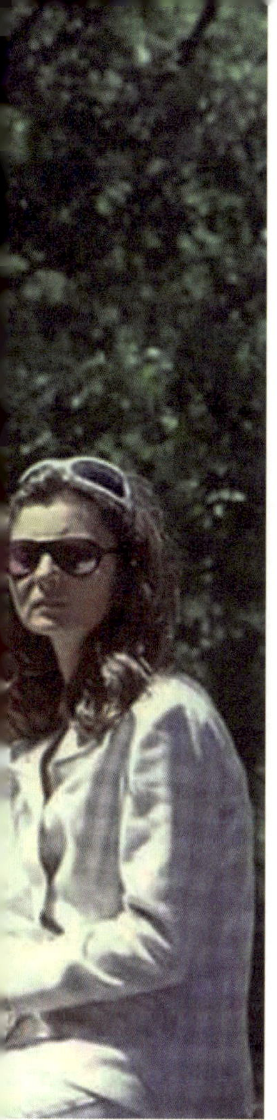

I met [Andy] Warhol on my first trip to NYC in 1963. . . . One night I invited a beautiful dancer, a classmate from Martha Graham School, and I took her to the El Quijote restaurant located in the Chelsea Hotel, the most emblematic hotel of the time, where a large part of the vanguard of New York City, Europe, and elsewhere stayed. At that time I didn't know it and I went because I was staying very close and since it was Spanish food and they spoke Spanish, I found it interesting because my English was not good. We arrived and sat at a table and very close to a large table was Warhol, with his group, Viva, Gerard Malanga, Ultra Violet, Nico, and others. At one point Gerard Malanga approached me and began to speak to me in English. I told him that my English was not very good, that I spoke Spanish and a little Italian. And he told me, no problem, we will mix Spanish and Italian. This is how we understood each other. He told me: "The person who is sitting with us is Andy Warhol, you caught his attention by the way you are dressed all in black with a cape and he wants to know if you are interested in participating in some film projects that we are planning." Of course I replied that yes, I was interested in him. I had already participated in theater and cinema in my country. I thought it was a good opportunity to enter the artistic world of New York City. After we finished dinner we went to their table and had some wine with them and they invited me to go to the Factory, where they worked and organized everything.

– Rolando Peña

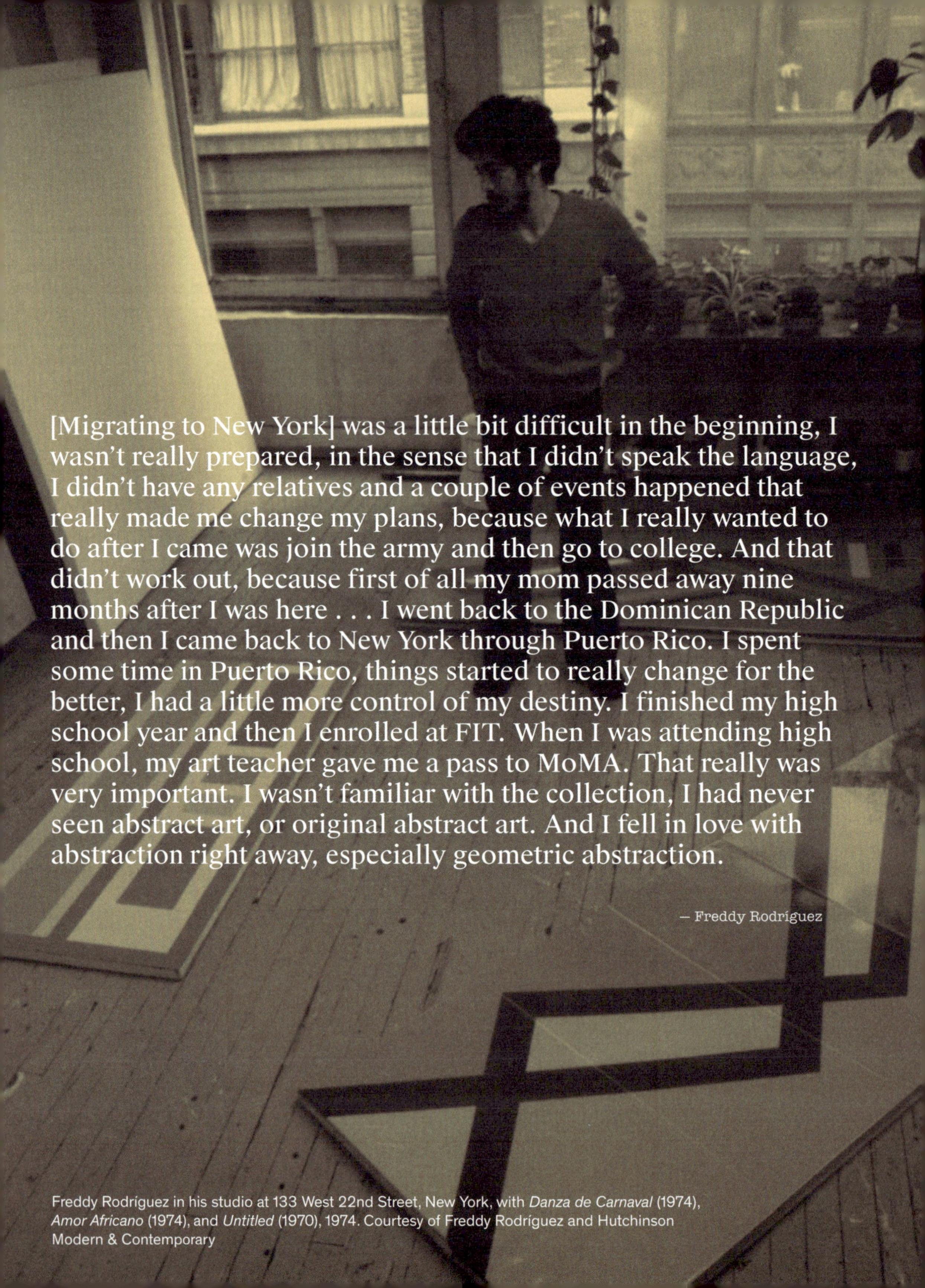

[Migrating to New York] was a little bit difficult in the beginning, I wasn't really prepared, in the sense that I didn't speak the language, I didn't have any relatives and a couple of events happened that really made me change my plans, because what I really wanted to do after I came was join the army and then go to college. And that didn't work out, because first of all my mom passed away nine months after I was here . . . I went back to the Dominican Republic and then I came back to New York through Puerto Rico. I spent some time in Puerto Rico, things started to really change for the better, I had a little more control of my destiny. I finished my high school year and then I enrolled at FIT. When I was attending high school, my art teacher gave me a pass to MoMA. That really was very important. I wasn't familiar with the collection, I had never seen abstract art, or original abstract art. And I fell in love with abstraction right away, especially geometric abstraction.

— Freddy Rodríguez

Freddy Rodríguez in his studio at 133 West 22nd Street, New York, with *Danza de Carnaval* (1974), *Amor Africano* (1974), and *Untitled* (1970), 1974. Courtesy of Freddy Rodríguez and Hutchinson Modern & Contemporary

New York is a mirage, a metropolis created by publicity. It looks like a stone made ship, anchored in the shadows, and whose skyscrapers I had to suffer for many long years. I live here out of masochism, almost to feed my desolation. And I would dare to say that its myth as a creative city is a thing of the past. It is a gigantic Narcissus in love with its own image reflected in the Hudson and East rivers, that does not listen to or observe the outside, because it is fooled by its own—rusty—blaze. Paris, on the contrary, is an essential city, profound. Their imagination left a crease, a mark, and life [is about] aesthetic pursuits. For the past few decades Paris had a tremendous decadence and the center of art seemed to shift toward the United States, but that was only an illusion.

— Omar Rayo

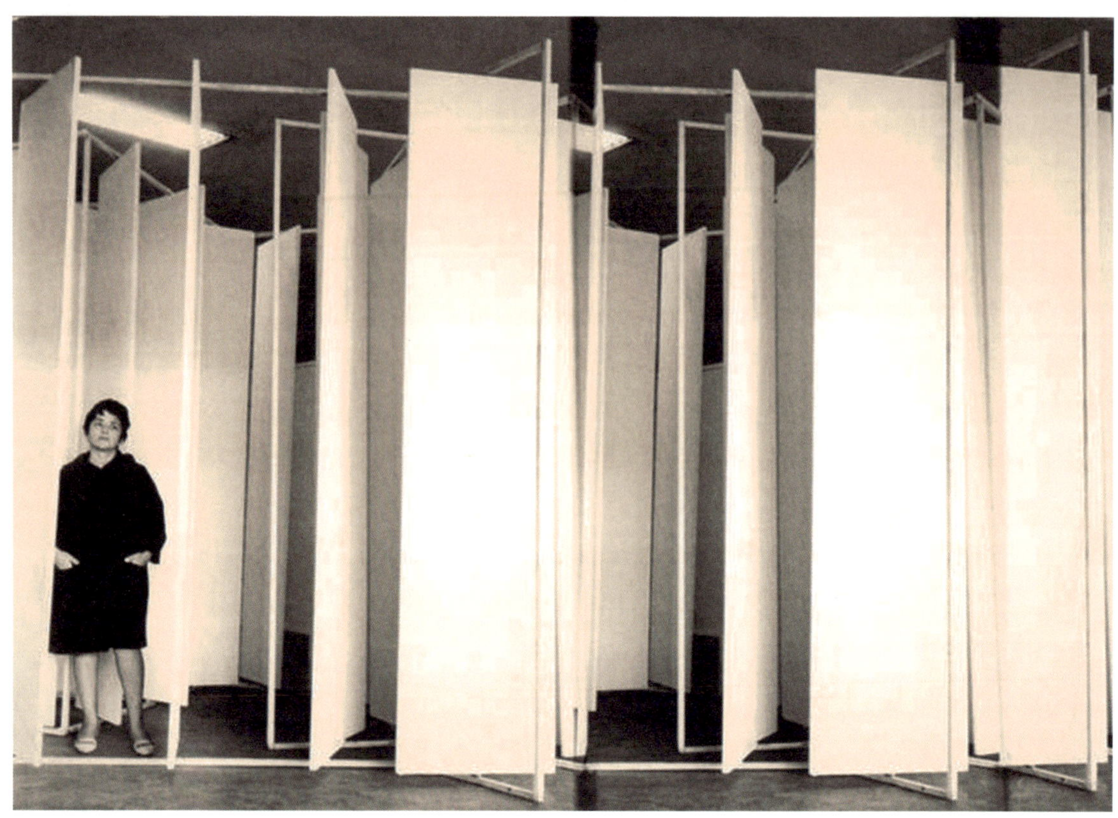

In New York I participated a lot in Conceptual art theory, although we could say that art was always conceptual . . . But in the modern conception of this trend the aesthetic pleasure is in the unification of the arts. Sometimes I've been represented by a photograph and a quote of my own. Not anymore with a picture or a sculpture. Sometimes I am represented by a letter or a recorded tape with a color or geometric background.

— Laura Márquez

Laura Márquez, *Puertas inútiles* (Useless doors), October 3, 1967.
Diario ABC Color. Courtesy of Exaedro

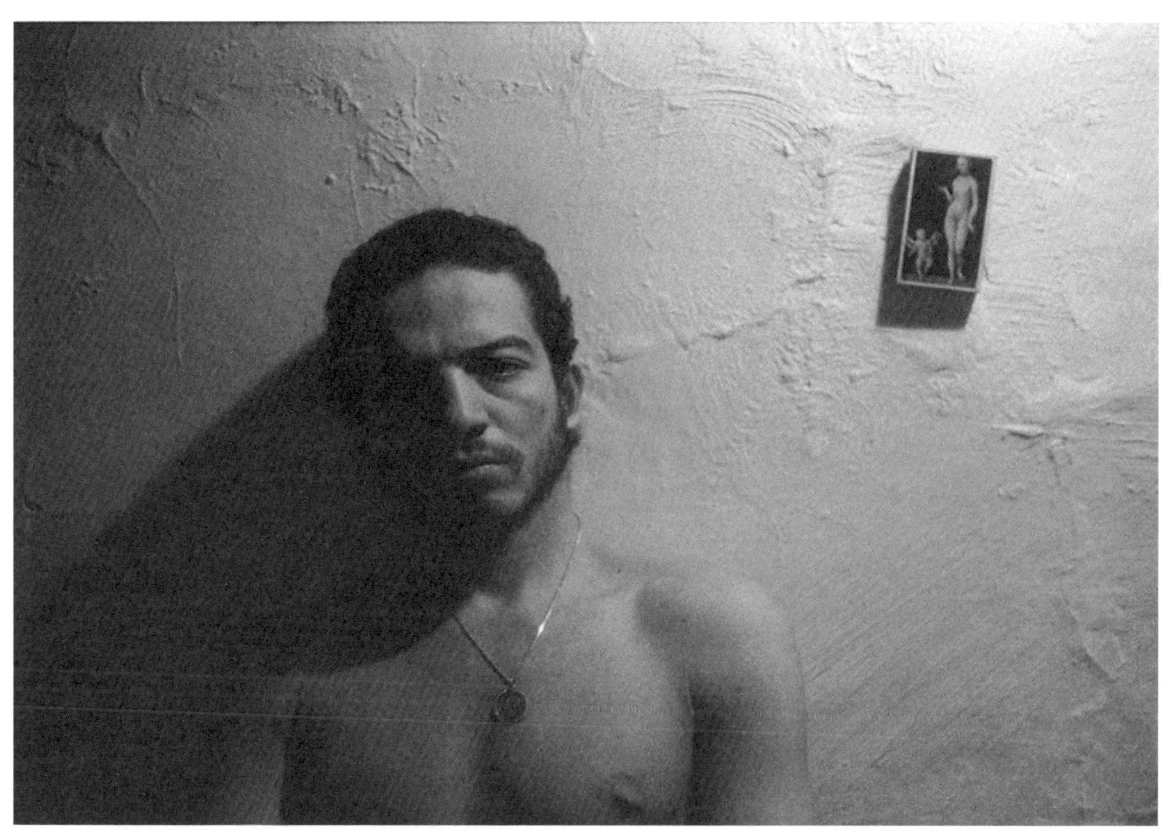

In 1965 I was in the sixth grade. . . . I had a lot of problems because I didn't speak English. Imagine. Leaving from Puerto Rico, where everything is green, and falling there in New York, which is a concrete jungle. My uncle used to tell me, "Men don't kiss. Children don't drink coffee." It was the first time I saw racism. . . . There is social upheaval. African Americans, Chicanos, in California, in Chicago. That experience of being aware at an early age of what was happening marked me forever. I have always cared about social issues, especially the anti-war movement. . . . When I got to school, whites would go to school to have "student deferment" from military service. I came to school as a challenge.

— Máximo Rafael Colón

Máximo Rafael Colón, *Self-Portrait*, 1974. Courtesy of the artist

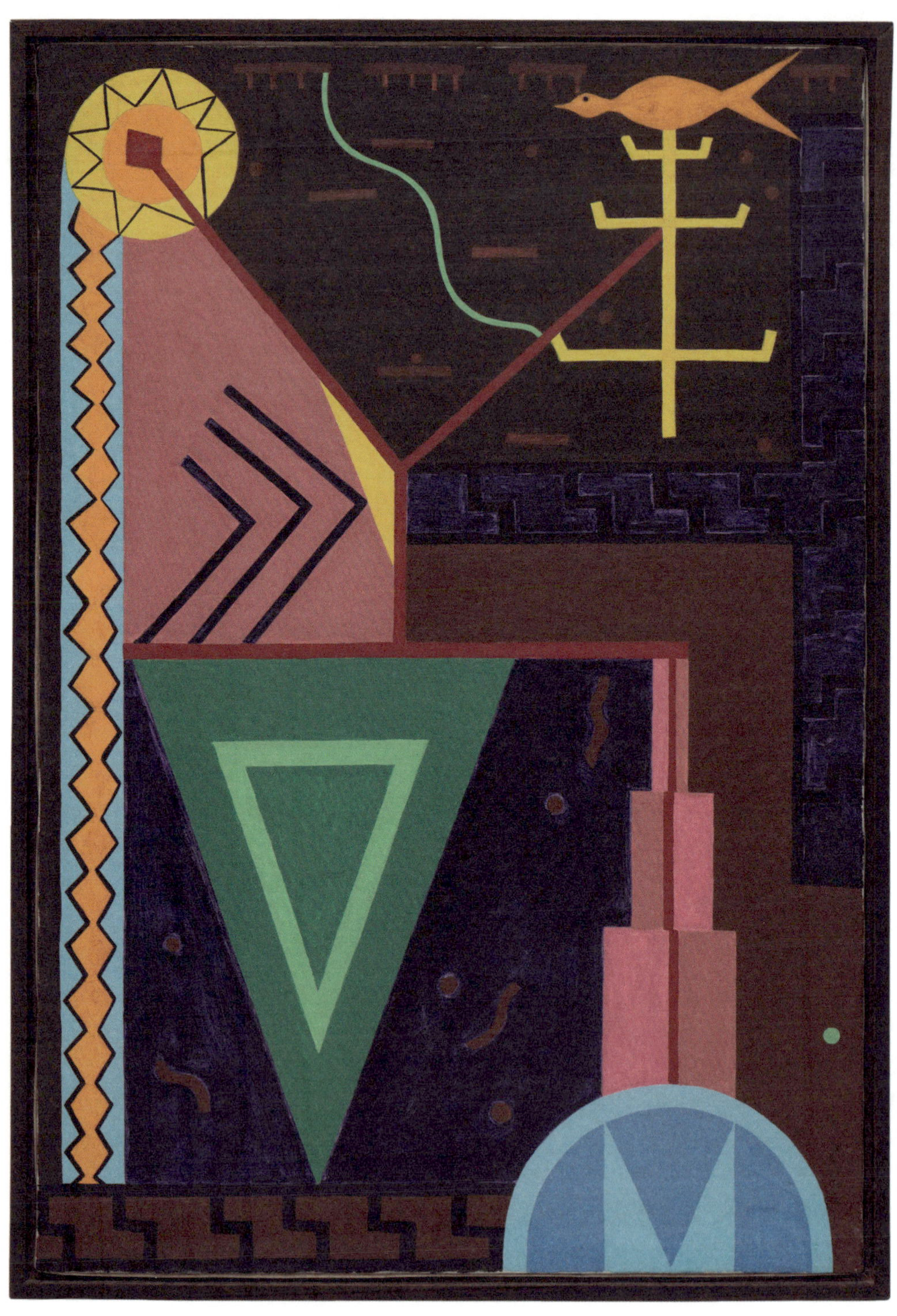

Abdias do Nascimento, *Composição no. 1* (Composition no. 1), 1971. Black Art Museum/ IPEAFRO, Rio de Janeiro. Courtesy of Fortes D'Aloia & Gabriel, São Paulo/Rio de Janeiro and Tanya Bonakdar Gallery, New York/Los Angeles

I have said, and I repeat, I have always been an exile in my own country, I do not have a “homeland.” Rather, I have Africa. Brazilian society refused my African roots, wanted to cut them off, tore them out by force, to make me uprooted. I had to hurl my roots from top to bottom, in a conscious effort, reaching the air like certain plants do. It was not the United States that created my exile. On the contrary: here I was able to express myself much better and continue to do what I was already doing, in another context.

A big difference is that, here in the United States, the value of my work was recognized, something I cannot deny. I left Brazil when I was fifty-four years old, always as an outlaw . . . . I arrived in the United States at the end of ’68 to stay for a month. I had started painting at that time, in my apartment in Copacabana. A department at Columbia University bought one of my paintings for a thousand dollars. A real joy. Not so much for the money itself, which I wasn’t counting on, but for the recognition. Then the Yale School of Drama invited me as a visiting lecturer. No theater school in Brazil has ever thought about my existence. Then Wesleyan University invited me as a visiting fellow, visiting professor. The next was the State University of New York at Buffalo offering me the position of associate professor in the department of Puerto Rican studies; within two years, they promoted me to full professor, with tenure.

— Abdias do Nascimento

The Loft and Living in the City

Carmen Beuchat, *Two Not One*, 1975. Carmen Beuchat Archive

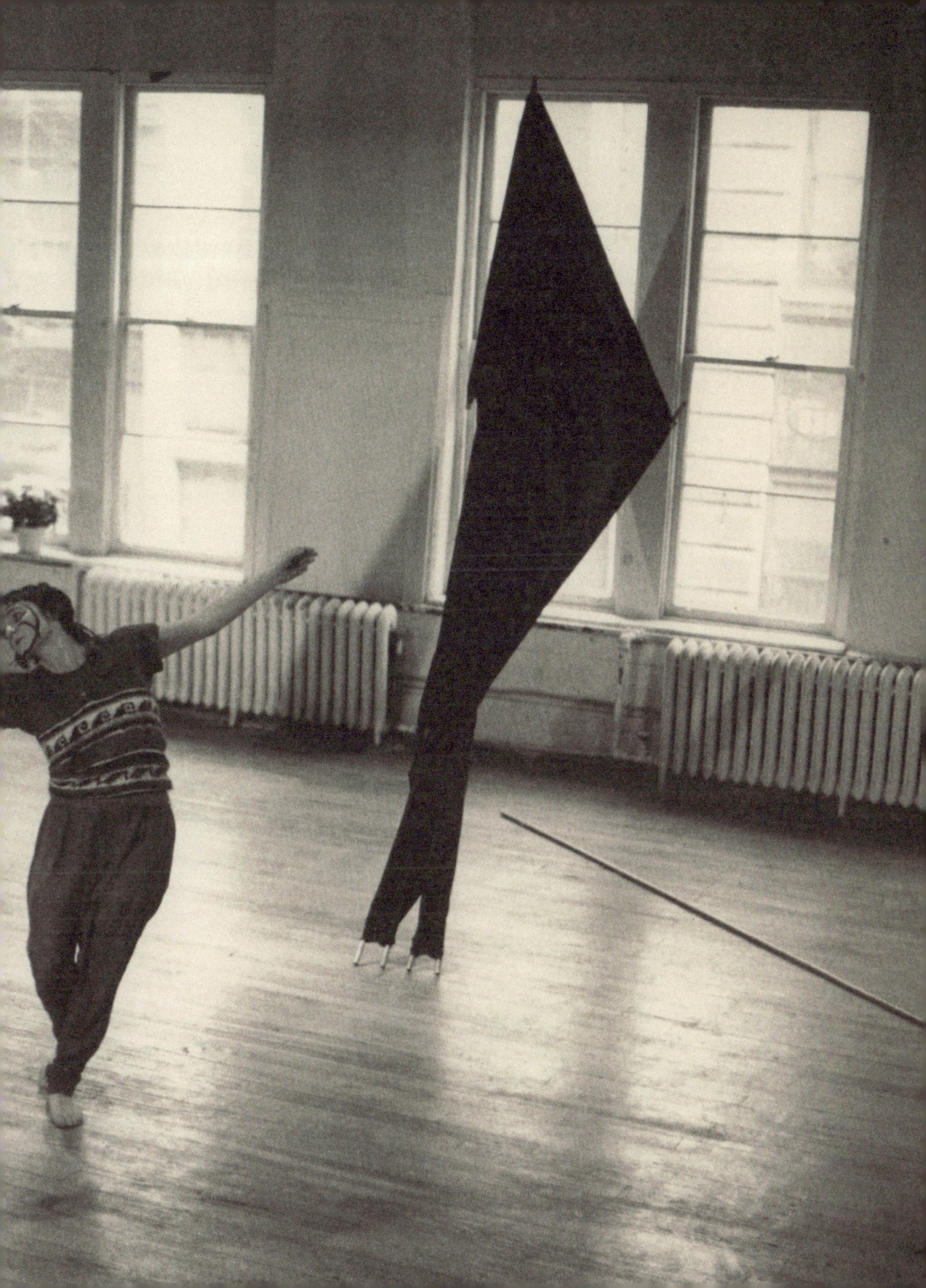

Many artists lived and worked in lofts located in Lower Manhattan, an area that was perceived as unsafe but was affordable for artists who came to the city without formal jobs or gallery representation. Entire buildings were inhabited by artists from all over the world who organized exhibitions and performances. In spaces of living and working, they interrelated art and life, addressing ideas of community, protection, precarity, and leisure. From Hélio Oiticica's Loft 4 to cooperative living experiences, Latin American artists joined their local and international peers in turning Lower Manhattan into a center of art experimentation in the 1960s.

Carmen Beuchat, *Steal with Style* (also known as *Steal with Style: We Are the One Who Sits at the Right and the One Who Sits at the Left*), with Irene Soler, Kei Takei, and Juliet Shen, The Kitchen, New York, January 1978. Carmen Beuchat Archive

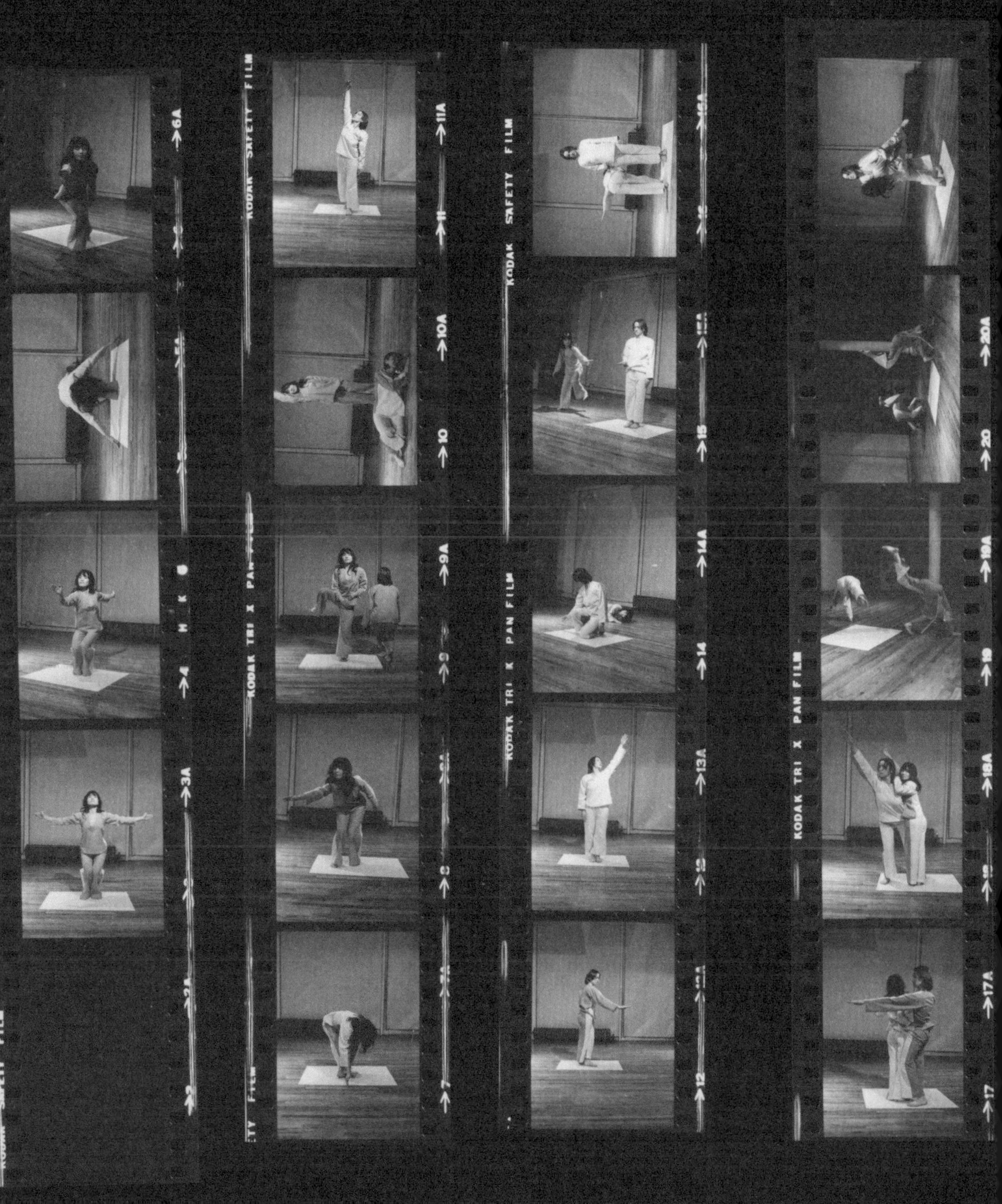

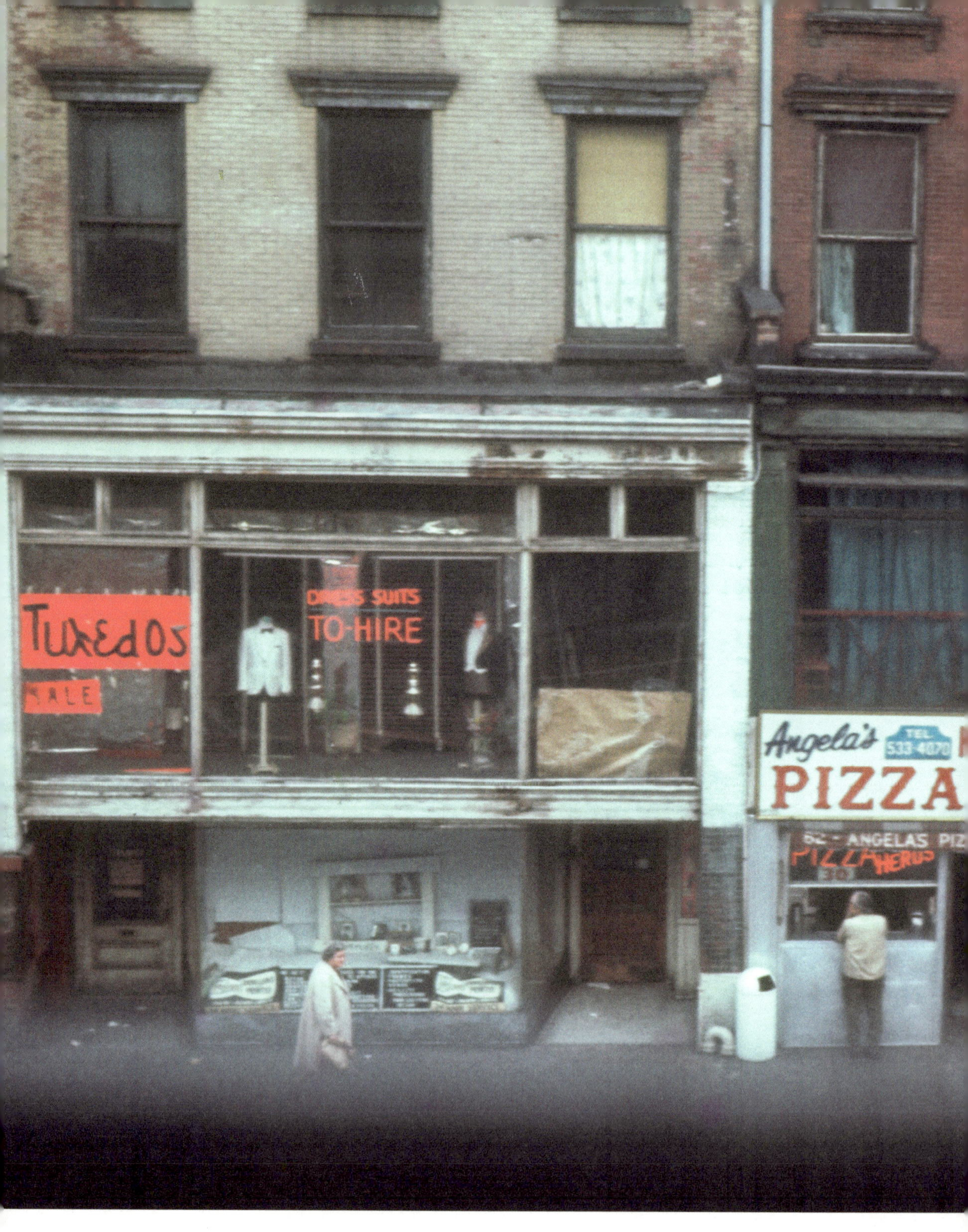

Andreas Valentin, *View from the Window of Loft 4 Overlooking Second Avenue*, 1972.
Courtesy of the artist

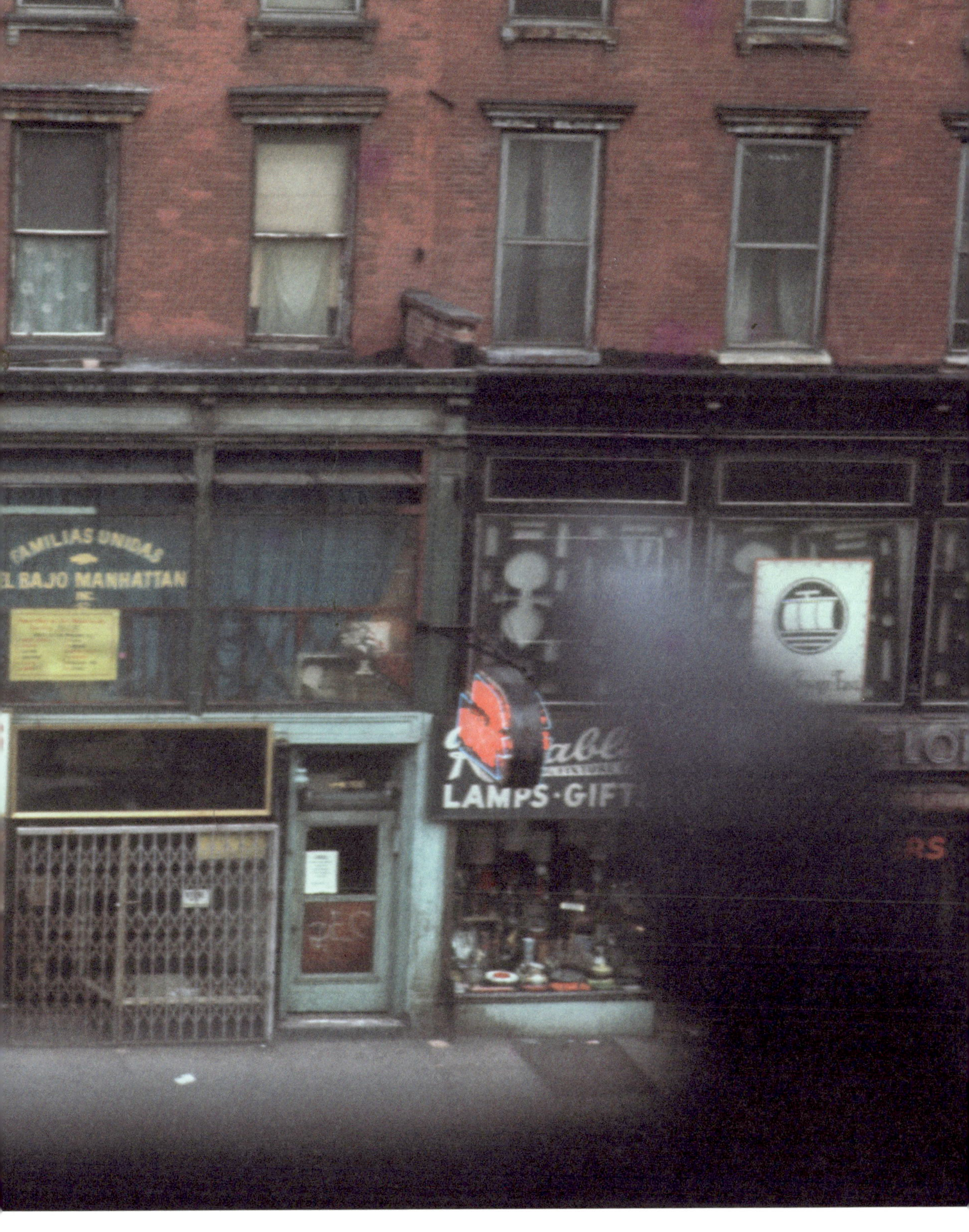
FAMILIAS UNIDAS
EL BAJO MANHATTAN
LAMPS · GIFT

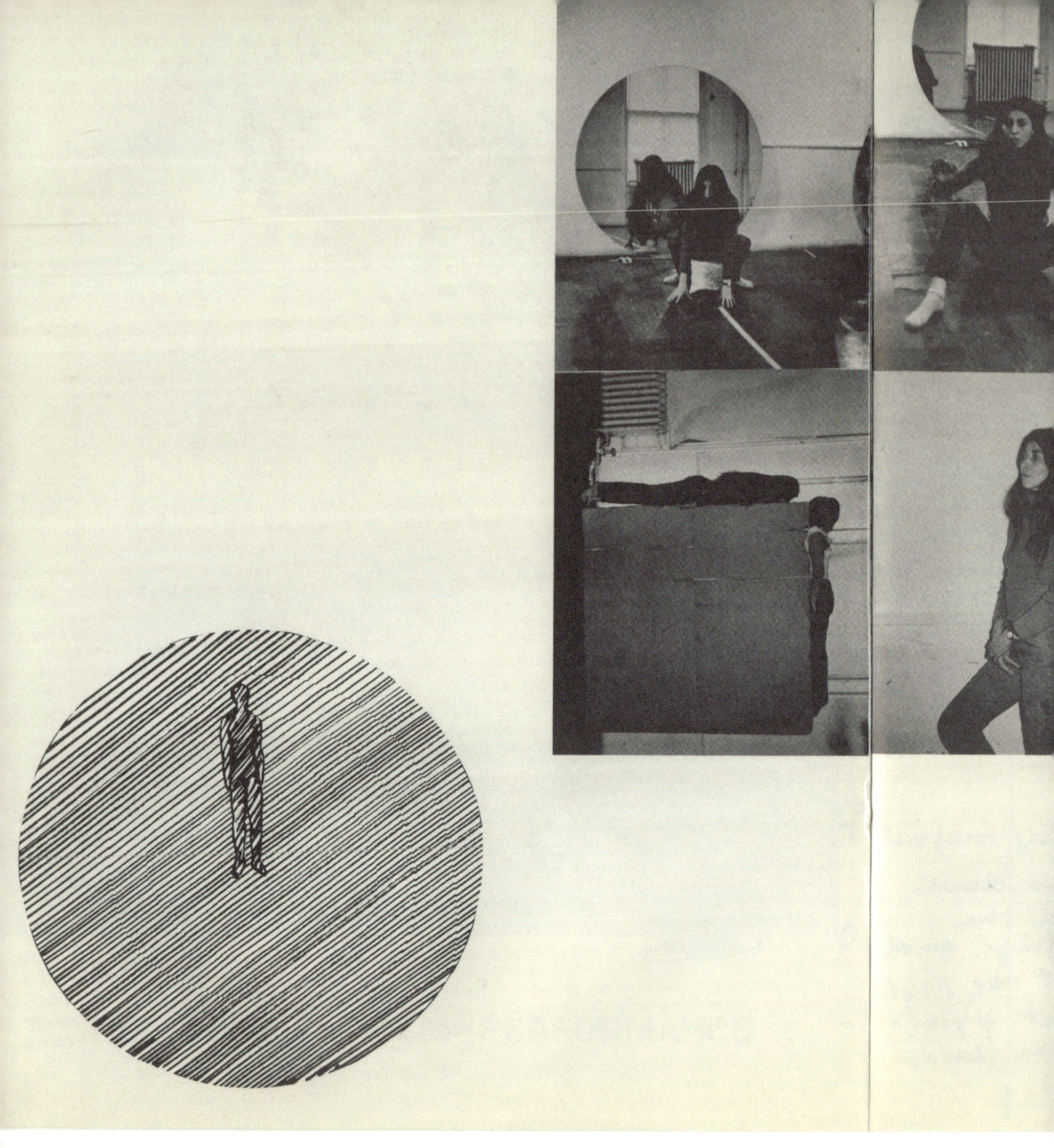

Catalogue for Sylvia Palacios Whitman, *Going*, Trisha Brown's studio, 541 Broadway, 1974. Sylvia Palacios Whitman Archive

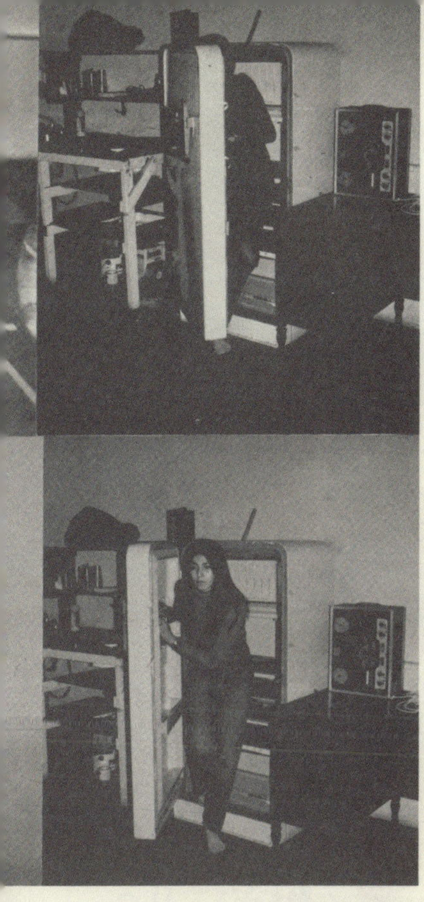

I never had an enormous studio but lived in lofts where you slept right next to the pieces that you were working on. In the bathroom there were always drawings on the floor, I just lived like that—like everyone at that time.

[T]he key venues for performances were the same for all of us: the Kitchen, the Idea Warehouse, and, once in a while, the Whitney downtown. Someone would call us, and we would do something downtown. And there were all these tiny, tiny places that had to be cleaned before getting anybody in there—lofts, mostly.

— Sylvia Palacios Whitman

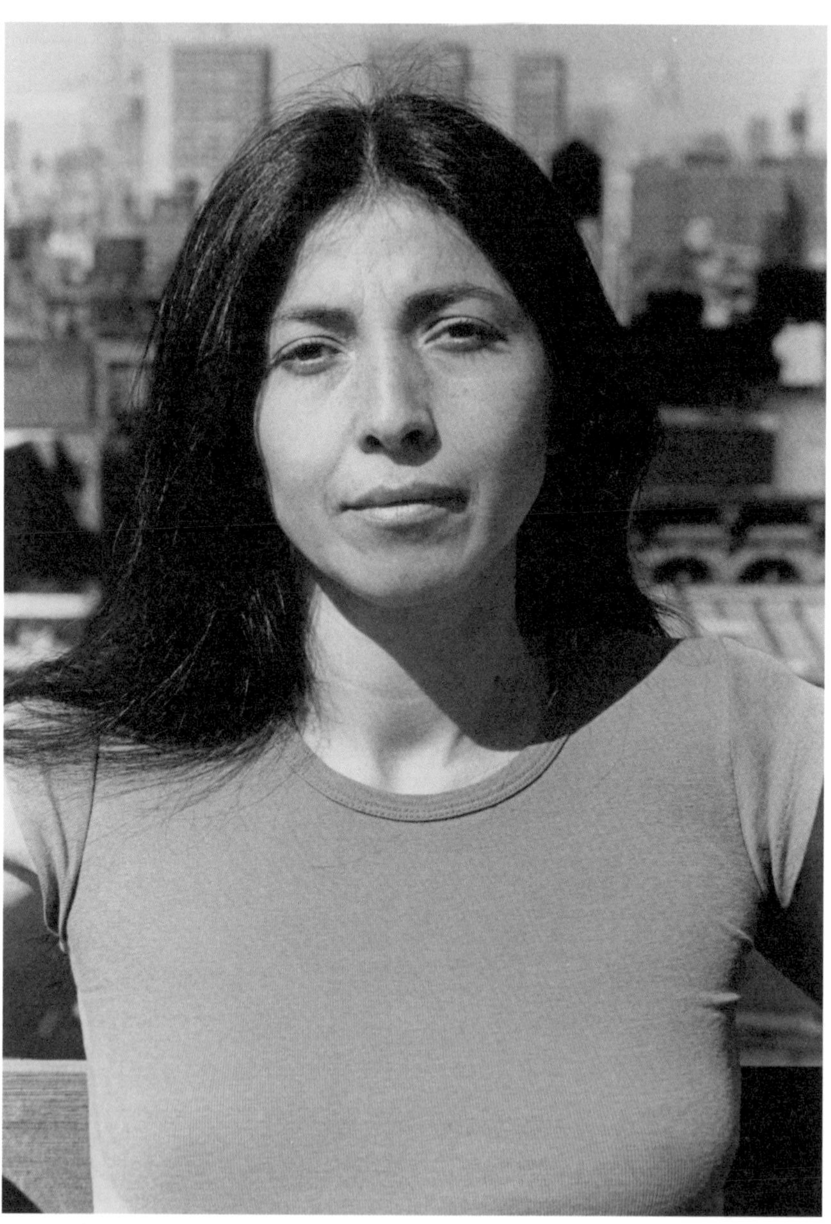

Sylvia Palacios Whitman on the rooftop of her White Street apartment, 1972. Sylvia Palacios Whitman Archive

We didn't have a penny when we arrived in New York. We didn't know anybody, and I didn't speak a word of English–my first husband [Chilean artist Enrique Castro-Cid] only spoke a tiny bit. My grandmother sent me what would now probably be $100, and I went out to buy something delicious or special. Then I saw this monkey in a window, and I walked in and I said to the lady, "How much is that monkey?" She told me, and I said, "Oh, that's too bad. I only have $100." I started to walk out, and she said, "Wait, wait, you can have it for $100." I took the monkey home to the Lower East Side where we were living in this tiny little place on Avenue A or B. I called this one Efraín. When I took the monkey out of the little box they had given me, Enrique said, "Why did you get a monkey? Now we are all going to starve." We were practically starving, and I thought he was right and this poor monkey was going to starve with us. Actually, because of the monkey we had good food for a while. I would take him out on the street and people would give me bananas. They thought it was for the monkey, but of course it was for us, too. Eventually one night the bar wouldn't give Enrique any more drinks–he liked to drink quite a bit–but that night he had to pay, so he took the monkey and gave it to the bartender in exchange for drinks.

– Sylvia Palacios Whitman

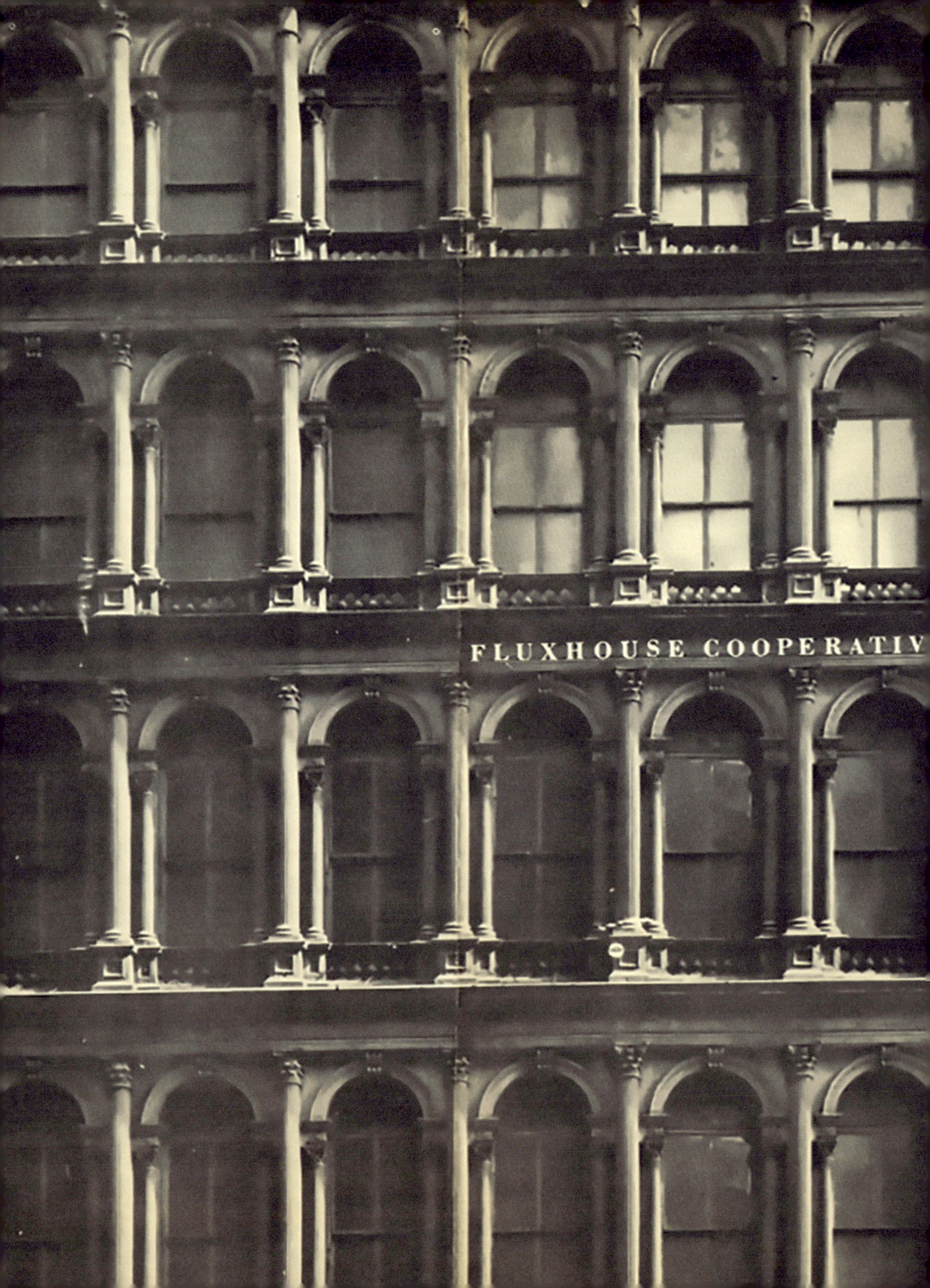
FLUXHOUSE COOPERATIV

You could purchase a loft from [George Maciunas], but without any legal documents to prove you owned the place. So it was a cash transaction, very friendly, and very much against the system . . . The whole concept was complete anarchy. No zoning. No guarantees of any kind. You gave money to somebody without officially owning anything and knowing that you were living there illegally. Today it's a big residential center, but in those days, it was a no-man's land. Maciunas would ask artists like Philip Glass, Lee Lozano, or different members of Fluxus to do the maintenance work. They borrowed tools from him and did the work without any expertise or knowledge of the building–no architectural drawings, nothing.

– Jaime Davidovich

Exterior view of a building converted by the Fluxhouse Cooperative Building Project at 80 Wooster Street, New York, 1966. The Gilbert and Lila Silverman Fluxus Collection Gift, Archives of the Museum of Modern Art, New York

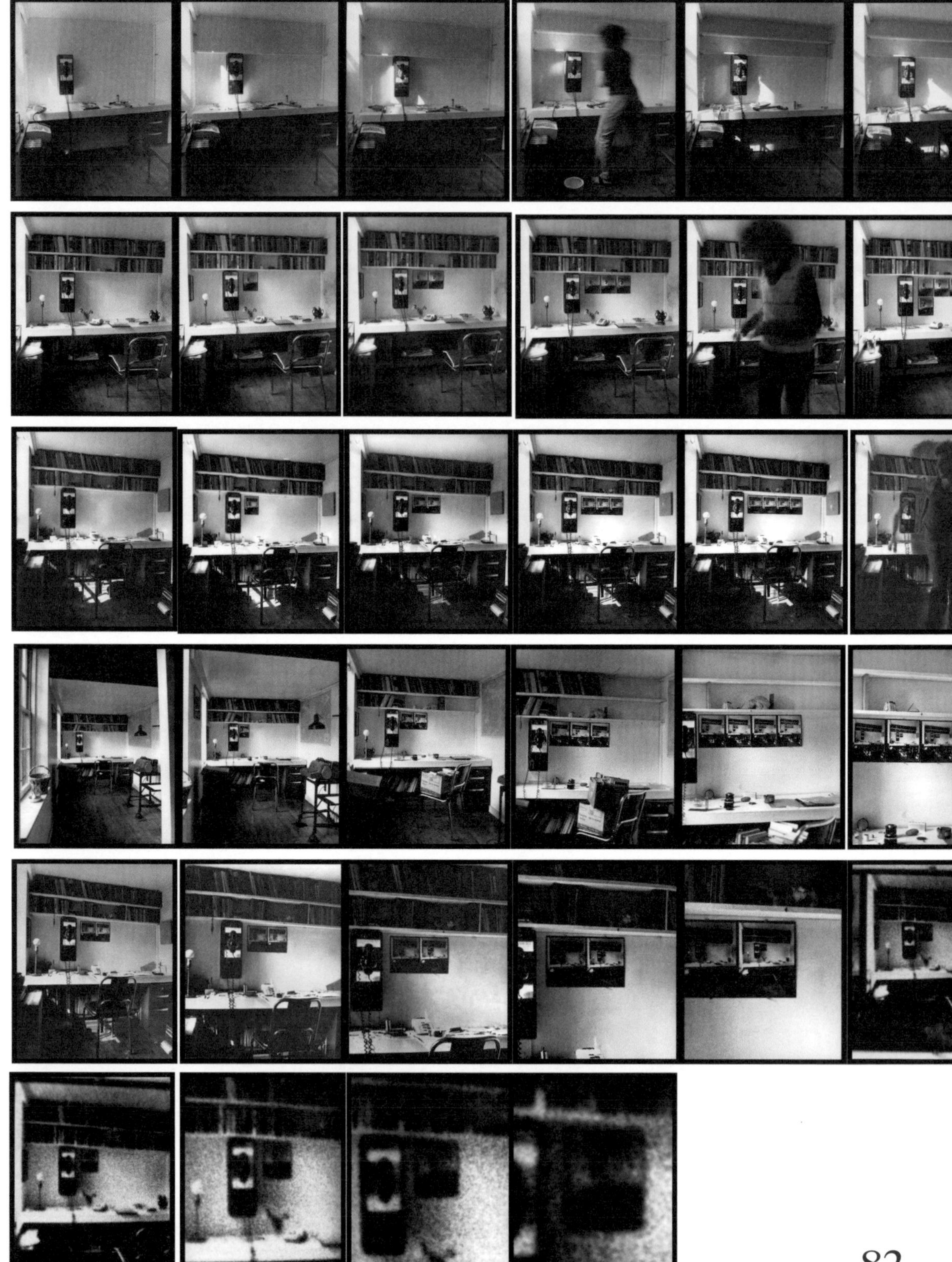

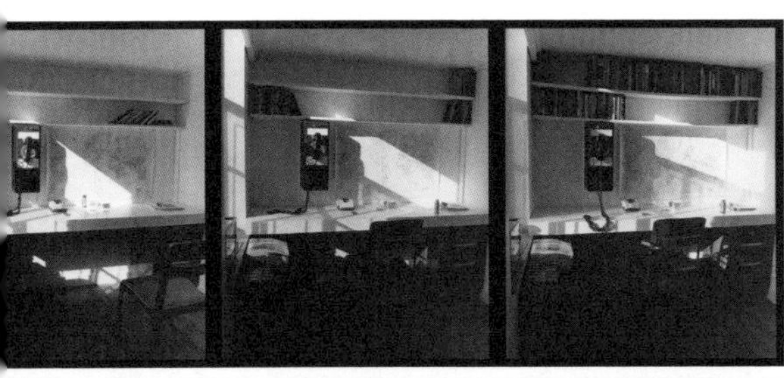

Leandro Katz, *S(h)elf Portrait*, 1972.
Gonzalo Parodi Collection, Miami

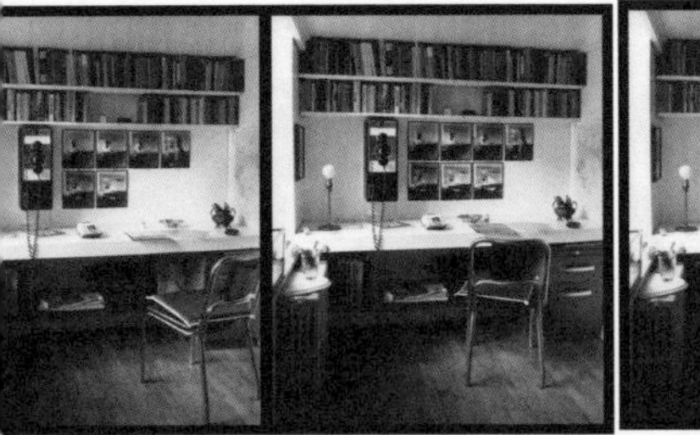
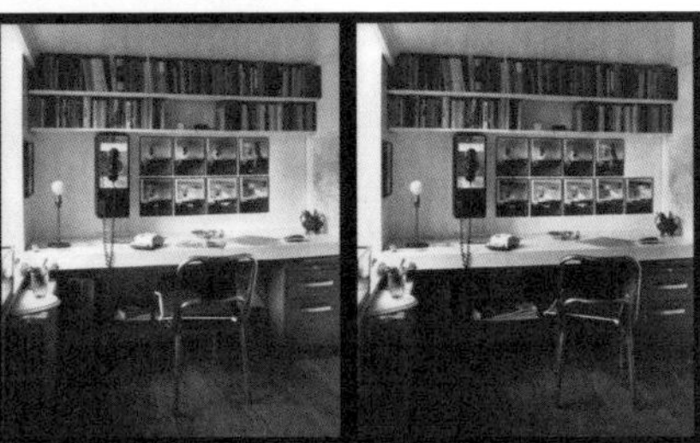
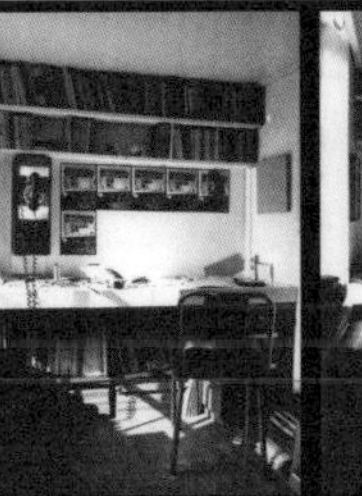
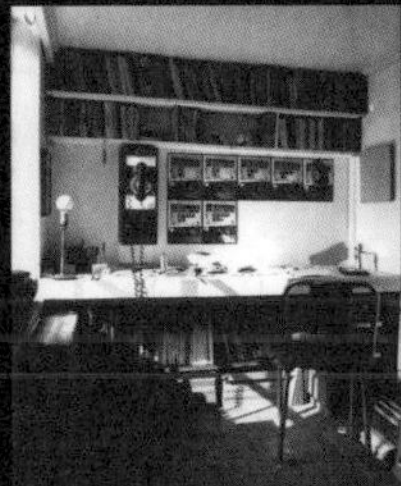
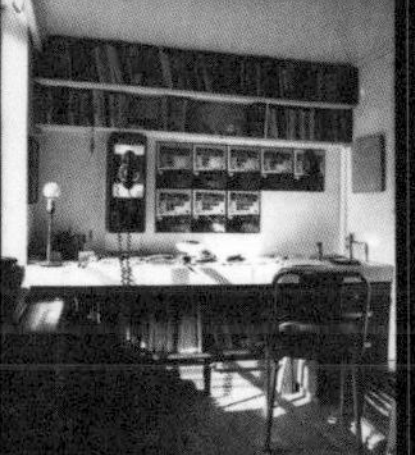
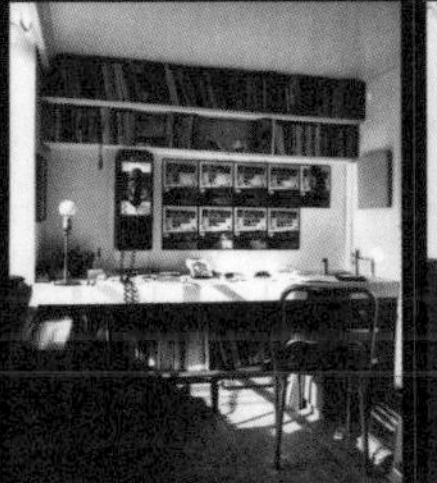
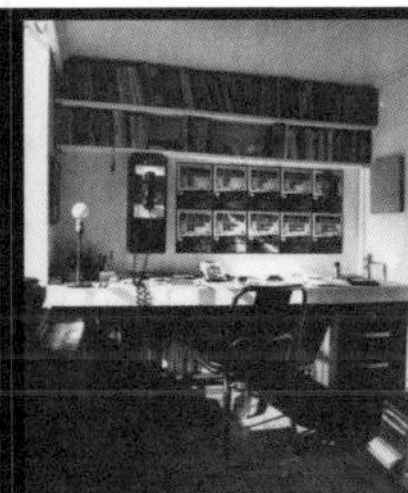
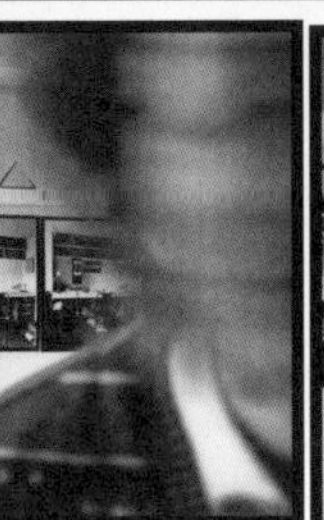
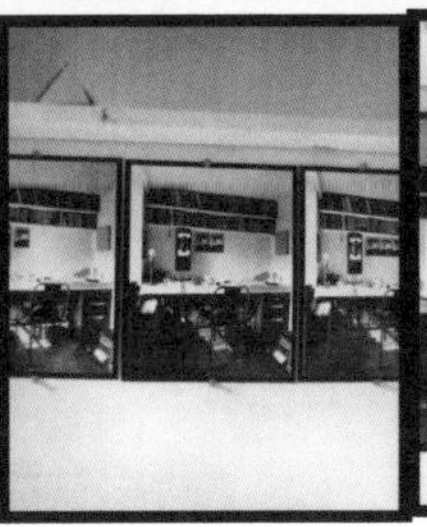
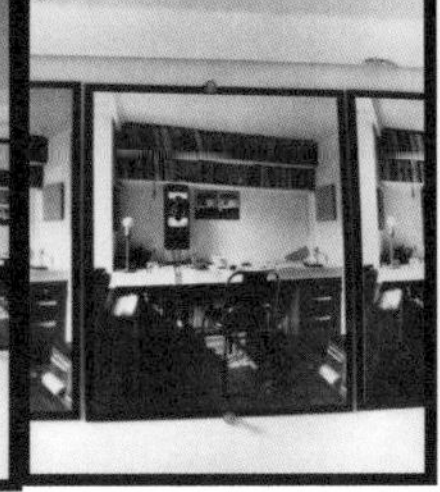
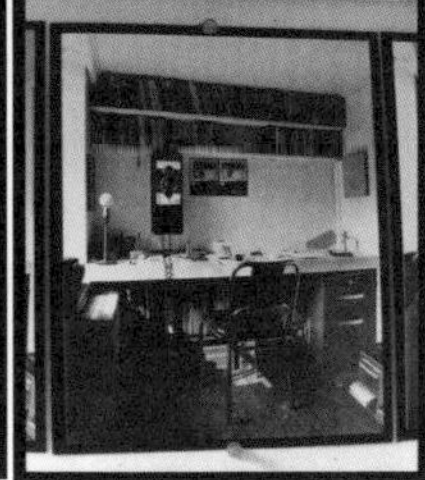

In his photo-installation *S(h)elf Portrait* (1972), Leandro Katz recorded the passing of time and used images of his room as self-portraits. From the fifty sequential photographs that register the construction of a workspace in his New York loft, four capture the artist as a phantasmagorical appearance, his body or face erupting accidentally into the photograph while escaping the frame.

Suddenly word would get around that Jack Smith was giving a performance in a loft at midnight. You'd get to some party in an empty loft where there was only music, beer, and mattresses on the floor, and as you entered you'd see people screwing on them, just like that! That was the climate of New York at that time . . . At the end of the sixties there was an environmental reason for the emergence of the lofts: they were forbidding small industries to stay in the city because of the pollution they created. The lofts were located toward the south, in what would later be called NoHo and SoHo, neighborhoods full of buildings with light industries that started to be evacuated and were empty. And there we artists started to find extremely cheap studios because the owners of those buildings were desperate to get anyone to rent those properties. I rented the loft I was to stay in for years, at 4th Street and Lafayette. It was a vast open space, with two small bathrooms, one that said ladies and the other that said gentlemen, two poky little rooms that had been for the workers. And electric outlets in the ceilings for the sewing machines, the tools, holes in the floor . . . It had been a sweatshop.

— Leandro Katz

Leandro Katz, *S(h)elf Portrait* (detail), 1972.
Gonzalo Parodi Collection, Miami

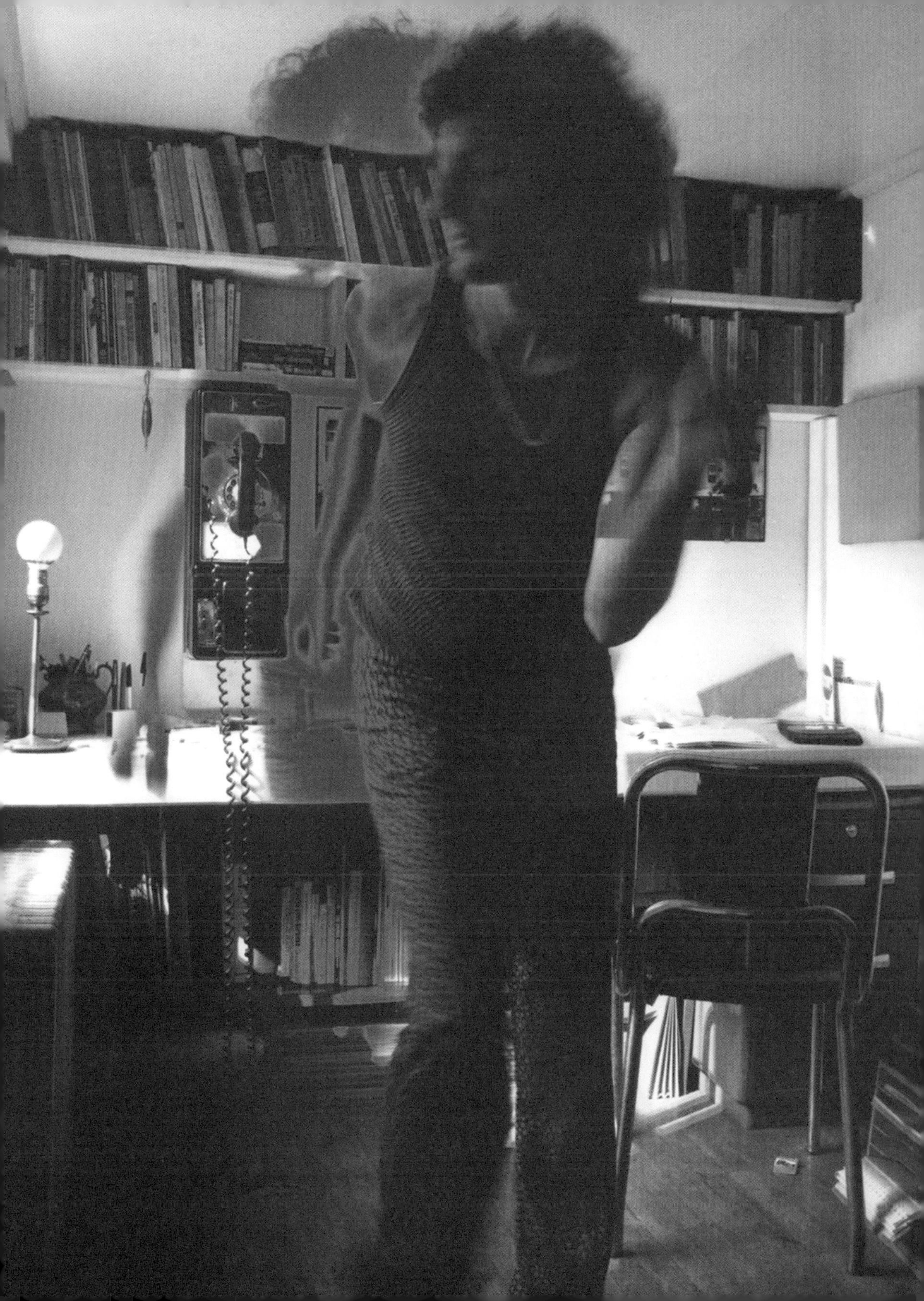

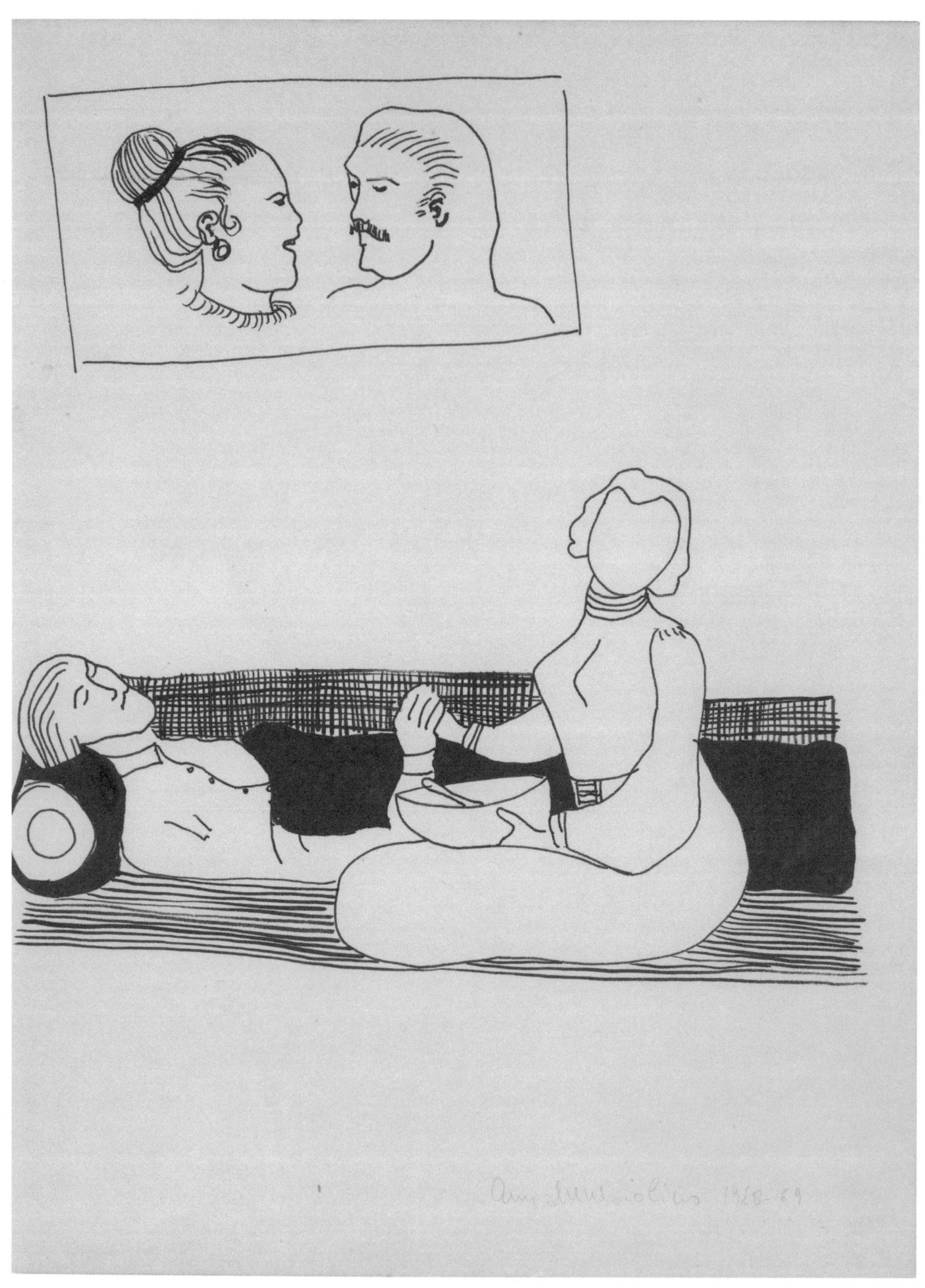

Anna Maria Maiolino, untitled drawing from the series *Entre Pausas* (Between pauses), 1968. Courtesy of the artist and Hauser & Wirth

Our loft is on the third floor, at 250 Bowery, almost on the corner of Spring Street. . . . I've often worried: What should I say to the children about the constant presence of groups of drunks staggering along the Bowery, their arms wound around one another to hold themselves up? . . . Even when unseen, the drunks are present. From a distance, we hear them talking loudly and disconnectedly. Their presence is also announced by the countless thin streams of urine which freeze in the winter, looking like veins in high relief on the asphalt. One more year left before returning to Brazil . . .

– Anna Maria Maiolino

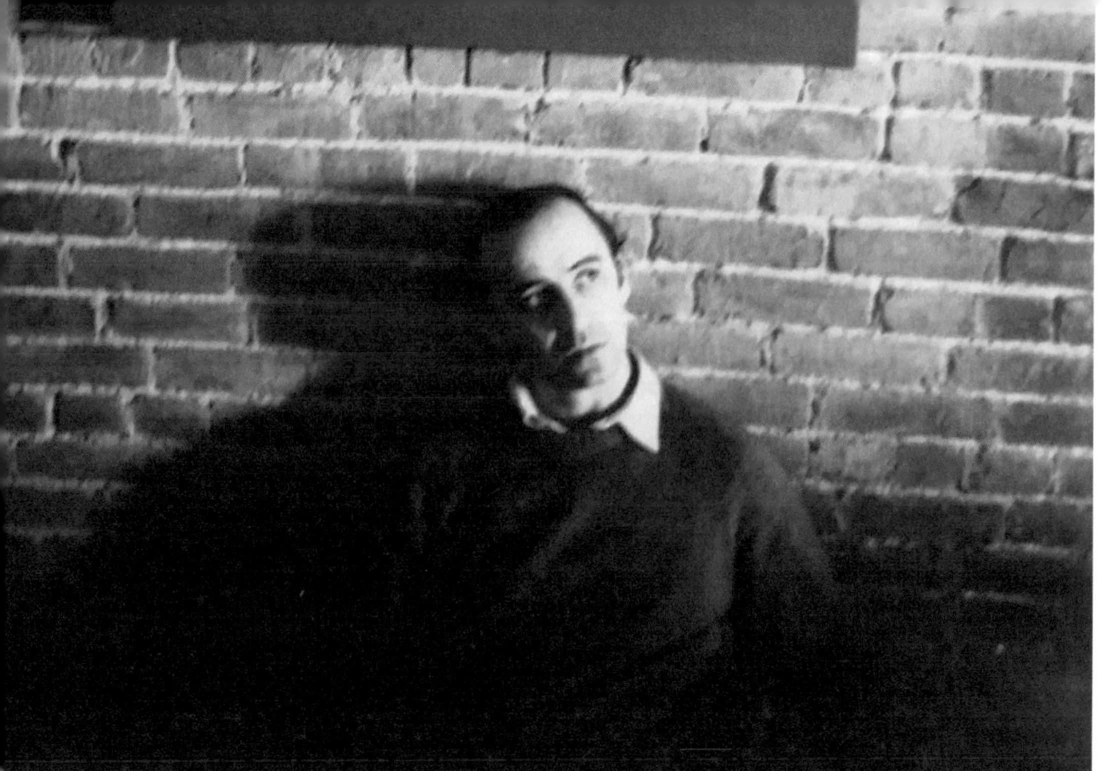

Alejandro Puente in his studio, 46 Grand Street, 1969. Estate of the artist

[Alejandro Puente and I] arrived in New York with a difference of months, we arrived almost at the same time. He arrived with the Guggenheim Fellowship and I arrived with a little money after selling everything, but the money soon began to evaporate. The crazy thing is that I had gone with my wife and two daughters. And the following year my wife became pregnant and in '68 my third daughter was born in New York.

— César Paternosto

→ César Paternosto in his studio, 248 Lafayette Street, New York, 1971. Institute for Studies on Latin American Art (ISLAA) Library and Archives

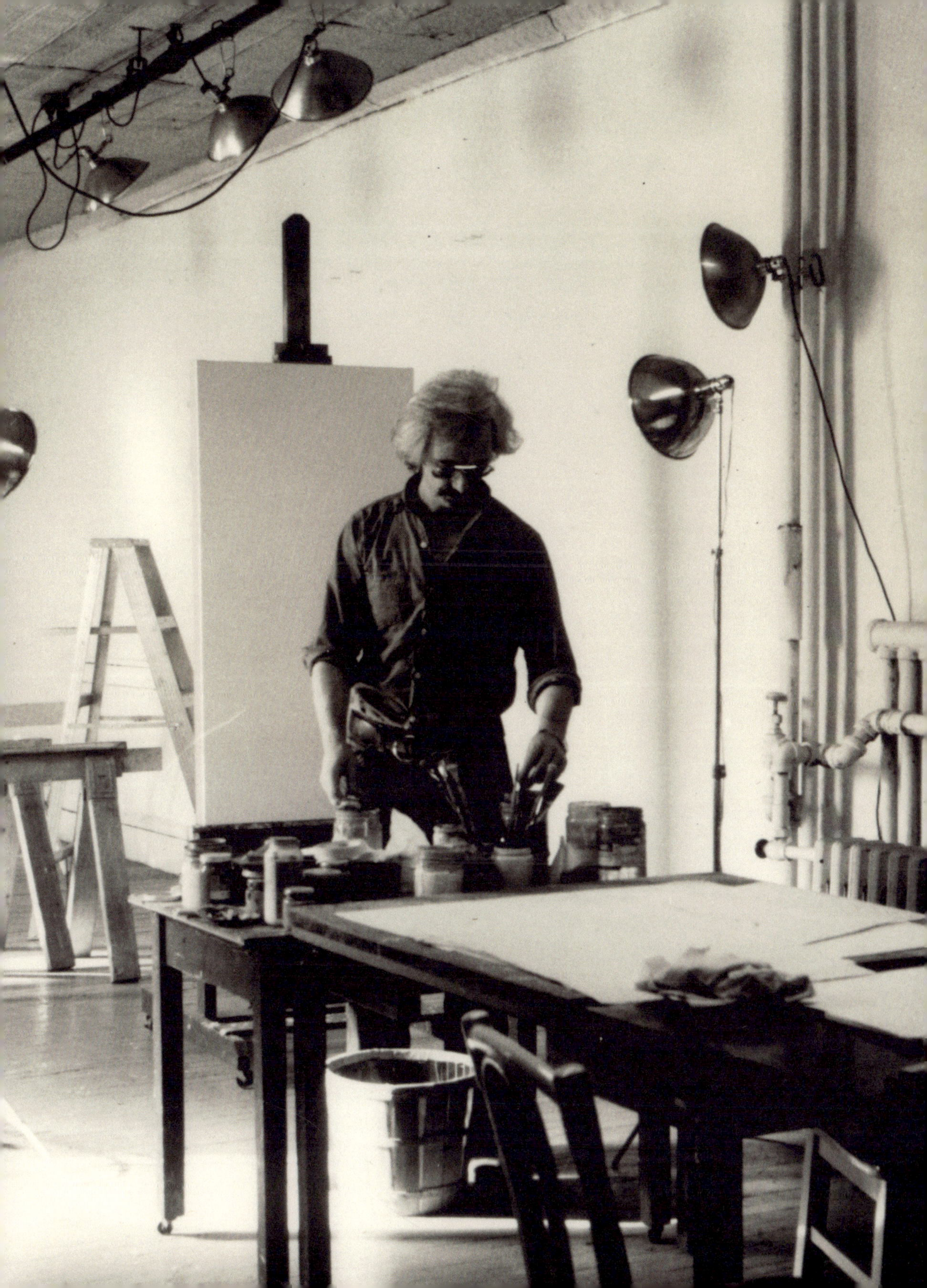

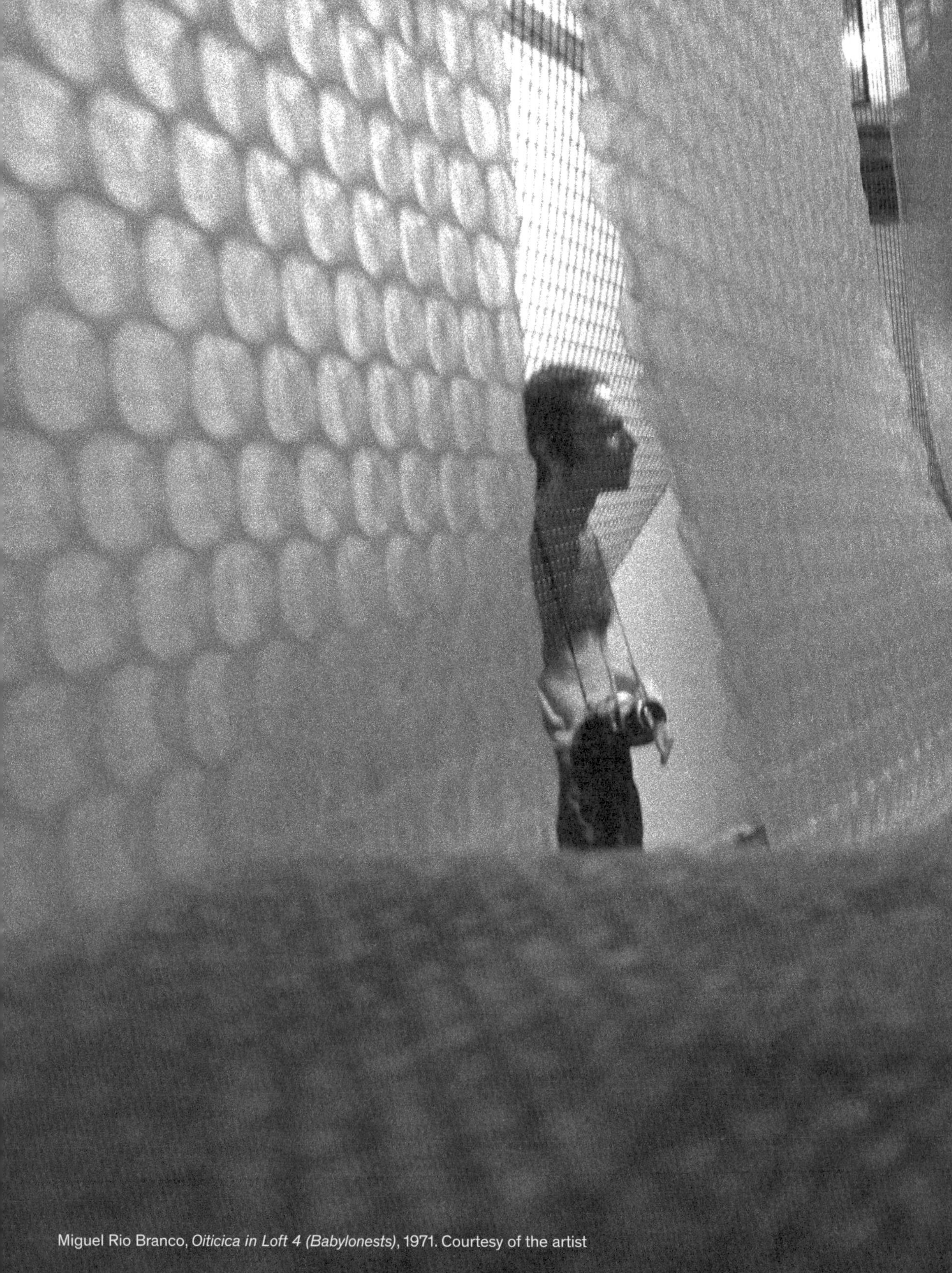

Miguel Rio Branco, *Oiticica in Loft 4 (Babylonests)*, 1971. Courtesy of the artist

The indefatigable lever or permanent spring that drove him nonstop into new orbits of experience made HO realize that the BABYLONEST (Babylon Nest) of Second Avenue was a compact cosmopolitan city. Kindergarten, playground, laboratory, motel, drug spot, a university campus contained in an environmental capsule. [Hélio's] NEST had a television and remote control zapping nonstop, newspapers, radios, recorder, cassette tapes, books, magazines, slide projector, viewer, boxes of labeled slides, paper tissue boxes, bottles and disposable cups, straws, agate cut into blades, etc. . . . NESTS and their archipelago structures neither solid nor linear or insular: like a television that transcoded the most secluded corner of private life into windows open to others and to the world: WORLD-SHELTER.

— Waly Salomão

During his time in the city, Hélio Oiticica began creating works inside his own apartment, which he called "world-shelter." Though a symptom of the difficulties he faced in exhibiting work in the mainstream art world, it also allowed him to develop more intimate practices, including writing, and transforming his own apartment into a site for experimental artworks. Waly Salomão, a close friend and collaborator, was a Brazilian poet who lived in New York in the 1970s. This excerpt is taken from an experimental book Salomão wrote on Oiticica, which includes biographical information and memories of the artist.

i have talked too much, as always; today is quite hot here; polluted as always; i live side by side with the fillmore east, and you can't imagine the freaky scenes going on on the sidewalk; thanks god i am on the fourth floor, of no easy reach; as it gets hotter, incredible things starts around this block (these blocks, to be more precise): east village is no joke; i am used to it now, but you can't fool around too much, specially during the night: everybody has guns or dogs to defend themselves from unexpected or expected attacks.

— Hélio Oiticica

Miguel Rio Branco, *Hélio Oiticica in Babylonests*, 1971. Courtesy of the artist

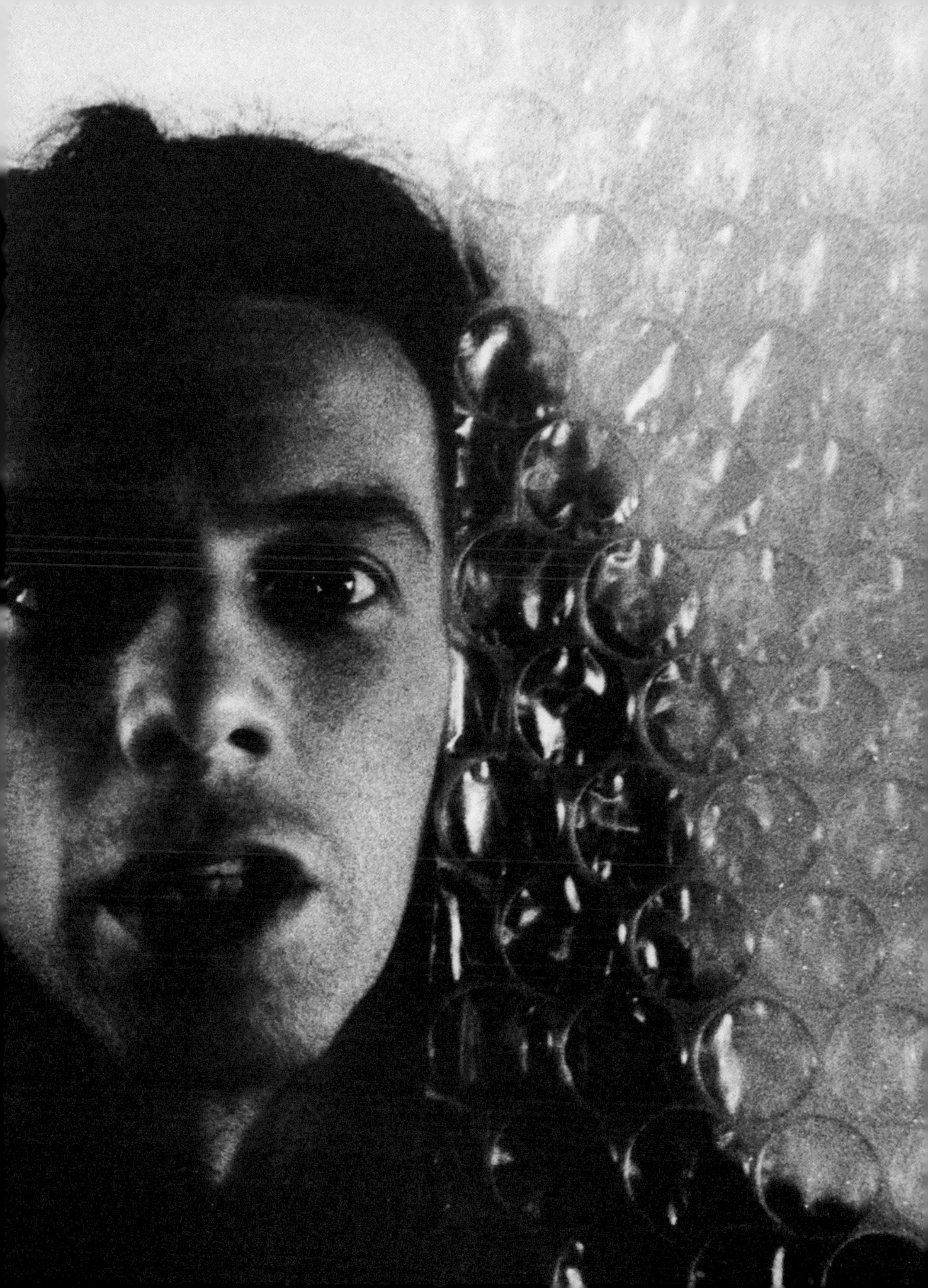

Regina Vater, *Cinematic Still for Mayakovsky*, 1974.
Galeria Jaqueline Martins

Views of the City

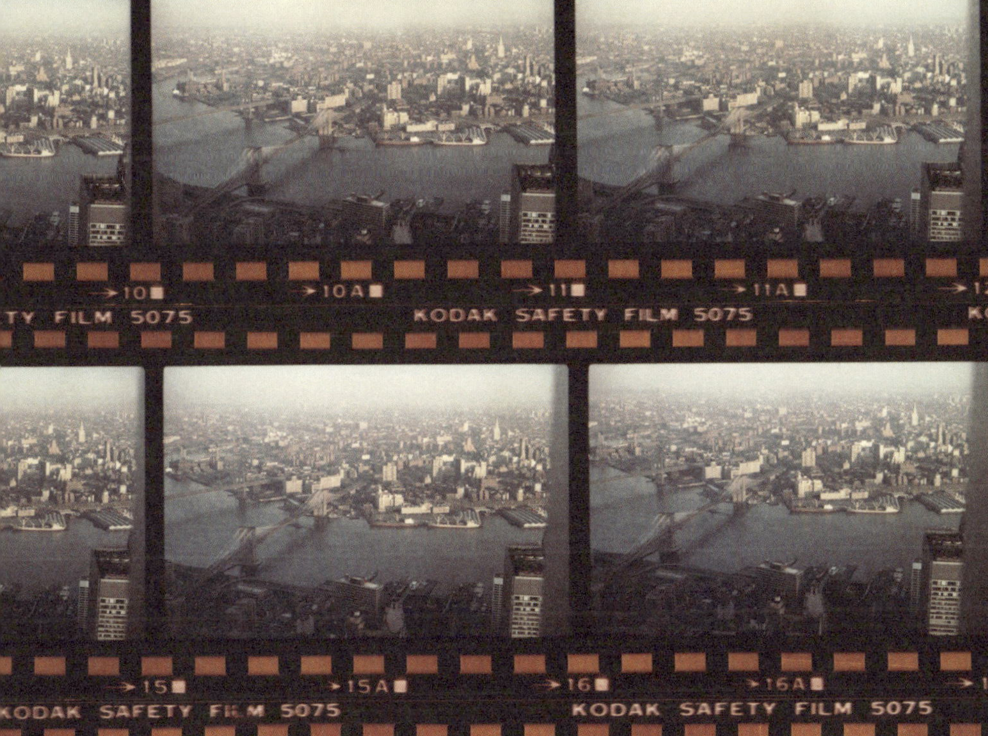

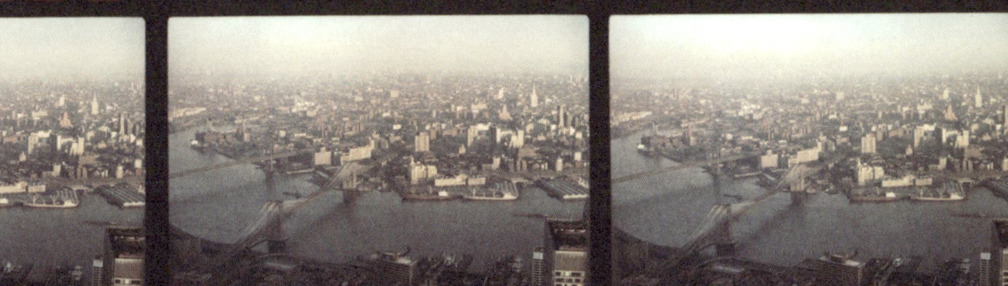

Conceptual and realistic depictions of the urban environment—like Leandro Katz's representation of the impossible experience of a sunset and the view of the horizon line in New York—point to the complex relationship these city dwellers established with their new home. From spectacular bird's-eye views of the city that try to grasp its monumentality to the collection and depiction of urban waste as a diaristic practice, Latin American artists captured the metropolitan landscape to reflect on capitalist accumulation, consumption, and the degradation of nature.

Leandro Katz, *Study for the Transcode Series*, 1978. Private collection

HEADQUARTERS

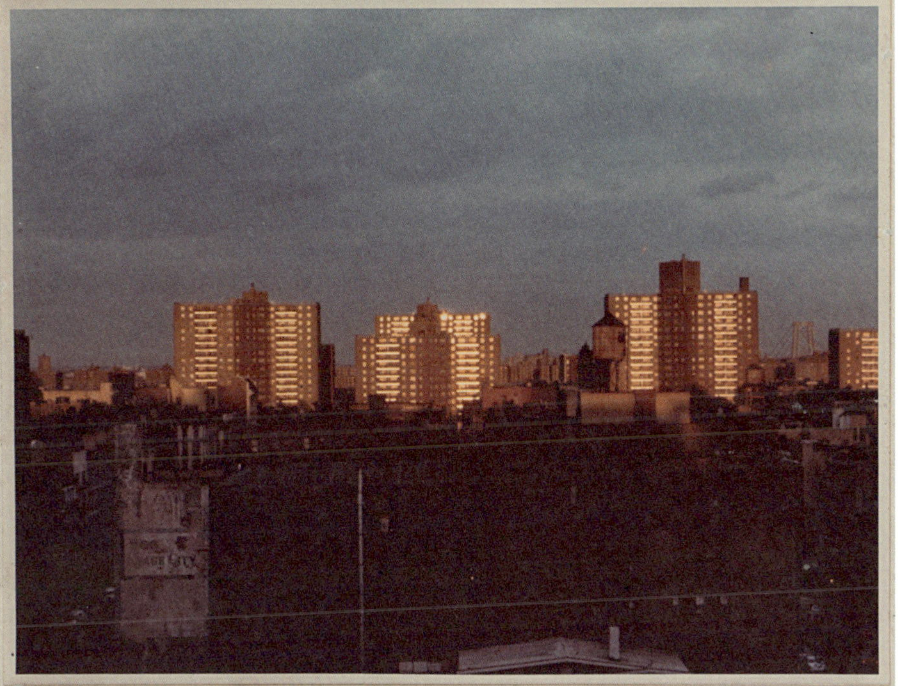

NOCTUARY ENVOY SAMENESS MOSQUE SWAYING WESTERN ALTERNATION SCALE SILLS QUOTIDIAN PAROXYSMS TOWER RAMPART ATTACK CULMINATION PEDIMENTS INERTIAL CONSEQUENCE PRESERVATION INTERPRETABLE POSITIVE TUTELAGE TRELLIS CONTROL LEARNED OPPOSITION QUALITATIVE LAWFUL SHIFT MOTION REGISTERED ATTITUDES DAWNS LIBERATION CRITICAL NORMS INTERNALIZATION DESIRES AUTONOMOUS TASK

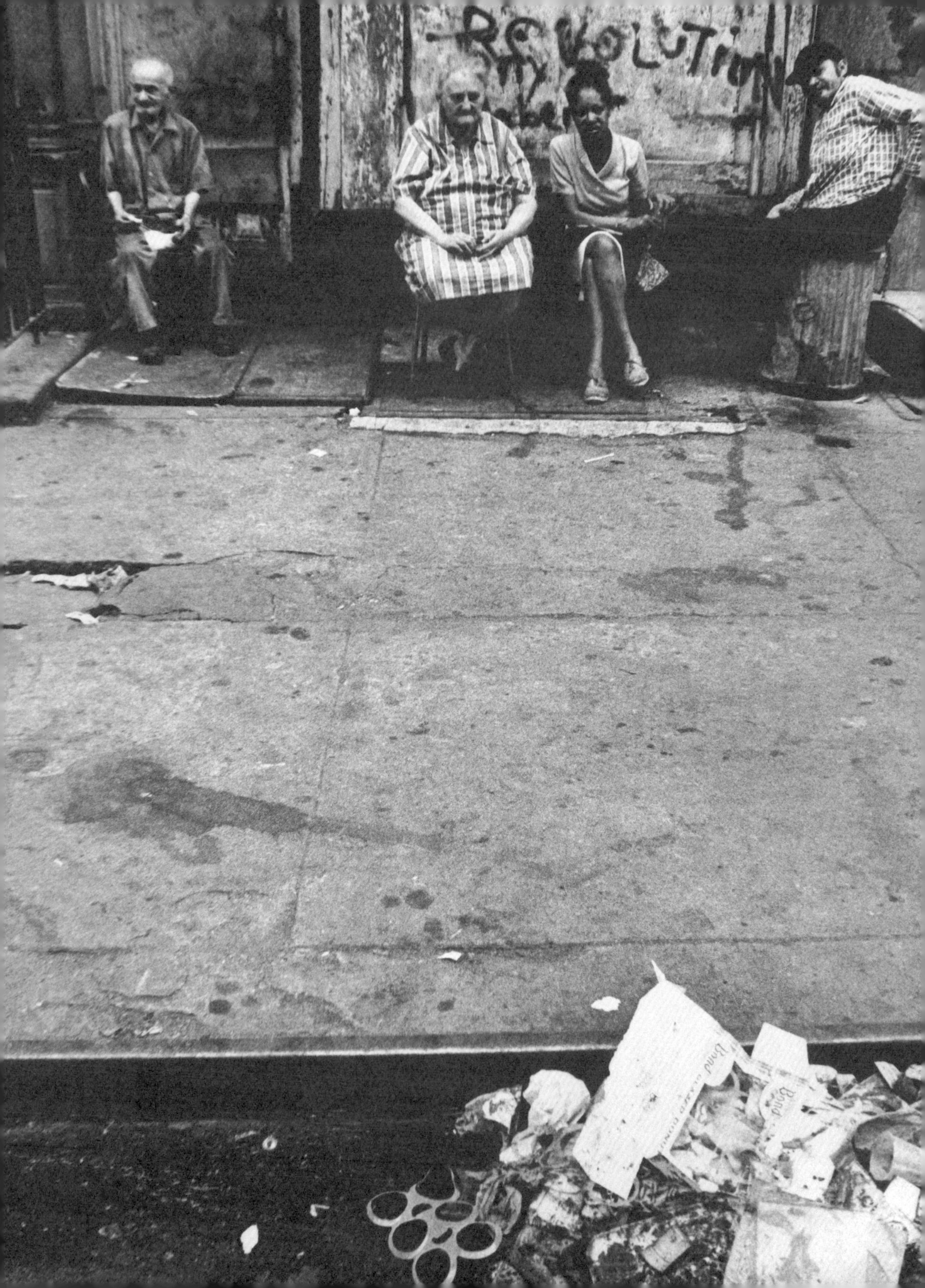
REVOLUTION

When I first arrived in 1973, I rented a sublet in SoHo and my first impression can be described in the concrete poem "Luxo/Lixo" by Augusto de Campos which was the theme of the work that I developed then.

— Regina Vater

Concrete poetry consists of language works whose meaning is informed by the visual aspect of words, as well as the spatial dimension of the poem's inscription. Brazilian concrete poet Augusto de Campos created the work "Luxo/Lixo" (Luxury/Trash) in 1966, a two-word poem that evidences two facets of capitalist accumulation.

Miguel Rio Branco, *Untitled*, from the series *New York Sketches*, 1970–72. Courtesy of the artist

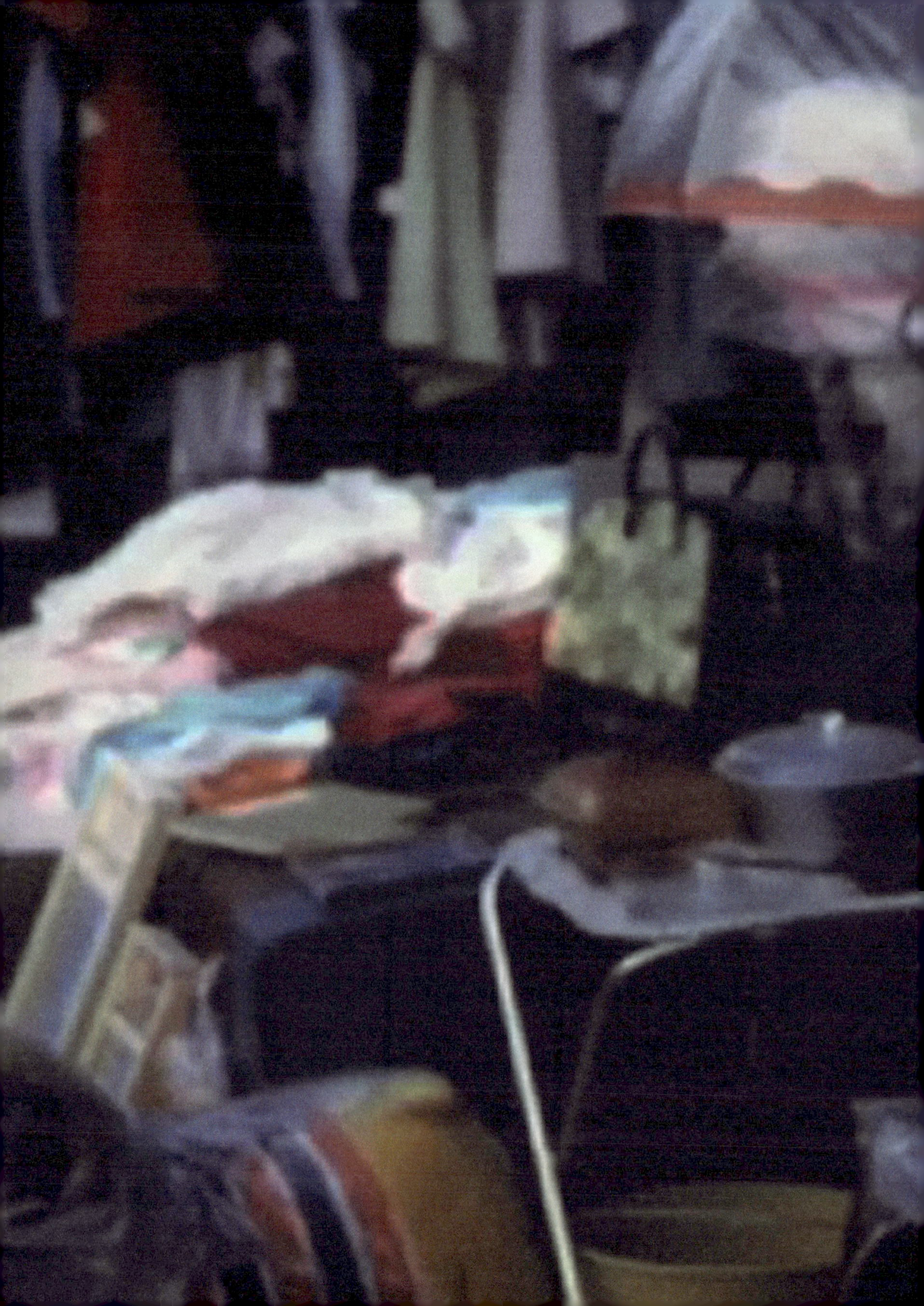

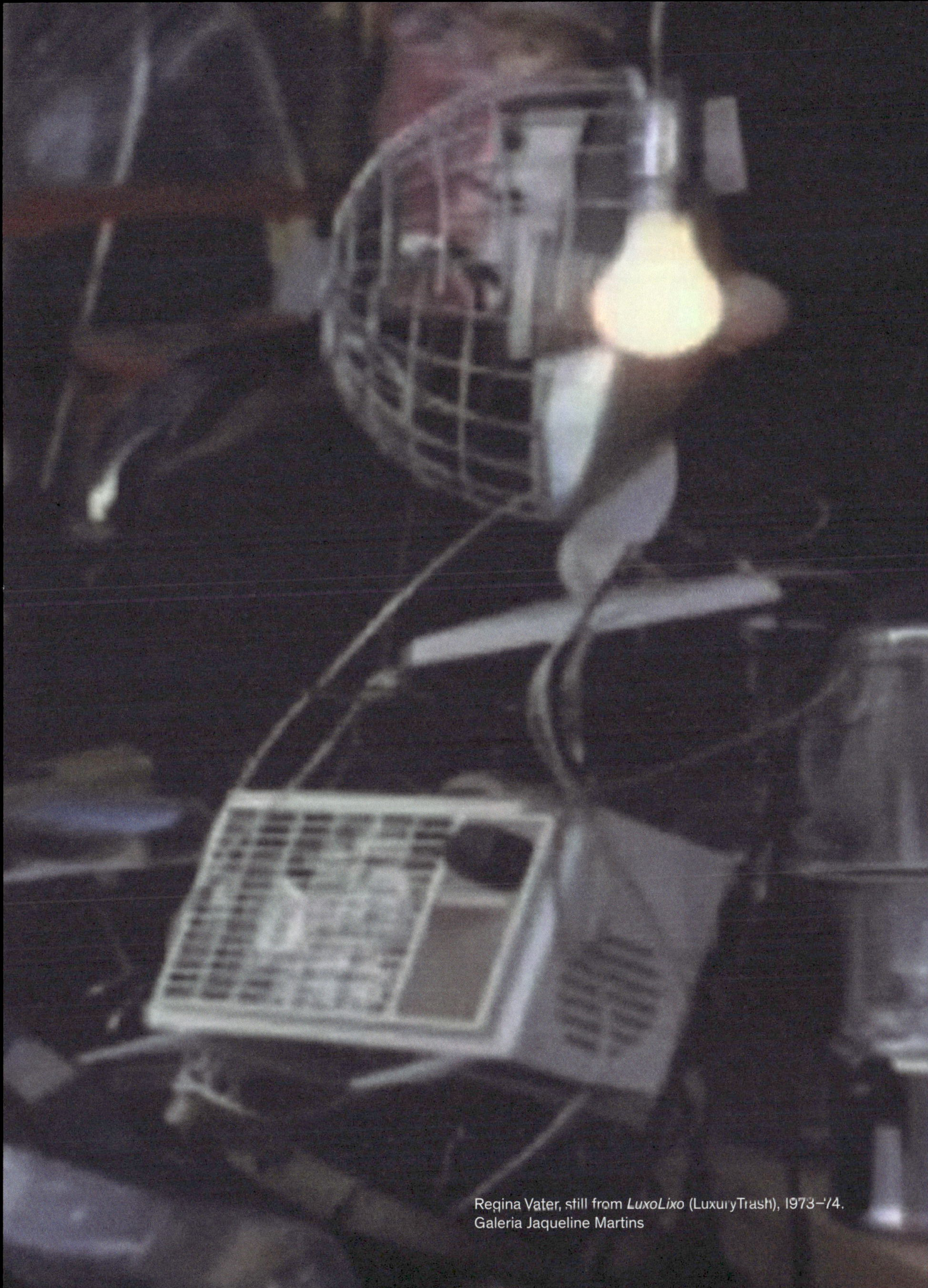

Regina Vater, still from *LuxoLixo* (LuxuryTrash), 1973–74. Galeria Jaqueline Martins

In 1970, aged 24, I went to New York City, to the School of Visual Arts where I stayed only one month before I decided to do my own explorations of New York with street photography. The neighborhoods I explored were the Bowery and the East Village, where I was living. My work during this time also included Super 8 experimental films, which I did while being hosted by Brazilian artist Hélio Oiticica, and working with American artists Gordon Matta-Clark and Lee Jaffe.

This was my first personal work, and was like a diary of my life in New York City. It was the beginning of my photographic practice. I didn't have a direction or a subject, my subject was my life around me: the streets, my girlfriend and the streets.

— Miguel Rio Branco

Miguel Rio Branco, *Untitled*, from the series New York Sketches, 1970–72. Courtesy of the artist

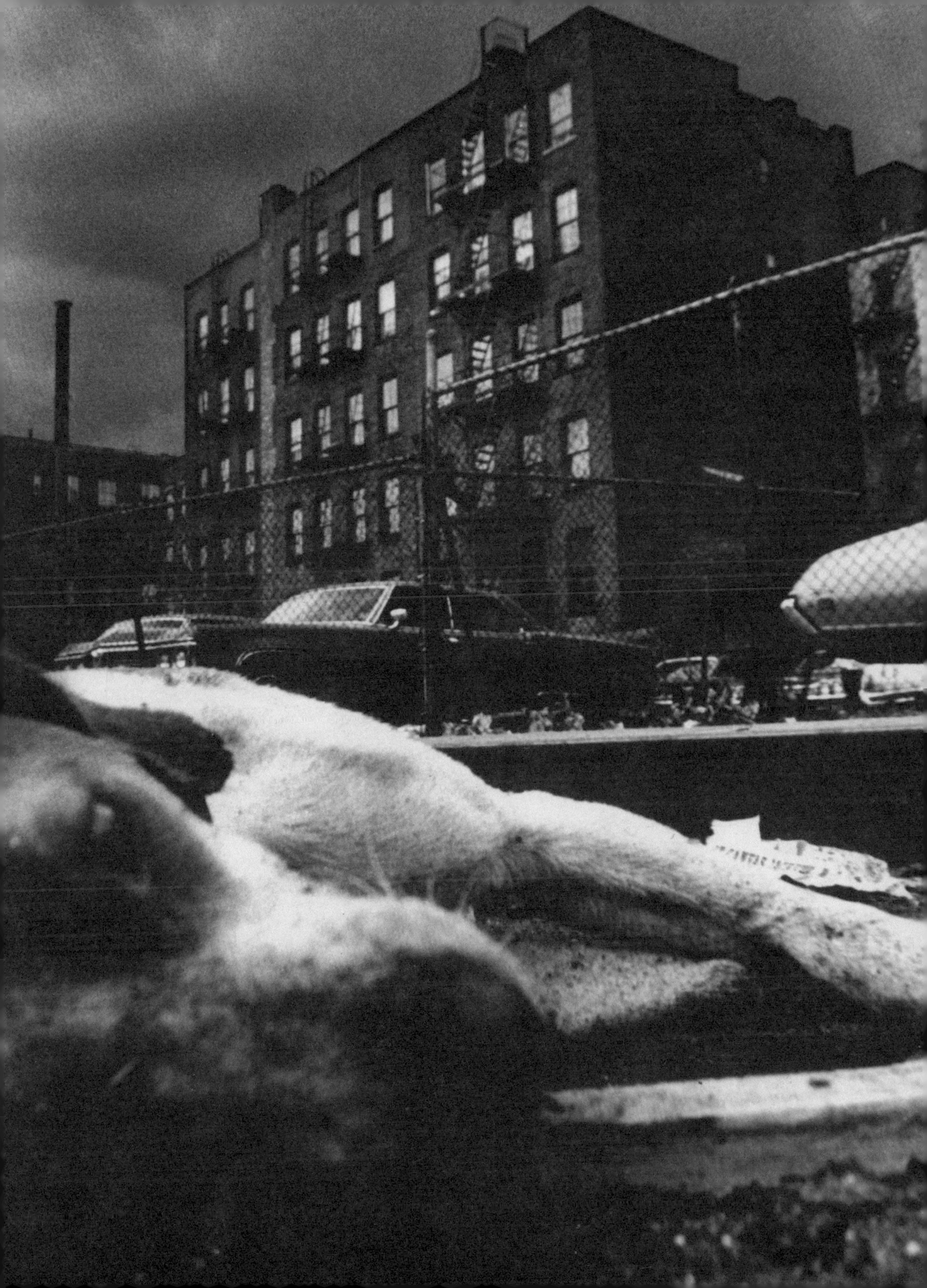

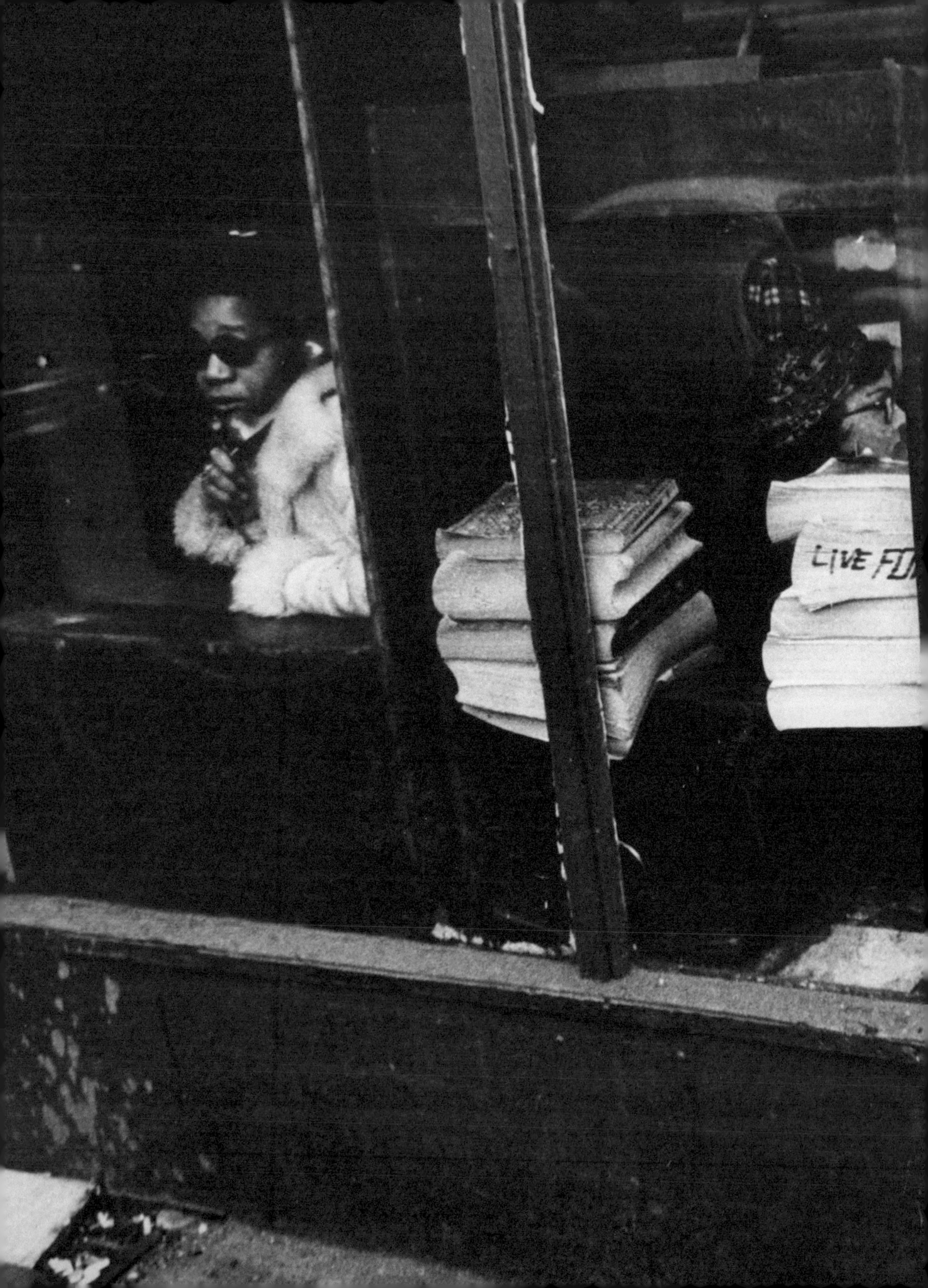
LIVE

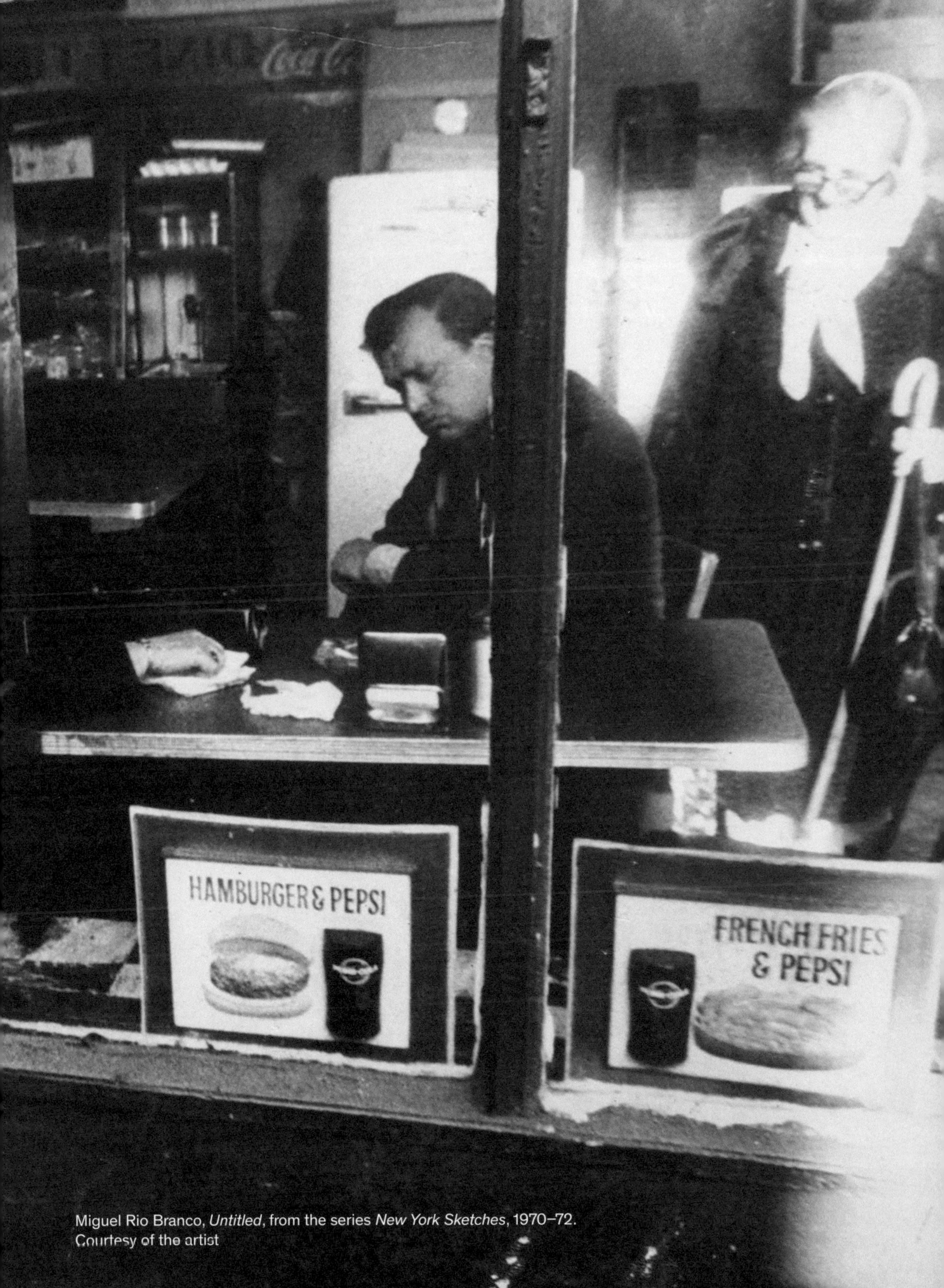

Miguel Rio Branco, *Untitled*, from the series *New York Sketches*, 1970–72.
Courtesy of the artist

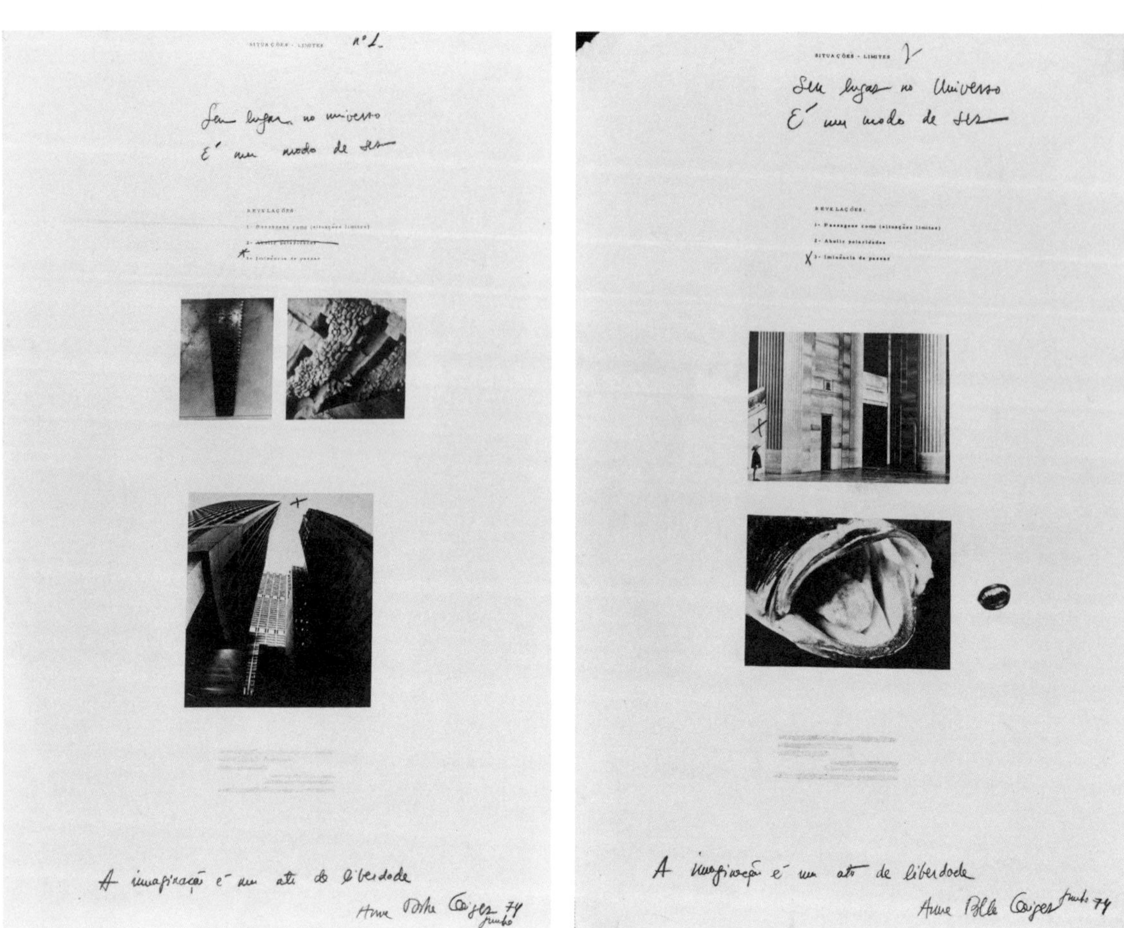

Anna Bella Geiger, *Situações-Limite* (Limit-situations), 1974.
Institute for Studies on Latin American Art (ISLAA)

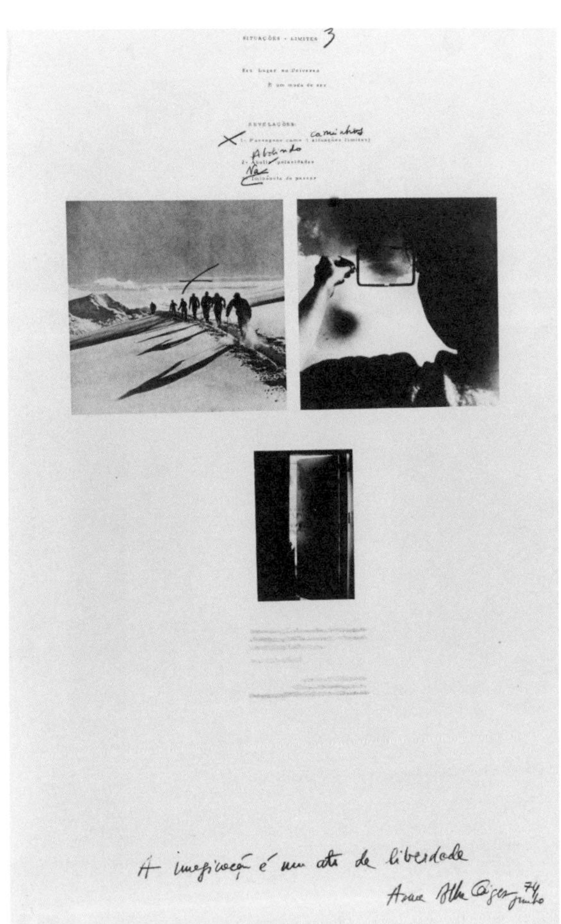

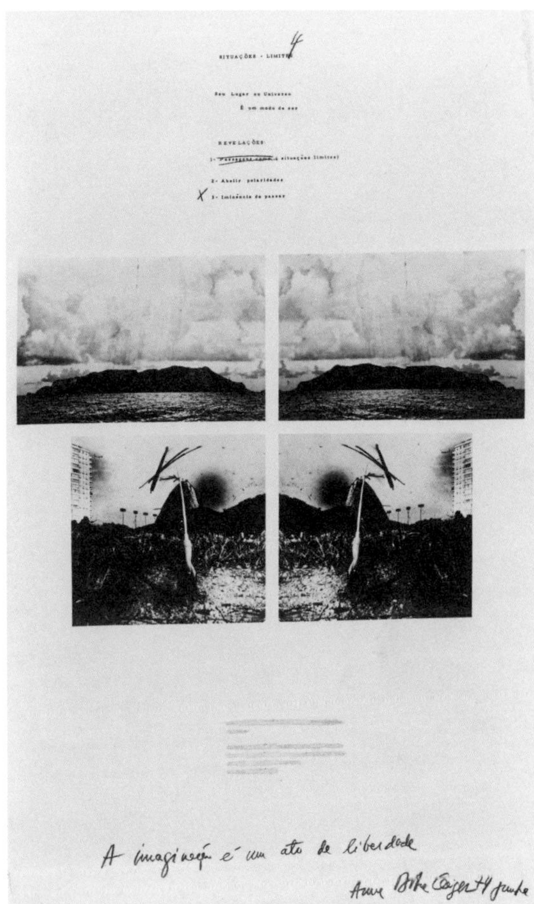

Living in the Village led me to draw [while] sitting for hours outside on the fire case stairs. At that time, several TV antennas started to pop up on the top of the roofs. The almost abstract scene contrasting the concrete cement and the graphic "landscape" of the antennas inspired me to draw much of my work. It meant to me an incredible new urban vision.

— Anna Bella Geiger

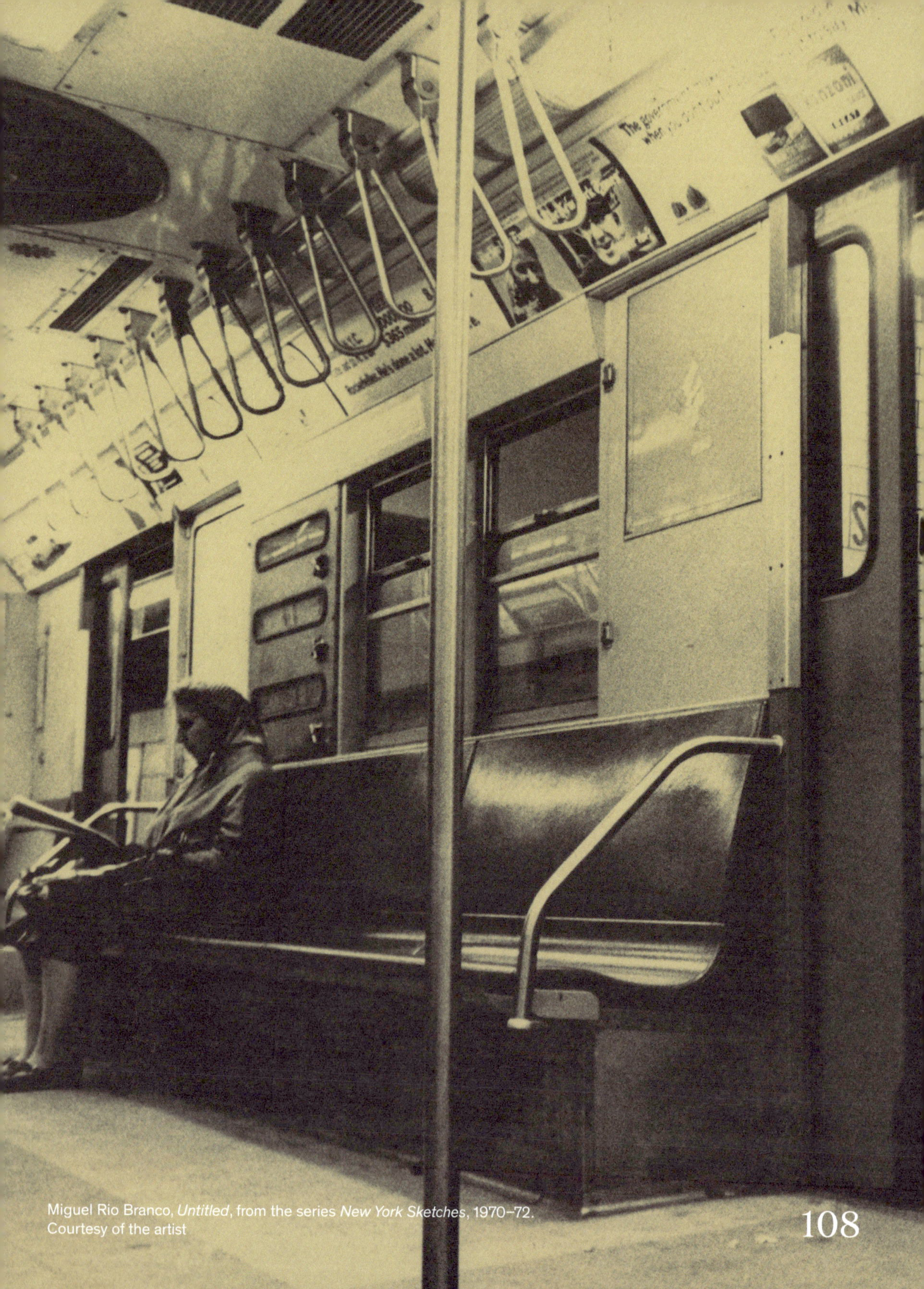

Miguel Rio Branco, *Untitled*, from the series *New York Sketches*, 1970–72.
Courtesy of the artist

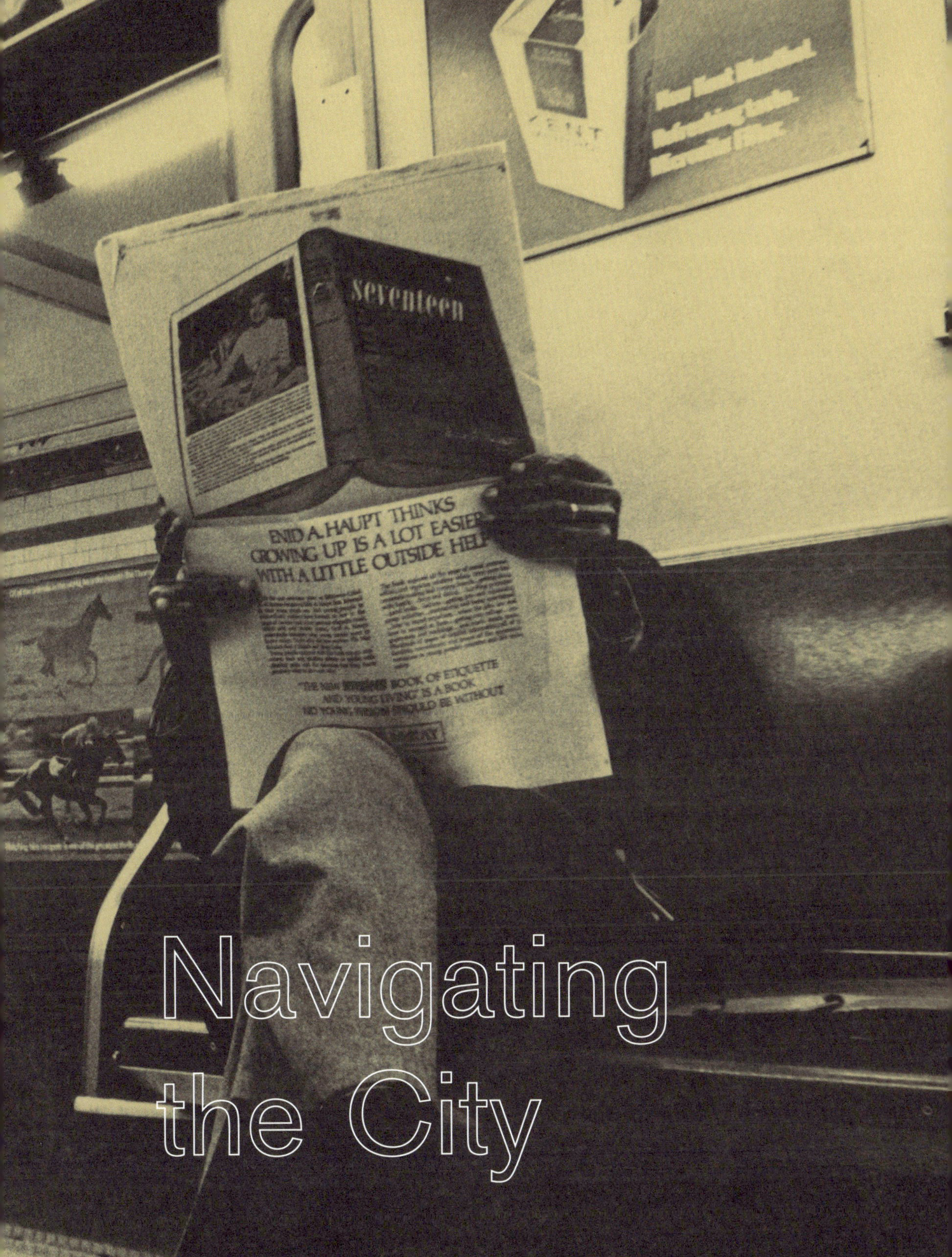

Navigating the City

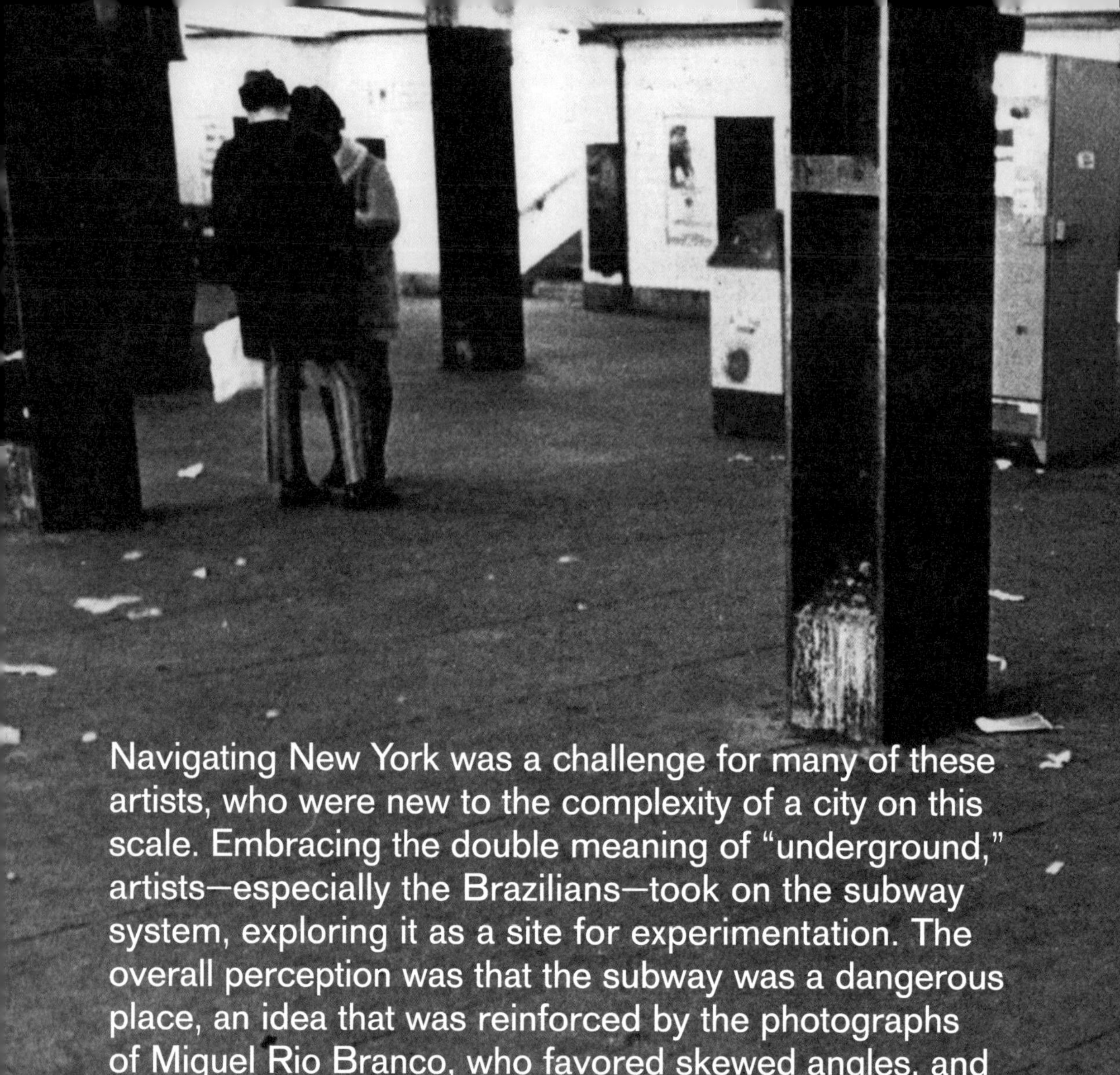

Navigating New York was a challenge for many of these artists, who were new to the complexity of a city on this scale. Embracing the double meaning of "underground," artists—especially the Brazilians—took on the subway system, exploring it as a site for experimentation. The overall perception was that the subway was a dangerous place, an idea that was reinforced by the photographs of Miguel Rio Branco, who favored skewed angles, and Anna Bella Geiger, who connected the implied sense of danger with the political situation in Brazil. Celebrating the violence of New York and his freedom to dislocate easily within it, Hélio Oiticica turned the subway into a space for dance and performance with his *Parangolé* cape.

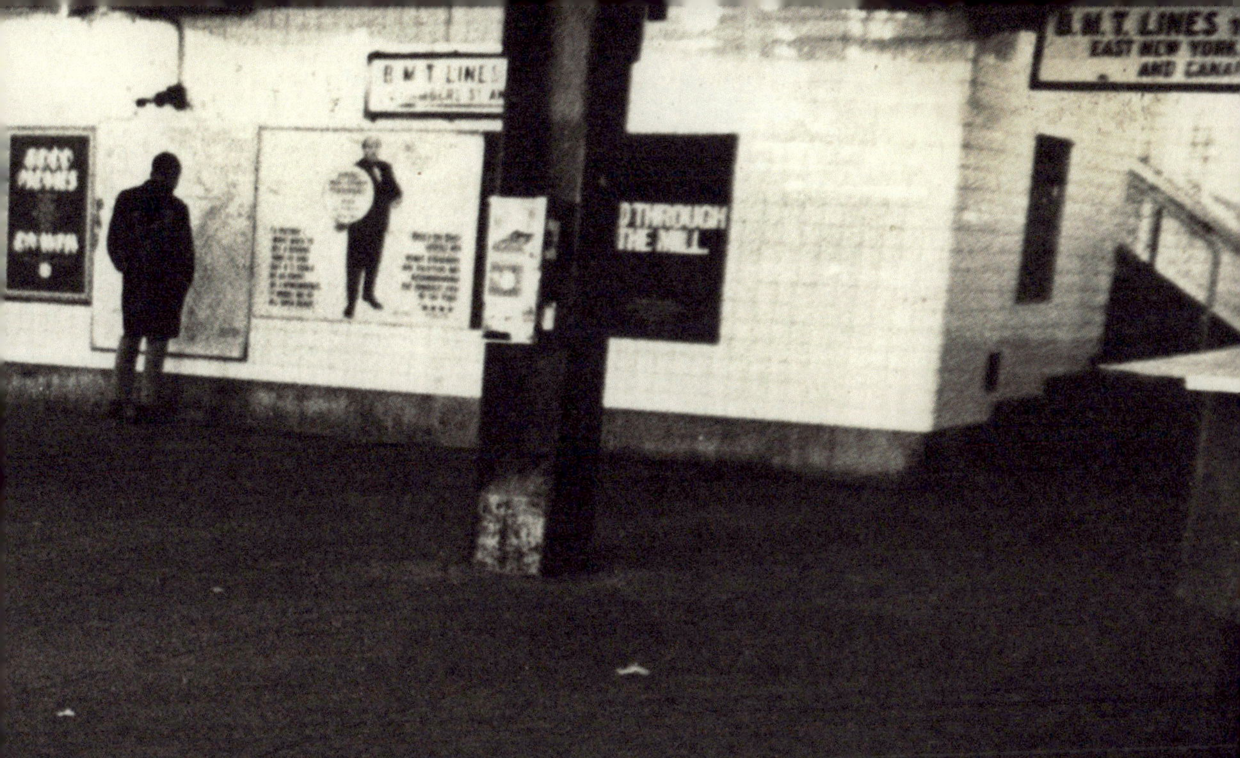

The subway fascinated me because of its hardness and above all because of the cold outside: most of [my photographs] were taken during my first winter spent in New York. Of course, in the subway, people's loneliness was much more evident.

— Miguel Rio Branco

Miguel Rio Branco, *Untitled*, from the series *New York Sketches*, 1970–72. Courtesy of the artist

Hélio Oiticica, *Parangolé Cape 30 in the New York City Subway*, 1972.
César and Claudio Oiticica Collection, Rio de Janeiro

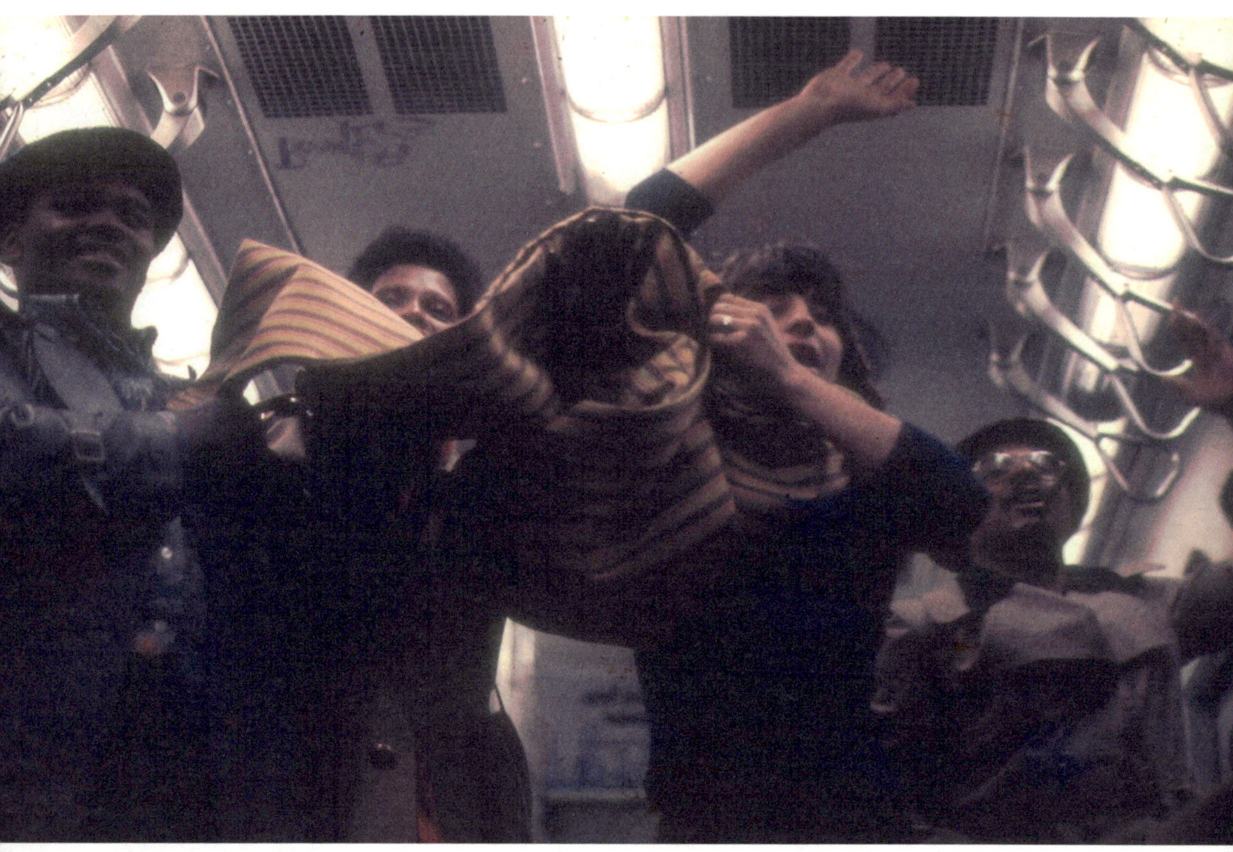

Hélio Oiticica created *Parangolé* capes as artworks that were intended to be worn by a performer who would dance in a public space, thus creating a dynamic of exchange between the wearer-performer and the people around them. In New York, Oiticica created one *Parangolé* cape, depicted in these photographs of a performance undertaken in the subway.

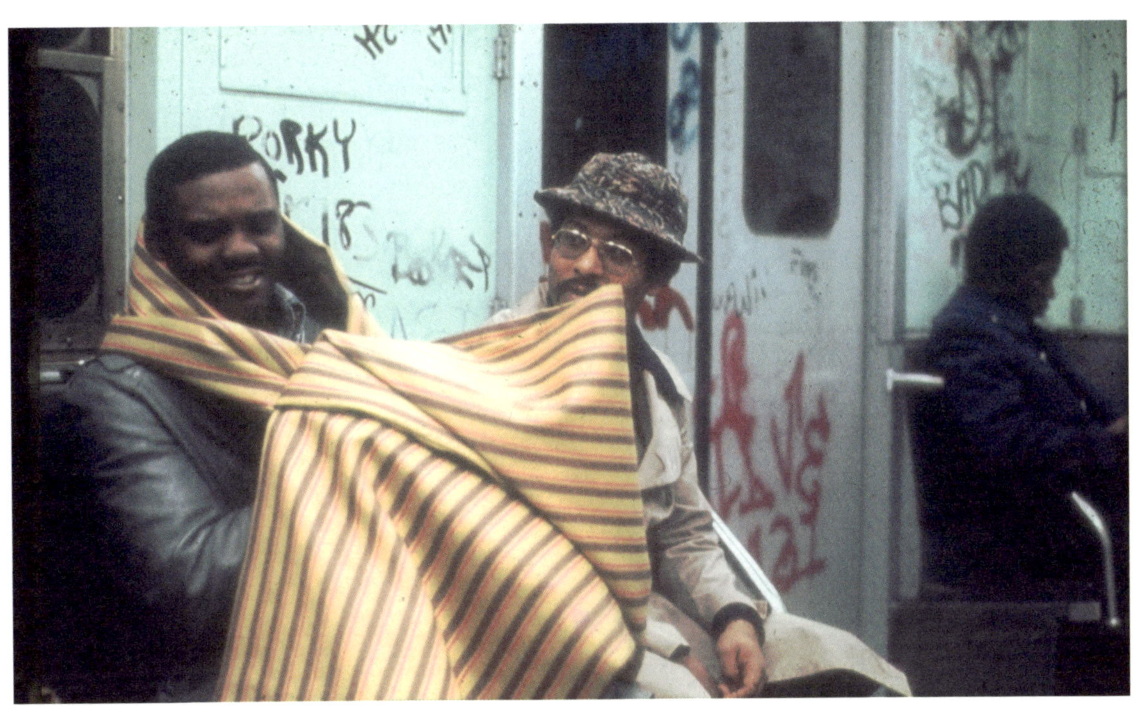

. . . we planned fun things: take the subway with PARANGOLÉ CAPES: it was really cool and part of one of my PARANGOLÉ-phases here: CAPES are made for specific contacts-events with random public in NEW YORK: programs of circumstances–ROMERO the "golden boy" of PARANGOLÉ acts as a PROPOSER first wearing and then offering CAPES for people to wear: we filmed (who is 20 years old and whom I've known since he was 6 when I taught painting when painting still existed, filmed in 16 mm some sequences of the encounter in the subway of the NEW LOTS AVE.).

— Hélio Oiticica

For my work's title *Situações-Limite* (Limit-situations) I used a term from anthropology, meaning, in a simplified dictionary, as an "extreme situation." I found that this term was a kind of metaphor for the dictatorship and its dangerous menacing time that we were living in since 1964 in Brazil. At that time there was not any laboratory to print these 4 large photographic papers—I ended up buying a whole roll of Kodak paper, and a photographer friend improvised a basin to develop it. The anonymous distorted photos of the New York buildings and other symbolic images where, for instance, like a child hesitating to cross a room. People in those images with dangerous passages to go through, such as snowy hills, where mountains almost crash, express "doubts." One cannot actually read some printed text messages that I deliberately scratched. In fact, I have censored myself out of fear.

— Anna Bella Geiger

Anna Bella Geiger, *Passagens* (Passages), 1975. Courtesy of the artist

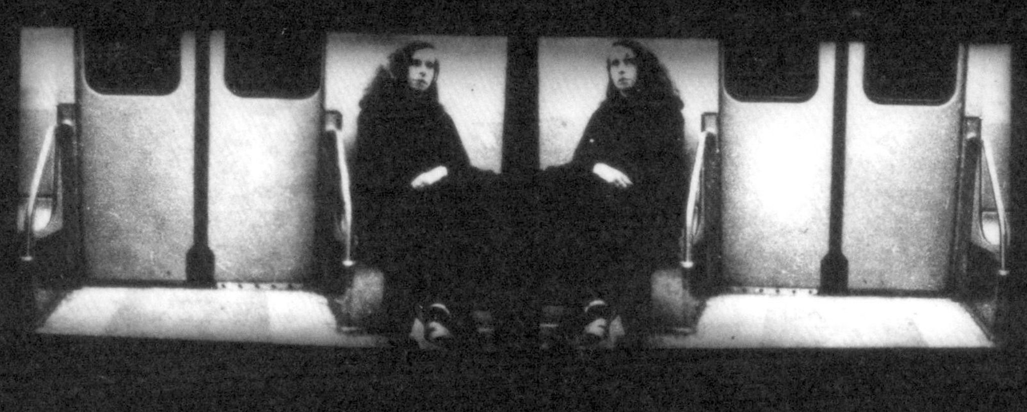

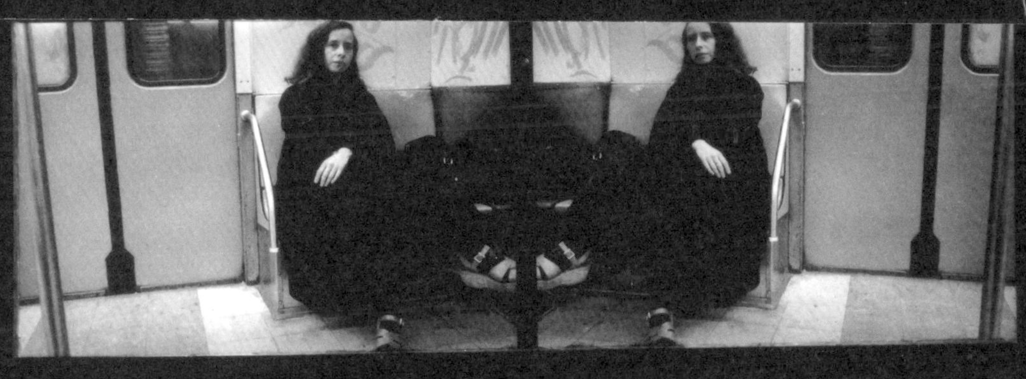

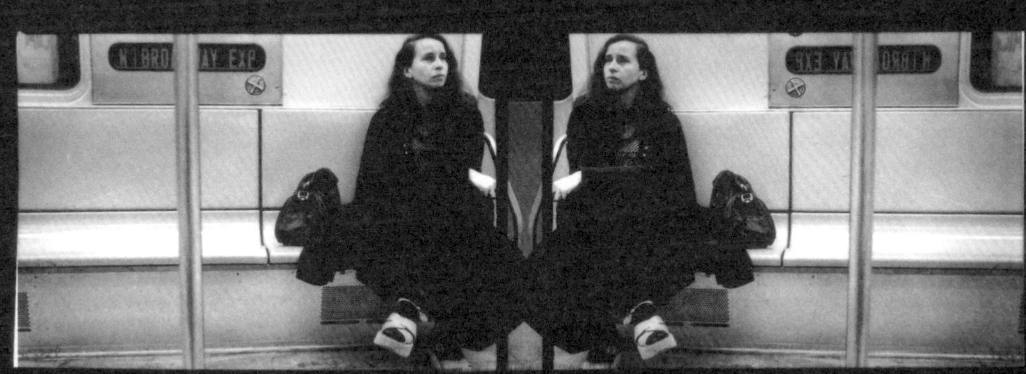

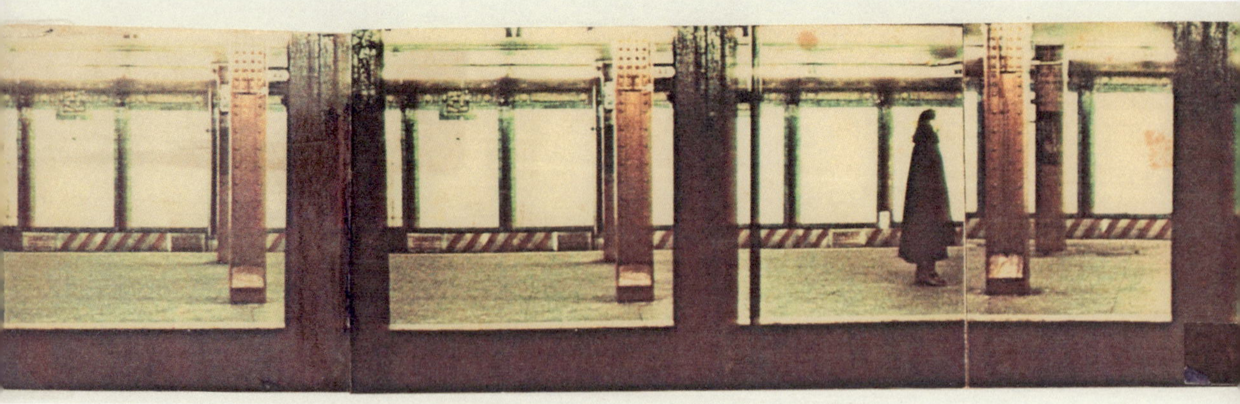

Anna Bella Geiger, *Passagens* (Passages), 1975. Private collection

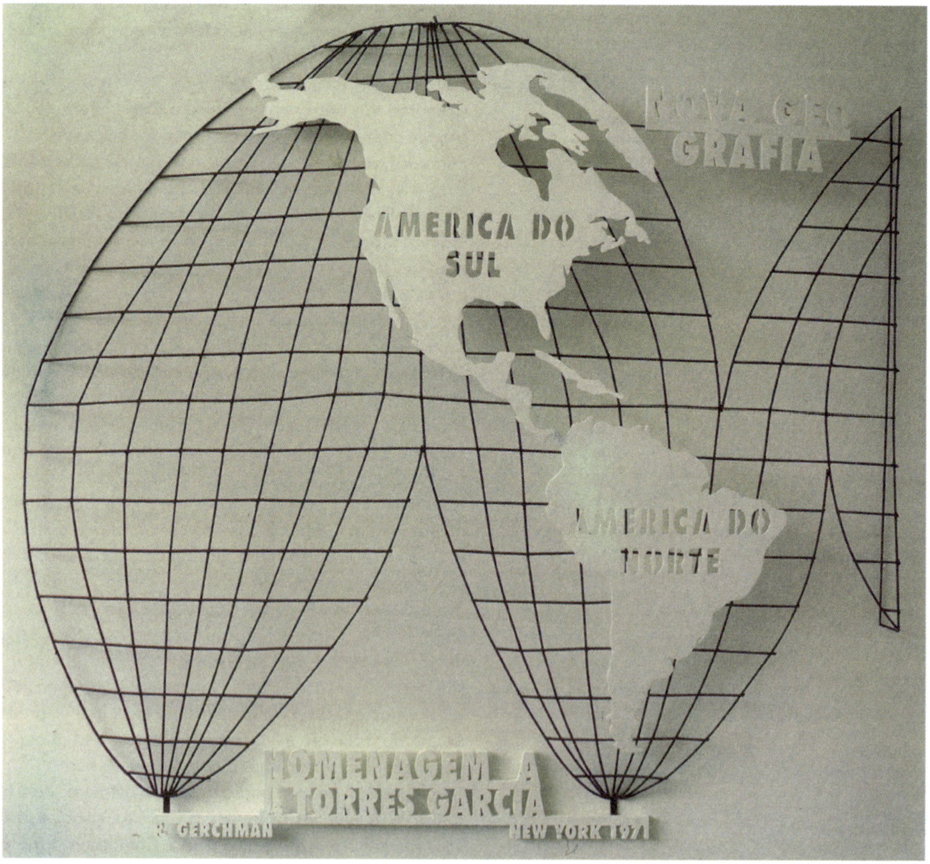

Rubens Gerchman, *A Nova Geografia / Homenagem à Torres-García* (The New Geography / Homage to Torres-García), 1971. Courtesy of Instituto Rubens Gerchman

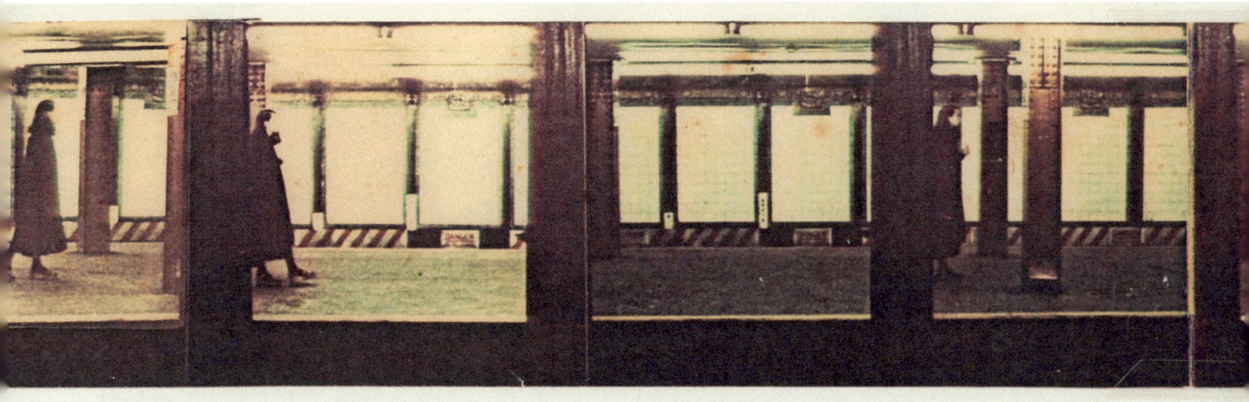

At the age of twenty I learned to navigate the maps of New York. I soon discovered the colorful maze of its transport system. In the subway, I remember Torres-García's overalls painted with the name of the streets of Manhattan. I quickly learned to get around with considerable speed and to reach the most distant places accurately. Gradually I arrived where I wanted. I was delighted with this easy mobility. I would take three or four different subway lines, changing levels several times, stopping in unknown stations to wait for new trains. I became a sort of "underground rat" and an avid reader of the colorful maps. I soon knew by heart the names of almost all stations, the difference between the A or F train.

Much later, when I was able to sell some works and get my life on track, I took a cab and went through the entire island of Manhattan, slowly, retracing the underground routes of the subway. Also later I realized that the reading of so many maps encouraged me to create Conceptual works like *Nova Geografia* (New Geography) of 1970 and *Você é cru ou cozido?* (Are you raw or cooked?) of 1972.

— Rubens Gerchman

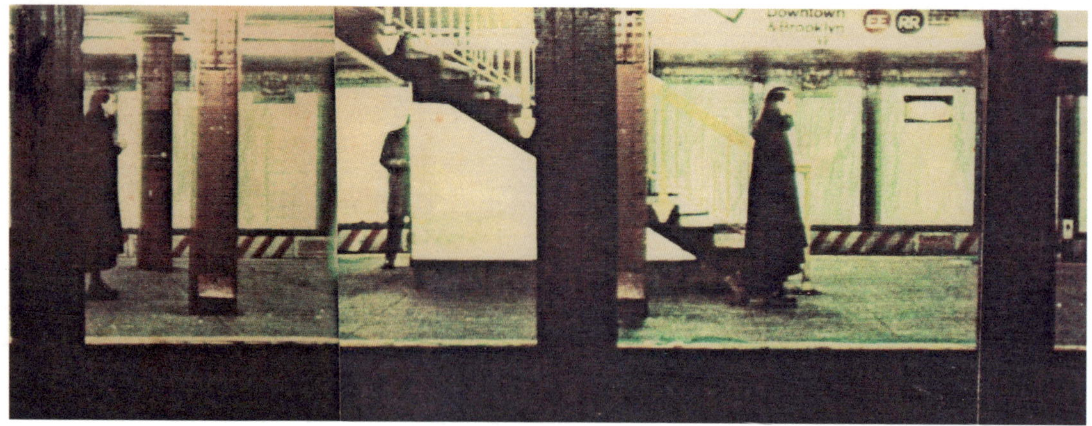

Anna Bella Geiger, *Passagens* (Passages), 1975. Private collection

ASSOMBRAÇÃO NO SUBWAY DA RUA 42. NYC.

A Figura fugidia
que passou por mim
levou consigo a alma
de um amigo
A Alma de muitos outros
que como essa figura que se ARRASTAVA
Rápido por entre vagões e portas
do subway
Arrastava também
uma parte de minha vida
A memória de amigos
que iam e vinham
companheiros definitivos que
se foram alguns para sempre
outros apenas desapareceram
Forever?
ou por temporada
os melhores eu sei que nunca
mais forever - que
Alguns por sua matéria não existe mais
De dor
De amor
De doença
ou desespero
Eles se foram e eu fiquei aqui
um sobrevivente

Desesperado
guardião de memórias vivas
ou dores permanentes
Nunca me abandonarão
Como os amigos que dentro
de mim ficam
para sempre.
nesses trilhos
o grito desesperado do subway
vejo o mesmo gorro
a mesma capa
o rosto embaçado
será ele
o Vestígio
o traço NOVA YORKINO
a sombra
o espectro ambulante.
Bleecker st
An emptiness in my head
A hollow of long friends
is gone forever.
Chambers. Spring. Astor Place
Canal Franklin Duane Tribeca
Downtown 14 street.

Rubens Gerchman, *Assombração no subway da rua 42 NYC* (A haunting in the subway, 42nd Street, NYC), 1942.
Text licensed by Instituto Rubens Gerchman. Collection Instituto Rubens Gerchman

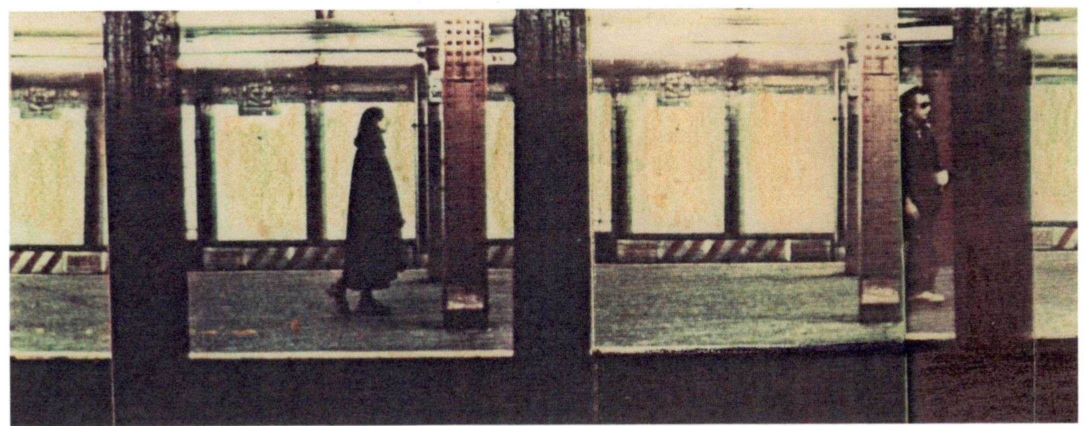

A Haunting in the Subway, 42nd Street, NYC

The fugitive figure
that passed me by
snatched the soul
of a friend
The soul of many others
alongside this figure which dragged
Fast through the carriages and doors
of the subway
swept part of my life as well
The memory of friends
that came and went
definitive companions that
were gone some forever
others just disappeared
Forever?
or for one season
the best ones I know I will never
see them again
Some because their matter no longer exists
Owing to pain
love
disease
or despair
They are gone and I stayed here
a survivor

Desperate
guardian of living memories
or permanent pains
they never leave me
like the friends that remain inside me
forever
on these tracks
the desperate cry of the subway
I see the same cap
the same cape
the blurry face
I wonder if it's him
the trace
the New York trait
the shadow
the wandering specter
Bleecker Street
an emptiness in my heart
A hollow of long friends
in some forever
Chambers. Spring. Astor Place. Canal.
Franklin. Duane Tribeca. Downtown.
14 street

— Rubens Gerchman

Intervening in the City

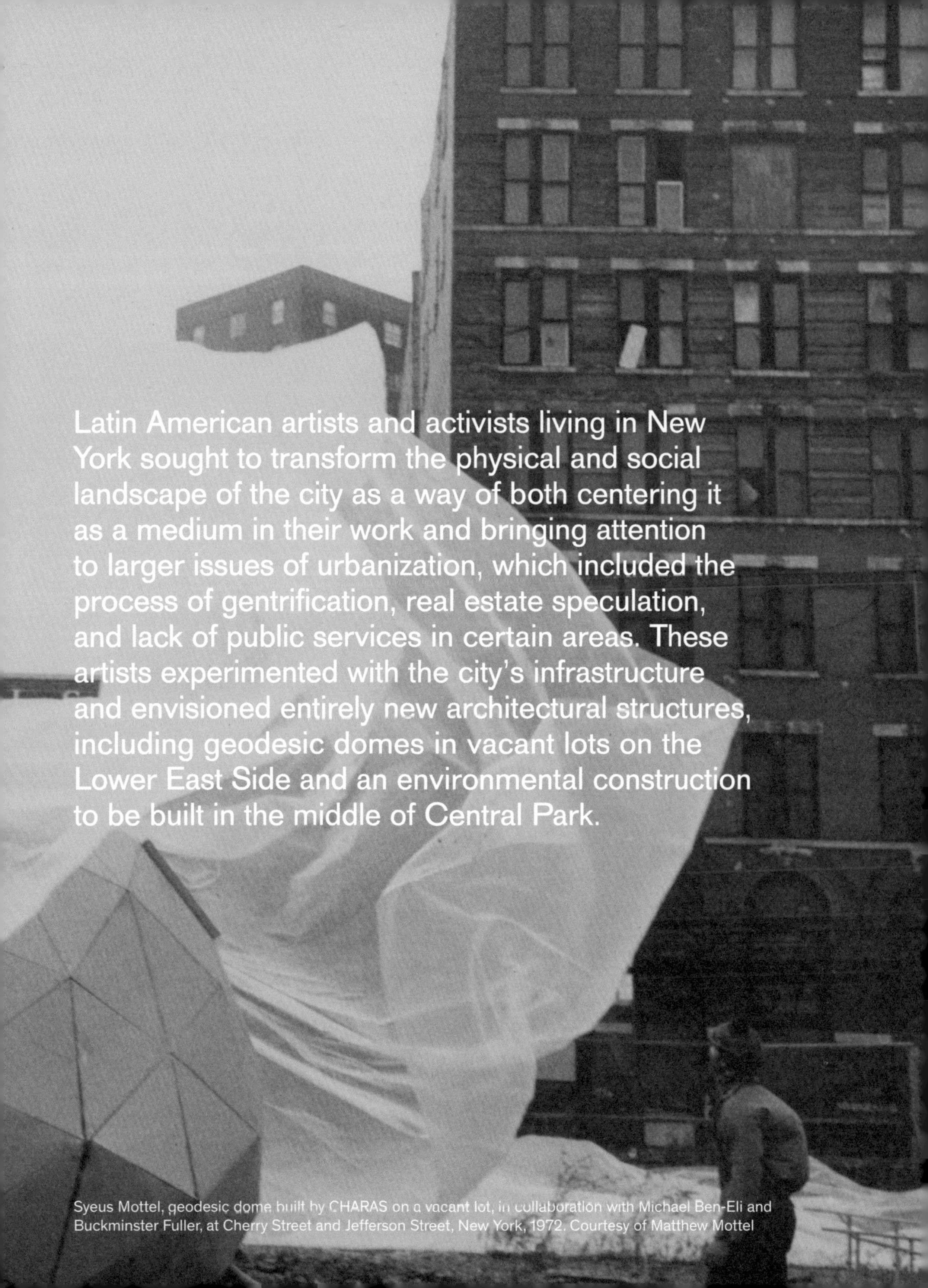

Latin American artists and activists living in New York sought to transform the physical and social landscape of the city as a way of both centering it as a medium in their work and bringing attention to larger issues of urbanization, which included the process of gentrification, real estate speculation, and lack of public services in certain areas. These artists experimented with the city's infrastructure and envisioned entirely new architectural structures, including geodesic domes in vacant lots on the Lower East Side and an environmental construction to be built in the middle of Central Park.

Syeus Mottel, geodesic dome built by CHARAS on a vacant lot, in collaboration with Michael Ben-Eli and Buckminster Fuller, at Cherry Street and Jefferson Street, New York, 1972. Courtesy of Matthew Mottel

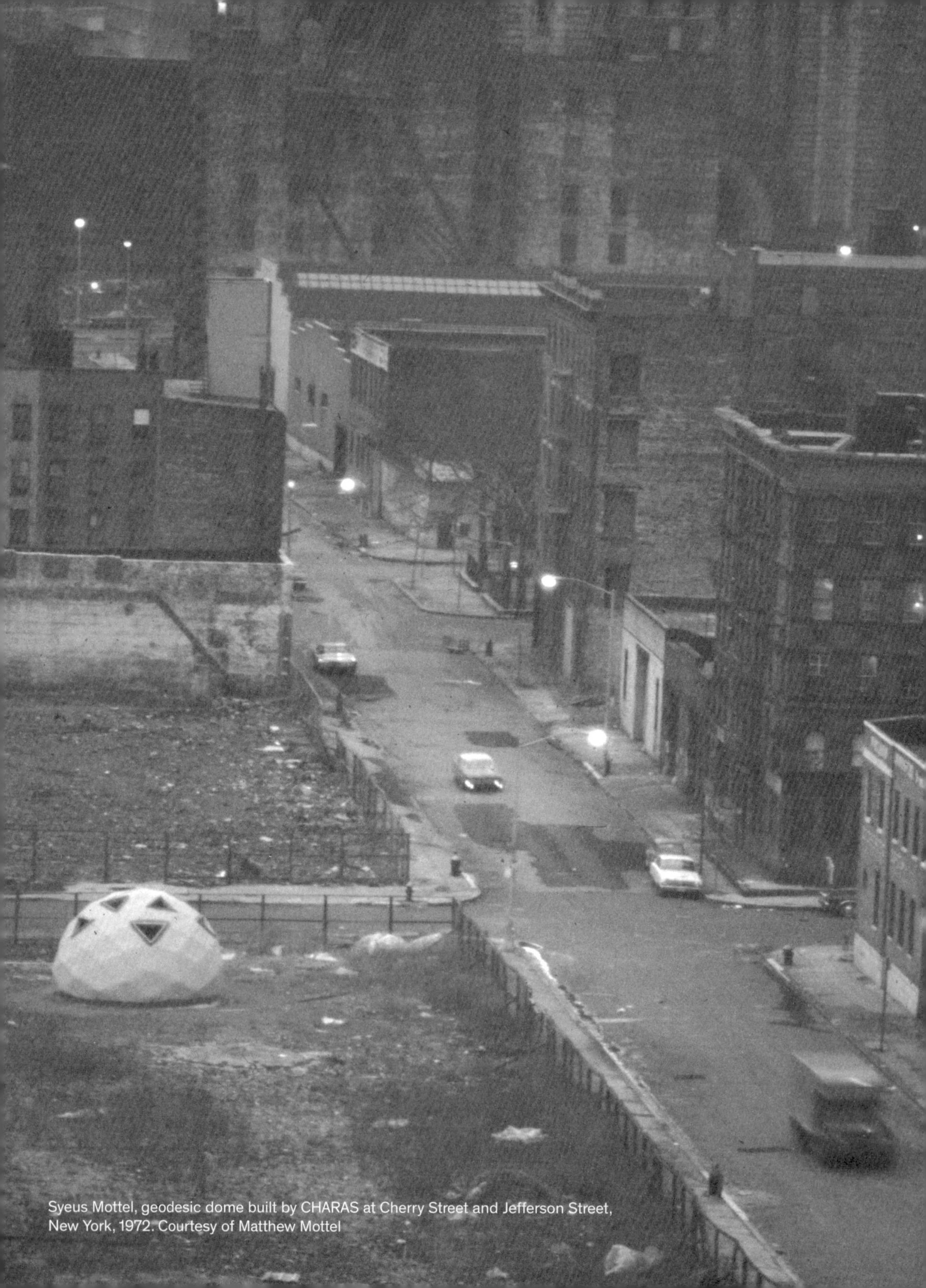

Syeus Mottel, geodesic dome built by CHARAS at Cherry Street and Jefferson Street, New York, 1972. Courtesy of Matthew Mottel

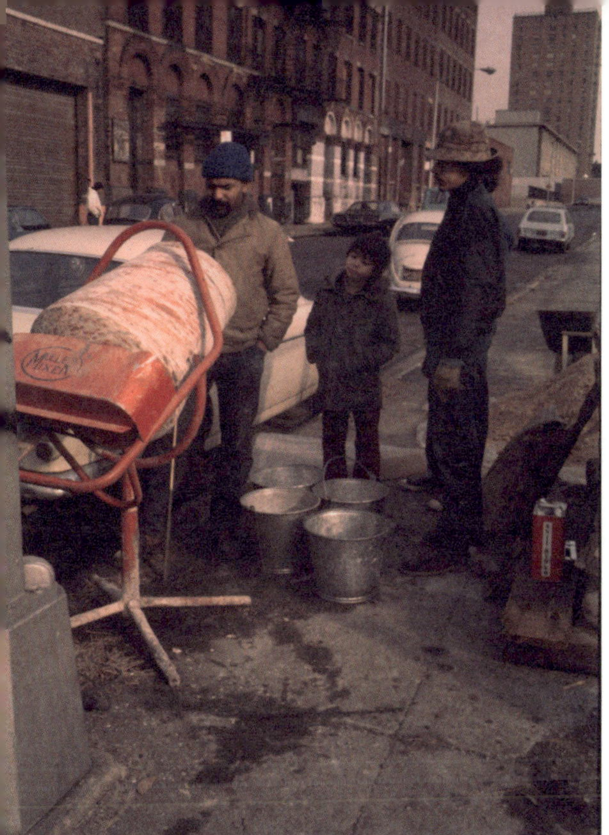

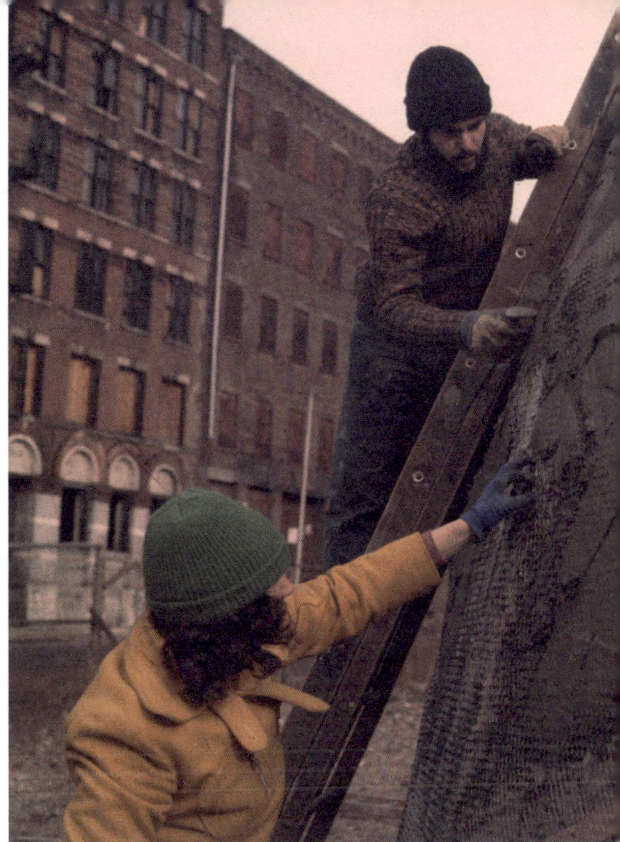

[It] was the beginning of abandonment by landlords. So how could we develop some of those buildings and do the most with less material? Basically we [CHARAS] became really interested in some of [Buckminster Fuller's] policies of design: how you do some of those designs, how you begin to design apartments or buildings, that sort of thing.

[W]hat was great about Bucky, that here he's meeting with a whole bunch of nuts from the Lower East Side—activists—we just have ideas. We don't have money, we don't have land. You know, *pero* the thing is, talking with him and that stuff. And him taking it seriously, where he would sit with us for hours.

— Carlos "Chino" Garcia

Syeus Mottel, CHARAS members at work on the dome at Cherry Street and Jefferson Street, New York, 1972. Courtesy of Matthew Mottel

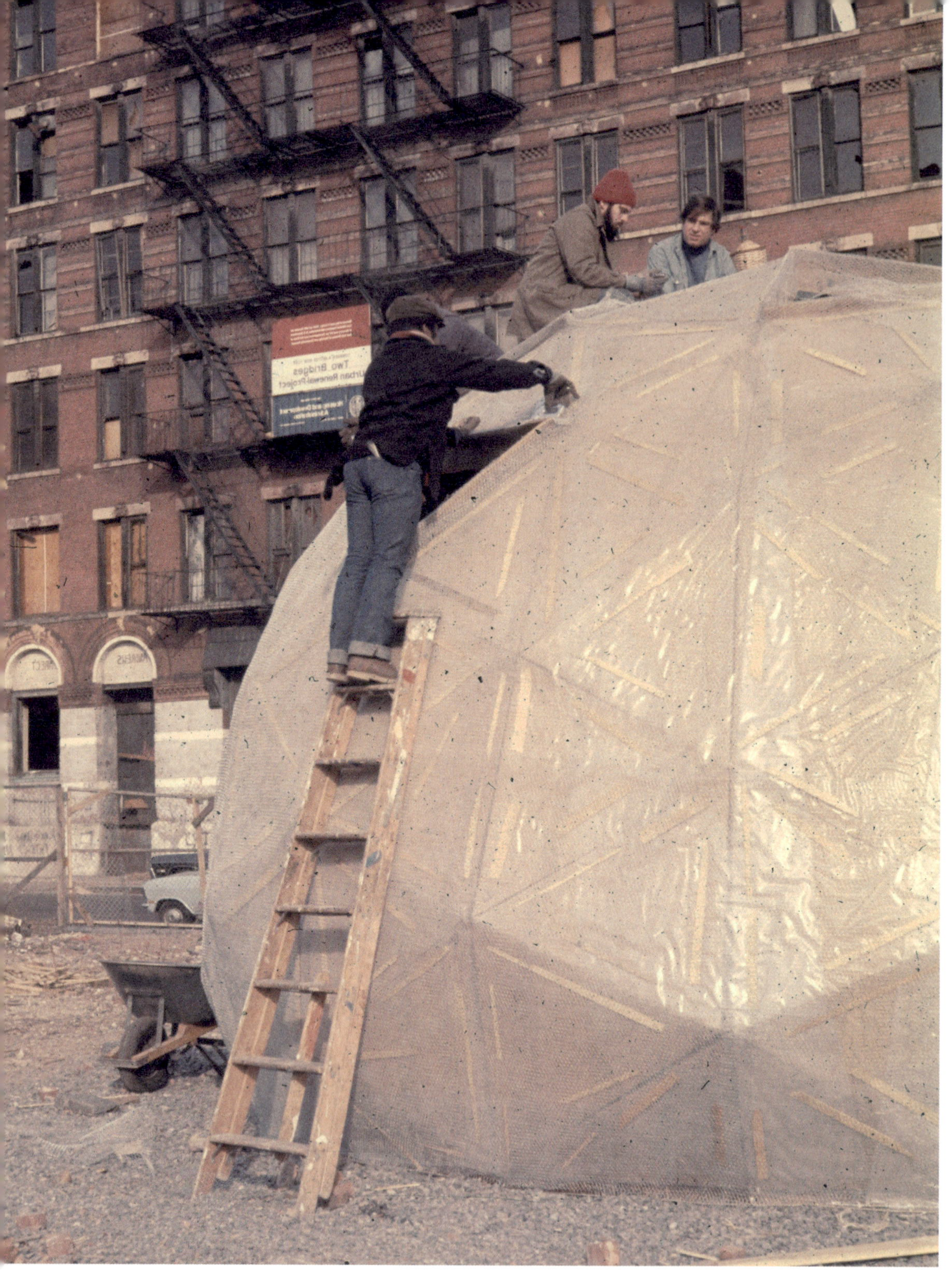

Syeus Mottel, members of CHARAS build a geodesic dome on a vacant lot at Cherry Street and Jefferson Street, New York, 1972. Courtesy of Matthew Mottel

We organized rent strikes against landlords and it worked. A lot of services got done. Then it came to the period in late '60s, early '70s, '80s, where the landlords started burning buildings in order to get rent. They would get more money from the insurance companies than they were getting from the tenants.

I think in 1979—no, '69, one of the first buildings that was vandalized was across the street [pointing across East Sixth Street] and we figured how to take the building and renovate it. It was all destroyed, the interior, and we started to have the idea of taking over city-owned buildings and began to fix them. Hopefully the City would cooperate with that, but we moved into buildings—we squatted into buildings even without their permission, because when you did ask them for permission, they gave you the runaround.

We actually started working on the buildings and then after that—together with other people from the community—after that particular building, that didn't work out for different reasons. Then together with the organization Adopt-A-Building, we decided to move on another building at 519 East Eleventh Street and that one worked. That was the first sweat equity building and that was in the early '70s that we started that project. So the housing rehabilitation started but a lot of the ideas started in '69, '70, '71, '72 and 519, I think we got in 1973, legally together in cooperation with the [John V.] Lindsay administration. And it became the first sweat equity building in any urban area of the United States. Then it also became the first solar energy building and the first wind-powered building in the United States in an urban area.

—Carlos "Chino" Garcia

On March 15, 1969, I introduced the initial two works in my series *Useful Art Works*, as part of Street Works performed in NYC by a group of artists and poets.

The first of these *Useful Art Works* consisted of placing in the right locations the missing street signs at the northeast corners of 42nd Street and Madison Avenue, 51st Street and Fifth Avenue, 49th Street and Fifth Avenue, 45th Street and Fifth Avenue, 44th Street and Fifth Avenue, and 51st Street and Sixth Avenue.

These signs replaced only some of the street signs missing in the area of Midtown Manhattan designated for the performance of Street Works. The signs read E 42nd St, E 51 St, E 49 St, E 45 St, E 44 St and W 51 St and might be considered as a discontinuous literary work with six lines.

The second Useful Art Work of the *Useful Art Works* series consisted of painting the subway station at 42nd St and Fifth Avenue on the Flushing line.

These two Works are intended to build a tradition where art does not have to be only beautiful or valuable in a philosophical, aesthetic, or vaguely social way. Art can also be directly useful to people in general, and should not aim at pleasing only the art audience. Useful art should result in a contribution to the improvement of living conditions for everybody.

Both Works were performed with the help of Scott Burton between 2:30 and 7:00 AM to avoid any problems with municipal laws.

The second Work could not be finished.

— Eduardo Costa

STREET WORKS

Saturday, March 15, 1969 (24 hours)

VITO HANNIBAL ACCONCI
ARAKAWA
GREGORY BATTCOCK
SCOTT BURTON
JAMES LEE BYARS
ROSEMARIE CASTORO
EDUARDO COSTA
JOHN GIORNO
BILL CRESTON
STEPHEN KALTENBACH
LES LEVINE
LUCY LIPPARD
BERNADETTE MAYER
MERIDITH MONK
BEN PATTERSON
JOHN PERREAULT
MARJORIE STRIDER
MR. T.
ANNE WALDMAN
HANNAH WEINER

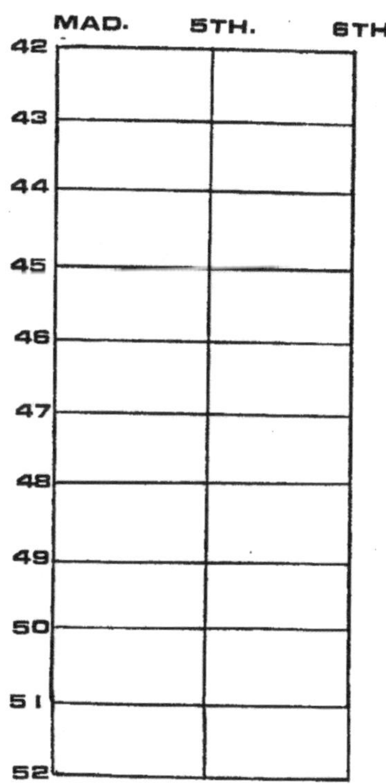

Flyer for *Street Works* events held between 42nd and 52nd streets and Madison and Sixth avenues, New York, March 15, 1969. Eduardo Costa Archive

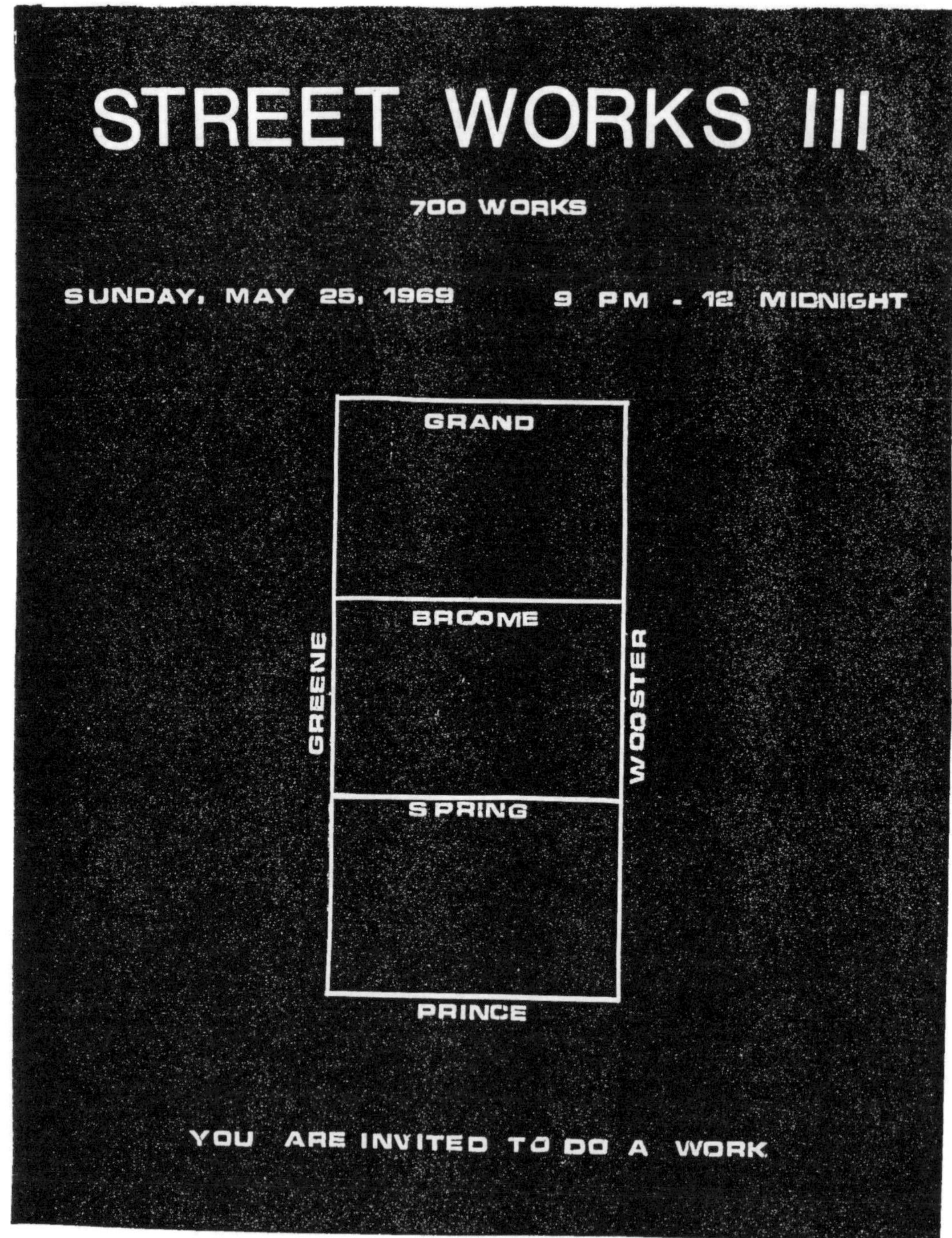

Flyer for *Street Works II* events held between Grand and Prince streets and Greene and Wooster streets, New York, May 25, 1969. Eduardo Costa Archive

STREET WORKS IV

Arakawa
Vito Hannibal Acconci
Scott Burton
Eduardo Costa
Stephen Kaltenbach
Abraham Lubelski
Bernadette Mayer
John Perreault
Marjorie Strider
Hannah Weiner

DATE: Fall 1969

Dept of Cultural
Doris Freeman

Les Levine

Part I: Opening night at The Architectural League. Street Workss by each of the above artists, to take place on E. 65th St. between Madison and Park during the opening.

Part II: Various street works each week for three weeks by the above artists at various times and at different locations throughout the city

Proposed budget: $200 per artist plus poster and mailings.

*****Some Of The Reasons We Have Been Doing Street Works (Street Works I, II, & III) Are:

1. To reach a broader cross-section of the public than the usual art audience. One of the ways of choosing this audience is geographically in terms of locations.
2. The unexpected appearance of "art works" in an everyday street context calls attention to the street itself as an environment.
3. A new situation such as Street Works engenders new ideas of the artist.
4. This new non-gallery, non-studio, non-museum situation with its new set of rules creates a sense of freedom for the artist. Becaus of the direct contact between audience and artist there is a situation of immodiate feedback that is not normally available.

*****Some Of The Reasons We Are Asking The Architectural League To Accept Our Proposal For Street Works IV Are:

1. Street Works use architecture and the city itself as a new context for art, therefore The Architectural League which is devouted to the inter-relationship between architecture and the other arts would be the ideal sponsor for such a project.
2. Sponsorhip of Street Works IV by the Architectural League would increase the kkkkk scale and impact of Street Works and thus promote a greater public awareness of the city as an architectural environment.

Please see the attached proposals which are not final but are included as an indication of some of the works we would likex to do.

Marjorie Strider
John Perreault
Hannah Weiner.

Proposal for *Street Works IV* events to be held on 65th Street between Madison and Park avenues, New York, fall 1969. Eduardo Costa Archive

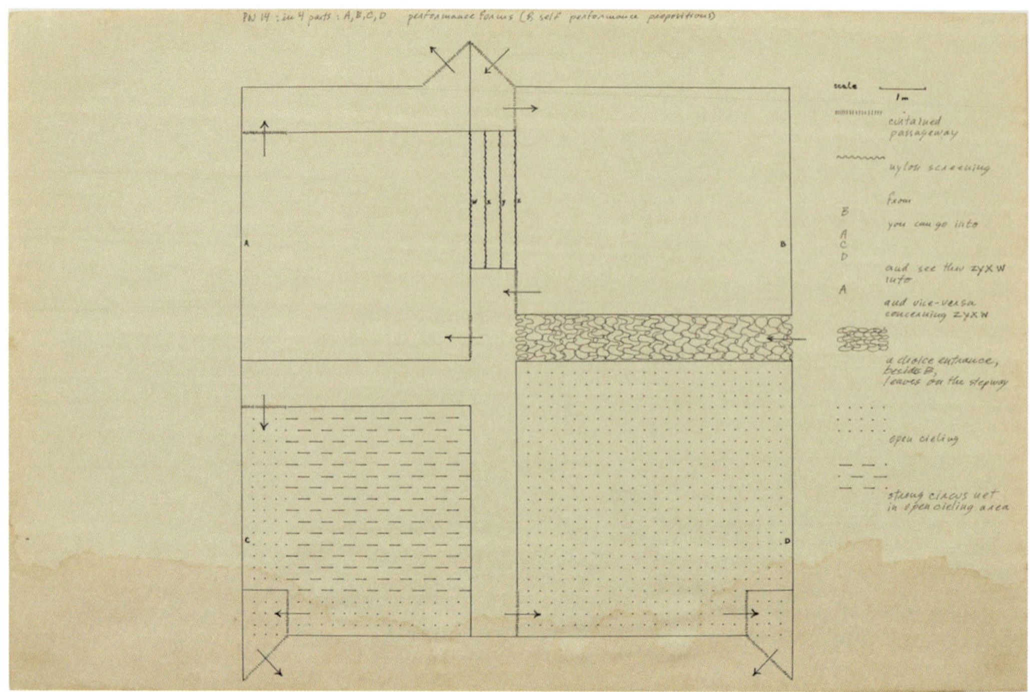

Hélio Oiticica planned the *Subterranean Tropicália Project* as a structure to be built in Central Park. Bringing together his ideas of a penetrable artwork—one in which viewers can physically enter the work and become immersed in space and color—with his desire to create a lasting intervention in the city, this work was never installed as the artist envisioned, even after it was reduced to smaller sizes. Oiticica, however, was able to circulate his plans in the underground magazine *Changes*.

Hélio Oiticica, *PN14*, 1971. César and Claudio Oiticica Collection, Rio de Janeiro

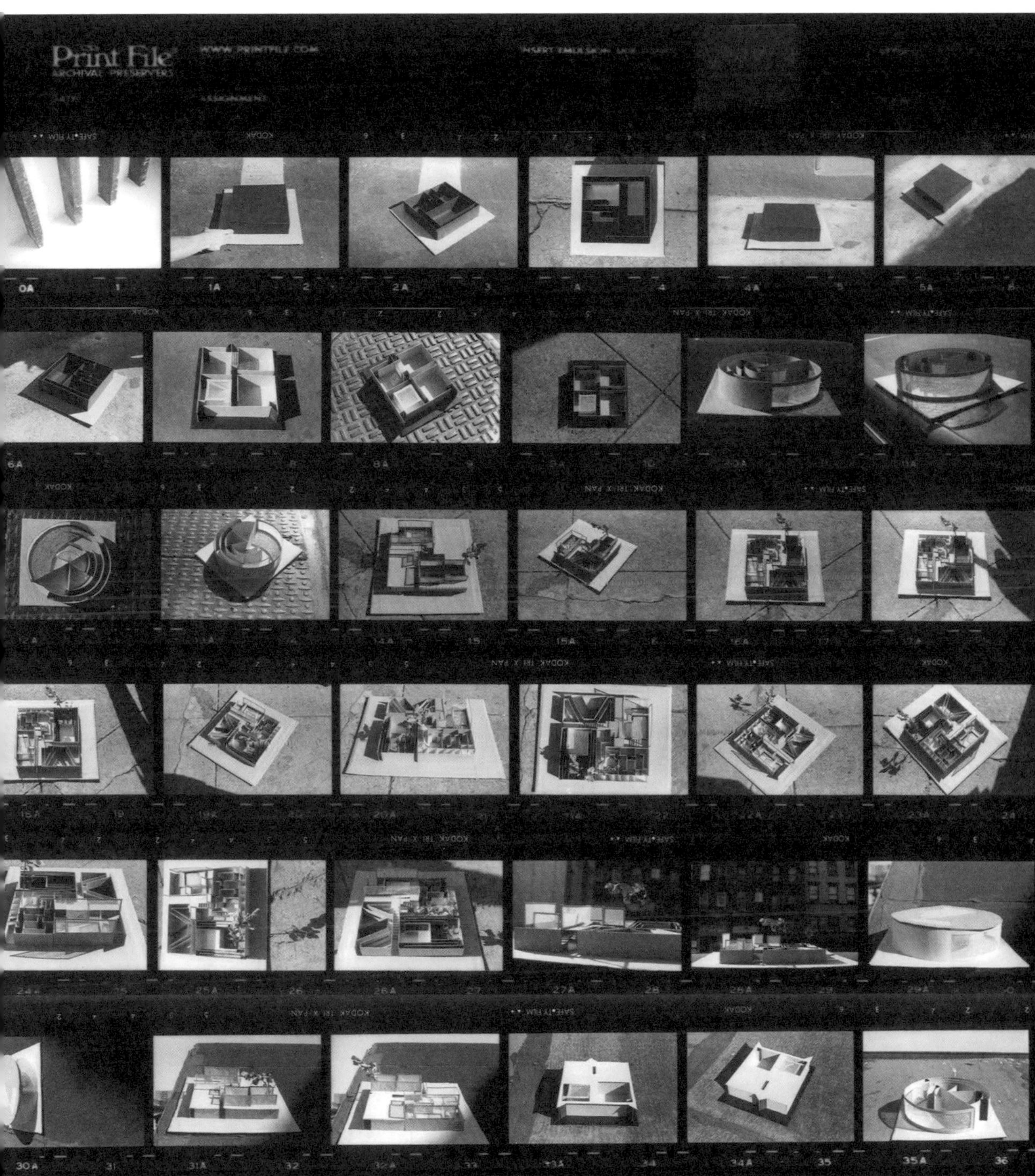

Miguel Rio Branco, *Oiticica's Subterranean Tropicalia Projects*, 1971.
César and Claudio Oiticica Collection, Rio de Janeiro

Marta Minujín created *Minuphone* in 1967 as part of her involvement with E.A.T. (Experiments in Art and Technology). *Minuphone* consisted of a telephone booth that acted unpredictably as the viewers entered it and dialed numbers, which would then trigger seven different special events inside the booth, including a sequence of psychedelic images, flashing lights, a TV set showing the participant via live closed-circuit video, and colored water that flooded the cabin from below. The work was first installed in the Howard Wise Gallery in New York in 1967.

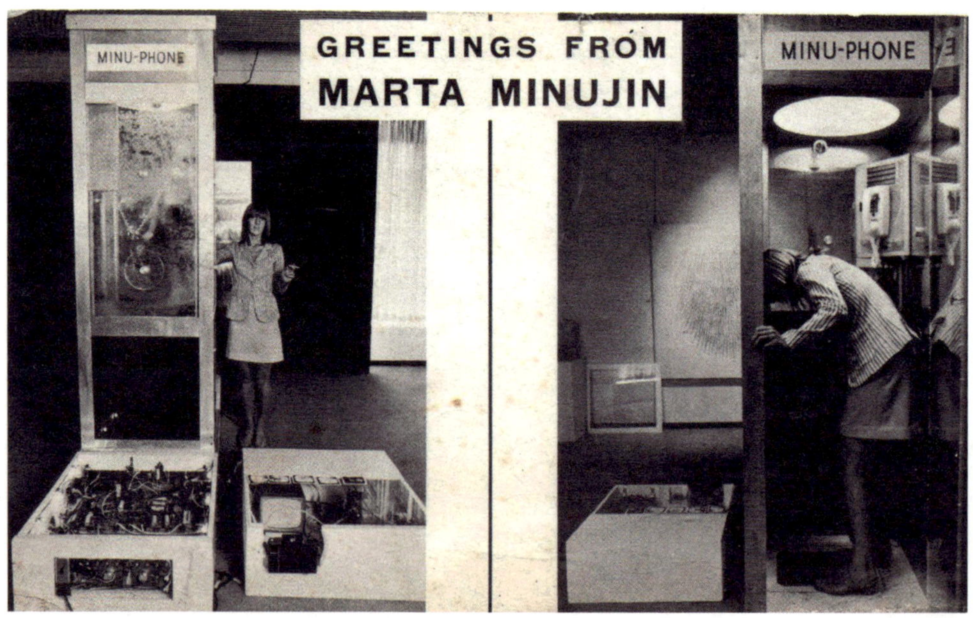

Postcard invitation for *Minuphone*, 1967. Marta Minujín Archive

NEW YORK REPORTER &

TOTAL ART IN A TELEPHONE BOOTH
(TAPE INSERTS AVAILABLE IN PROGRAM DOCUMENTATION UNIT)

ANNCR: IF YOU WENT INTO A TELPHONE BOOTH TO MAKE AN ORDINARY TELEPHONE CALL AND FOUND CEILING LIGHTS CHANGING COLOR, THE WALLS TURNING BLACK OR BLUE, AND BUZZING AND RUSHING NOISES FILLING YOUR EARS, YOU WOULD WONDER WHAT WAS WRONG WITH THE TELEPHONE COMPANY -- OR WITH YOUR OWN MIND. WELL, THERE IS ONE SUCH TELEPHONE BOOTH AND IT IS THE PROTOTYPE OF WHAT ITS INVENTOR HOPES WILL BE THE PHONE OF THE FUTURE. HERE WITH THAT STORY IS ----------.

NARR: IT LOOKS JUST LIKE AN ORDINARY TELEPHONE BOOTH -- BUT WHEN YOU DIAL YOU GET MORE THAN TELEPHONE NUMBERS, AND THAT$ THE IDEA, SAYS THE ARTIST-INVENTOR, MARTA MINUJIN (MINUIN)...

TAPE:--MINUJIN: "WHEN YOU DIAL THE NUMBER, ALL KINDS OF THINGS HAPPEN TO YOU."

NARR: WHAT HAPPENS TO YOU, ACCORDING TO MISS MINUJIN, IS AN ARTISTIC, CREATIVE EXPERIENCE APPROPRIATE TO THE AGE OF TECHNOLOGY IN WHICH WE LIVE. MACHINES PLAY A VITAL PART IN OUR DAILY LIVES: COMMUNICATION,PARTICULARLY MASS COMMUNICATION, IS AN EQUALLY IMPORTANT PART OF OUR EXISTENCE AND IT IS HER CONCEPT THAT ART SHOULD BE A FUNCTION OF MASS COMMUNICATION THROUGH ELECTRONICS. TO MAKE THIS IDEA CLEARER SHE POINTS OUT THAT WHEN YOU USE HER TELEPHONE IF THE LINE IS BUSY OR THERE IS NO ANSWER AND THERE IS NO COMMUNICATION, NOTHING HAPPENS...

TAPE: MINUJIN: "...JUST HAPPENS WHEN THE PEOPLE REALLY TALK AND THE PEOPLE HAVE FIVE EFFECTS TO GET INFORMATION ABOUT THEM-SELVES...LIKE THEY CAN HEAR (SEE) THEMSELVES ON A TELEVISION SCREEN (IN THE FLOOR) THEY CAN GET A PICTURE BY POLAROID CAMERA, THEY CAN RECORD THEIR VOICE WHILE THEY ARE TALKING AND IT PLAYS BACK FORTY-FIVE SECONDS LATER AND SO WHEN THE PEOPLE ARE TALKING THEY CAN HEAR WHAT THEY SAID BEFORE."

NARR: THERE IS ALSO AN ECHO, THE FEEL AND THE SOUND OF WIND, THE WALLS OF THE PHONE BOOTH FILL UP WITH COLORED WATER AND THE CEILING LIGHT CHANGES COLOR ACCORDING TO THE VIBRATIONS OF THE VOICE. IF THIS SOUNDS CONFUSING -- PARTICULARLY IF YOU WERE TRYING TO MAKE AN APPOINTMENT OR WRITE DOWN A COMPLICATED ADDRESS -- WELL, UNDOUBTEDLY IT WOULD BE. THE KEY TO MISS MINUJIN$ IDEA IS THAT A TELEPHONE CALL, LIKE MANY OF OUR ROUTINE ACTIONS, IS IMPERSONL. BY MAKING IT PERSONAL SHE GIVES AN INDIVIDUAL A DIFFERENT, AND, HOPEFULLY, ILLUMINATING IMAGE OF THEMSELVES. MARTA MINUJIN, A YOUNG WOMAN WITH A PIXYISH FACE FRAMED IN LONG BLOND HAIR, WAS BORN IN BUENOS AIRES AND HER FIRST EXPERIMENTS IN THIS KIND OF IMPROVISED, ENVIRONMENTAL ART WERE CARRIED ON IN ARGENTINA.

(OPT) ONE SUCH PROJECT INVOLVED RANDOM COMMUNICATION BETWEEN THREE COUNTRIES -- ARGENTINA, THE UNITED STATES AND GERMANY -- THROUGH RADIO, TELEPHONE AND TELEPRINTER, EVERY HOUR ON THE HOUR FOR A TTOTAL OF FORTY-EIGHT HOURS. (END OPT)

MISS MINUJIN STARTED WORK ON THE TELEPHONE, WHICH SHE CALLS "MINUPHONE," IN HER OWN COUNTRY BUT CAME TO THE U.S. AT THE BEGINNING OF THIS YEAR ON A GUGGENHEIM GRANT BECAUSE TECHNICAL FACILITIES HERE WERE MORE READILY AVAILABLE. WHILE SHE IS HERE, SHE WILL BE WORKING ON OTHER PROJECTS INVOLVING ART AND COMMUNICATION -- WHAT SHE CALLS "GIVING A NEW SHAPE TO INFORMATION." (OPT) ONE OF THESE IS A PUBLIC TELEVISION BOOTH.

TAPE -- MINUJIN: "YOU ENTER A TV BOOTH...YOU ARE WAITING FOR SOMEBODY AND YOU LOOK AT TELEVISION FIFTEEN MINUTES, TEN MINUTES, YOU SEE THE NEWS AND THEN YOU GO OUT. SO THAT PEOPLE WILL NOT MEET ANY MORE ON THE CORNER (OF THE STREET) THEY WILL MEET IN THE BOOTH." (END OPT)

NARR: MEANWHILE, SHE SEES INNUMERABLE POSSIBILITIES FOR EXTENDING THE EFFECTS IN THE MINUPHONE, VARYING THEM IN MANY WAYS, BECAUSE, AS SHE SAYS, THE EFFECTS THEMSELVES ARE NOT IMPORTANT, ONLY THE EXPERIENCE THEY PRODUCE. (OPT) TO HEAR HOW THIS EXPERIENCE AFFECTS THE AVERAGE PERSON, LET$ LISTEN IN ON PART OF A CONVERSATION FROM THE MINUPHONE...

TAPE--BUZZING, FOLLOWED BY MAN$ VOICE: AS DESIRED: "HELLO, IM IN A WEIRD PHONE BOOTH...YOU WOULDNT BELIEVE IT IF I TOLD YOU...IT$ A COMPUTER DEVICE...IT$ A PHONE BOOTH WITH CLOSED

"Total Art in a Telephone Booth," review of *Minuphone* by New York reporter, July 18, 1967. Marta Minujín Archive

MARTA MINUJIN'S MINUPHONE BOOTH
IN COLLABORATION WITH PER BIORN, TECH. ASST.

Lift the phone off the hook. Touch-dial a local number. Call someone whom you wish to speak with for at least three minutes. Do not hang up the Minuphone for three minutes, no matter what happens.

When the screen comes down behind you, place your hand in front and against it, so that a neat shadow is formed, and do not move it until the light goes off. You may move your hand now; your shadow will remain there.....This sequence will repeat three times.

At times you will not see anything happening, keep talking because your voice will be recorded to be played back later, or you will get a true echo effect.

If the white light on the ceiling turns redddish-blue, sing, yell, etc., because the colors will change according to the pitch of your voice.

If all the lights go off and only the one on the floor goes on, look down until you see yourself perfectly centered in the TV screen (trying moving your face to the left). Then, stand still, until the image fades. If you would like a Polaroid snapshot of your TV image, inquire in the office. Charge is 50 cents.

\# \#

Instructions for *Minuphone*, 1967. Marta Minujín Archive

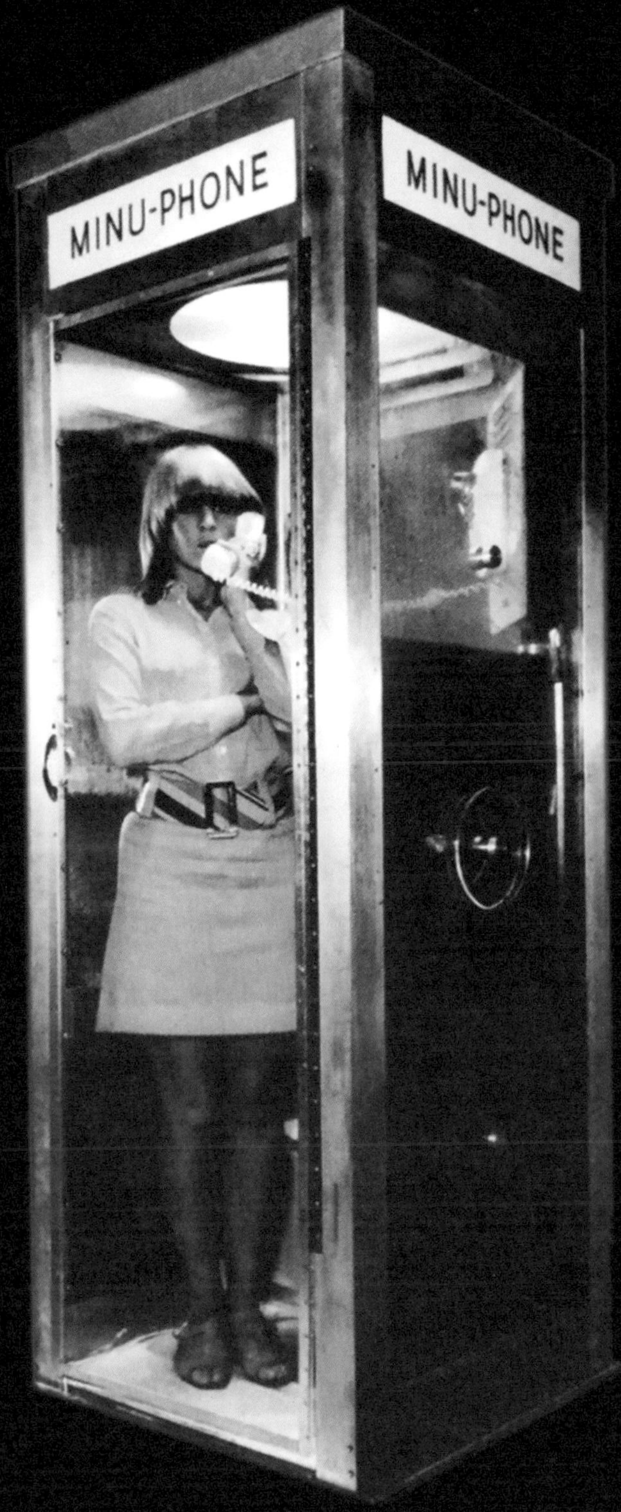

Marta Minujín inside *Minuphone*, 1967. Marta Minujín Archive

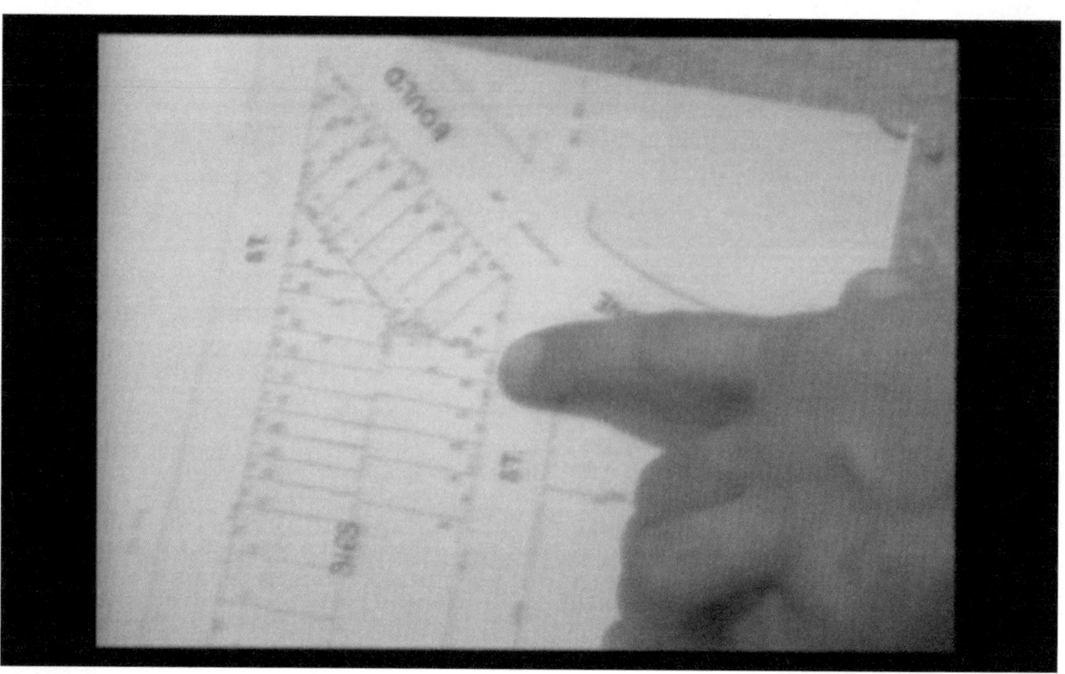

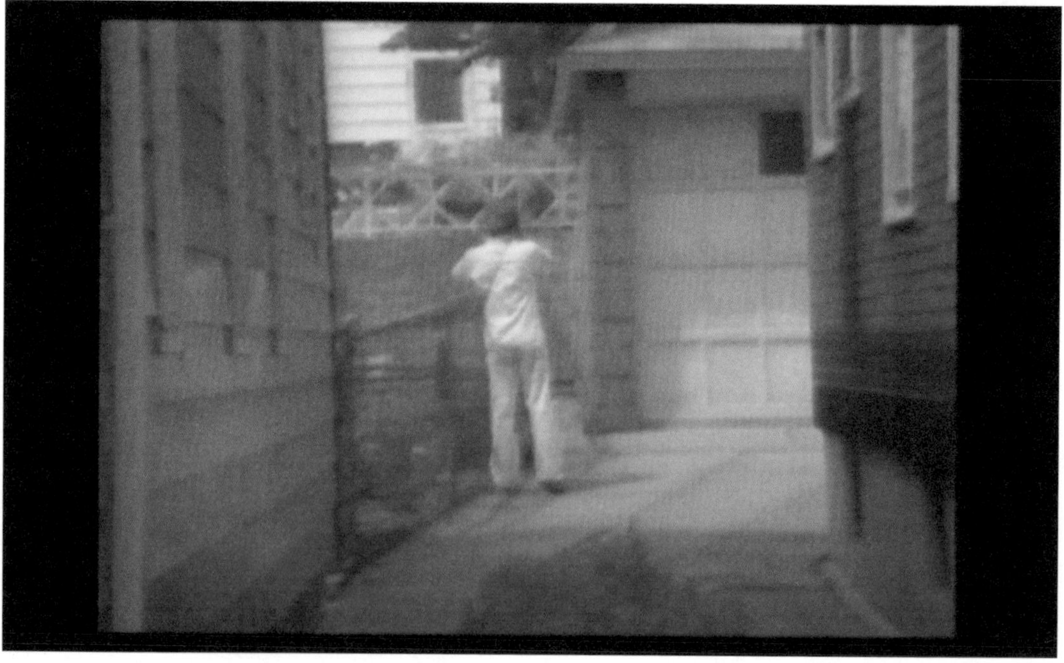

Jaime Davidovich (with Gordon Matta-Clark), *Reality Properties: Fake Estates (Queens Project)*, 1975.
Jaime Davidovich Foundation

When [Gordon Matta-Clark] learned that I was using video, he said, “I’m buying these slivers of land in Queens,” and I said, “I’m very interested in that.” He went and got the blueprints and he gave me three; they were maybe ten dollars each. He said, “Let’s go to Queens to find my pieces,” but the guy who owned the rest of the property would not let us in because the piece of land was inside his warehouse, in a corner. The size of that little piece was maybe one foot–he didn’t even know that it wasn’t his! It belonged to the city. In other places, however, we were able to go and see the pieces. I went there with my Portapak and made a video.

— Jaime Davidovich

I was not interested in covering a wall in an exhibition space with tape. I was interested in using spaces that were not considered appropriate frameworks for an artwork–for instance, in doing a tape project on a sidewalk, which is a public space, or on a billboard . . .

— Jaime Davidovich

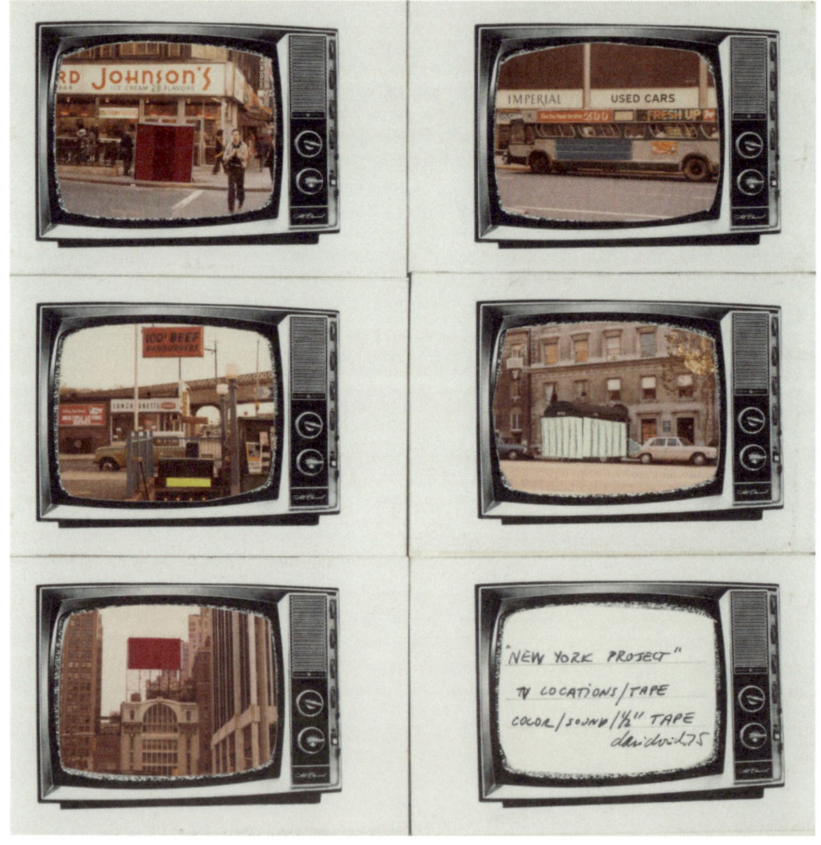

Jaime Davidovich, *New York Project: 6 Monitors*, 1975. Private collection

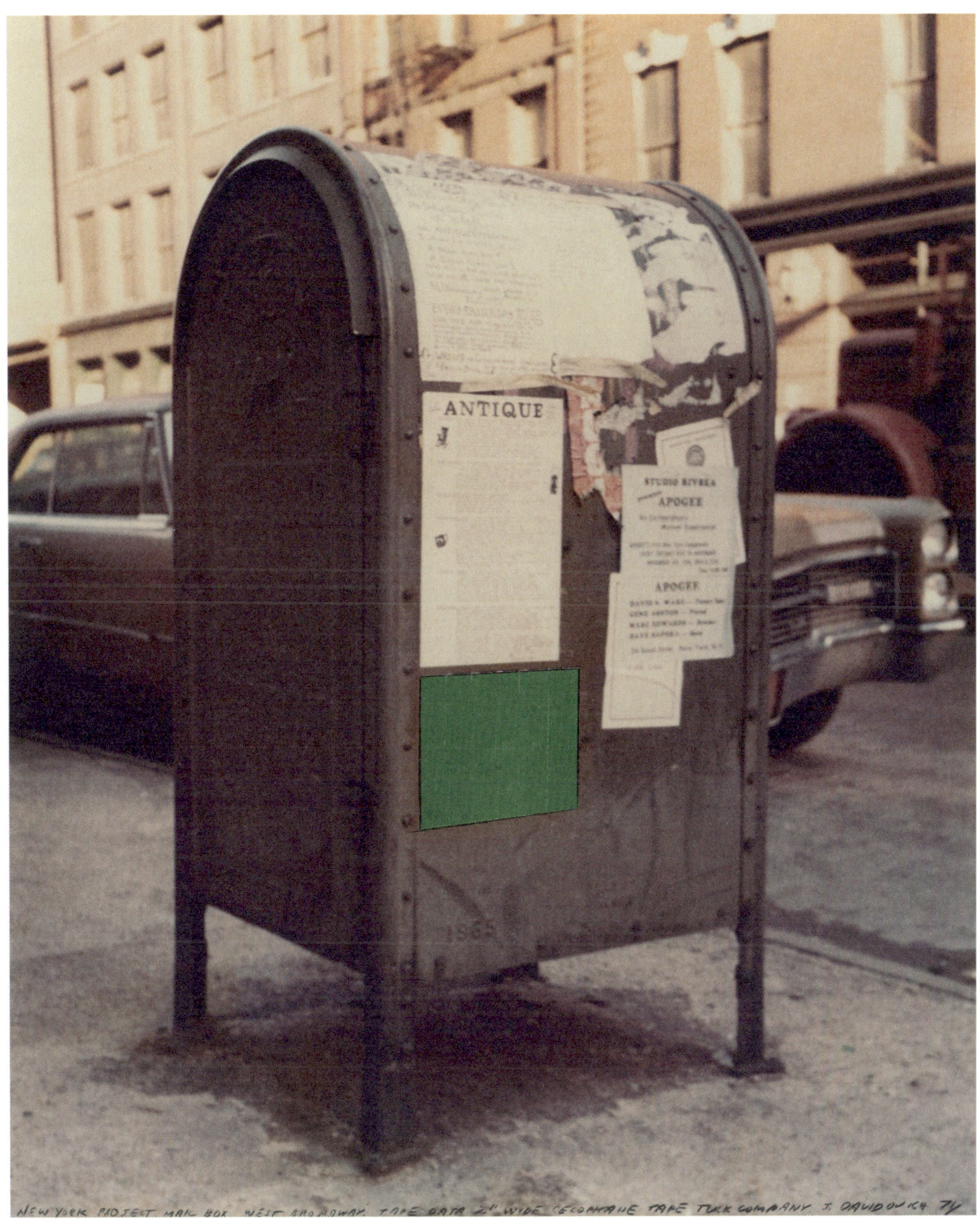

Jaime Davidovich, *New York Project: Mailbox. West Broadway*, 1974. Private collection

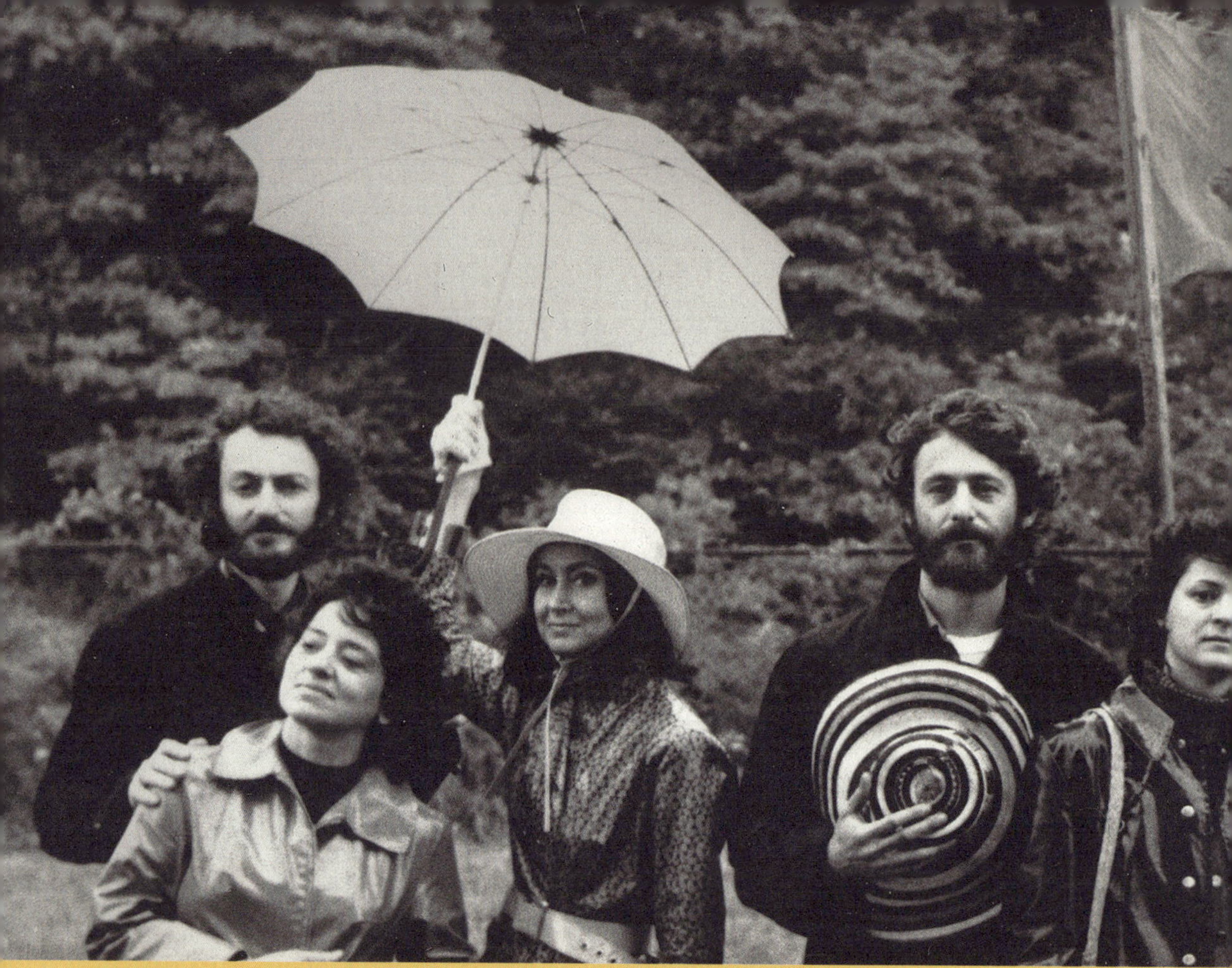

The prospect or the expectation of visiting land or ground designated for a special purpose by properly appointed persons gathered to come together and convene in the immanent act and probable exercise of the faculty of sight, the power and nature of vision, in relation to the possibility of seeing something of a distinct and vivid kind or unusual beauty, the visual appearance, aspect and view of a landscape, the extended scene of an area covered by the eye from one point but which nevertheless may multiply itself consequently or simultaneously so as to adorn a surface or picture of each self or to fancy and represent dramatically or to represent with words and describe graphically, setting forth in a concrete or a collective sense a solid image, representation, type, likeness, similitude and portrait

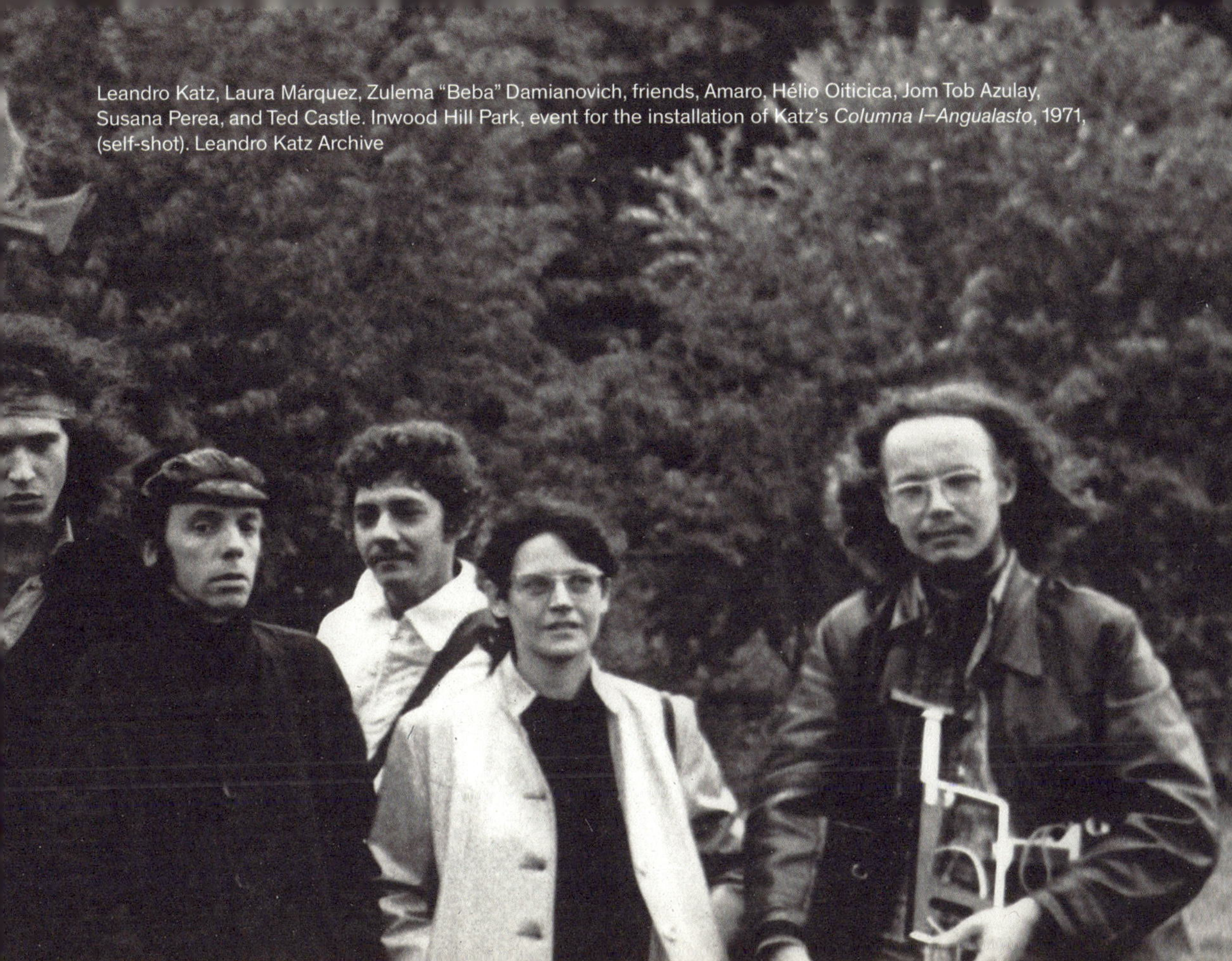
Leandro Katz, Laura Márquez, Zulema "Beba" Damianovich, friends, Amaro, Hélio Oiticica, Jom Tob Azulay, Susana Perea, and Ted Castle. Inwood Hill Park, event for the installation of Katz's *Columna I–Angualasto*, 1971, (self-shot). Leandro Katz Archive

of a happy rural seat of many diverse views, mobile or immobile beings, mental contemplation or visions in the place, position, location and site of *Column I* in relation to its surroundings in the northwest corner of Inwood Hill Park at the Northwest extreme of the island of Manhattan, county of New York in the State of New York, and also, in relation to its given name Angualasto meaning "water from the heights," actual name of the site and terrain of a town by the Chilean frontier in the Western province of San Juan, Republic of Argentina, once occupied by communities of people tributary to the Inca empire, and probably later occupied by Incas fleeing South at a certain period of bracketed time and gardens of meaning.

— Leandro Katz

2. Community and Institutions

We were getting money from the establishment, so we knew that there were certain things of which you could not talk about in workshops and activities. The thing was how to deal with that, and get the money, and still do the job.

— Nitza Tufiño

Between 1965 and 1975, Latin American artists countered the exclusionary practices of major museums and galleries in New York by forging their own spaces to create and exhibit artworks and forming artist-led initiatives that sought to challenge simplistic, stereotypical views of Latin American art. This chapter highlights spaces that fostered community, collective practice, and friendship, such as the artists-run New York Graphic Workshop and the Pratt Graphics Center, alongside galleries and institutional spaces dedicated to Latin American art and artist-led initiatives that promoted artistic self-representation in the United States.

A small number of galleries and alternative art spaces dedicated to Latin American art emerged in the city, including Galería Sudamericana, Galería Bonino, and Cayman Gallery. Along with other institutional spaces dedicated to promoting Latin American art in New York, such as the Center for Inter-American Relations (CIAR, today's Americas Society), they helped shape the category of Latin American art for the North American public.[1] Founded in 1967 by David Rockefeller, CIAR was the first exhibition space in the city—and the second in the United States, following the gallery of the Organization of American States in Washington, DC—to promote Latin American art. The goal of CIAR was to create transnational exchanges of policy, arts, and culture throughout the Americas.

Artists protested CIAR's inaugural exhibition, deeming it conservative and creating stereotypical views of Latin American art. Some saw CIAR as a tool for North American cultural diplomacy in Latin America—mainly through art exhibitions—that served the interests of the state and corporations during the Cold War. Others created works disguised as social events held at CIAR that opened it to more experimental practices while mocking its seriousness, such as Marta Minujín's *Minucode* (1968) and Eduardo Costa, John Perrault, and Hannah Weirner's *Fashion Show Poetry Event* (1969). One instance of the overt denunciation of North American power caused controversy: in the exhibition *Energy Systems* at CIAR (1975), Juan Downey included the work *Anaconda*, criticizing North American corporations' exploitation of resources in Chile. The work included a live anaconda, which was removed following complaints by animal rights activists. Its suppression was perceived as censorship and proof that the artist had effectively touched an institutional nerve.[2]

Incited by political and artistic activism, two key art institutions emerged in 1969: El Museo del Barrio and Taller Boricua. Founded by artists who were already participating in different activist movements against the marginalization of the Puerto Rican communities and who were invested in creating spaces to disseminate Puerto Rican art and culture in New York, these institutions served as educational and cultural centers for the East Harlem Puerto Rican community.[3]

In the spirit of resistance, Latin American artists also embraced Institutional Critique, a form of art practice that revealed and questioned the multifarious power dynamics operating within art institutions, to create works targeting such major museums and cultural centers as MoMA, the Whitney Museum of American Art, and even the CIAR.

NOTES

[1] For the history of spaces for Latin American and Latino art in New York during the period, see Taína B. Caragol Barreto, "Boom and Dust: The Rise of Latin American and Latino Art in New York Exhibition Spaces and the Auction House Market, 1970s–1980s" (PhD diss., City University of New York, 2013).

[2] Americas Society restaged Minucode in an exhibition curated by José Luis Blondet and Gabriela Rangel in 2010. The work was also presented at MoMA in 2021. For more on Marta Minujín's *Minucode* and Eduardo Costa's *Fashion Show Poetry Event*, see Alexander Alberro, "Media, Sculpture, Myth," in *A Principality of Its Own: 40 Years of Visual Arts at the Americas Society*, ed. José Luis Falconi and Gabriela Rangel (New York: Americas Society, 2006), 160–79; Daniel Quiles, "Marta Minujín: talks about *Minucode*, 1968," *Artforum* 48, no. 8 (April 2010): 156–9; and Gabriela Rangel, Alexander Alberro, and Inés Katzenstein, *Marta Minujín: Minucodes* (New York: Americas Society, 2015). For more on Juan Downey's Anaconda, see Julia Bozer, "Juan Downey's 'Anaconda' Map of Chile, 1975," in *Shift: Graduate Journal of Visual and Material Culture*, no. 11 (October 2019), accessed January 4, 2022, https://shiftjournal.org/issue-11/bozer/.

[3] For more on the history of each of these spaces, see Yasmín Ramirez, "The Activist Legacy of Puerto Rican Artists in New York and 'The Art Heritage of Puerto Rico,'" *ICAA Documents Project Working Papers*, no. 1 (September 2007): 46–53; *Voces y Visiones: Highlights from El Museo del Barrio's Permanent Collection, 1969–2004*, ed. Fatima Bercht and Deborah Cullen, vol. 1 (New York: Museo del Barrio, 2003).

Art Spaces

Several commercial art galleries and institutional spaces promoted the works of Latin American artists between 1965 and 1975 (and beyond). Spaces such as Galería Sudamericana, Galería Bonino, and Cayman Gallery were important sites for the exhibition and circulation of Latin American art in the city, bringing visibility to these artists and contributing to the establishment of a more complex notion of Latin American art in the United States, a niche that not all artists embraced because of the potential for stereotyping. Other artist-led initiatives, most of them taking the form of publications, created their own methods of communicating the issues that Latin American artists faced while living in the United States.

Luis Camnitzer, José Guillermo Castillo, and Liliana Porter (New York Graphic Workshop). Exhibition catalogue. Galería Colibrí, San Juan, Puerto Rico, November 6, 1970. Liliana Porter Collection

Galería Sudamericana, founded in 1953 by the Chilean writer and critic Armando Zegrí, was an important venue—and one of the earliest—for Latin American artists in the city. Galería Bonino, founded by Italian-Argentinian gallerist Alfredo Bonino, had branches in Buenos Aires, Rio de Janeiro, and New York, and played a fundamental role in facilitating artistic exchanges between these three cities in the 1960s. Bonino's influential exhibition *Magnet: New York* (1964) featured Latin American artists working in the city and set an important precedent, touring the United States and Mexico with the support of the CIAR.

PRINTS

1 Tuba and Chorus
2 Obese and Harmonic Soprano
3 Seated Woman
4 Semi-sympathetic Cement Mixer
5 Huge Cement Mixer
6 Rug
7 Councilman
8 Hero
9 Two in A Box
10 Fat Women in A Mirror
11 "Go back now, thou who can," the river said, crying.
12 Para Musch

ALSO DRAWINGS

GALLERY HOURS: Monday through Saturday 11 to 6:30, Friday evenings to 9:30

GALERIA SUDAMERICANA

10 EAST 8th STREET, NEW YORK 3, N. Y. • GRamercy 3-7510

Luis Camnitzer – N.Y., 1962. Exhibition brochure. Galería Sudamericana, New York, March 19–30, 1963. Institute for Studies on Latin American Art (ISLAA) Library and Archives

Armando Zegrí had been a war correspondent for the United Press. When he retired, he invested his savings in his Galería Sudamericana and maintained his press contacts. The gallery was open to all South American artists who came to New York. His press contacts served so that with each exhibition in the artist's country the press would publish a news item about the success of both the artist and the show. In addition, Zegrí had contacts with museums, taking advantage of the institutional need to demonstrate a certain degree of inclusiveness. Because of that a work of mine entered the collection of the Metropolitan Museum. Zegrí was probably the most dedicated and honest gallery owner of his day. I am still ashamed that in the first meeting I asked him for a receipt for the consignment of the works. He gave it to me, but with such a look of hurt because of my lack of confidence that it remained etched in my memory.

At the time of the Museo Latinoamericano and MICLA, the artists who were part of these groups wanted to organize a tribute exhibition at the Bonino Gallery following Zegrí's disappearance in 1972. Bonino was the gallery in New York that, in a more pretentious way, had inherited Zegrí's mission and that seemed the most appropriate place to acknowledge the importance of his achievements. The project was unfortunately not accepted. Meanwhile Bonino also disappeared, but the image of Zegrí lives on.

—Luis Camnitzer

The Zegrí Gallery was founded in June 1953 with the express purpose of devoting itself exclusively to the presentation of contemporary Latin American art in New York. At the time almost no Latin American artists exhibited in New York. Most galleries openly admitted a total lack of interest in Latin American art. They didn't believe there was any, and when confronted with work by any Latin American artist who dared to venture into the city they refused to touch it. . . . The absence of Latin American art in New York affected me deeply. In New York, where the best and the worst art of the world was represented, why not Latin American art?

—Armando Zegrí

11th ANNUAL EXHIBITION

LATIN AMERICAN PRINTS

JANUARY 5
FEBRUARY 4
1965

SUDAMERICANA

ARMANDO ZEGRI
DIRECTOR

10 EAST 8th ST., N. Y. 3 • GR 3-7510

Fifty artists from eleven countries with a total of more than a hundred works in varied graphic media are represented in our 11th Annual Exhibition of Latin American Prints. Again in 1965 we introduced new names along with new work by artists included in previous annuals. Because of the number of artists participating, the quantity of prints and the quality and variety, this exhibition offers a panoramic view of the graphic work now being done in Latin America.

Armando Zegri, Director

ARTISTS AND COUNTRIES IN THIS EXHIBITION:

ARGENTINA
Alda María Armagni, Carmen Gracia, Mabel Rubli, Daniel Zelaya, Jorge G. Luna Ercilla, Carlos Scannapiesco, Osvaldo Romberg, Albino Fernandez, Liliana Porter, Delia del Carril

BRAZIL
Marina Caram, Roland Cabot, Livio Abramo

CHILE
Roser Bru, Dinora, Florencia de Amesti, Simone Chambelland, Mario Toral, Eduardo Vilches, Lea Kleiner, Jaime Cruz, Juan Downey, Eugenio Tellez, Carlos Ortuzar, Jorge Gonzales Tornero

COLOMBIA
Omar Rayo, Enrique Sanchez

CUBA
Emilio Sanchez, Wilfredo Lam, Daniel Serra-Badué, Guido Llinas

GUATEMALA
Roberto Cabrera

MEXICO
Francisco Dosamantes, Raul Anguiano, Reyes Mesa, Hector Xavier, Rufino Tamayo

PANAMA
Julio Augusto Zachrisson

PARAGUAY
Edith Jimenez

PERU
Francisco Espinoza, Maria Scholten

PUERTO RICO
Lorenzo Homar, Rafael Tufiño, José Alicea, Myrna Baez, John Balossi, Antonio Martorell, R. Ferrer, Cesar Irizarry, Luis Hernandez, Rivero

URUGUAY
Luis Camnitzer, José Gamarra, Giancarlo Puppo

We are grateful for their cooperation in this exhibition to:

Sr. Hugo Parpagnoli, Director of Museum of Modern Art, Buenos Aires, Argentina

Sr. Enrique Gomez, Director of Galeria de Arte, Montevideo, Uruguay

Sr. Luigi Marrozzini, Director of Galeria Colibri, San Juan, Puerto Rico

GALLERY HOURS:
Tuesday through Saturday 11-6:30
Friday evenings to 9:30
Closed Sunday, Monday

11th Annual Exhibition of Latin American Prints. Exhibition catalogue. Galería Sudamericana, New York, January 5–February 4, 1965. Museo de Arte Moderno, Buenos Aires. ICAA Record ID 777359

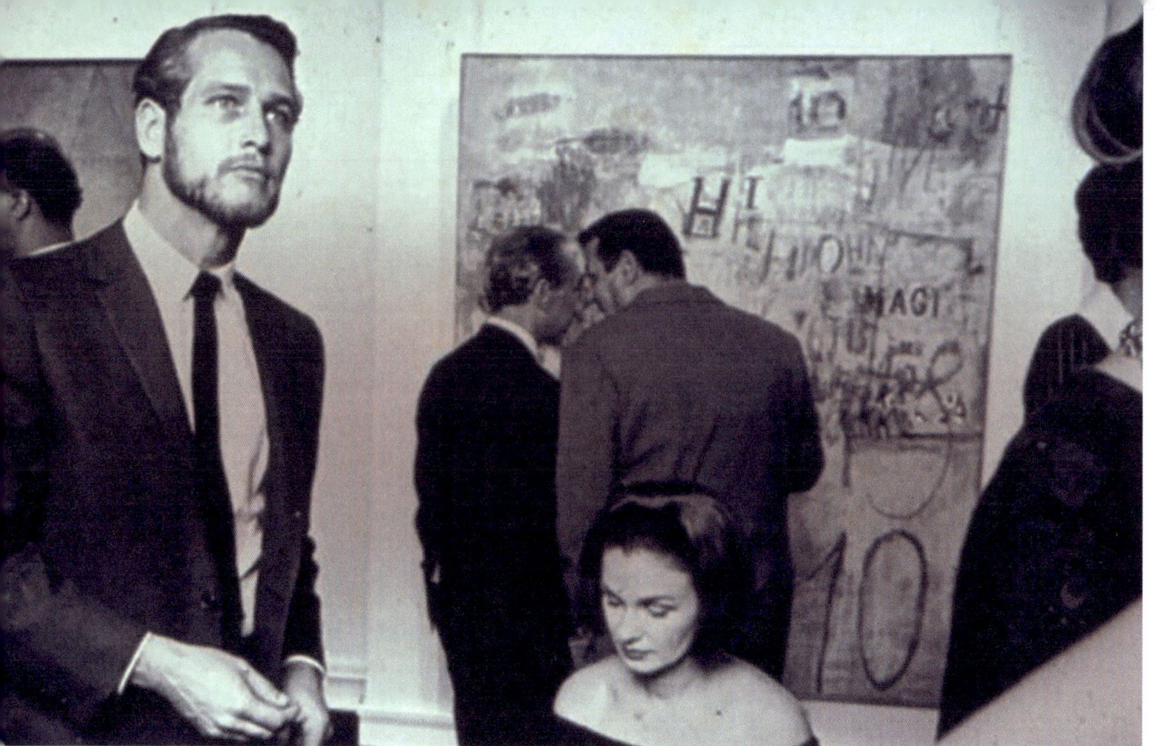

It is not exactly an invasion, but there is at least a strong Latin-American infiltration into the international strongholds so largely cornered by New York galleries. The exhibition currently at the Galería Bonino, 7 West 57th Street, arranged by the Inter-American Foundation for the Arts, might have been called "Target: New York," in which case the comment would be in order that a sound hit, although not a bull's-eye, has been scored.

But the exhibition is more tactfully called "Magnet: New York," since all the 28 artists represented have been lured from their homelands to residence in this wonderful and terrible city. The list includes 12 Argentines, 3 Colombians and 3 Cubans, 2 artists each from Guatemala, Uruguay and Bolivia, and single representatives of Mexico, Chile, Venezuela and Nicaragua.

—John Canaday, The New York Times

Paul Newman and Joanne Woodward at the opening of *Magnet: New York*, Galería Bonino, New York, September 21, 1964. A work by Sarah Grilo, *Charge* (1964), is in the background. Colección Centro de Estudios Espigas - Fundación Espigas

Magnet: New York. Exhibition catalogue. Galería Bonino, New York, September 21–October 10, 1964.
Colección Centro de Estudios Espigas - Fundación Espigas

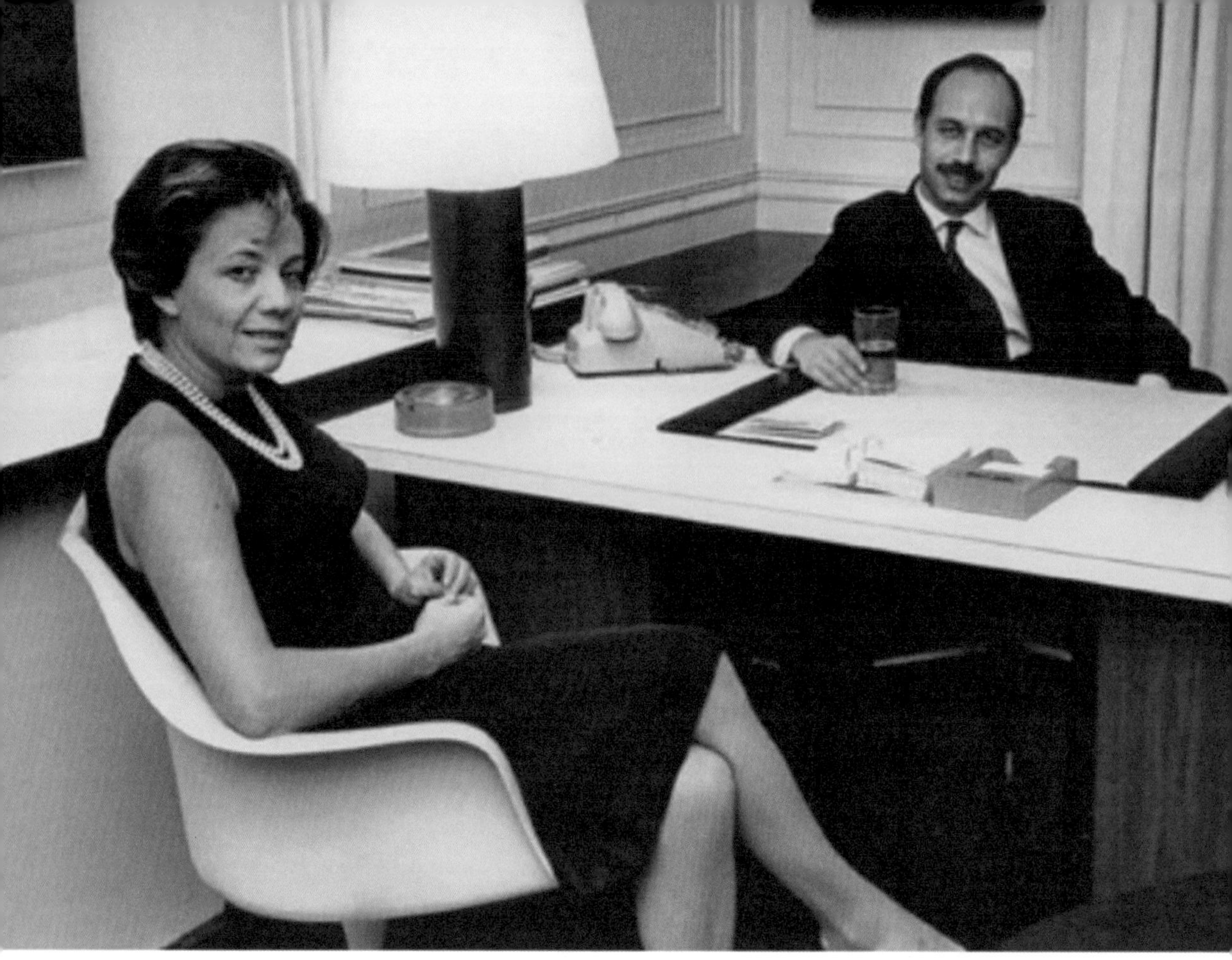

Fernanda and Alfredo Bonino at Galería Bonino, New York, ca. 1965.
Fernanda Bonino Archive

We arrived to New York in 1963 with plans to open a gallery. Andrew Morris was closing his space at 7 West 57th street, and we took it over. We did more than fifty exhibitions there . . . The contacts I had from that first trip to New York were a good start and over the years, we added many loyal collectors to our portfolio. In a way, it was always the same people. Most were from the United States, and then there were Europeans that lived in New York. We also had some regular buyers from abroad. Naturally, there were some from Argentina, like Guido Di Tella, and also from Italy.

The Rockefeller family–Nelson, David, Rodman, all of them–were also clients of ours . . . David Rockefeller became a friend; he was buying a lot of Latin American art . . . In 1964, we organized a very successful exhibition of all the Latin American artists living in the city. It was called *Magnet: New York*, and that opened up the market to Latin American art. Alfredo had come up with the idea for that show, which later traveled to Mexico. He called up the curator Stanton Catlin and organized it with the support of the Inter-American Foundation for the Arts, a nonprofit founded by the Rockefellers. When the show was up, we made an appointment for Nelson Rockefeller to see it. That day the phone rang, and when I picked up, a young woman said, "This is Mr. Rockefeller's secretary. He is a little bit delayed. Is it all right if he gets there at six fifteen instead of six?" I laughed and said, "Mr. Rockefeller can come at any time he wants." That day, he bought six or seven pieces, including two works by Liliana Porter.

— Fernanda Bonino

In the '60s, New York was consolidating the geopolitical power of its art and Latin America was, particularly with regard to visual arts, more than ever "the backyard." And a Latin American artist, especially if he or she aspired to make avant-garde art in New York, was perceived as an annoyance or as an intruder. . . . The category of "Latin American" was very much present. It was a label that they would stick on you as soon as you arrived. A label of discrimination. And the decisive factor that led to the formation of the so-called Museo Latinoamericano was the discrimination of galleries, curators and the establishment in general. In other words, discrimination meant lack of access to galleries, meaning the development of a career. And one would feel the discrimination because most Latin American artists already had earned a name in their home countries, and they rightfully aspired to continue their professional life in New York.

— César Paternosto

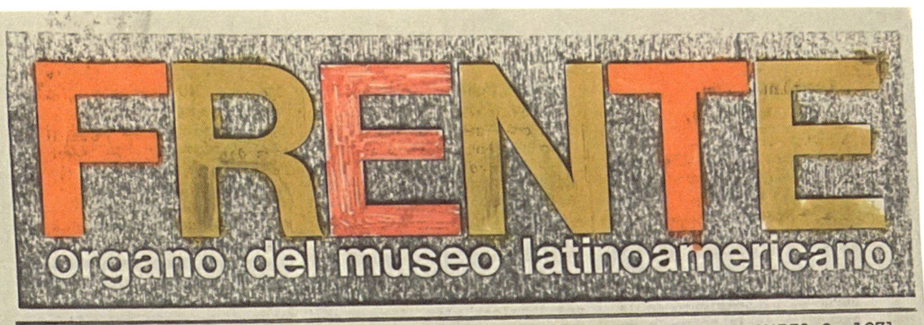

AÑO I VOLUMEN I NEW YORK MARZO 2 1971

carta a latinoamerica

Un grupo de artistas e intelectuales latinoamericanos residentes en EE.UU., acabamos de formar en MUSEO LATINOAMERICANO. Esta agrupación se propone representar y difundir la cultura de nuestros países, actualmente falseada y utilizada con fines políticos por las instituciones que se atribuyen dicho objetivo, y de las cuales es un excelente ejemplo el center for interamerican relations. Este centro, aprovechando nuestra ignorancia respecto de su verdadera naturaleza, ha logrado que contribuyéramos en el pasado a justificar su existencia con el aporte de nuestro trabajo y la posible significación de nuestros nombres en el mundo de la cultura. Pero la corta distancia y en algunos casos el trato frecuente nos ha permitido ajustar la visión ingenua que posibilitó nuestro acercamiento al c.i.r., y nos ha decidido a rechazar totalmente toda perspectiva de colaboración con esta institución, o cualquier otra de características similares. Y hemos tomado esta decisión a pesar de las supuestas ventajas económicas que implicaría nuestra asociación con el center, porque sentimos el deber de tomar algunas precauciones mínimas en defensa de nuestra identidad intelectual.
En efecto, el c.i.r. y su antepasado la interamerican foundation for the arts han hecho lo posible por destru

sigue en pag.2

PLATAFORMA

EL MUSEO LATINOAMERICANO propone una transformación para lograr un amplio nucleamiento de latinoamericanos envueltos en la tarea de difundir el nuevo fenómeno cultural que está emergiendo.
Se hace indispensable para dicha tarea la identidad social de todos sus componentes para una efectiva acción dentro del medio que conforma nuestra cotidianeidad.
Artistas plásticos, músicos, escritores, cineastas, gente de teatro, etc., buscan expandir por todos los medios posibles el resultado de su trabajo fuera de los medios e instituciones que distorsionan el verdadero contenido de su mensaje.
La unión de todos estos intelectuales promoverá una mayor comunicación entre ellos y consecuentemente logrará la proyección a que se aspira:

1) Operar fuera del control de fundaciones, corporaciones, u otros organismos que codifican arbitrariamente una jerarquía cultural y poner en evidencia la situacion de discriminacion hacia el arte latinoamericano en los Estados Unidos.
2) Desocultar el verdadero fenómeno cultural latinoamericano e informar.
3) Diseminar el nuevo fenómeno en forma autónoma desheredándolo del sojuzgamiento socio-cultural.
4) Hacer consciente la función de trabajadores de la cultura en situación de integrar los nuevos "conocimientos" adquiridos, para el trabajo en libertad en los propios países de origen.

La efectividad de esta acción hermanada logrará que el esfuerzo individual no sea absorbido por el medio, no se desgaste en una tortuosa subsistencia, en muchos casos, y obtener una verdadera representatividad.

New York, Febrero 2, 1971.

Frente, no. 1 (March 1971). Museo Latinoamericano, New York. Private collection

Show Is Suspendec

By GRACE GLUECK

Dissent by a number of artists has caused the indefinite postponement of a show organized by the Art Gallery of the Center for Inter-American Relations, 680 Park Avenue.

The show, scheduled for April 29 through June 30, was intended to give exposure to "outstanding" Latin-American artists living in New York. The plan was to exhibit their works for one week at 15 to 20 local galleries, with a simultaneous group show at the center that would last through June.

The show was suspended after 25 of the prospective artists drew up a list of "conditions" for their participation in it and in the center's future programs. The first condition called for "a drastic revision" of the center's board of directors, with removal of those "who symbolize United States imperialist activity in our hemisphere."

The directors specifically mentioned, as "politico-financial personalities," were Lincoln Gordon, who recently resigned as president of Johns Hopkins University; John R. White, vice president and director of the Standard Oil Company (New Jersey), George Meany, president of the labor federation, and Sol M. Linowitz, chairman of the National Urban Coalition, former chairman of the Xerox Corporation, and onetime United States Ambassador to the Organization of American States.

Other conditions set by the artists specified that the center refrain from establishing relations with state or private organizations serving "as instruments of repression against social, political, economic and cultural liberation of our countries"; and that it open to the public its ad hoc meetings and study groups "where such subjects as 'U. S. Military Assistance to Latin America,' 'United States-Cuban Relations,' 'U. S. Private Investments in Latin America' and 'Current Events in Brazil' have been discussed in the past."

In reply to the artists' charges, William D. Rogers, a member and former president of the board, said:

"The issues raised by the artists' statement obviously go so directly to the central purpose and structure of the center that the board itself would have to set policy with respect to it. I doubt if any individual would be able to comment until the board has had a chance to consider it—except to express a note of personal regret that the statement indulges in personalities."

Aided by Foundations

The center, a private organization set up in 1966 to strengthen the ties of commerce and culture between the United States and Latin America, is supported by a number of foundations and corporations, as well as by dues from individual members. Three of its biggest donors are the Ford Foundation, the Rockefeller Brothers Fund and the Tinker Foundation.

Its art gallery has carried on a program of Latin-American shows. In 1967 a group of artists—some of them also involved in the present protest—wrote a letter published in The Times criticizing the opening exhibition, "Artists of the Western Hemisphere: Precursors of Modernism, 1870-1930," as "identifying both Americas in their worst aspects."

Hans van Weeren-Griek, director of the center's visual arts department, said that although other artists were willing to cooperate with the show, he had postponed it "to cool the situation." "I don't want to polarize the Latin-American art community," he said. "But the show is definitely not canceled."

Mr. van Weeren-Griek, who took over the directorship of the visual arts department from Stanton Catlin and has been meeting regularly with the dissident artists, recently sent them a letter outlining a program he intended to undertake at the center. The proposed program was partly prompted by criticisms made by the artists.

The letter listed a number of steps the department would take to expand its activities from "a sometime showcase of painting and sculpture to a broadly based dialogue between the creative minds of Latin America and the people of the United States."

Several of the artists who signed the statement have said, however, that they want no further connection with the center. "It's lamentable that it's the only organization to speak for us here," said Arnold Belkin, a painter from Mexico now living in New York. "Culture for them is an afterthought, like brandy and cigars after dinner. They specialize in

Artists Dissent

misrepresenting Latin America."

He added that the artists felt the center should carry out such activities as building up collections of Latin-American art, making grants to artists, and presenting shows of younger Latin-American artists. "But it's a hopeless task to get them to change," he said.

Mr. Belkin, Leonel Góngora, a Colombian painter, and Rubens Gerchman, a sculptor from Brazil, said that they and other artists were involved in setting up an alternate project, the Museo Latinoamericano.

An information center and gathering place for the Latin-American creative community, it would develop a program of cultural activities, help to set up courses in Latin-American art at universities, and disseminate "moral information" about censorship and suppression of cultural activities.

Board members of the Center for Inter-American Relations, in addition to those already mentioned, are:

Dr. James A. Perkins, chairman of the International Council for Educational Development and board chairman of the center.

William E. Barlow, president, Vision, Inc.

Leonard Goldenson, president, American Broadcasting-Paramount Theaters, Inc.

Andrew Heiskell, chairman, Time Inc.

Edgar F. Kaiser, president, Kaiser Industries.

Antonie T. Knoppers, senior vice president, Merck & Co.

Bayless Manning, dean, Stanford School of Law.

George S. Moore, chairman, First National City Bank of New York.

Forrest Murden Jr., president, Murden & Co.

Miss Martha Muse, president, Tinker Foundation.

David Rockefeller, chairman, Chase Manhattan Bank.

David S. Smith, associate dean, Columbia University School of International Affairs.

Arthur Ochs Sulzberger, president and publisher, The New York Times.

Charles Wagley, director, Institute for Latin American Studies, Columbia University.

Rawleigh Warner, president, Mobil Oil Corporation.

Grace Glueck, "Show Is Suspended as Artists Dissent," *New York Times*, March 20, 1971, 13

Between 1967 and 1971, a group of artists including Luis Camnitzer, Eduardo Costa, Leandro Katz, Rubens Gerchman, Carla Stellweg, César Paternosto, and Liliana Porter, among others, formed the Museo Latinoamericano. In 1971, part of the group splintered into a more politically radical faction, Movimiento de Independencia Cultural Latinoamericana (MICLA). These groups protested against the CIAR for its ties with corporations and governmental entities that had interventionist agendas in Latin America, publicly challenging the institution with letters to the *New York Times* that detailed their objections to its representation of Latin American art and their demands for changes to its administration.

Liliana Porter, Memory of the first MICLA meeting, New York, April 3, 1971.
Carla Stellweg Archive

NUEVA YORK,
Abril 3
11:00 a 15:00 Hs.

VITA
LEONEL
LUIS
LUIS
CARLA
TEDDY
YO

Liliana Porter, Memory of the first MICLA meeting, New York, April 3, 1971.
Carla Stellweg Archive

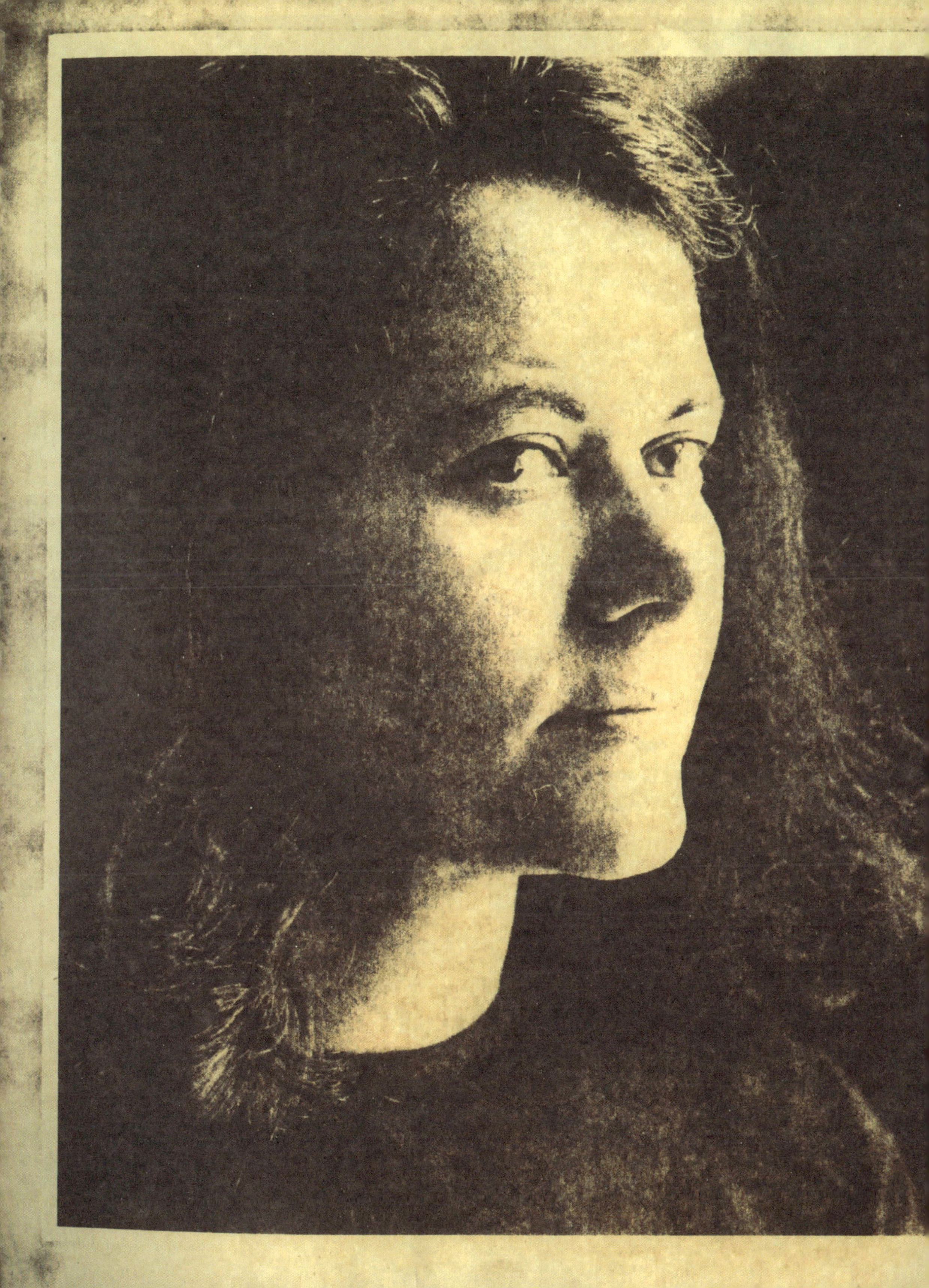

CHA/CHA/CHA

A MAGAZINE OF ART CRITICISM DEDICATED TO THE INVESTIGATION OF THE LATIN -AMERICAN ARTISTIC PRODUCTION

At the present time there are in the United States thousands of Latin-American artists whose work melts into the production of American art while remaining unknown to the countries of origin of these artists.

To restore this cultural patrimony and to make it known in all Latin-America and within the Latin community in the United States and in Europe is precisely one of the principal tasks of CHA/CHA/CHA. At the same time the magazine will provide these artists working in the United States with informative material concerning the artistic activities taking place in Latin-American countries and Europe.

Apart from this exchange of information intrinsic to the nature of the magazine, CHA/CHA/CHA will serve as a critical document for the investigation of the significance of the Latin-American artistic production in the countries of origin as well as as in the United States and Europe.

CHA/CHA/CHA will thus be an instrument of criticism of Latin-American creation as well as its vehicle of information. The magazine will cover literature, sculpture, painting, film, television, video-tape, radio and music besides the publishing of original works of poetry, criticism and literature.

Marta Minujín, Julián Cairol, and Juan Downey, opening pages of *Cha/Cha/Cha: A Magazine of Art Criticism Dedicated to the Investigation of the Latin-American Artistic Production*, New York, 1974. Marta Minujín Archive

In order to preserve the form of Latin-American critical thought as well as to convey it authentically, CHA/CHA/CHA will be published exclusively in spanish. For those investigators, critics and artists who are not aquainted with the languag the magazine will provide upon request literal translations of the material as a guide line for their work.

CHA/CHA/CHA will reach approximately 100.000 copies which will be distributed in universities, museums, schools, libraries, bookstores etc. It will be also sent at a minimum cost to all those people in Latin-America, The United States and Europe who wish to subscribe.

CHA/CHA/CHA will be edited in New York by three Latin-American artists and critics now residing in the United States in collaboration with outstanding critics ... artists and intellectuals living in Latin-America, the United States and Europe.

We expect CHA/CHA/CHA to fulfill the urgent necessity of creating a magazin which will reunite without descrimination all the Latin-American cultural forces and to reflect their character and thought throughout the world.

In 1974 Marta Minujín, Julián Cairol, and Juan Downey created *Cha/Cha/Cha: A Magazine of Art Criticism Dedicated to the Investigation of the Latin-American Artistic Production* to promote the work of Latin American artists living in the United States. Although it was never published as a magazine, it circulated as a typewritten document among their network of friends. Beyond the immediate goal of sharing information, the document reveals the artists' desire to redefine and highlight the significance of Latin American art in the context of the country's cultural production.

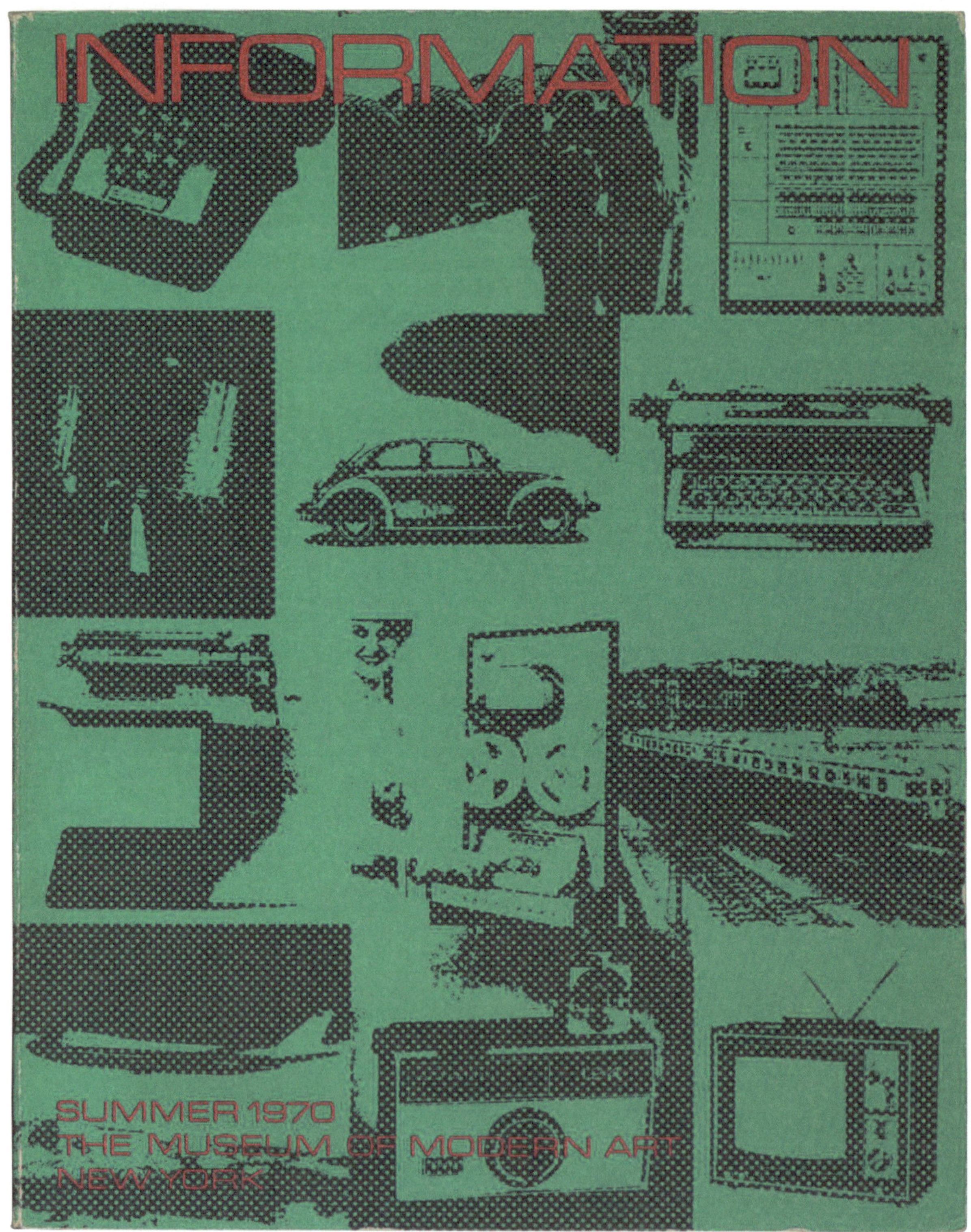

Cover of *Information*, edited by Kynaston L. McShine, 1970. The Museum of Modern Art Library, New York

Our participation in *Information* was thanks to Lucy Lippard. We were invited as a group—the New York Graphic Workshop, with Liliana and José Guillermo—and we did a team project naively designed to be in the show without being corrupted by it.

— Luis Camnitzer

> The exhibition *Information* took place at MoMA between July 2 and November 20, 1970. Curated by Kynaston McShine, it included more than one hundred artists from all over the world, with works that reflected on the information age. *Information* marked the institutionalization of Conceptual art in the United States. Many Latin American artists participated in the exhibition, among them Hélio Oiticica, Marta Minujín, Artur Barrio, and Alejandro Puente.

I am not here representing brazil; or representing anything else: the ideas of representing-representation-etc. are over.

— Hélio Oiticica

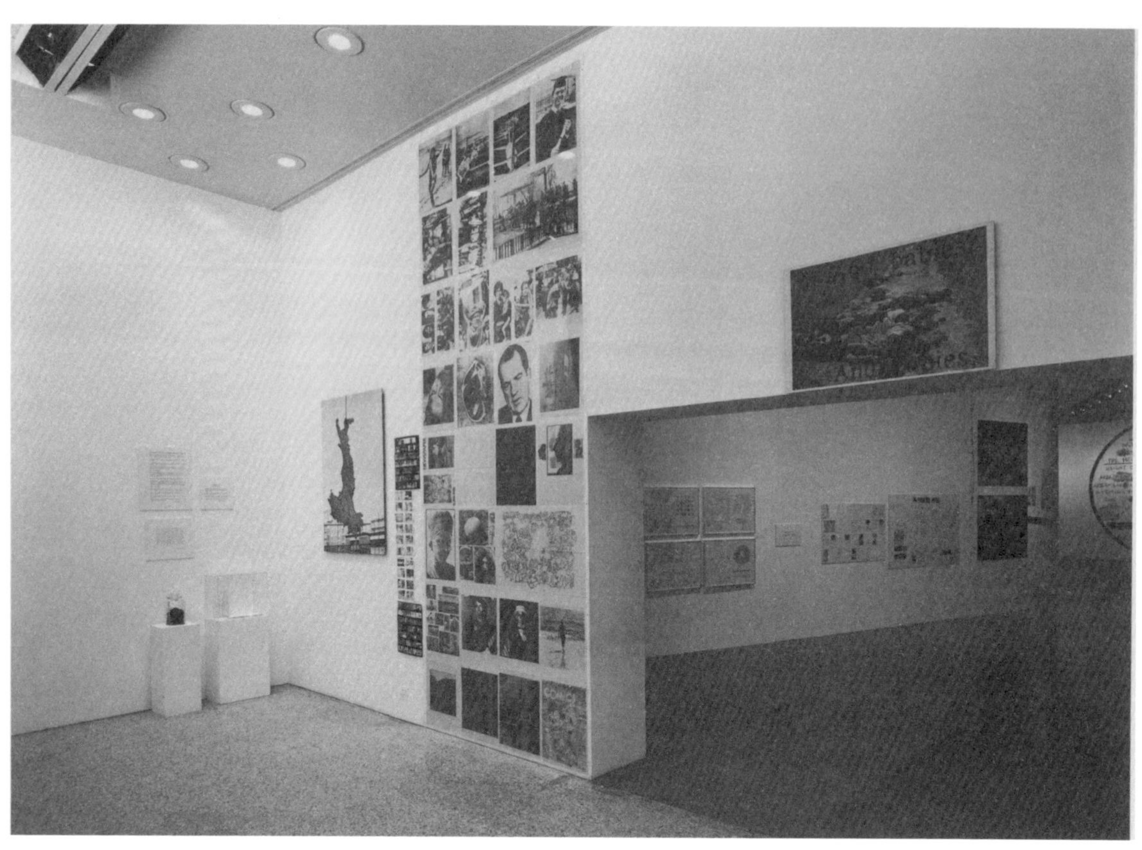

Installation view of the exhibition *Information*, The Museum of Modern Art, New York, July 2–November 20, 1970. Photographic Archive. The Museum of Modern Art Archives, New York

Cildo Campos MEIRELLES
Born 1948, Rio de Janeiro, Brazil
Lives in Rio de Janeiro

I am here, in this exhibition, to defend neither a career nor any nationality.

I would rather speak about a region which does not appear on official maps, a region called the SOUTHERN CROSS. Its original inhabitants never divided it. Others came, however, who for some reason did it. Such a division remains to this day.

I believe every region to have its boundary lines, imaginary or not. The line I am referring to is called Tordesilhas. Its Eastern side you know rather well through post cards, pictures, descriptions and books.

I would like, however, to speak from the other side of this border, with my head under the Equator line, hot and buried in the ground, the very opposite of skyscrapers, their roots in the ground, about all constellations. The wild side. The jungle in the head, deprived of the brilliancy of intelligence and brains. About this people, about the heads of these people, they who searched, or were forced, to bury their heads in the ground or in the mud. In the jungle. Therefore, their heads within their very own heads.

A circus: ways of thinking, capabilities, specializations, styles, all ends. What remains is what always existed: the ground. The dance to be performed begging for rain. And the swamp. And from the swamp worms will be born, and again life. Another thing: always believe in rumors. In the jungle there are no lies, only very private truths.

The precursors. But who dared to intuit, West of Tordesilhas, other than its own inhabitants? Hard luck on the hippies and their sterilized beaches, their disinfected lands, their plastics, their emasculated cults and their hysterical intelligence. Hard luck on the East. Hard luck on those who compromise: willfully or not, they take the side of the weak ones. Worse for them. For the jungle will grow and spread out to cover their sterilized beaches, their disinfected lands, their lazy sexes, their buildings, their roads, their earth-works, think-works, nihil-works, water-works, conceptual-works and so on, East of Tordesilhas and in each and every East of no matter what region. The jungle will go on spreading itself over the East of no matter what region. The jungle will go on spreading itself over the East and over those who compromise, until all those who have forgotten, or no longer know, how to breathe oxygen will die, infected with health. Cat bed.

Within its womb it still bears the shy end of the metaphor: since metaphors have no intrinsic value West of Tordesilhas. It is not that I myself am not fond of metaphors: I want someday all works to be looked at as hallmarks, as remembrances and evocations or real and visible conquests. And whenever listening to the History of this West, people will be listening to fantastic legends and fables and allegories. For a people who can transform its History into fantastic legends and fables and allegories, that people has a real existence.

April 1970

85

Cildo Meireles, artist statement, *Information*, ed. Kynaston L. McShine (New York: The Museum of Modern Art, 1970), 85

INSTALLATION
FREDDY RODRIGUEZ
&
PHOTOGRAPHS
ROBERT LEITH
MARCO KALISCH

CAYMAN GALLERY
Friends of Puerto Rico
381 West Broadway
New York, N.Y. 10012

OPENING: Nov. 21, 6 p.m.
Gallery Hours: Wed.-Sat. 11 a.m.-6 p.m.

druk wim schoot amsterdam

Cayman Gallery, later known as the Museum of Contemporary Hispanic Art, was founded in 1973 by the nonprofit organization Friends of Puerto Rico—whose leadership included Luis Cancel, Jack Agüeros, and Nilda Peraza—as a space dedicated to showcasing the work of Puerto Rican and other Latin American artists in New York.

Installation Freddy Rodríguez & Photographs Robert Leith Marco Kalisch. Exhibition postcard. Cayman Gallery, New York, November 1978. Courtesy of Freddy Rodríguez

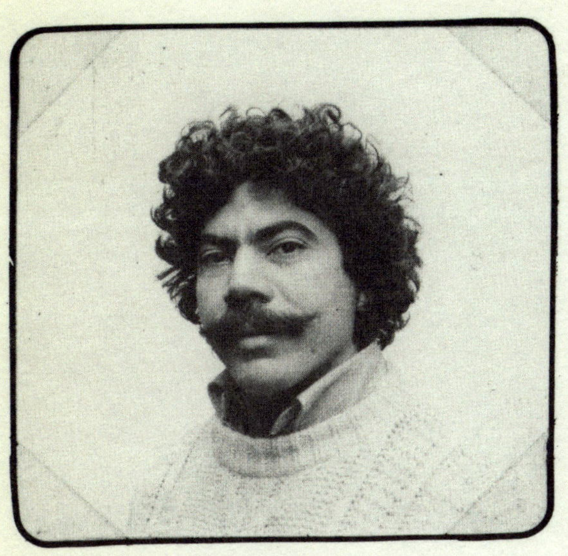

Publications:

Hiperrealismo Dominicano
Nuestro Museo de Arte Moderno.
Concurso Independencia de la casa Espana
o la Masacre del Jaragua.
Guillo Perez: XIII Exposicion Individual,
with Diogenes Cespedes).
Written statement for the environmental piece
"Mil Imagenes Plus."
Lecture on Contemporary Art, Casa de Teatro,
Santo Domingo, Dominican Republic.
Lecture on Arts in Santo Domingo, Escuela de
Artes Plasticas, San Juan, Puerto Rico.

Freddy Rodríguez portrait and CV. Cayman Gallery, New York, 1978. Courtesy of Freddy Rodríguez

El Museo del Barrio

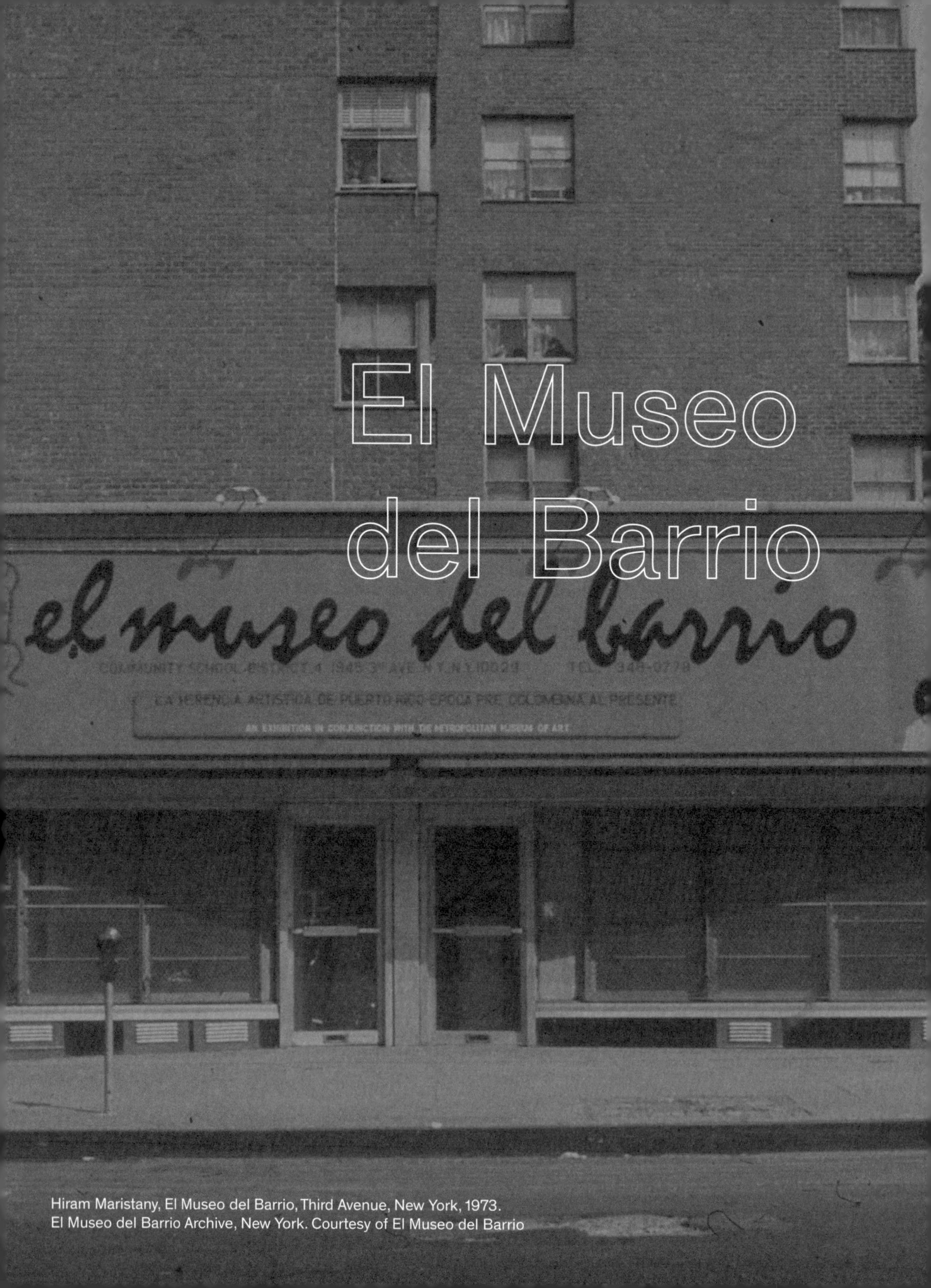

Hiram Maristany, El Museo del Barrio, Third Avenue, New York, 1973.
El Museo del Barrio Archive, New York. Courtesy of El Museo del Barrio

Taller Boricua and El Museo del Barrio are two cultural institutions founded in 1969 to serve the Puerto Rican community of East Harlem. These spaces were created against the backdrop of the political and artistic activism of the period, as well as the underrepresentation of cultural minorities in major art institutions in the city. El Museo del Barrio was conceived as the first Puerto Rican Museum in the country, and Taller Boricua was created as an artist-run printmaking workshop and cultural space for artists and poets.

and Taller Boricua

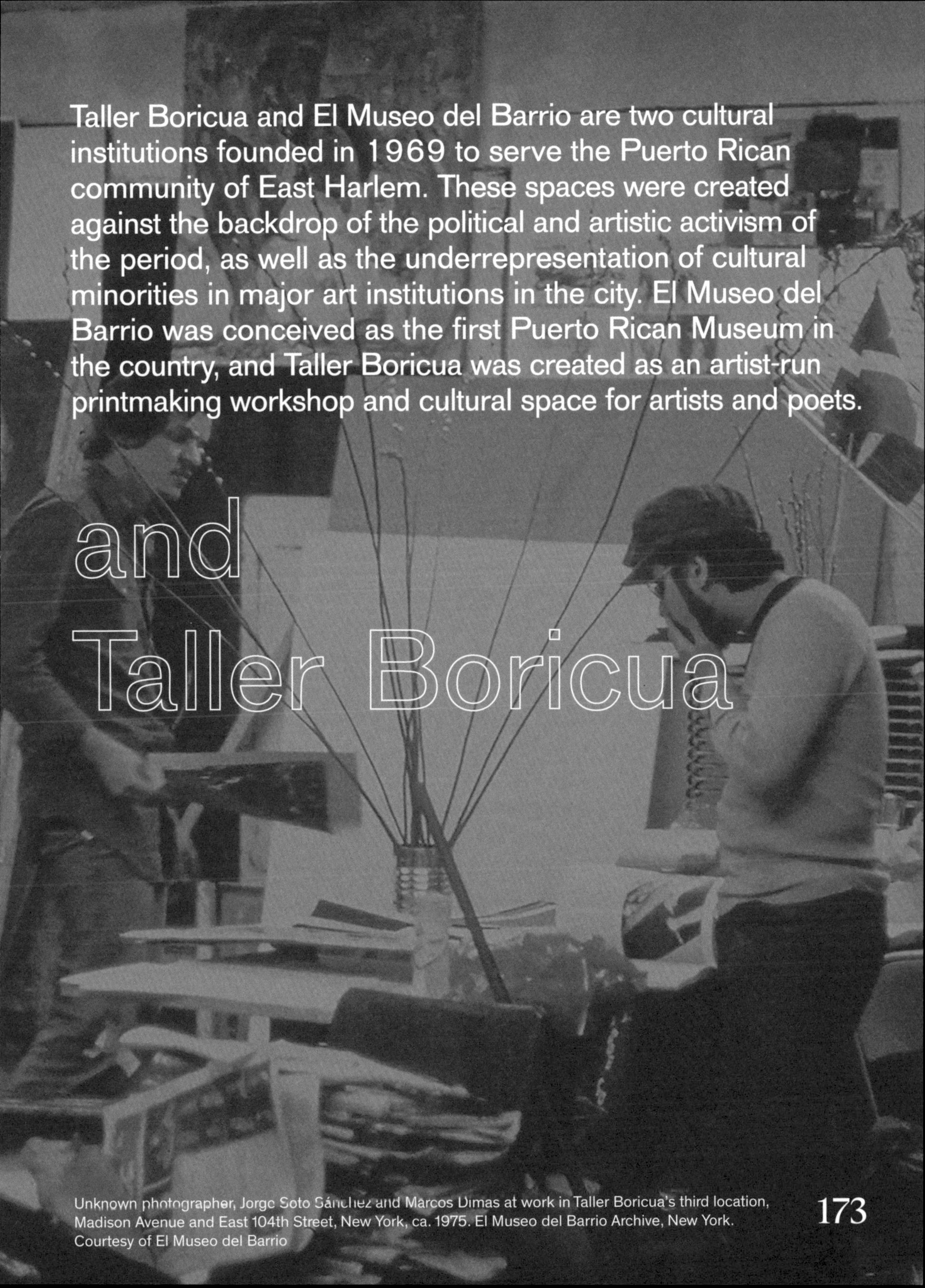

Unknown photographer, Jorge Soto Sánchez and Marcos Dimas at work in Taller Boricua's third location, Madison Avenue and East 104th Street, New York, ca. 1975. El Museo del Barrio Archive, New York. Courtesy of El Museo del Barrio

The cultural disenfranchisement I experience as a Puerto Rican has prompted me to seek a practical alternative to the orthodox museum, which fails to meet my needs for an authentic ethnic experience. To afford me and others the opportunity to establish living connections with our own culture, I founded Museum del Barrio, a nonprofit educational corporation.

To us at El Museo, the museum as a treasure house of objects is a distortion of the cultural process; culture is embalmed in a way that makes it inaccessible to every approach but the elitist esthetic. The alternative "museum" is museumless; it uses slides, tapes, films and television to produce a powerful multisensory experience relevant to the people's needs. It can be seen as an anthropological team of interviewers, photographers, sound technicians and communication technologists whose aim is to collect live cultural experiences from their own communities rather than dead objects.

This concept was not arrived at easily. It resulted in part from prolonged attempts to combat cultural neglect by such mammoth institutions as the Metropolitan Museum and such smaller ones as the Museum of the City of New York. I–and others–protested this neglect from the podium of the American Association of Museums' conference in early 1970. The bigotry of such institutions in our society will not end until public needs are heeded over private interests. Such bigotry . . . consists of institutionalizing the notion that one *people* (or race or sex) is inferior or superior to another. This manifests itself in museums in many ways. Few Puerto Ricans (or Blacks, or Chicanos) hold administrative or curatorial posts in our museums.

– Raphael Montañez Ortiz

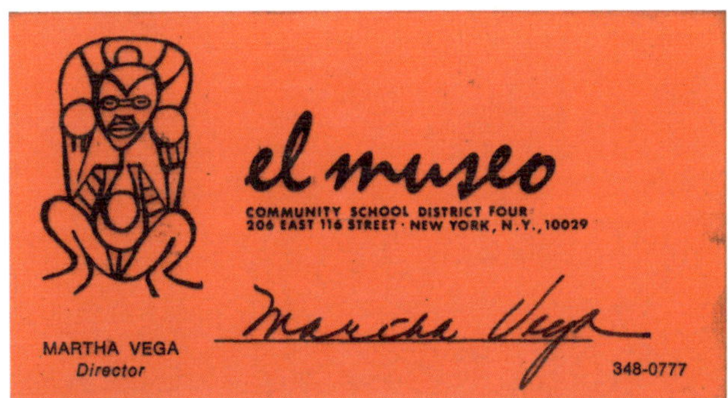

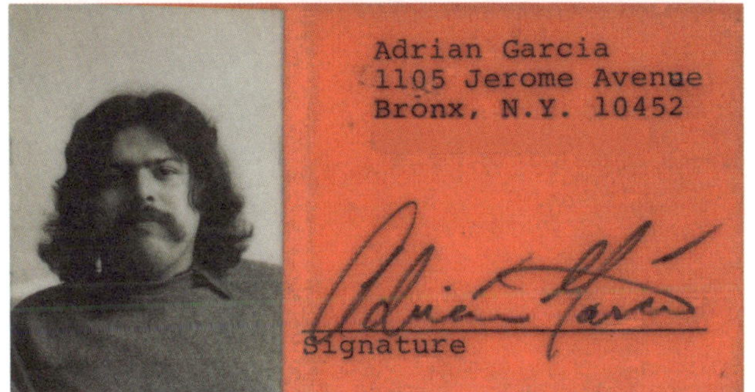

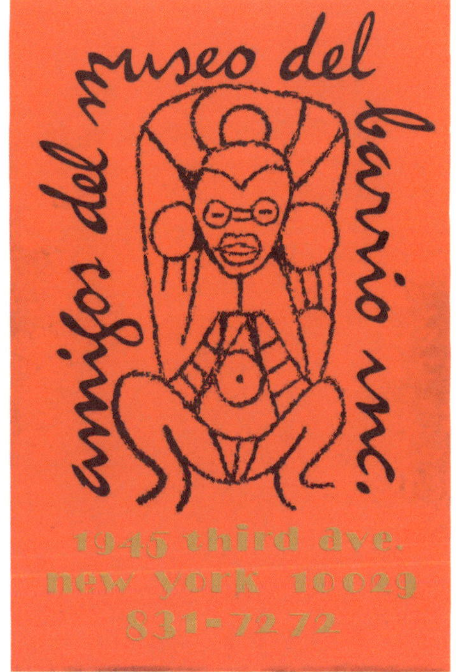

Founded by Raphael Montañez Ortiz with other educators, artists, and activists, El Museo del Barrio countered the exclusionary practices of large art institutions against cultural minorities by creating space for the dissemination of Puerto Rican culture and identity.

El Museo del Barrio, identification cards, ca. 1972 (above left) and Amigos del Museo del Barrio, Inc., ca. 1972–74 (above right). El Museo del Barrio Archives, New York. Courtesy of El Museo del Barrio

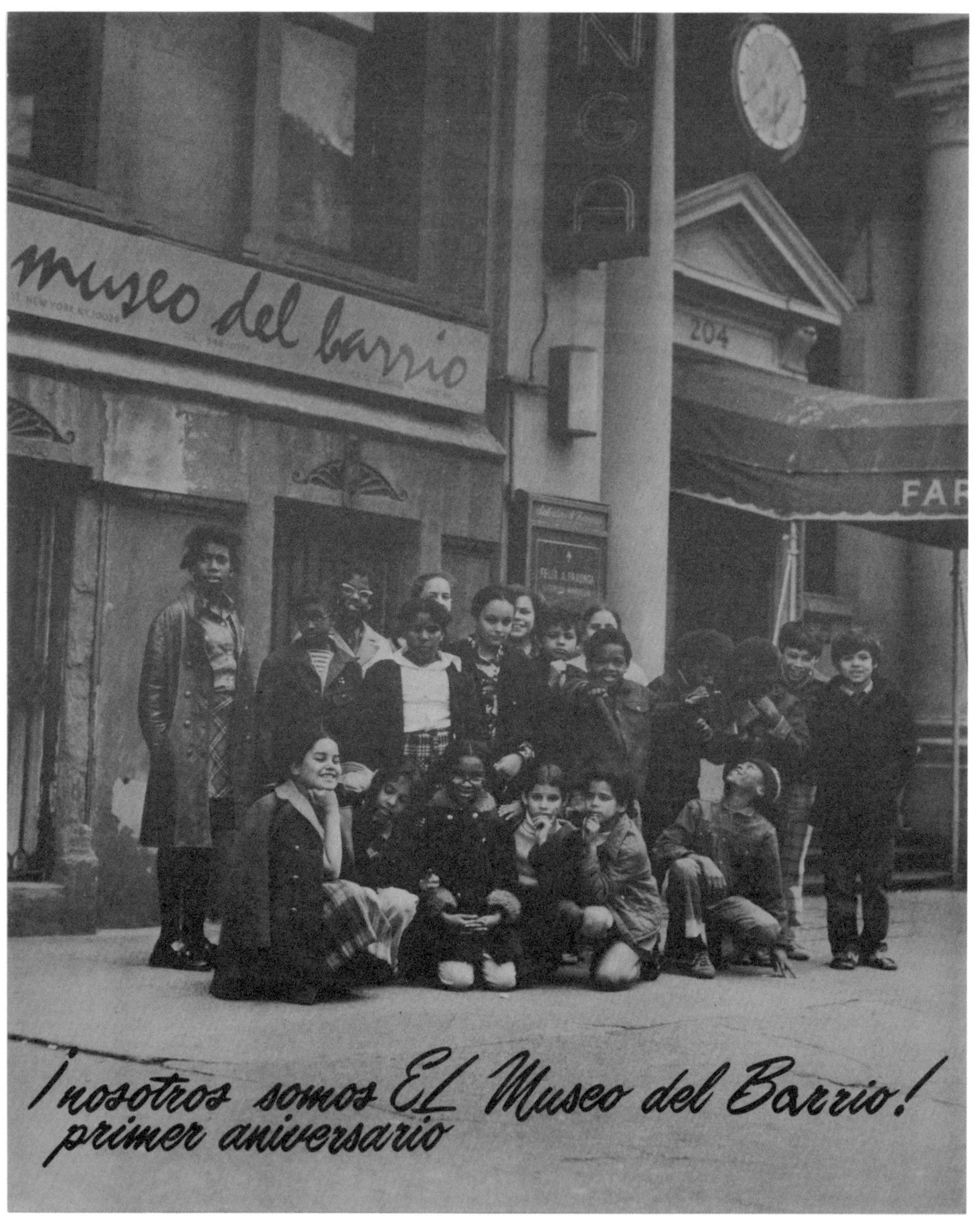

¡Nosotros somos El Museo del Barrio!: Primer aniversario (We are El Museo del Barrio!: first anniversary), ca. July 1972. Photo: Hiram Maristany. El Museo del Barrio Archive, New York. Courtesy of El Museo del Barrio

Barrio Museum: Hope Si, Home No

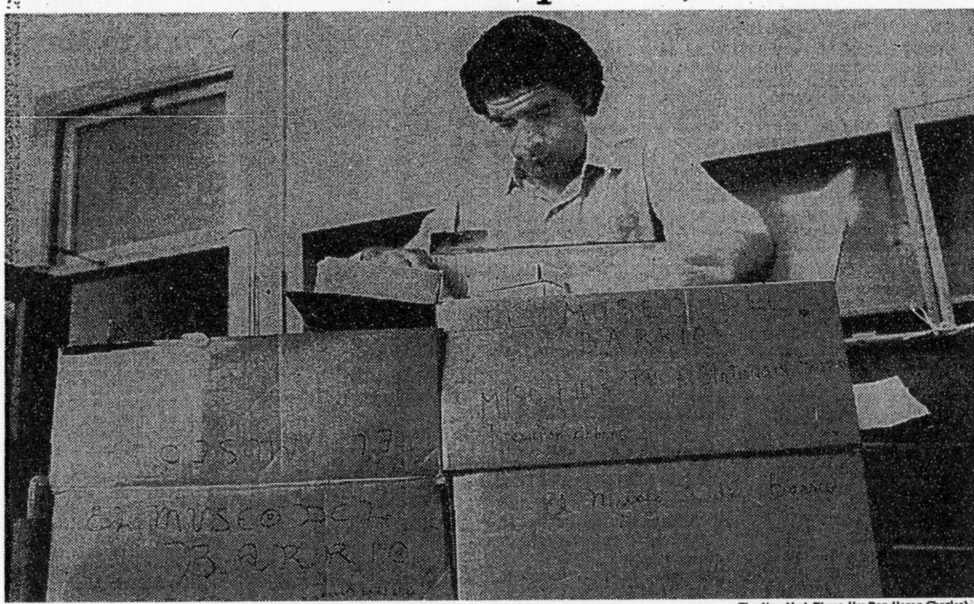

The New York Times (by Don Hogan Charles)

Ralph Ortiz, director of El Museo del Barrio, packing cardboard boxes in preparation for move to new headquarters

By GRACE GLUECK

El Museo del Barrio, the city's first museum of Puerto Rican culture, has no building, no collection, no guards. And right now, all its belongings are stashed in cardboard boxes, awaiting a move to another site from its present headquarters in P.S. 125 at 425 West 123d Street.

But the museum, whose name is intended not only to reflect El Barrio, the Puerto Rican ghetto in East Harlem but all mainland Puerto Rican communities, is very much in business. It has a staff of 10, and has already mounted two exhibitions. And it is bravely girding itself to meet, in the words of its director, Ralph Ortiz, "the needs of Puerto Ricans for a cultural identity."

"As a people, Puerto Ricans have been disenfranchised economically, politically and culturally," he says. "As a group like the Young Lords was born to deal with the political and economic disenfranchisement, so Museo is an attempt to begin to come to terms with our cultural disenfranchisement.

"But I want it to be more than a stuffy museum—I want it to be a working thing that will give folk culture as much value as fine culture."

So far, because of budgetary limitations, Museo has worked mostly through the public schools. Its two exhibitions—one of needlework by Puerto Rican women, the other of paintings and graphics by contemporary Puerto Rican artists—have been held at P.S. 206 on East 120th Street.

It also has a research program, whose purpose is to provide educational materials for the schools on Puerto Rican history, culture and folklore (one result will be a collection of island folk tales for distribution to children). Another project makes films on Puerto Rican life and culture available to schools and other organizations.

But the museum has more far-ranging plans. For one, it hopes to find a permanent building where, like any museum, it can mount exhibitions and re-create "historic environments and situations." It would also like to establish workshops in Puerto Rican culture, teaching theater, music, painting, dance, poetry, needlework and the making of musical instruments. And it wants to find money—at least $100,000 to start—to buy examples of Puerto Rican arts, past and present.

"We also plan to go into the community as anthropologists, with cameras and tape recorders," says Mr. Ortiz, a 36-year-old artist who grew up in a Puerto Rican community on the Lower East Side.

"What we want are the folk tales of the elders, the music played and the poetry read at festive occasions, the games, the food. Our aim is not to deal with high Puerto Rican culture, in its European derivations, but with the culture of the folk. There's a tendency to overlook our powerful African and Indian roots."

Museo was born in June, 1969, the brainchild of Martin W. Frey, superintendent of School District 4—then covering Central and part of East Harlem, now changed to cover only the latter.

"There were a number of black culural facilities but nothing for Puerto Ricans," says Mr. Frey. When funds for such a project came through from the Community Education Center, a locally operated, state-financed program that provides supplementary services for children and adults, Mr. Frey went into action.

He approached Mr. Ortiz, then teaching nearby at the High School of Music and Art, and working toward his doctorate in education at Columbia. "He filled the bill perfectly," says Mr. Frey. "He was an artist, had a background in education, and was Puerto Rican himself." To soak up ideas for the project, the two made a tour of museums in Puerto Rico last summer.

Mr. Ortiz sees Museo, administered by a community advisory board, as one of many viable alternatives to big central institutions.

"The trouble with central cultural institutions is that they give more dollar than spiritual value to culture," he says. "But culture originally was the symbolic realization of ethnic emotional needs. The only way to get back to that is to give each community its own museum allowing these indigenous expressions."

"Take needlework, for instance," he continued. "I remember my mother and aunt crocheting beautiful things to decorate the house because they couldn't afford to buy them. They, and other women like them, began by meeting the needs of a life style and developed an art form."

Right now, El Museo is having budget troubles. Though it is scheduled to get $93,554 from the Community Education Center to cover salaries and programs for fiscal 1971, changes in school district lines and a cutback in funds by the Board of Education may reduce the promised sum or eliminate it altogether. Meanwhile, the museum has applied to the New York State Council on the Arts for additional money—over $300,000—to help realize some of its goals.

"We need El Museo," says Mr. Ortiz, "to help Puerto Ricans in New York develop a sense of pride in their community."

Grace Glueck, "Barrio Museum: Hope Si, Home No," *New York Times*, July 30, 1970, 32

At the Museo . . . besides doing the exhibits, we used to make these exhibitions at Cayman [Gallery]. There were a couple of galleries in SoHo, that's the beginning when SoHo starts changing. The factories start leaving, the artists started moving in because they wanted to have more space . . . and then the galleries started moving in. You have Leo Castelli, OK Harris, Paula Cooper, Galería Bonino . . . There was another one, Tibor de Nagy, which was on 57th Street. They were more contemporary, so they brought artists from Puerto Rico: Rafi Ferrer, Eli Barreto, Domingo Lopez. The critic Marta Traba talks a lot about some of those artists' works because she went a lot to Puerto Rico.

We helped each other. When I was at El Museo, I was running the education [department] . . . Some of these artists, like Mario Toral from Chile, Gómez Quiroz, couldn't get papers to stay here in the States. So El Museo was very instrumental, by hiring [them] to teach classes and then filling out papers and telling the government, "Listen, we don't have anybody to do this that speaks Spanish, and they know the culture and we need that."

— Nitza Tufiño

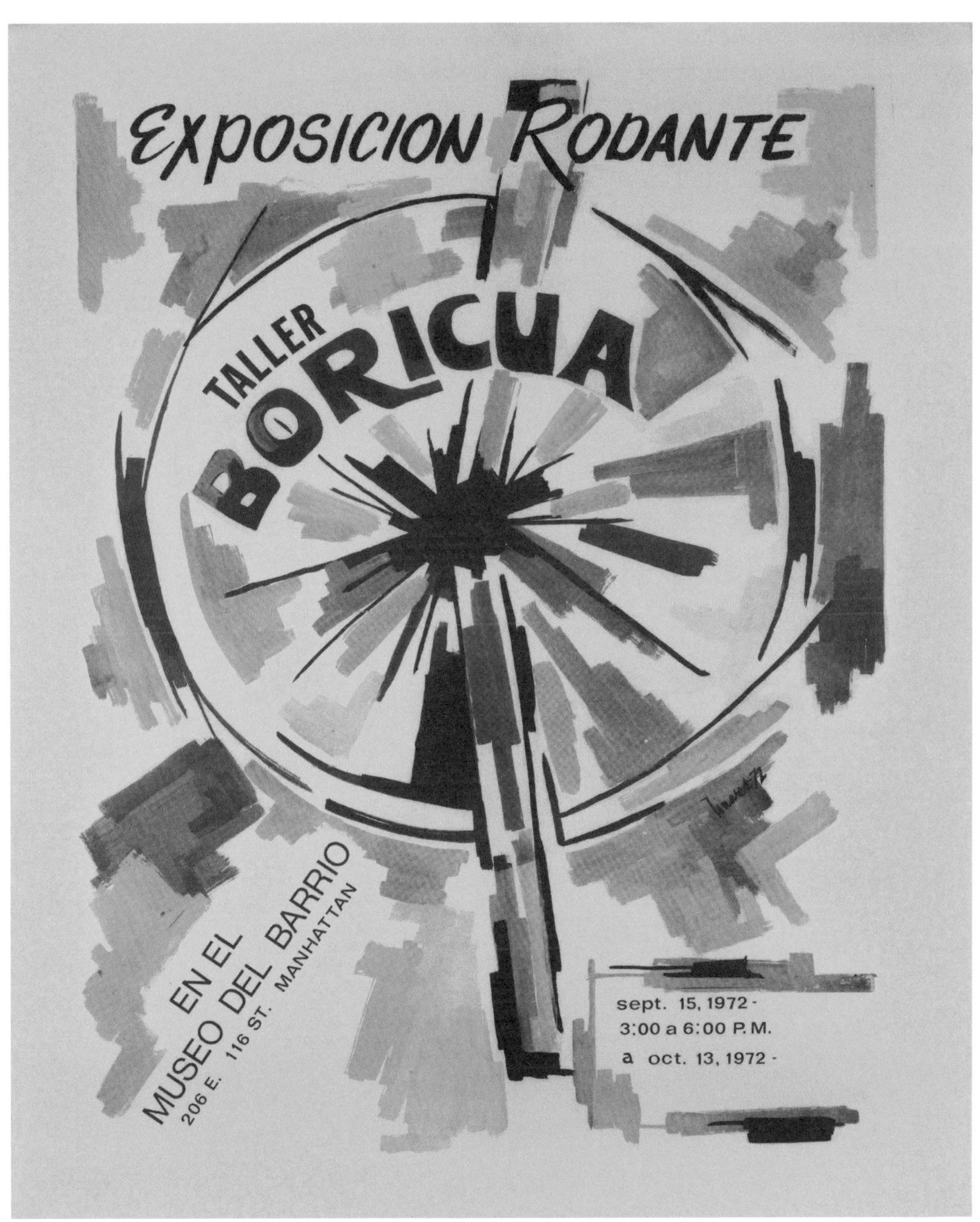

Exposición Rodante: Taller Boricua en El Museo del Barrio (Rolling exhibition: Taller Boricua at El Museo del Barrio), September 15–October 13, 1972. Design by Victor Linares. El Museo del Barrio Archive, New York. Courtesy of El Museo del Barrio

We moved to our second location on Second Avenue between 110th and 111th streets. El Taller Boricua became a multifaceted endeavor, fostering appreciation for our natural culture and supporting our collaborators. There we were, drawing spiritual and abstract concepts from African, Native American, and other traditions, assimilating authentic forms that flourished without the benefit of "European history." American art has had an affair with what some refer to, or classify as, anthropological art–whose examples range from earthworks, like Robert Smithson's *Spiral Jetty*, which are reminiscent of pre-Columbian earth carving, stretching for miles in the deserts of South America, to the sanitized graffiti, which simulates hieroglyphics or codices, drawn with chalk by Keith Haring in the catacombs of the New York City subway system.

– Marcos Dimas

Jorge Soto Sánchez, *Rostro de muerte (Tito)* (Face of death [Tito]), 1976. Collection of El Museo del Barrio, New York. Gift of the artist, 1984. W91.635. Courtesy of El Museo del Barrio

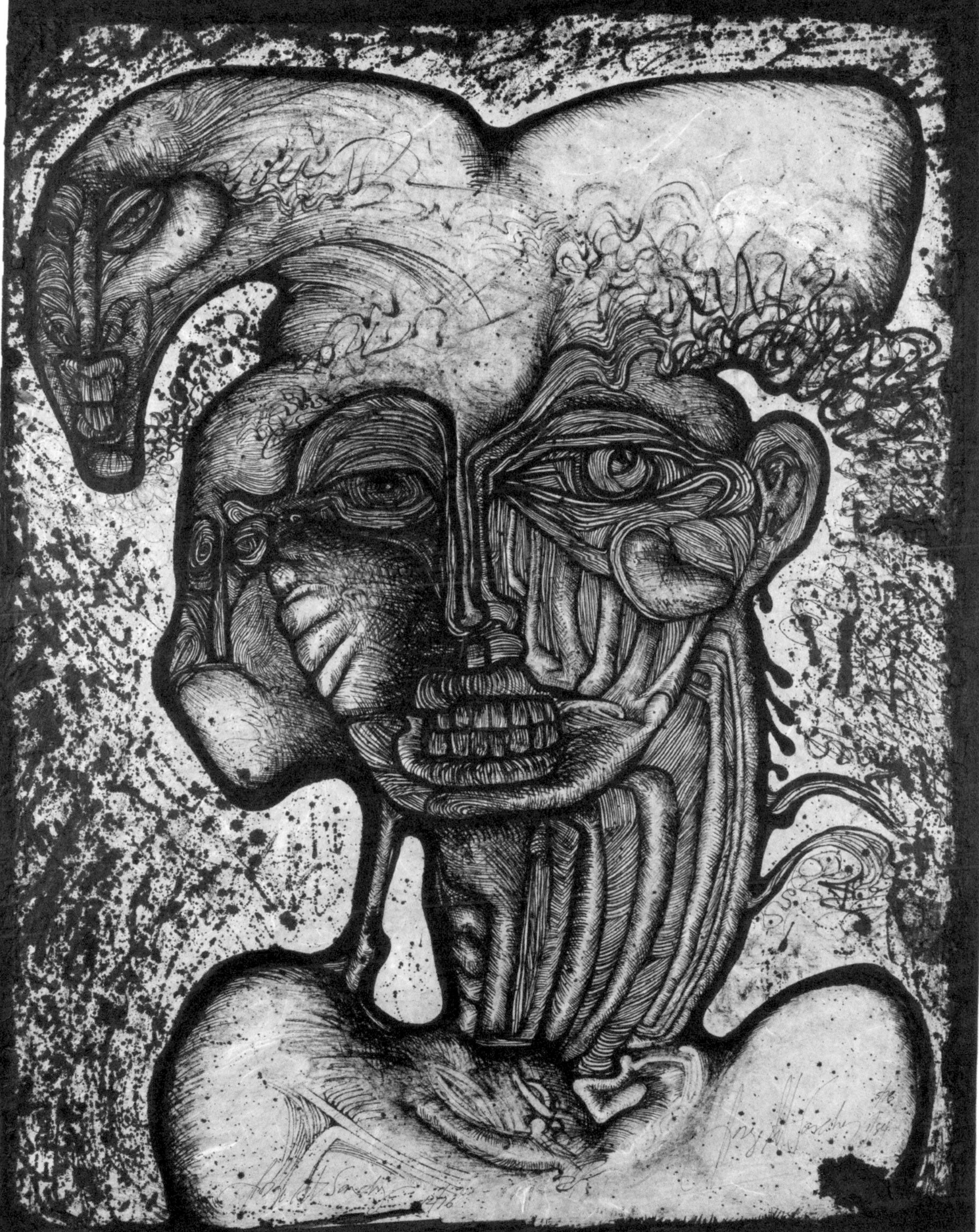

Founded by artists and activists including Marcos Dimas, Adrian Garcia, and Armando Soto, Taller Boricua is a cultural and educational center for New York's Puerto Rican community. It became a primary educational and cultural center for the Latino and Boricua community in New York during the 1970s, and its members organized events and created artworks, especially prints, that highlighted the history and lived experiences of Puerto Ricans in the city.

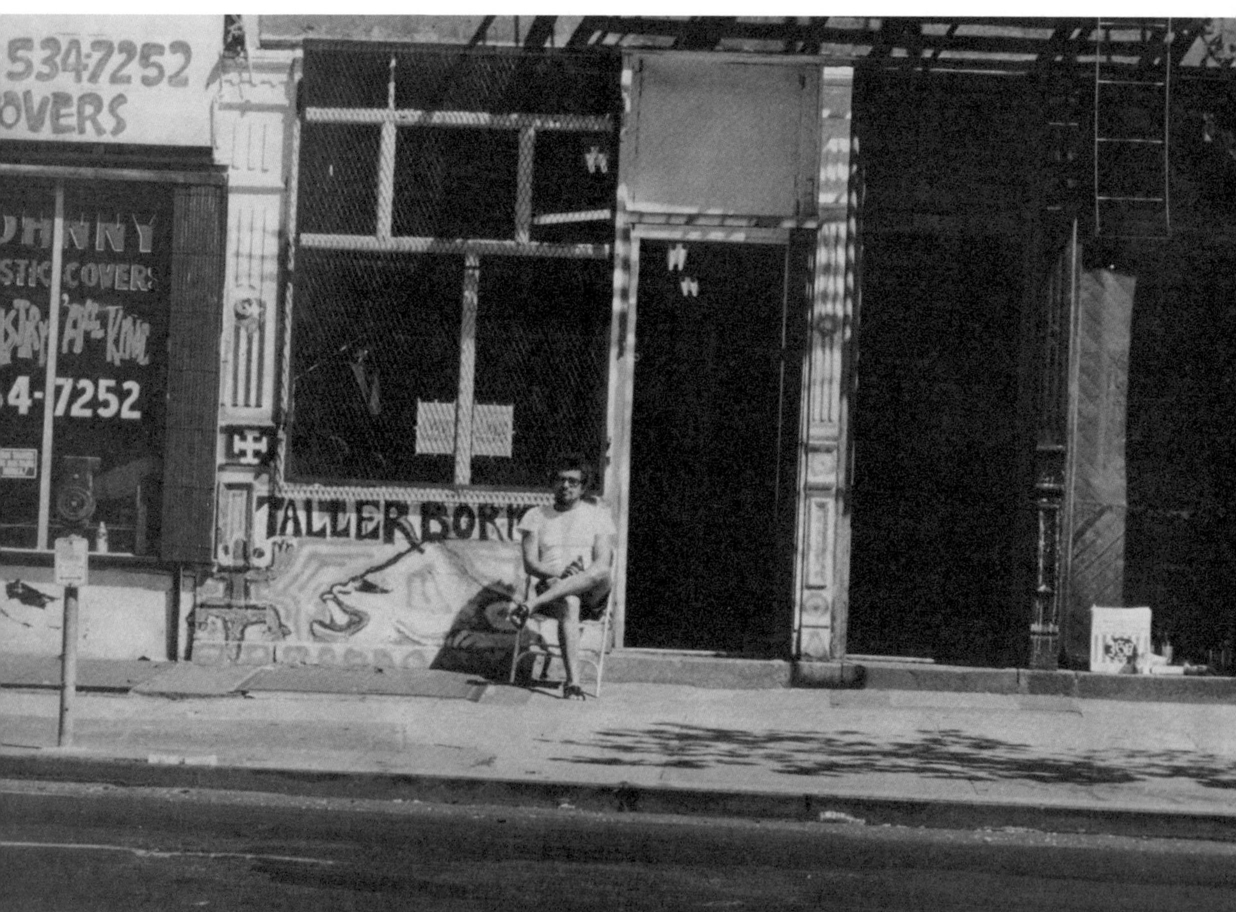

Hiram Maristany, Carlos Osorio at Taller Boricua, 2156 Second Avenue, New York, ca. 1971.
El Museo del Barrio Archive, New York. Courtesy of El Museo del Barrio

Following the citywide action, organized by the Art Workers' Coalition to boycott and close all city museums in solidarity with the Kent State University massacre, our group's core membership, which included Armando Soto, Adrian Garcia, Martin Rubio, Manuel (Neco) Otero, Carlos Osorio, and myself, created El Taller Boricua in East Harlem.

We decided to do this for a variety of reasons, but I think we could all agree that there existed a cultural void in the Puerto Rican community. El Taller became a forum on culture and the arts, a place where artists could share ideas, workspace, and materials. As a gesture of solidarity and union, we adapted and personalized Taíno images, which became insignias that symbolically linked us with our ancestral root culture.

Our first workshop space was located at the corner of 111th Street and Madison Avenue. It was a four-story building we inherited from the Real Great Society, Inc. We became squatters. Across the street was the headquarters for the Young Lords political party. From this location we started to exhibit in the streets, created and donated works for and to the community, and initiated educational workshops. Later, we were driven out of that building by a series of uncontrollable circumstances, including the shutdown of water service. Then, the last straw was when Con Edison turned off the power for the building, and, as a result, it also turned off, temporarily, our "art to the people" movement.

— Marcos Dimas

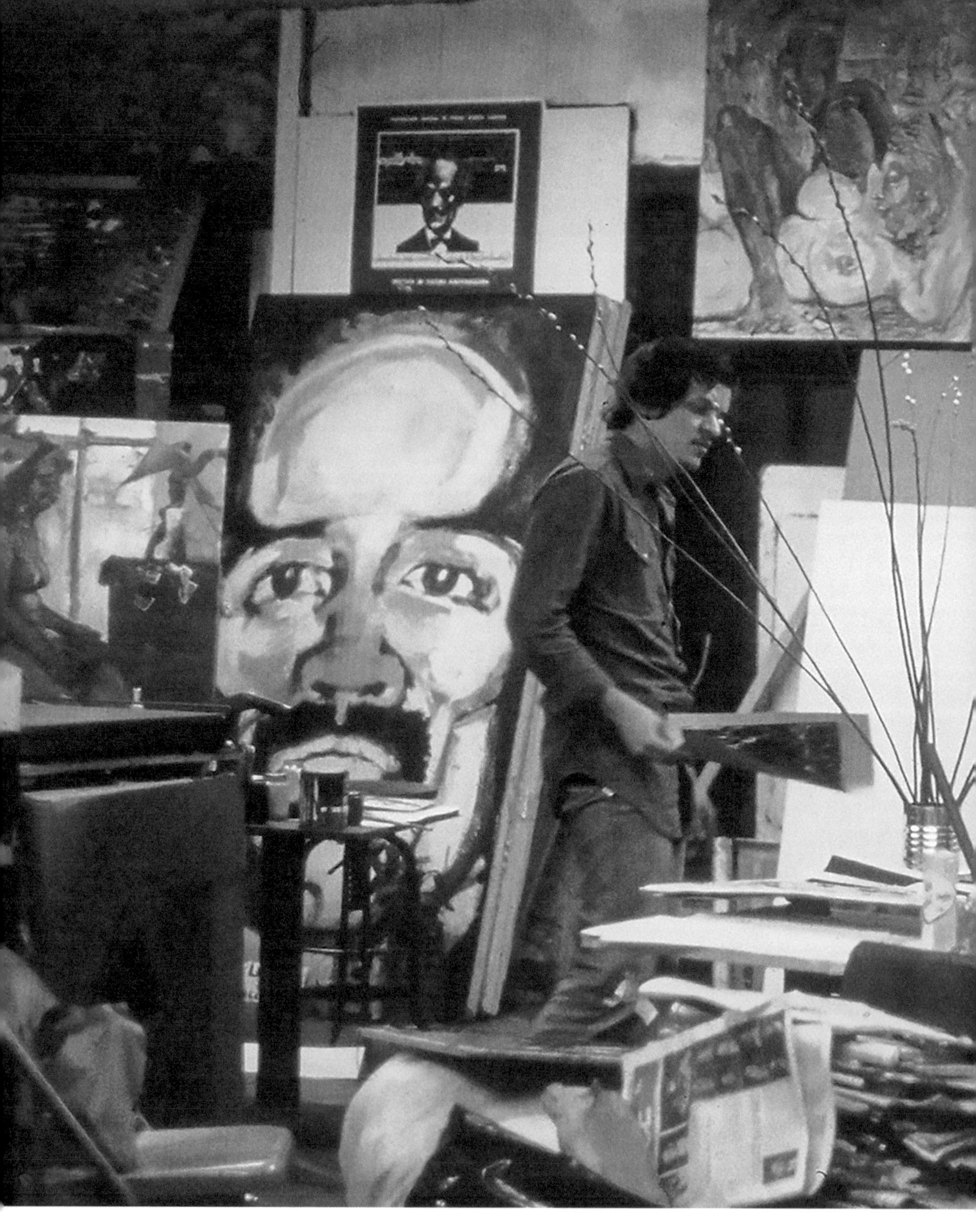

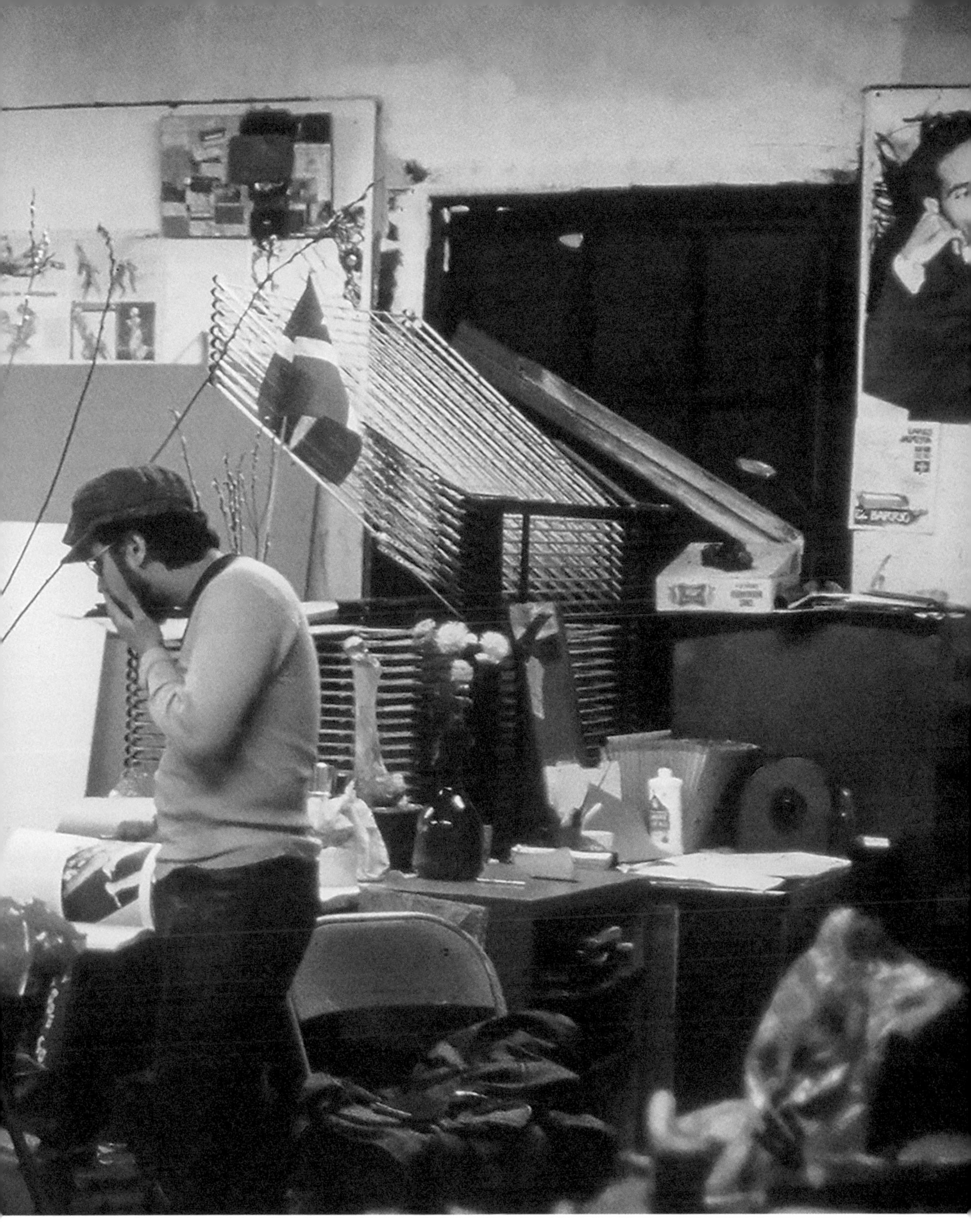

Unknown photographer, Jorge Soto Sánchez and Marcos Dimas at work in Taller Boricua's third location, Madison Avenue and East 104th Street, New York, ca. 1975. El Museo del Barrio Archive, New York. Courtesy of El Museo del Barrio

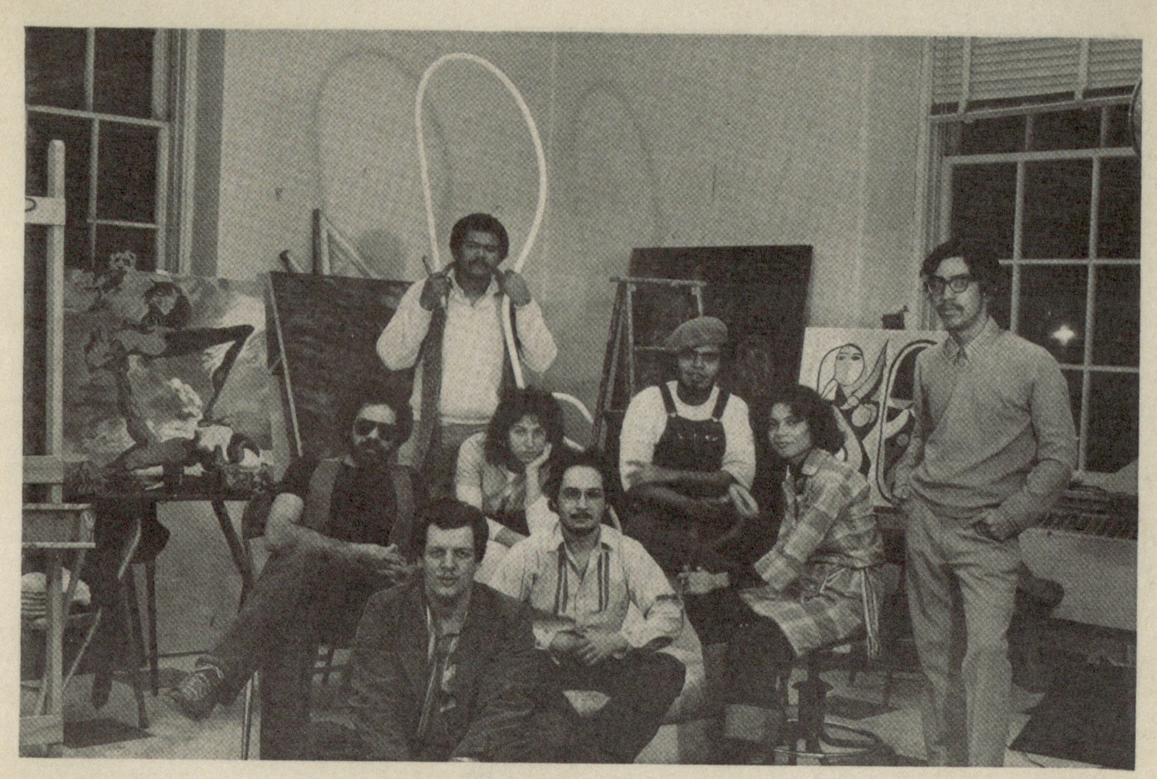

El Taller has always served as a springboard for emerging artists, continually maintaining a sense of exploration with media, materials, and concepts. The underlying current of the eclectic body of work created there has been a combination of searching and a stubborn refusal to lose our identity. We also refused to be classified in “isms” or to be rediscovered every few years by a new crop of liberal critics. Visual art at its best is nonverbal, non-narrative communication, retinal literature that requires us to learn to look and see by feeling.

— Marcos Dimas

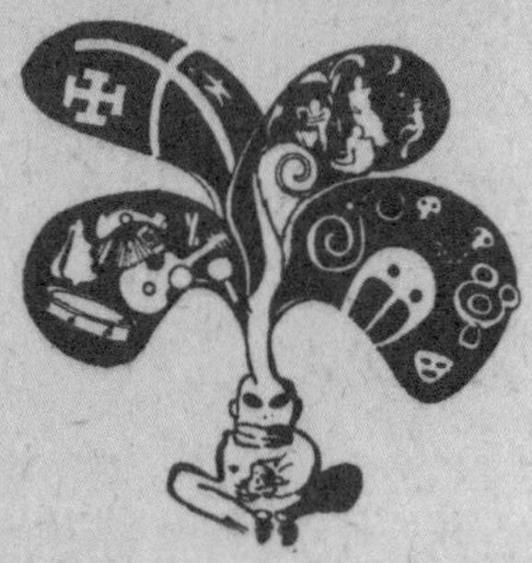

We at "EL TALLER BORICUA" (Puertorriquen Art Workshop) Cordially Invites You To Our Open House, in our presently new location at the East Harlem Arts and Educational Complex.

This special event will take place: Friday, March 23, 1979 at 6:00pm - Until ????

We will also preview the first collective silk screen portfolio of Puerto Rican Contemporary Art.

"EL TALLER"; JORGE, MARCOS, FERNANDO, GILBERTO, WANDA, & ROSANNE

ADDRESS: 1 EAST 104th Street 2nd Fl.

Taller Boricua, Open House invitation card, 1979. El Museo del Barrio Archive, New York. Courtesy of El Museo del Barrio

Pratt Graphics Center and the

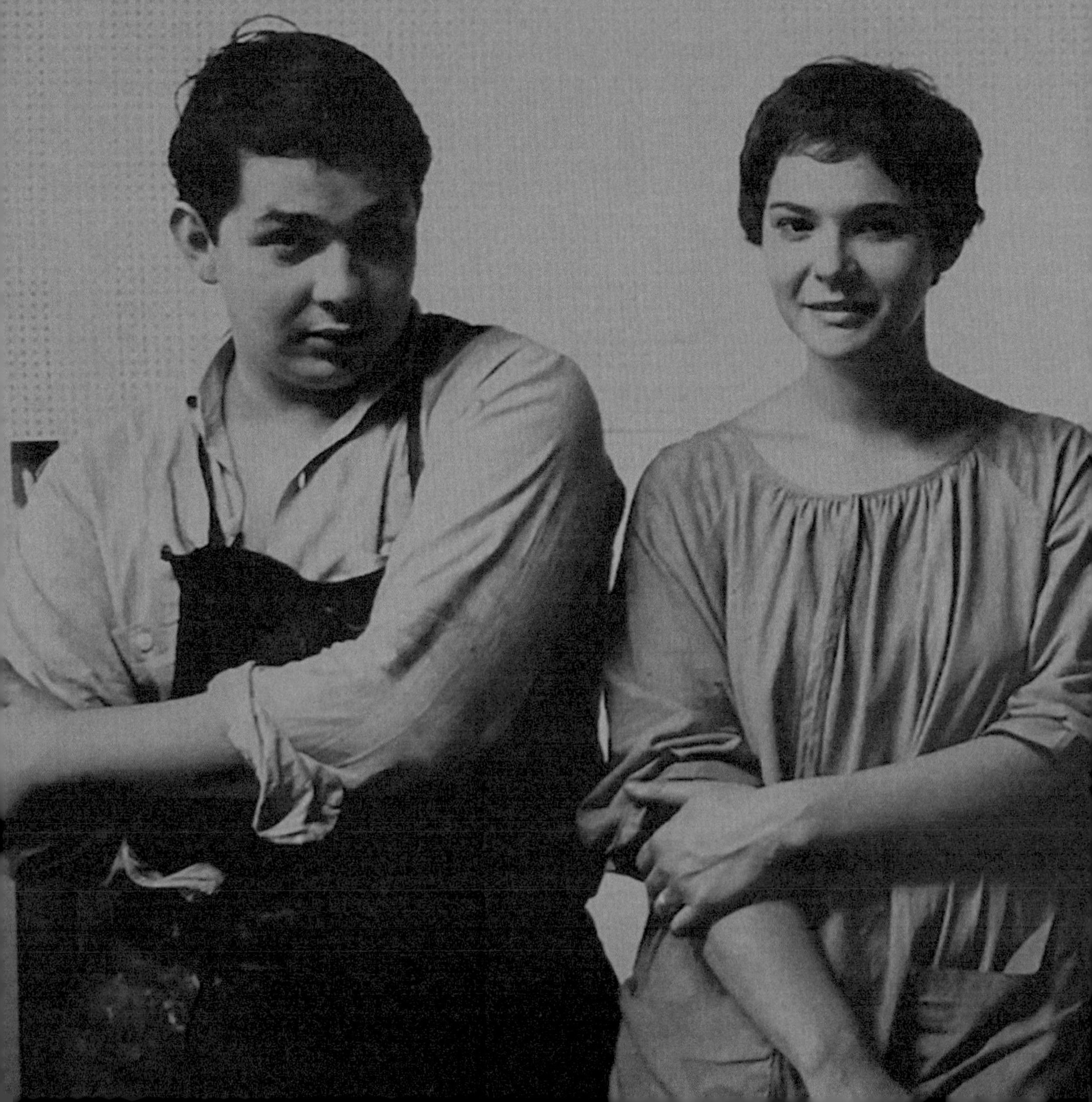

New York Graphic Workshop

José Guillermo Castillo, Liliana Porter, Luis Camnitzer, and Gabriel Morera at the New York Graphic Workshop, 1965. Liliana Porter Collection

Part of Pratt Institute, Pratt Graphics Center was founded in 1956 as a graphic workshop and educational center that promoted different printmaking techniques. International in scope, Pratt Graphics Center has welcomed many artists from Latin America, including Anna Maria Maiolino, Lydia Okumura, Alicia Barney, Liliana Porter, Luis Camnitzer, and José Guillermo Castillo, and has functioned as a hub for connection.

When you graduate in the arts, I believe you are not ready to become a professional artist. It is necessary to know and learn more. I believe that in this sense, Pratt was an ideal place. I had always felt unsatisfied and my anxiety was almost becoming anguish. Pratt was extremely competitive. It was necessary for me to develop my ego and begin to defend myself. Silence was used as a way of protest; that was a terrible thing to do. It was like saying "I am so good at this that I am above any product." I began to rebel. This is when I began making the "Object-diary," which emerged to give a new meaning to my life. It was autobiographical.

— Alicia Barney

Alicia Barney: Object Diary, MFA thesis exhibition, Pratt Institute, New York, March 21–26, 1977. Courtesy of the artist

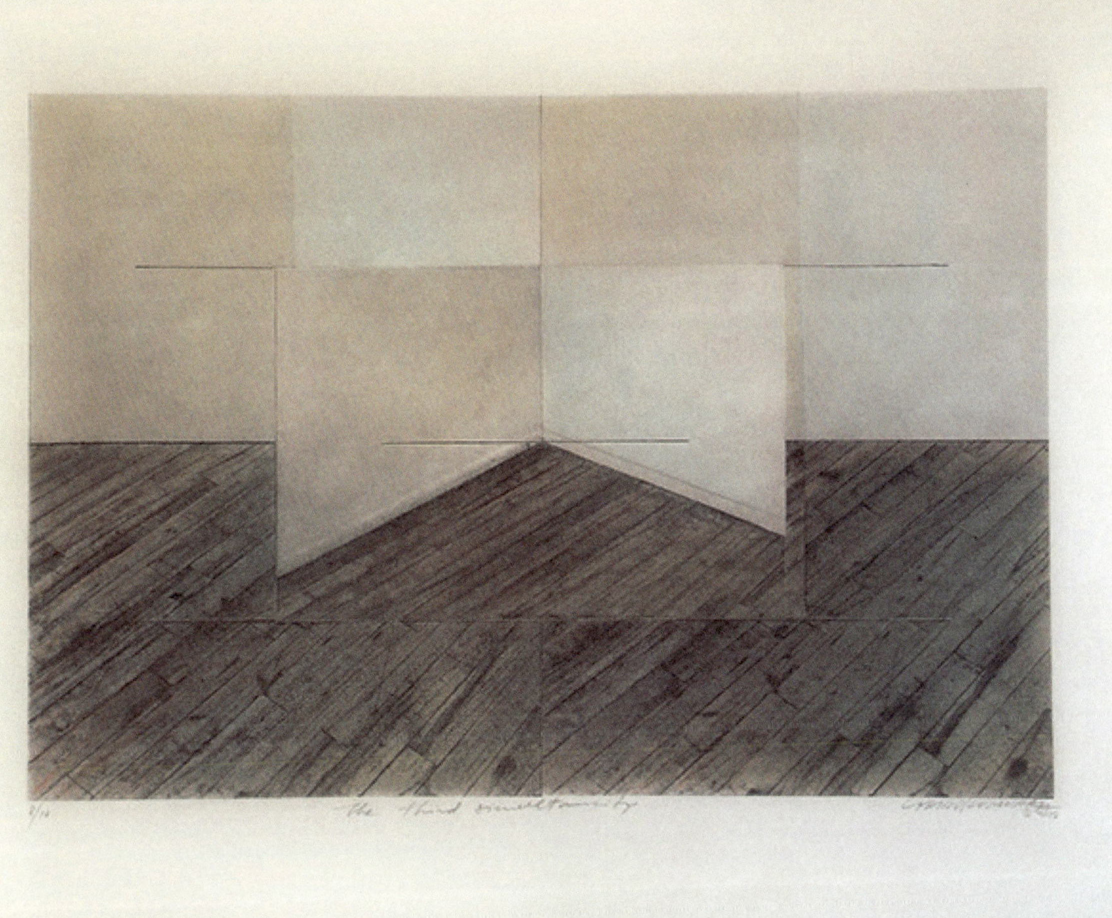

In New York I was admitted with a scholarship to Pratt Graphics Center, in Manhattan, from 1974 to 1978. I produced silkscreens based on the images of my installation from the Biennial of São Paulo, and photographs in sequence of constructions I was making, and I received the Annual Pratt Graphics Center Award in 1976. Seeing the exhibition, Earl Willis, the owner of Nobé Gallery on 57th Street, invited me for a solo exhibition of graphics in the same year.

— Lydia Okumura

Lydia Okumura, *The Third Simultaneity*, 1977. Galeria Jaqueline Martins

What happened was that one day Rubens showed some of my wood engravings from the sixties to Luis Camnitzer, a Uruguayan artist who had come to visit him, and he liked them. He immediately got me a grant from Pratt Graphics Center, where he was teaching. They had studios for foreign artists. That's when I abandoned figuration and started doing metal engravings: *Escape Point* and *Escape Angle*. This return to work after such a long period of inactivity helped me to redefine my life. I decided to leave Rubens and to return to Brazil.

— Anna Maria Maiolino

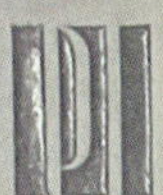

PRATT INSTITUTE BROOKLYN · NEW YORK 11205

OFFICE OF
ASSISTANT TO THE PRESIDENT

December 1, 1970

Mr. Luis Camnitzer
The Fandso Foundation
33 Ash Street
Locust Valley, N.Y. 11560

Dear Mr. Camnitzer:

We too were advised of your generosity providing partial funds for the tuition of Ana Maria Maiolino Gerchman at Pratt's Graphic Center which will be matched by them to cover sixteen weeks of tuition for the artist.

I would like to add the Institute's appreciation for this assistance and to assure you that scholarship grants for both our students of the Graphics Center as well as the Institute as a whole, are among the most pressing needs of this School.

Thank you,

Sincerely,

Neal G. Raska

Neal G. Raska
Assistant to the President

CC: Mr. Stasik

NGR:ak

Pratt Institute, letter to the Fandso Foundation (New York Graphic Workshop), December 1, 1970. Private collection

[Pratt Graphics Center] had been recommended to me as the best and most specialized place for printmaking. This was probably true in the technical sense. There were many Latin American artists working there–Armando Morales, Enrique Castro-Cid, Marcelo Bonevardi, and others. Hans Haacke was there making dots consistent with his Group Zero period. I floundered at cutting wood, and took advantage of working with people like [Ansei] Uchima and [Shikō] Munakata.

Meanwhile, I met frequently with another Uruguayan printmaker, Antonio Frasconi. I believe he was the first Uruguayan Guggenheim Fellow (Jorge Damiani was the second and I the third), and he was considered the most important woodcut artist in the States. We had met in Uruguay at one of his exhibitions in 1961 or early 1962, and he told me to call him when I arrived in New York. Antonio took me all over the city, and introduced me to William Lieberman, then curator of prints at the Museum of Modern Art. Out of deference to Antonio, Lieberman took two of my prints for the collection. This was my second museum now, and I was very proud. The prints were fifty dollars each (I don't know who helped me price them), and MoMA paid me half of that. I always mention this event as the beginning of my career in philanthropy. In my semicolonial (though rebellious) frame of mind, I figured that I pretty much had now accomplished everything I ever would, and that upon my return everybody would have to listen to my opinions.

— Luis Camnitzer

THE NEW YORK GRAPHIC WORKSHOP

THE FANDSO FOUNDATION
33 Ash street
Locust Valley
N.Y. 11560
Luis Camnitzer

Mr. Andrew Stasik
PRATT GRAPHIC CENTER
831 Broadway
N.Y.C.

November 19, 1970

Dear Andy:

Enclosed please find a check for $82.50, covering tuition and workshop fees for Ana María Maiolino Gerchman, from Brazil.
I hope that the P.G.C. will again be able to match funds and therefore extend Ana María's working period to sixteen weeks.
Some_when during next Wednesday I intend to come with her in order to introduce her to you.

Again thank you very much

for the FANDSO FOUNDATION

Luis Camnitzer

The Fandso Foundation (New York Graphic Workshop), letter to Pratt Graphics Center, November 19, 1970. Private collection

The New York Graphic Workshop (NYGW) was founded in 1964 by Liliana Porter, Luis Camnitzer, and José Guillermo Castillo as a printmaking workshop. There, they taught printmaking classes and experimented with Conceptual art strategies. Not only did the NYGW connect artists specializing in different media, inviting them to create prints, but it also put pressure on traditional ideas of art-making by questioning issues of authorship in art production and putting forward alternative exhibition formats, such as mail art.

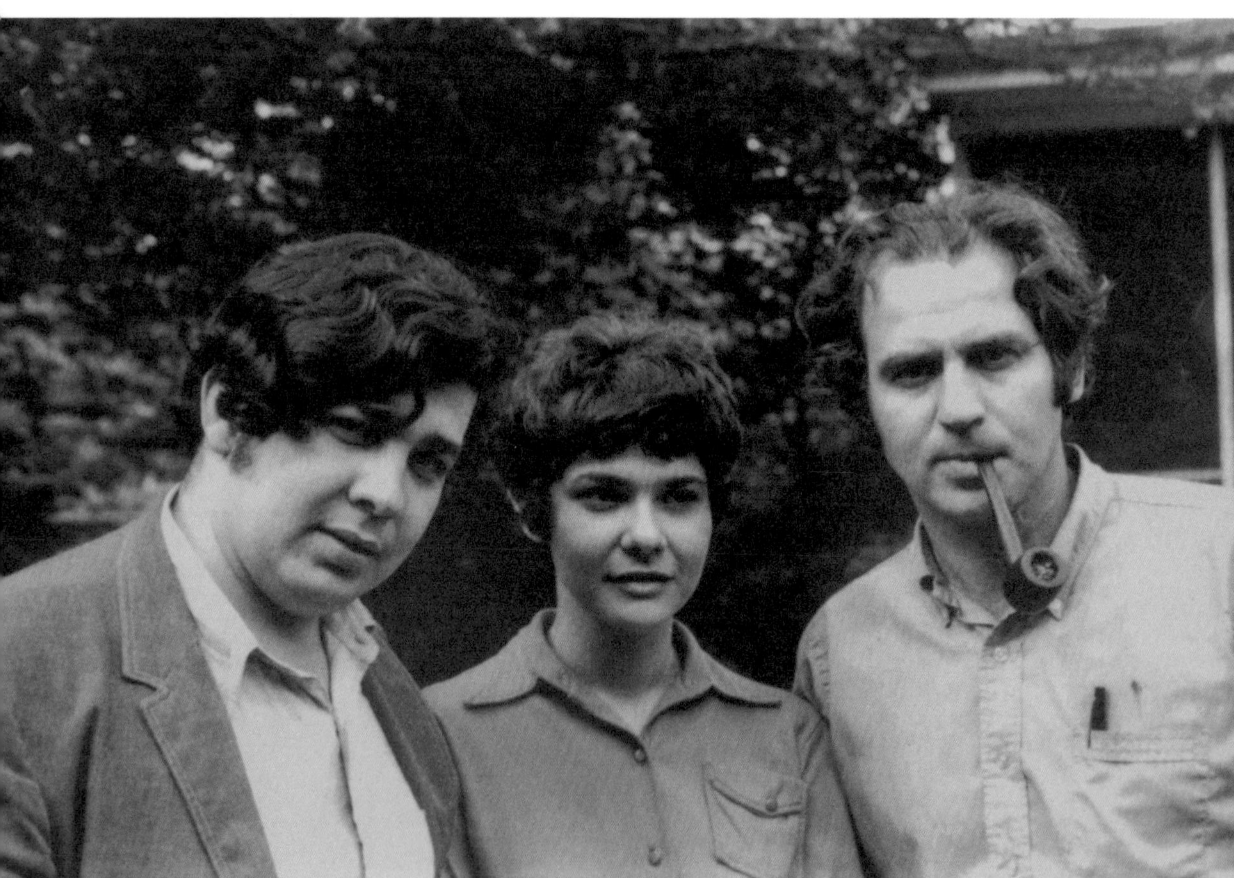

José Guillermo Castillo, Liliana Porter, and Luis Camnitzer, 1969.
Liliana Porter Collection

The New York Graphic Workshop was an accident. During the opening of a show of hers in 1965, Liliana Porter met Dr. Julian Firestone, a dentist whose hobby was etching. He had a big press in his apartment and offered to let her use it. It sounded like one up on "come and see my etchings," and Liliana quickly introduced me to him to protect herself. The offer was totally honest and real. Firestone liked her work, and he had also seen mine. He wanted to learn more about printmaking in exchange for letting us use his studio. Eventually he rented a phenomenal space on West 3rd Street. The space was fully installed for printmaking and had been set up and used by Leo Kalapai, a known printmaker at the time. There was an apartment in the back, which Firestone moved into. Together with Venezuelan artist José Guillermo Castillo and Sharon Arndt (an American artist we had met at Pratt Graphics), we planned the workshop. Sharon left the group very shortly after, and the remaining three of us started to organize an alternative to Pratt Graphics Center, with a more up-to-date approach to printmaking.

The whole thing started from the point of view of three printmakers who were dissatisfied with the constraints given by the traditional definitions of printmaking, which hadn't changed much since the sixteenth century. So we decided to revise the definitions and break the limits. But we definitely started as printmakers who wanted to access art at large, and not as artists who were making prints. In the process of those revisions, we shifted views and started to downgrade printmaking to the status of a craft that was useful for the production of art. In that shift, we maintained the notion of dissemination and tried to de-commodify it (it was, in retrospect, a totally utopian aim, but one to which we aspired).

— Luis Camnitzer

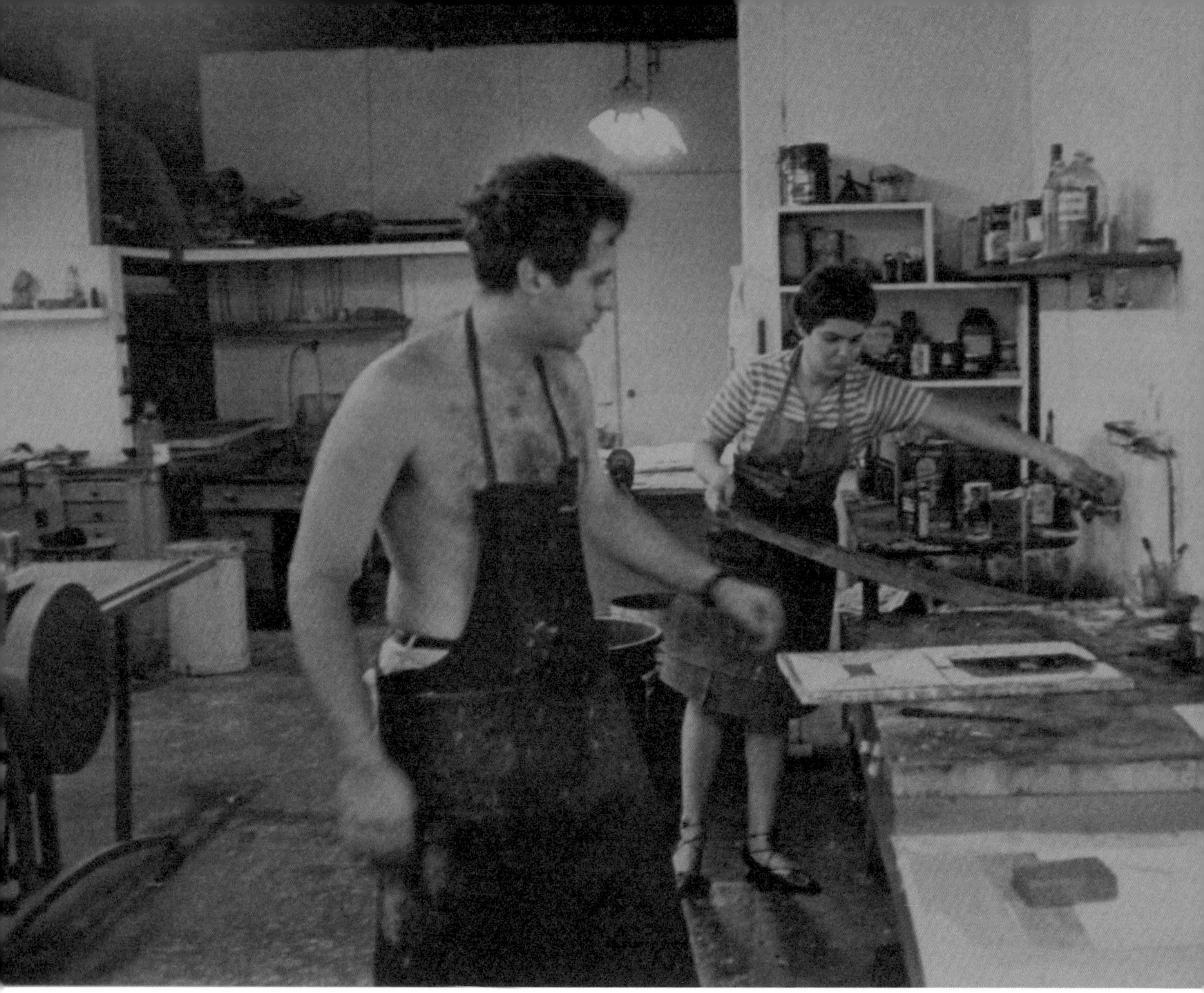

There were many friendships. But there weren't many that I can point to as influential for my art, beyond Noé and the small circle of the New York Graphic Workshop that was formed by Liliana Porter, José Guillermo Castillo, and me. Serious mutual critiques were reduced to those few people.

— Luis Camnitzer

Luis Camnitzer and Liliana Porter at the New York Graphic Workshop, 1965. Liliana Porter Collection

Letter announcing the opening of the New York Graphic Workshop, 1966. Liliana Porter Collection

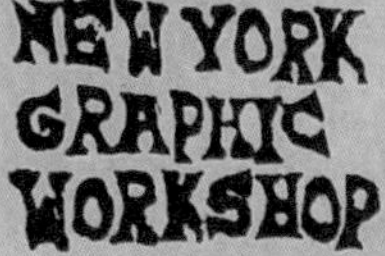

82 west 3rd. street , n.y. 10012 , new york · tel · 228-9100

The New York Graphic Workshop, a workshop dedicated to advanced printmaking, teaching and research, has opened this month.

In the field of teaching, the aim is to help the pupil to express himself through printmaking, but without being limited by traditional methods.

In the field of research, it is trying to promote the seeking of a creative relationship between the matrix and the printable material. New techniques, such as three dimensional printmaking, use of plastics, assemblage, etc., are explored.

We firmly believe that printmaking is today's medium, from a technological and a social point of view. The Workshop, therefore, intends also to organize cultural events through which printmakers may become aware of their role in our time.

→ Poster for New York Graphic Workshop exhibition at Galería Plástica, Buenos Aires, October 10–29, 1966. Liliana Porter Collection

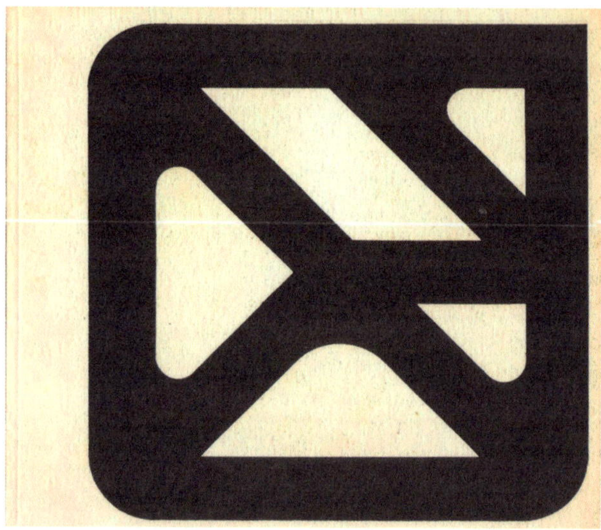

New York Graphic Workshop: Luis Camnitzer, José Guillermo Castillo, Liliana Porter. Exhibition catalogue, Museo de Bellas Artes, Caracas, January 1969. Liliana Porter Collection

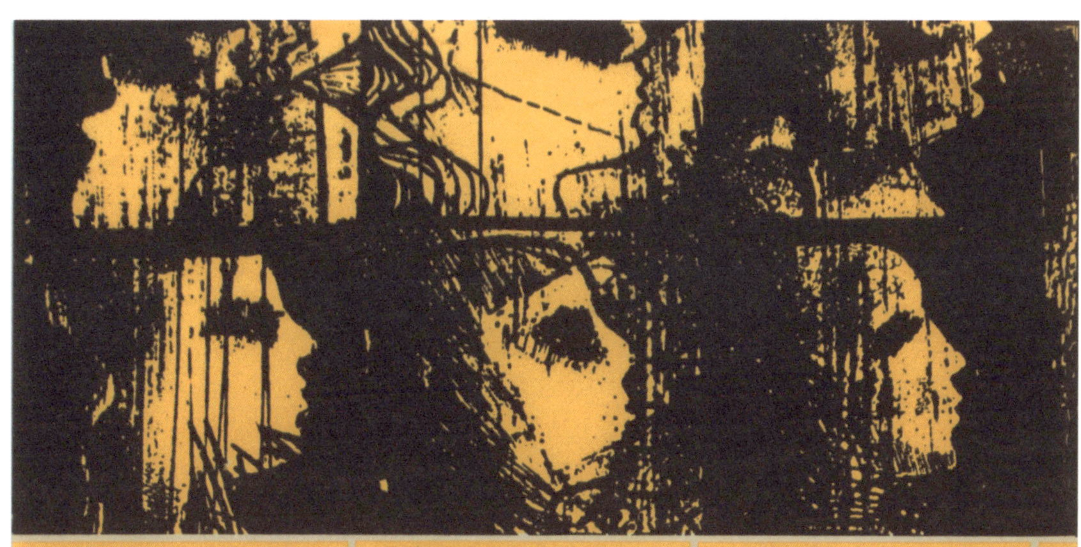

NEW YORK GRAPHIC WORKSHOP

NEW YORK GRAPHIC WORKSHOP

NEW YORK GRAPHIC WORKSHOP

NEW YORK GRAPHIC WORKSHOP

NEW YORK GRAPHIC WORKSHOP

NEW YORK GRAPHIC WORKSHOP

AUSPICIA MUSEO DEL GRABADO

EXPOSICION EN
PLASTICA GALERIA DE ARTE
10 AL 29 DE OCTUBRE 1966

Obras de Porter, Noé (Argentina)
De Lamónica (Brasil)
Dalí (España)
Campbell, Celentano, Goff, Kogan, Sims, Smith (EE.UU.)
Camnitzer (Uruguay)
Castillo, Morena (Venezuela)

FLORIDA 588 - BUENOS AIRES

NEW YORK GRAPHIC WORKSHOP

NEW YORK GRAPHIC WORKSHOP

NEW YORK GRAPHIC WORKSHOP

NEW YORK GRAPHIC WORKSHOP

The main ideas of the New York Graphic Workshop placed an emphasis on the edition, on the multiple work, which involved a desire to make a more democratic art form. On the other hand, we were very aware of the need to emphasize the concepts and proposals, not the technical prowess. Printmakers have always been very rigid with respect to the laws of the métier, and we sought to broaden the possibilities that were offered by the prospect of multiple-work production. That was what led us to environmental pieces, mail art, three-dimensional art, the use of nontraditional materials for printmaking, and ideas like editing a gesture—for example, the act of folding in *Wrinkle* [Arruga] from 1968.

— Liliana Porter

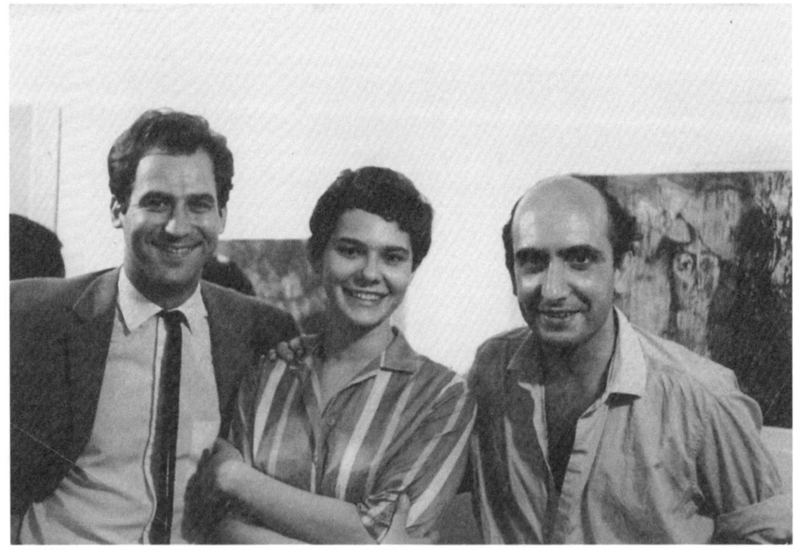

Luis Camnitzer, Liliana Porter, and Luis Felipe Noé, ca. 1965.
Liliana Porter Collection

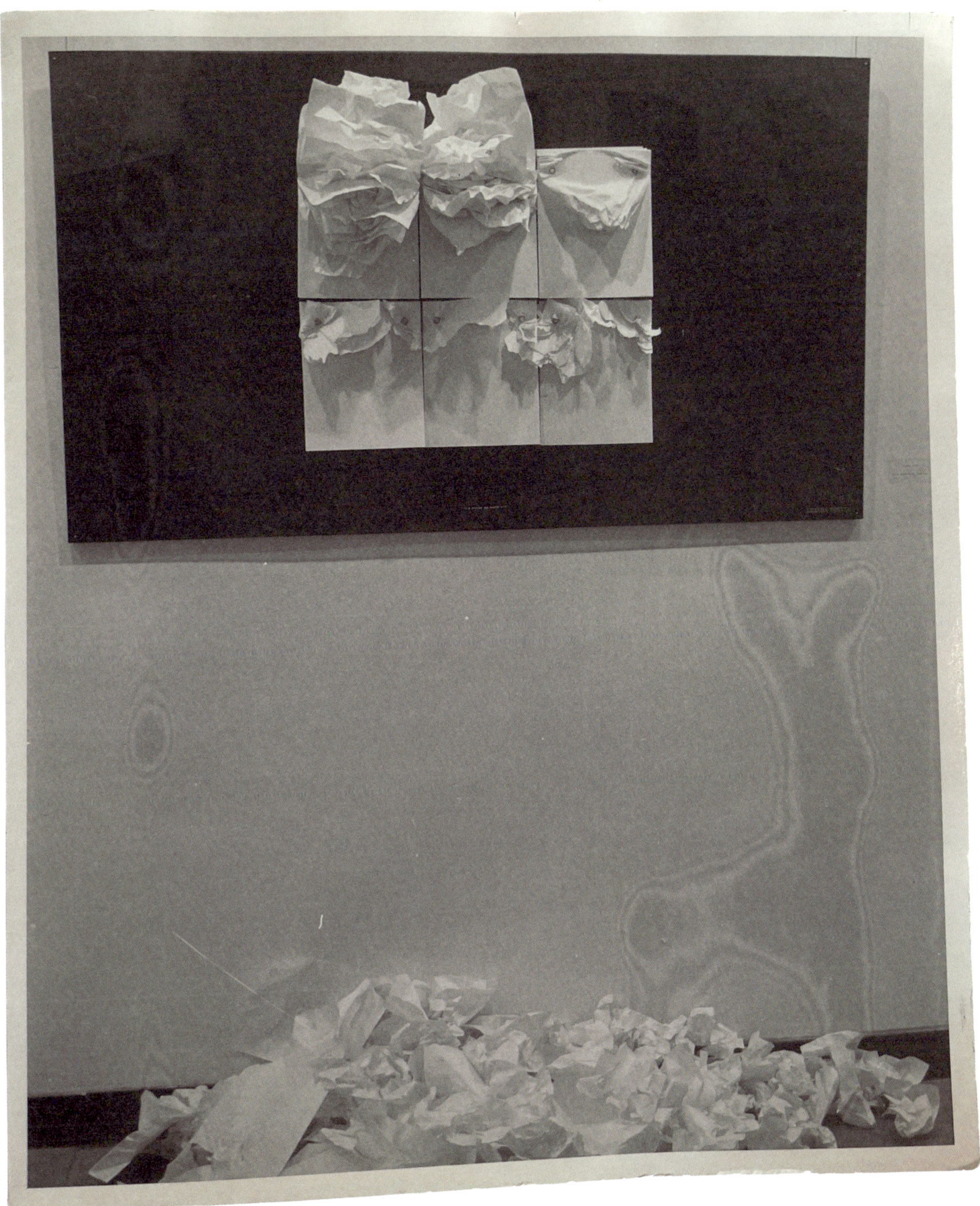

Liliana Porter, *To Be Wrinkled and Thrown Away* (front), installation view at the Institute of Contemporary Arts, Philadelphia, 1969. Liliana Porter Collection

Liliana Porter, *To Be Wrinkled and Thrown Away* (back), installation view at the Institute of Contemporary Arts, Philadelphia, 1969. Liliana Porter Collection

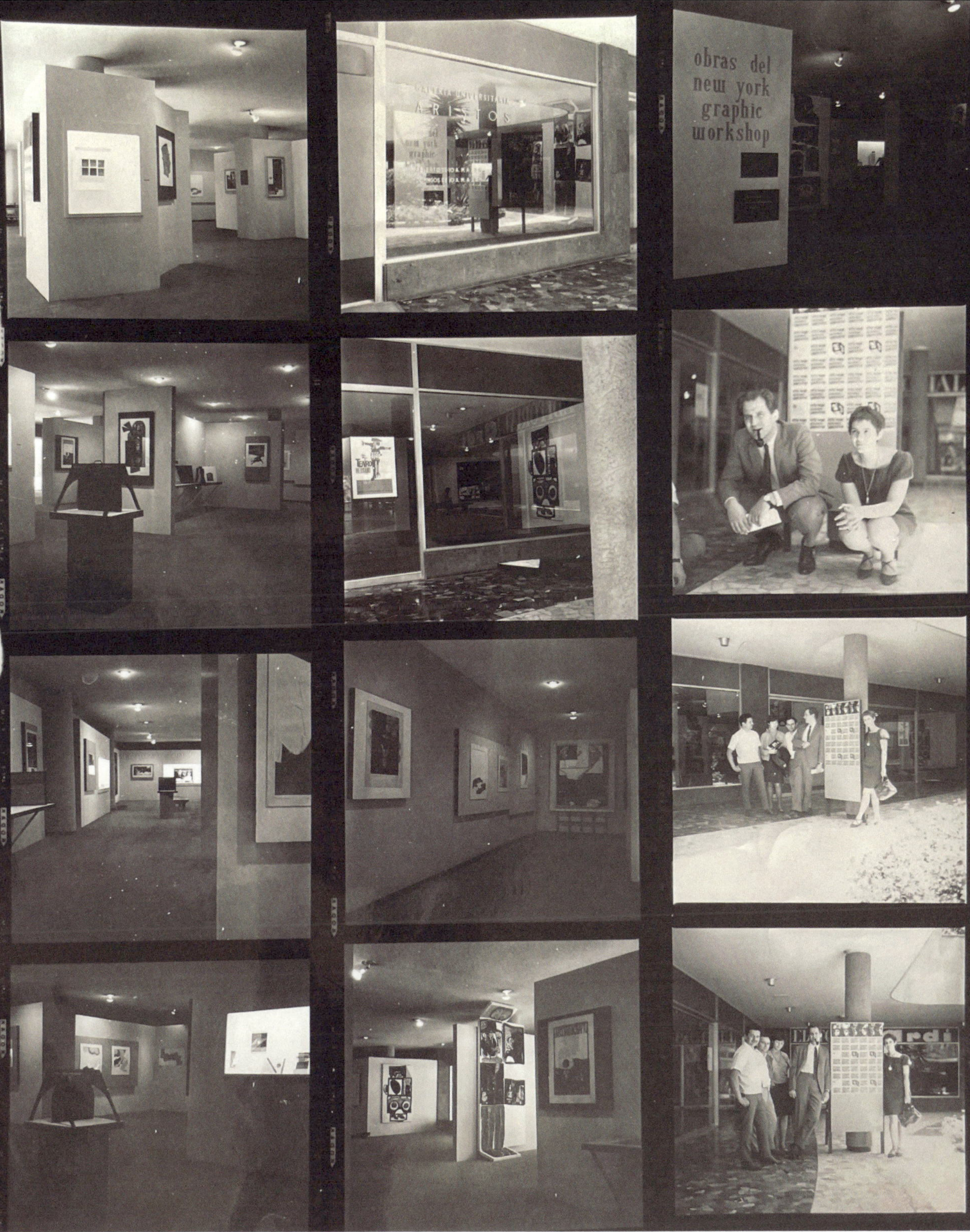

Opening of *Obras del New York Graphic Workshop* at Galeria Universitaria Aristos, Mexico City, 1966. Liliana Porter Collection

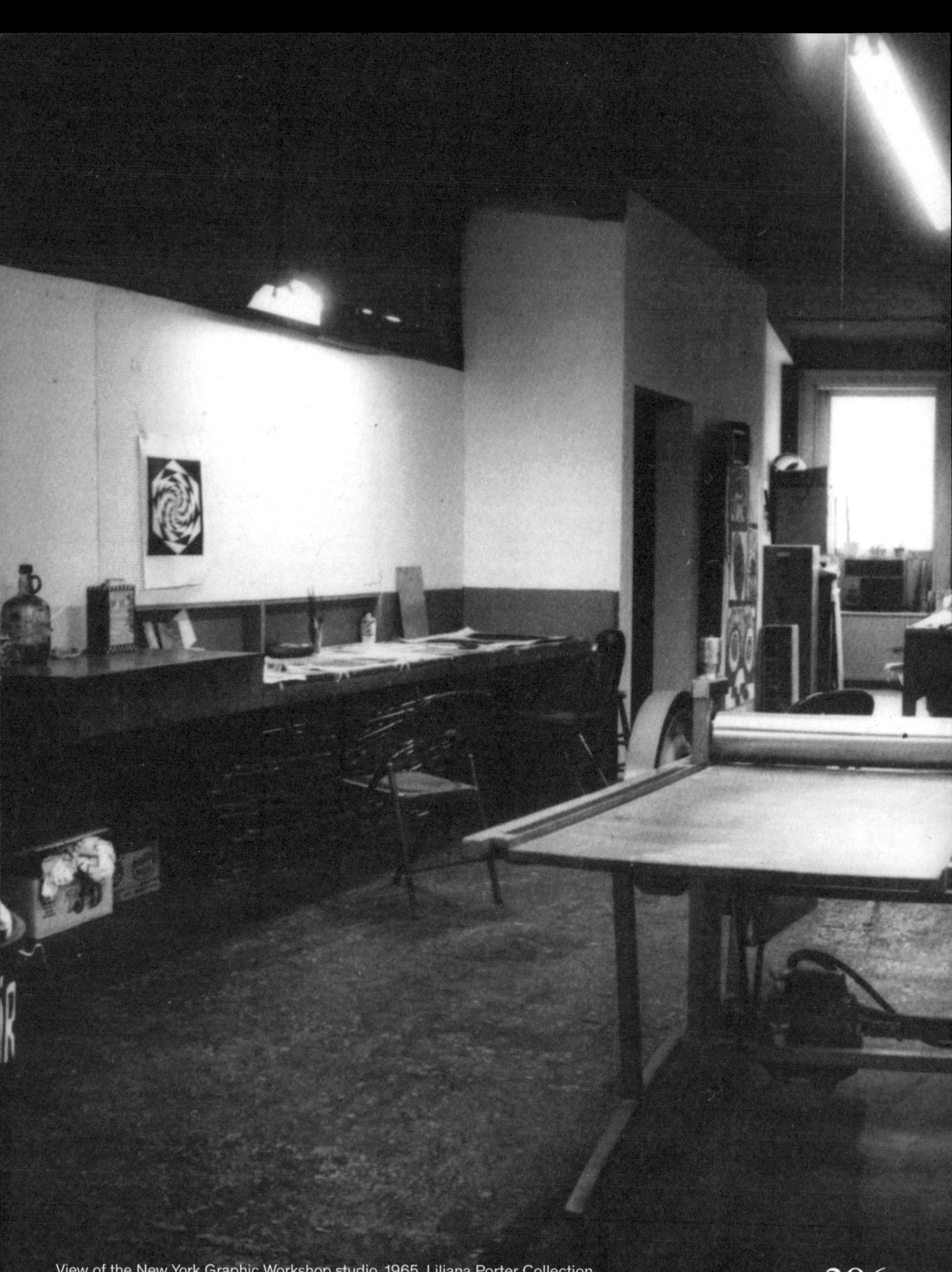

View of the New York Graphic Workshop studio, 1965. Liliana Porter Collection

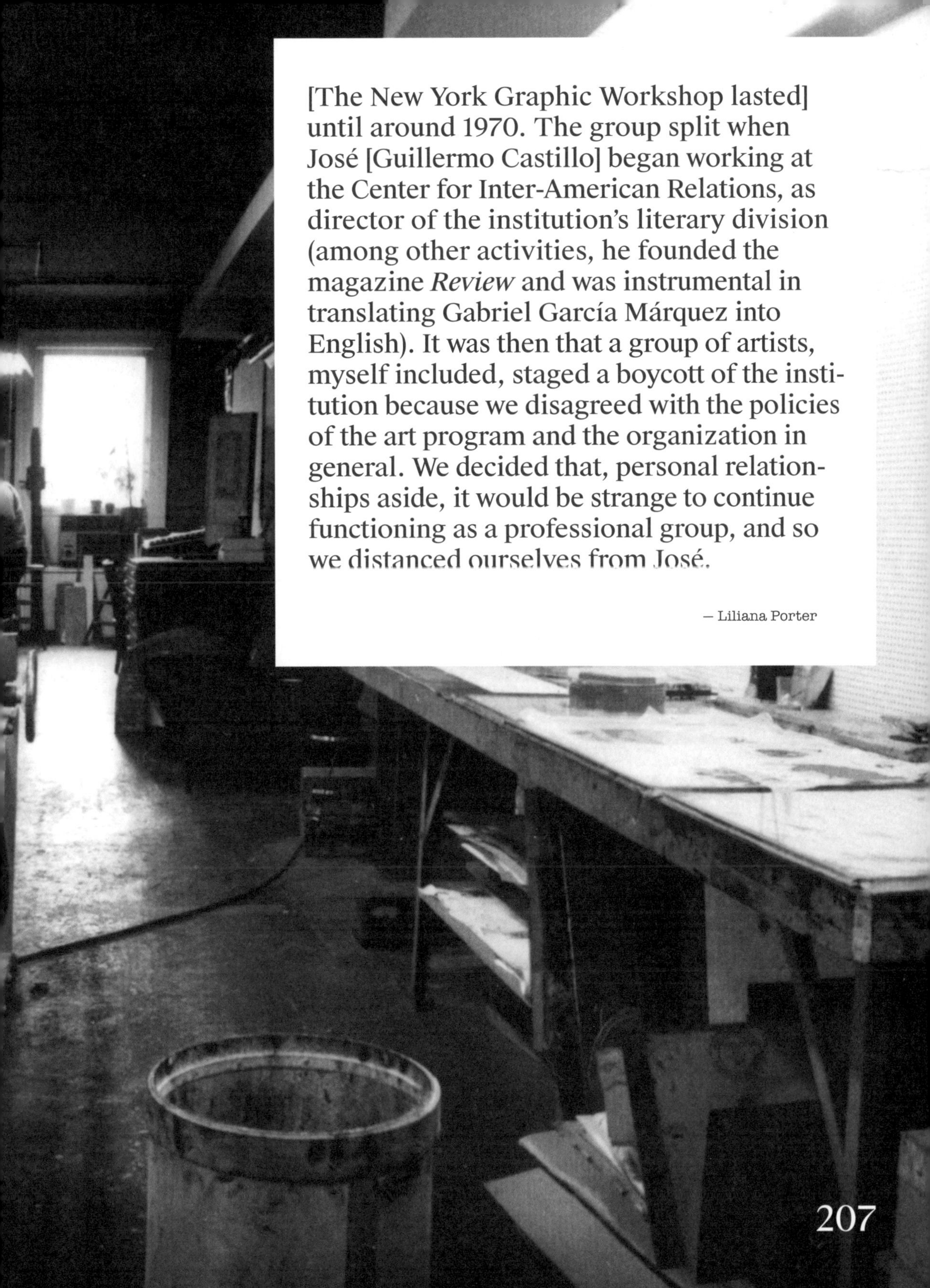

[The New York Graphic Workshop lasted] until around 1970. The group split when José [Guillermo Castillo] began working at the Center for Inter-American Relations, as director of the institution's literary division (among other activities, he founded the magazine *Review* and was instrumental in translating Gabriel García Márquez into English). It was then that a group of artists, myself included, staged a boycott of the institution because we disagreed with the policies of the art program and the organization in general. We decided that, personal relationships aside, it would be strange to continue functioning as a professional group, and so we distanced ourselves from José.

— Liliana Porter

Several Latin American artists created works that engaged with Institutional Critique, a form of art practice that questions and reveals the dominant ideologies and power dynamics operating within art institutions, including spaces like MoMA and the CIAR. To challenge institutional narratives, other artists created alternative exhibition models and other forms of art dissemination, including publications, mail art, and commercial initiatives to sell ephemera and multiples for accessible prices.

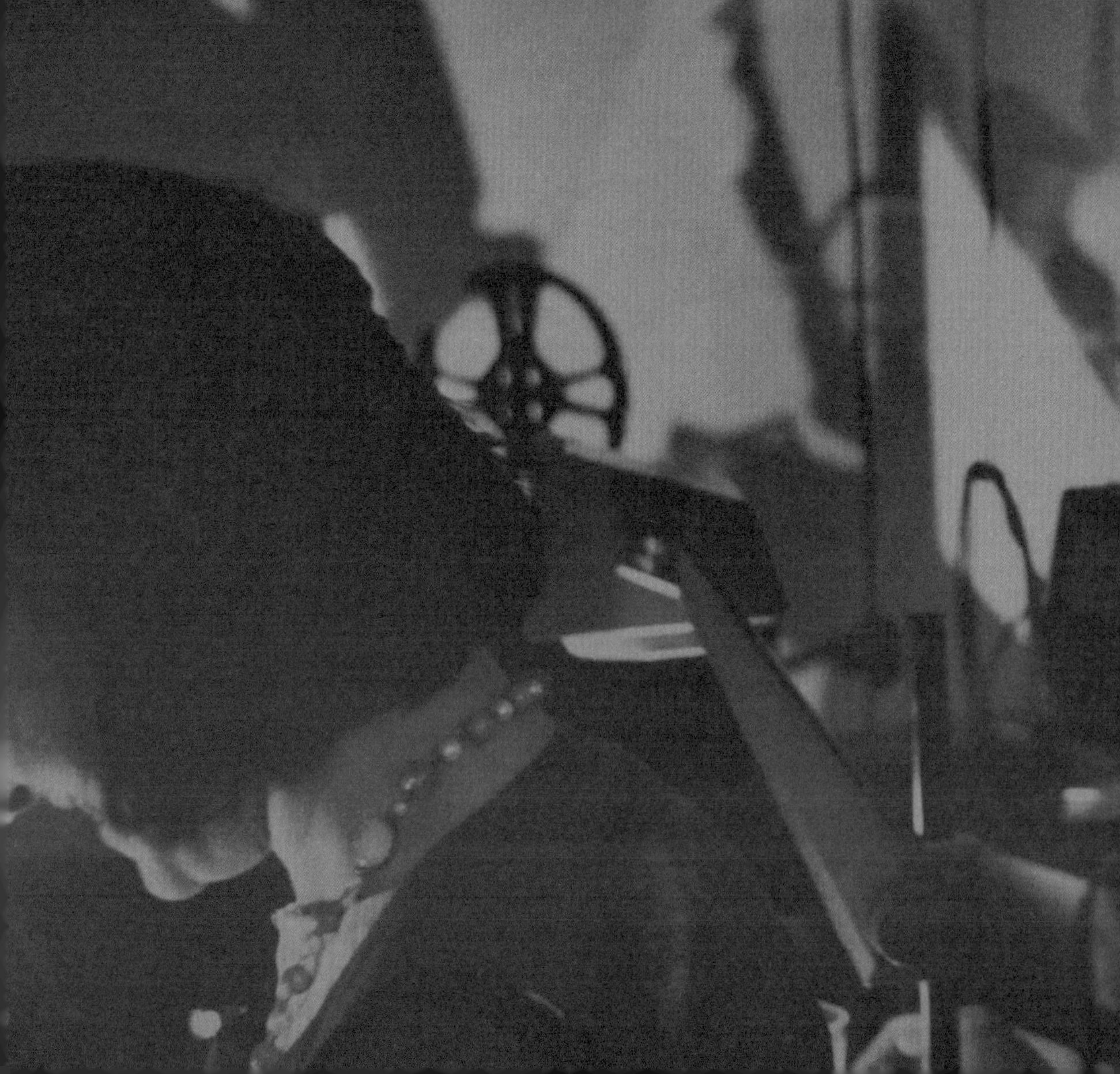

Critique of Institutions

Marta Minujín, *Minucode*, 1968. Happening at the Center for Inter-American Relations. Marta Minujín Archive

Juan Trepadori was a fictional character invented by the founders of the New York Graphic Workshop (NYGW). Trepadori was a self-taught artist from Paraguay. Because prints signed by Trepadori faired relatively well in the North American art market, he became an alternative source of income for the NYGW artists, who shared that income with any artist who needed extra money. Challenging traditional views of artistic authorship, Trepadori also functioned as an avenue for these artists to create without the pressure of making a single authorial work, thus opening space for experimentation.

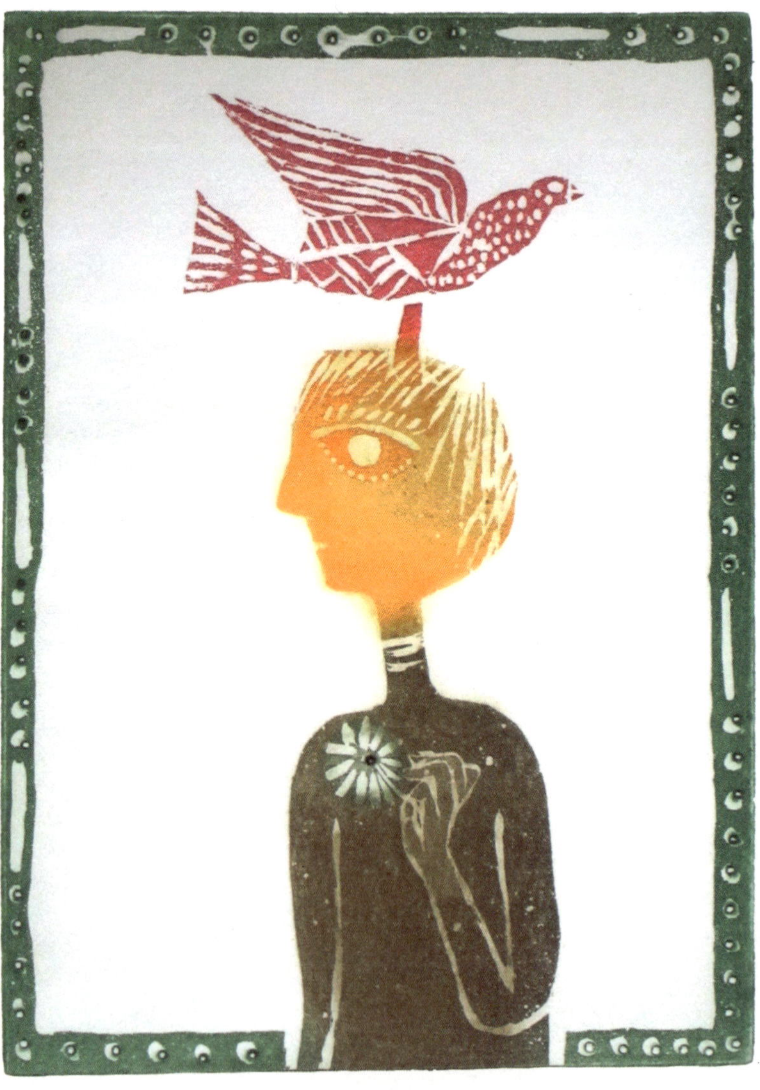

Juan Trepadori, *Niño e idea* (Boy and idea), 1969. Liliana Porter Collection

Juan Trepadori was an artist we invented at the [New York Graphic] workshop. This is the story: in the beginning, when our work was still somewhat expressionist and we were making prints with color and texture, there were publishers who would buy entire series of prints. But when we began to be more "ascetic" in terms of form, the works turned out to be unsellable, much less in full editions. So one time, when an artist friend had run into financial trouble, we decided to invent a printmaker artist who could respond to the aesthetic/commercial desires of a publisher named Barton, who was thrilled with the work by this invented artist from Paraguay, Juan Trepadori. They were modern works, but comprehensible, sophisticated, and at the same time happy pieces—in other words, ideal. So any friend who came by and needed money would make a Trepadori. The work would sell and the artist would win their little Trepadori grant, which served, among other things, to free works of art that were being held up in customs (that was the situation with the first Trepadori), to cover the costs of an art class, or to pay for materials. Lots of artists made Trepadori pieces because it was a very easy style to follow. The beauty of all this was that our "accomplices" (from the very first one, whose own work was dramatic, Francis Bacon-style work) got into the Trepadori spirit and actually had a great time when they made these prints, even though they were the exact opposite of their own personal aesthetics. As time went by, Trepadori became more and more human, and quite adored. He was basically a derivative, not at all brilliant artist who, curiously, gave the artists who participated in the enterprise the freedom to create without pressure and to experience an unprecedented, almost unspeakable kind of pleasure.

— Liliana Porter

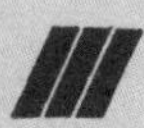

Francisco Sanguiñedo
Escuela de Bellas Artes
Martí 3328
Montevideo , URUGUAY

Instituto Torcuato Di Tella
Centro de Artes Visuales

Florida 936
Buenos Aires, Argentina

Contenido: Exhibición N° 3
Luis Camnitzer

When we devised the idea of mailing exhibitions, we weren't really thinking about what is now known as mail art, or about Fluxus. It was sort of a logical solution to the fact that we didn't really have access to New York galleries.

— Luis Camnitzer

PARA PARAR DE CANTO
Y APLASTAR,
COMO EJERCICIO DE PODER

Luis Camnitzer, *Exhibición n. 3*, 1969. Private collection

What most captivated me [about doing mail exhibitions] was the poetry of sending something like a shadow by mail. Today Luis says (and I don't know where he gets this from) that we made mail art because we couldn't get a gallery, but I think that we were trying to get by without the galleries, they seemed antiquated and we were against the idea of making objects. You see, the great thing about NYGW was that different visions of art were able to coexist without friction.

— Liliana Porter

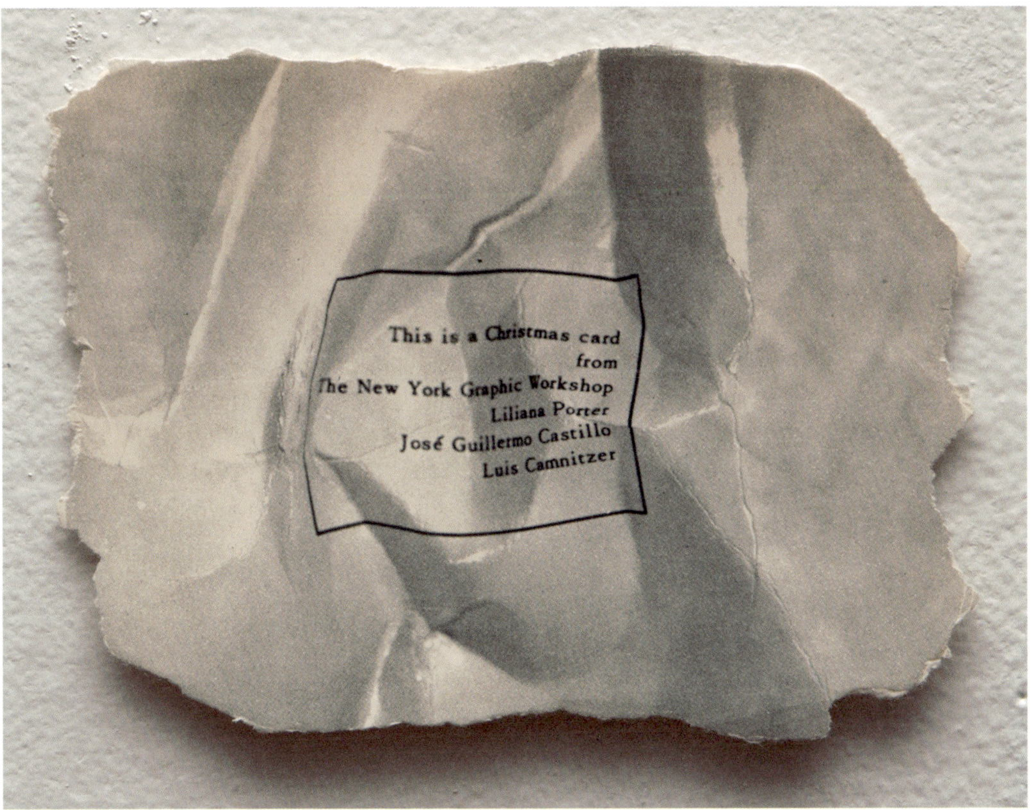

New York Graphic Workshop, Christmas card, ca. 1968. Liliana Porter Collection

In 1971, Rubens Gerchman created Integralia Corporation in partnership with other artists, such as Luis Camnitzer and Luis Wells, and critic Jorge Romero Brest. Integralia produced small art objects for people to carry around as keepsakes in everyday life.

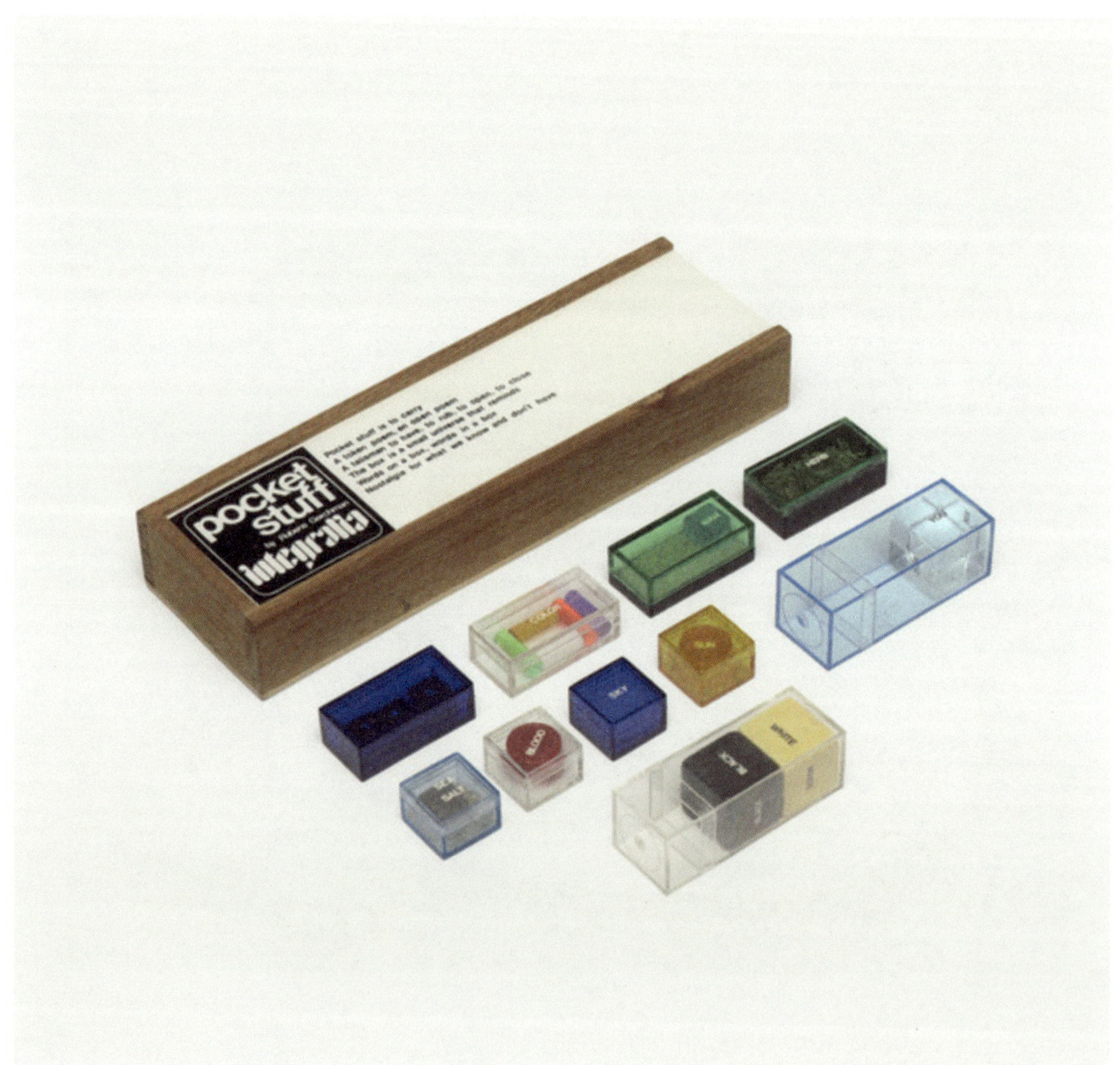

Rubens Gerchman, *Pocket Stuff*, 1971. Courtesy of Instituto Rubens Gerchman

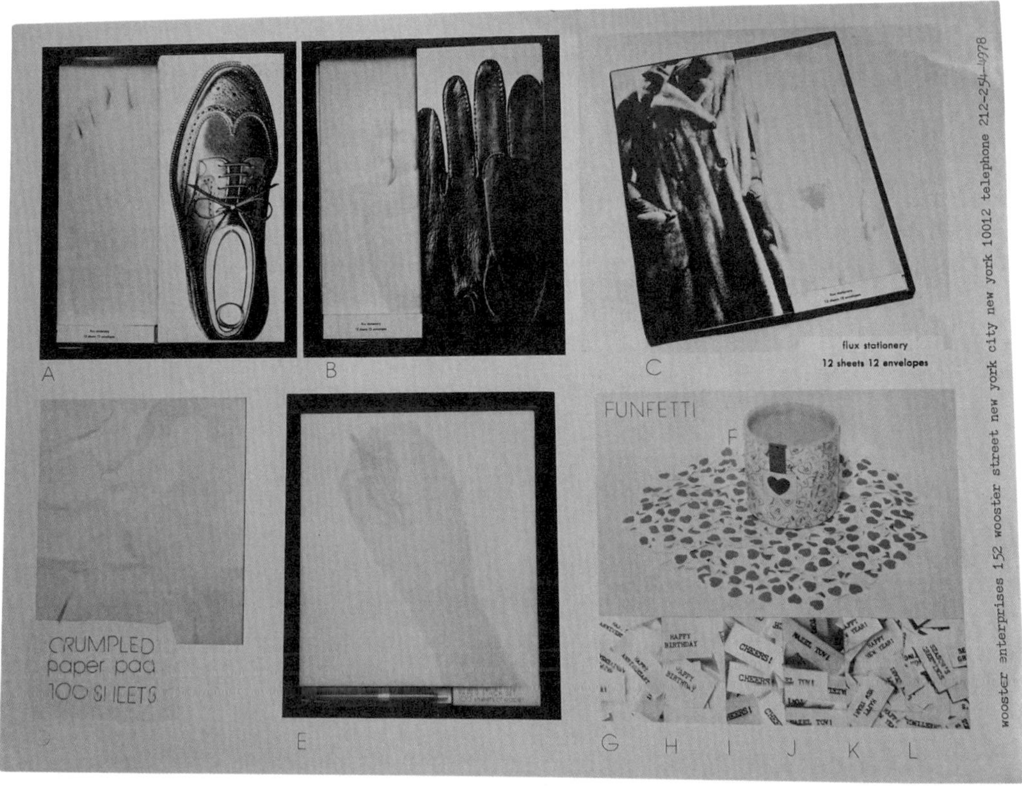

Wooster Enterprises was a stationery business created in 1976 by artists Jaime Davidovich and Judith Henry, who were then married. Blurring the boundaries between art and life, the artists created works that were meant to be sold at low prices as common merchandise, not high-value artworks. These included postcards, writing paper, masks, and notepads, among other objects.

Flyer for Wooster Enterprises, ca. 1977. Institute for Studies on Latin American Art (ISLAA) Library and Archives

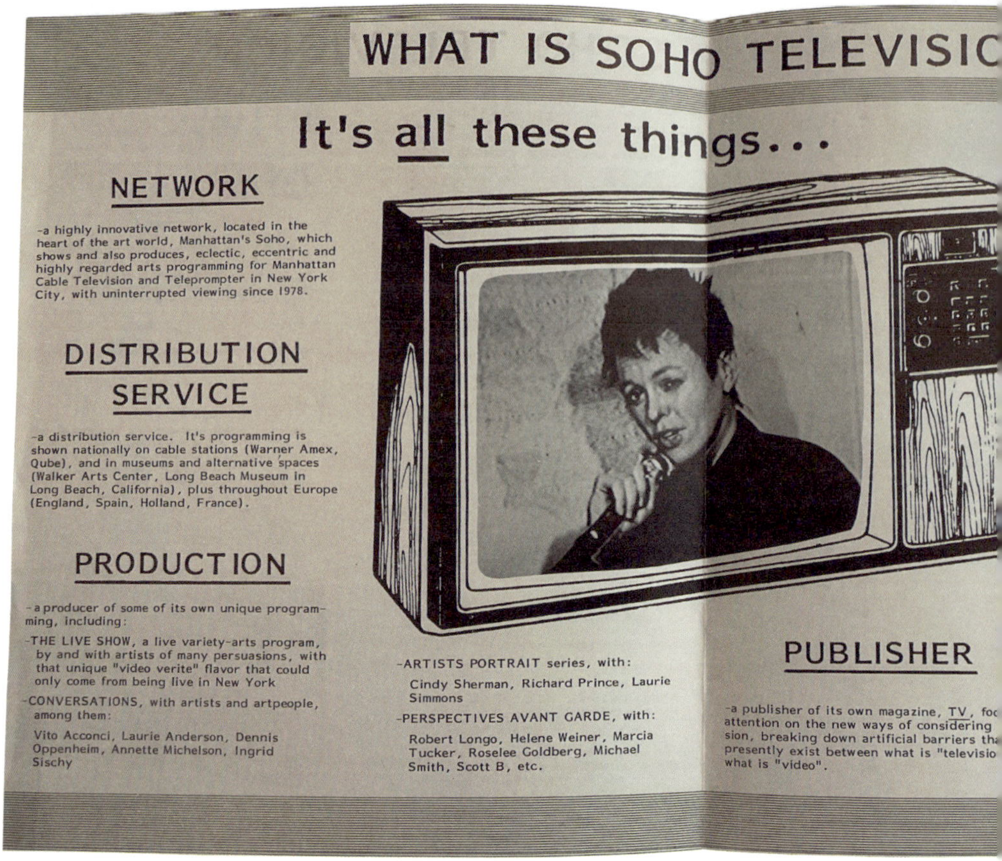

WHAT IS SOHO TELEVISIC

It's all these things...

NETWORK

-a highly innovative network, located in the heart of the art world, Manhattan's Soho, which shows and also produces, eclectic, eccentric and highly regarded arts programming for Manhattan Cable Television and Teleprompter in New York City, with uninterrupted viewing since 1978.

DISTRIBUTION SERVICE

-a distribution service. It's programming is shown nationally on cable stations (Warner Amex, Qube), and in museums and alternative spaces (Walker Arts Center, Long Beach Museum in Long Beach, California), plus throughout Europe (England, Spain, Holland, France).

PRODUCTION

-a producer of some of its own unique programming, including:

-THE LIVE SHOW, a live variety-arts program, by and with artists of many persuasions, with that unique "video verite" flavor that could only come from being live in New York

-CONVERSATIONS, with artists and artpeople, among them:

Vito Acconci, Laurie Anderson, Dennis Oppenheim, Annette Michelson, Ingrid Sischy

-ARTISTS PORTRAIT series, with:

Cindy Sherman, Richard Prince, Laurie Simmons

-PERSPECTIVES AVANT GARDE, with:

Robert Longo, Helene Weiner, Marcia Tucker, Roselee Goldberg, Michael Smith, Scott B, etc.

PUBLISHER

-a publisher of its own magazine, TV, foc attention on the new ways of considering sion, breaking down artificial barriers th presently exist between what is "televisio what is "video".

Brochure for SoHo Television, 1976. Institute for Studies on Latin American Art (ISLAA) Library and Archives

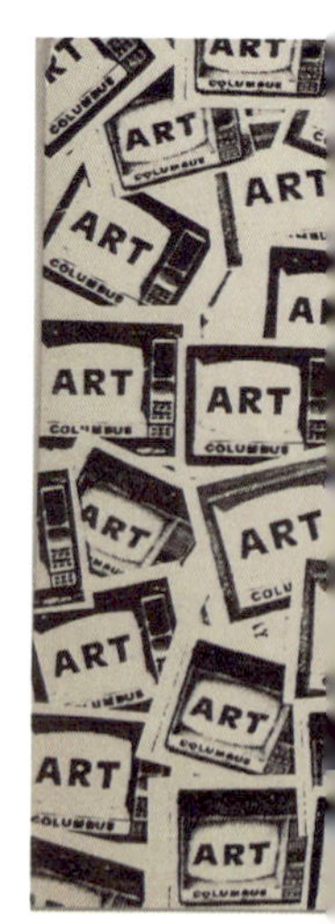

Jaime Davidovich experimented with video to create works that reflected on the city of New York and the political situations in the United States and Argentina, his home country. In the late 1970s, Davidovich embraced public access cable television as a medium for artistic experimentation and the dissemination of art with the creation of *Cable SoHo* (1976) and *The Live! Show* (1979–84).

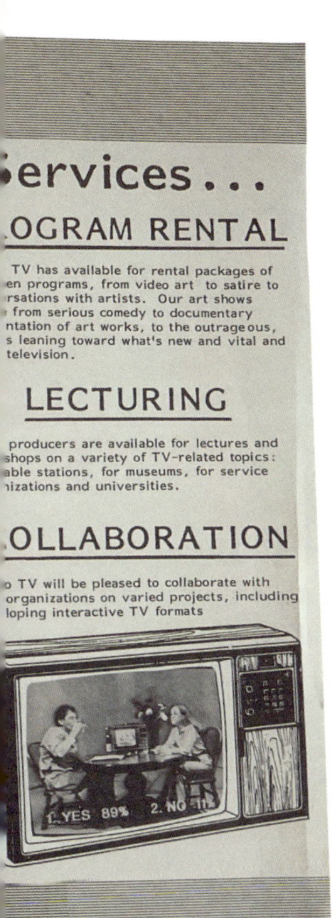

In SoHo, there was a movement against the gatekeepers of culture going on—the galleries, museums, and collectors. Artists were trying to do work outside the gallery system, ephemeral works. In 1976 a group of artists and arts organizations formed a nonprofit called Cable SoHo. It included Anthology Film Archives, The Kitchen, Franklin Furnace, Global Village, and others. We wanted to create a television station for arts programming. Between all the different organizations, there was enough to fill a channel. The idea was to get a mobile production unit, in a truck that could go around to the different art spaces in SoHo and cablecast live events to the rest of the city.

[M]y group saw cable as a way to intervene in television. To go inside the TV and do something directed at people at home.

— Jaime Davidovich

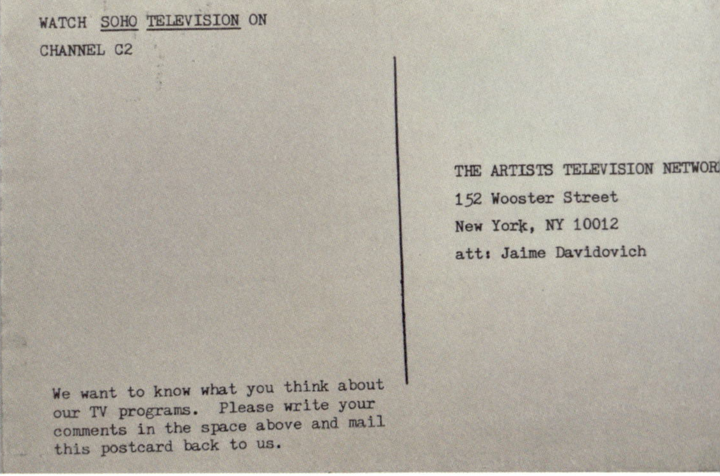

Front and back of Artists Television Network postcard, 1977.
Institute for Studies on Latin American Art (ISLAA) Library and Archives

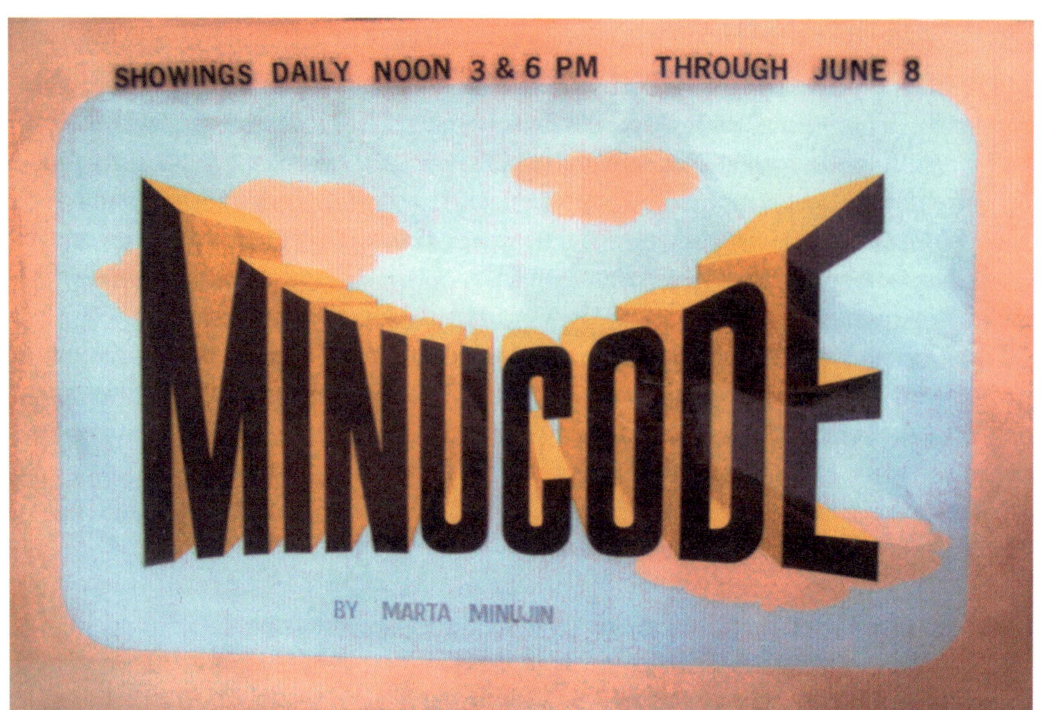

Poster for *Minucode*, 1968. Marta Minujín Archive

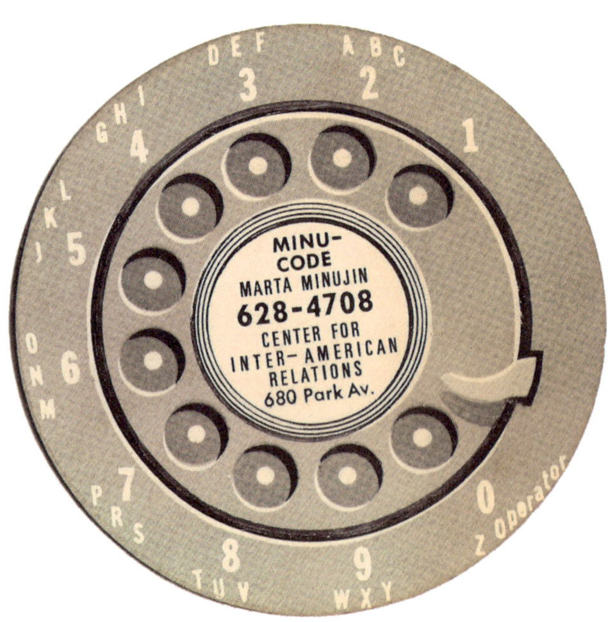

Marketing sticker for *Minucode*, 1968. Marta Minujín Archive

The MINUCODE consists of four different social environments that involve Wall Street executives, politicians, artists, and people of the fashion world. In the case of the MINUCODE, I separate the four groups, which, in an affluent society, appear melted among themselves, especially in what is called social interaction; for example, a cocktail party. But the fact that we can see a politician talking to an artist at a party does not mean that, in reality, a relationship exists between them. The frames in which each group develops its activities are rigorous and, since their interests are different, they only mix in an apparent or illusory way. So I emphasize this point. But at the same time, I have chosen these four different groups just for the hidden relationships that exist, functionally-wise, among them: economy, political direction, entertainment, and ornamentation.

– Marta Minujín

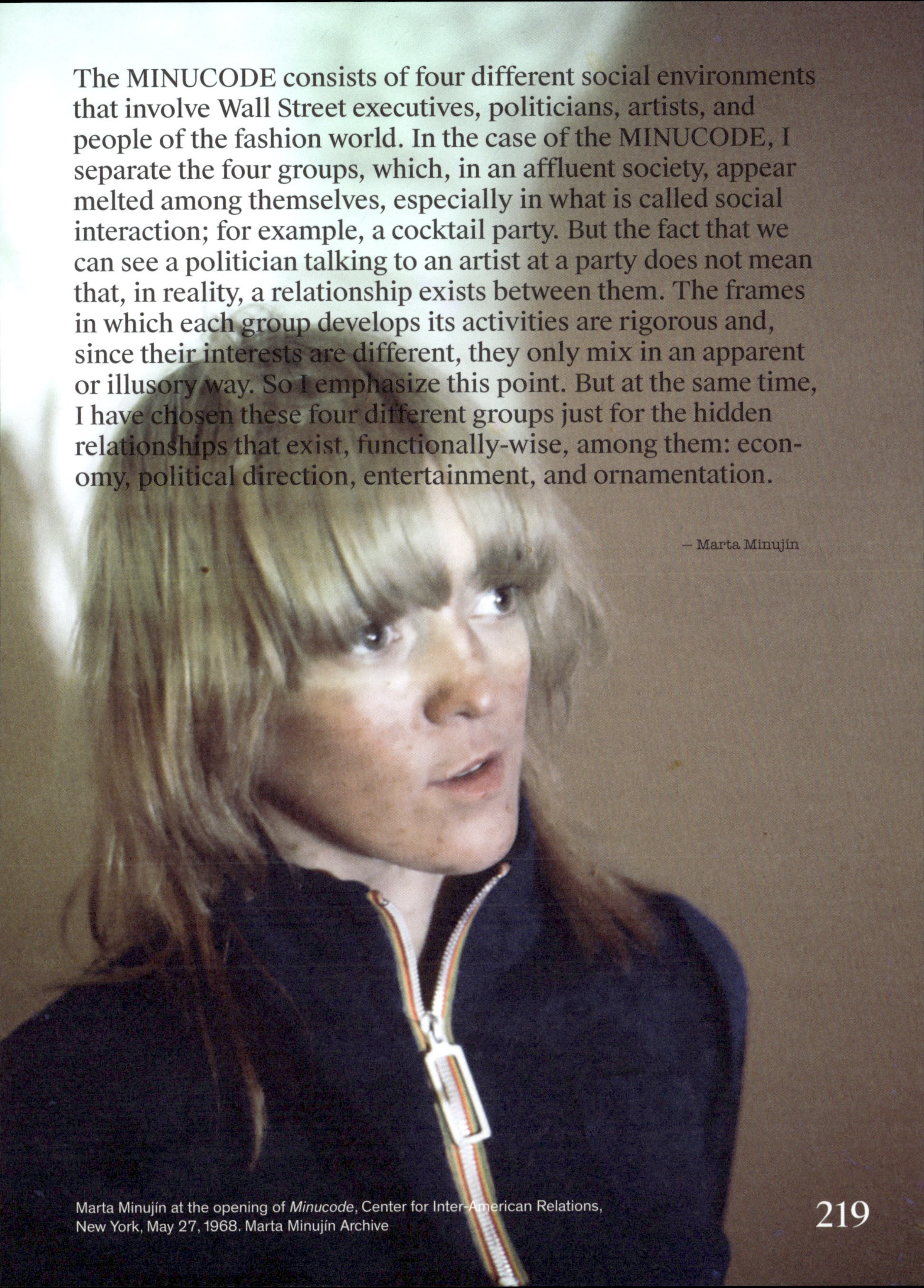

Marta Minujín at the opening of *Minucode*, Center for Inter-American Relations, New York, May 27, 1968. Marta Minujín Archive

Marta Minujín, statement for *Minucode*, 1968. Marta Minujín Archive

M I N U C O D E

A Multi-social and Media Environment Experience
Created and Produced by Marta Minujin

MINUCODE statement

"320 people belonging to four different social groups, selected from answers to a questionnaire published in several metropolitan newspapers, were invited to four 'group' cocktail parties. During the cocktail parties, which were filmed, eight representatives of each group were asked to create a second environment or light show in an adjoining room.

"Now you are going to have an audio-visual experience which consists in the projection of each of the cocktail parties' films and the re-creation, at the same time, of the light show created by the eight representatives of each cocktail party. This experience is the MINUCODE.

"For MINUCODE's realization, I followed the procedure described above, seeking only to provide it with a function, that of re-establishing confidence in the possibilities of the public 'show'.

"The sociological connotations that surround the project--since the four social groups represent basic parts of the social system: economy, politics, entertainment, and ornamentation--have been used as the main element of MINUCODE's realization, and deliberately used to create a social-scientific atmosphere.

"Those groups which have meaning only in relation to other groups of the same system, now become the 'sub-plot' in the reality of the films. For this, I can say that the 'code' used in the MINUCODE is sociological, but its message is strictly artistic."

Marta Minujin

May 28 - June 8, 1968
40-minute presentations: noon, 3 and 6 p.m.

Sponsored and presented by the Art Gallery
Center for Inter-American Relations
680 Park Avenue, New York, N.Y. (68th Street)

Marta Minujín, questionnaire sent to *Minucode* participants, 1968. Marta Minujín Archive

MINUCODE QUESTIONNAIRE

COMPLETE AND RETURN BEFORE MAY 13TH TO MINUCODE; ART GALLERY OF THE CENTER FOR INTER-AMERICAN RELATIONS, 680 PARK AVENUE, NEW YORK 10021

NAME: ______________________ PHONE: __________

ADDRESS: ______________________

IN WHICH OF THE FOLLOWING AREAS ARE YOU INVOLVED? (CHECK ONE)

BUSINESS __________ ART ______

FASHION __________ POLITICS ______

DESCRIBE YOUR ACTIVITY IN THIS AREA: ______________________

____

TO WHAT EXTENT ARE YOU ACTIVE IN THE OTHER THREE AREAS? __________

____

WHAT MATERIALS TURN YOU ON?

LIGHTS __________ MOVING SCREENS __________

SOUNDS __________ SLIDE PROJECTION __________

MOVIES __________ T.V. __________

OTHER ______________________

IF YOU ARE SELECTED FOR MINUCODE, WOULD YOU PREFER TO BE A (CHECK ONE)

PARTICIPANT __________ LEADER __________

(IF SELECTED, YOU WILL RECEIVE AN INVITATION TO THE COCKTAIL PARTY FOR YOUR GROUP AT THE CENTER FOR INTER-AMERICAN RELATIONS ART GALLERY)

Opening of *Minucode* at the Center for Inter-American Relations, New York, May 27, 1968. Marta Minujín Archive

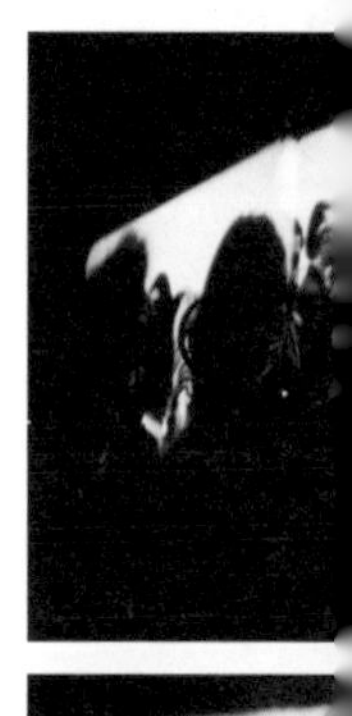

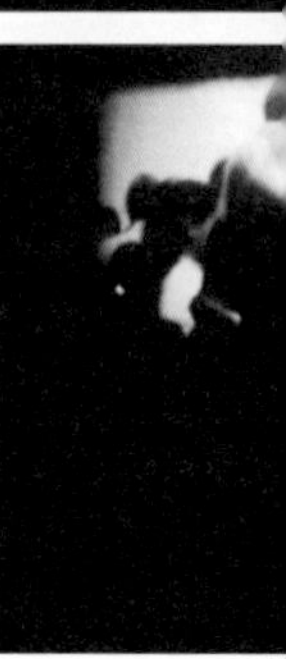

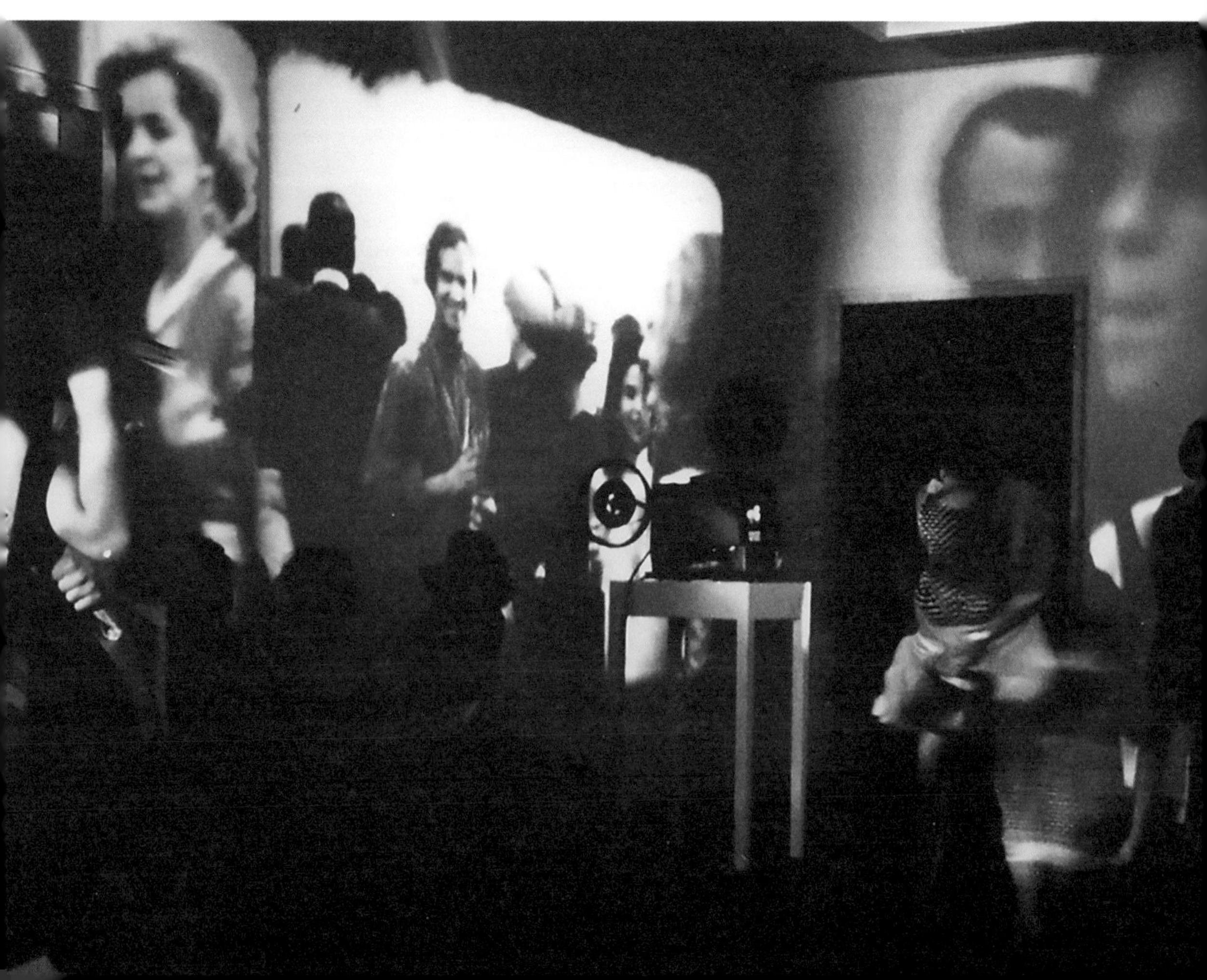

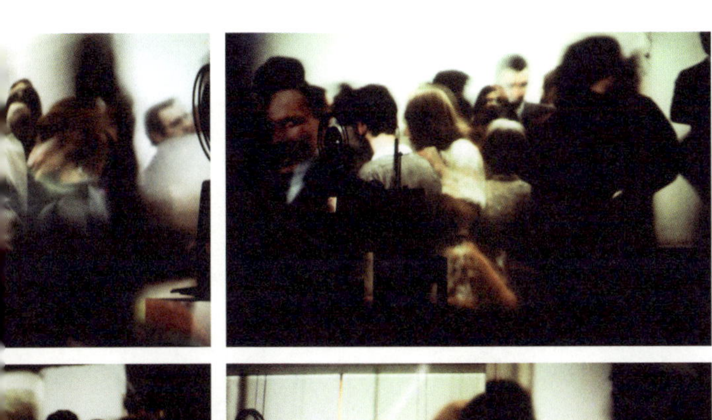
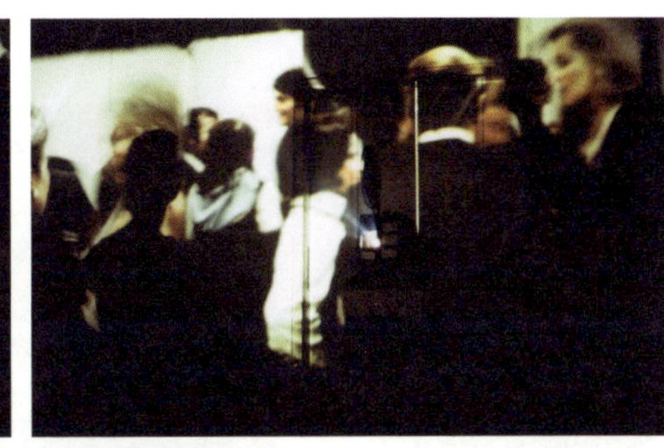
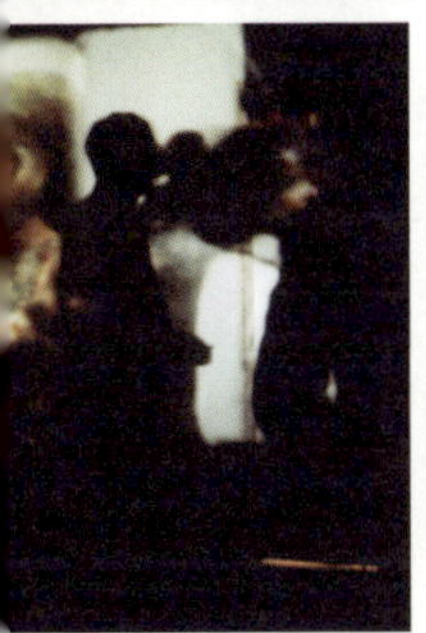
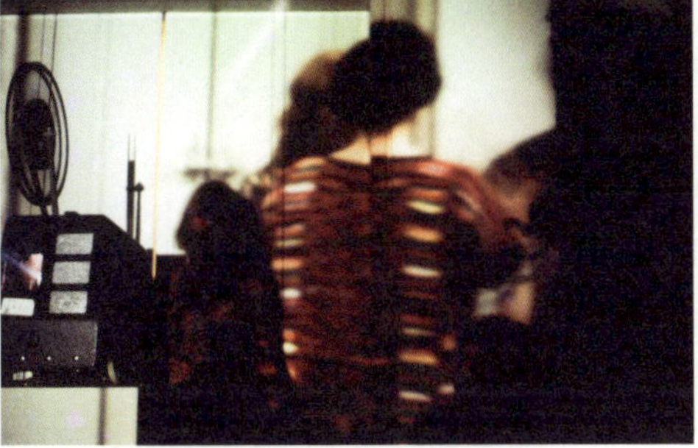
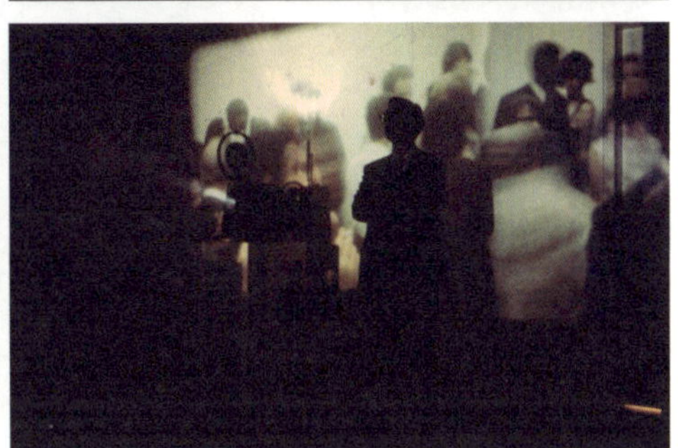
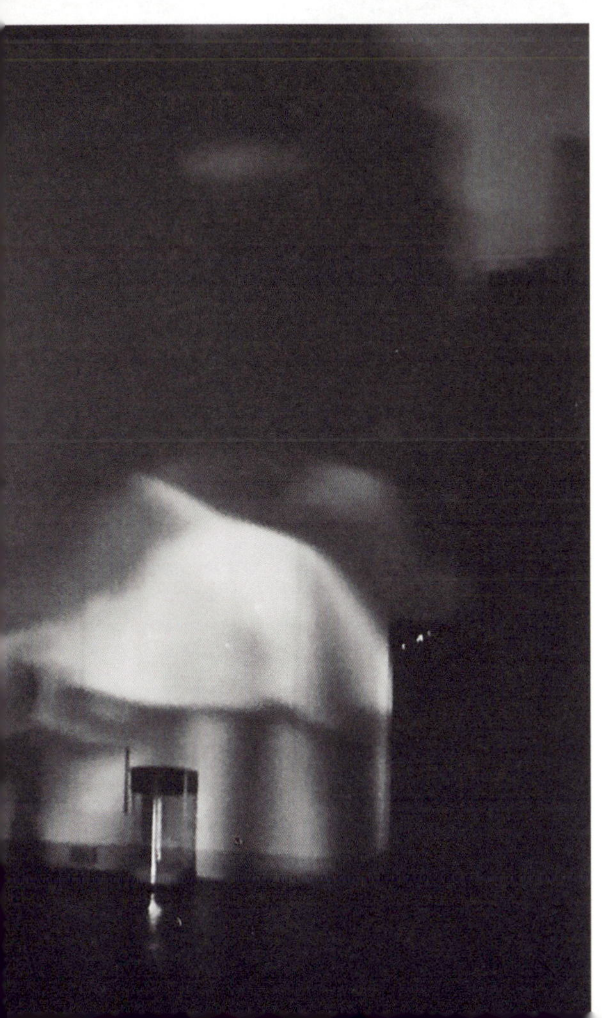

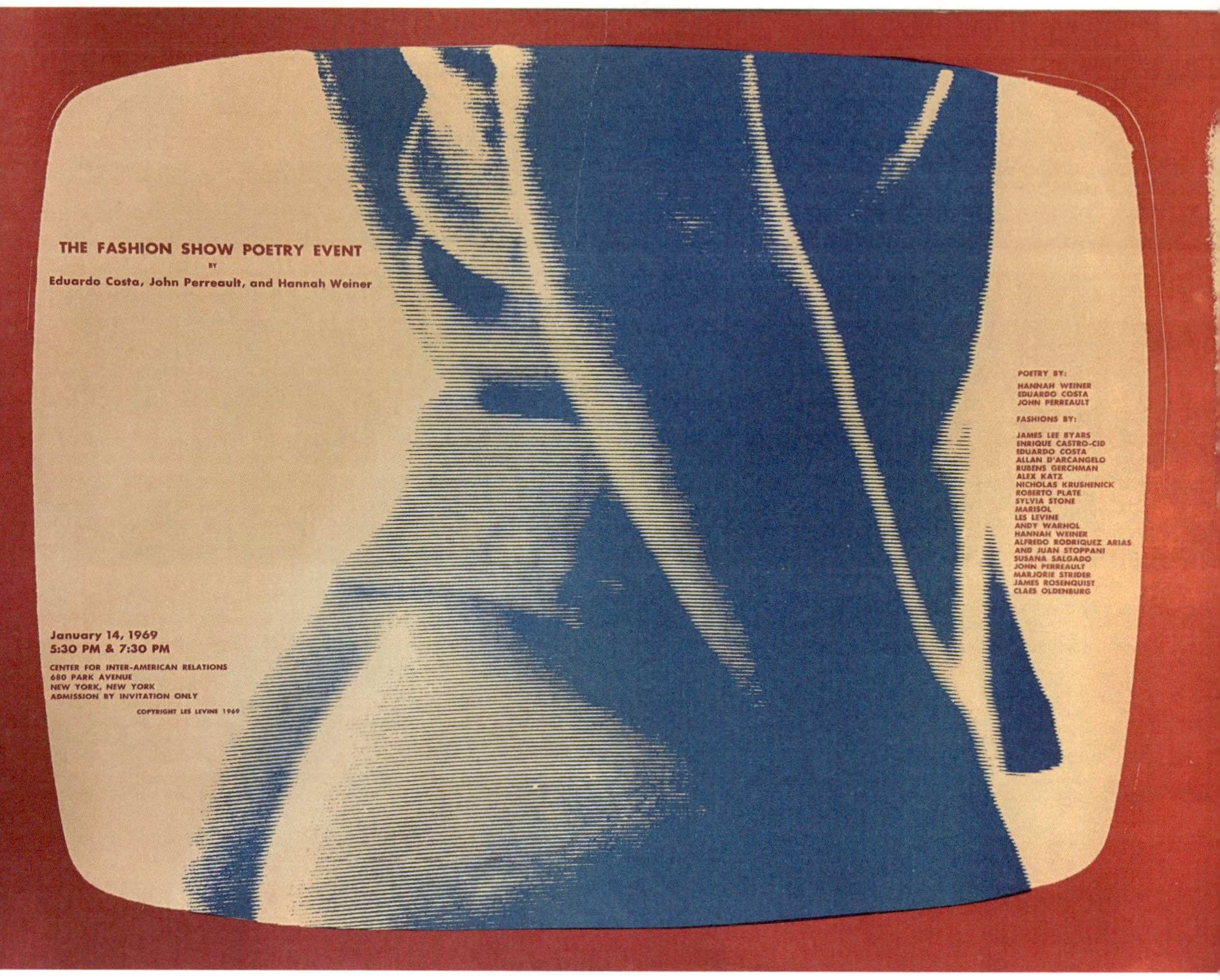

The Fashion Show Poetry Event was an experimental event organized in 1969 by Eduardo Costa, John Perreault, and Hannah Weiner at the CIAR. The event, which spoke to Eduardo Costa's long-standing interest in the interrelation between fashion, mass media, and consumerism, brought together twenty-four artists and poets, including Andy Warhol, Marisol, and Carolee Schneemann, to create artworks to be displayed in the form of garments modeled on a catwalk.

Poster by Les Levine for *The Fashion Show Poetry Event*, Center for Inter-American Relations, New York, January 14, 1969. Eduardo Costa Collection

The Fashion Show Poetry Event managed to do something no other fashion-media event, TV, film documentary, or otherwise has ever done or dared to do. Through its pure creativity it managed to slash through fashion's heavy bullshit, smack into the essence of it all, which unfortunately is merely more of the same.

— Blair Sabol, The Village Voice

You are cordially invited to
The Fashion Show Poetry Event
at the Center for Inter-American
Relations, 680 Park Avenue.
Our capacity is limited;
there are two showings: 5:30 &
7:30 PM on January 14, 1969.

RSVP stating time choice
249-8950
Ext. 60

This card admits two.

Invitation for *The Fashion Show Poetry Event*, Center for Inter-American Relations, New York, January 14, 1969. Americas Society Archive

THE FASHION SHOW POETRY EVENT
by
Hannah Weiner, John Perreault, and Eduardo Costa

artists .... models

1. Rubens Gerchman..John Bulfair, Susan Blanchard, Katrin Tralongo

"Yellow and green structures...combine the latest in fashion with the latest in architecture. Wear your home." *

2. Alex Katz..Jerry Jacquette

"The ten minute dress...signed by Alex Katz...Voila! An original work of art!"

3. Allan D'Arcangelo..Sylvia D'Arcangelo

"Stop! Look! Listen!...Super-chic barrior dress."

4. Marisol..Rene Ricard

"Slightly insolent creation...for the young man about town."

5. Jim Rosenquist..Frank DeGroote

"Are you too attached to your environment? Is it hard to get up and go?"

6. Eduardo Costa..Sheyla Limax, Haru Wells

"Ears, fingers, and breasts made of pure gold...Wear the shape of your own beauty!"

7. Hannah Weiner..Bernadette Mayer

"Taking a trip? Wear your luggage don't carry it!"

8. John Perreault..Anne Waldman

"'HAIR' Line...chic primitivism...bold, bold new look."

9. Alfredo Rodríguez Arias and Juan Stoppani...............Marucha Bo

"...let the designer in you create the dress you have always dreamed of."

10. Les Levine..Susan Blanchard, Rex Lau, Patty Ford, Katrin Tralomgo, John Bulfair, Jerry Jacquette, Joy Bang

"Plastic-man strikes again!"

- 4 -

11. Marjorie Strider.......................................Deborah Hay

 "Have you ever thought of yourself as a work of art?"

12. Allan D'Arcangelo.......................................Sylvia D'Arcangelo

 "...the excitement of high art with the body-consciousness of high fashion!"

13. Claes Oldenburg.......................................Carolee Schneemann

 "'The poets will provide her clothes.'"

14. Enrique Castro-Cid.......................................France Raysse

 "For those difficult transitional moments when your clothes are being altered."

15. Roberto Plate.......................................Marucha Bo

 "...doll-look, complete with matching make-up."

16. Sylvia Stone.......................................Donna Dennis

 "...delicious black and white creation."

17. Andy Warhol.......................................Gerard Malanga

 "The ultimate Pop solution to the question: Is life a drag?"

18. Susana Salgado.......................................Jean Ferreyra

 "Gigantically ultra-feminine..."

19. James Lee Byars.......................................Rex Lau and the audience.

 "Group therapy...Group living...And now group clothing."

* All quotes are from The Fashion Show Poetry Event Poems.

Note: All the garments presented are for sale. The artists may be contacted directly or through their galleries..

Checklist for *The Fashion Show Poetry Event*, Center for Inter-American Relations, New York, January 14, 1969. Eduardo Costa Collection

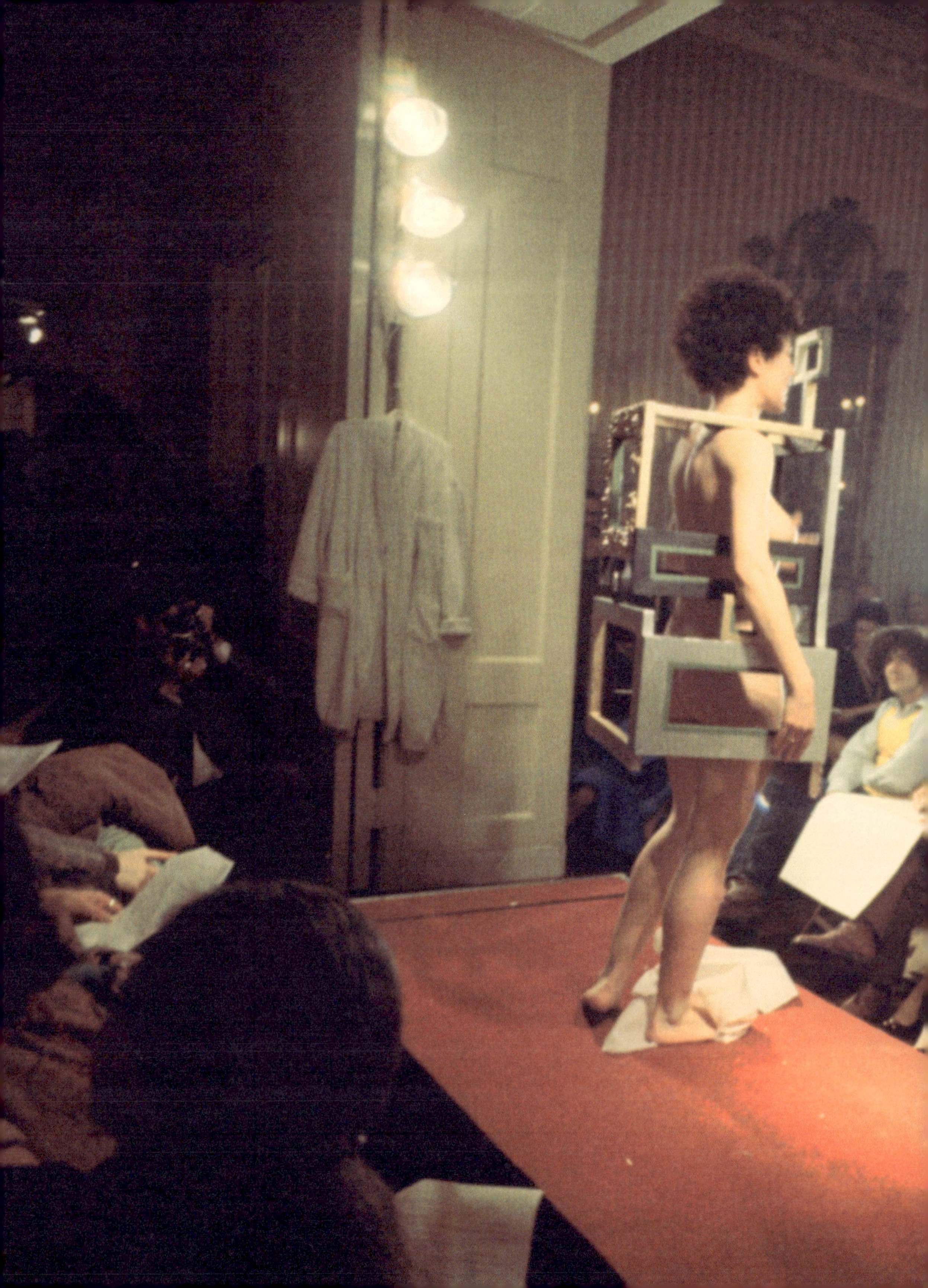

Eduardo Costa (with John Perreault and Hannah Weiner), *The Fashion Show Poetry Event*, Center for Inter-American Relations, New York, January 14, 1969. Peter Moore Photography Archive, Charles Deering McCormick Library of Special Collections, Northwestern University Libraries

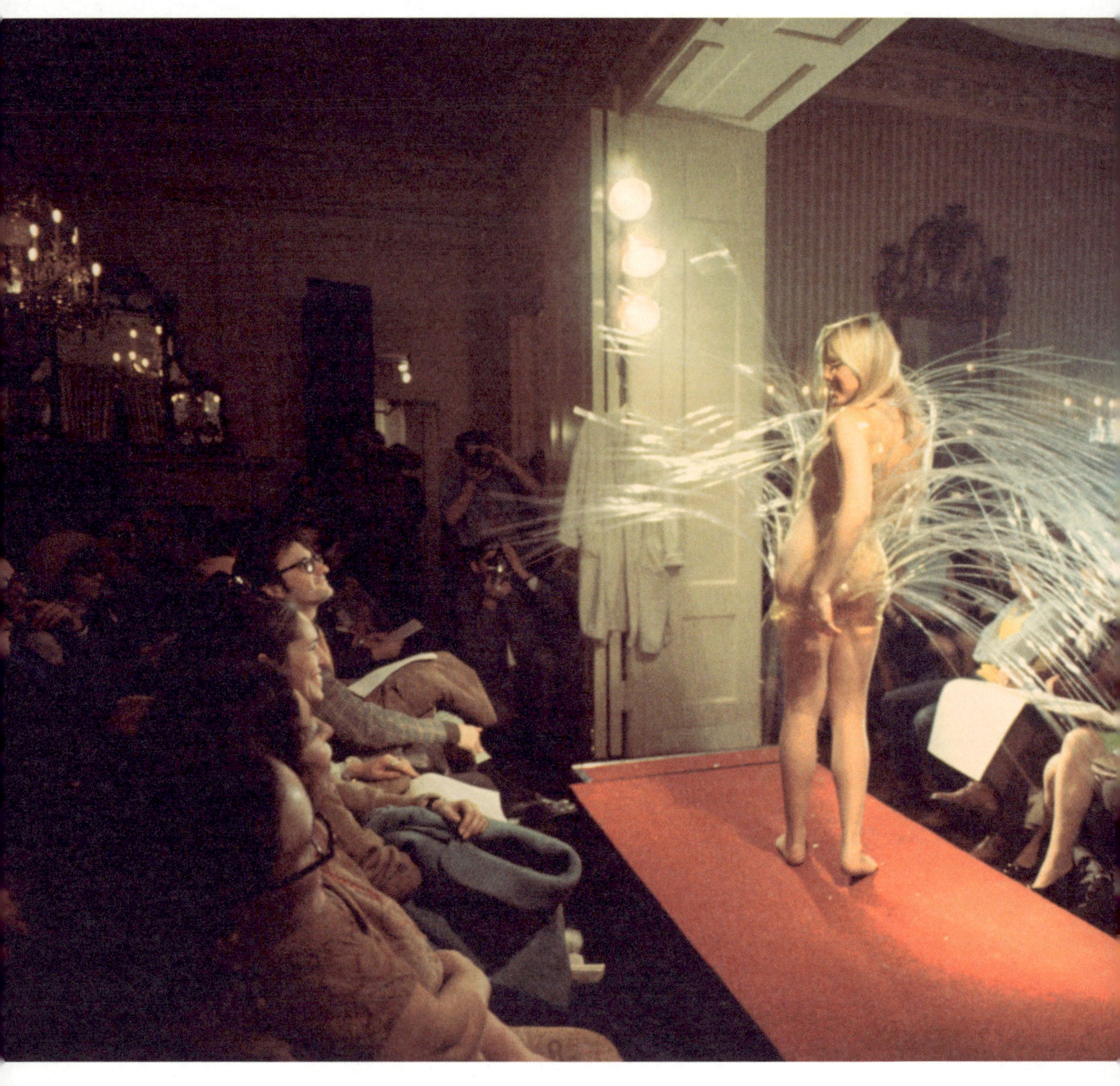

Eduardo Costa (with John Perreault and Hannah Weiner), *The Fashion Show Poetry Event*, Center for Inter-American Relations, New York, January 14, 1969. Peter Moore Photography Archive, Charles Deering McCormick Library of Special Collections, Northwestern University Libraries

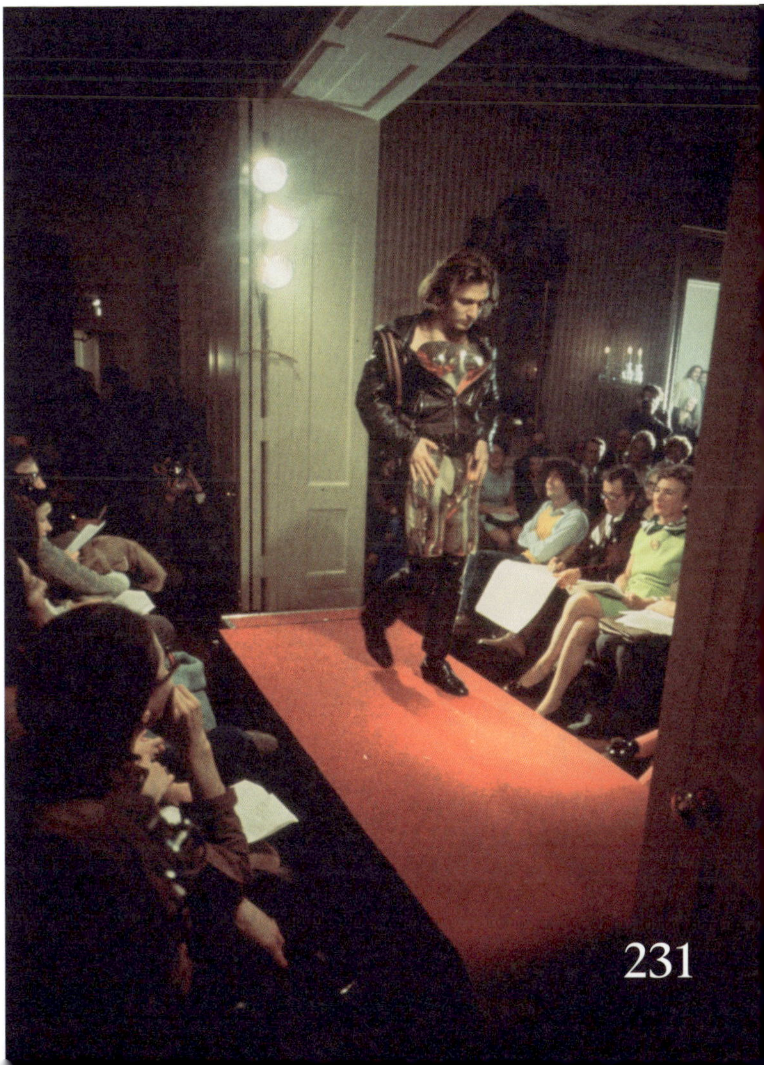

In 1975, Juan Downey had a solo exhibition at CIAR titled *Energy Systems*. At the center of the gallery space, he placed *Map of Chile* (1973), a work consisting of a rectangular box with a plexiglass top and a map of Chile drawn on its inner base. Inside the box, the artist added a live anaconda, referencing the name of the United States–based Anaconda Copper Mining Company, which extracted copper in Chile. A critique of the economic exploitation of Chile by North American companies, as well as the institutional role of CIAR itself in protecting North American interests in Latin America, the snake was ultimately removed from the exhibition because of complaints from animal rights activists, an act that was interpreted by the artist as censorship.

Juan Downey with *Map of Chile* at the Center for Inter-American Relations after being asked to remove the live anaconda from the installation, 1975. The Juan Downey Foundation, New York

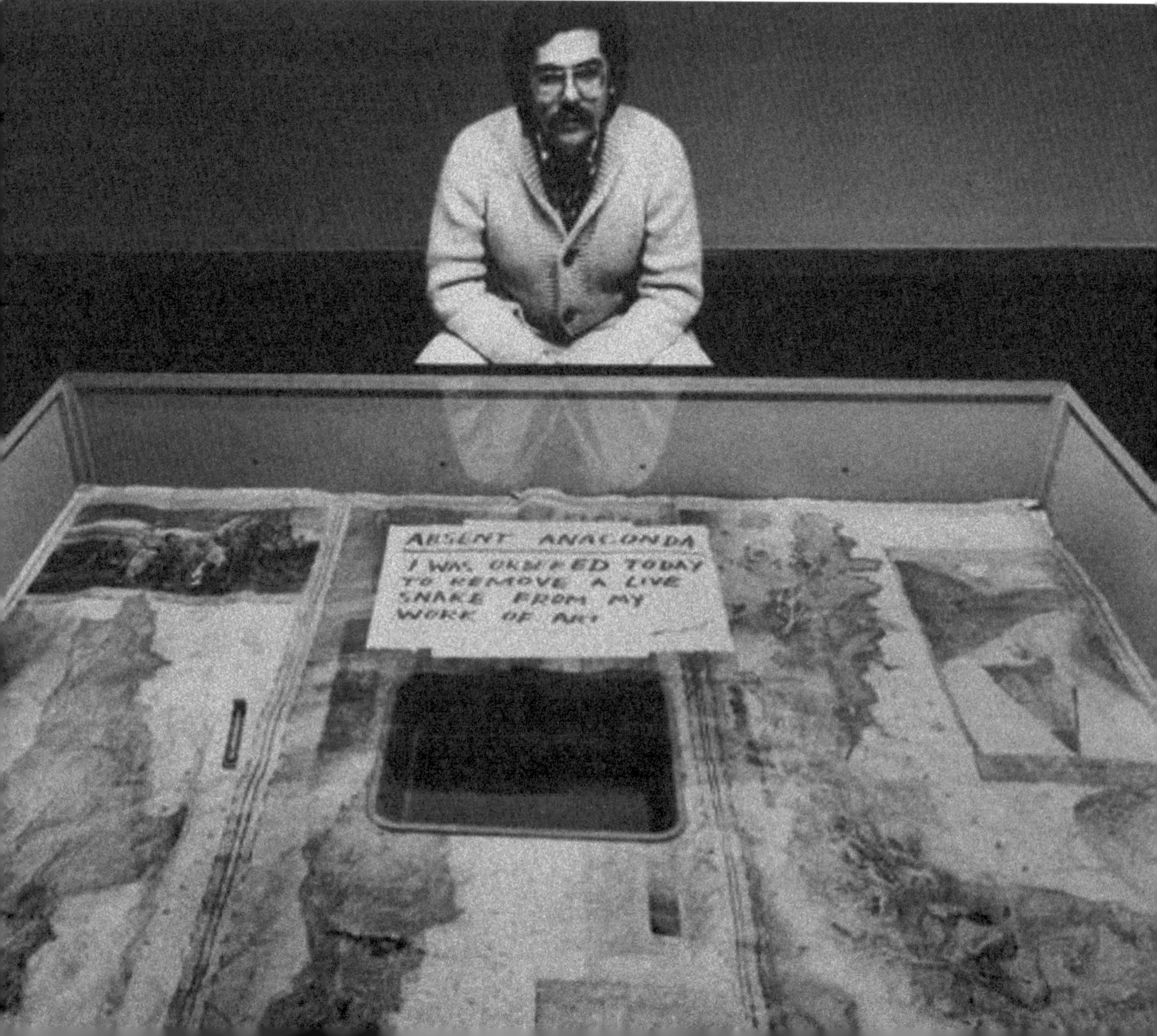

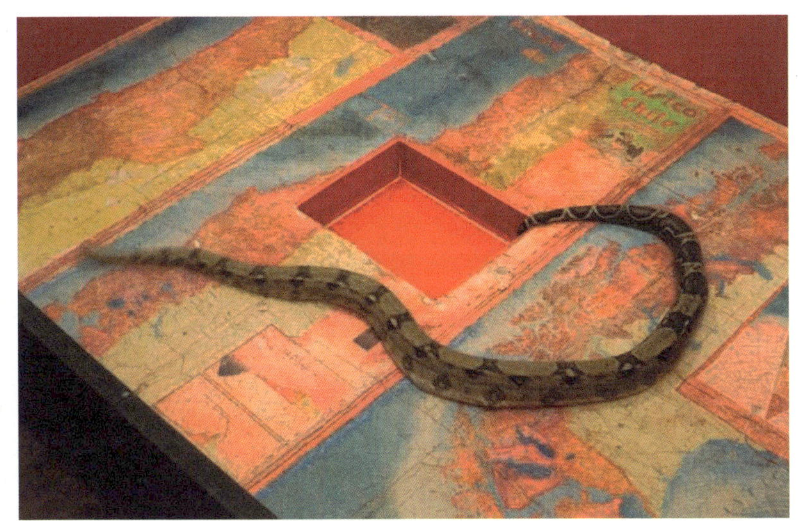

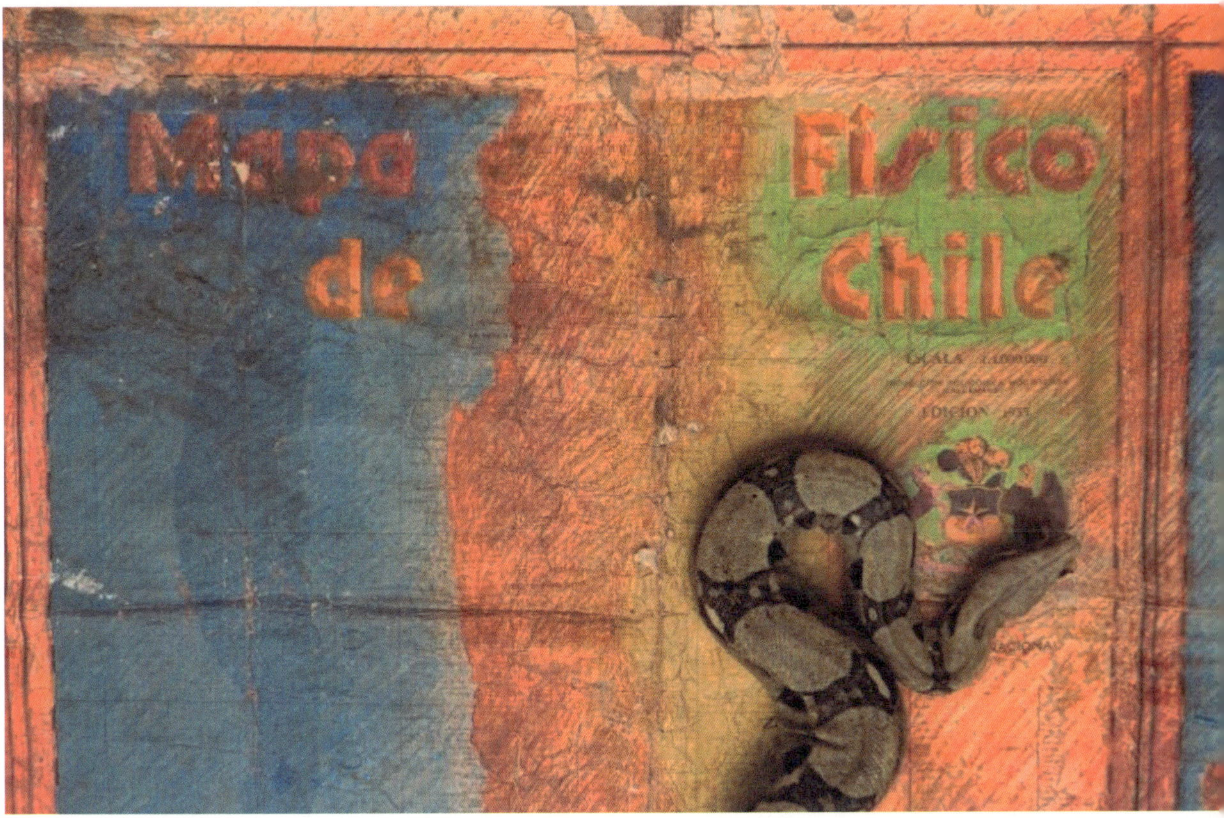

Juan Downey, *Map of Chile* (details), 1975. Juan Yarur Collection, Fundación AMA, and the Juan Downey Foundation, New York

Picasso had passed away, his death shocked me and I wanted to pay tribute to him. Who knows when a creator of the universal dimension that he had will be born again. I had an invitation from the Museum of Modern Art in New York to do a garden show in the summer events section. The museum would provide me with $400 for expenses, and the rest would have to come from the "impossible or miraculous," but since I had been working with very low budgets lately, I didn't worry too much and let my imagination wander to let ideas begin to flow.

I started the organization of the "event." I had little money and needed costumes, a lot of makeup, and, above all, the thirty cars that would drive the thirty blindfolded people and their "kidnapper" each night.

— Marta Minujín

In 1973, Marta Minujín created *Kidnappening*, an "opera-cantata-happening" that took place as part of MoMA's Summer Garden program. Directed by Gary Glover, the piece paid homage to the recently deceased Pablo Picasso and involved more than forty performers, their faces painted as Cubist compositions. While dancing, the performers sang poems citing modern artists, philosophers, politicians, and poets. The lyrics were selected by Minujín with the help of Claudio Badal, a Chilean poet living in New York City.

For the work's main act, performers surrounded the audience while chanting the word "kidnappening." They grabbed fifteen spectators—most of whom had previously agreed to participate in the action—and removed them from the event without further explanation. The "kidnapped" audience members were blindfolded and taken in taxis to different New York locations, including a concert, an apartment on the Upper East Side, the French Consulate, a barbershop, and the Brooklyn Bridge. Participants were then invited to share their impressions in writing with the artist, some of which are presented in the following pages. While the act of taking people outside MoMA was an invitation to merge art and life, it also functioned as a critique of the sterile experience of art in museums.

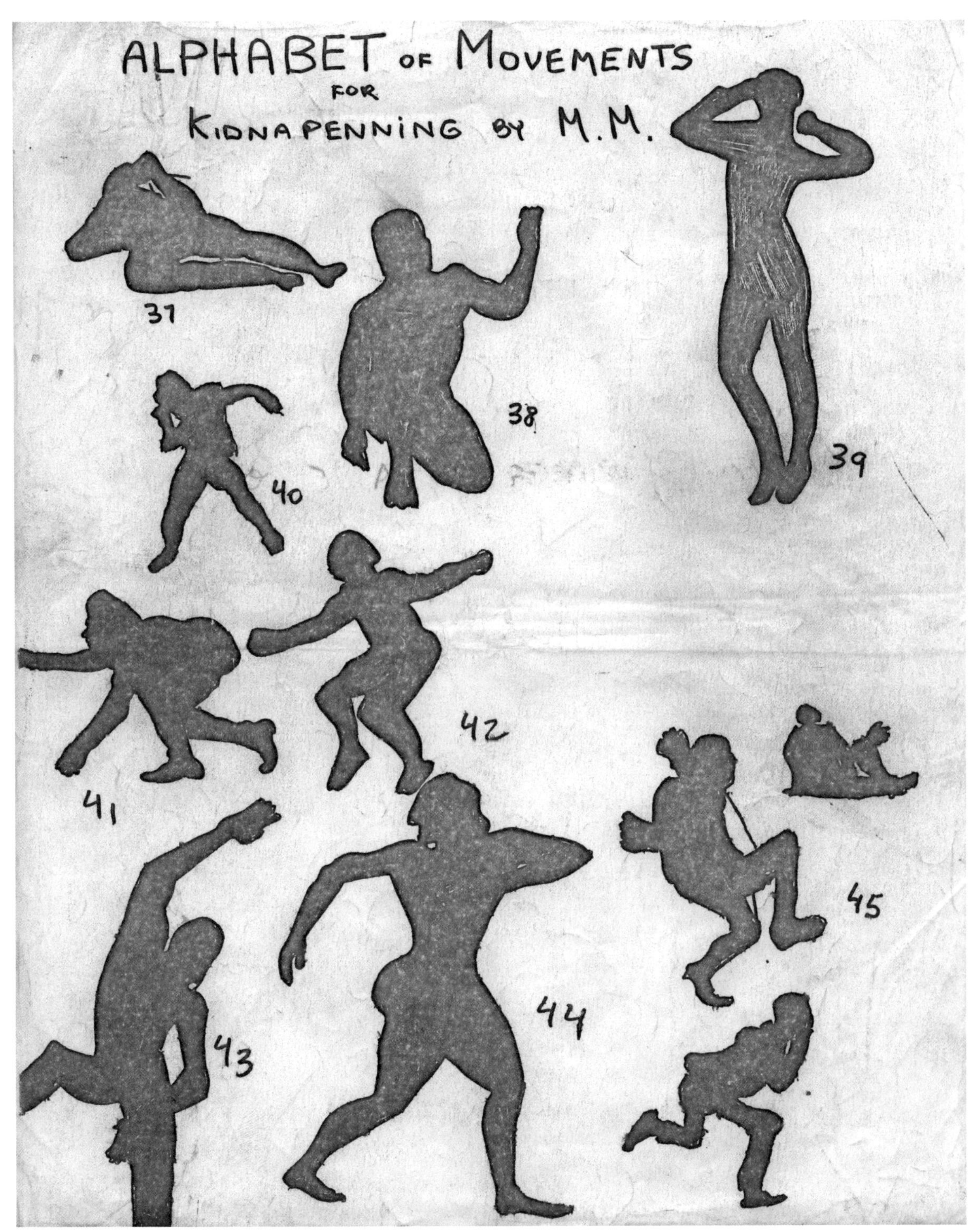

Marta Minujín, "Alphabet of Movements," choreographic instructions for *Kidnappening*, 1973.
Marta Minujín Archive

It was like an opera-Happening. It turns out that Picasso had died, and Dalí, whom I knew well, threw a big party to celebrate the death of Picasso. So I wanted to do that opera with Picasso, with the images of Picasso, all the painted faces of Picasso. At the same time, as in Argentina at that time many people were kidnapped, I invented the theme that twenty or thirty people, I don't remember, were kidnapped and taken to an unknown destination.

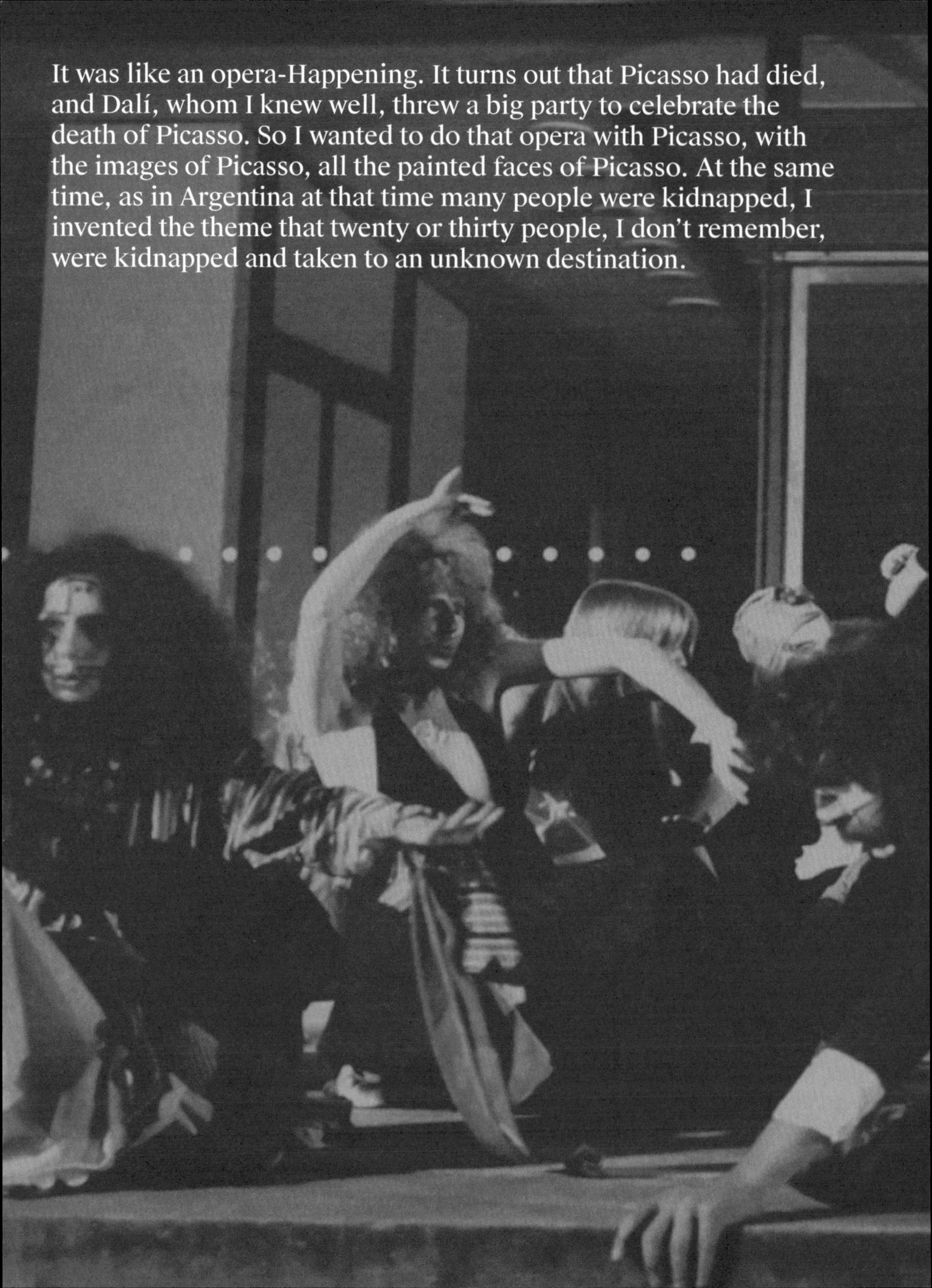

It was a brutal production: at night we were rehearsing at MoMA and they gave me the key to the museum to rehearse. And during the day we would go to the places that were going to receive the abductees so the host (someone with a big loft) could prepare for the visitors . . . For instance, one made an edible table of products arranged to look like a Picasso painting; another at the French Consulate created a meal in which people were walking around all the time naked when people were eating . . . Others were abandoned on the Brooklyn Bridge, in the middle of the bridge. The plan was for each actor–with their face painted in Picasso style–to grab people when the opera ended. They had consented to be kidnapped and had to sign a document saying I was the one responsible if anything happened. The museum didn't take over.

– Marta Minujín

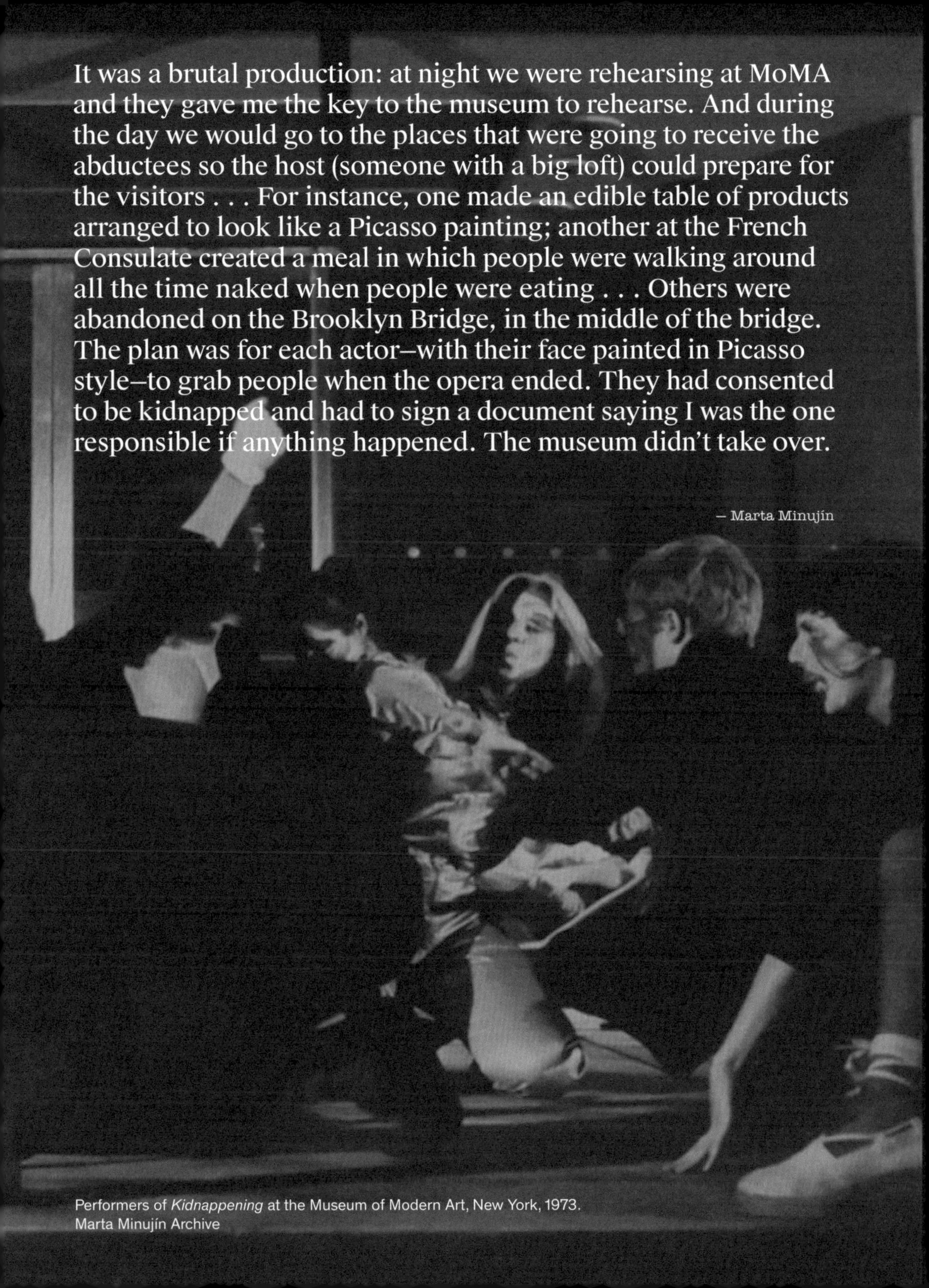

Performers of *Kidnappening* at the Museum of Modern Art, New York, 1973.
Marta Minujín Archive

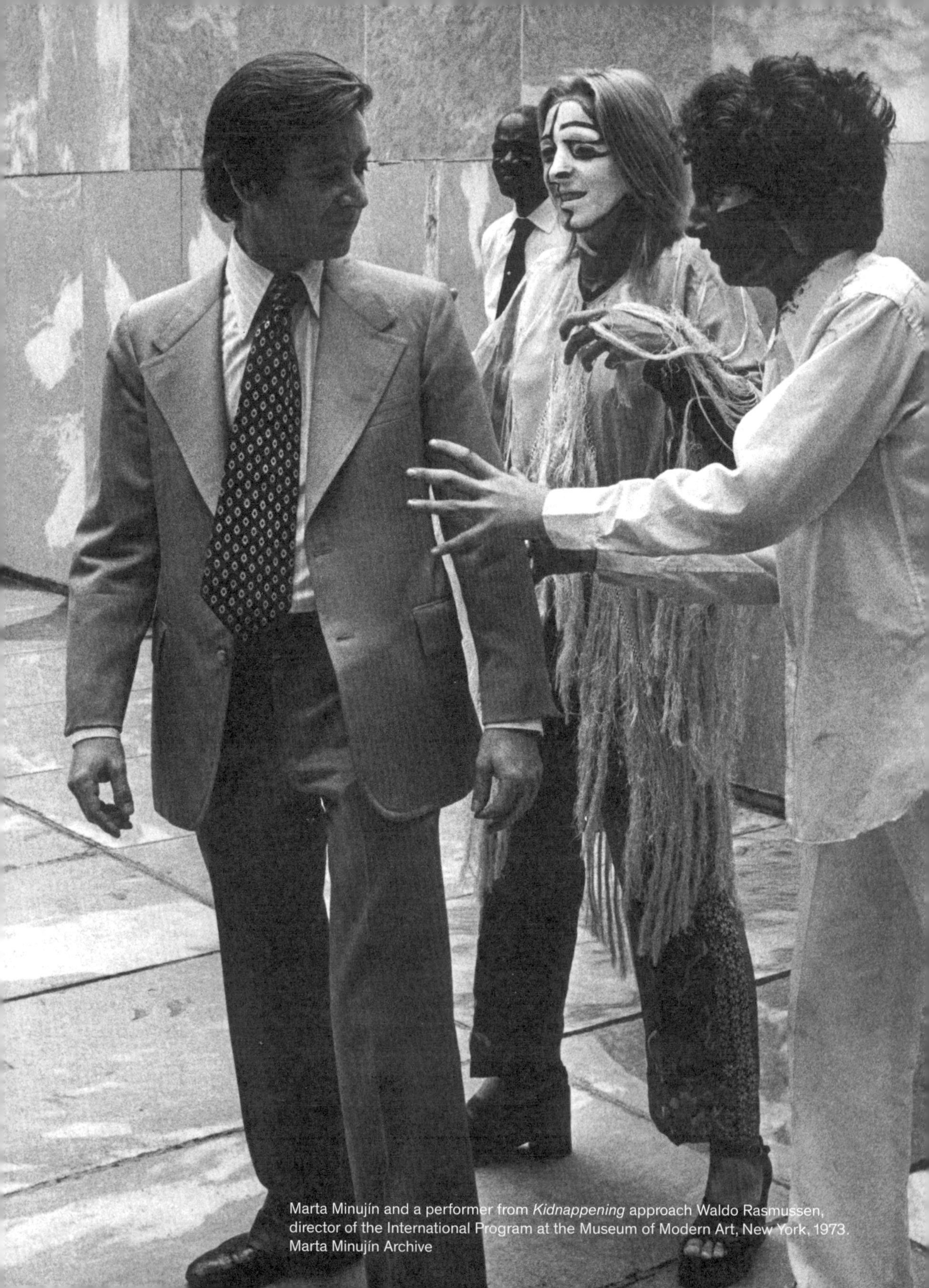

Marta Minujín and a performer from *Kidnappening* approach Waldo Rasmussen, director of the International Program at the Museum of Modern Art, New York, 1973. Marta Minujín Archive

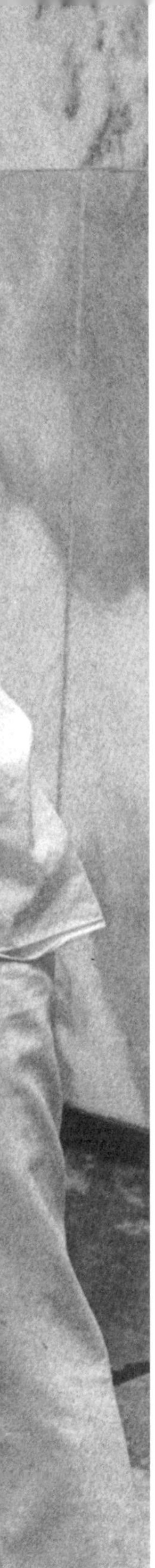

The following is a really beautiful letter, which I received a short time after [the Happening]:

"Dear Marta: I have to thank you for your creation, you have changed my life, it turns out that that was my first night in New York and also the only one, since I had only come from Chicago for the weekend. On the noon news, on TV, I saw you announcing your show and inviting the public to be kidnapped to an unknown destination. I had nothing to do and wanted to see the museum. As you entered the garden, you approached me and asked if I wanted to be kidnapped, which I naturally accepted, I love adventures. I was impatient the entire time the show lasted, eager to know what my surprise was. All I can tell you is that you sent me to my destiny: I was taken to the studio of photographer Anton Pelli, and as soon as I saw him, I fell in love, and the same thing happened to him, and now we are determined to get married. I quit my job in Chicago and I am truly happy. I wish that all the artists in the world would dedicate themselves to crossing fates."

– Marta Minujín

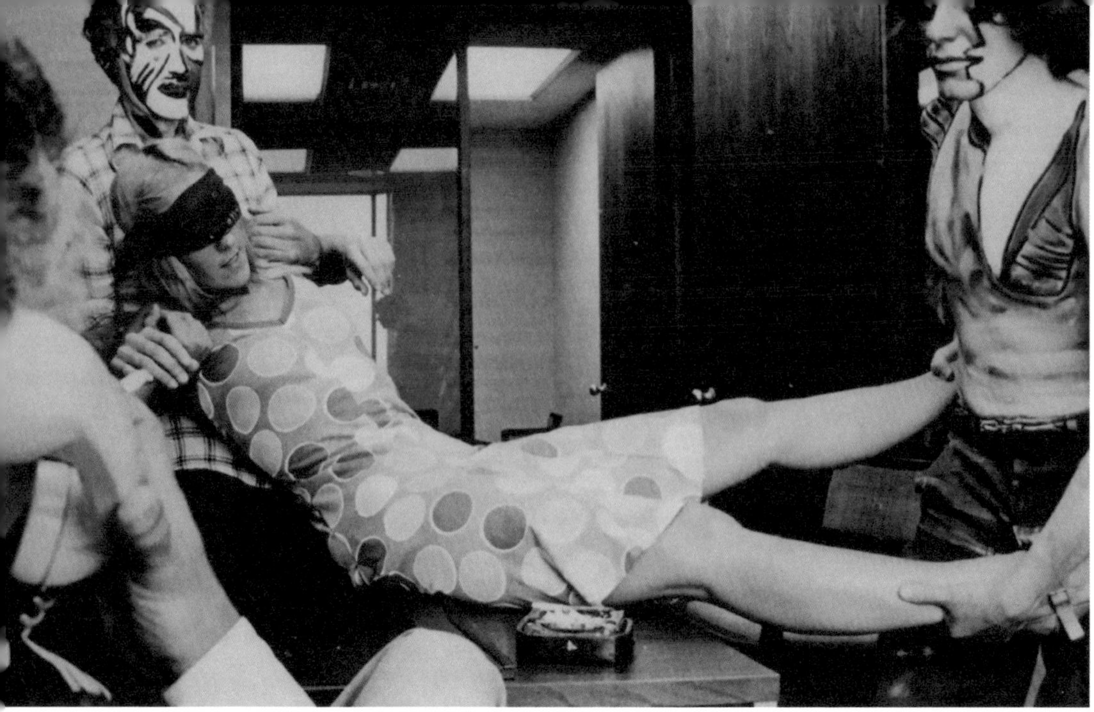

Marta Minujín and performers of *Kidnappening* at the Museum of Modern Art, New York, 1973. Marta Minujín Archive

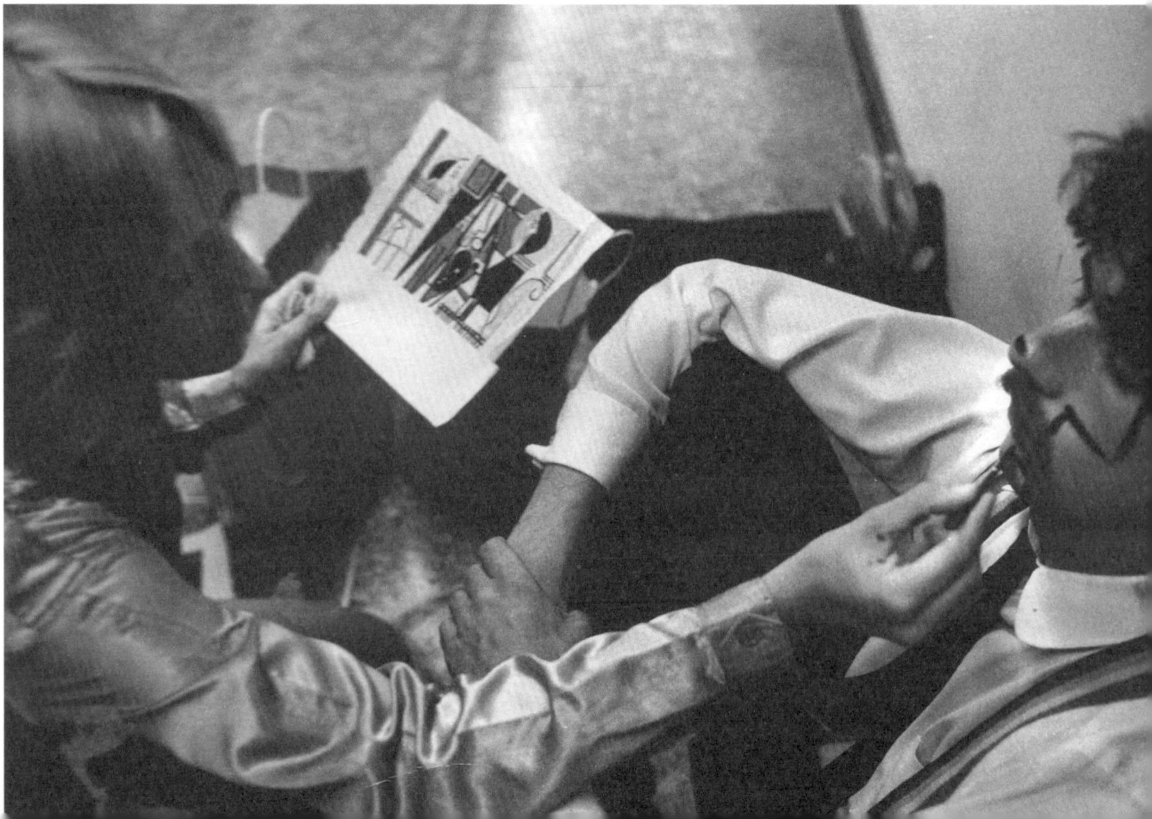

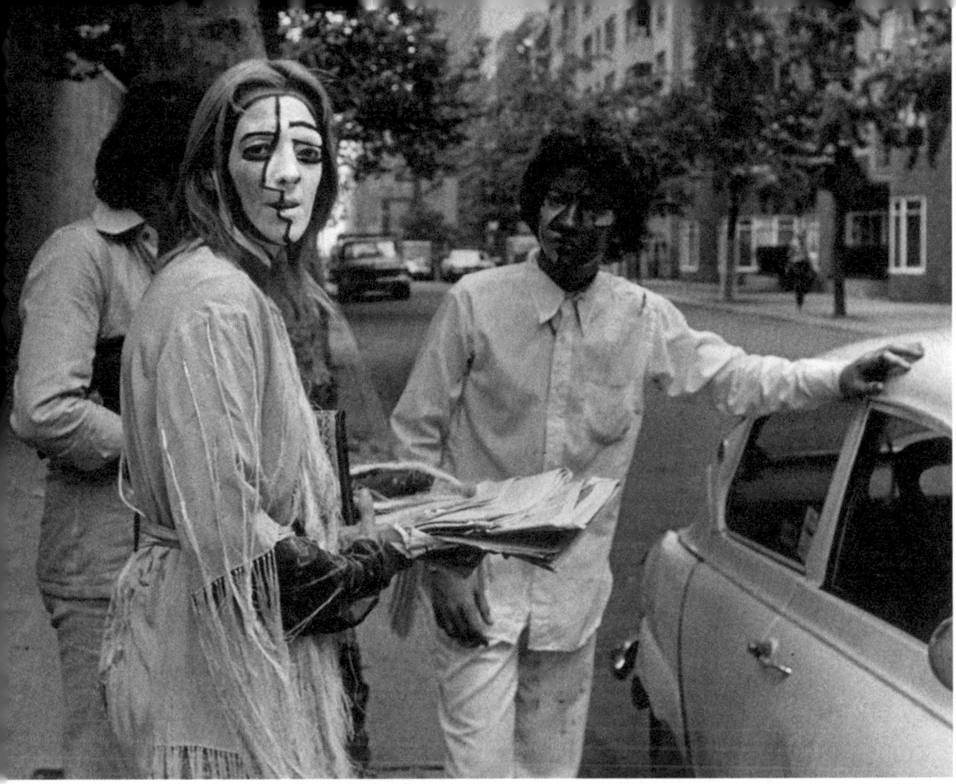

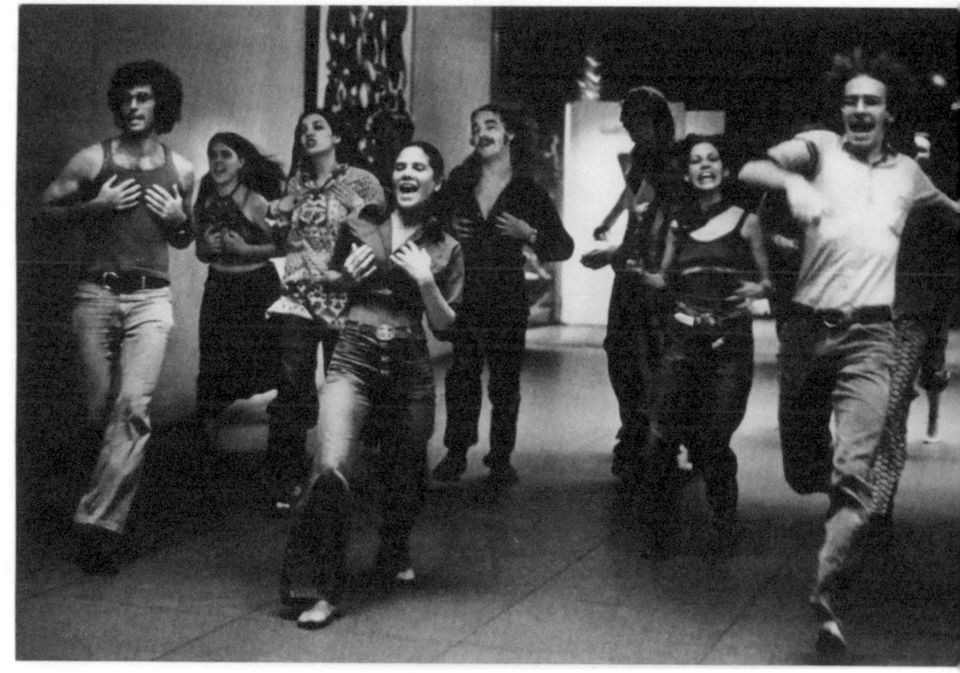

Performers of *Kidnappening* at the Museum of Modern Art, New York, 1973.
Marta Minujín Archive

On Saturday night I was kidnapped along with a young man named Doug. After waiting outside the garden for our kidnapper, who decided to stay at the party in the Garden, Doug and I were instructed to go to [artist] Joe Logiudice's place. He didn't expect us when we showed up, but he and Patsy were very cordial to us. We sat on his unique couch, drank coffee, played with their South American adorable monkey, and chatted, about TV, about boycotting banks, about how far behind the times he felt the museum is—not avant-garde enough, not enough avant-garde young American painters. He has a fabulous loft. After a while, four other people showed up. Again we chatted. At about 12:30 a.m. we left. It was a very pleasant evening.

— Ruth Kleiman , Happening participant

Performer and participant in *Kidnappening* at the Museum of Modern Art, New York, 1973. Marta Minujín Archive

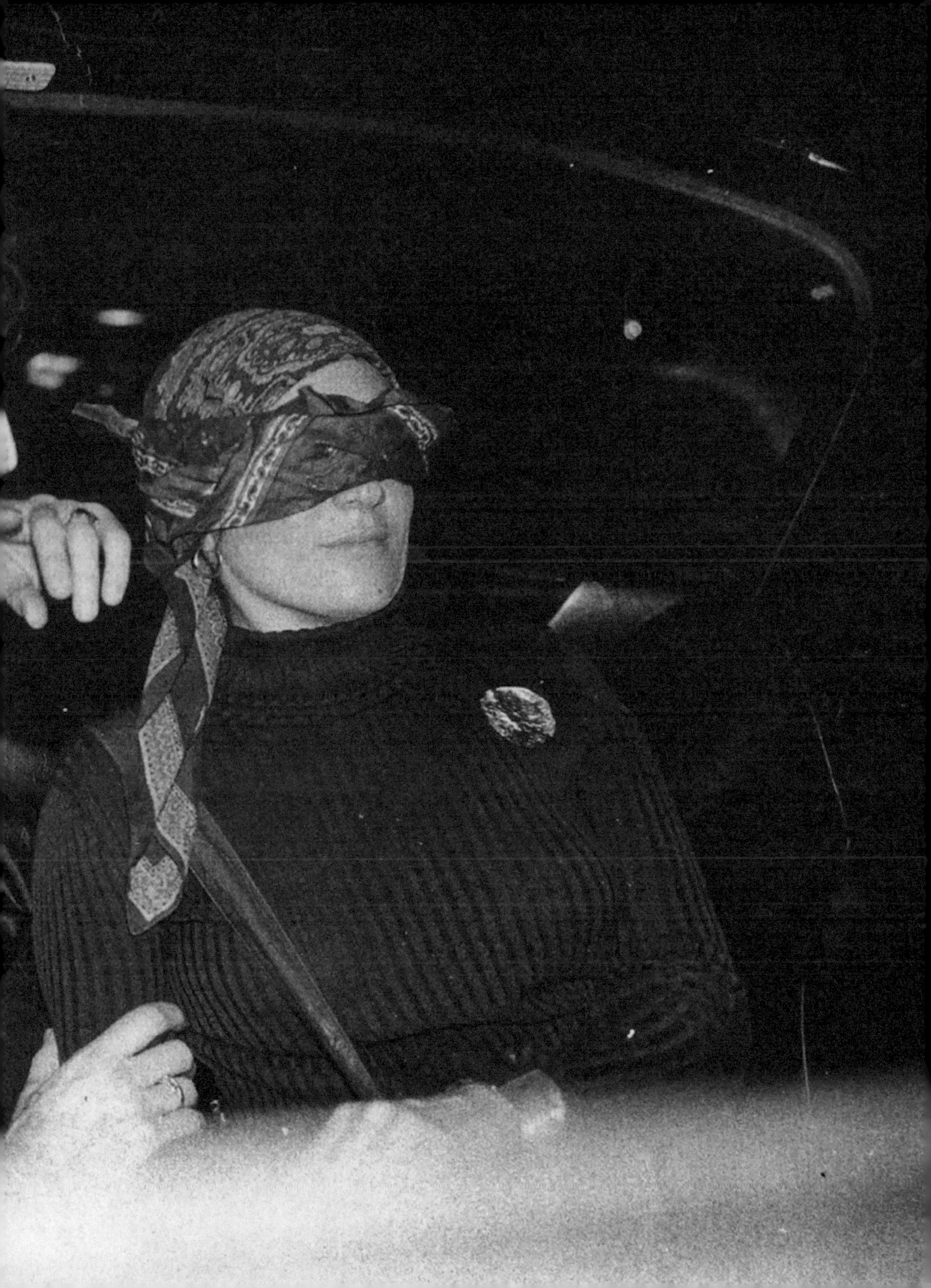

3. Politics, Identity, and the Body

It was in New York that I discovered that I was Latin American.

— César Paternosto

In 1972, the TV program *Camera Three*, a WCBS-TV show dedicated to the arts, presented an episode about the Latin American Fair of Opinion, a cultural event directed by Brazilian playwright Augusto Boal in New York (see 264–67). The episode featured samples of music, theater, and film by different Latin American artists and culminated with Boal speaking about the humanitarian consequences of the actions of South American military regimes backed by the North American government. Boal concluded his speech by addressing the audience directly, stating: "You can't say 'I didn't know.' You have to know, and you have to do something." He aimed to shift the perception held by North American audiences of Latin America—for instance, by challenging the imaginary of it as an exotic paradise—and to transform public opinion about North American politics in the southern hemisphere. Strategies like Boal's form the heart of this chapter, which features works by Latin American artists living in New York that reflect on the interconnection between mass media, national and international politics, representation, and identity (including its relationship to language, race, and sexuality), as well as how these elements are tied to subject formation. These broad and complex topics are divided into subsections: political actions and solidarity initiatives; identity and representation; and the body and performance.

The history of North American political and economic intervention in Central and South America dates from the early nineteenth century.[1] During the 1960s and 1970s, news reporting and activist work shone a light on the contradictory nature of a country that boasted its democratic values and traditions while actively sponsoring coups and wars around the world. Specifically in South America, the United States offered direct and indirect support to military coups in Brazil and Chile, which were followed by state-sponsored violence and repression, including the torture and assassination of political opponents.[2] Artists, scholars, and activists based in the United States took part in human rights activism and organized campaigns pressuring the government to take a stand against rather than support those regimes. These campaigns also helped to bring information to the North American public, inciting solidarity initiatives. These efforts included the Latin American Fair of Opinion (1972); the reconstruction of Brigada Ramona Parra murals in New York (1973); and the concert "An Evening with Salvador Allende" (1974).[3] Artistic activism against the Brazilian dictatorship includes the creation of *Contrabienal* (1971), a book that called for the international boycott of the XI São Paulo Biennial because of the ongoing violence of the dictatorship. The book functioned as a counter-exhibition, with contributions by more than sixty artists and hundreds of signatures of support.[4]

Issues of visibility and representation were at the core of activist and artistic practices in the period: from the demonstrations by groups, such as the Young Lords, which attracted media attention to important issues in the Puerto Rican community, to the practice of self-representation fostered by the Young Filmmakers Foundation, which provided film equipment to Latinx youth on the Lower East Side so they could record their own realities. Representation was key to these practices—and central to the recognition of citizenship status by mainstream culture and politics.

While all Latin American artists living in New York were—on different levels—marginalized by mainstream cultural institutions, their varying experiences of the city were informed by their unique identities in terms of nationality, class, and race. Many South American artists, for example, migrated to New York as adults in search of opportunities to develop their artistic careers, lived in Lower Manhattan, and often came with the support of families and fellowships. While these South American artists mostly funneled their political critique to the dictatorial regimes in their home countries, artists from Puerto Rico experienced a different kind of marginalization that was informed by a long history of migration to the United States shaped by colonialism. Many Puerto Rican artists left their home country only to take up residence in New York neighborhoods where city infrastructure and public services were lacking, such as Harlem. As a result, many embraced activism, creating works that reflected both on the political reality in Puerto Rico and the marginalized status of their communities within the United States.

Practices centered on the body, such as performance and dance, also played an essential part in discussions of selfhood and identity. This chapter highlights the practices of Chilean dancers Sylvia Palacios Whitman and Carmen Beuchat, who collaborated not only with each other but also with a range of artists from Latin America and the United States, including Trisha Brown, Kei Takei, and Juan Downey. Other artists, inspired by the technological discourse of the Cold War, questioned the limits and definitions of the body itself by experimenting with robotic beings. Embracing video technology or merely presenting themselves in ephemeral performances, these artists shed light on how a person's body (and, ultimately, how it exists in this world) is informed by the technological advancements of its time, from drugs produced by the pharmaceutical industry to representations of people disseminated in mass media as standardized ideals linked to consumerist agendas.

NOTES

[1] For a comprehensive list of interventions and historical writing on inter-ventions, see C. Neale Ronning, ed., *Intervention in Latin America* (New York: Alfred A. Knopf, 1970).

[2] For more on US support for the Brazilian coup—the "Brother Sam Operation"—see Phyllis R. Parker, *Brazil and the Quiet Intervention*, 1964 (Austin: University of Texas Press, 1979). For more on American support for the Chilean coup, see Lars Schoultz, *Human Rights and United States Policy Toward Latin America* (Princeton, NJ: Princeton University Press, 1981).

[3] For more on Brigada Ramona Parra, see Florencia San Martín, "Aesthetics of Disobedience, Part II: Reconstruction of a Chilean Mural in New York," *Archives of American Art* (blog), *Smithsonian Institution*, August 9, 2018, https://www. aaa. si.edu/blog/2018/08/aesthetics-of-disobedience-part-iireconstruction- of-chilean-mural-new-york.

[4] For more on *Contrabienal*, see Aimé Iglesias Lukin, "Contrabienal: Art, Politics, and Identity in New York, 1969–1971," *Artl@s Bulletin* 3, no. 2 (Fall 2014): 68–82.

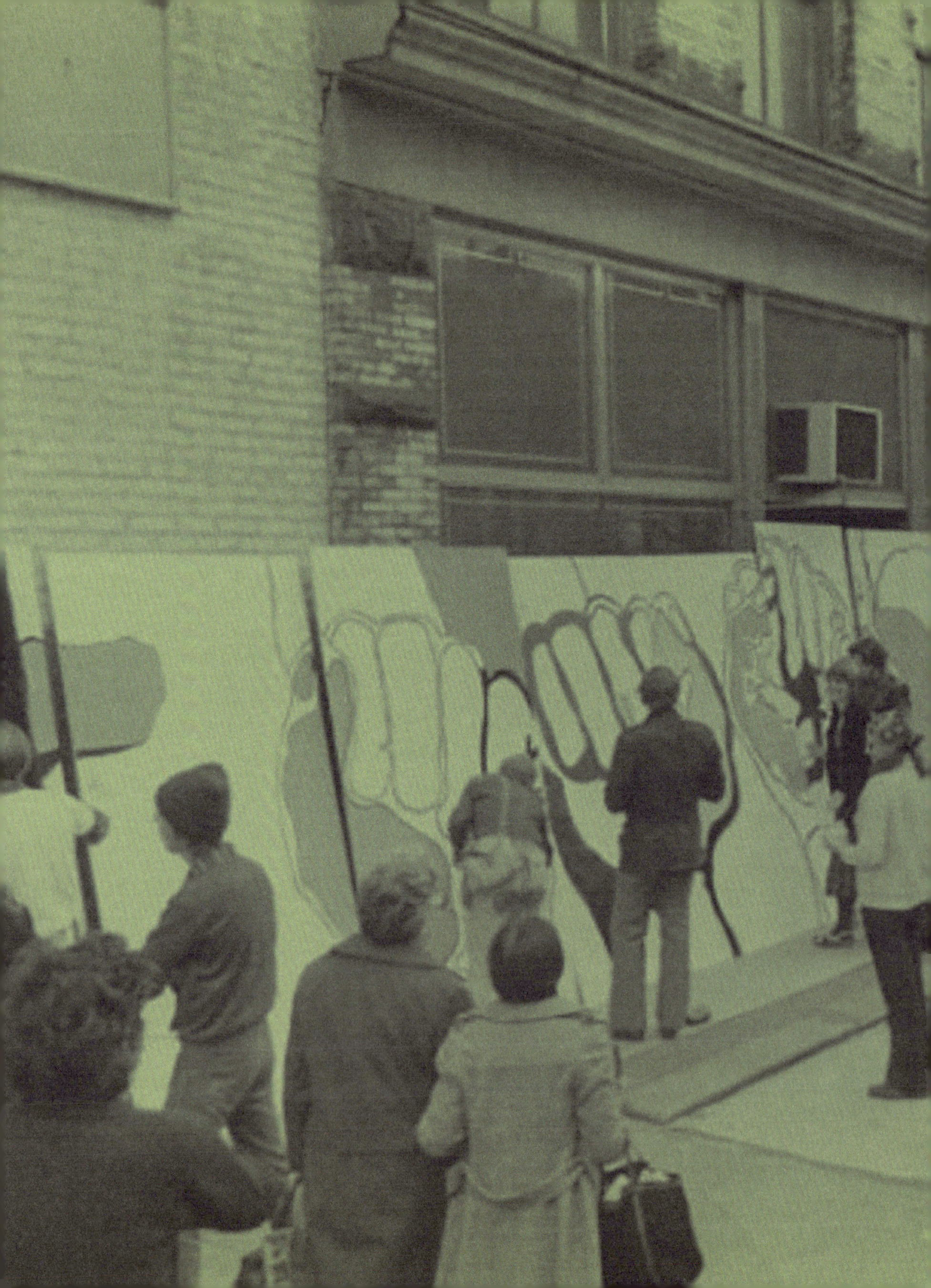

Political Actions and Solidarity Initiatives

The revolutionary energies of the 1960s and 1970s led many artists to embrace activism and form solidarity initiatives, including those organized in New York against dictatorships in South America. From Puerto Rican activist groups such as the Young Lords, which organized demonstrations and actions in the city, to artists from Taller Boricua who created prints to galvanize demonstrations against the marginalization of their communities, the aim was to effect social change. Some artists embraced the vocabulary of guerrilla political actions to create impromptu performances in public spaces with the goal of shocking viewers out of the mundanity of their lives.

Recreation of a Brigada Ramona Parra mural in New York, October 20, 1973. Lucy R. Lippard papers, 1930s–2007, bulk 1960–1990. Archives of American Art, Smithsonian Institution

># CHILEAN MURAL PROTEST: PART II <

100' MURAL DESTROYED IN CHILE BY THE JUNTA + RECREATED ON WEST BROADWAY LAST SATURDAY WILL BE TAKEN TO CHILEAN NATIONAL AIRLINES THIS SATURDAY.

MEET TO MARCH* UP FIFTH AVE. WITH THE (VERY LIGHT) PANELS. JOIN ARTISTS PROTESTING MILITARY REGIME

SAT. OCT. 27 AT 10 AM.

WEST BROADWAY + HOUSTON ST.

Flyer for Chilean mural protest: part II, October 27, 1973. Lucy R. Lippard papers, 1930s–2007, bulk 1960–1990. Archives of American Art, Smithsonian Institution

Formed in Chile in the late 1960s, Brigada Ramona Parra was a left-wing organization that created murals in public spaces countrywide, spreading messages against different forms of social and political repression. After the military coup in 1973, a group of activists, intellectuals, and artists in the United States organized in solidarity with resistance movements against the dictatorship in Chile to recreate—in New York—a mural by Brigada Ramona Parra that had been erased by the regime.

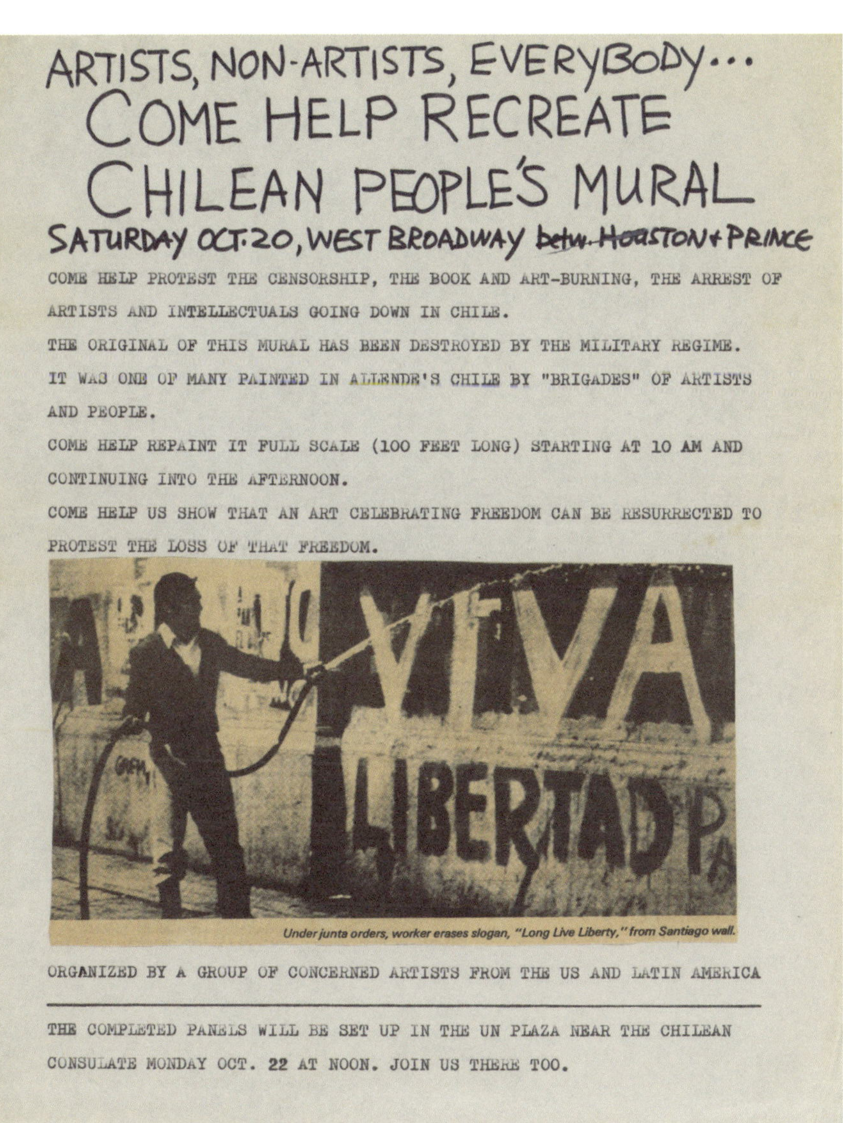

ARTISTS, NON-ARTISTS, EVERYBODY...
COME HELP RECREATE
CHILEAN PEOPLE'S MURAL
SATURDAY OCT. 20, WEST BROADWAY betw. HOUSTON + PRINCE

COME HELP PROTEST THE CENSORSHIP, THE BOOK AND ART-BURNING, THE ARREST OF ARTISTS AND INTELLECTUALS GOING DOWN IN CHILE.

THE ORIGINAL OF THIS MURAL HAS BEEN DESTROYED BY THE MILITARY REGIME.

IT WAS ONE OF MANY PAINTED IN ALLENDE'S CHILE BY "BRIGADES" OF ARTISTS AND PEOPLE.

COME HELP REPAINT IT FULL SCALE (100 FEET LONG) STARTING AT 10 AM AND CONTINUING INTO THE AFTERNOON.

COME HELP US SHOW THAT AN ART CELEBRATING FREEDOM CAN BE RESURRECTED TO PROTEST THE LOSS OF THAT FREEDOM.

Under junta orders, worker erases slogan, "Long Live Liberty," from Santiago wall.

ORGANIZED BY A GROUP OF CONCERNED ARTISTS FROM THE US AND LATIN AMERICA

THE COMPLETED PANELS WILL BE SET UP IN THE UN PLAZA NEAR THE CHILEAN CONSULATE MONDAY OCT. 22 AT NOON. JOIN US THERE TOO.

Flyer for the recreation in New York of a mural originally created by Brigada Ramona Parra by the Mapocho River in Chile, October 20, 1973. Lucy R. Lippard papers, 1930s–2007, bulk 1960–1990. Archives of American Art, Smithsonian Institution

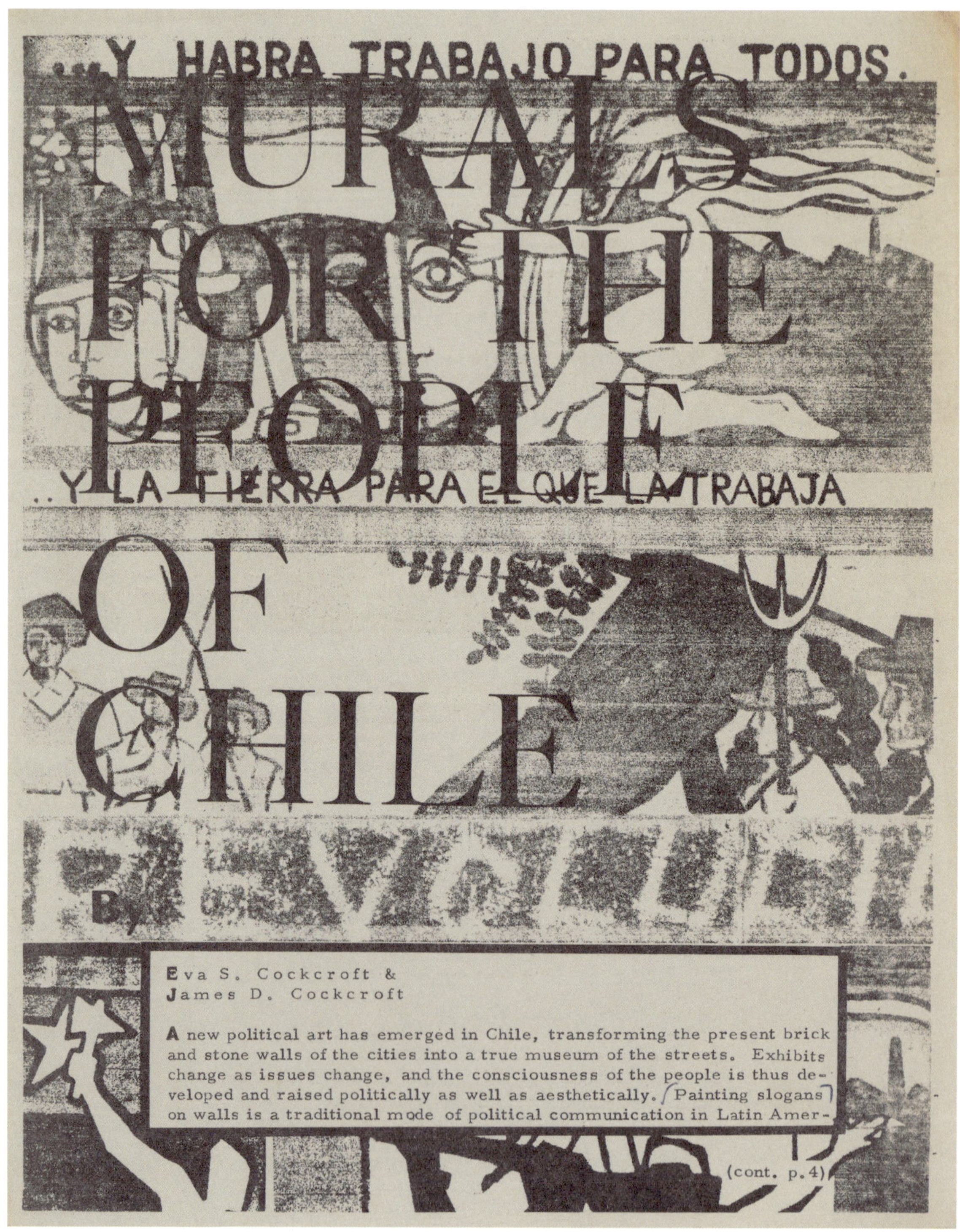
...Y HABRA TRABAJO PARA TODOS.

MURALS FOR THE PEOPLE OF CHILE

..Y LA TIERRA PARA EL QUE LA TRABAJA

By

Eva S. Cockcroft &
James D. Cockcroft

A new political art has emerged in Chile, transforming the present brick and stone walls of the cities into a true museum of the streets. Exhibits change as issues change, and the consciousness of the people is thus developed and raised politically as well as aesthetically. Painting slogans on walls is a traditional mode of political communication in Latin Amer-

(cont. p.4)

Eva S. and James D. Cockcroft, "Murals for the People of Chile," in *Toward Revolutionary Art*, no. 4 (1973): 2–11. Lucy R. Lippard papers, 1930s–2007, bulk 1960–1990. Archives of American Art, Smithsonian Institution

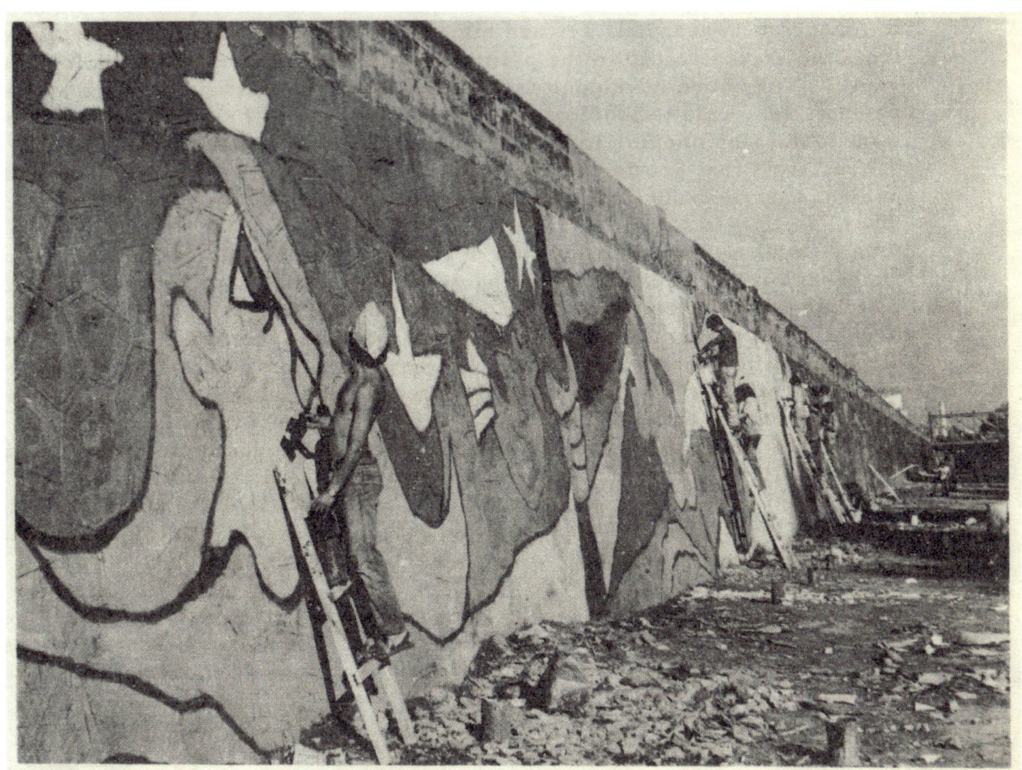

Today the majority of intellectuals and artists are struggling against the cultural deformations of the capitalistic society and are trying to introduce the fruits of their creation to the workers and trying to link themselves with their historical destiny; in the new society they will have a place in the vanguard to continue their action. The new culture will not be created by decree. It will arise from the struggle between brotherhood and individualism, the valuation of human work and its deprecation, national values and cultural colonization, and the access of the popular masses to art, literature and the means of communication and their commercialization.

— Program of the Popular Government of Chile

View of the original mural by Brigada Ramona Parra at the Mapocho River, Chile, 1972, reproduced in Cockcroft, "Murals for the People of Chile," 9.

Jaime [Barrios] moved in 1977 to a loft that [Silvia] Doris [Dillems Quezada] and I rented in SoHo, where we had art-political evenings. At the beginning they were very social, social-political. This was what was called *veladas* [evenings], a monthly meeting in two parts. In the first part there were speeches and political proposals, the information coming from Chile, more or less official, generally, official in the sense that it was someone who for instance just came from Chile and told how things were there, or a representative of a party, who had come to the United Nations and then participated in the evenings. Then there was an intermission where people drank wine that we bought at that time, a Polish wine, because we were boycotting Chilean wine. And in the second part there was music, Chilean musicians or guests, in general the vast majority were of the folklore style, especially from Latin America and Chile; and later, when it finished, people stayed up late, they did not want to leave because it was the opportunity they had to get together with other Chileans. And as time went by, Nicaraguans began to arrive, they began to arrive from Salvador, Honduras, and this began to transform into a meeting that was more Latin American than Chilean.

– Marcelo Montealegre

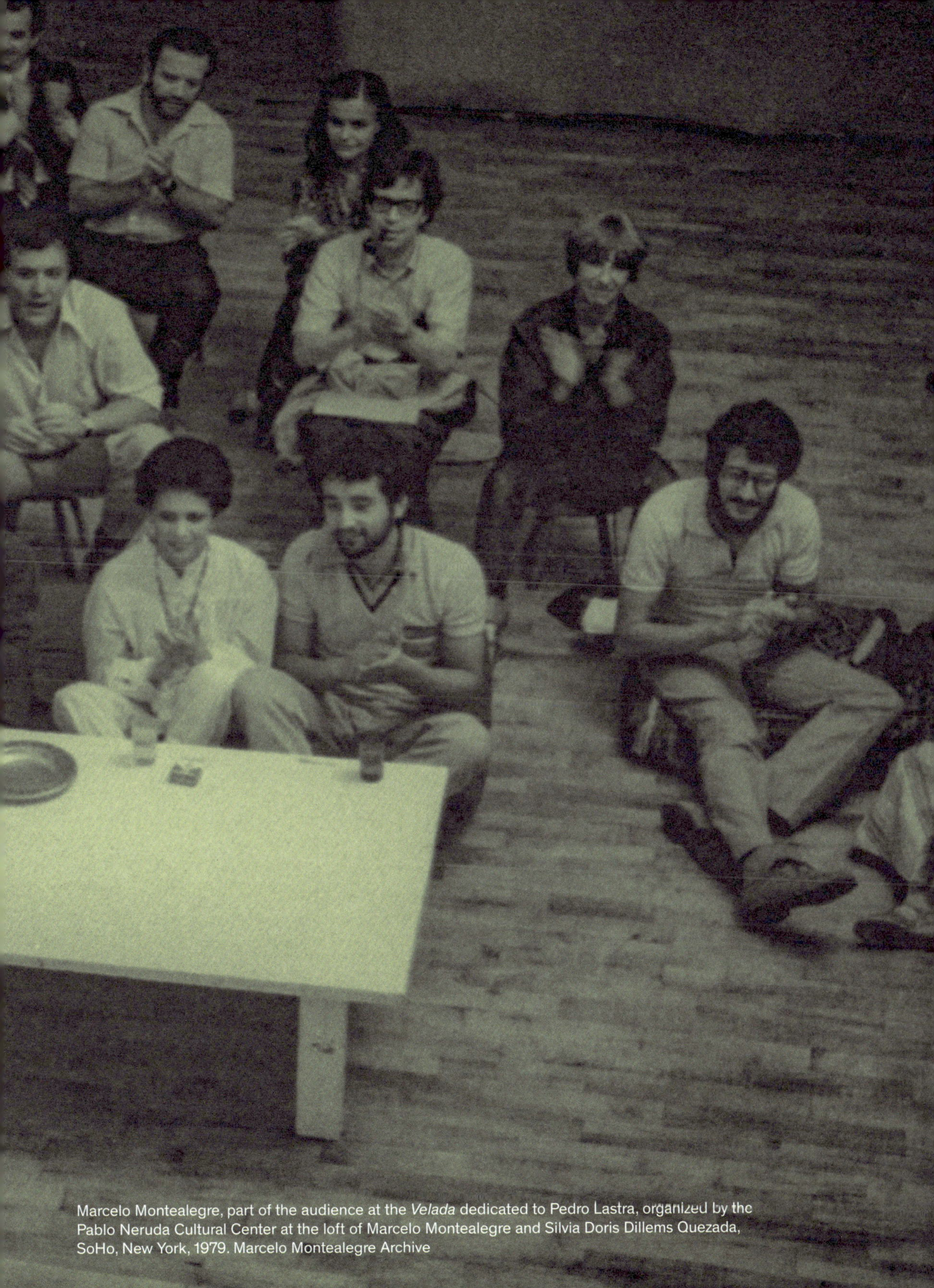

Marcelo Montealegre, part of the audience at the *Velada* dedicated to Pedro Lastra, organized by the Pablo Neruda Cultural Center at the loft of Marcelo Montealegre and Silvia Doris Dillems Quezada, SoHo, New York, 1979. Marcelo Montealegre Archive

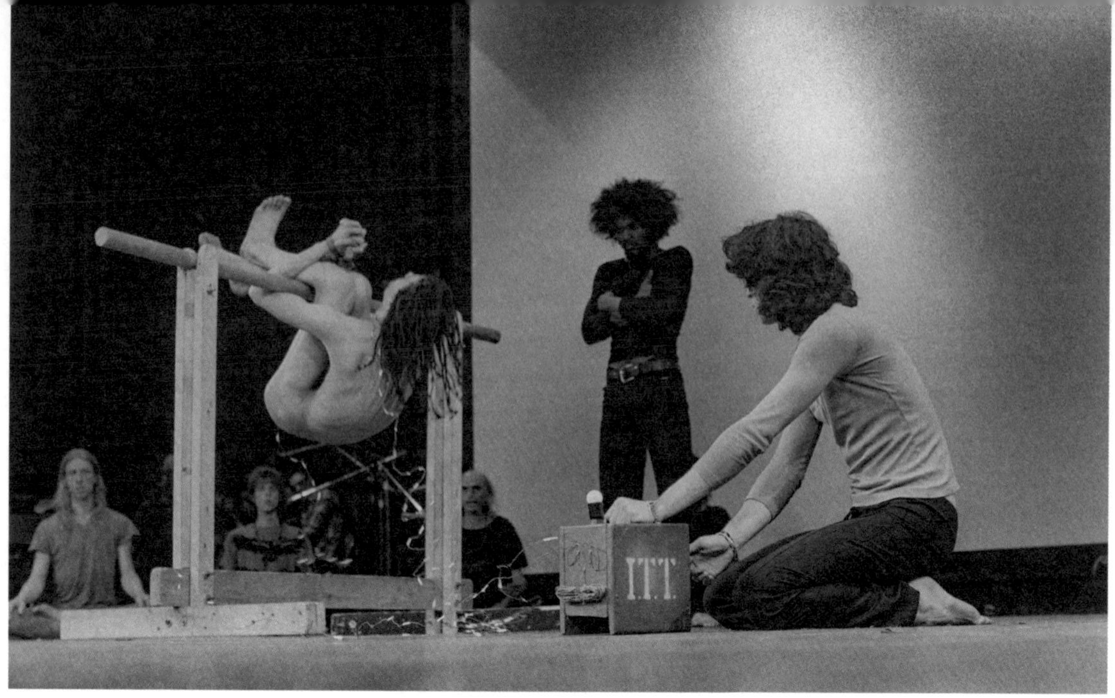

Marcelo Montealegre, Julian Beck, and Judith Malina's Living Theatre reenact torture onstage at "An Evening with Salvador Allende," organized by Phil Ochs with Friends of Chile, Felt Forum at Madison Square Garden, New York, May 9, 1974. Marcelo Montealegre Archive

At the beginning [my participation in the Chilean resistance in New York] was quite slow, the first photos I took of an event were in 1974, at the concert that was organized with Phil Ochs at Madison Square Garden, where Pete Seeger came, Bob Dylan, the monsters of American music.

— Marcelo Montealegre

"An Evening with Salvador Allende" was a concert held on May 9, 1974, in Madison Square in solidarity with Chileans and their resistance movements against the dictatorship. Organized by American protest singer Phil Ochs with the group Friends of Chile and documented by New York–based Chilean photographer Marcelo Montealegre, it featured performances by artists and musicians. The Living Theatre also presented a performance about violence and torture in Latin America, which featured a recreation of the "pau de arara" torture technique (image above).

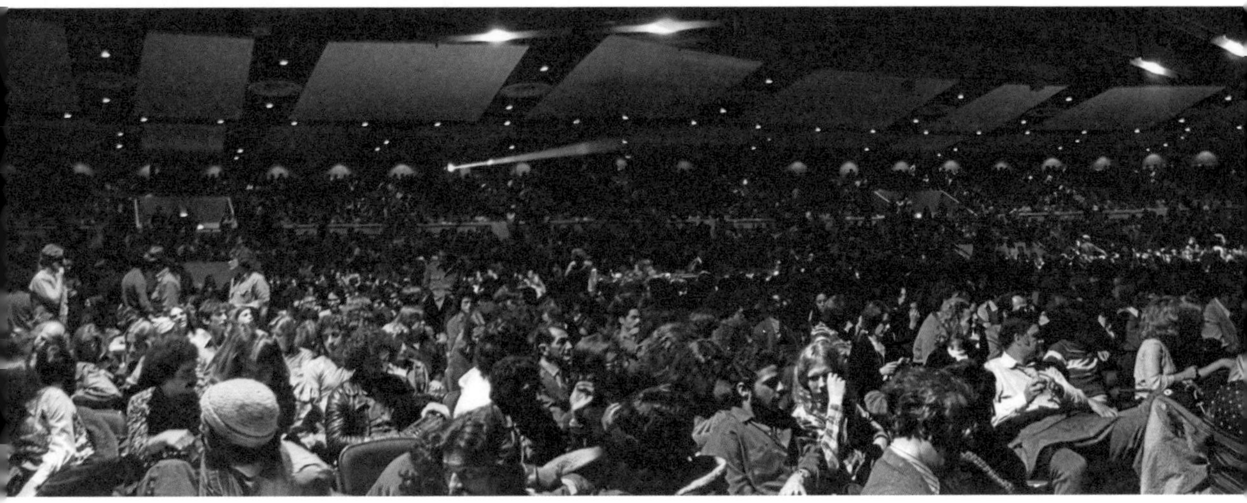

Marcelo Montealegre, audience at "An Evening with Salvador Allende."
Marcelo Montealegre Archive

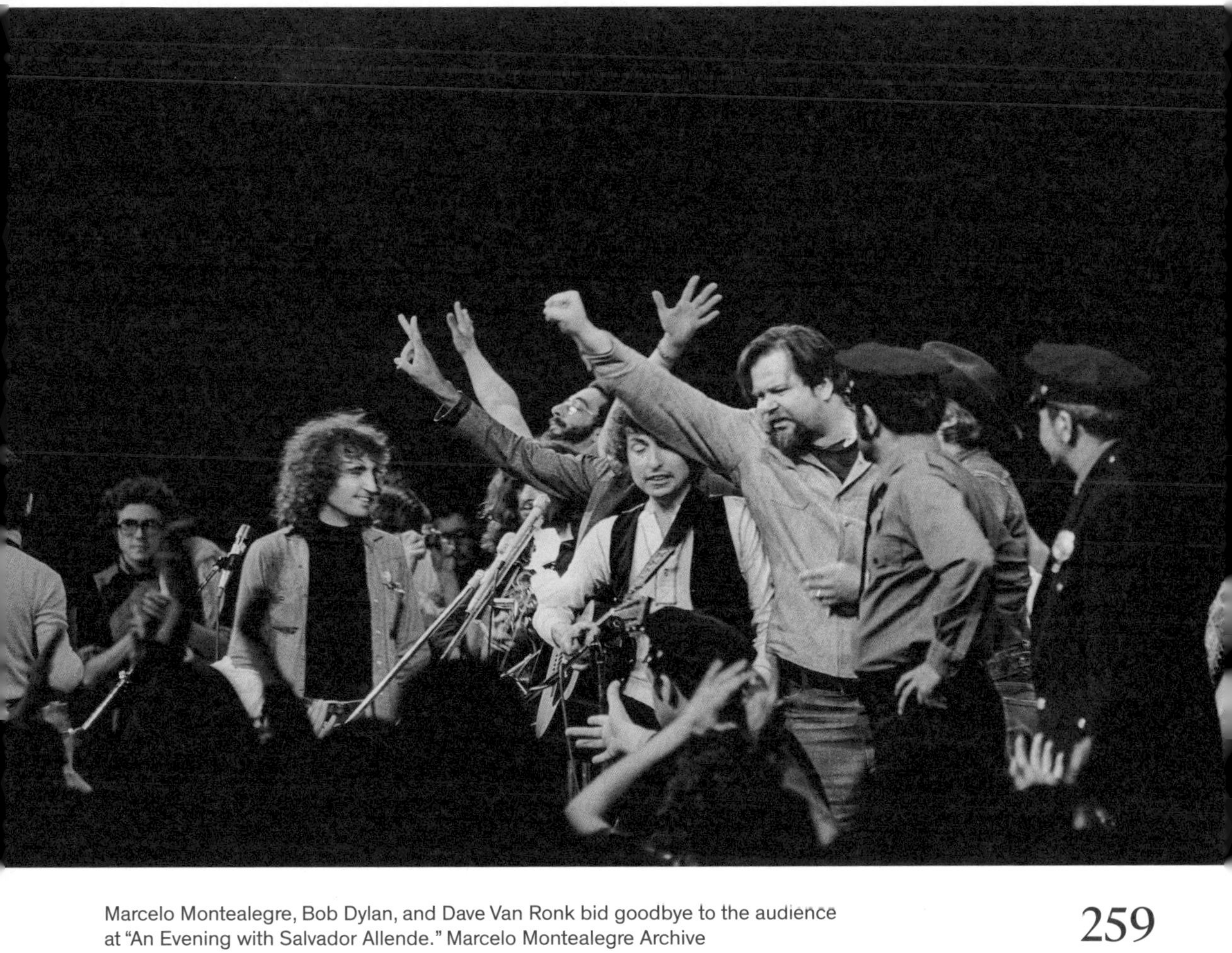

Marcelo Montealegre, Bob Dylan, and Dave Van Ronk bid goodbye to the audience at "An Evening with Salvador Allende." Marcelo Montealegre Archive

Orlando Letelier was a Chilean politician and diplomat during the tenure of President Salvador Allende. After the 1973 military coup, Letelier was arrested and tortured by the military. He was able to escape the country and became a political exile in the United States. In 1976 he was assassinated in a bomb attack in Washington, DC, by Pinochet's secret police. The attack also killed his assistant, Ronni Karpen Moffitt, an American citizen. This photograph by Marcelo Montealegre depicts Letelier delivering a speech at the Felt Forum in Madison Square Garden on September 10, less than two weeks before his assassination.

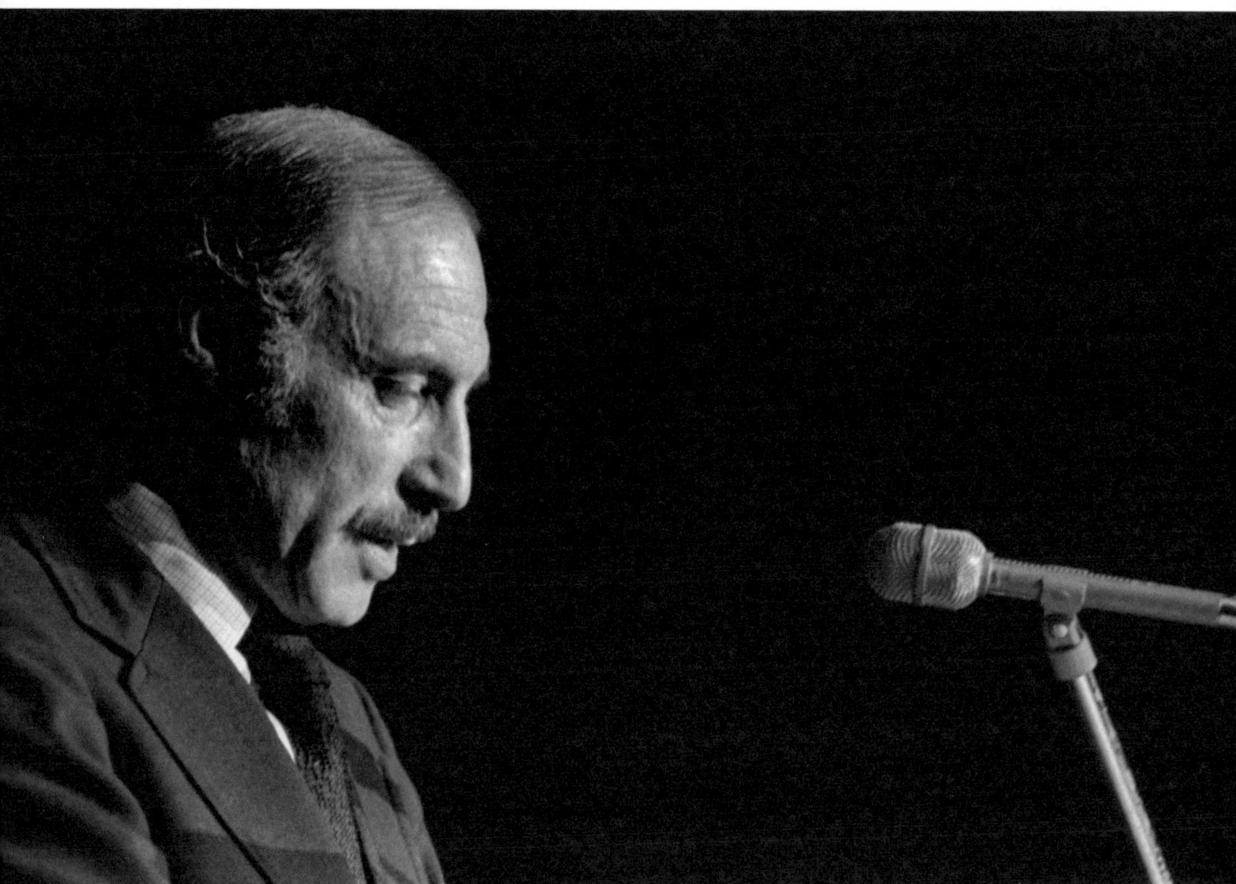

Marcelo Montealegre, Orlando Letelier, on the stage of the Joan Baez and Aparcoa concert in the Felt Forum, Madison Square Garden, New York, September 10, 1976. Marcelo Montealegre Archive

SOLIDARITY WITH CHILEAN DEMOCRACY A MEMORIAL TO ORLANDO LETELIER

On September 22, 1976, Orlando Letelier was brutally murdered by agents of the Chilean junta in Washington, D.C. The unresolved crime which took the life of a young American as well as Letelier, ambassador of the first democratically elected socialist government in the world, once again remind us of the abysmal crimes of Pinochet's regime.

EXHIBITION AND BENEFIT FOR THE CHILE COMMITTEE FOR HUMAN RIGHTS IN MEMORY OF ORLANDO LETELIER, ORGANIZED BY THE U.S. AD HOC COMMITTEE OF THE MUSEO INTERNACIONAL DE LA RESISTENCIA 'SALVADOR ALLENDE'
WORKS BY LEADING UNITED STATES AND LATIN AMERICAN ARTISTS
THE CAYMAN GALLERY, 381 WEST BROADWAY, NEW YORK, N.Y. 10012
APRIL 30 THROUGH MAY 7, NOON TO 6 PM OPENING APRIL 30, 5—8 PM
ADDRESS BY ISABEL LETELIER CHILEAN MUSICAL-CULTURAL PROGRAM

Card for *Exhibition and Benefit for the Chile Committee for Human Rights in Memory of Orlando Letelier*, Cayman Gallery, New York, April 30–May 7, 1977. Nitza Tufiño Archive

Four-Master From Chile Is Called 'Torture' Ship

By LESLIE MAITLAND

The four-masted barquentine Esmeralda, Chile's envoy to Operation Sail, has become the object of protests here by groups charging that political prisoners were tortured aboard the ship after a military coup overthrew President Salvador Allende in 1973.

The protesters, who are seeking to have the ship turned away from this country's shores, say that if the Esmeralda is permitted to dock in New York they will demonstrate at the pier.

The ship, the second-largest of 228 scheduled to take part in the July 4 Bicentennial event on the Hudson River, was cited "with significant unanimity" as a place of torture by inmates of 12 different prisons in Chile who had been interviewed by a five-nation investigating team.

Chile's General Consul, Sergio Crespo, said, however, "It's not fair to think we use a ship for that purpose. We are not going to answer those lies. We are not going to change our schedules or our plans."

He said that the Esmeralda had been on her way to Japan at the time that the torture was said to have occurred.

'Politics' Deplored

And Frank Braynard, the founder and general manager of Operation Sail, said he had no intention of excluding the Esmeralda from the flotilla that will bring ships from more than 30 nations into New York Harbor for the Bicentennial celebration.

"She's one of the finest sailing ships in the world, and one of the most desired to have in any port," Mr. Braynard said, adding that he had never heard of the ship's being used as a place of torture. "We're trying to do something positive, not dwell on past horrors," he said. "It's too bad to hamper a good ceremony by bringing politics into the picture."

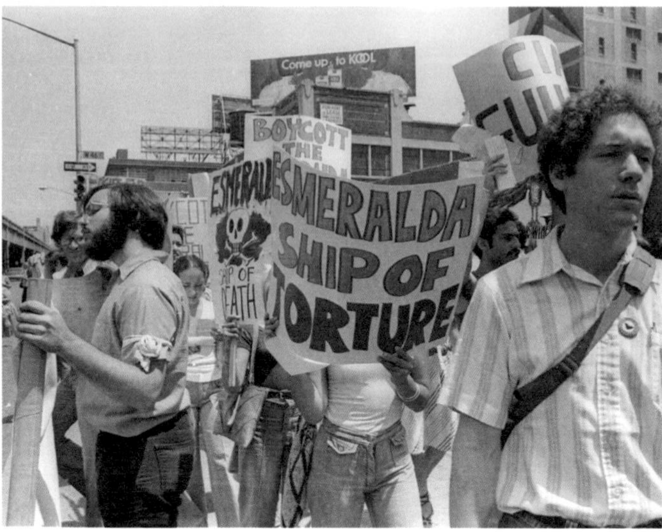

The philosophy of Operation Sail, Mr. Braynard said, is that, "just as seamen are international citizens, we are all seamen on this spaceship earth and must learn to live together."

He added: "We've invited everyone — South Africa, both Chinas, Russia—everyone that might conceivably have a sailing vessel. Operation Sail is nonpolitical."

'7 of Us Were Tortured'

The investigators, sent to Chile by the Inter-American Commission on Human Rights of the Organization of American States, noted in a report issued in 1974 that the country's military government had denied it permission to inspect the Esmeralda on the ground that she had been designated a "military area."

In its report, however, the commission included testimony from prisoners who described their treatment aboard the ship, which was built in Spain for Chile more than 20 years ago and has been used as a naval training vessel.

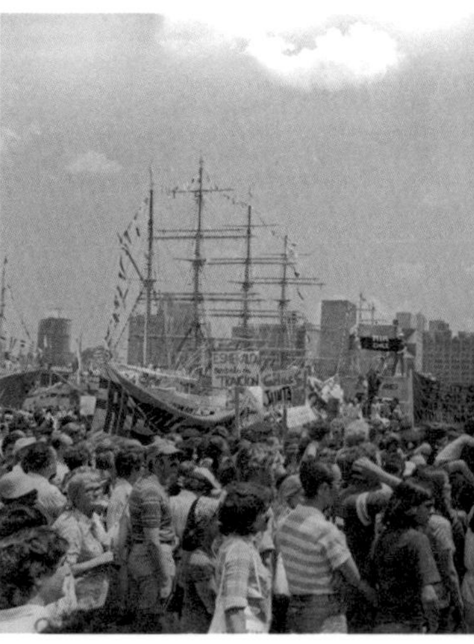

Marcelo Montealegre, Esmeralda Ship protest, 1976. Marcelo Montealegre Archive

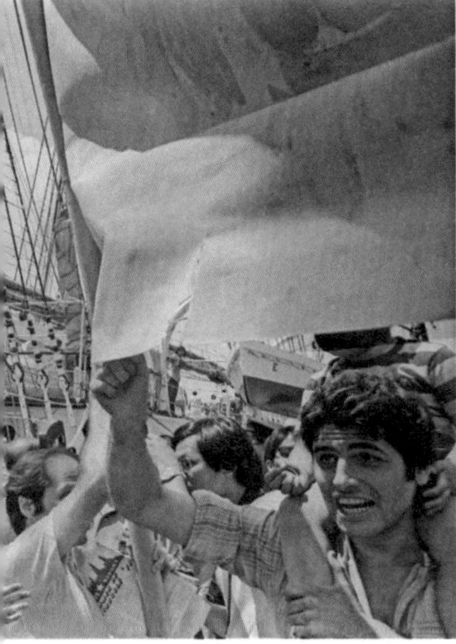

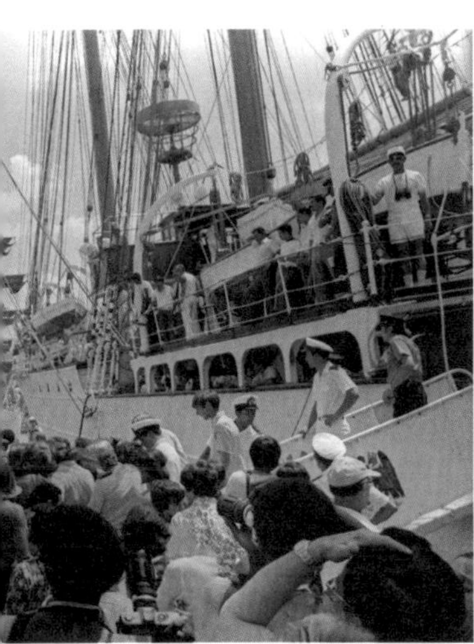

One prisoner said:

"The seven of us were tortured on the ship Esmeralda for nine days. They applied electric shock on my skin, on my testicles, on my chest and back. Also, the officers who were interrogating me hit me 50 times in this part with their fists. . . . And all this was done by both men and women in the training ship of the Chilean Navy."

'Arbitrary Jailings' Cited

The commission—which said in a follow-up report issued earlier this month that "arbitrary jailings, persecutions and torture" were continuing in Chile—also cited testimony from prisoners who said they had been beaten so badly that they had urinated blood, and from other prisoners who said their tongues had been burned.

"There would be good reason to protest any Chilean ship coming here," said Susan Borenstein of the National Coordinating Center in Solidarity with Chile, an umbrella organization that represents several of the groups protesting against the Esmeralda's scheduled arrival here. "Its presence would make a mockery of the very principles of democracy and human decency our nation is celebrating in this Bicentennial year," she said.

In addition to many citizen groups—Action for Women in Chile, Amnesty International, American Committee for Cultural Change, Women's International League for Peace and Freedom — several religious groups have become involved in expressing their opposition, Miss Borenstein said.

O'Dwyer's Aid Sought

William Whipfler, director of the Latin America department of the National Council of Churches, said he had written to the City Council President, Paul O'Dwyer, and to the city's Congressional delegation, asking for help in persuading Operation Sail to reconsider the invitation to have the Esmeralda participate.

"It would be like having the Germans bring mobile gas units here for an automobile show in the 1940's," Mr. Whipfler said. "We are very concerned."

To the dissenters, who say they will demonstrate at Pier 86, at 46th Street and the Hudson River, where the Esmeralda will be on display to visitors, the invitation to the ship is itself a political gesture.

Mr. O'Dwyer, who was invited by the Chilean Embassy to attend a July 8 reception at the pier in honor of the Esmeralda, agrees with those who would prefer not to see her here.

"We've drafted a resolution to introduce to the City Council on Tuesday, calling upon the Mayor to deny access to Esmeralda to any city-owned facility," said James Callaghan, Mr. O'Dwyer's assistant.

Other Visits Scheduled

A spokesman for the Port Authority of New York and New Jersey said that Pier 86 is owned by the city, which gave it to the New York City Convention and Exhibition Center Corporation as a possible site on which to build.

According to Mr. Callaghan, this means that, although the situation is a complicated one, "if the Mayor wanted to say, 'No, we don't want them here,' he could."

New York, however, is not the only city that will have to face the problem. The Esmeralda is scheduled to visit Newport, R.I., on July 1 and Baltimore, Md., on July 12. And Miss Borenstein—who said that San Francisco had successfully barred the use of city piers to the Esmeralda on a visit there two years ago — added that demonstrations were being planned, at least in Baltimore.

In Keyport, N.J., where a yacht club is to be host at a reception for the Esmeralda's crew, the Mayor and five of the community's six Councilmen have decided not to attend.

Leslie Maitland, "Four-Master From Chile Is Called 'Torture' Ship," *New York Times*, June 20, 1976, 34

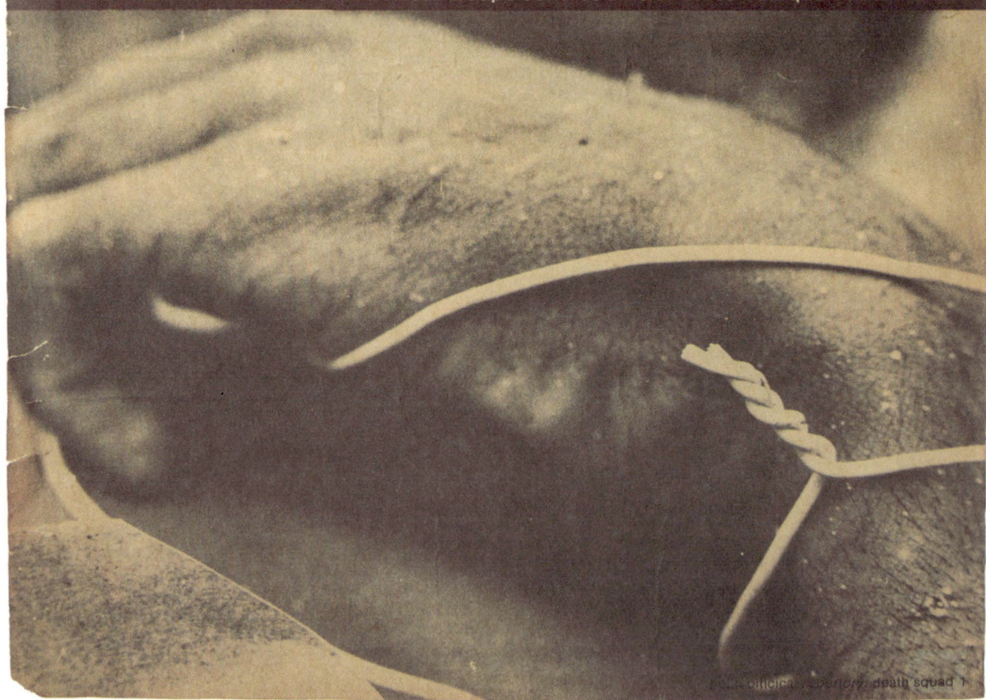

Poster by Hélio Oiticica for the Latin American Fair of Opinion, produced by the Theatre of Latin America (TOLA)/Joanne Pottlitzer, March 15–April 9, 1972. Courtesy of Andreas Valentin

The Fair of Opinion begins with a questioning. It was my own questioning in Brazil when I was arrested, and questioned, and tortured by our police. The audience enters into a very small place. And there she is going to suffer also a kind of questioning. From there, Jonas goes to another place where they can look at the people singing and hear people singing. And from that place, they go upstairs and that they can choose–like in a fair–three different places to see from all over Latin America. And then we concentrate on the question of the audience. And from that point on, we have a few more places, which give a precise idea of what's going on–what's happening to us. And at the same time, we also pose the question, to you the American artist, what are you doing now? What are we doing now in relation to us? And what are you doing now in relation to yourselves?

I remember that a few months ago the United States Senate was held a subcommittee hearing about the relation between the United States and Brazil, in particular, and some other countries. And then which way could the United States, or would the United States, be helping some regimes that were not supposed to be helped. And that same way in which way as one of the songs said, the Latin America helps New York to be such a glowing city. Well, it's about this that Latin American Fair of Opinion is.

– Augusto Boal

latin american fair of opinion

repertory.

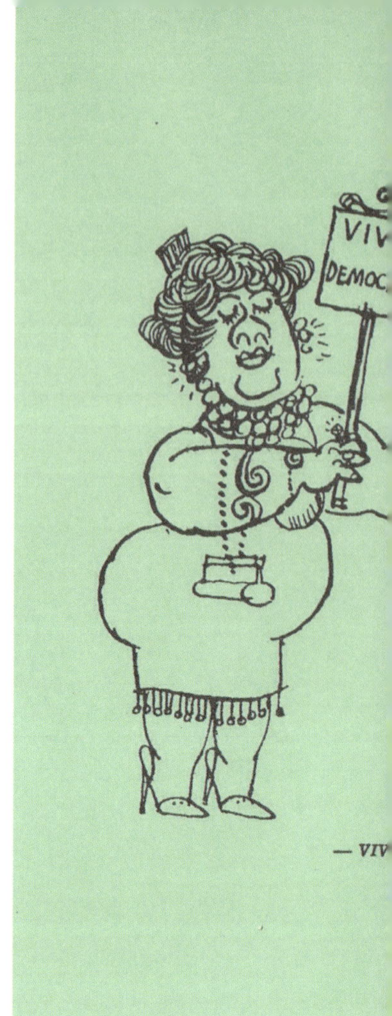

Pages from the program of the Latin American Fair of Opinion, 1972. Courtesy of Instituto Augusto Boal and Joanne Pottlitzer

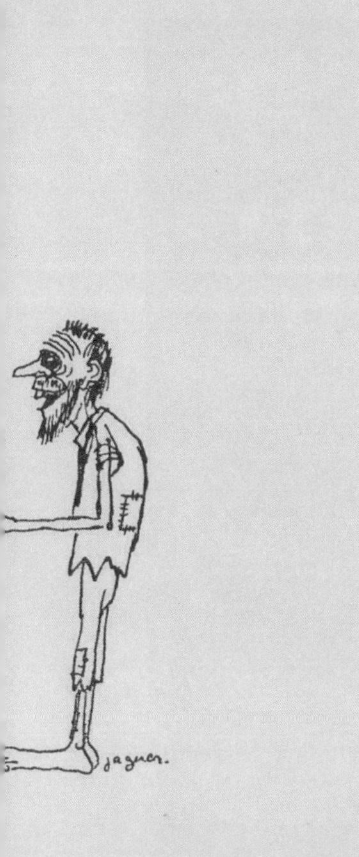

LATIN AMERICAN THEATRE FAIR

directed by

AUGUSTO BOAL

A kaleidoscope of Latin American points of view
through theatre and music

THE BLACK AIRPLANE (Argentina) by Roberto Cossa, German Rozenmacher, Carlos Somigliana, Ricardo Talesnik

THE COCK (Peru) by Victor Zavala

THE AUTOPSY (Colombia) by Enrique Buenaventura

TORQUEMADA, Prologue (Brazil) by Augusto Boal

GUARDIAN ANGEL (Brazil) by Augusto Boal

MAN DOES NOT DIE BY BREAD ALONE (Chile) by Jorge Diaz

ANIMALIA (Brazil) by Gianfrancesco Guarnieri

COLLAGE adapted by Augusto Boal

translations by Joanne Pottlitzer & Susan Rudge

....

The audience may attend the first four plays as they wish, as they will play simultaneously throughout the church; the audience will watch the remaining four pieces in sequence.

....

There will be no intermission

The idea of presenting a Latin American Fair of Opinion here in New York is to present a kaleidoscopic view of our problems and our relationship to the United States. We don't want to be folkloric. We don't want to give you just a travelogue on Latin America—that's not the point. We went through the different points of view of the different artists and present to you exactly what do you think about ourselves and what we think about you, also.

— Augusto Boal

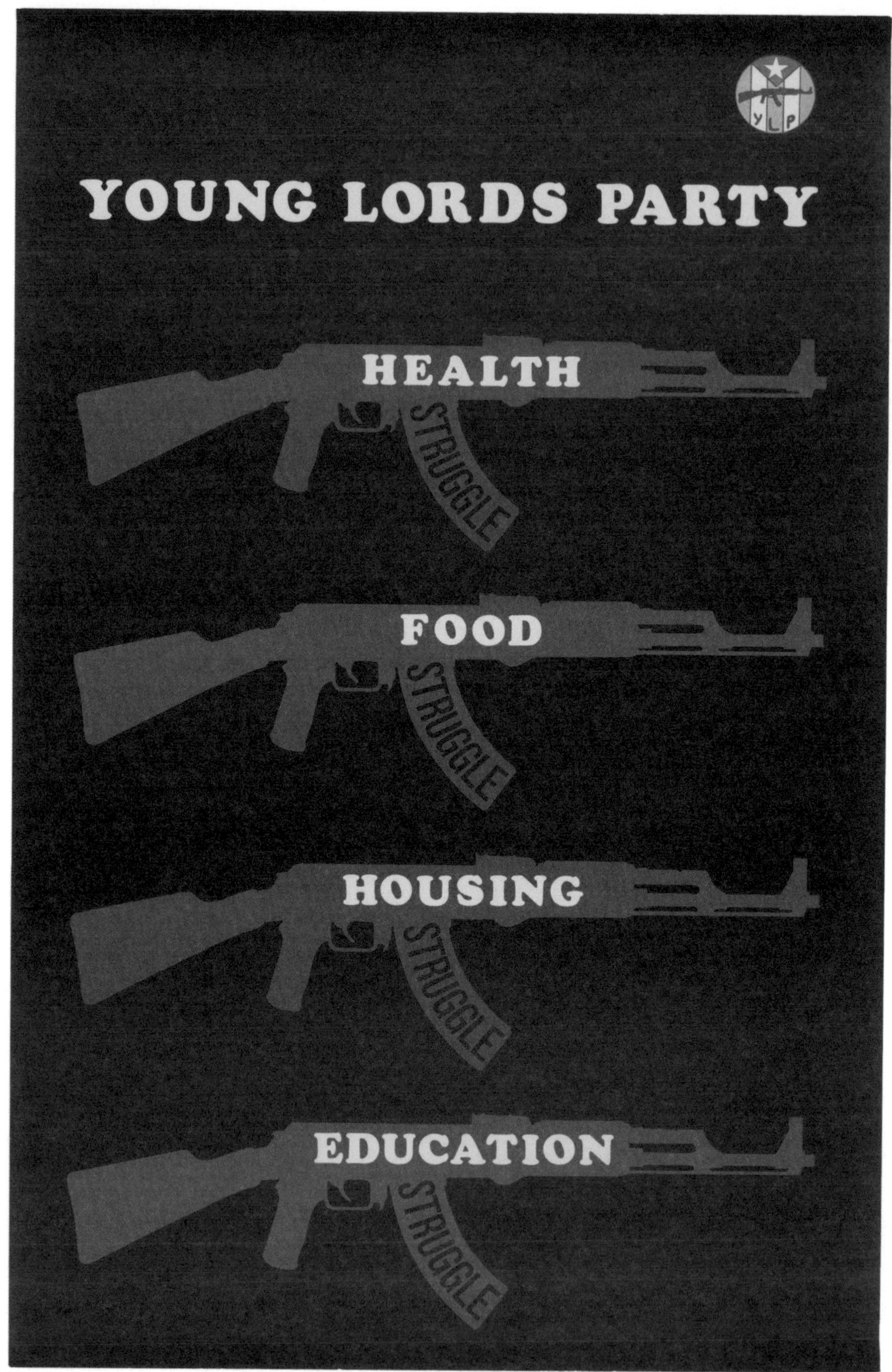

Young Lords Party, *Health, Food, Housing, Education, Struggle*, ca. 1970

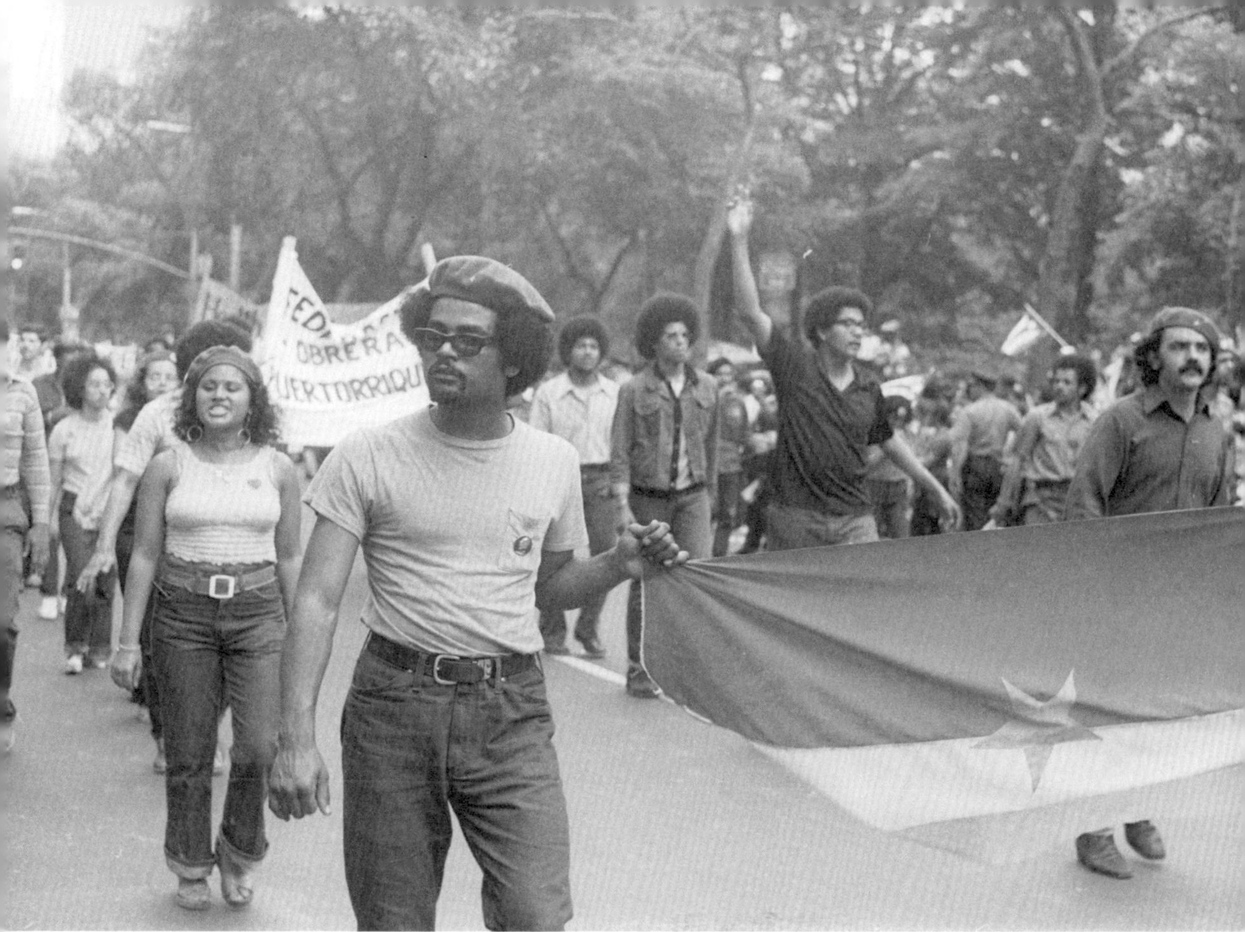

The Young Lords Organization was an activist group of working-class Puerto Rican youth that formed in the 1960s in Chicago in the context of the civil rights movement, later expanding to New York. The Young Lords organized demonstrations against structural and social issues that affected their community, such as police brutality, unemployment, lack of housing, and poor access to education and health care. Their actions spurred legislative progress, such as the passing of a new housing law, as well as key changes in city infrastructure, such as the building of a new hospital in the Bronx. A memorable action led by the group was the Garbage Offensive, which demanded improvements to city sanitation services in East Harlem.

Máximo Rafael Colón, *Untitled (Puerto Rican Day Parade)*, 1972.
Máximo Rafael Colón Archive

Young Lords Block Street with Garbage

(From the newspaper *Young Lords Organization* 1, no.4 [October 1969])

In a display of community strength and support of the YOUNG LORDS ORGANIZATION, the people of East Harlem (El Barrio), and the YLO closed the streets of Third Ave. from 110th, across to 112th and down to Second Ave. on Sunday, July 27.

For two weeks previously, the YOUNG LORDS had been cleaning garbage from the streets and into garbage cans to show the people that the department of garbage (Lindsay's department of sanitation), or D.O.G., does not serve them. At first, communication with the people was slow. Then, as the barriers broke down and everyone got their thing together, the people saw that even a nothing department like D.O.G. looks upon Puerto Ricans and Blacks as though they are something lower than garbage. These dogs at D.O.G. have forgotten that they must SERVE THE PEOPLE. And it all blew up on Sunday.

By July 27, the original operation had grown to such a large number of people, not just including LORDS, that the brooms and shovels we were using were not enough. So four LORDS—the Deputy Minister of Finance, Information and Education and an information photographer—went to the nearest D.O.G. hole at 108th St. After some Bureaucratic Bullshitting they steered us to the D.O.G. hole at 73rd St. Dig it! Two miles away, while a hole is sitting three blocks away. After playing the man's game of red tape, the LORDS brought it all back home. We ran it down about what happened and a course of action was developed. As fast as it takes a streetlight to change, all the People—Lords, mothers, Li'l Lords—placed cans of garbage across Third Ave. at 110th St. The pigs, who have been eyeing the LORDS for the past few weeks in New York, came to the scene in a matter of seconds. Sources on the blocks say the pigs had trucks waiting a few blocks away. But the pigs found out that the spirit of the people is greater than all the man's pigs. At least 1,000 Puerto Ricans turned out to cheer the LORDS on as they woofed the pigs to their pens. Brothers and Sisters on 111th and 112th caught that old revolutionary spirit, last seen in '66, and blocked their streets, too.

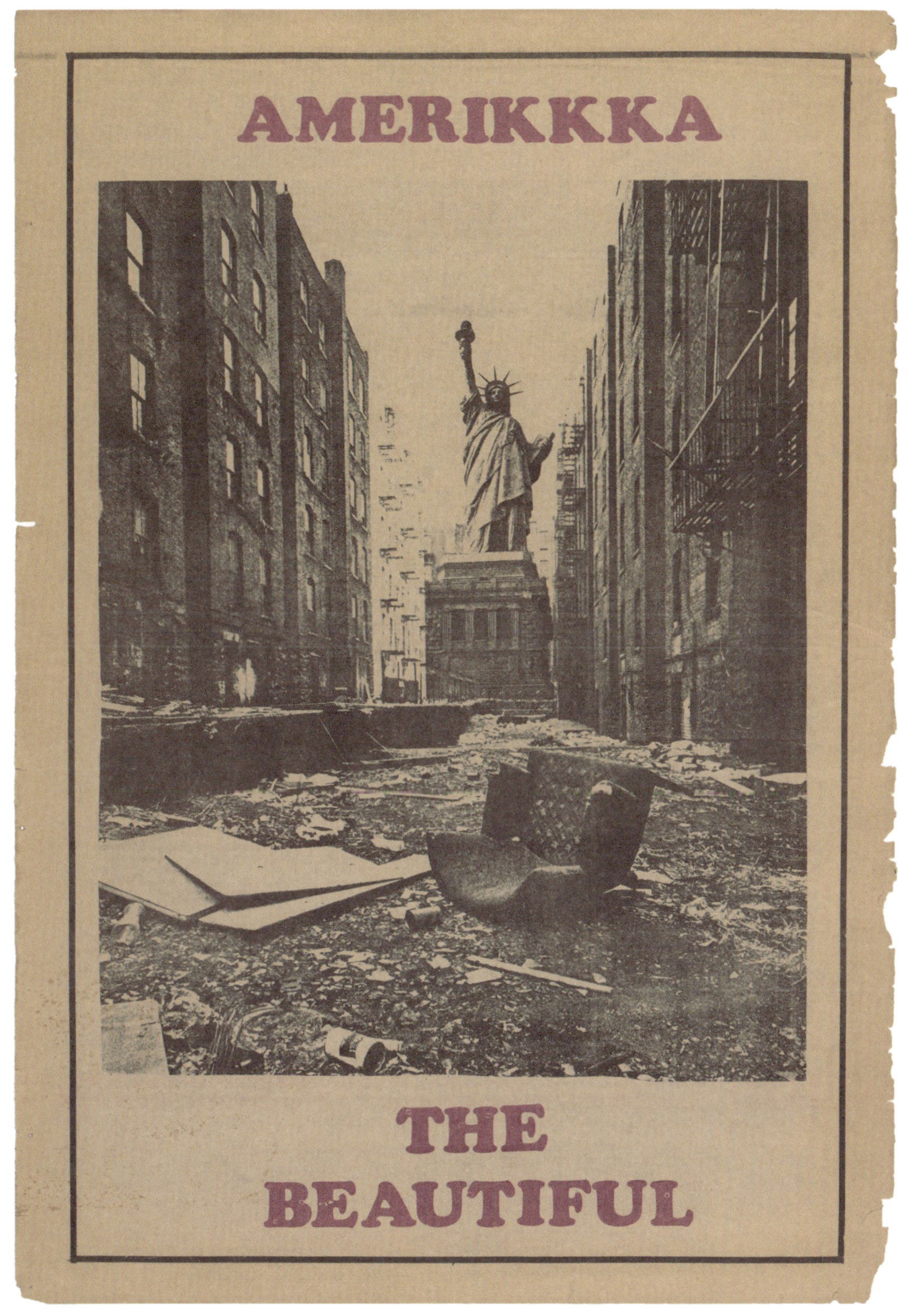

Back cover of *Palante* 2, no. 13 (October 16, 1970). Boxed Newspaper Collection, Tamiment Library/Robert F. Wagner Labor Archives, New York University

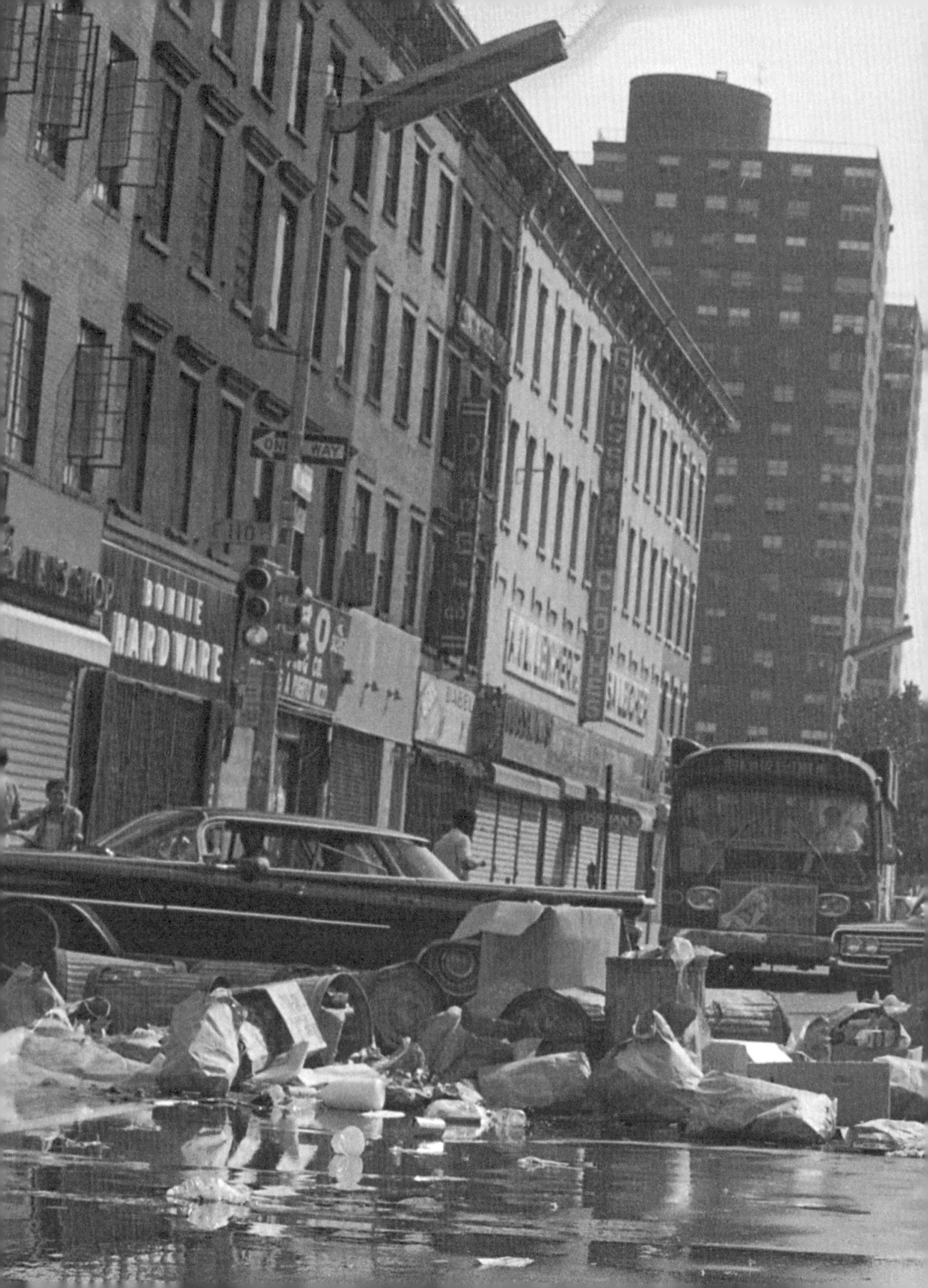
BONNIE
HARDWARE

[A]fter the Garbage Offensive, we trusted our people in El Barrio and they trusted us. They would now support and protect the Young Lords. There was also a practical lesson for all parties involved: when a community stands together and makes a strong statement, it will be heard. On this occasion, something had been done to address the problem. . . . [T]he experience helped us to understand the relationship between the political, the underground, the people, and the media that was needed to get our story told.

— Miguel "Mickey" Melendez

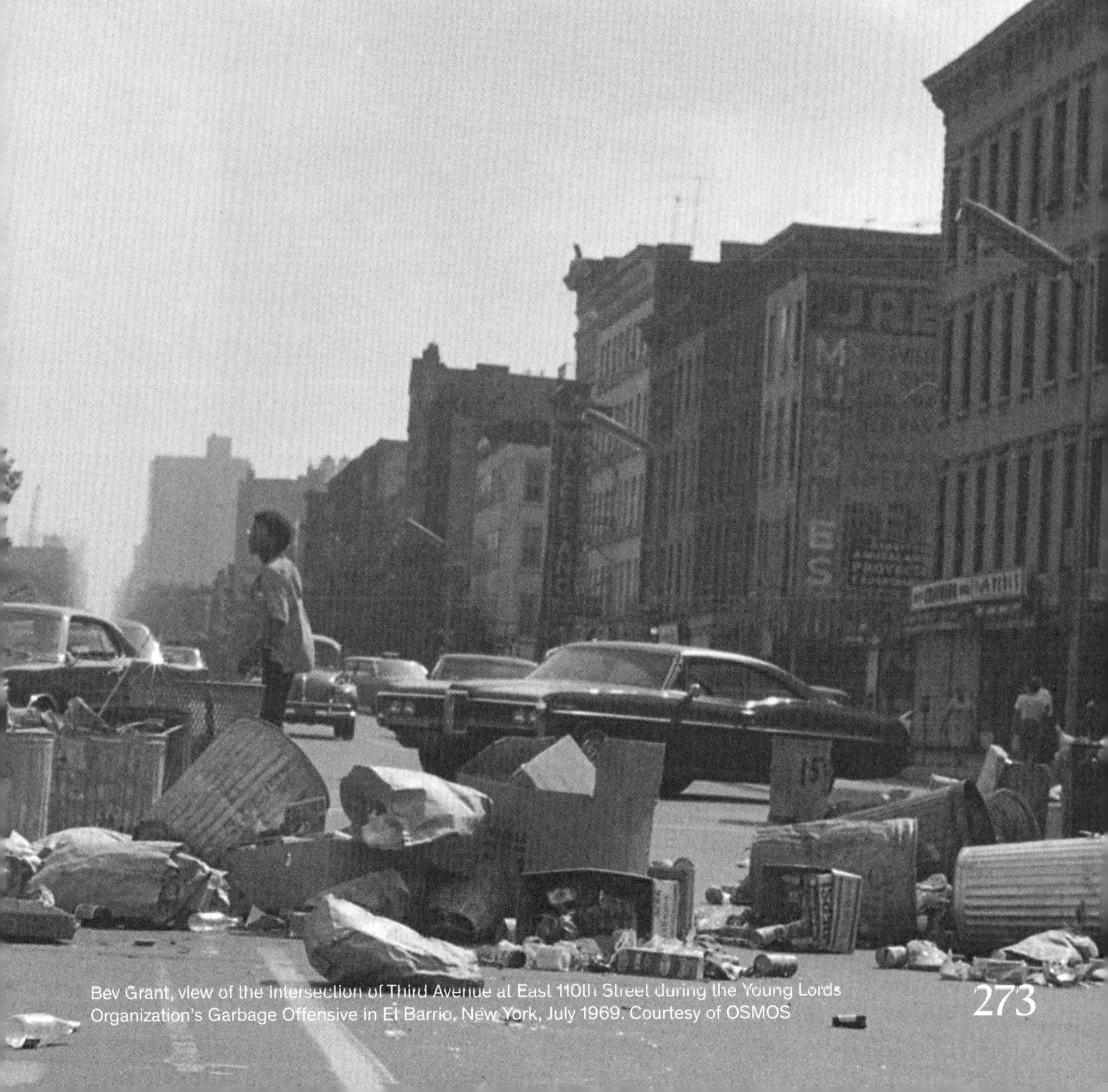

Bev Grant, view of the intersection of Third Avenue at East 110th Street during the Young Lords Organization's Garbage Offensive in El Barrio, New York, July 1969. Courtesy of OSMOS

Puerto Rican activists organized many actions that involved the takeover of public buildings and spaces. In 1977 a group from the NY Committee to Free the Nationalist Political Prisoners took over the Statue of Liberty and demanded the release of four political prisoners who had participated in a 1954 protest against the colonial status of Puerto Rico. This typewritten document, titled "Why We Took the Statue of Liberty," summarizes their grievances and demands. It was presented by the committee in court in the same year.

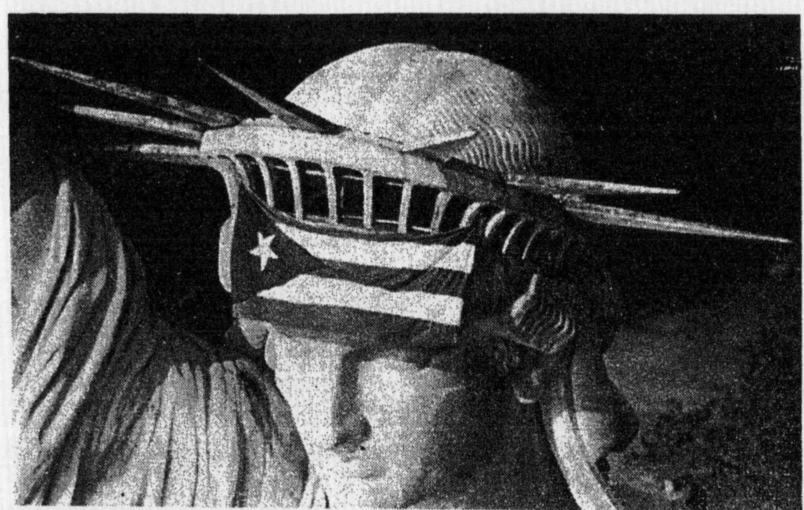

The New York Times/Neal Boenzi

Puerto Rican flag hanging from the Statue of Liberty after it was occupied by nationalist group yesterday

30 in Puerto Rican Group Held in Liberty I. Protest

By MARY BREASTED

Thirty Puerto Rican nationalists demanding freedom for four Puerto Rican terrorists occupied the Statue of Liberty for eight hours yesterday, chasing tourists out of its inner passageways and locking themselves inside.

Eight hours after occupying the statue and draping a Puerto Rican flag from its crown and a banner calling for the independence of Puerto Rico across its pedestal, the group was arrested by Federal authorities without violence. A spokesman for the United States Park Police indicated that members of the group would be charged with trespassing on Federal property.

Deputy Chief Hugh Groves of the United States Park Police, commander of field operations, flew to New York City from Washington to supervise the arrest of the demonstrators. He said that when the statue was retaken by Park Police the demonstrators had been very cooperative and that the only damage had been the breaking of a glass door.

"If there's such a thing as being a pleasure to work with, why those people were," he said.

Park police said that the demonstrators had been given seven offers of amnesty by the Federal authorities before they were finally arrested, at around 6 P.M.

Cutting Off Traffic

Shortly after the takeover began, at 9:30 A.M., the Park Police and the Coast Guard moved quickly to cut off all tourist traffic to the island, and vessels occupied by reporters were kept 500 yards away.

cording to plan. Supporters of the group told reporters, who had been summoned to the scene by repeated phone calls from the group, that they had intended to invite the press to a news conerence on Liberty Island shortly after the statue was occupied.

But, because a quick blockade by the authorities thwarted that plan, it was the support group at the Battery that held a news conference and numerous press briefings to speak on behalf of the Liberty Island protesters.

They were expressed most often by Vicente Alba, a former member of the Young Lords political party. He was arrested last August on what later turned out to be misinformation that he might be connected with the F.A.L.N., which has claimed responsibility for setting off bombs in New York City.

Mr. Alba said that he and the Liberty Island protesters, known as the Committee to Free the Five Puerto Rican Nationalists, wanted the four nationalists still in jail for shooting up the House of Representatives in 1952 set free.

The 91-year-old statue has been the site of several other protest demonstrations in recent years.

Mary Breasted, "30 in Puerto Rican Group Held in Liberty I. Protest," *New York Times*, October 26, 1977, 30

I have been asked to speak on behalf of the 28 people arrested at the Statue of Liberty. I would like to begin by offering my own apologies to all of the people here in court because the words of one person can never express fully the anger that all of us feel inside of us, and the commitment we have to the liberation of Puerto Rico. I want to try to do as best as I can.

We are members of the New York City Committee to Free the Nationalist Political Prisoners and supporters of the Puerto Rican independence movement. We are the sons and daughters of the Puerto Rican workers who were forced to migrate to this country in order to survive because the United States was sucking the wealth out of Puerto Rico and leaving our people impoverished. We are the sons and daughters of Albizu Campos and Lolita Lebron, and these are the people that set the standards by which we judge our own actions.

The history of the Puerto Rican people for us is one of oppression and resistance and we see ourselves as a continuation of that history, not isolated from it.

We took the Statue of Liberty because the United States government has left the Puerto Rican people no choice. We are not going to stay quiet in the face of the continuous and growing repression in Puerto Rico and in the United States. It is our responsibility to the people who came before us--to our mothers and fathers who slaved in Puerto Rico and in the United States, and to those who come after us--our younger brothers and sisters, who are being denied every opportunity in this country and in Puerto Rico to develop as a Puerto Rican people with a proud history and a proud heritage.

You say that we are guilty of the occupation of the Statue of Liberty. We say tha the American government is guilty of occupying Puerto Rico since 1898, an occupation that has been maintained through the use of brutal force to crush all of those people who have opposed that occupation and the plundering of the wealth of Puerto Rico and the exploitation of the Puerto Rican workers.

Today the American government is moving to consolidate its control even further on Puerto Rico by imposing statehood on the island; and just as in 1950 when the United States was planning to change the status of Puerto Rico to the status of Commonwealth, it was forced to move to silence the voices of opposition, most notably the voices raised by the Nationalist Party who spoke not only with words, but through bullets, because that's what history has proven that oppressors understand.

Today, freedom fighters are also being persecuted both in this country and in Puerto Rico. In the prisons, Puerto Rican freedom fighters like Lolita Lebron, Rafael Cancel Miranda, Irvin Flores and Oscar Collazo continue to be tortured; and we don't use the term "torture" lightly. We think it is a serious term. And when Lolita Lebron is subjected to an internal examination that leaves her hemorraging--that is torture. When Andres Figueroa Cordero is left in solitary confinement for six months complaining of bleeding from the rectum and no medical care is given to him, and then later on he is told that he has cancer of the rectum, we say that is torture. Then later on he is told he has cancer in his lungs, and one of his lungs is cut out--we say that is torture. Later on, after everyone is saying that all of his cancer has been cured, the cancer spreads into his bronchial tubes and he is told that he is going to die--we say that is torture.

Not only are <u>we</u> taking this position, but the people of the world also understand it, and we are not in an isolated position.

The suffering that the Nationalists are experiencing in prison is burned into our hearts. And we feel it very, very deeply; and in our actions we try to convey that as long as they suffer, there will not be that kind of peace in Puerto Rico or in the United States.

NY Committee to Free the Nationalist Political Prisoners, "Why We Took the Statue of Liberty," statement presented in court, November 22, 1977. Richie Pérez Papers, 1918–2006. Archives of the Puerto Rican Diaspora, Center for Puerto Rican Studies, Hunter College, CUNY

We would also like to raise that the exact week that we took the Statue of Liberty, in Puerto Rico the body of one of our labor leaders was found strangled and murdered in El Yunque, Juan Rafael Caballero. The Puerto Rican people have testified that he was murdered by a police execution squad; very similar to those that have roamed throughout Latin America persecuting the freedom-loving people and who have now openly raised their head in Puerto Rico.

Are we imagining that there is a conspiracy? Are we imagining that on the part of the United States government there is a concerted effort to smash the Puerto Rican independence movement and the Puerto Rican workers movement?

We don't think we are imagining these things. We think that the revelations about the COINTELPRO (Counter-Intelligence)Program , about the FBI programs of disruption and kidnapping of militants in this country, the frameups and the setups of the Black Panther Party have already been proven by history--as well as the revelations about government misdeeds, covering the aggressive policies of the U.S. in the Vietnam War, that all of those things have been proven before the people of the world. We are not paranoid. That is what's taking place. We understand it fully well.

In the United States our situation has not improved. Contrary to the myths raised in this country of upward mobility and that we would--all minorities would be integrated into the economy of the system--that's a lie. The U.S. Civil Rights Commission has been forced to admit that the future of Puerto Ricans in this country is "uncertain" (report of Oct. 1976).

So what is being asked of the Puerto Rican people? That we sit back and allow our "uncertain future" to be smashed in our very faces. Our children play in empty lots, that's their playground. We can't accept that, and we will never accept that. And that's why we took the Statue of Liberty.

Our sisters are sterilized in butcher shops like Lincoln Hospital, and we will never accept that. And that's why we took the Statue of Liberty.

Our Puerto Rican and Black youth are murdered in the streets by the real terrorists, by police terrorists, who are then set free--and we will never accept that either.

We will never forget Clifford Glover, Tito Perez, Randolph Evans, Israel Rodriquez and many more. Israel Rodriguez was beaten to death by the police in front of his wife. They beat him so severely that they broke his spleen in half. The policeman who murdered him was given -- was found supposedly "guilty" on a charge of "negligent homicide." Now, how was that "negligent homicide"? That's an example of the distortions and the use of the law to protect the oppressor and to, you know, to come down against the oppressed.

The murders of our people are also burned in our hearts. And their suffering and the suffering of their loved ones is our suffering too. We can't rest until we end the system that brings that suffering on our people.

That's why we took the Statue of Liberty.

And in addition to all of these open terrorist and racist attacks, we have the disguised "legal" attacks. Through the use of grand juries in this country, the United States government has attempted--has intensified its attempts to crush the Puerto Rican independence movement. Today, nine of our people are in prison for refusing to collaborate with what we consider to be police state tactics. It is our responsibility to free them, and we will free them. The taking over of the Statue of Liberty was part of a movement not only to free our imprisoned Nationalist brothers and sisters, but to free our people who have been imprisoned throughout this country.

We recognize, whether or not anyone else in this courtroom cares to recognize, the rising tide of fascism in this country, and we refuse to be silent and to passively cooperate with our own destruction.

By your law you may say we are guilty, but we also know that this law has historically served to protect only the ruling class of this country. It is used to legitimize the exploitation and oppression of our people and all Third World people. But the people's law also exists and the people will have their justice also. By the people's law it is the United States who is guilty of terrorism and the violation of our rights.

We stand with the world's people who have clearly stated that Puerto Rico is a colony of the United States and has the right to self-determination. The world's people have stated this in the United Nations. We understand that stating it is not enough, that we have to fight for it. We stand for freedom and liberation for all oppressed people, not only for Puerto Ricans, not only for the four Nationalists who are still in prison, but also for other freedom fighters, like Assata Shakur, who is on trial today.

Regardless of what happens to us here today, we will never consider ourselves to be criminals, because we consider ourselves to be freedom fighters for our people. Our people will never consider us to be criminals, because the people and history will prove (just as the forward march of history and the struggle of the people in Vietnam proved) who is the real criminals are.

The slight inconvenience that we may have caused to some tourists can never be compared to the genocide committed by the U.S. government in the sterilization of 35% of the Puerto Rican women of child-bearing age.

We make no apologies for our actions. We want to make that very clear. We took the action. We are proud that we took the action. We say that the Puerto Rican people have the right to be free.

We know that we are not on trial for taking over the Statue of Liberty. What is on trial here, what is being attacked here is the right of the Puerto Rican people to struggle for self-determination.

What we say is: we will be free -- as Malcolm X said, we will be free by any means necessary.

QUE VIVA PUERTO RICO LIBRE!

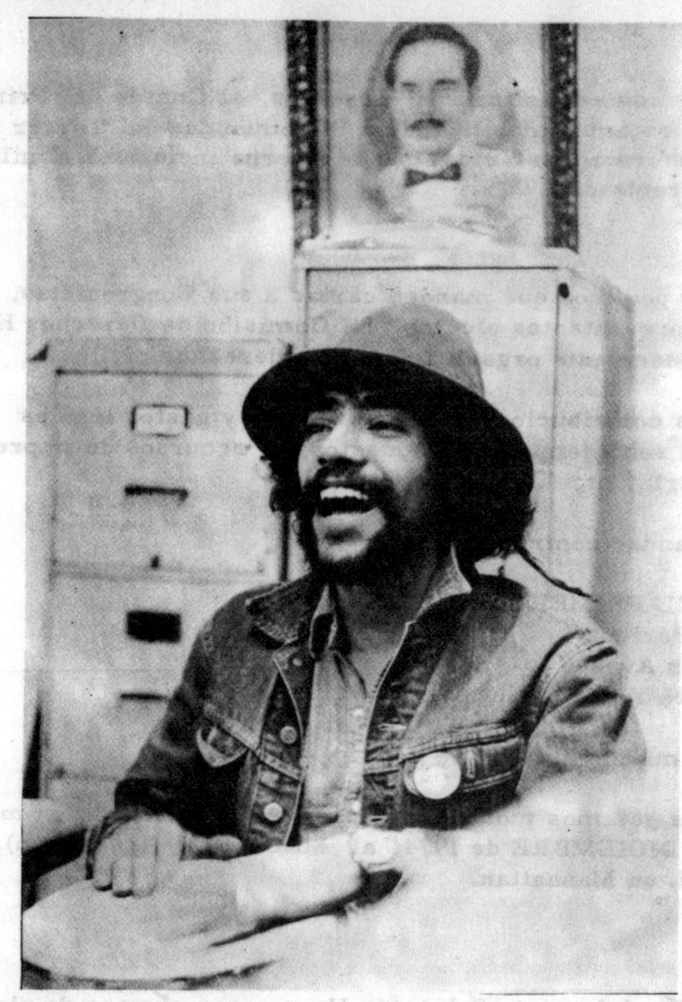

HOMICIDIO, NO SUICIDIO

El primero de Diciembre de 1974 a las 10:30 pm, Martin "Tito" Perez fué arrestado por la Policía de Tránsito por "conducta desordenada". El arresto tomó lugar en la plataforma de la estación de la calle 125 en el Lexington Ave. subway. Dos horas más tarde Tito estaba muerto.

Este no es un incidente aislado dentro de la comunidad Puertorriqueña. Nosotros, el Comité del Primero de Diciembre, creemos que Tito fué asesinado y dejado ahorcado en las barras de la celda para crear un ambiente de suicidio.

El precinto 25 tiene una larga historia de brutalidades y atentados suicidios de los presos. Estas situaciones son comunes y ocurren amenudo contra Afroamericanos, Latinos, Asiaticos, y Nativoamericanos (Indios) - la comunidad del Tercer Mundo, en este caso El Barrio en East Harlem, Nueva York.

Homicide, Not Suicide, 1974. El Museo del Barrio Archive, New York. Courtesy of El Museo del Barrio

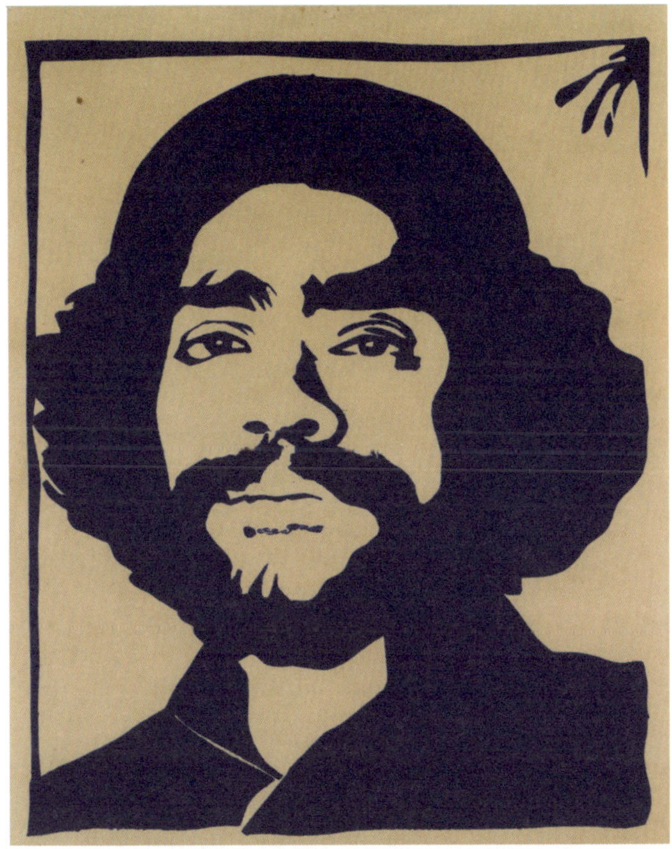

Martín "Tito" Pérez was a Puerto Rican artist and musician involved with Taller Boricua. On December 1, 1974, Pérez was arrested by the New York City police for "disorderly conduct" while playing drums in the subway. He was killed while in custody; the police reported that he hanged himself in his cell. Taller Boricua members organized protests in response to his death and against the police brutality that deeply affected their community.

Jorge Soto Sánchez, *Martin "Tito" Pérez*, ca. 1974. Collection of El Museo del Barrio, New York. Gift of Pedro Pedraza. Courtesy of El Museo del Barrio

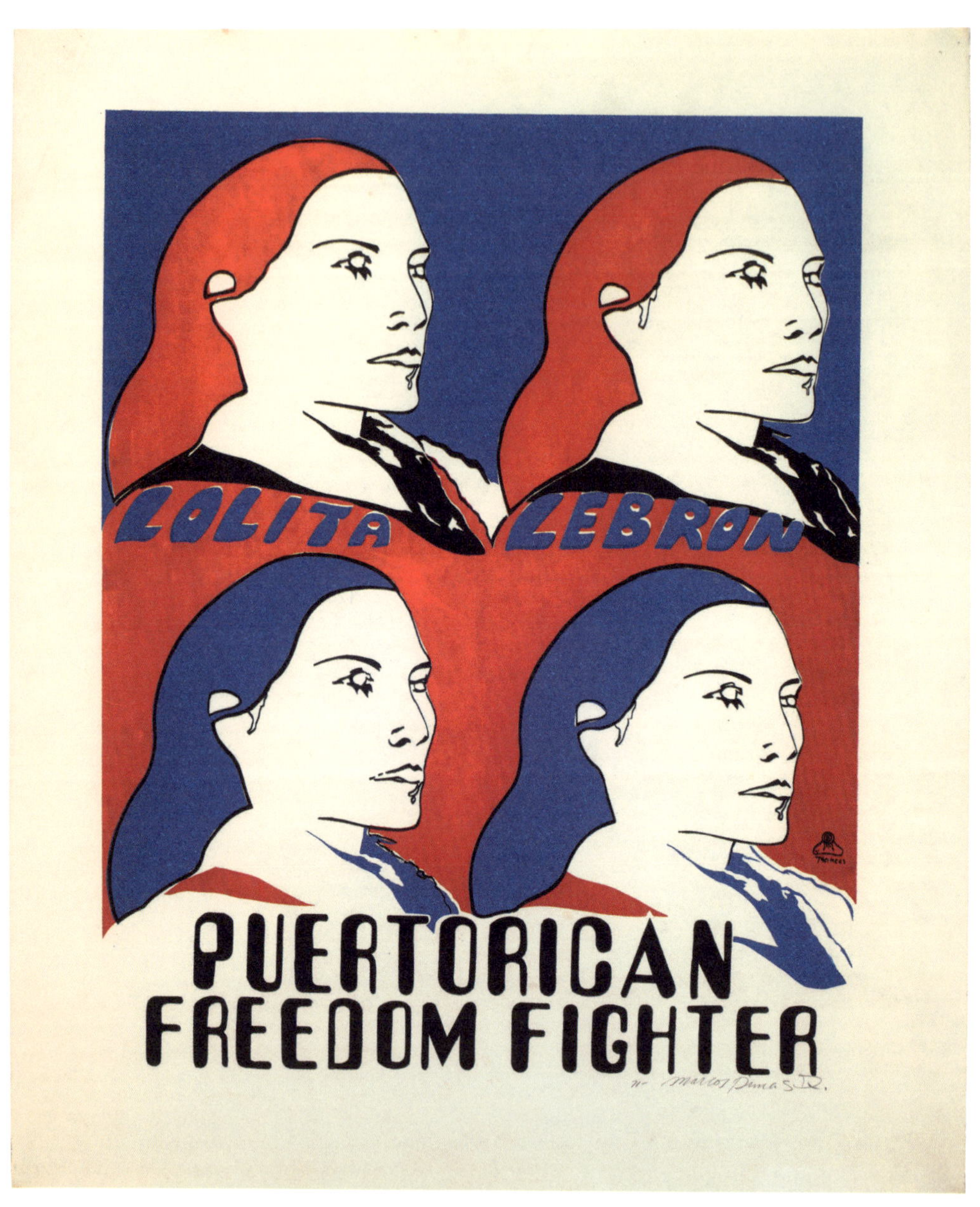

Marcos Dimas, *Lolita Lebrón: Puerto Rican Freedom Fighter*, 1971. Collection of El Museo del Barrio, New York. Courtesy of the artist and El Museo del Barrio

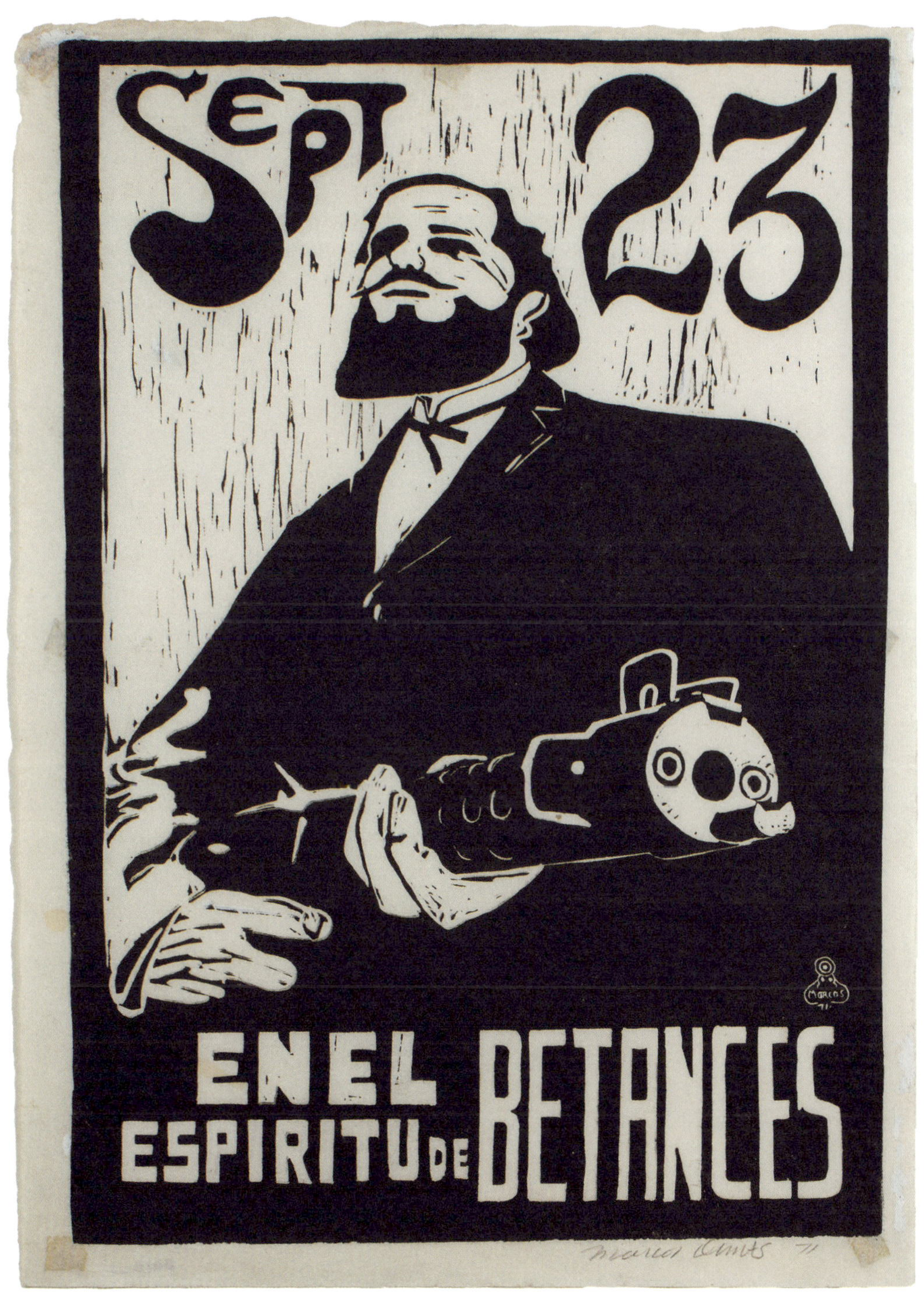

Marcos Dimas, *En el espiritu de Betances* (In the spirit of Betances), 1971. Collection of El Museo del Barrio, New York. Courtesy of the artist and El Museo del Barrio

In 1979, during an American Airlines flight from Washington, DC, to Puerto Rico, Puerto Rican artist Carlos Irizarry threatened to explode the airplane. He gave a message to the flight attendant titled "This is an explosive message," demanding the liberation of Puerto Rican nationalist prisoners. For this act, the artist was imprisoned by the United States for four years. In his court defense, he and his lawyer argued that the threat had been a work of Conceptual art.

Carlos Irizarry, *My Son, the Soldier, Part I*, 1970.
San Juan Racing Association Fund, The Museum of Modern Art, New York

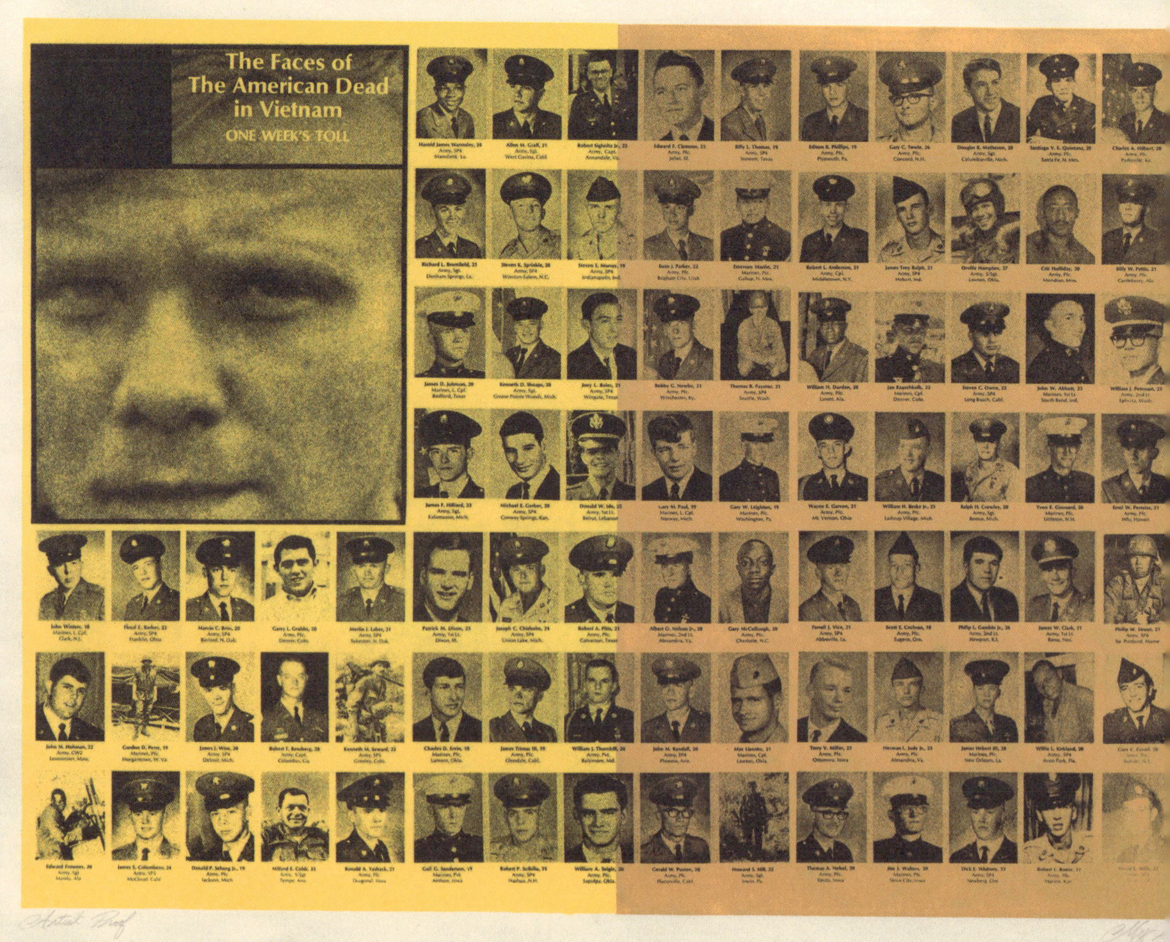

Puerto Rican Artist Held In Threat Against Plane

Carlos Montes Irizarry, a 40-year-old commercial artist from Puerto Rico, was held in $500,000 bail in Federal Court in Brooklyn yesterday after he allegedly threatened to blow up a plane that had just left Kennedy International Airport for San Juan.

Federal authorities charged that Mr. Irizarry, one of the 136 passengers aboard the American Airlines DC-10, sent a written message to the captain of the plane saying: "Call the White House and tell President Carter we are going to blow up this plane if he doesn't follow through with demands of the Puerto Rican liberation army."

The message was sent, through a flight attendant, shortly after midnight yesterday, about 20 minutes after the plane had left Kennedy. The pilot, who was unidentified, immediately returned to Kennedy, where Mr. Irizarry, surrendered to authorities, without resistance. He was found to have no explosives or weapons.

Gavin W. Scotti, an assistant United States attorney, said that the Federal Bureau of Investigation knew of no terrorist group called the Puerto Rican liberation army. An F.B.I. spokesman said that Mr. Irizarry was believed responsible for anonymous written threats make earlier this week in Washington, Newark and New York City, to blow up an unspecified airplane and harm President Carter.

Mr. Irizarry was arrested in Puerto Rico in 1976 after allegedly threatening the life of President Gerald R. Ford, Mr. Scotti said. That case was subsequently dismissed.

"Puerto Rican Artist Held In Threat Against Plane," *New York Times*, August 16, 1979, 7

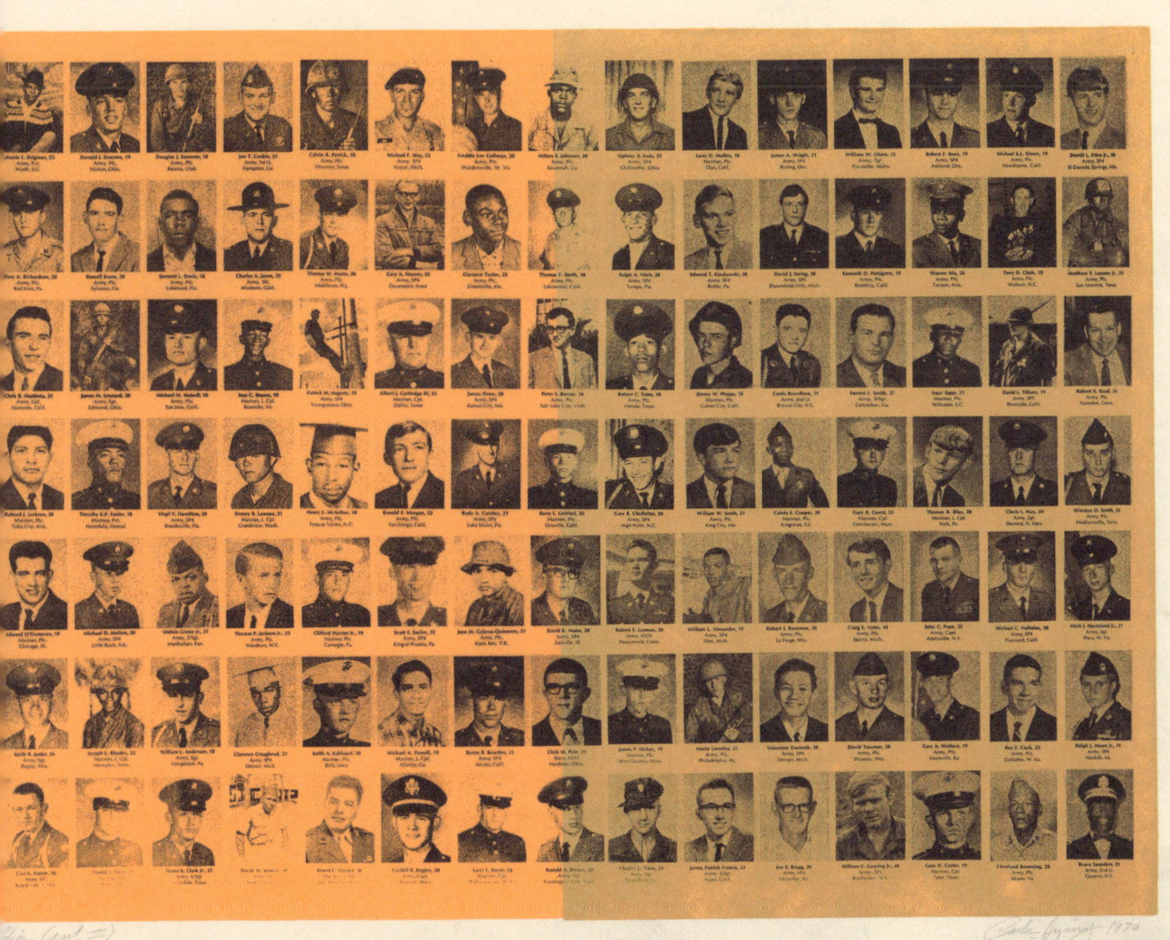

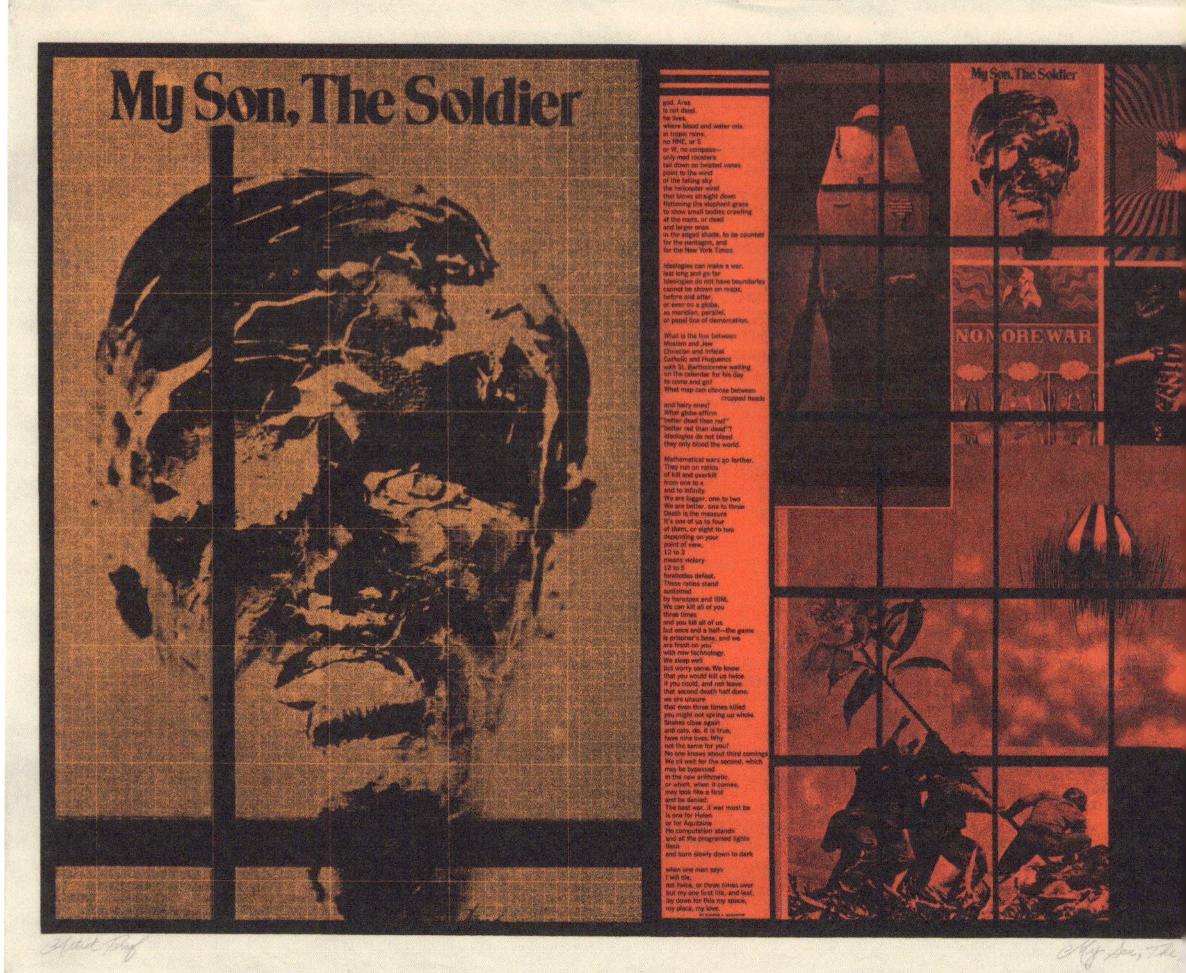

Carlos Irizarry, *My Son, the Soldier, Part II*, 1970.
San Juan Racing Association Fund, The Museum of Modern Art, New York

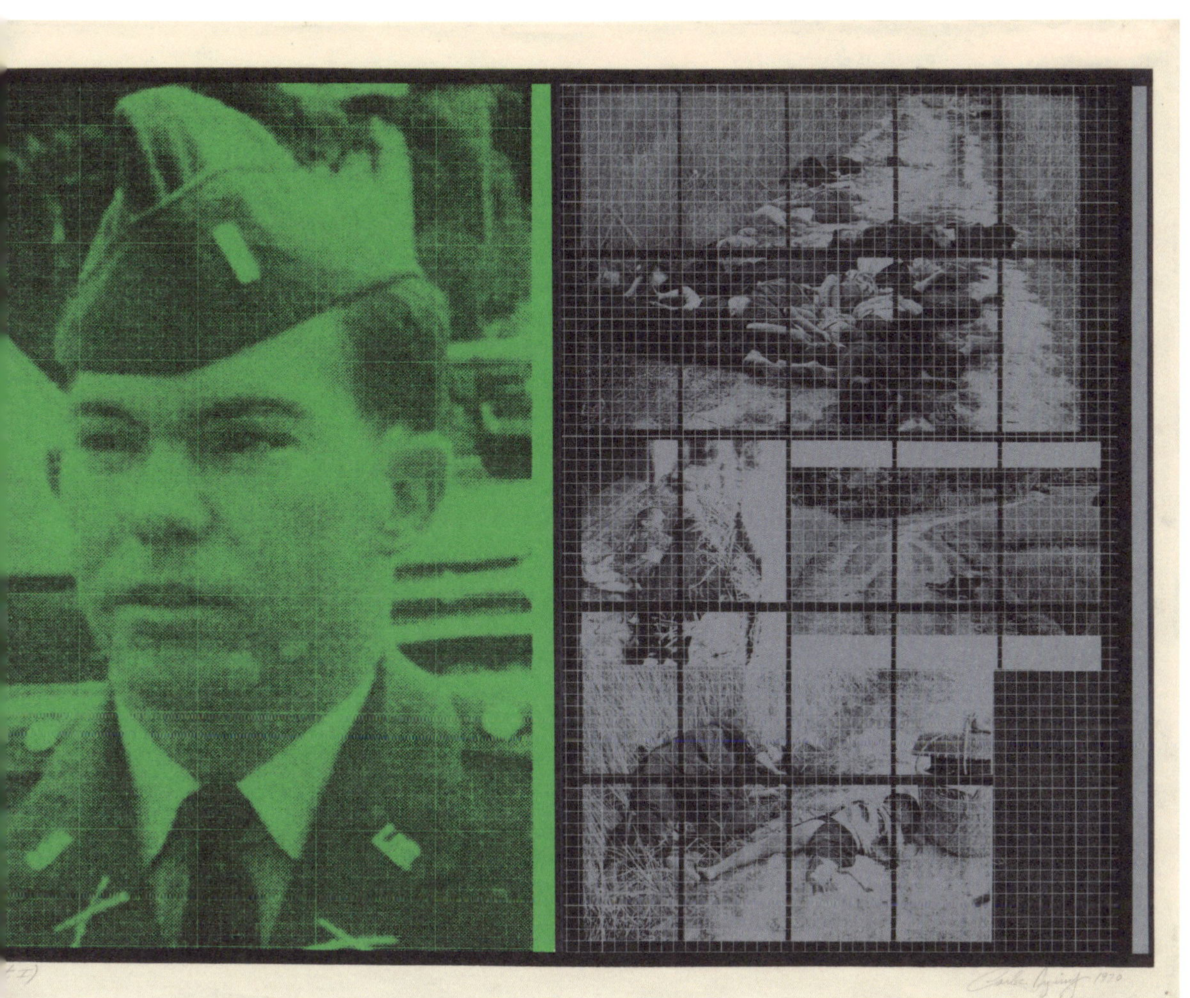

The Art Workers' Coalition (AWC) was formed by a group of artists who organized with the goal of putting pressure on major New York cultural institutions, such as the Metropolitan Museum of Art, the Whitney Museum of American Art, and the Museum of Modern Art, on issues of discrimination and inequality in their curatorial and collection practices. It was especially concerned with the lack of representation of women and artists of color in museums. In its list of demands, the AWC demanded the inclusion of programming that would be not only dedicated to but also created by African Americans and Puerto Ricans. A subgroup of the AWC, the Puerto Rican Art Workers' Coalition (PRAWC), was created by Raphael Montañez Ortiz and artists from Taller Boricua.

Jan van Raay, Protest by the Art Workers' Coalition, Black Emergency Cultural Coalition, and Guerrilla Art Action Group (GAAG) at the Museum of Modern Art, New York, May 2, 1970

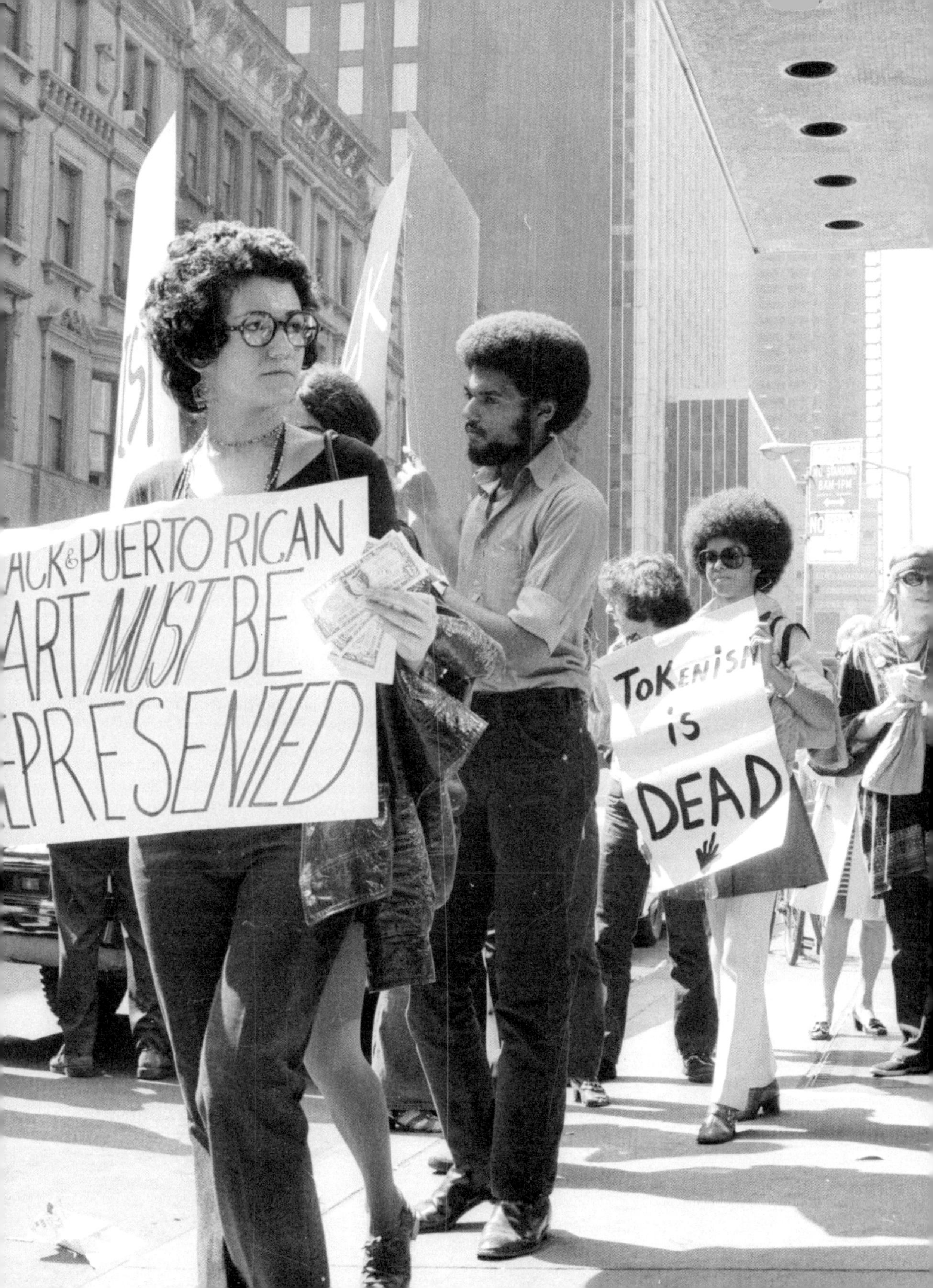

ACK&PUERTO RICAN
ART MUST BE
EPRESENTED
TOKENIS
is
DEAD
NO STANDING
8AM-1PM

STUDENTS AND ARTISTS UNITED FOR A MARTIN LUTHER KING JR. WING FOR BLACK AND PUJERTO RICAN ART AT THE MUSEUM OF MODERN ART IN NEW YORK CITY

FAITH RINGGOLD 345 W 145th St. NYC 862-5876
TOM LLOYD 154-02 107th Avenue Jamaica NY 657-6433

THE MUSEUM OF MODERN ART EXCLUDES BLACK AND PUERTO RICAN ART
The Museum is the international pace-setter of the modern art movement. Its exclusion of the work of black and Puerto Rican artists has denied them recognition, support, and the impetus for development which every art school and movement requires. It stands as the redoubt of the only great cultural empire in America which, however unwittingly, perpetuates total and unrelenting racism in America. Music, dance, theatre, literature, and audio-video communications have made themselves great by enriching themselves with the cultural wealth of black and Puerto Rican heritage; they have shared the prestige of artistic regeneration through a new and dynamic cultural infusion. In order to develop as a maovement, black and Puerto Rican art requires national and international exposure. Either it will receive it, or the decaying effects of a society already weighted with war and racism will crush what little hope remains that art is not indeed dead in America. But Black and Puerto Rican art are alive! In search of museum retrospectives! Of major exhibitions, International representation, and all the exposure which museum publications, commissions, grants, and sponsorship can give!

THE MARTIN LUTHER KING JR. WING WILL BE SEPARATE--BUT ONLY AS THE YOLK IS SEPARATE FROM THE SHELL. Black determination has never failed to provide creative leadership to surmount every hurdle to freedom. We cannot be free until our art is free! We would gladly be free in any way. But we have been 34 years at the Museum waiting to be free without being separate, and there have been no retrospectives for Jacob Lawrence or Romare Bearden, no publications devoted to their work, no group shows for our younger artists. If our art is not to be mixed with the art of whites, well, so be it! Give us our own wing, where we can show our black and Puerto Rican artists, where we can proclaim to the world our statement of what constitutes value and truth and the spirit of our people! Give it to us, or tell us that we have no place at all in your museums, just as we have no place in your churches and clubs and cooperatives! Can the Museum of Modern Art at least be that honest about it? We ask Governor Rockefeller and Mr. Philip Johnson of Johnson's Wax--trustees of the Museum--to make reason prevail. We will have our art, and we will have our wing. We have our own thing to do, something that grows out of our different experience as a people, coupled with the unceasing need of black and Puerto Rican people to give reason and vitality to existence. Modern Art needs a new direction and impetus--away from the "Cool School" emphasis of use of materials in the hope of avoiding the revolution. Black and Puerto Rican Art proclaims to the world: "We are the revolution! We are 25 million strong, very much alive and very seldom cool! Our art is not dead, and we will not let it die, because to kill our art is to kill the spirit of our people! That is why we <u>must</u> have the Martin Luther King Wing----NOW!!!!!"

AT 12 NOON AT THE MUSEUM OF MODERN ART, 21 W 53 St., in the AUDITORIUM, SUNDAY, April 13, we will conduct an evaluation of the Museum in its default of cultural responsibility to the public and cultural integrity to itself and the artistic community. TAKE PART. CARE. SAVE BLACK AND PUERTO RICAN ART FROM CULTURAL GENOCIDE. SAVE AMERICAN ART FROM THE FOLLY OF RACIST SUICIDE!

A MESSAGE TO THE BLACK AND PUERTO RICAN COMMUNITY ABOUT THE IMPORTANCE OF PORTRAYING THE CONTRIBUTIONS OF OUR CULTURAL HERITAGE

WHY IT IS IMPORTANT

Although we are all members of the same human family, our experience as a people has helped to make us different from other groups, just as our individual experiences make us as indivuduals different from one another. That differentness is a right; it makes us who and what we are, and that differentness has a right to be respected and preserved. The differentness of other Americans is recorded and preserved in the art of their group; their children and our children see it, and this fosters identification and a sense of worthwhilaness. Our children and we ourselves are entitled to this same identification, respect, and sense of worthwhileness enjoyed by others. The public vehicle for helping to sustain and encourage all of this is the museum. For people alive, developing and contributing today, the foremost vehicle in the world for telling the story of cultural contribution is the Museum of Modern Art.

IS IT BEING DONE ?

We want you to find this out for yourselves. On Sunday, April 13th, at 12 Noon, 200 black and Puerto Rican students will assemble in the Auditorium of the Museum of Modern Art for a brief orientation on methods of evaluating whether orf not the Museum of Modern Art is usefully fulfilling its obligation to portray the cultural contributions of black and Puerto Rican artists and to determine whether that portrayal could be better served by the establishment of a black and Puerto Rican wing at the Museum. Cultural leaders of the community will speak to the group. We urge you to support this work either by personally attending, or by encouraging others to attend, or both.

WHY A SEPARATE WING?

The Museum maintains wings for the exhibition of Dutch, Russian, Italian, Austro-Germanic, and other ethnic and national cultural contributions. Blacks and Puerto Ricans amount to more than 25 million Americans--one out of every eight! Our distinctiveness as a people is clearly recognied in the many laws, practices and customs within the American society which declared and even today declare such a difference. In short, we are different for purposes of unequal treatment, but not different for purposes of equal recognition of our cultural individuality. If we are different--and we are among the first to insist that we are--then we ought to be able to present that difference through our art and other cultural contributions in a Martin Luther King, Jr. Wing of the Museum of Modern Art.

SUPPORT YOUR CHILD'S RIGHT TO KNOW, ENJOY AND UNDERSTAND HIS RICH CULTURAL HERITAGE. HELP TO FREE BLACK AND PUERTO RICAN ART FROM THE CULTURAL GENOCIDE PRACTICED BY THE MUSEUM OF MODERN ART TODAY. WITHOUT A MARTIN LUTHER KING, JR. WING, BLACK AND PUERTO RICAN ARTISTS WILL HAVE TO WAIT ANOTHER 100 YEARS FOR FREEDOM, IF CULTURAL GENOCIDE DOES NOT IN FACT, AS IT SEEKS TO DO, WIPEOUT OUR CULTURE ENITRELY. BRING THIS PAPER WITH YOU TO THE MUSEUM THIS SUNDAY, OR MAIL IT TO A MEMBER OF OUR COMMITTEE!

Faith Ringgold 345 W. 145th St., New York, N.Y.
Tom Lloyd 154-02 107th Ave., Jamaica, N.Y.

STUDENTS & ARTISTS FOR A MARTIN LUTHER KING, JR. WING FOR BLACK ART AT THE MUSEUM OF MODERN ART

65

Flyer from Students and Artists for a Martin Luther King, Jr. Wing for Black and Puerto Rican Art at the Museum of Modern Art, New York, 1969. Courtesy of Primary Information

Let me tell you about the first Whitney Counterweight. Because there was a small museum of the Whitney that opened up in SoHo, American art and all of that. And they left the American Indians out, the African Americans, the Puerto Ricans, a lot of Latin Americans. And we started picketing . . . the museums during the '60s . . . The system was colonizing and also creating more marginalized situations, so that it could keep you there and you can't move out from that square.

— Nitza Tufiño

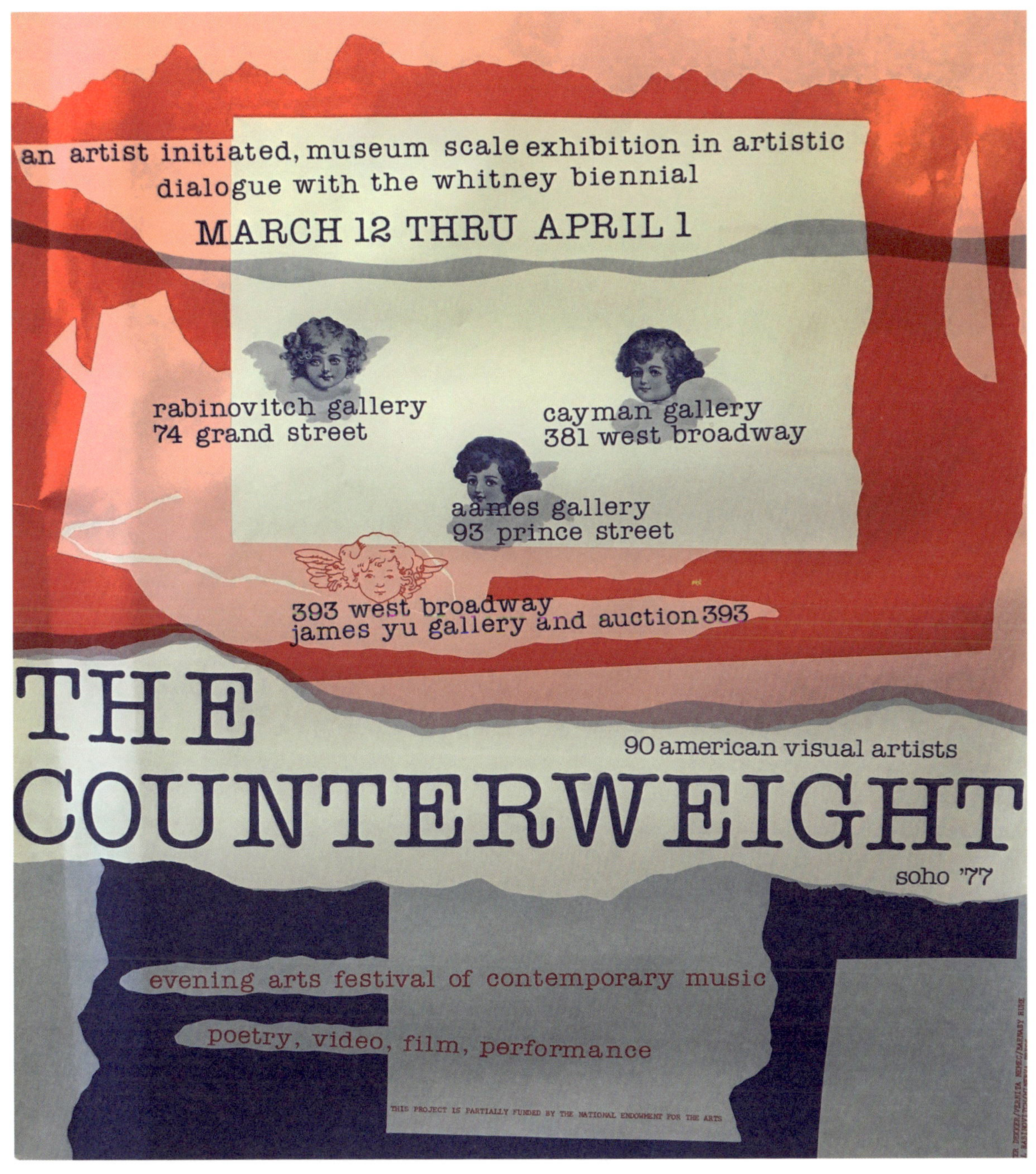

Poster by Peter Dekker, Vernita Nemec, Barnaby Ruhe, and Bill Rabinovitch for the *Counterweight*, 1977. Private collection

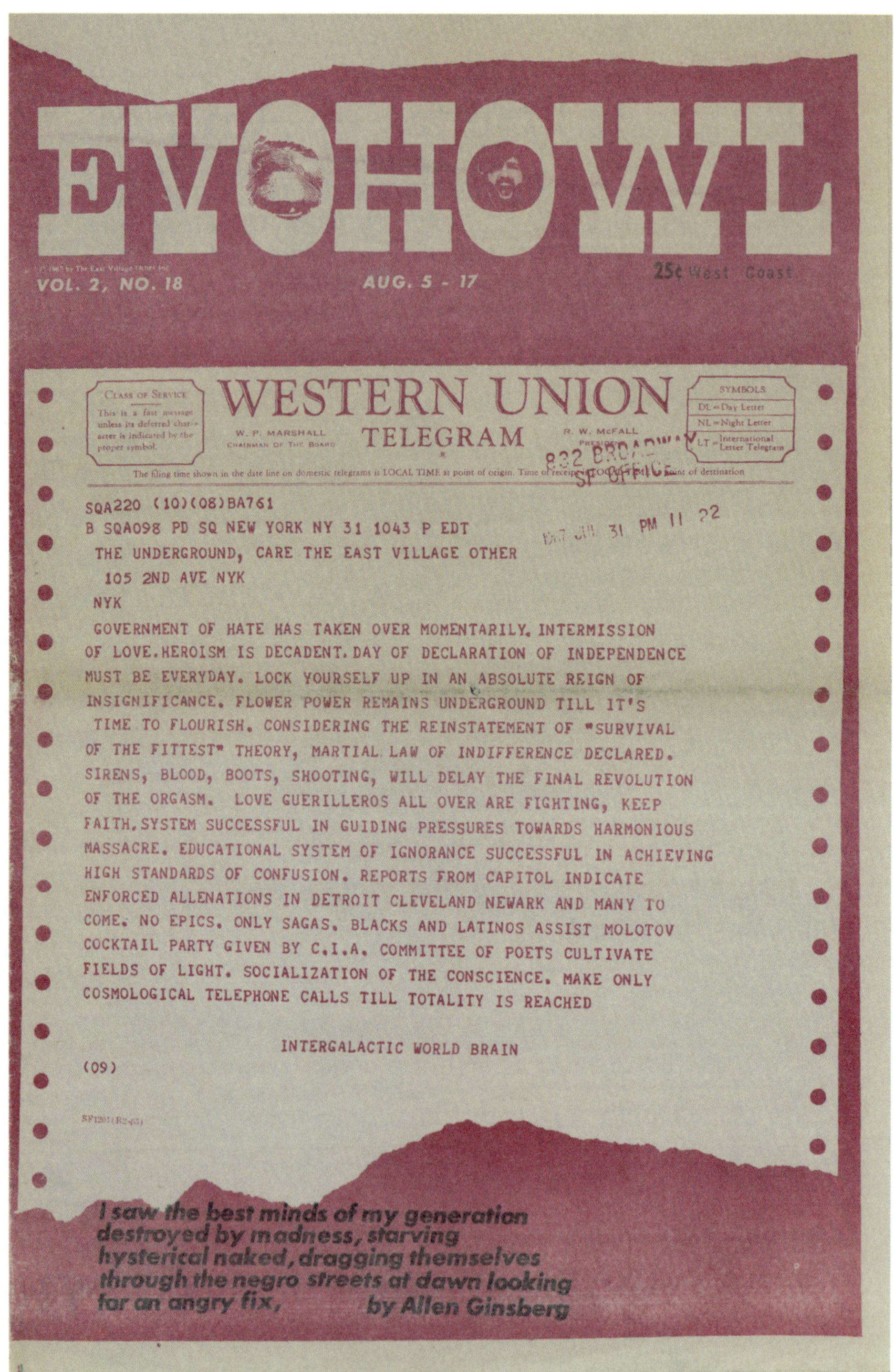
EVOHOWL

VOL. 2, NO. 18 AUG. 5 - 17 25¢ West Coast

WESTERN UNION TELEGRAM

W. P. MARSHALL CHAIRMAN OF THE BOARD

R. W. McFALL PRESIDENT

CLASS OF SERVICE: This is a fast message unless its deferred character is indicated by the proper symbol.

SYMBOLS: DL = Day Letter; NL = Night Letter; LT = International Letter Telegram

The filing time shown in the date line on domestic telegrams is LOCAL TIME at point of origin. Time of receipt is LOCAL TIME at point of destination

832 BROADWAY SF OFFICE

SQA220 (10)(08)BA761

B SQA098 PD SQ NEW YORK NY 31 1043 P EDT

THE UNDERGROUND, CARE THE EAST VILLAGE OTHER

105 2ND AVE NYK

NYK

GOVERNMENT OF HATE HAS TAKEN OVER MOMENTARILY. INTERMISSION OF LOVE. HEROISM IS DECADENT. DAY OF DECLARATION OF INDEPENDENCE MUST BE EVERYDAY. LOCK YOURSELF UP IN AN ABSOLUTE REIGN OF INSIGNIFICANCE. FLOWER POWER REMAINS UNDERGROUND TILL IT'S TIME TO FLOURISH. CONSIDERING THE REINSTATEMENT OF "SURVIVAL OF THE FITTEST" THEORY, MARTIAL LAW OF INDIFFERENCE DECLARED. SIRENS, BLOOD, BOOTS, SHOOTING, WILL DELAY THE FINAL REVOLUTION OF THE ORGASM. LOVE GUERILLEROS ALL OVER ARE FIGHTING, KEEP FAITH. SYSTEM SUCCESSFUL IN GUIDING PRESSURES TOWARDS HARMONIOUS MASSACRE. EDUCATIONAL SYSTEM OF IGNORANCE SUCCESSFUL IN ACHIEVING HIGH STANDARDS OF CONFUSION. REPORTS FROM CAPITOL INDICATE ENFORCED ALLENATIONS IN DETROIT CLEVELAND NEWARK AND MANY TO COME. NO EPICS. ONLY SAGAS. BLACKS AND LATINOS ASSIST MOLOTOV COCKTAIL PARTY GIVEN BY C.I.A. COMMITTEE OF POETS CULTIVATE FIELDS OF LIGHT. SOCIALIZATION OF THE CONSCIENCE. MAKE ONLY COSMOLOGICAL TELEPHONE CALLS TILL TOTALITY IS REACHED

INTERGALACTIC WORLD BRAIN

(09)

I saw the best minds of my generation destroyed by madness, starving hysterical naked, dragging themselves through the negro streets at dawn looking for an angry fix, by Allen Ginsberg

Foundation for the Totality, "Manifest," *East Village Other* 2, no. 18 (August 5–17, 1967).
Archives and Special Collections at the Thomas J. Dodd Research Center, University of Connecticut

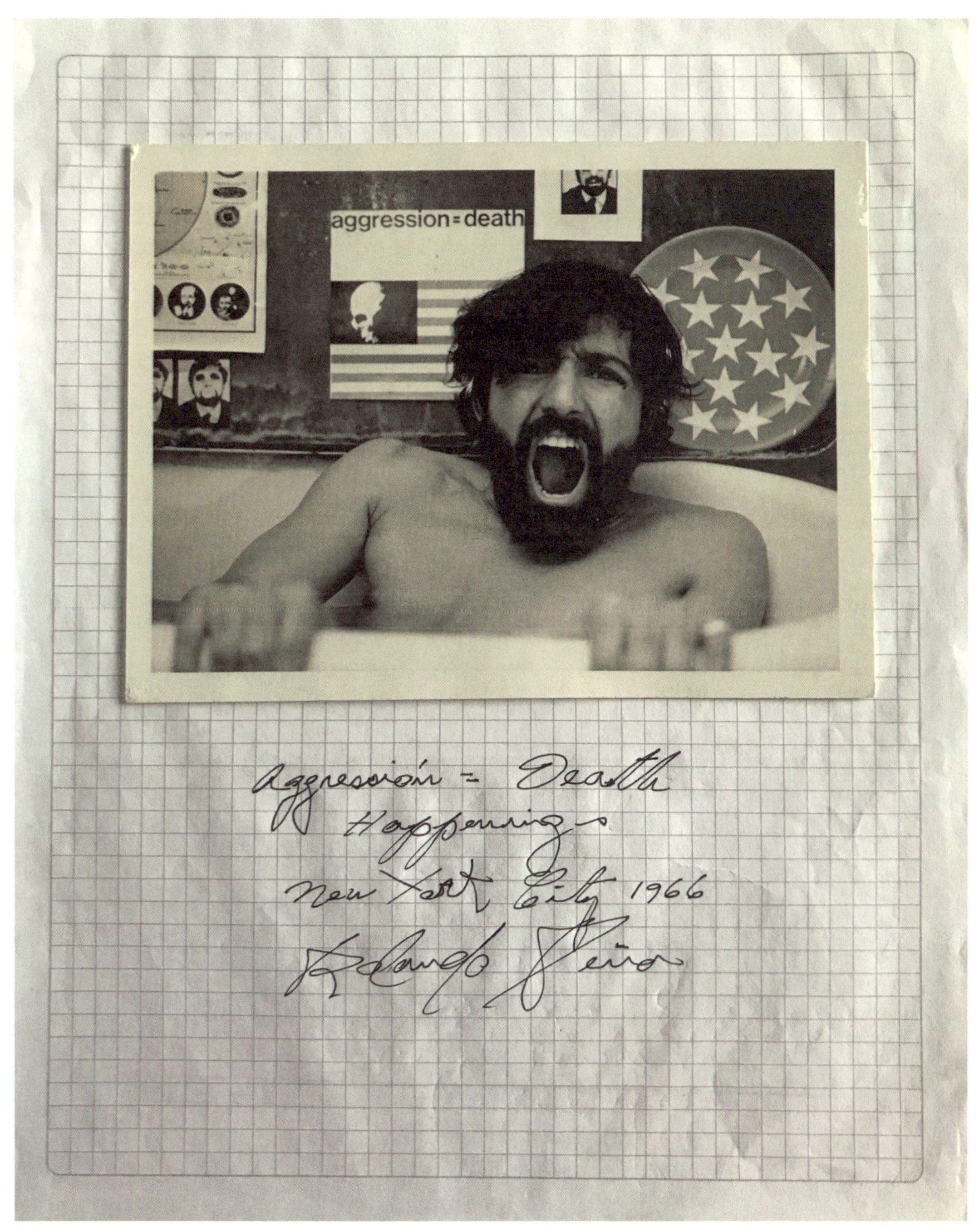

Rolando Peña (Foundation for the Totality), *Aggression = Death*, 1966.
Rolando Peña Studio

Foundation for the Totality was a group that I founded and led in NYC in 1966. Juan Downey, Manuel V (Manuel Vicente Peña), Jaime Barrios, Waldo Díaz Balart, Carmen Beuchat, Alfonso Barrios (Palito), Ana Maria Fuenzalida, Vicky Larraín, José Rodríguez-Soltero accompanied me on this crusade. I had some wonderful collaborators, Gregory Battcock, Walter Bowart, Andy Warhol, Joseph Aliaga, Marisol Escobar, Chuck Federman, Aldo Vigliarolo, Isabel Morrison, Allen Ginsberg, Edie Sedgwick, Carla Rotolo, and many more. . . . We carried out and collaborated on many happenings, guerrilla theater, videos, movies and we organized many demonstrations against the Vietnam War. We baptized the group in a bathtub, and the godfather was Andy Warhol. For the event we read a MANIFESTO published on the cover of the *East Village Other*, NY, 1967.

— Rolando Peña

Rolando Peña (Foundation for the Totality), *Totality vs. Capitan USA*, 1967.
Rolando Peña Studio

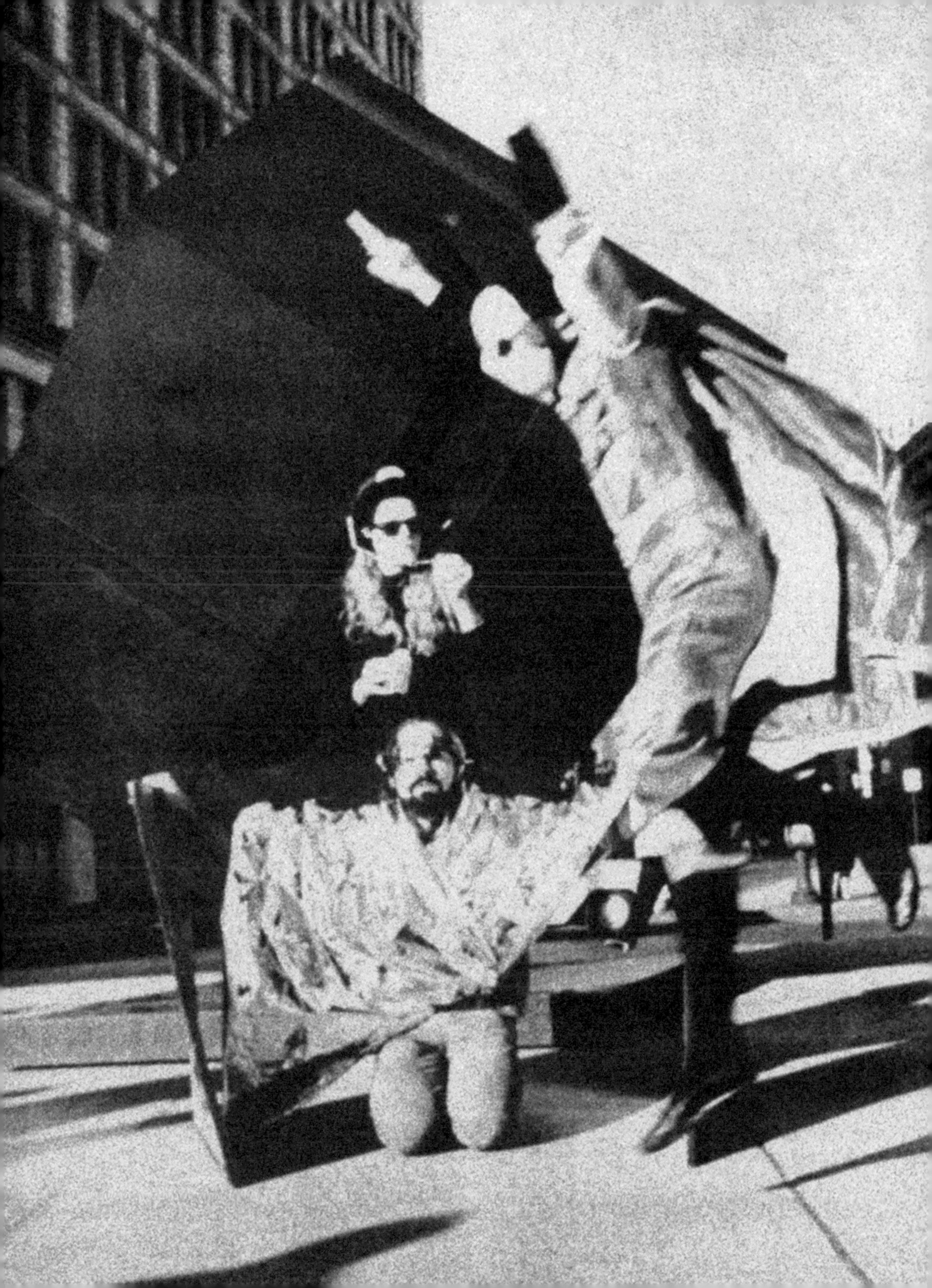

In the late 1960s, Carlos "Chino" Garcia, Humberto Crespo, Angelo Gonzalez, Jr., Roy Batiste, Moses Anthony Figueroa, and Sal Becker came together to form CHARAS, a group whose name is an acronym formed from the first letters of its founders' names. Their goal was to foster cultural activities such as concerts, plays, exhibitions, and after-school activities on Manhattan's Lower East Side. In 1970, inspired by a meeting with architect and urban theorist Buckminster Fuller, the group began building geodesic domes in the neighborhood, filling empty lots with the new structures through community building initiatives.

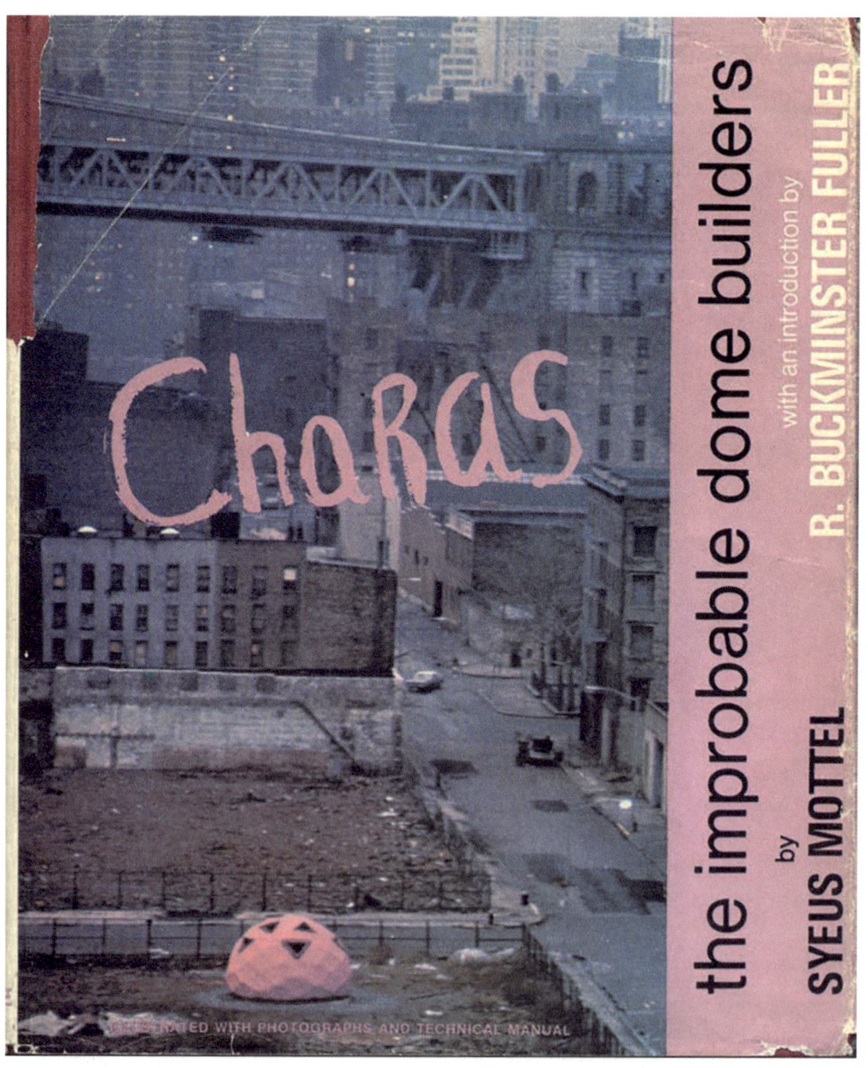

Cover of *CHARAS: The Improbable Dome Builders* by Syeus Mottel. New York: Drake Publishers, 1973. Courtesy of Matthew Mottel

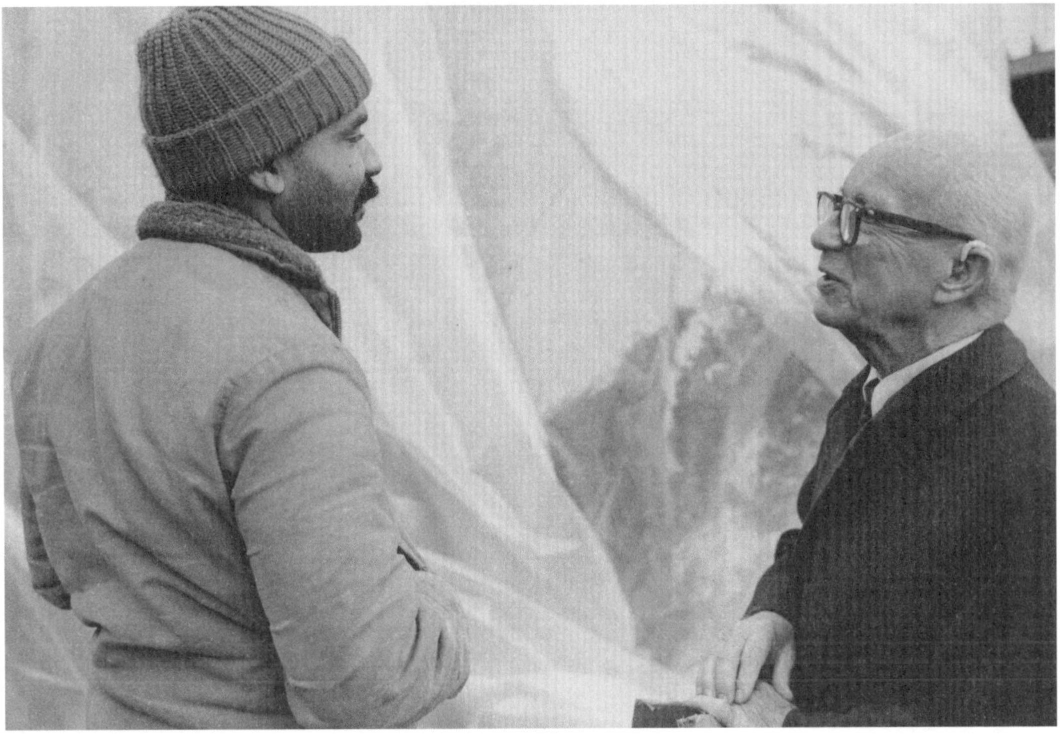

Syeus Mottel, Carlos “Chino” García and Buckminster Fuller next to the geodesic dome built by CHARAS on a vacant lot at Cherry Street and Jefferson Street, New York, 1972. Courtesy of Matthew Mottel

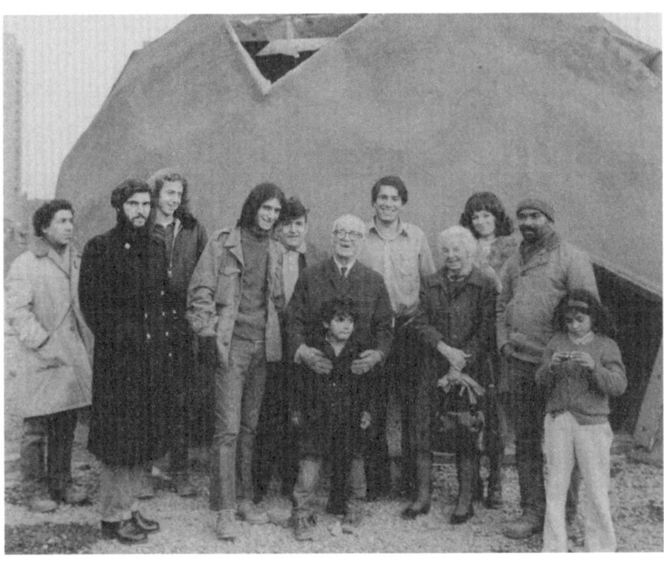

Syeus Mottel, members of CHARAS and community volunteers with Buckminster Fuller next to the geodesic dome at Cherry and Jefferson streets, New York, 1972. Courtesy of Matthew Mottel

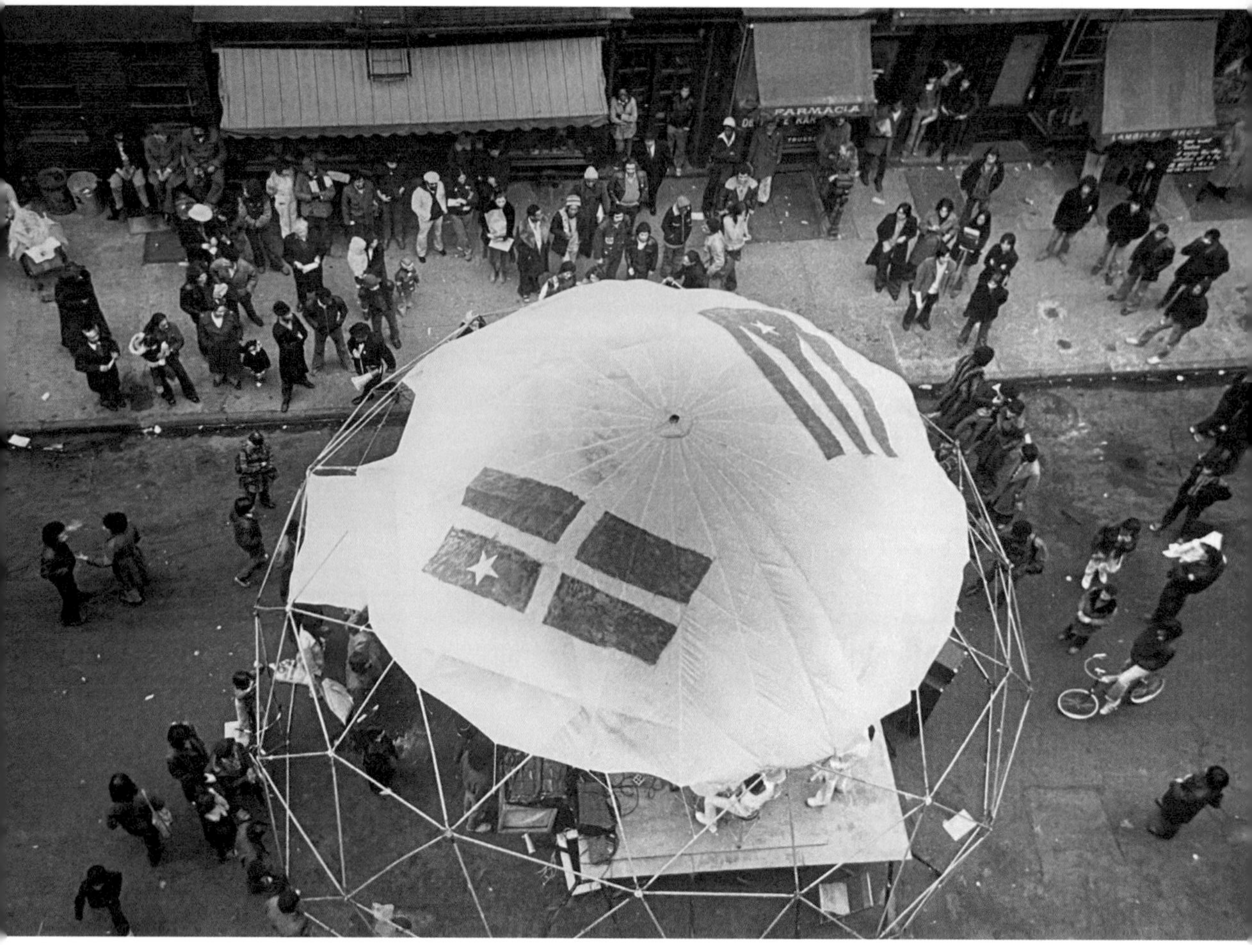

Máximo Rafael Colón, CHARAS dome on East 6th Street, New York, 1974.
Courtesy of the artist

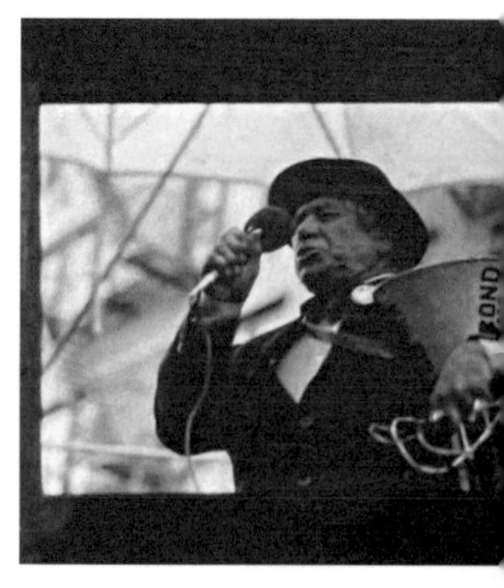

One of the things that we had, we used to have a traveling theater group, and we did street theater. Bimbo [Bittman John "Bimbo" Rivas] called it El Teatro Ambulante, the Ambulatory Theater it would be in English. Basically we did plays in different locations throughout the city, for political–most of all our plays had a political touch to it–in a lot of the festivals and that kind of stuff.

— Carlos "Chino" Garcia

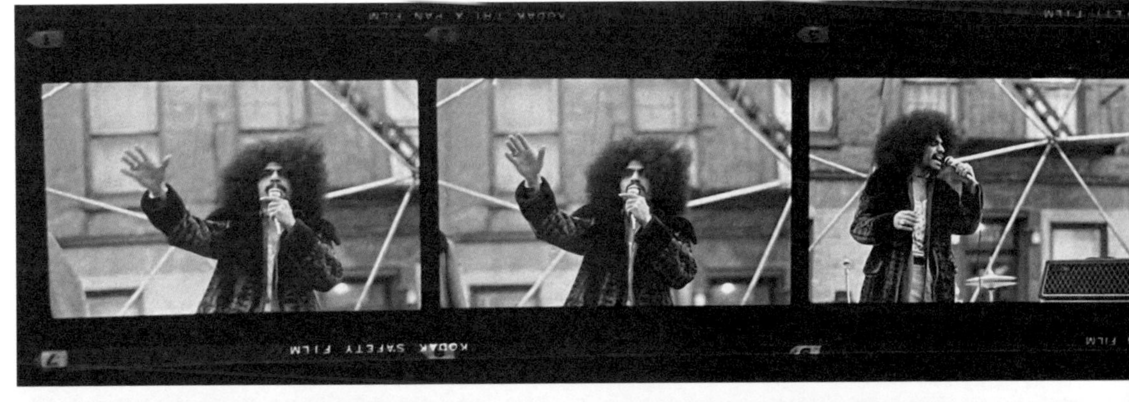

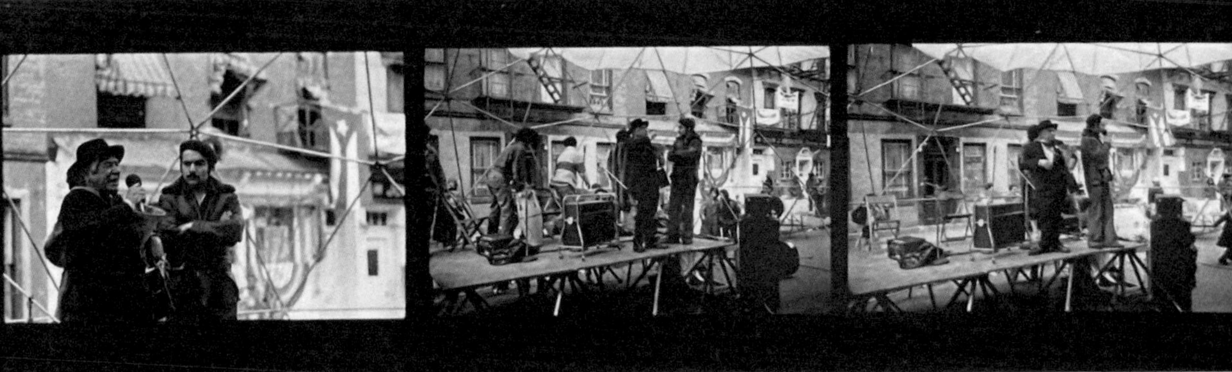

Máximo Rafael Colón, poet Bimbo Rivas, activists, and musicians at the CHARAS dome on East 6th Street, New York, 1975. Courtesy of the artist

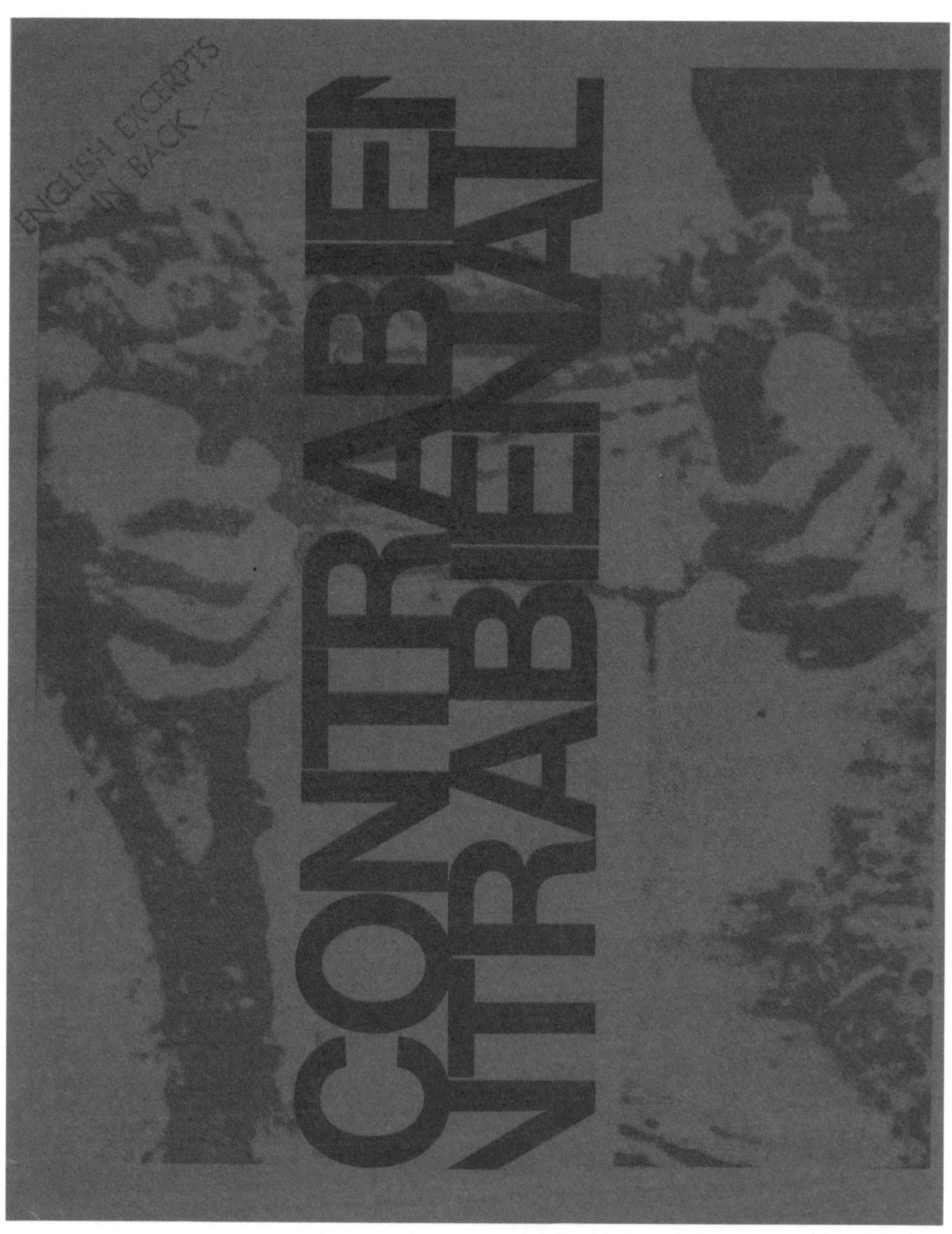

Museo Latinoamericano and Movimiento de Independencia Cultural Latinoamericana, cover (above) and interior pages (opposite) of *Contrabienal*, 1971. Institute for Studies on Latin American Art (ISLAA) Library and Archives

Produced and distributed in 1971, the artists' book *Contrabienal* promoted an international call to boycott the XI São Paulo Biennial in protest of censorship and violence under the Brazilian military dictatorship. The publication, organized by Museo Latinoamericano and Movimiento de Independencia Cultural Latinoamericana (see 160), was originally created to express opposition to the cultural politics of the Center for Inter-American Relations. In addition to contributions from sixty-one artists and letters of support from artists across the Americas and Europe, it included a report denouncing the torture methods of the Brazilian dictatorship and submissions from Latin American artists and collectives from all over the world. *Contrabienal* represented a key moment of intersection between Conceptualism and the nascent identity politics emerging in New York's Latin American community.

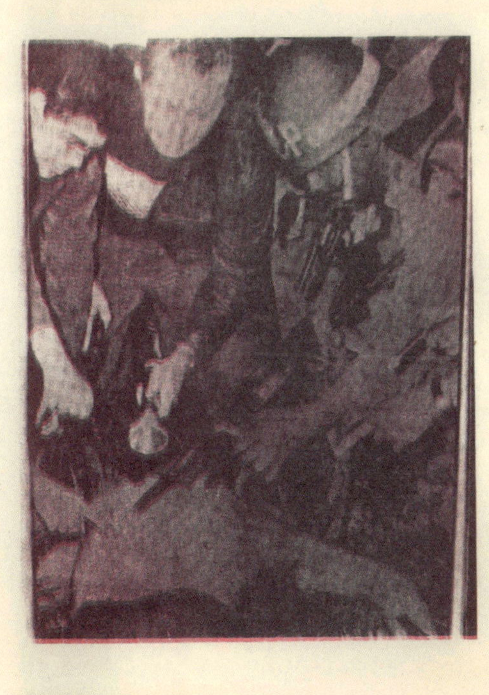

Ficha técnica:
El Pau de Arara es el instrumento más usado en el curso de las torturas. Se distingue por su simplicidad de empleo: Una barra que reposa sobre dos soportes elevados; sillas, mesas o cajones.
La barra puede ser de madera o de hierro, vigueta o caño. Tiene dos o tres centímetros de diámetro para el buen funcionamiento del sistema, que se basa en la detención de la circulación de la sangre debido a la contracción muscular y nerviosa.
El prisionero, desnudo, es atado de las muñecas y los tobillos y es sentado en el suelo de forma que abrace sus rodillas; la barra entonces es deslizada entre las rodillas y los antebrazos y es elevada sobre los soportes.
Todo el peso de la víctima queda entonces soportado por las articulaciones de las rodillas y los antebrazos; los efectos se comienzan a sentir luego de unos treinta minutos, los pies y las manos enrojecen, se vuelven insensibles después de un estado de hormigueo; la hinchazón progresa y la víctima tiene la sensación que sus dedos van a estallar; el dolor aumenta cuando el prisionero es hamacado de atrás para adelante.

The members of Museo Latinoamericano, visual artists living in New York, consider that, even though the dissemination of the work is one of the main functions of an artist, it is necessary to have the option of rejecting some Biennials and official exhibitions, which, in our opinion, do not conform to our social and ethical principles.

We regard the São Paulo Biennial, due to the characteristics it has shown in the past, and because it is located in a country where there is a disgraceful regime of repression, torture and humiliation of its citizens, as an example of a contest that we must censor energetically, not participating in it, and encouraging other artists to do the same.

The visual artists of the Museo Latinoamericano think that showing our work is the vital condition that inspires it. We advocate for communication, the dissemination of our knowledge and the awareness of our culture.

The position adopted broadens and gives more meaning to this rejection.

— Museo Latinoamericano (Latin American Museum)

MICLA (Movement for Latin American Cultural Independence) by undertaking the realization of this "Contrabienal," has no intention to substitute an exhibition for another, nor of changing ways of expression by substituting a show for a publication. We are using a publication to try and sketch the outlines of one possibility of action against cultural imperialism.

We don't constitute a social class, but it is up to us to make the choice within which social class we militate: the exploiter's or the exploited's . . .

The São Paulo Biennial is an excuse for our publication . . . The vehicle we use is only one of many to learn of other groups and/or individuals that wish to unite, because of a common consciousness, and to help discover and inform our realities. Brazil is just a "vanguard" of what could await all of us . . . Therefore, it's important to underline and denounce time and again these "cultural activities." They pretend, while colonizing our people, to project an image of well-being, and at the same time serve as a "decorative frosting" to the daily crimes of some of the bloodiest dictatorships . . .

This Counterbienal intends to open another breach, documenting the refusals to complicity, valuing moral positions above sale or conspiracy.

– MICLA (Movement for Latin American Cultural Independence)

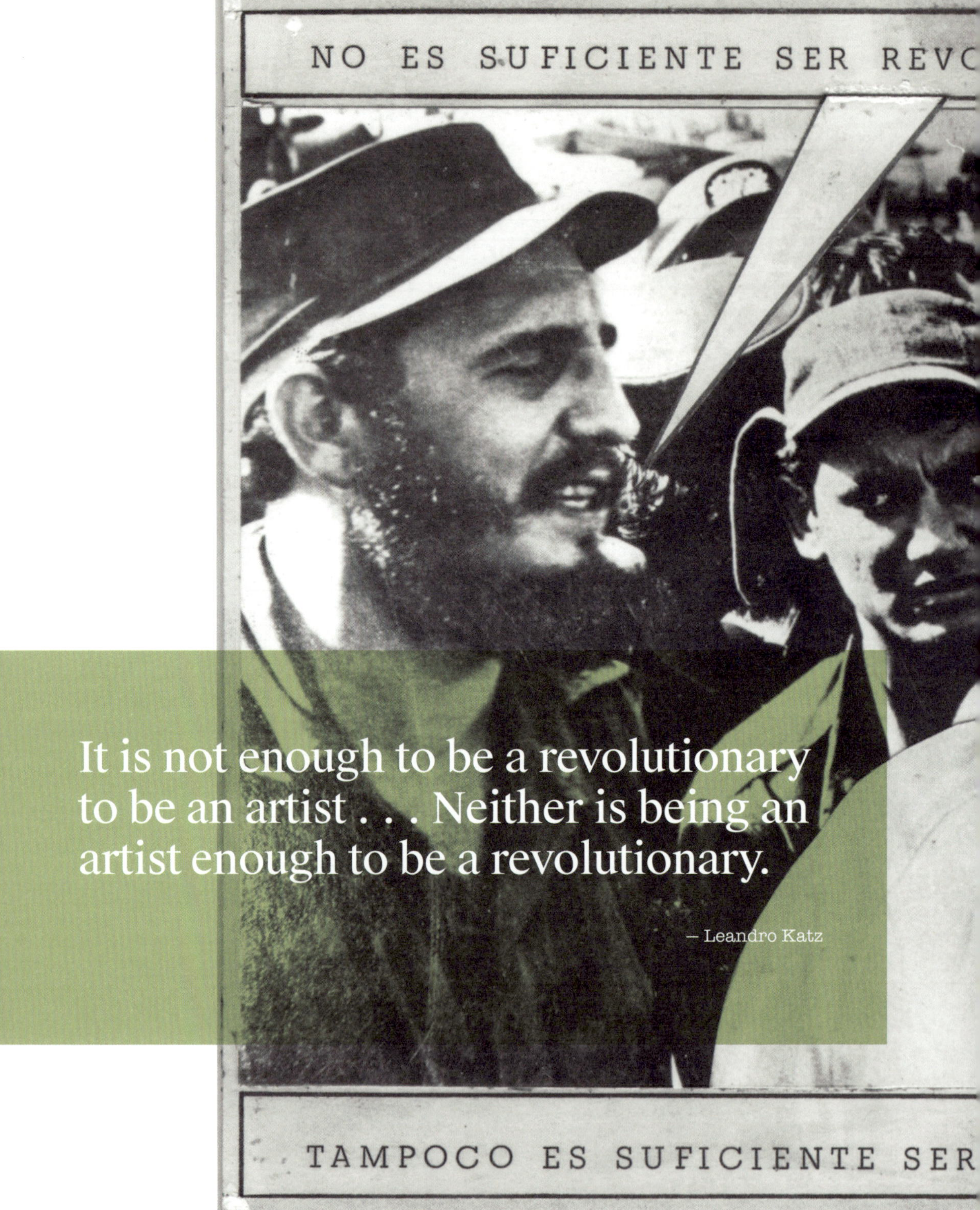

It is not enough to be a revolutionary to be an artist . . . Neither is being an artist enough to be a revolutionary.

— Leandro Katz

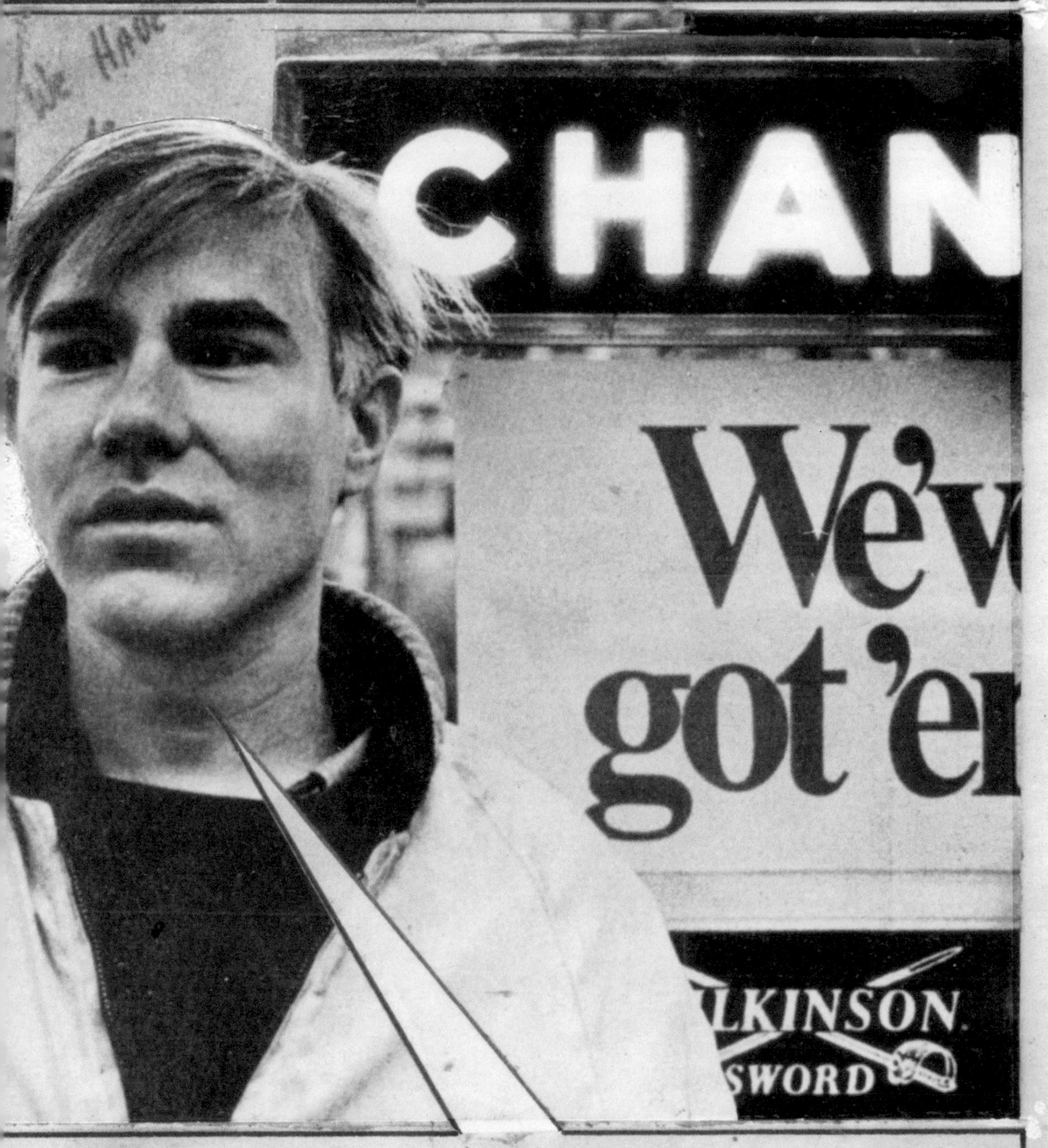

Leandro Katz, original collage for back cover illustration for *Negación y consumo en la cultura* (Negation and consumption in the cultural sphere) by Guy Debord. Translated by Leandro Katz (New York: The Vanishing Rotating Triangle), 1972. Leandro Katz Archive

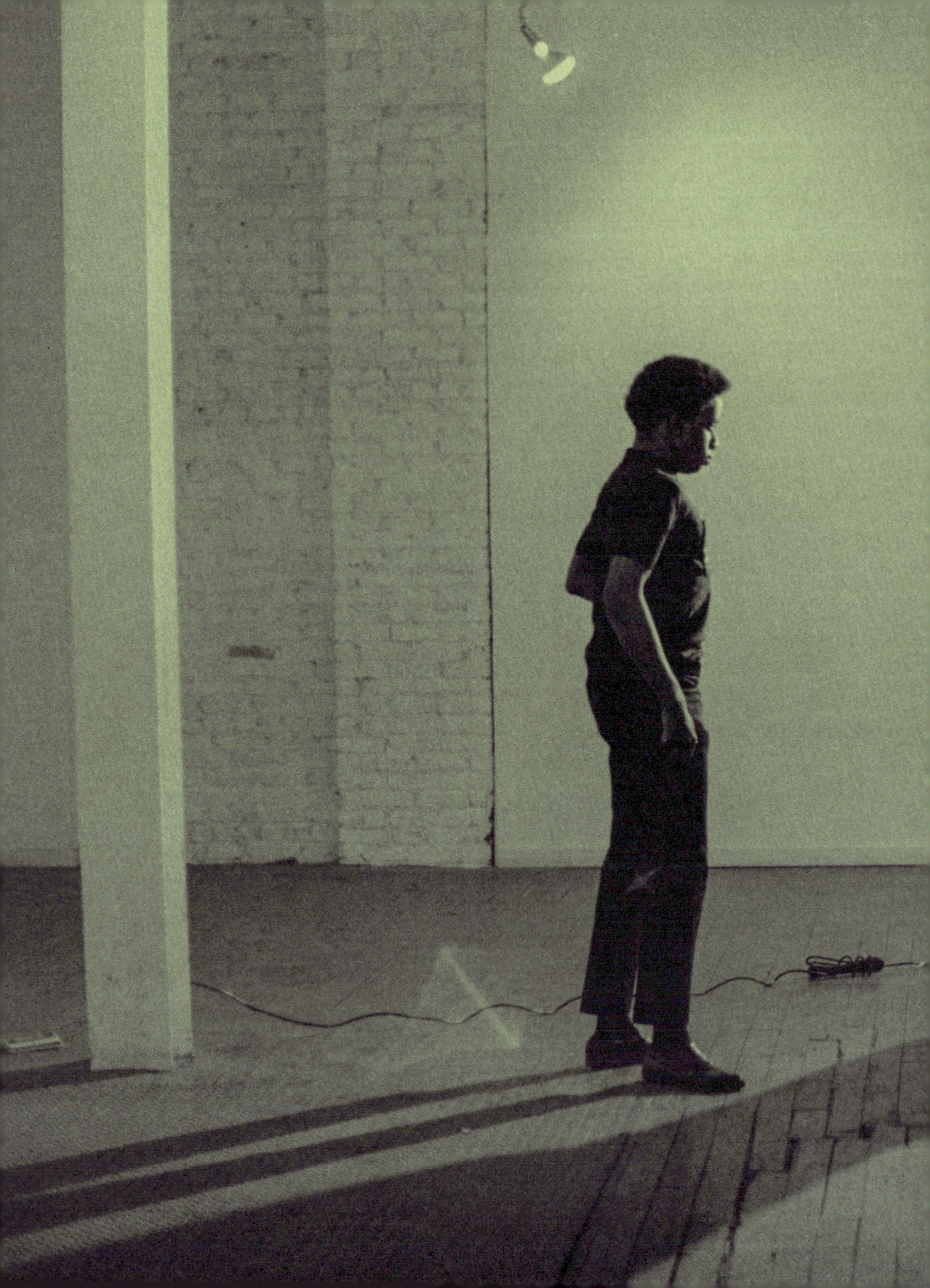

Identity and Representation

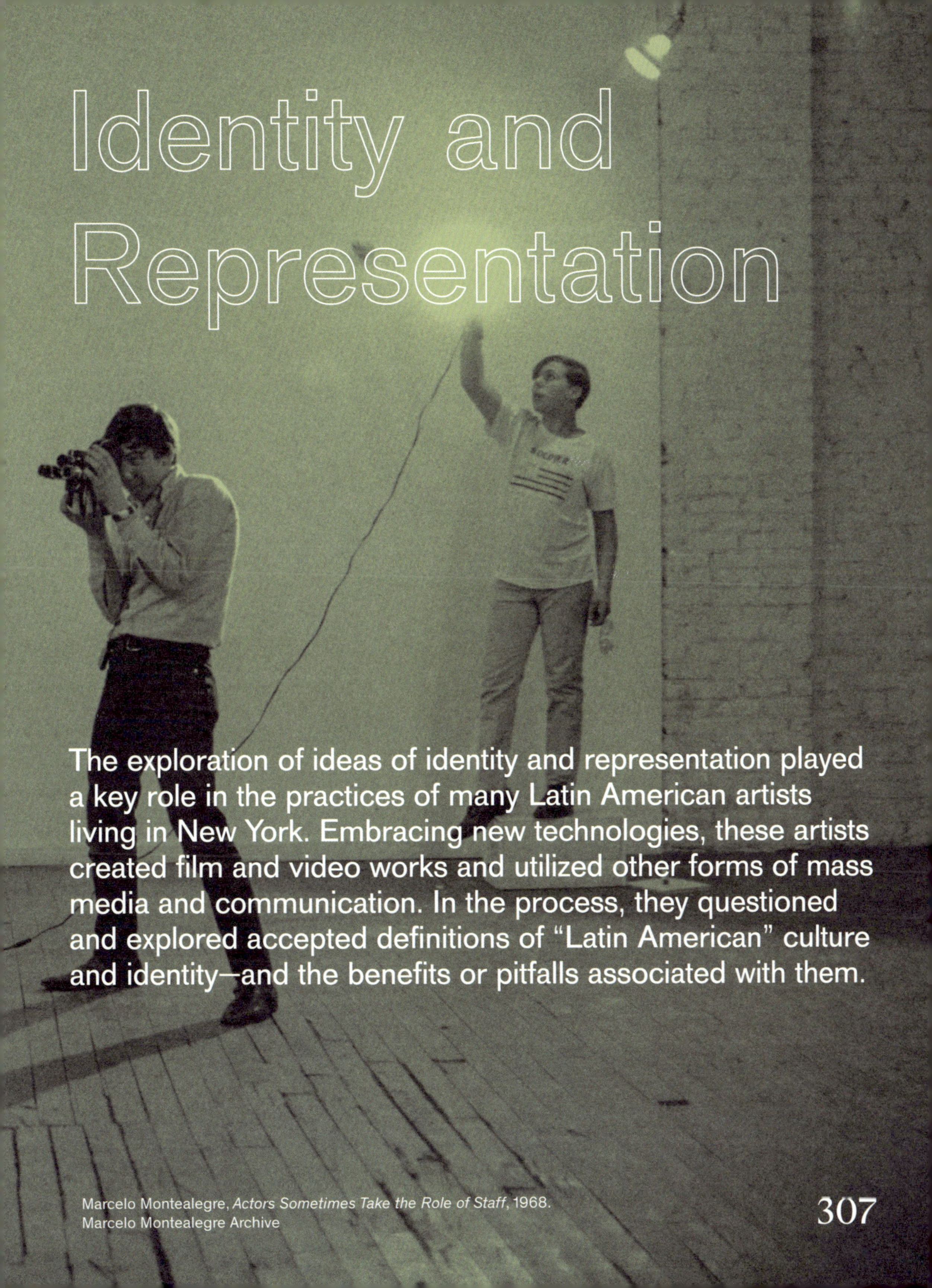

The exploration of ideas of identity and representation played a key role in the practices of many Latin American artists living in New York. Embracing new technologies, these artists created film and video works and utilized other forms of mass media and communication. In the process, they questioned and explored accepted definitions of "Latin American" culture and identity—and the benefits or pitfalls associated with them.

Marcelo Montealegre, *Actors Sometimes Take the Role of Staff*, 1968. Marcelo Montealegre Archive

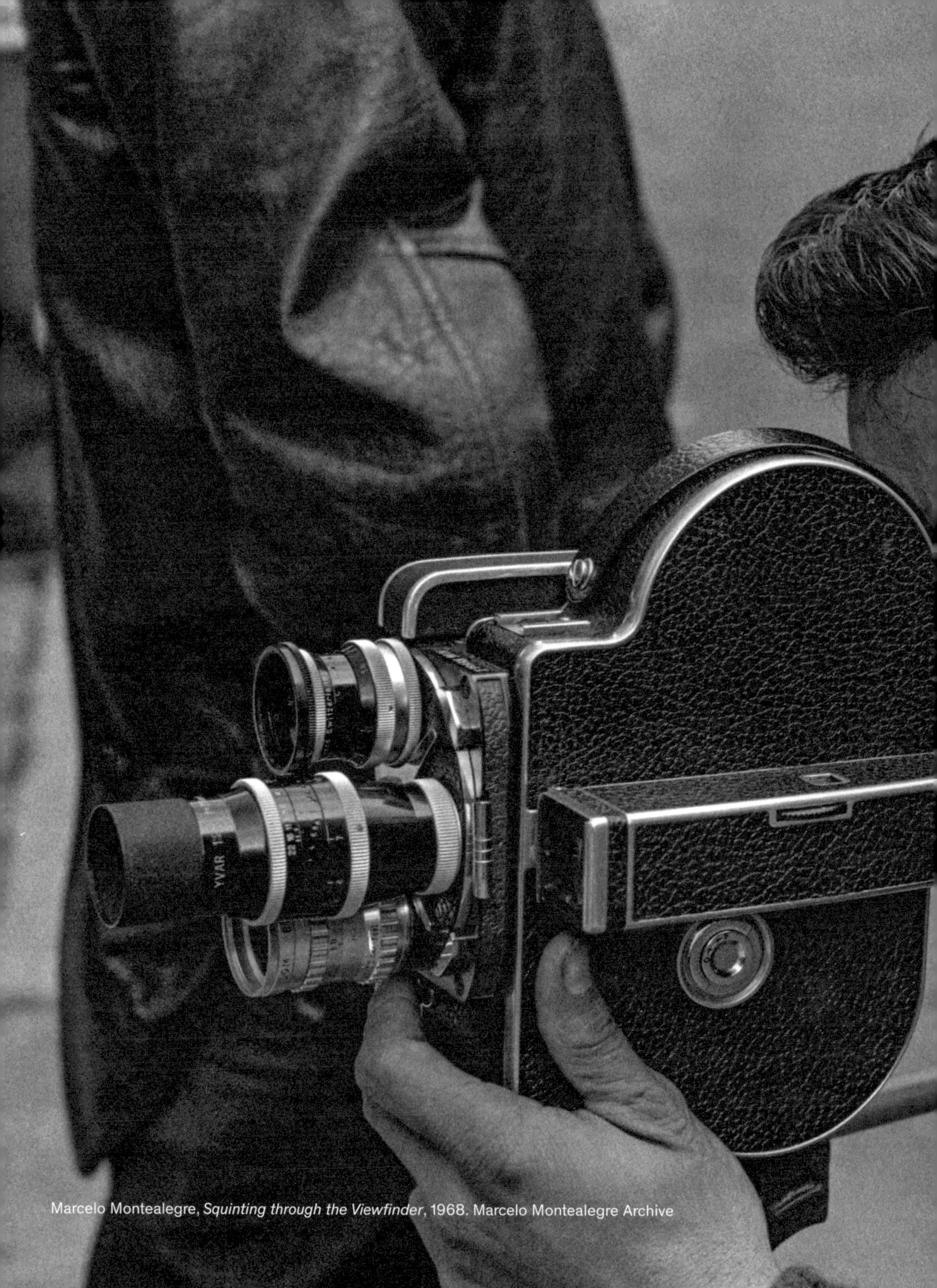

Marcelo Montealegre, *Squinting through the Viewfinder*, 1968. Marcelo Montealegre Archive

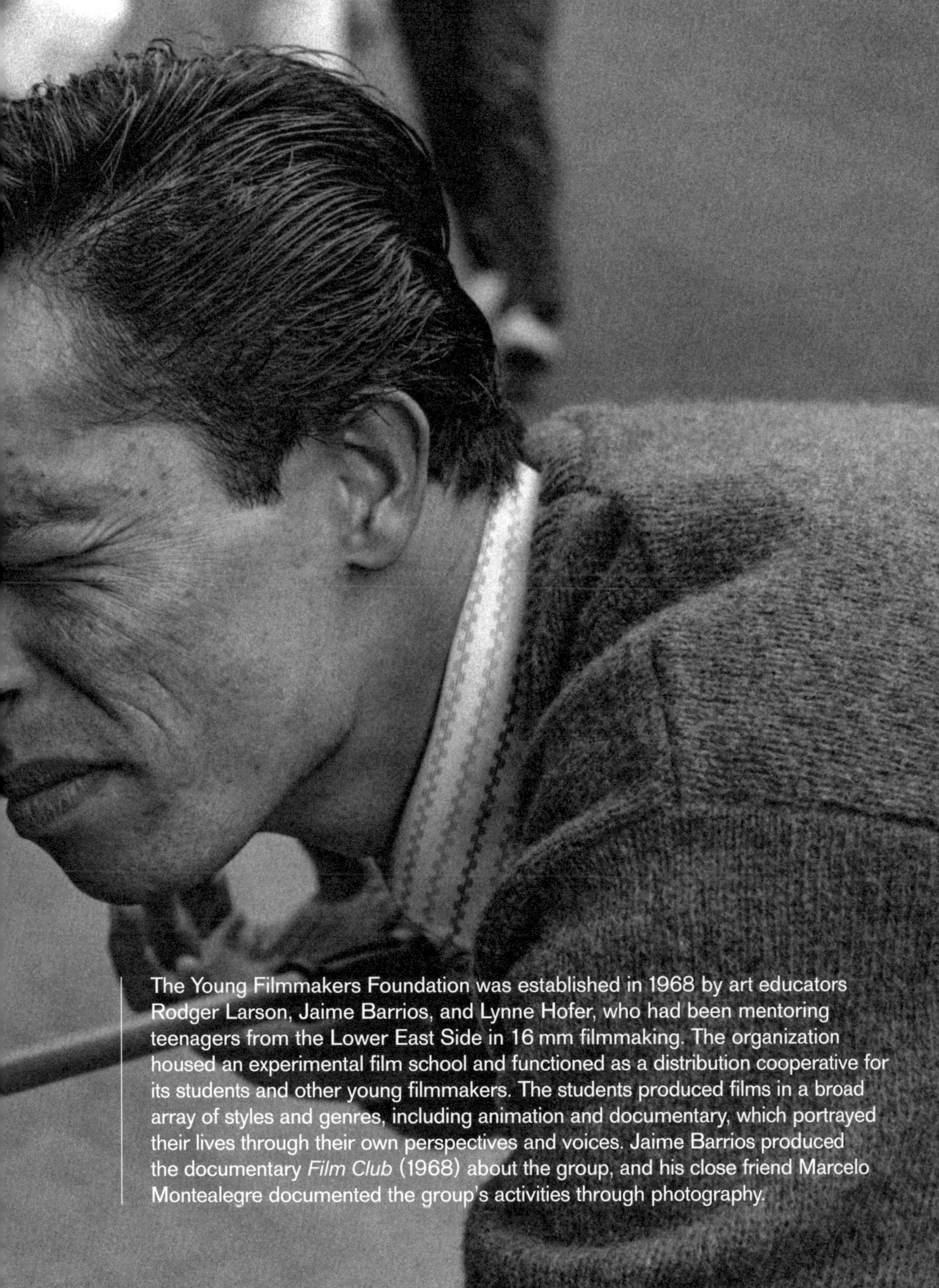

The Young Filmmakers Foundation was established in 1968 by art educators Rodger Larson, Jaime Barrios, and Lynne Hofer, who had been mentoring teenagers from the Lower East Side in 16 mm filmmaking. The organization housed an experimental film school and functioned as a distribution cooperative for its students and other young filmmakers. The students produced films in a broad array of styles and genres, including animation and documentary, which portrayed their lives through their own perspectives and voices. Jaime Barrios produced the documentary *Film Club* (1968) about the group, and his close friend Marcelo Montealegre documented the group's activities through photography.

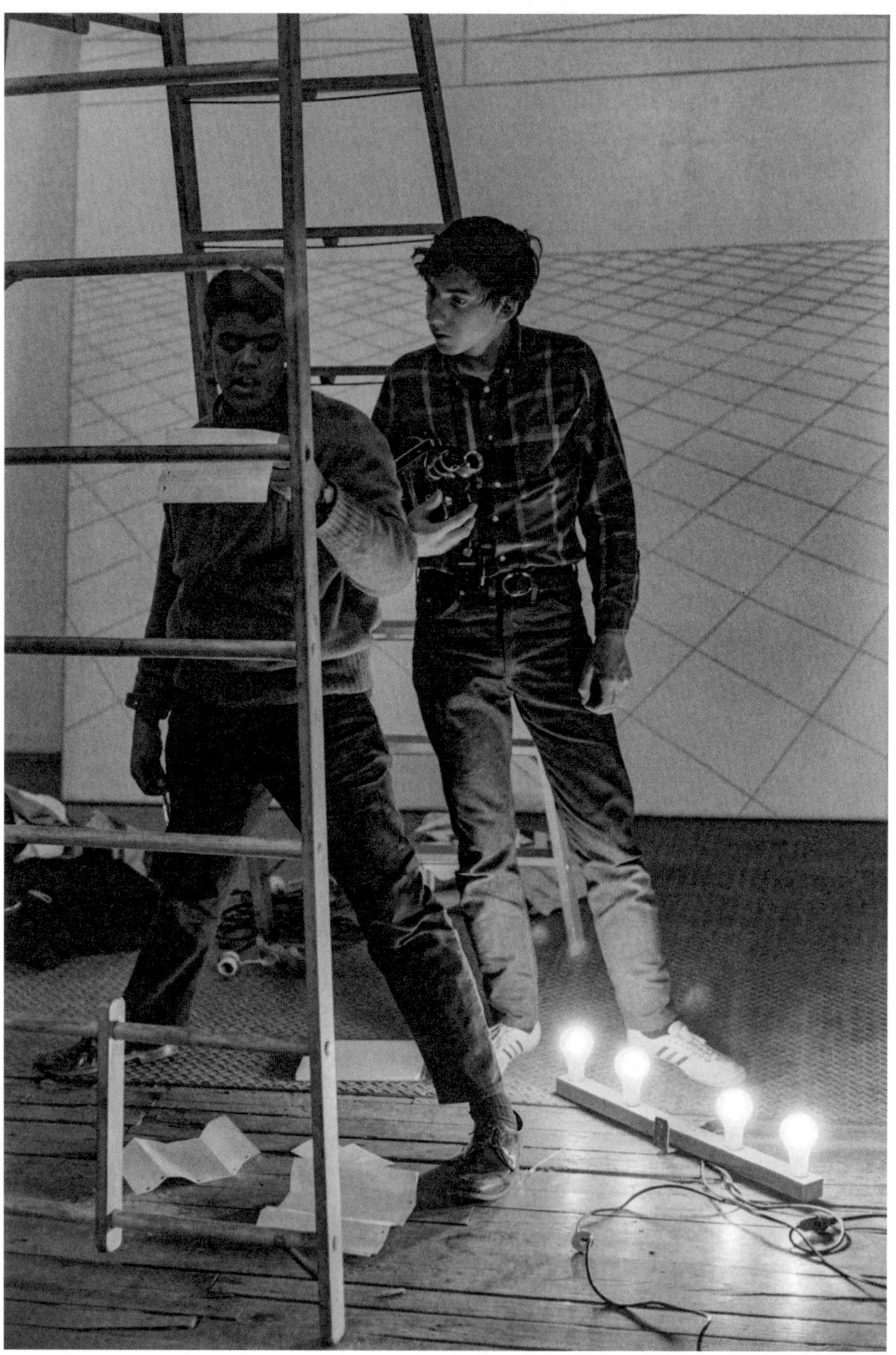

Marcelo Montealegre, *Consulting the Script* (above) and *Picking a Scene to Include in the Film* (opposite), 1969. Marcelo Montealegre Archive

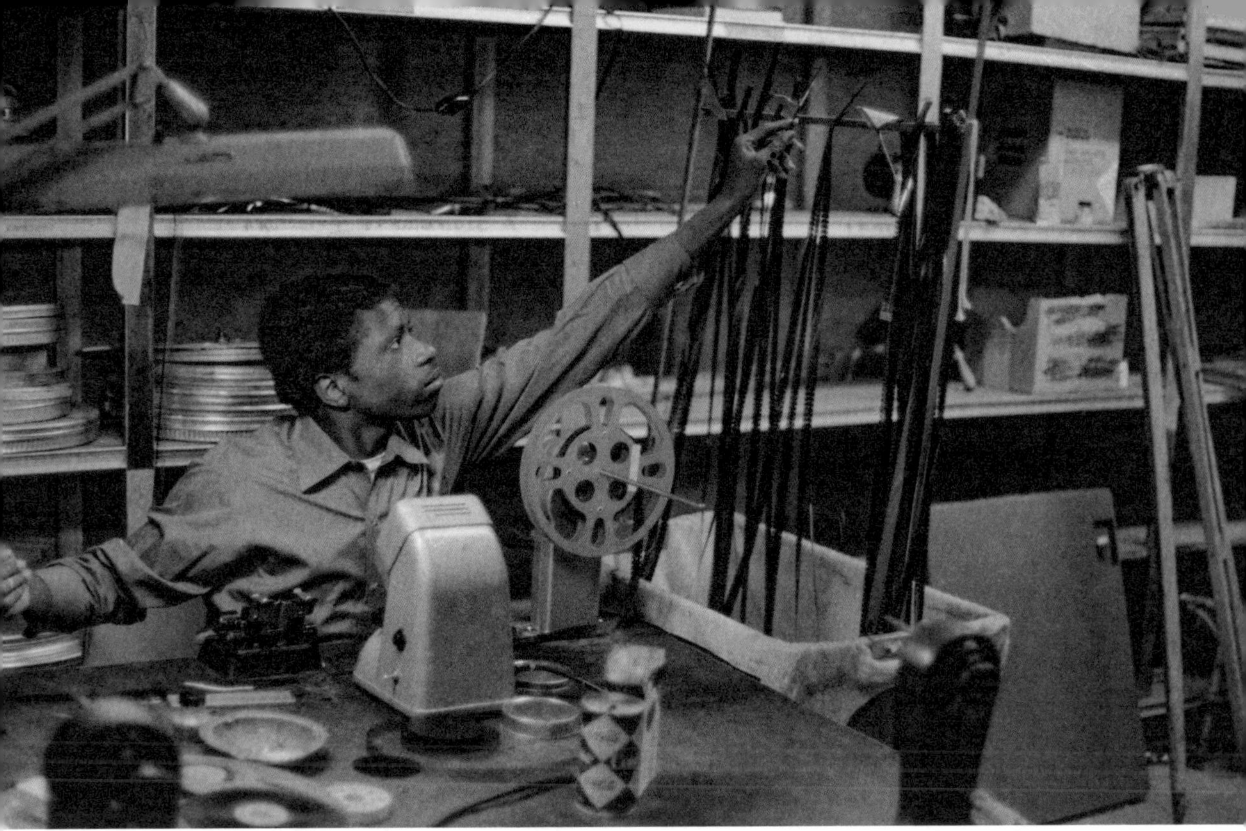

Jaime [Barrios] had come to New York with the intention of studying film at the School of Visual Arts, but dropped out because he thought the program was too conventional. That summer he was working at the Film Club, part of the Young Filmmakers Foundation that he had founded with Rodger Larson in 1968. The idea was based on Larson's theory of the importance of films as a way of self-expression for teenagers. In practice, it was a matter of letting interested children and teenagers create their own films with instructions and equipment that the Film Club provided. The Film Club was in the Bowery area of Lower Manhattan, a neighborhood known as one of New York's "ghettos." They kept their door open all the time, with the intention that the youth of the neighborhood would come to ask. When they were told that it was a club where they could make movies their interest grew, and even more so when they found out that to shoot their own movie they just had to say so.

– Marcelo Montealegre

Rally Demonstration
Wednesday June 27, 11<u>00</u> AM

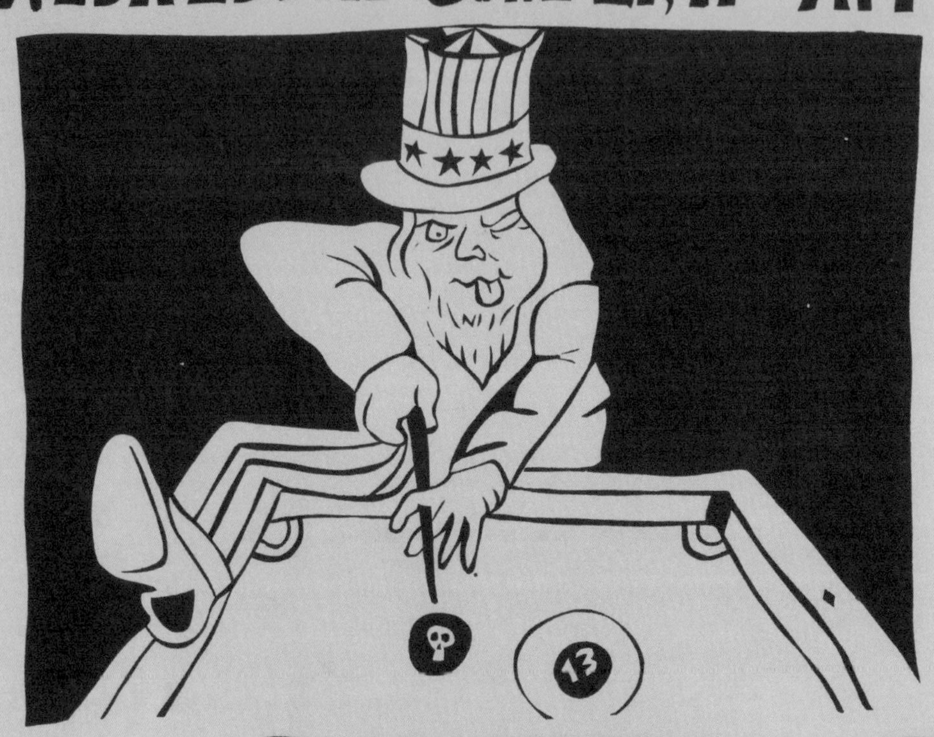

SUPPORT FOR
REALIDADES → WNET (13)

First and Only Bilingual, Puerto Rican + Latino Television Program Series on Major Station, 304 W 58 ST, Between 8TH and 9TH Ave.

BE THERE! HELP BRING BACK REALIDADES

Realidades and the activism around didn't come out of thin air. The Puerto Rican community was in an uproar, with the Young Lords, the Garbage Offensive, [the occupation of] the church in the Upper West Side . . . Wherever there was a pocket of Puerto Ricans in this city, in New Jersey or Connecticut, Puerto Ricans were organizing, saying "basta ya," enough. This activism comes in the middle of this fight for Puerto Ricans naming themselves and redefining who we were and demanding the powers to be an equitable program. It wasn't easy . . . the organizing that it took to mobilize the Puerto Rican community. I don't use the word "Latino" because it wasn't the Latin American community . . . I was in El Comité, a community-based socialist organization. I was also part of Taller Boricua, I am an artist. I used to do sculpture classes in the streets of East Harlem for the kids, wonderful work.

— Esperanza Martel

Realidades was the first bilingual (English and Spanish) TV series in the United States. Broadcast on WNET's Channel 13 from 1971 until 1977 in twenty-week series of half-hour programs, the show included entertainment and educational and cultural content focused on civil and social rights relevant to Nuyoricans, Chicanos, and other Latino communities in the United States.

Martín "Tito" Pérez, Poster for Rally Demonstration: Support for *Realidades* – WNET 13, 1971. Collection of El Museo del Barrio, New York. Courtesy of El Museo del Barrio

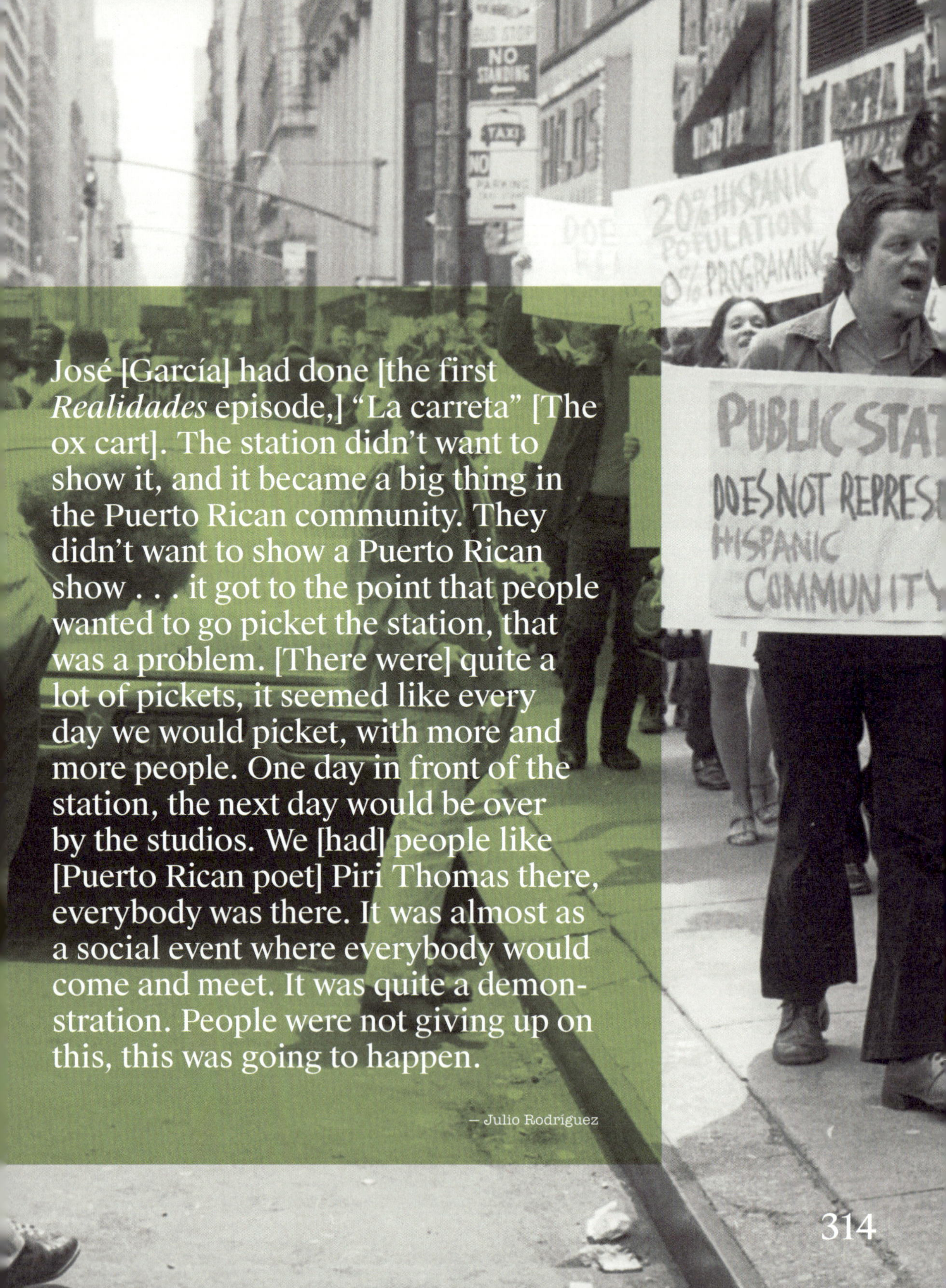

José [García] had done [the first *Realidades* episode,] "La carreta" [The ox cart]. The station didn't want to show it, and it became a big thing in the Puerto Rican community. They didn't want to show a Puerto Rican show . . . it got to the point that people wanted to go picket the station, that was a problem. [There were] quite a lot of pickets, it seemed like every day we would picket, with more and more people. One day in front of the station, the next day would be over by the studios. We [had] people like [Puerto Rican poet] Piri Thomas there, everybody was there. It was almost as a social event where everybody would come and meet. It was quite a demonstration. People were not giving up on this, this was going to happen.

— Julio Rodriguez

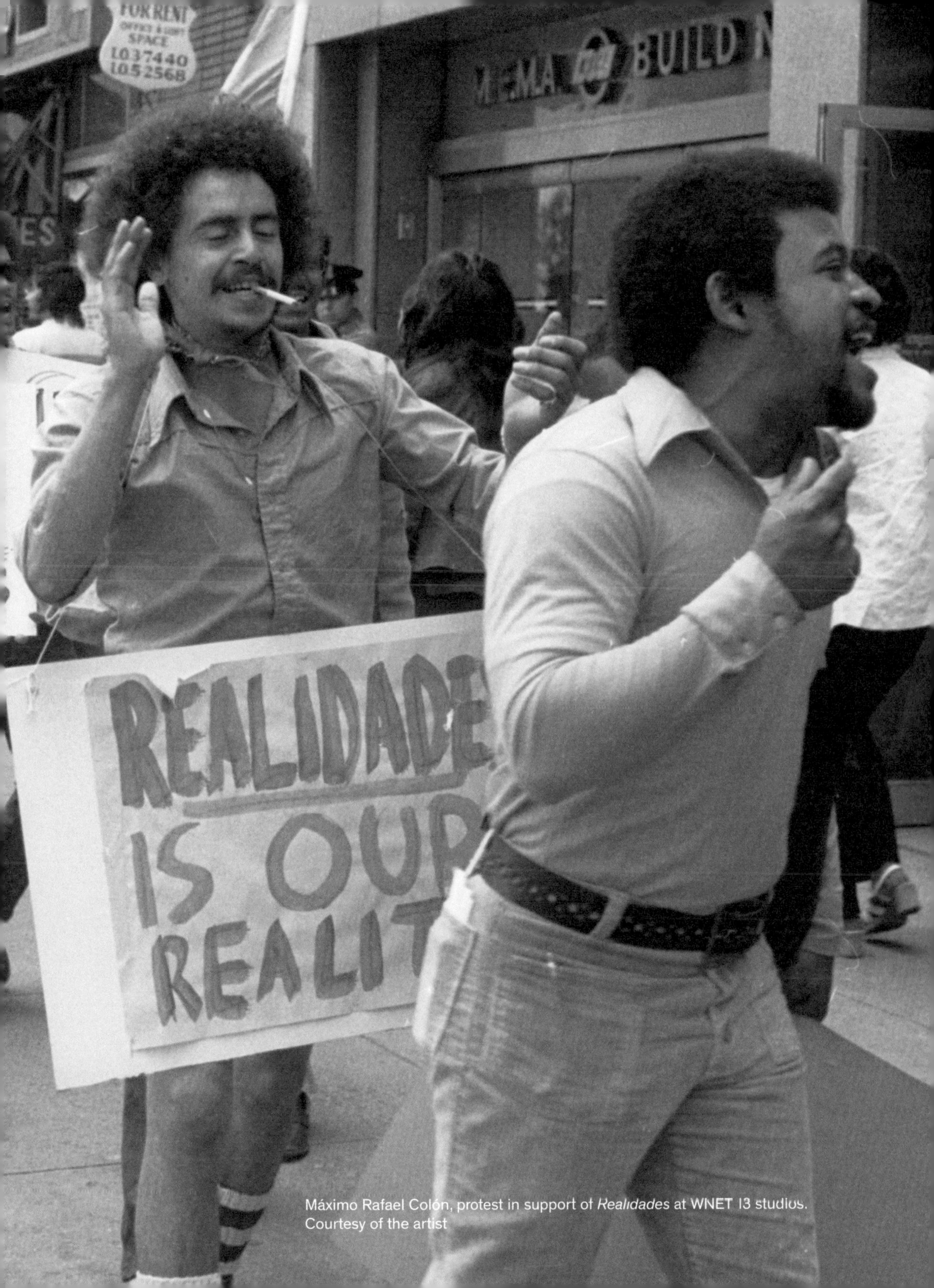

Máximo Rafael Colón, protest in support of *Realidades* at WNET 13 studios. Courtesy of the artist

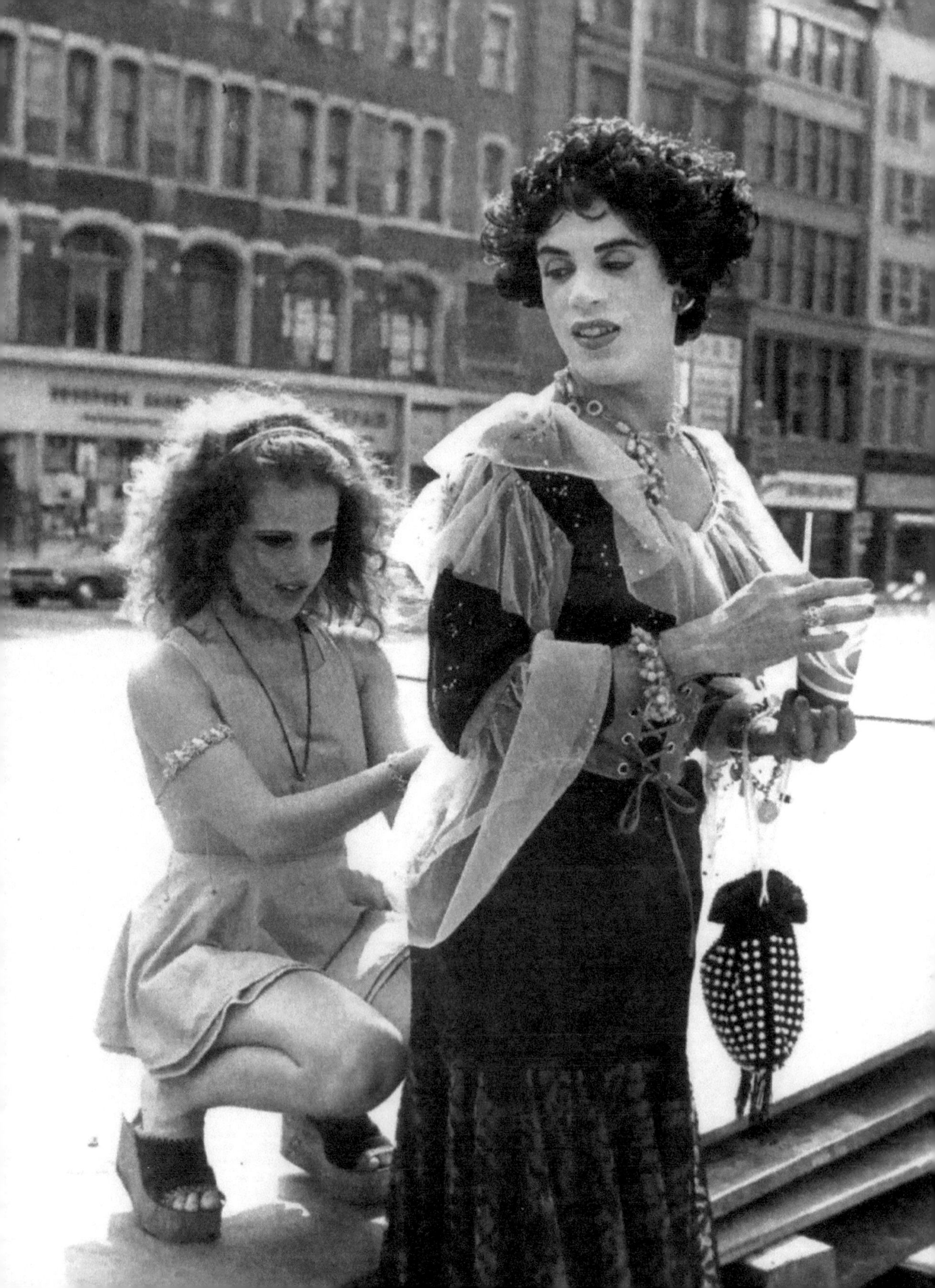

Mario Montez (born René Rivera) was a Puerto Rican actor and drag performer who collaborated with many artists from the New York experimental scene in the 1960s and 1970s, including José Rodríguez-Soltero, Jack Smith, Hélio Oiticica, Leandro Katz, and Andy Warhol. Montez adopted his name as a camp version of and homage to Maria Montez, a 1940s cinema actress from the Dominican Republic. A key figure in the city's underground scene, Montez was featured in Hélio Oiticica's 1972 film *Agrippina é Roma-Manhattan* (Agrippina Is Rome-Manhattan), which tells the story of Agrippina, a reference to the Ancient Roman aristocrat-widow, and her pimp, amid the neoclassical buildings of Lower Manhattan.

Mario Montez in a production still from Hélio Oiticica's *Agrippina Is Rome-Manhattan*, 1972.
Projeto Hélio Oiticica

Probably [my most successful work is] *Lupe* by José Rodríguez-Soltero. He was one of the best directors I've had. I worked very hard. At times I felt like I was in Hollywood because I had so many things to do—four location shots—walking in the street in costume; I was scared about that, but it had to be done, and since I was wearing the red wig, I looked like his sister.

— Mario Montez

José Rodríguez-Soltero, stills from *Lupe*, 1966.
The Film-Makers' Cooperative/The New American Cinema Group

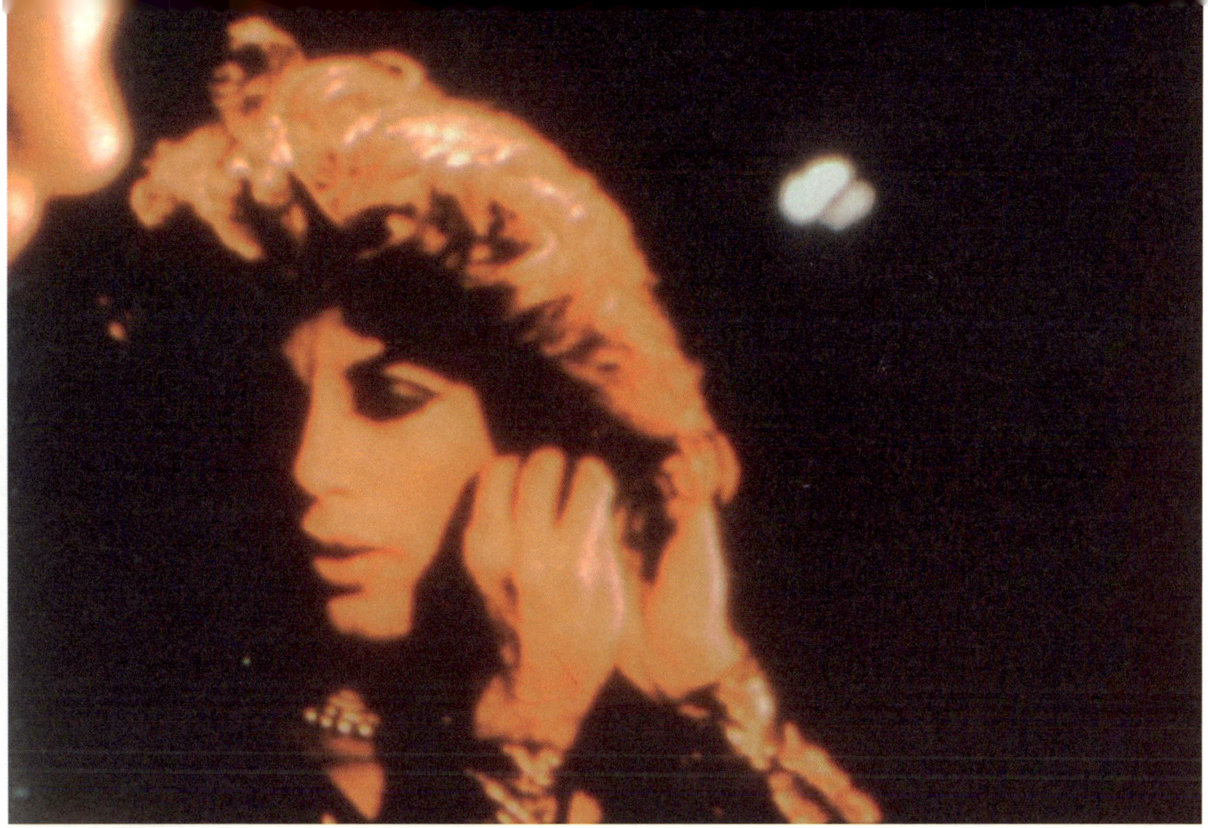

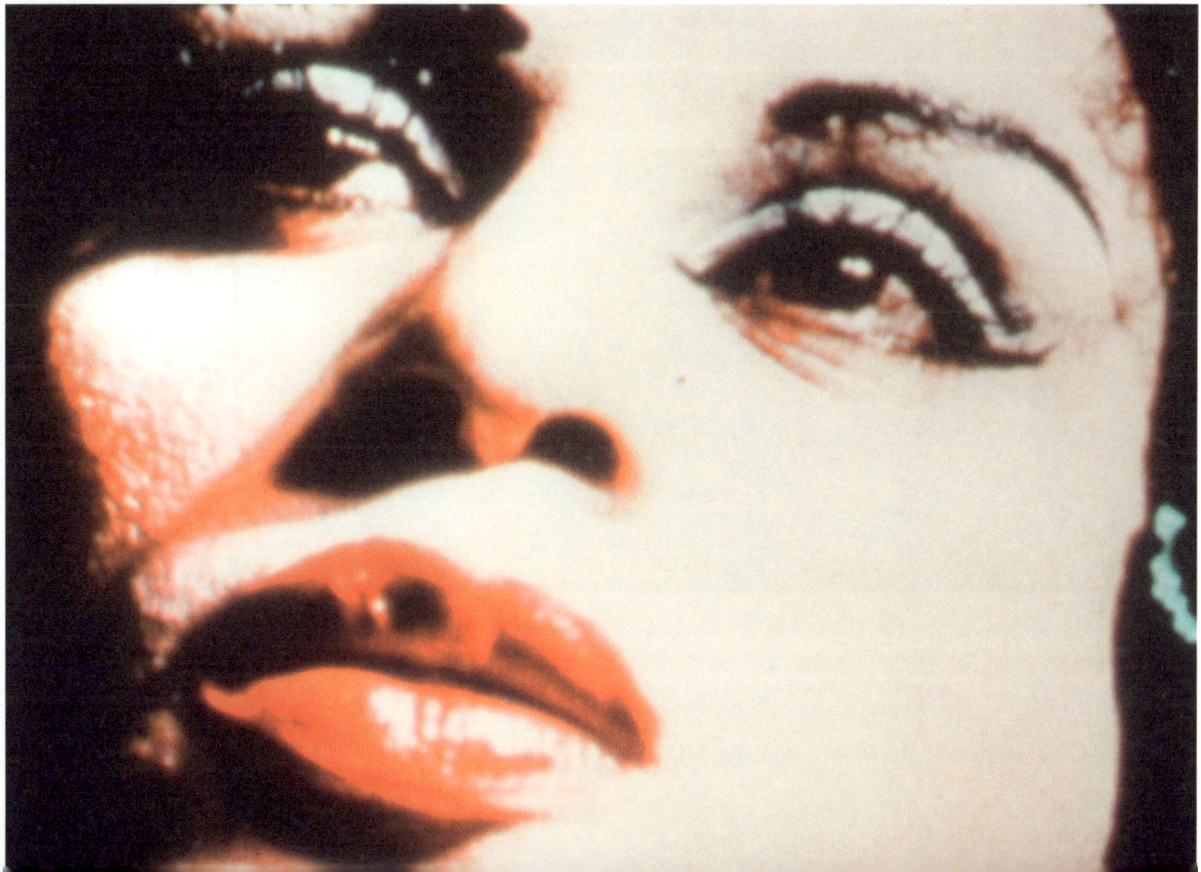

The Ridiculous Theatrical Company (RTC) was founded by Charles Ludham in 1967 in the context of the queer underground culture of Lower Manhattan. Drawing from experimental theater, camp aesthetics, and drag culture, the RTC presented performances that mocked and subverted both popular and "high" culture to critique the status quo. Actor Mario Montez performed with the group and designed costumes as "Montez Creations." Argentinian artist Leandro Katz served as the photographer and lighting designer for the company between 1968 and 1975.

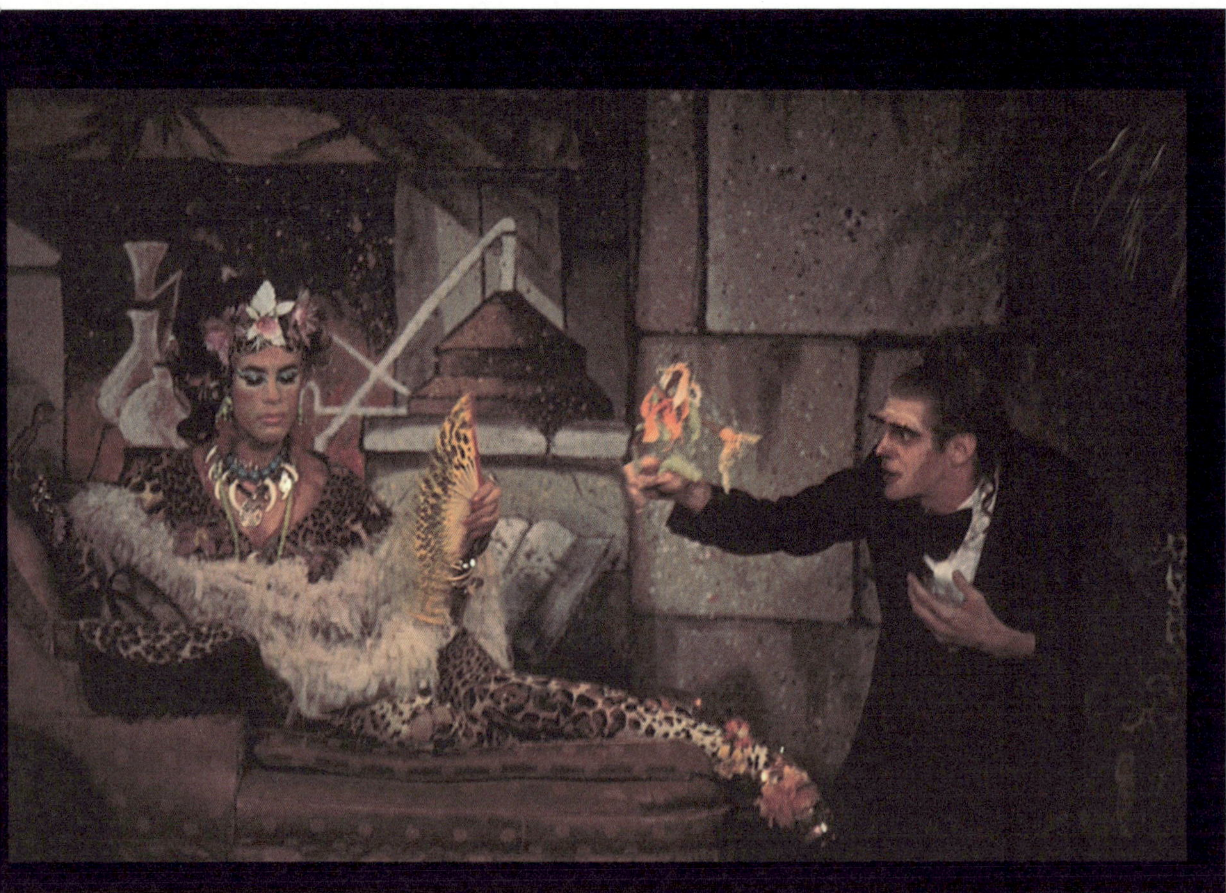

The Ridiculous Theatrical Company, *Bluebeard*, 1970. Leandro Katz Archive

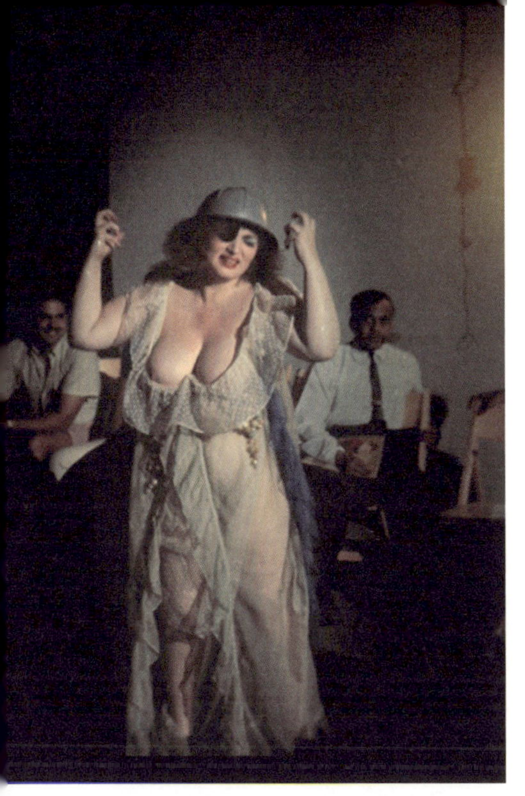

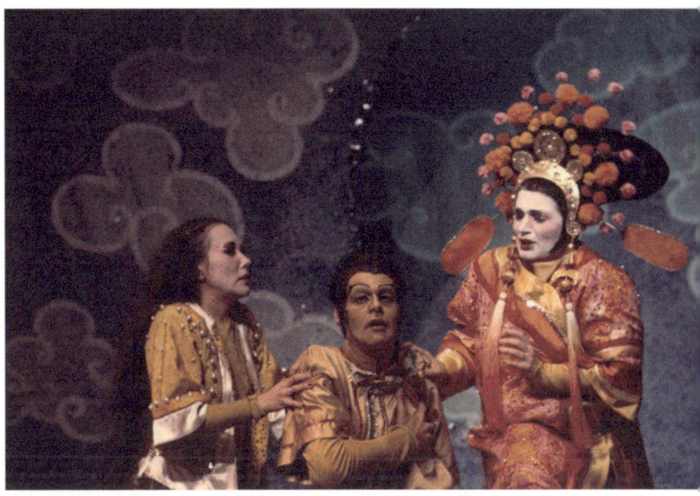

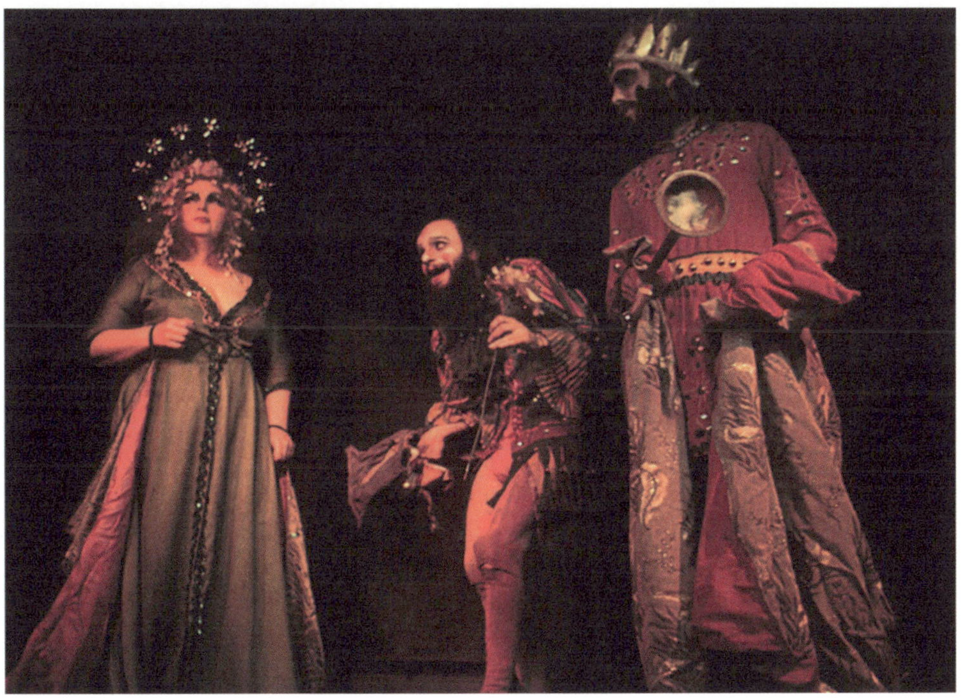

The Ridiculous Theatrical Company, (clockwise from top left) *When Queens Collide*, 1967, *Forbidden City*, 1971, and *The Grand Tarot*, 1969. Leandro Katz Archive

When we made the film *Dialogue with Che*, José Rodríguez-Soltero and myself were twenty-something years old. At that moment it seemed very unfair to us how they killed him and the film is based precisely on those final moments of his life. We were naive and well intentioned. I proposed to José the idea of making the film in a very improvised and natural way, like cinéma vérité, which was controversial. He agreed with me and I got the Che Guevara diary that had just been published. A small group of friends collaborated with us, including Taylor Mead, who, at the time, was one of Andy Warhol's superstars. The film was an absolutely improvised Happening, filmed by José. At one point I look at the camera and say to José, "José, I'm not really Che Guevara and I have nothing to do with him," and I began to improvise a dialogue with José about who we were, what we represented, and about our situation as Latinos in New York City and in Latin America. The film belongs to that underground spirit of the time.

— Rolando Peña

José Rodríguez-Soltero, stills from Diálogos con el Che (Dialogues with Che), 1967.
The Film-Makers' Cooperative/The New American Cinema Group

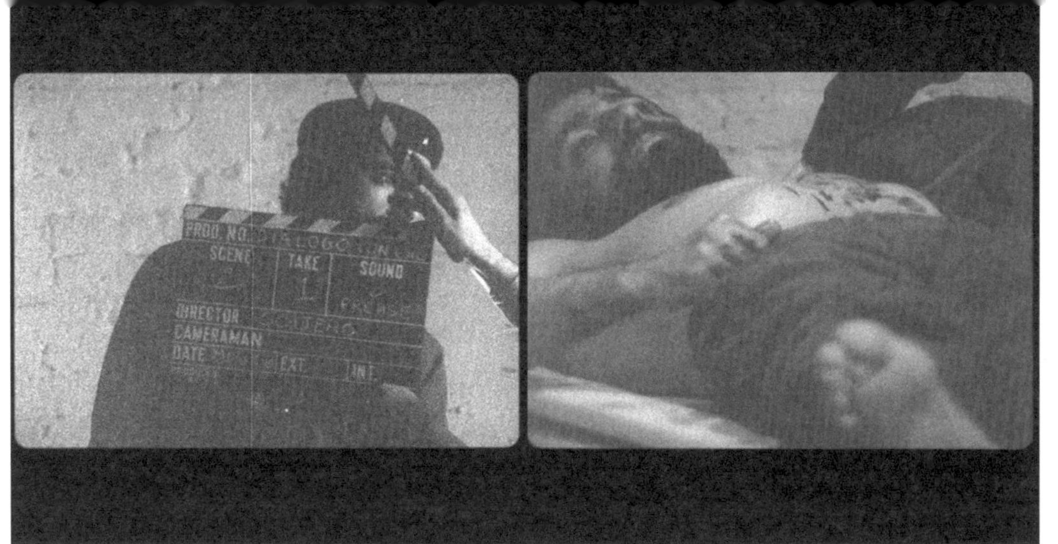
PROD. NO.
SCENE
TAKE
SOUND
1
DIRECTOR
CAMERAMAN
DATE
EXT.
INT.

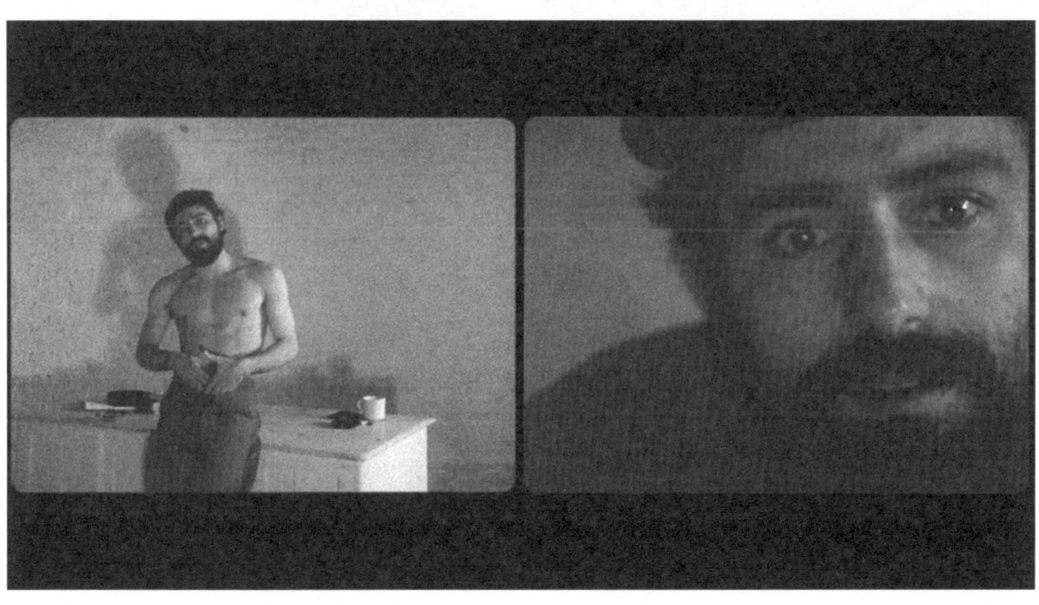

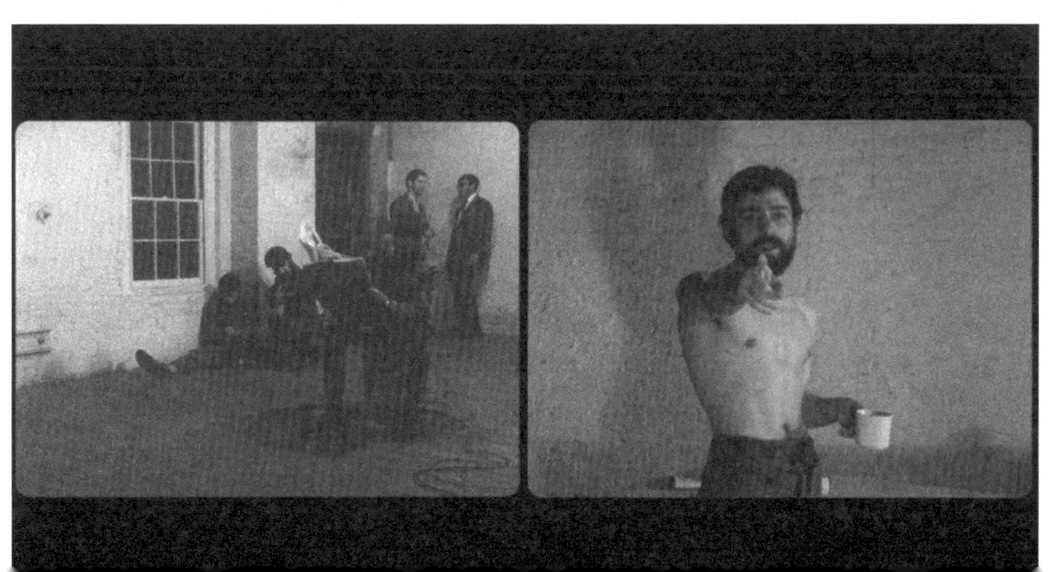

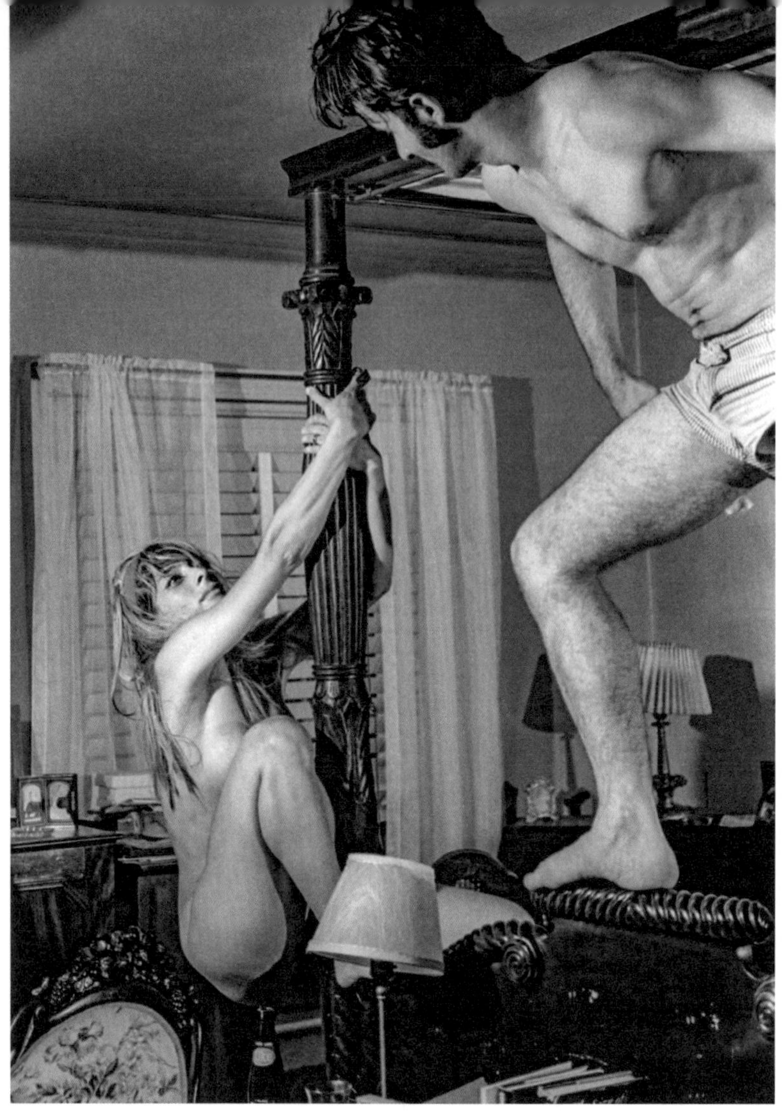

Virginia Cows was an experimental film directed by Chilean filmmaker Jaime Barrios in 1969. Filmed in Virginia on a farm that belonged to the family of a friend of Barrios's, it had no predetermined script; all the acting—done by friends—was improvised. The film has been lost since the 1970s. Marcelo Montealegre documented the entire process of shooting it in photographs that reveal moments of subversion of social conventions and a liberal stance toward sexual norms, which reflected the sexual liberation ethos of the 1960s. Scenes included a dinner in which actors and actresses end up removing their clothes and sitting on top of the dining table, explicit sexual acts, and carefree moments in nature.

Marcelo Montealegre, production stills from Jaime Barrio's *Virginia Cows*, 1969.
Marcelo Montealegre Archive

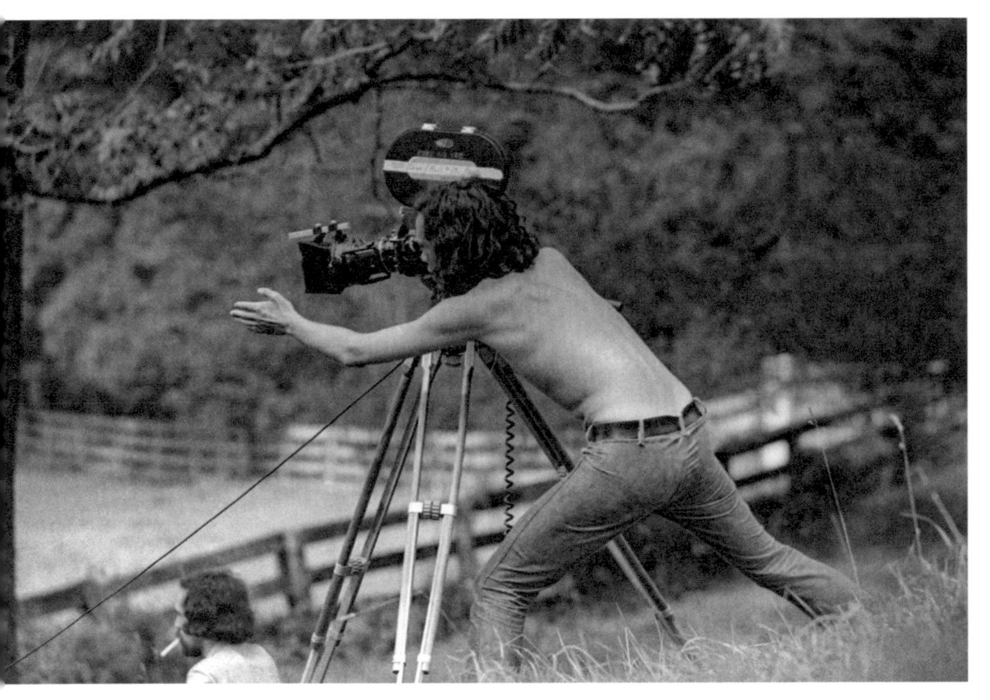

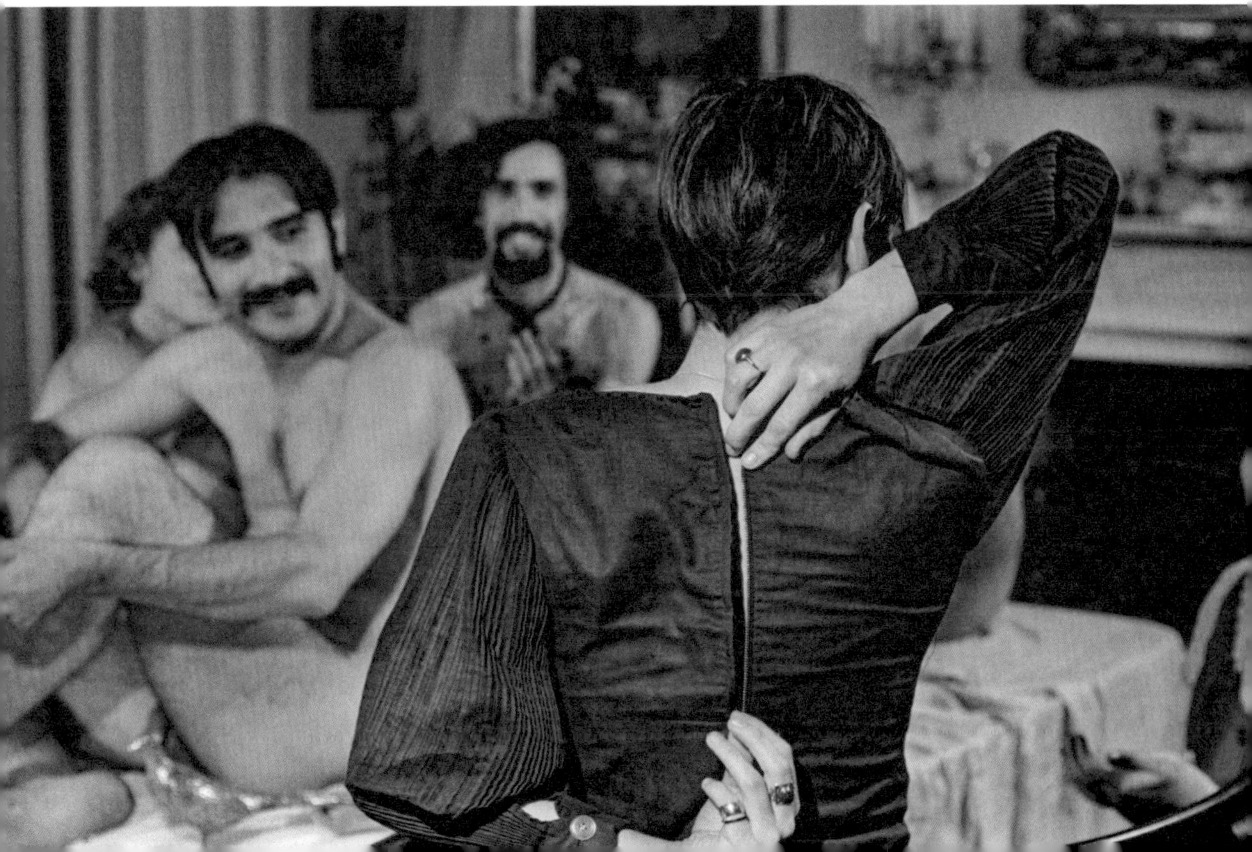

Born in a certain space and time, carrying a certain color in the face, learning about lines and borders of these spaces in different languages. Everyone having a personal history, obviously belongs to the same space, the Earth. Types of misunderstandings, prejudices, or privileges among people are invented by people, not by nature. I believe art is a way of surpassing those barriers, by seeking humanness, awareness, and freedom of individuals belonging to one nature.

— Lydia Okumura

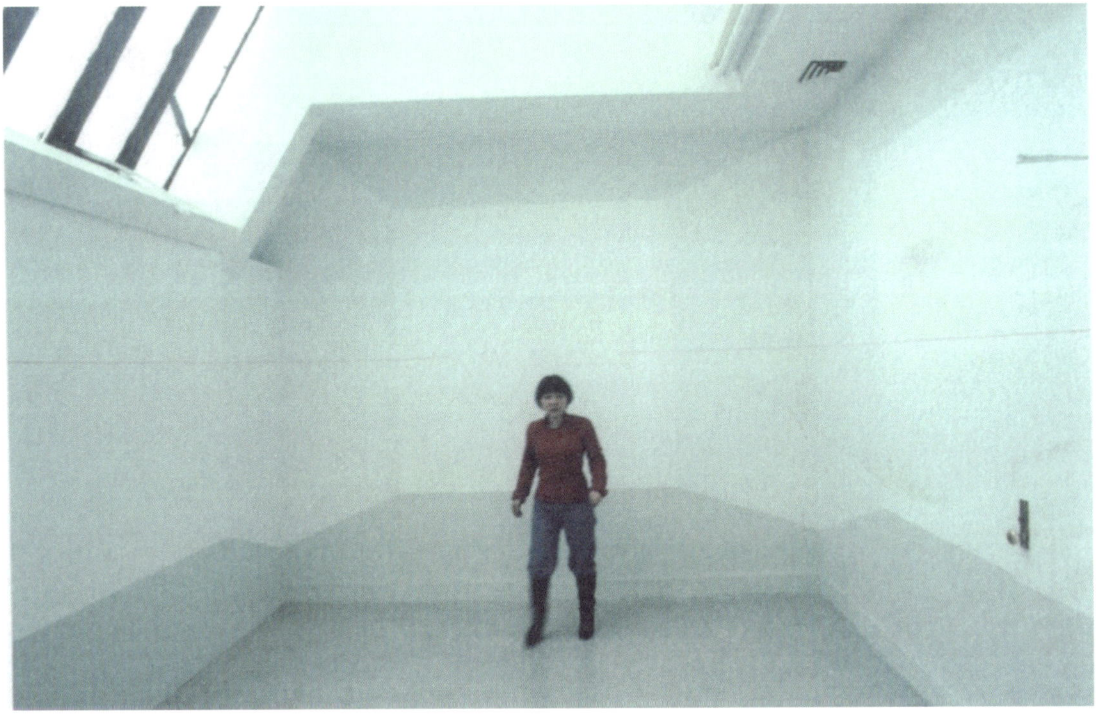

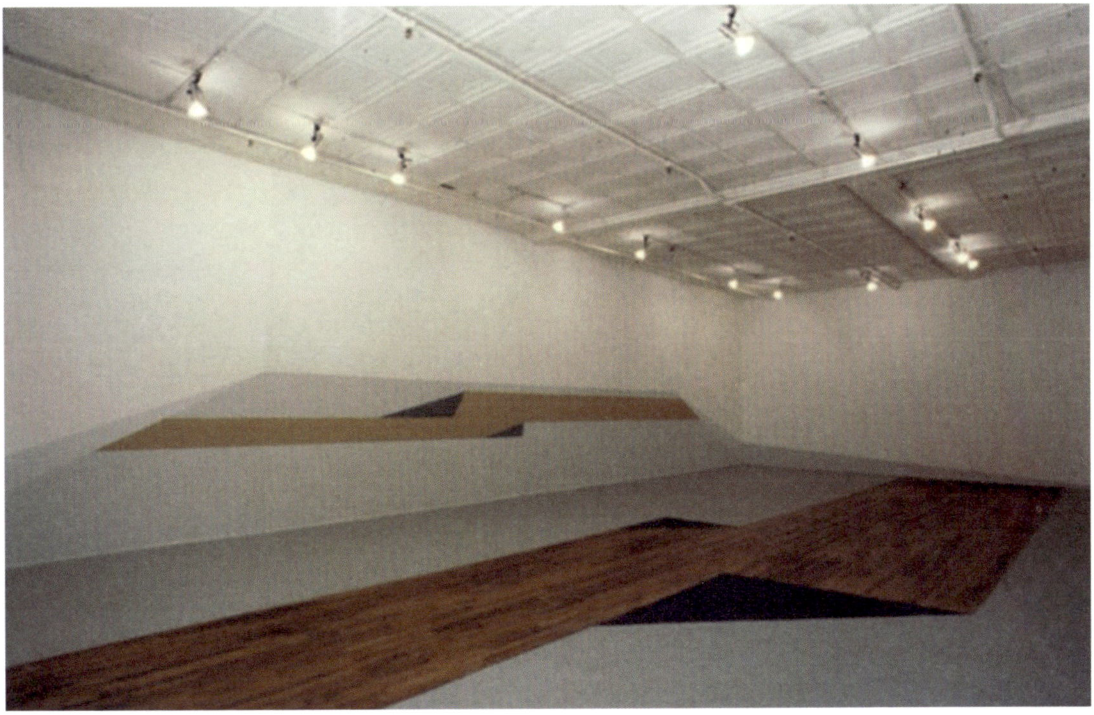

Lydia Okumura at Nobe Gallery, New York, 1979 (top) and view of Lydia Okumura's *Installation/ Instalação* at Cayman Gallery, New York, 1978 (bottom). Galeria Jaqueline Martins

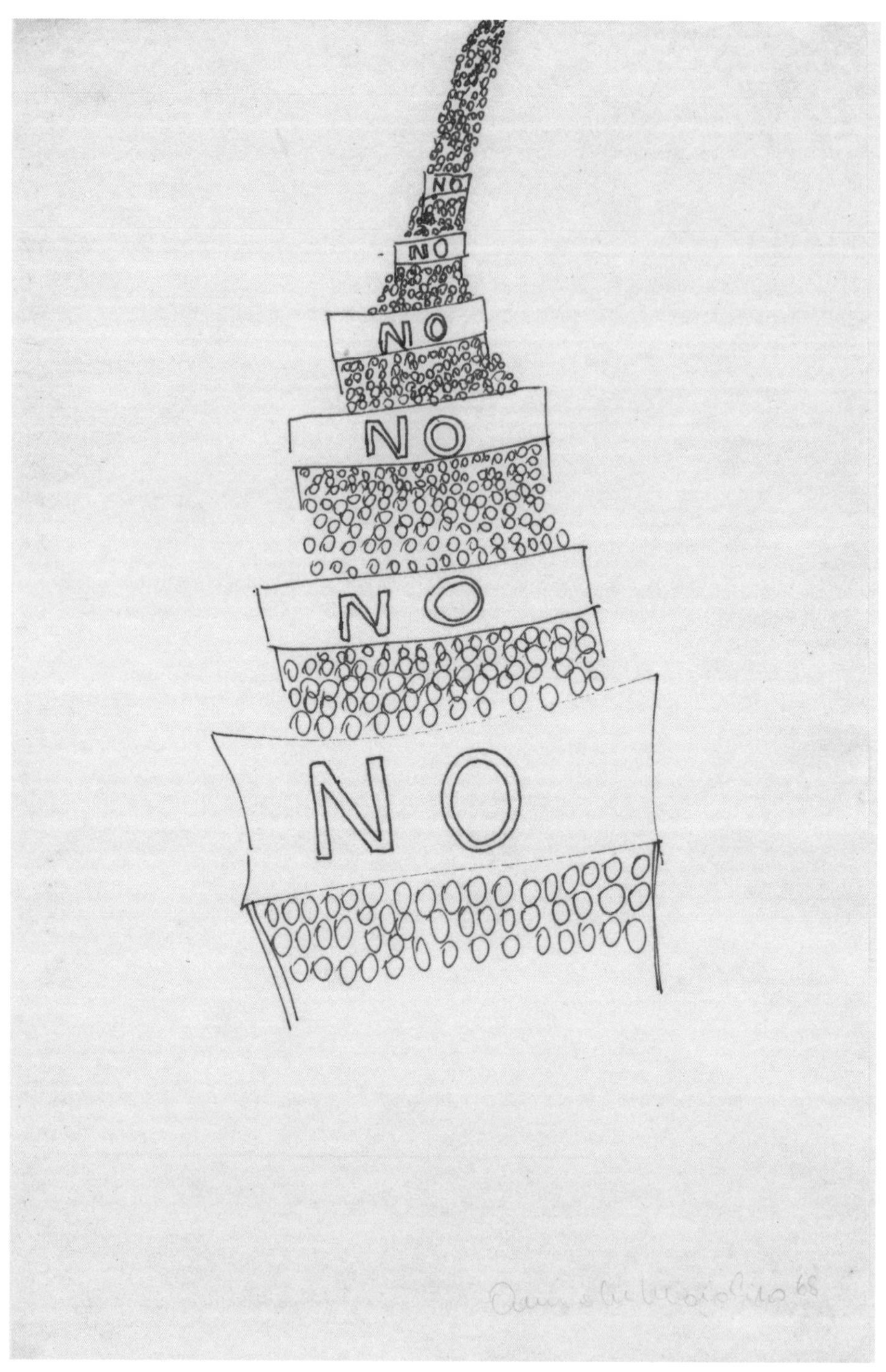

Anna Maria Maiolino, untitled drawing from the series
Entre Pausas (Between pauses), 1968. Private collection, Boston

In a sense, all of us, the South American artists who are living in the city, are in exile. We are ideologically ambiguous, guests in the very country that is the mentor of alien dictatorships and protector of generals of our countries far away.

– Anna Maria Maiolino

The excerpts on the following pages come from interviews with artists from South America in which they reflect on their positionalities as Latin Americans living and working in the United States and their critical views about North American culture. The quotes also include these artists' contrasting opinions about "Latin American" as a marker, whether rejected or embraced, of their identities.

INTERVIEW WITH ENRIQUE CASTRO-CID

Interviewers: Julián Cairol, Claudio Badal, Marta Minujín.
Edited by Marta Minujín

Enrique Castro-Cid points out at an "Interest in a higher order of synthesis" "An art without examples" - "The intensity of the surface."

Enrique Castro-Cid: In all creative processes there is an interest, in the end, to create a higher order of synthesis—which implies that art can't be generated without such examples. Thus the paradigmatic Arts. That is what is done here in the USA, a false culture, a paradigmatic culture, an exemplifying culture of what art should be. Art does not point to anything. I point out this as a fundamental aspect of the concept that I have of what the artist is.

Cha/Cha/Cha: The Latin American artist incorporated into the forces of American cultural production as well as the meaning of his work constitutes the subject of our investigation. Let us begin by considering some questions that place the Latin American artist beyond that universal status conferred by his profession and, unlike other foreign artists, in a position that, because it is traditionally antagonistic, suggests at first glance a problem of conscience, their confrontation with a society that for political and economic reasons is recognized by all Latin Americans as hostile to their interests, what effect such a situation has on the artist and in what way.

ECC: The question comprises issues of political and cultural orders. The question, which is quite general, would have to be deciphered in two ways. In the order of what is political and in the order of what is cultural.

CCC: But the political and the cultural play at an ideological level.

ECC: You are asking me for an idiosyncrasy more than an answer.

The Westbury-NewYork -30 de Marzo de I974-I2-Am-

Entrevista a Enrique Castrocid

Entrevistadores Claudio Badal-Julian Cairol-Marta Minujin-

Editado por Marta Minujin

Enrique Castrocid puntualiza un "Interes en un orden superior de sintesis"

"Un arte sin ejemplos"-"La intensidad de la superficie".

Enrique Castrocid:Con respecto a la pregunta-abandonar la tecnologia,diria, que en todos los procesos creativos hay un interes finalmente,de crear un orden superior de sintesis,lo que implica que un arte se puede generar sin ejemplos.
Asi las artes paradigmaticas.
Esto es lo que se hace aqui,una falsa cultura,una cultura paradigmatica.
Una cultura ejemplificadora de lo que el arte debiera ser-
El arte no senala nada-esto lo senalo yo,como un aspecto fundamental,del concepto que Yo tengo de lo que es el artista.
Pregunta Cha Cha Cha:El artista latinoamericano incorporado a las fuerzas de la produccion cultural americana asi como el significado de su obra constituye la materia de nuestra investigacion-comenzemos por considerar algunos interrogantes que situan al artista latinoamericano mas alla,de ese status universal que le confiere su profesion y a diferencia de otros artistas extranjeros, en una posicion que por ser tradicionalmente antagonica-sugiere a primera vista un problema de conciencia,su enfrentamiento con una sociedad que por razones politicas y economicas es reconocida por todo latinoamericano como hostil a sus intereses,que efecto tiene tal situacion en el artista y de que manera Voz pensas que se manifiesta en su obra?-.
EC La pregunta entiende,cuestiones de orden politico y cultural.
Habra que descifrar la pregunta que es bastante general,de dos maneras, en el orden de lo que es politico y en el orden de lo que es cultural.
Cha Cha Cha-Pero lo politico y lo cultural juegan a un nivel ideologico.
EC-Me piden una idiosincracia mas que una respuesta.
Cha Cha Cha-Nos interesa saber si de alguna manera Voz encontras que existe una tercera posicion-

Marta Minujín, Julián Cairol, and Juan Downey, pages from *Cha/Cha/Cha: A Magazine of Art Criticism Dedicated to the Investigation of the Latin-American Artistic Production*, New York, 1974. Marta Minujín Archive

Juan Downey-interroga a Julian Cairol-

-J.D.- Julian a mi me parece que publicar una revista latinoamericana,cultural- es una falta de responsabilidad,pues el movimiento latinoamericano debe ser total-debe ser politico.

_JC-Bueno,precisamente-la revista aspira a unificar esa totalidad al analizar-investigar el trabajo de los artistas que viven en new York- y se plantea inmediatamente un problema de conciencia-esa desintegracion permanente-pues no esta ni integrado aqui ni integrado alla-en eso que todavia no sabe que es y que es su arte- esa posicion critica debe ser analizado para que no se lo trague en la vida americana-

A ese sentimiento de alienacion que de alguna manera implica una internacionalizacion como Marck lo senalo.Con la revolucion nos internacionalizamos porque el hombre ha llegado a la universalidad-

Lo importante es;al nivel de la investigacion cientifica- observar el producto,el trabajo del artista latinoamericano,visto desde el lenguaje latinoamericano ,no criticado al nivel del arte-sino en si misma-

Ese es el problema principal-lo que la revista se propone analizar-la situacion del artista latinoamericano que por todas las razones que se puedan dar se aliena una vez mas y se lo come la alienacion.

Asumir una cierta imagen,que nosotros tenemos frente al capitalismo-

Lo que sifnifica la imagen de un mexicano durmiendo en un rincon-

La cultura siempre es traducida a travez de esa imagen-por ser inautentica esa imagen es antimitica-

JD La revista se trata en realidad de presentar un mito que esta ahi-el mito no se hace aparente porque esta en el lugar equivocado.

JC-Esa inautenticidad del mito en este momento puede ser usado-porque precisamente hay algo mitico-en el trabajo de los artistas aqui-esto mitico es inautentico-porque los mitos estan basados en realidades concretas-y es por eso que el mito se expresa de otra manera-

Porque nosotros coincidimos en ese pensamiento-~~que no cree en nada de eso que hace.~~

El ultimo de mi entrevista deberia decir lo siguiente-
En lo que es cultura hay tres capitulos lo que es definicion de cantidad lo que es definicion cualidad lo que es intensidad.
Esos aspectos de la cultura son los mas importantes porque estan relacionados con todo el mundo.
Y Yo estoy en *la intensidad de la Superficie* SIGUE en O
.

cantidad
cualidad
intensidad { cultura - { son los tres porque se relacionan con todo el mundo

Si yo descubro que en una elaboracion abstracta una categoria concreta, entonces vuelvo al mundo-
Hay un gran mito cuando entran los muchachos en la tribu en la edad de la pubertad ese mito está basado en categorias domesticas de la cultura lizacion- Levi Strauss compara la musica con el mito,es porque con el mito nunca podemos llegar a esas categorias abstractas que podemos intuir en la musica-
La naturaleza del mito es un acto cultural-
En el caso mitologico cocinar la comida y ese mito implica otra imagen de cosa, esa imagen es en la cual nos reflejamos- esa imgen es la que nosotros pensamos que es el mundo ideal-
Hay que sacar a los poetas y hechar a los pintores.del Parnaso platonico porque ellos creen falsas realidades.
EC No estoy de acuerdo-
Picola Miranda dijo-Consco todo lo que es existente en el conocimiento humano
San agustin le pregunta_qu es el tiempo

I realized that the cultural shock I suffered [in the United States] could possibly be the seed of a work of art, and I understood that it was important to return to my roots, to what was strictly Latin American.

New York is fabulous: ideas coexist, interact, copulate, rip off and proliferate. Nevertheless, there is nothing in New York that I wish to remember now. The essence and tenderness are in Latin America.

— Juan Downey

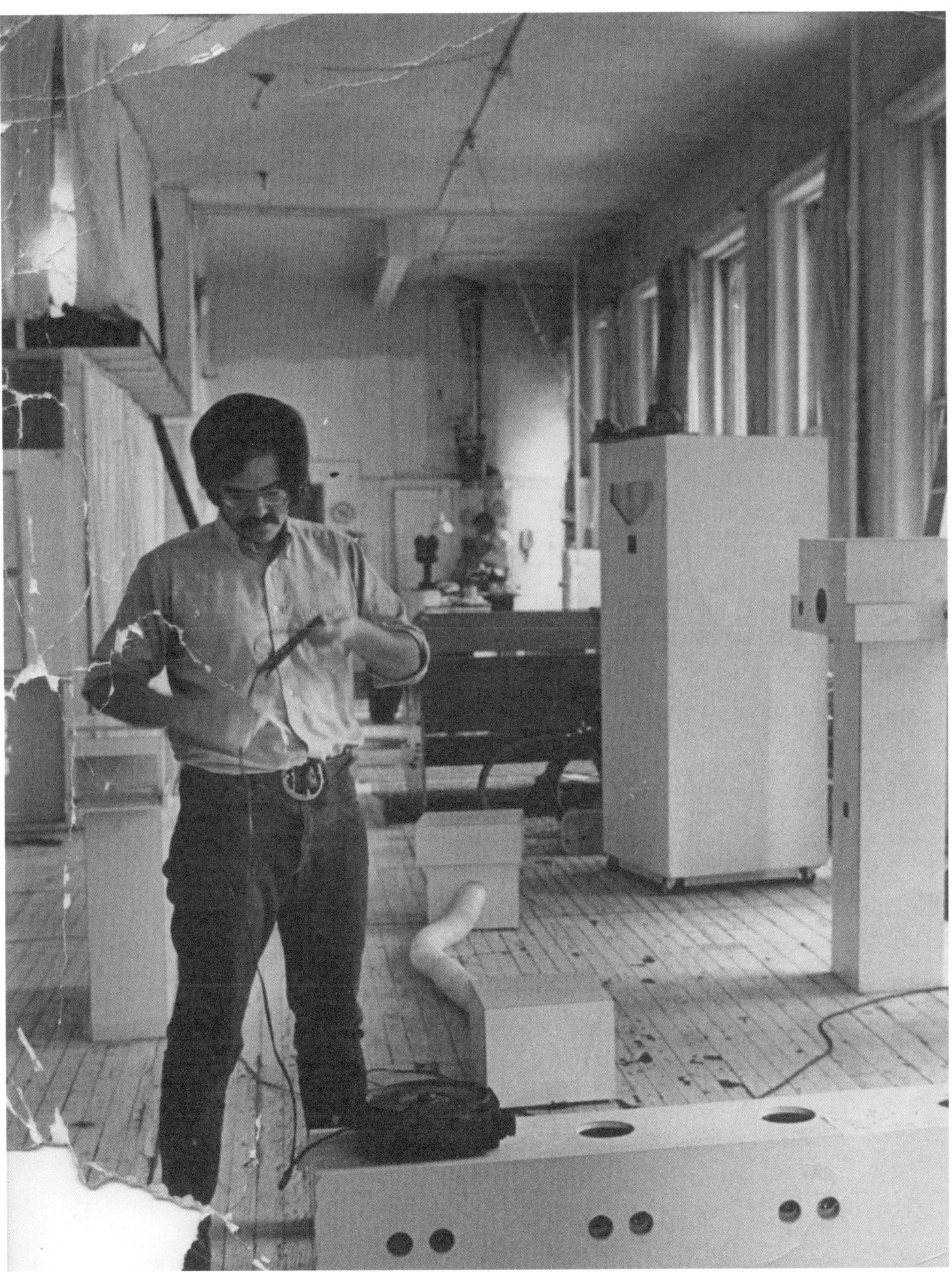

Juan Downey in his studio at East 20th Street, New York, ca. 1969.
The Juan Downey Foundation, New York

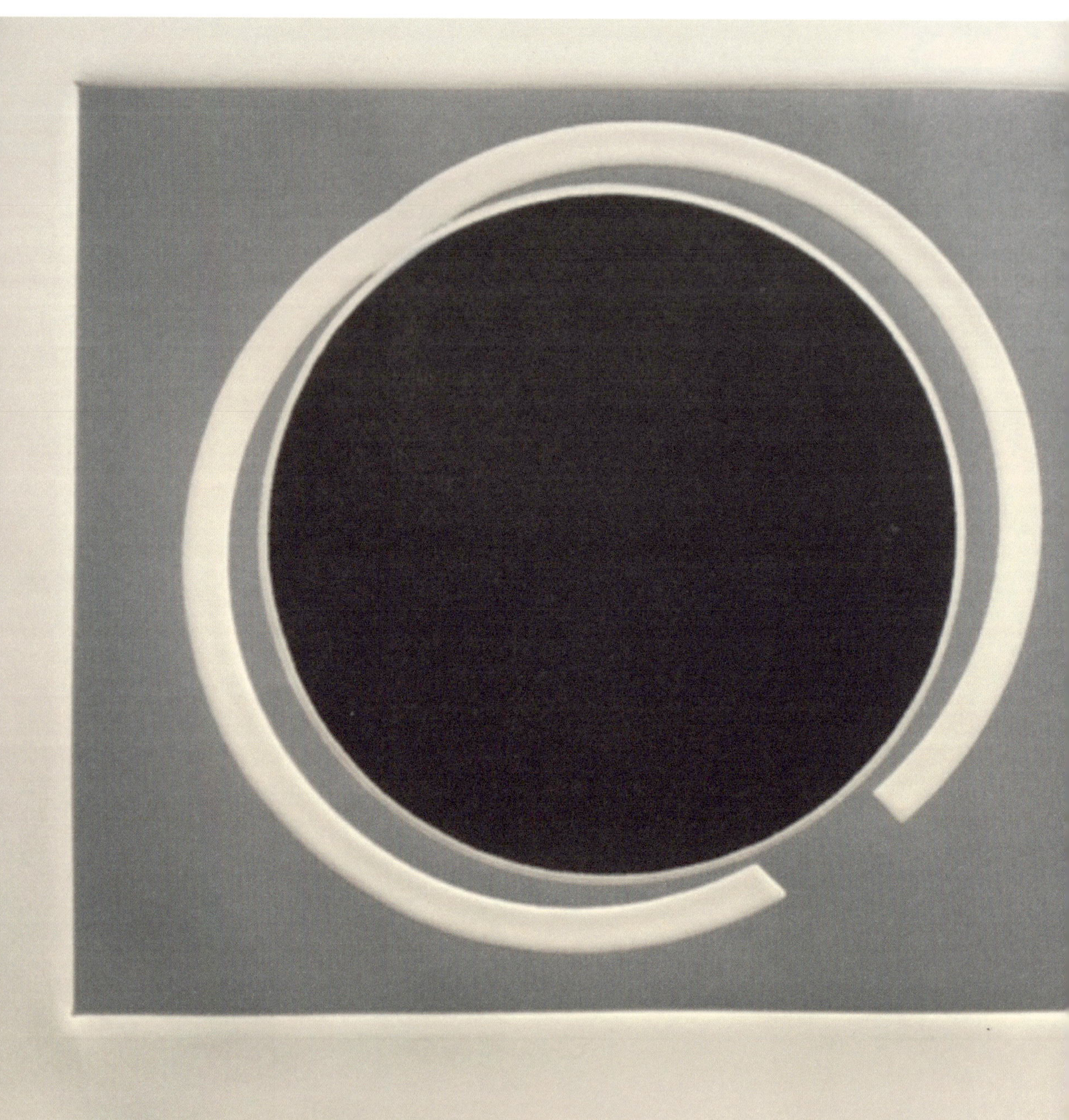

Laura Márquez, *Presión/represión* (Pressure/repression), ca. 1970.
Private collection

At some point in New York, as I did in Asunción, I tried to nucleate a group of Latin American artists in an entity that we called: Latin American Museum of New York. The original idea was to create an entity that would reflect the Latin American life and thought. Facts and circumstances of our reality. And as in previous experiences I verified that to pretend this kind of nucleation is utopic.

Soon artist colleagues pretended that the museum rather be a representative of paintings and sculptures and a site to offer conferences. I think the idea is not reprehensible, but the project first was to take this entity to a more abstract question. But, accordingly with the time we live in, what we need the most is to transmit ideas and idiosyncrasies as soon as possible and in the most graphic and economical way.

— Laura Márquez

ABAIXO DO EQUADOR

ULTRA AEQUINOXIALEM NON PECCARI (ditado do século XVII)

Como se o Equador não sòmente dividisse o mundo em dois hemisférios
mas também separasse o Bem do Mal. (Barlaeus, século XVII)

AMÉRICA DO SUL
ÁFRICA
ÁSIA

O NORTE foi criado pelo Colonizador.
Proposição: uma cultura que fôsse não-branca
não-européia
não-colonial
não-geográfica

Arte Internacional não é Arte Internacional; Arte Internacional é Imperialismo Cultural.

Um astronauta vindo do espaço sideral não poderia distinguir sem nenhum preconceito
qual a parte da Terra que está voltada para baixo.

O NORTE É ABAIXO
O SUL É ABAIXO
O NORTE É ACIMA
O SUL É ACIMA

Vivemos uma cultura transplantada.

MEMÓRIA

perfume queimado

poema queimado

Rubens Gerchman
New York, 1971

Rubens Gerchman, *Abaixo do Equador* (Below the Equator), New York, 1971.

BELOW THE EQUATOR

ULTRA AEQUINOXIALEM NON PECCARI (17th century saying)

As if the Equator not only divided the world in two hemispheres, but also separated the Good from the Evil. (Barlaeus, 17th century)

SOUTH AMERICA
AFRICA
ASIA

THE NORTH was created by the Colonizer.
Proposition: a culture that is non-white
non-european
non-colonial
non-geographic

International Art is not International Art; International Art is Cultural Imperialism

An astronaut coming from outer space could not distinguish without biases which part of the Earth is below.

THE NORTH IS BELOW
THE SOUTH IS BELOW
THE NORTH IS ABOVE
THE SOUTH IS ABOVE

We live in a transplanted culture.

MEMORY

burned perfume

burned poem

Rubens Gerchman
New York, 1971

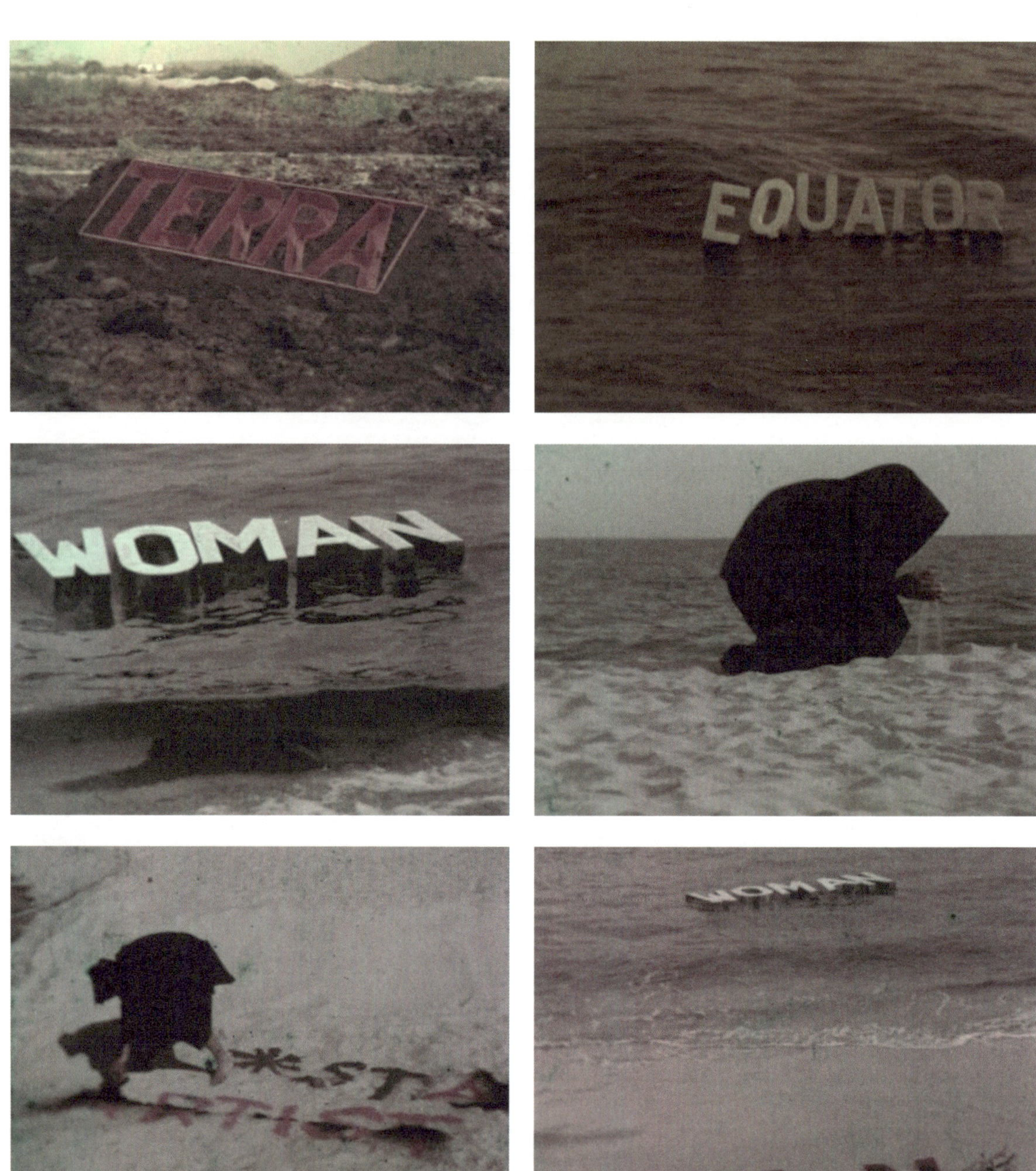

Rubens Gerchman, stills from *Triunfo Hermético* (Hermetic Triumph), 1972.
Courtesy of Instituto Rubens Gerchman

I never liked the separation of Latin American art as some isolated thing because of several reasons. One is that I wouldn't want to be included in it. Another is that I think the way this is done is very provincial. Also, the fact is that Latin America is made up of heterogeneous things and [this category] makes everything very problematic. For example, Brazil has nothing to do with Peru and other countries. I think it is an artificial thing, a forced way, and in fact it is forced. In New York, I was already against it, because I thought it was a manufactured minority. Latin American art kept artists apart in a fabricated minority, in a country that is already full of minorities. So, it is a very reactionary thing, in my opinion. But all this is in relation to the situation in New York, which has nothing to do with Brazil. But I think Brazil has more to do with the United States than with other Latin American countries.

— Hélio Oiticica

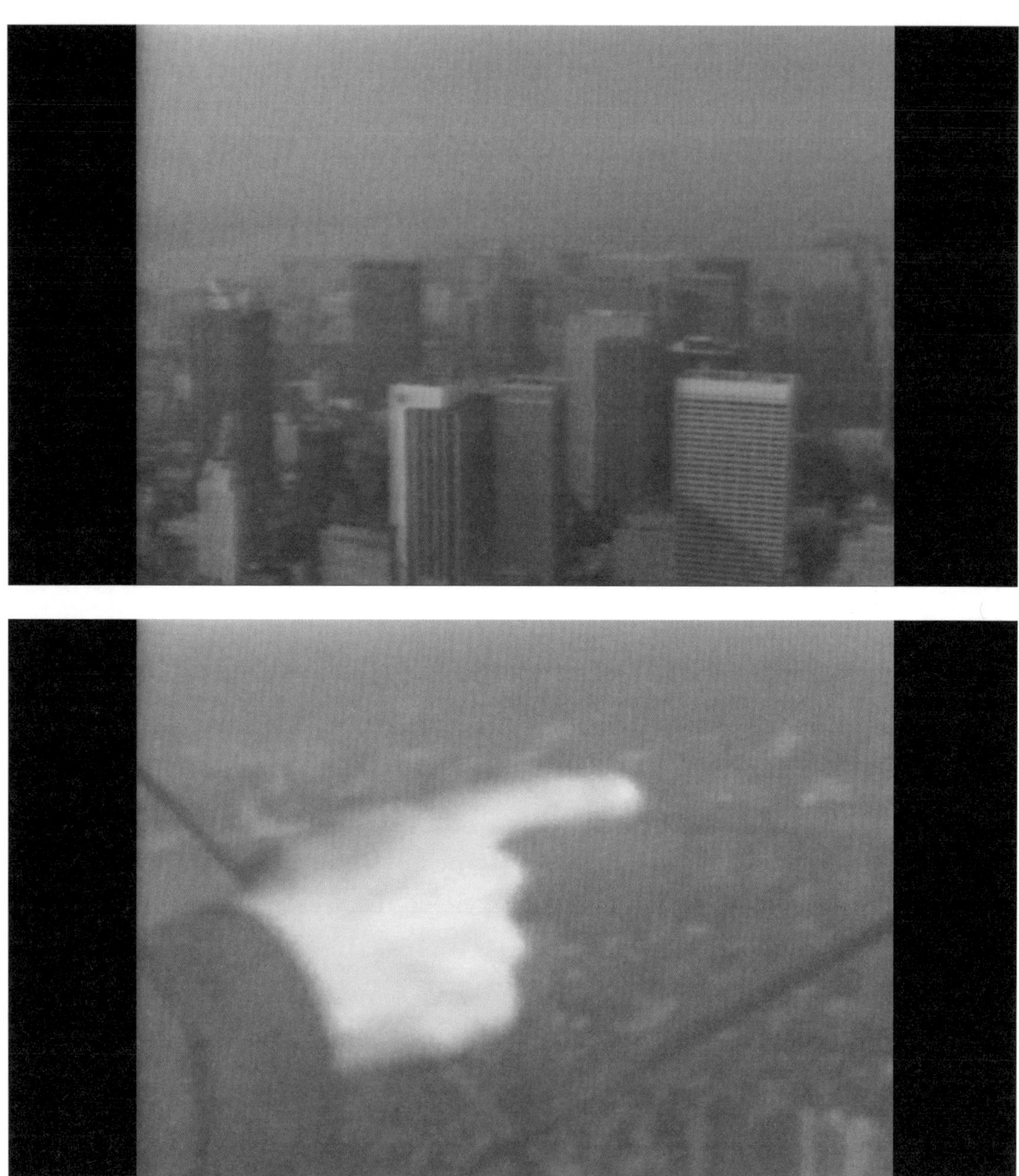

Sonia Miranda (with José Roberto Aguilar), stills from *Where Is South America?*, 1974.
Courtesy of the artist

Sonia Miranda's 1974 video *Where Is South América?*, created with José Roberto Aguilar, begins with the artists asking visitors to the Empire State Building the titular question, inviting them to point toward where they think the continent is. Following the opening scenes, the artists present other views of South America, specifically Brazil, showing imagery of carnival, Candomblé, poetry readings, and other cultural phenomena.

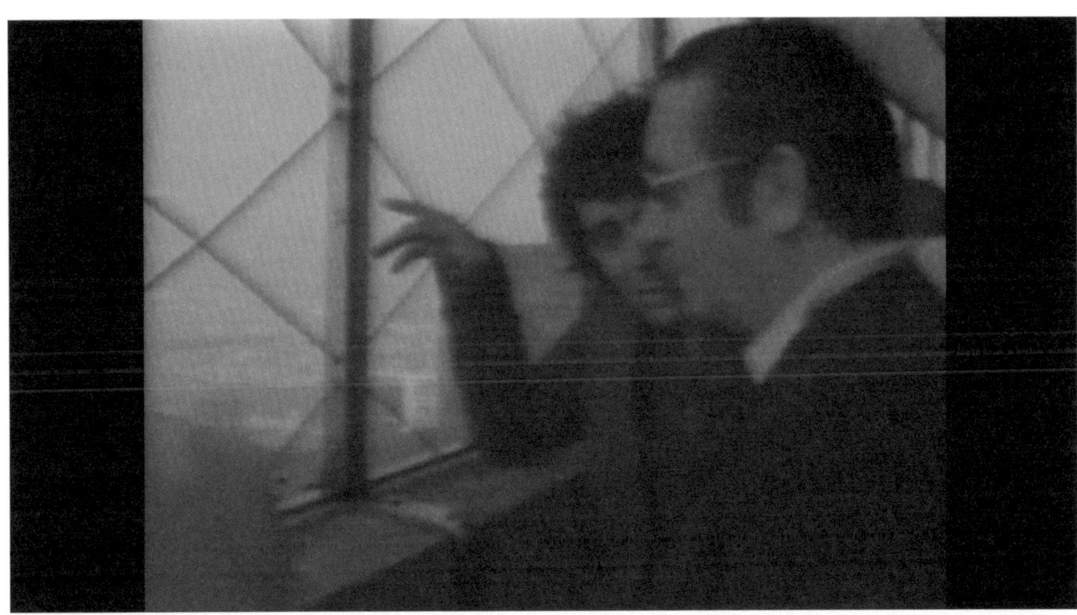

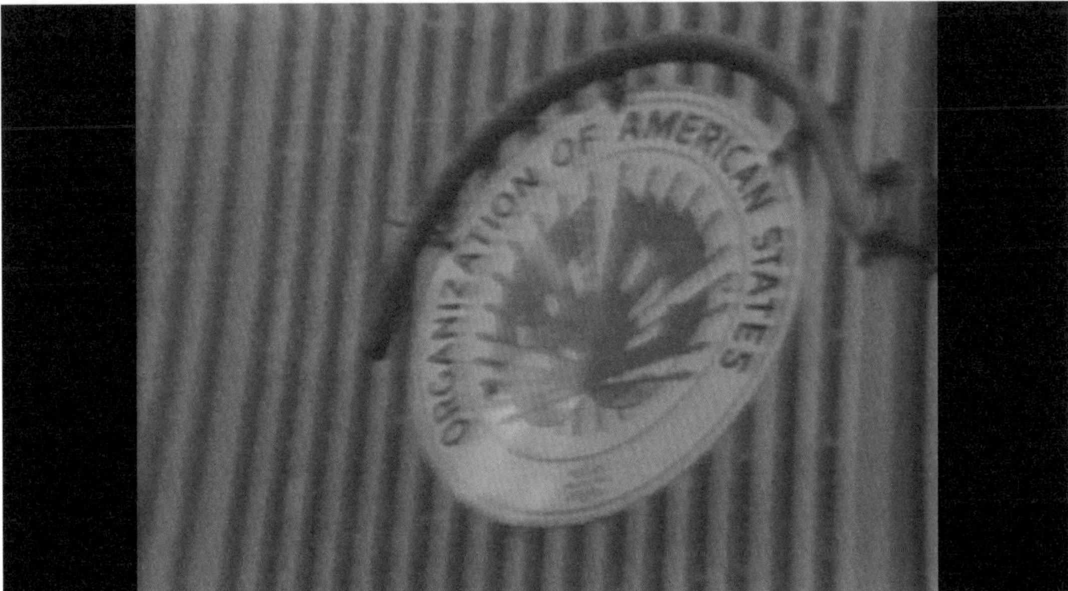

Something amazing happened to me in the USA. Limited by the English language, I developed a new form of communication. Instead of learning to speak another language well, I found out that I had another form of language inside me: I discovered that I could paint; and through painting I would be able to show what no words would ever say. This is a difficult experience to explain. It is even more appropriate to say that the deities have descended upon me and that I paint in a state of intimate communication with the deities. I don't do conventional or ritual painting. Nor is it an arbitrary invention. I express a deep experience of Afro-Brazilian culture. I apprehend certain visions, certain fantasies, above all certain revelations configured in the symbols of Candomblé. This is not folkloric, I am against what white society usually labels "primitives."

— Abdias do Nascimento

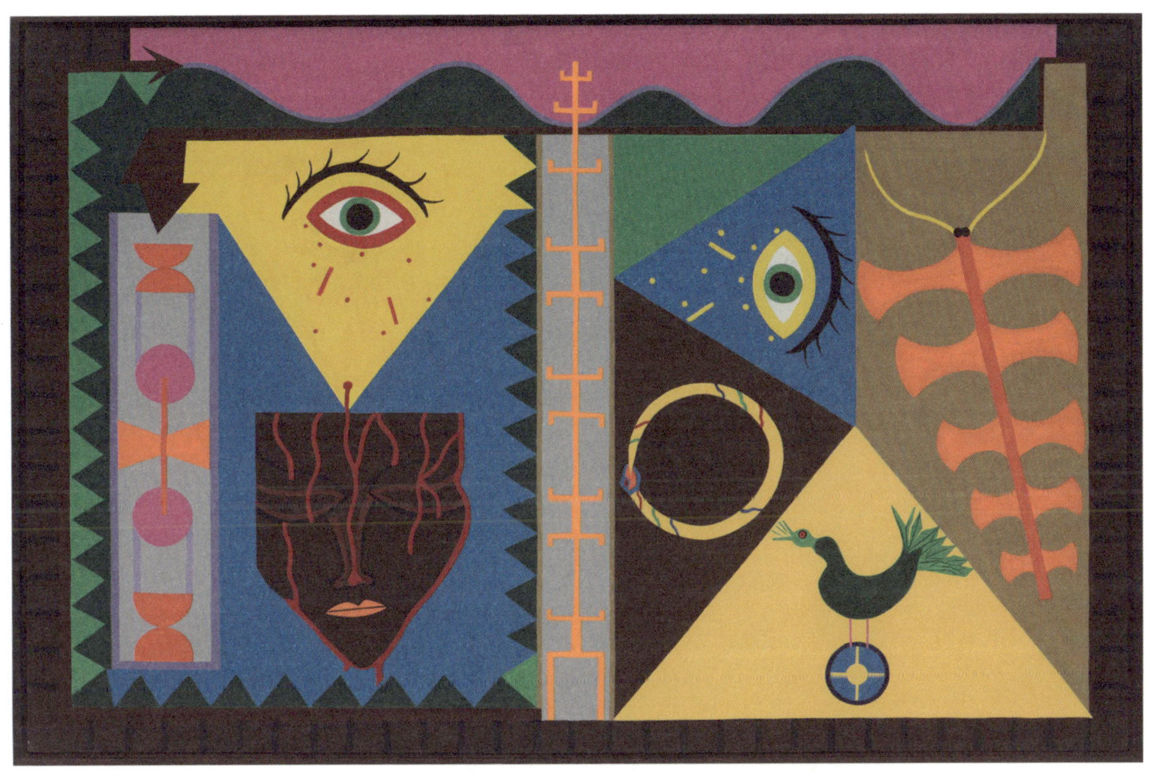

Abdias do Nascimento, *Frontal de um templo* (Front of a temple), 1972. Courtesy of Fortes D'Aloia & Gabriel and Tanya Bonakdar Gallery, and Black Art Museum/ IPEAFRO, Rio de Janeiro

Working in the 1970s, Dominican artist Freddy Rodríguez embraced geometric abstraction in his paintings and collages. Countering ideas of abstract art as works devoid of meaning—especially in the North American and European traditions—Rodríguez's abstractions reference specific aspects of his own cultural background, such as music and dances from the Dominican Republic.

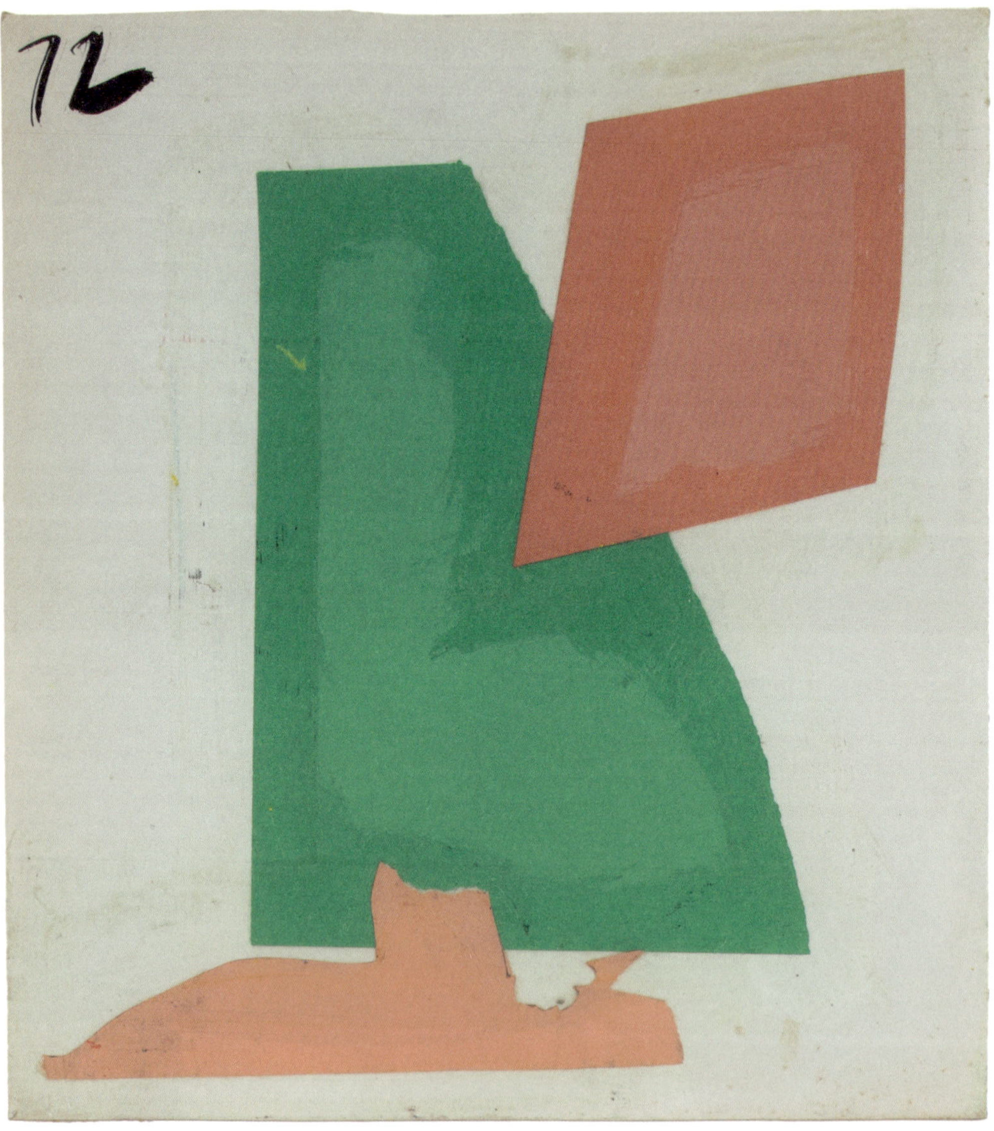

Freddy Rodríguez, *Untitled*, 1971. Courtesy of Hutchinson Modern & Contemporary

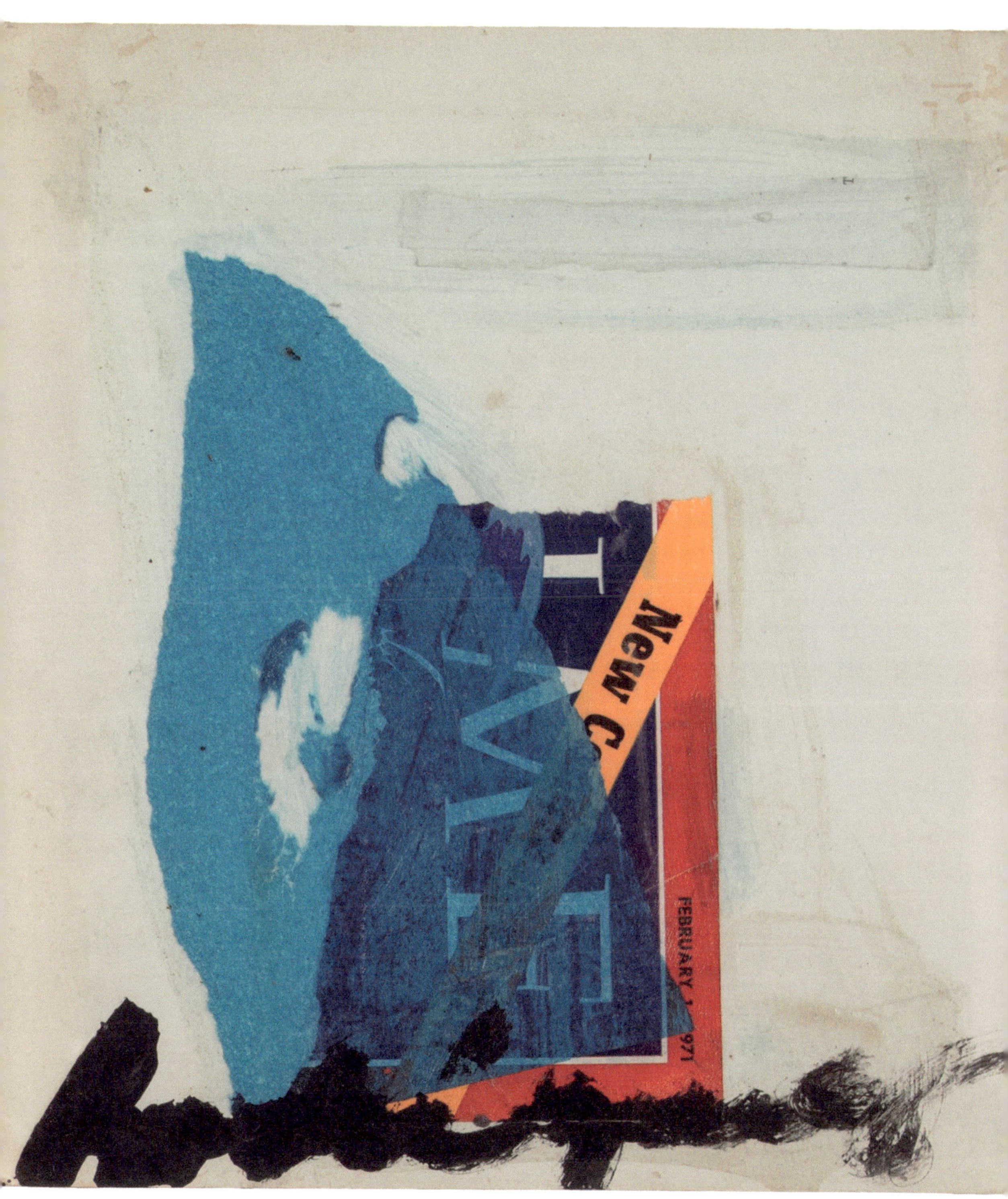

Freddy Rodríguez, *Untitled*, 1972. Private collection, New York.
Courtesy of Hutchinson Modern & Contemporary

A "painter to the core" who went after a radical reaffirmation of the specificity of the (easel) painting medium, vis-à-vis the prevailing Minimalists' and Conceptualists' dismissal of it. On the other hand, silencing the traditional screen meant, fifty years ago, a premonitory rejection of the numbing visual noise of the all-embracing consumer society, today even more hypertrophied by the hugely available digital photography and social media. Within this visually suffocating climate, yes, there is a (slight) possibility that a blessed soul might stop before the white front of one of my paintings and experience a flight of his/her imagination or else a projection of self.

— César Paternosto

César Paternosto's large-scale abstract works invite viewers to walk around the paintings in order to perceive details applied in unexpected places, such as the sides of the canvas (traditionally covered by a frame). In this way, the artwork not only welcomes bodily movement, but also provides a moment of silence for the viewer's own reflection and projection onto the canvas.

César Paternosto, *Who Was in Last Night's Dream*, 1970. Private collection

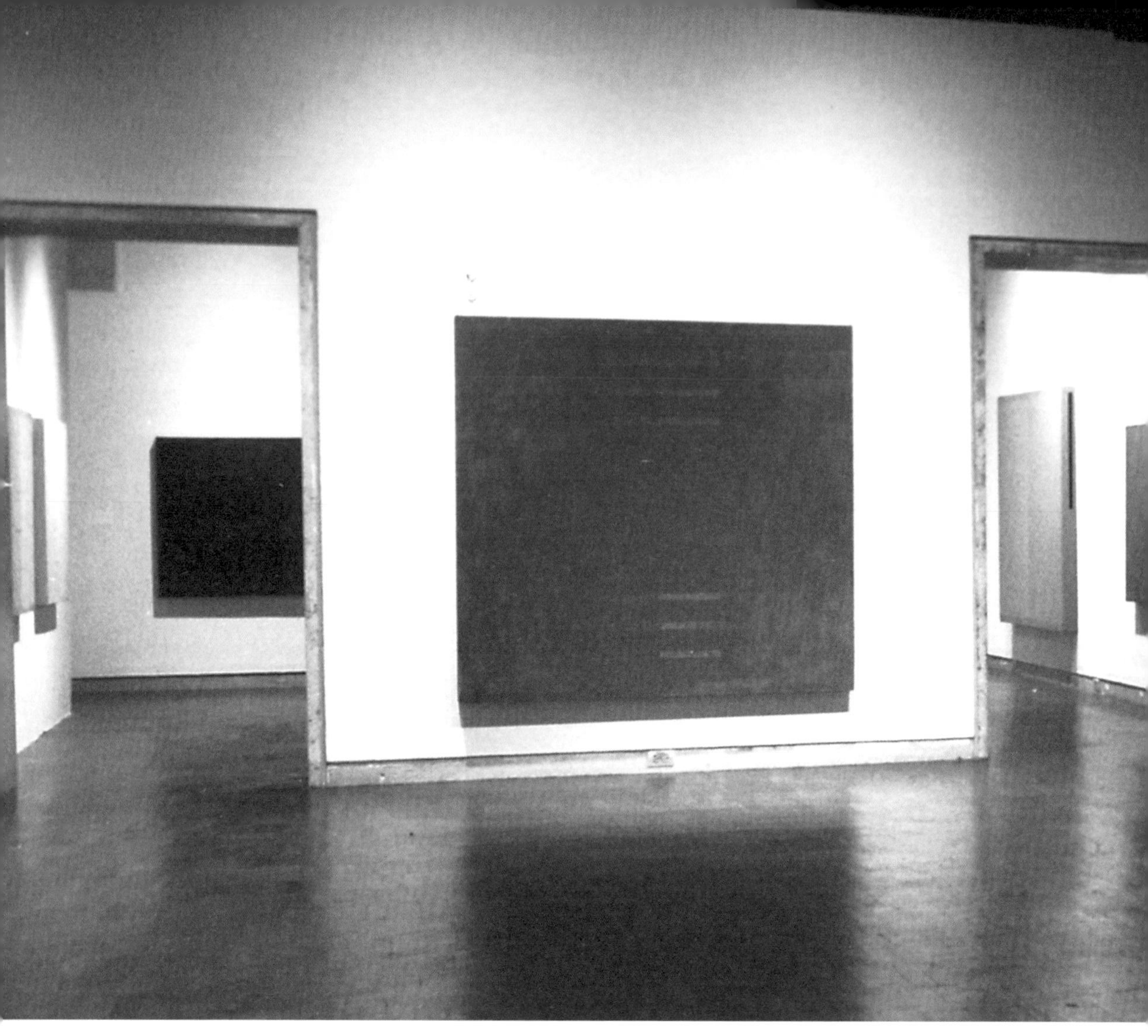

View of *César Paternosto, Paintings: 1969–1980* at the Center for Inter-American Relations, New York, 1981. Americas Society Archives

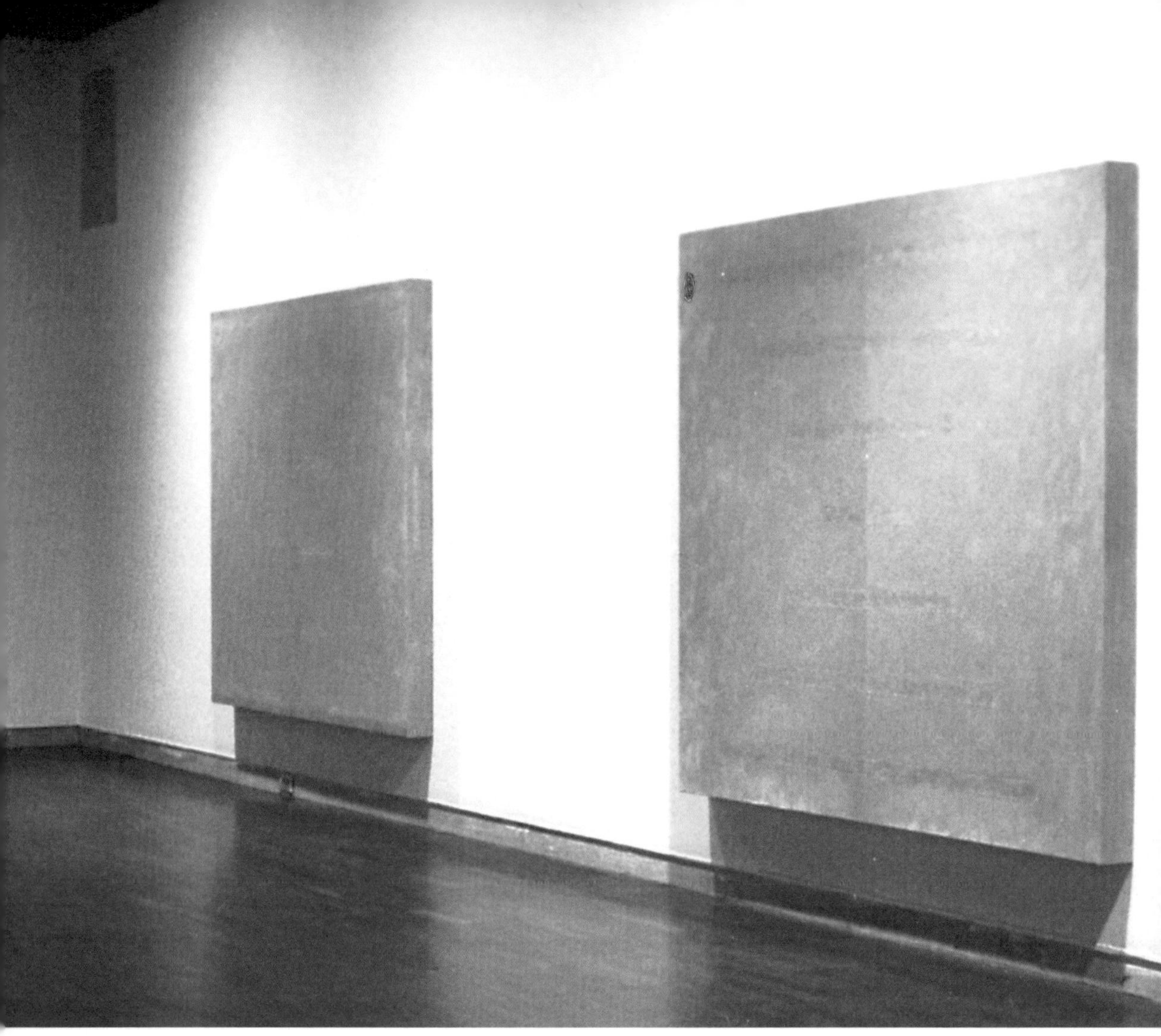

[In my paintings] my primary concern was the materialization of a proposal to reorder the viewer's gaze before my work. Inevitably, that involved the viewer's body animation, an animation that, in the end, was not alien to the body movement required to create the work. The ages-old stance before the traditional screen, either laying pigment or contemplating it, was altered in order to embrace either physically or visually the totality of this new painting that articulated its object quality.

— César Paternosto

The Body and Performance

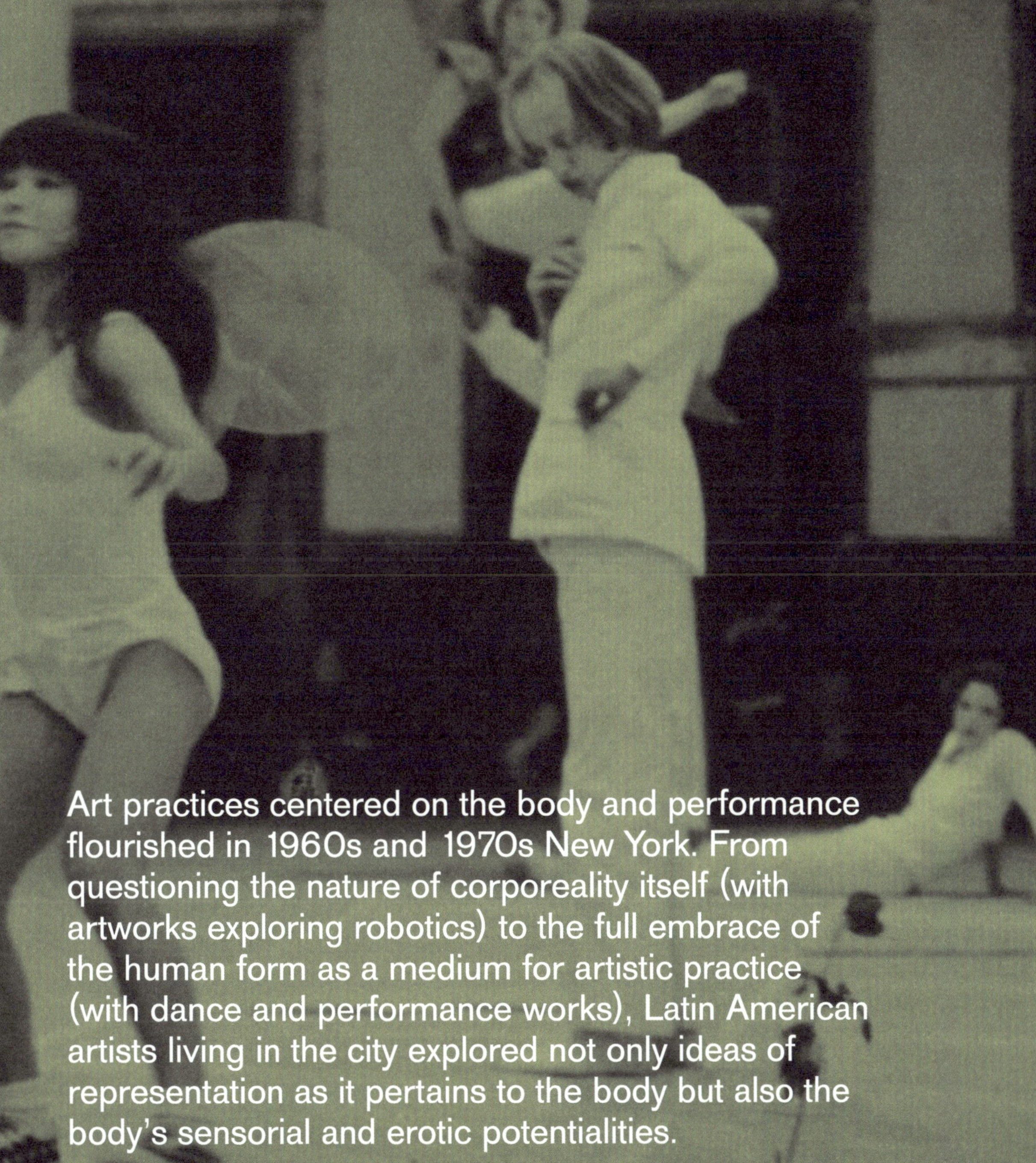

Art practices centered on the body and performance flourished in 1960s and 1970s New York. From questioning the nature of corporeality itself (with artworks exploring robotics) to the full embrace of the human form as a medium for artistic practice (with dance and performance works), Latin American artists living in the city explored not only ideas of representation as it pertains to the body but also the body's sensorial and erotic potentialities.

Carmen Beuchat, *Mass in CBS Minor, or the Brown Table* (also called *Cupid*), 112 Greene Street, New York, November 1972. Carmen Beuchat Archive

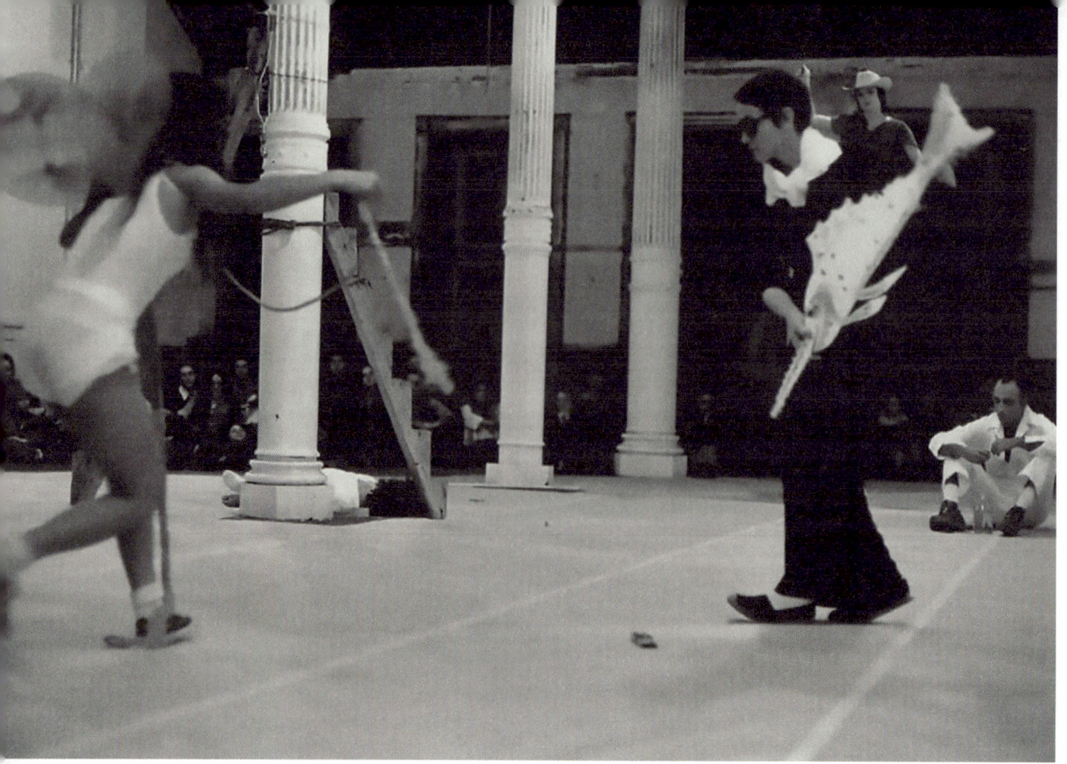

Carmen Beuchat, *Mass in CBS Minor, or the Brown Table* (also called *Cupid*), 112 Greene Street, New York, November 1972 (above and opposite). Carmen Beuchat Archive

Mass in C. B. S. Minor
or
The Brown Table

NOVEMBER 9, 1972
8:00 P. M.

Carmen Beuchat

Claudio Badal
Suzanne Harris
Barbara Lloyd

Emmett Murray
Penelope
Kei Takei

112 GREENE ST. GALLERY
NEW YORK CITY 10012

CONTRIBUTION

CARMEN BEUCHAT

Invitation for Carmen Beuchat, *Mass in CBS Minor, or the Brown Table* (also called *Cupid*). Carmen Beuchat Archive

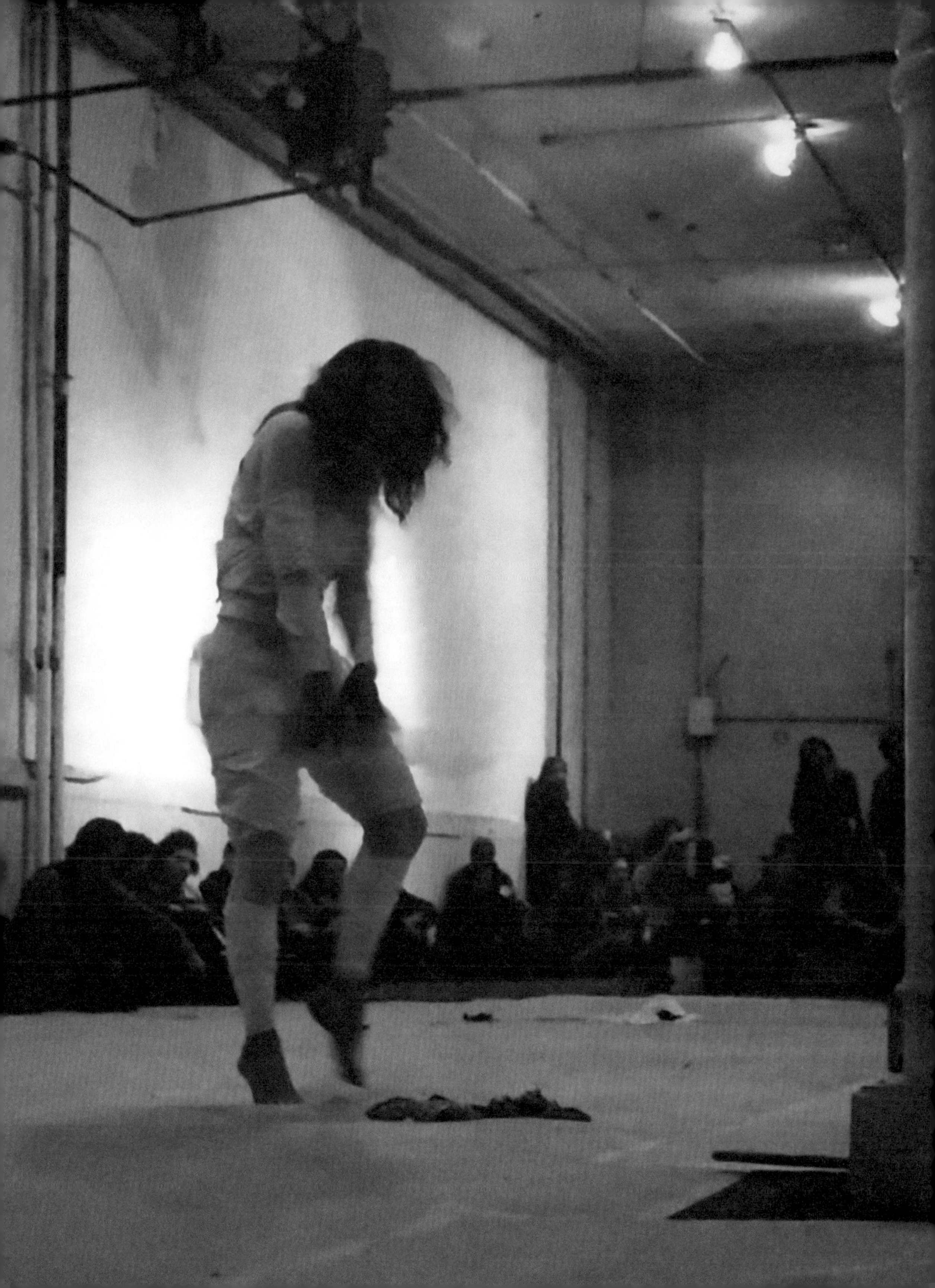

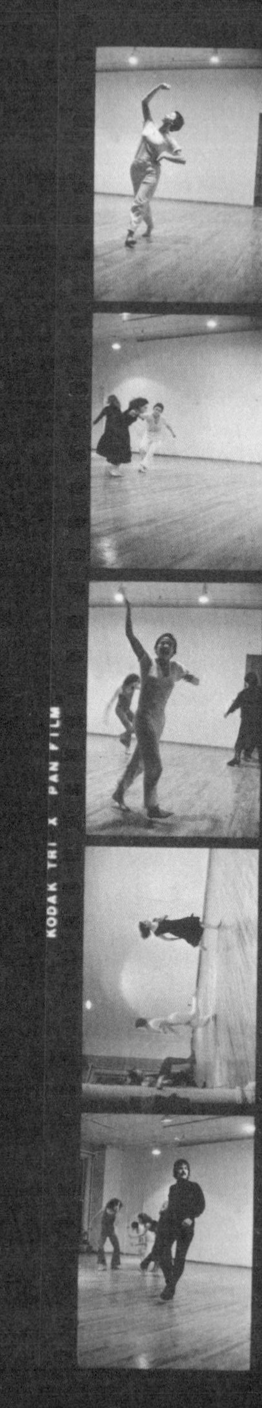
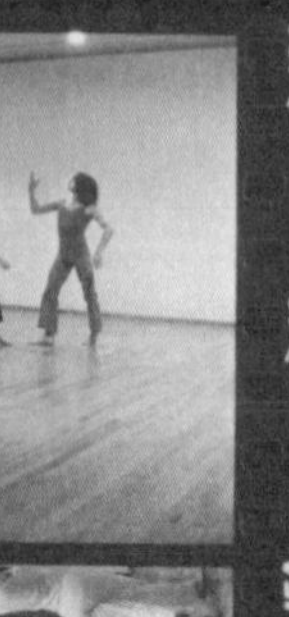
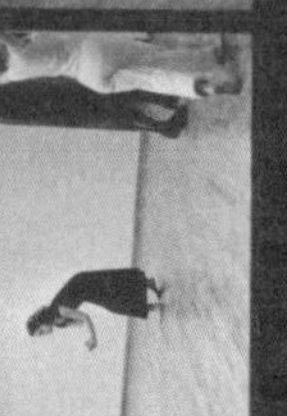
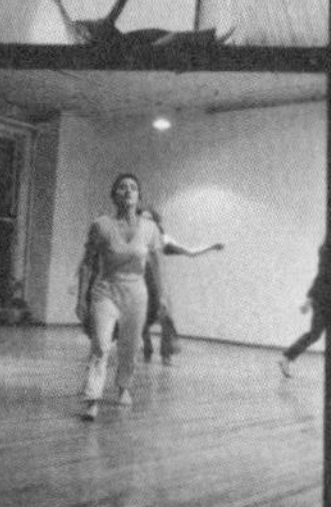
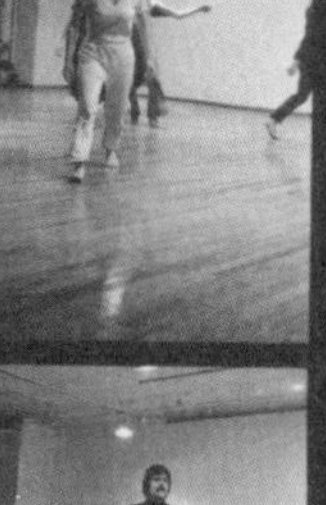
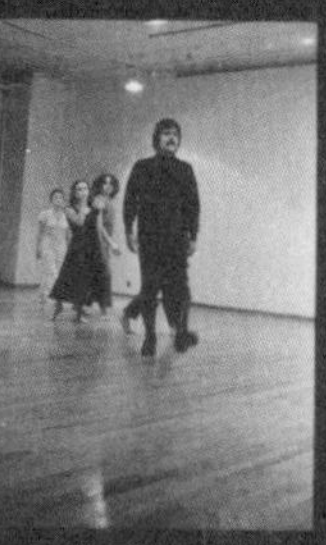
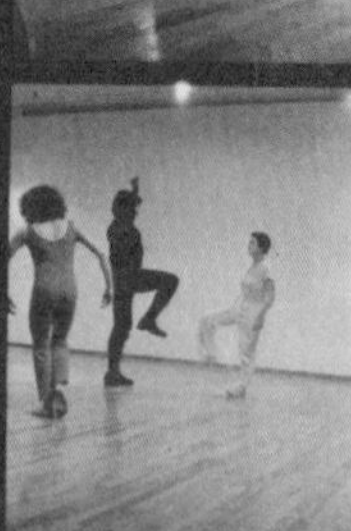
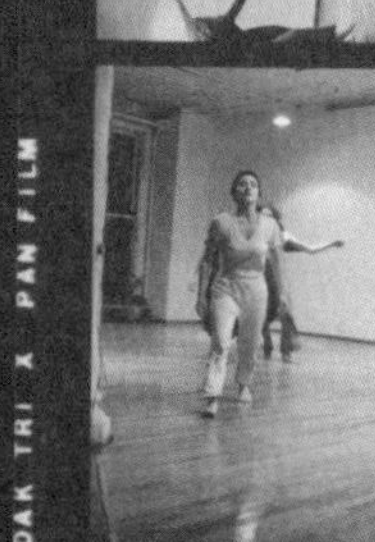
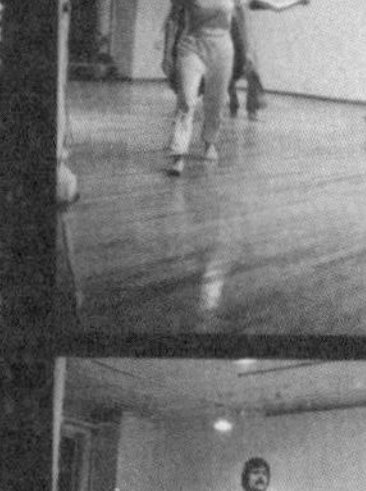
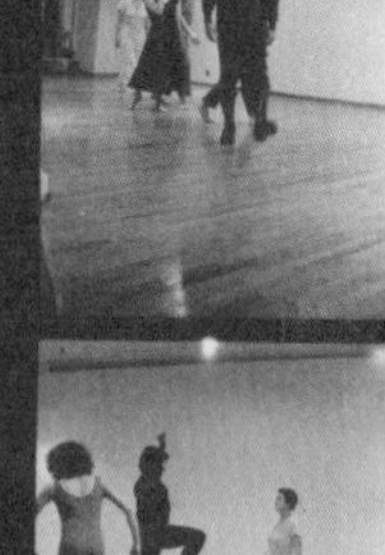
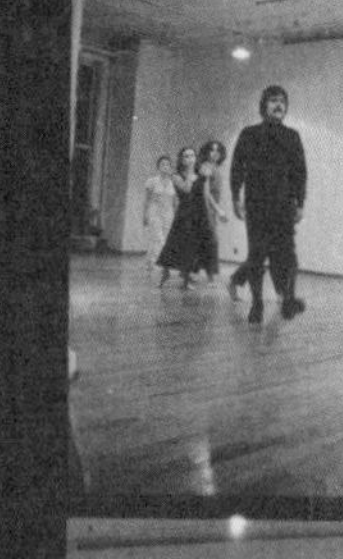
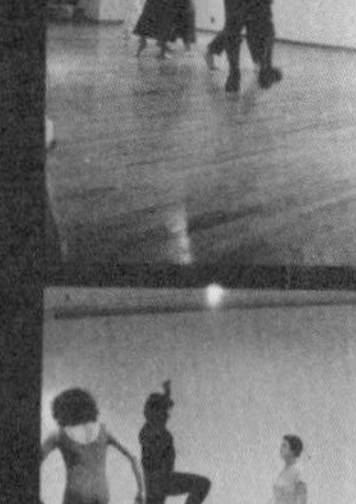
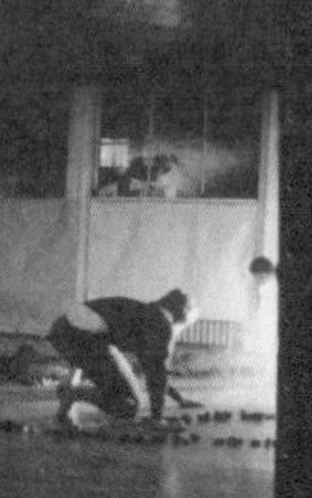
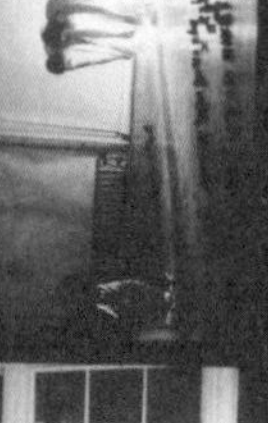
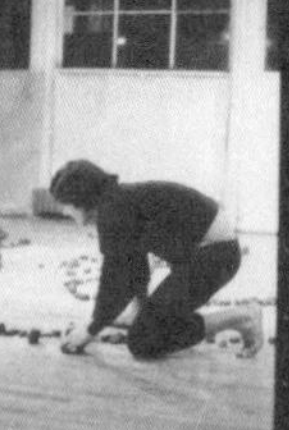
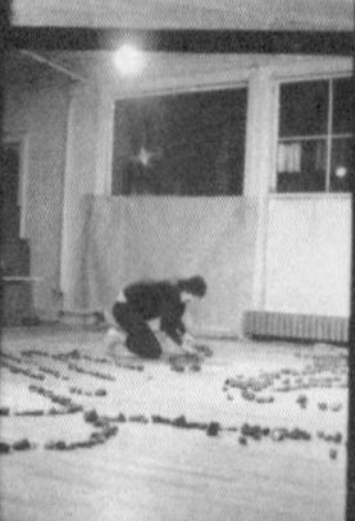

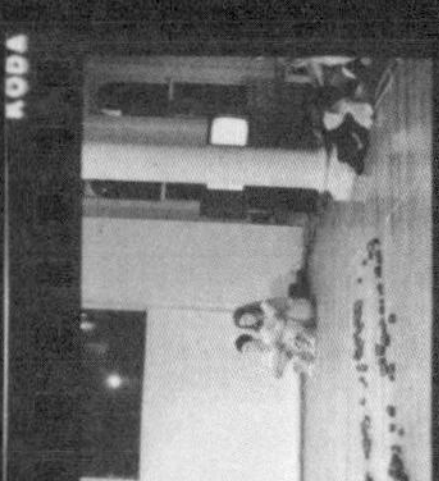
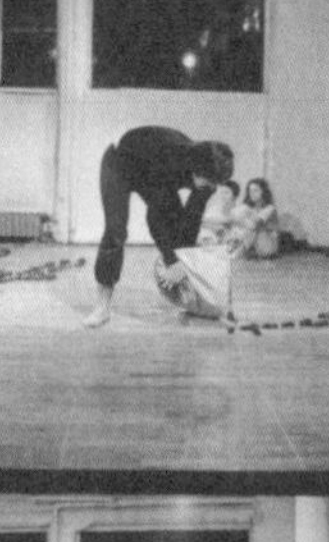
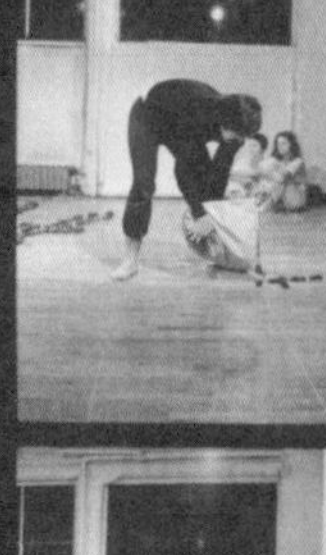
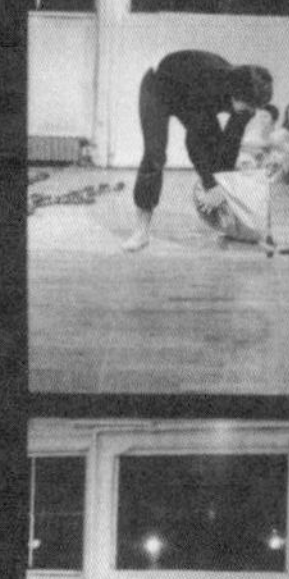
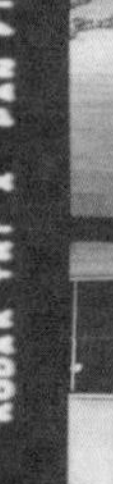

[Even after so many years away from the country, my] entire work has Chilean elements, because they are in my personality and in my life experience. I like the children's games, children's songs, and [Pablo] Neruda.

— Carmen Beuchat

Carmen Beuchat, *Nazca*, video dance performance in collaboration with Juan Downey, The Kitchen, New York, 1972. Carmen Beuchat Archive

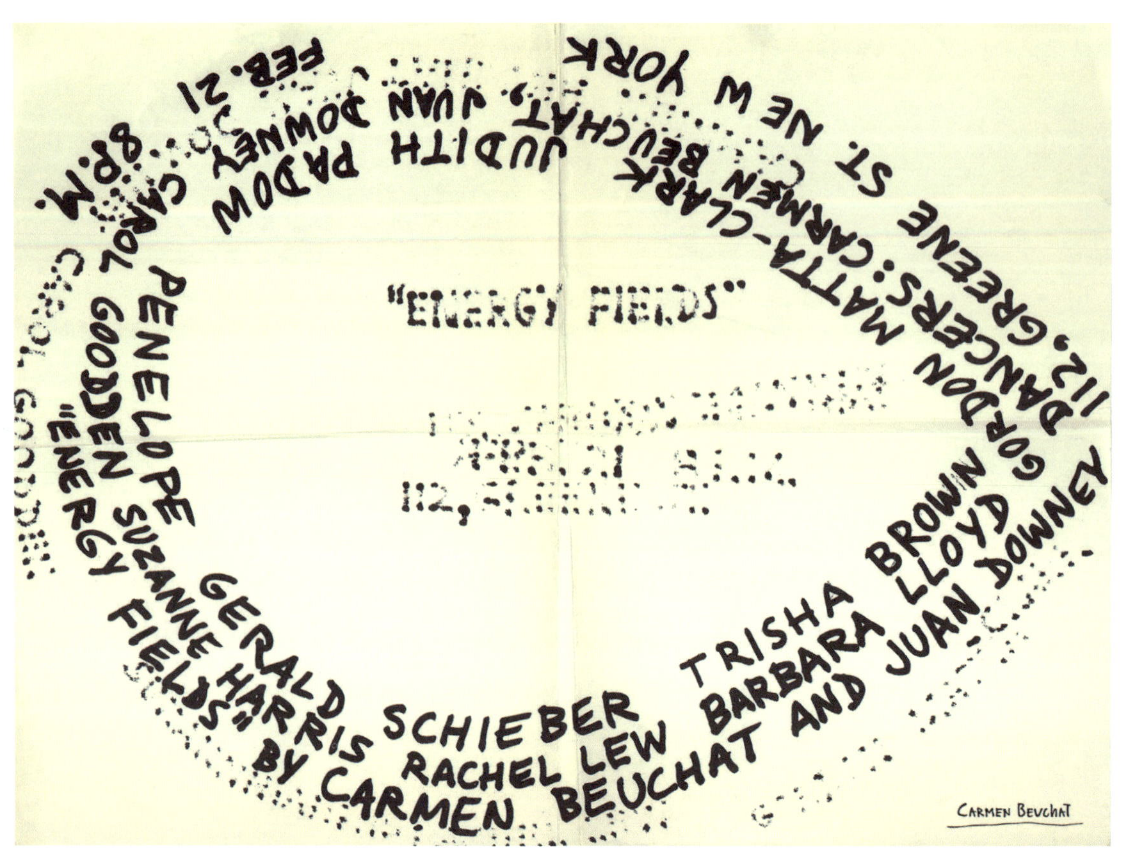

Dancer and choreographer Carmen Beuchat collaborated with fellow Chilean artist Juan Downey for several performances, including the piece *Nazca* (1974), which was performed at the Kitchen by Downey, Beuchat, and Suzanne Harris. A direct reference to the monumental geoglyphs created by the ancient Nazca civilization, *Nazca* involved the placement of pieces of coal on the floor according to the shapes of the ancient lines as part of a contemporary dance performance.

Poster for Carmen Beuchat and Juan Downey's performance *Energy Fields*, with Trisha Brown, Gerald Schieber, Penelope, Judith Padow, Gordon Matta-Clark, Carol Goodden, Suzanne Harris, Rachel Wood (Lew), and Barbara Dilley (Lloyd), 112 Greene Street, New York, 1972. Carmen Beuchat Archive

Poster for *Video Trans Americas*, a video series by Juan Downey, and *Nazca* and *The Flag*, two performances, The Kitchen, New York, 1974. Dancers: Carmen Beuchat, Suzanne Harris, Missie Zollo, and Gregorio Fazzler. Technician: Juanfi Lamadrid. Electronic Arts Intermix. Carmen Beuchat Archive

Sylvia Whitman Playful, Funny In an Hour-Long Dance, 'Going'

By ANNA KISSELGOFF

Fun is beautiful is what Sylvia Whitman seemed to be saying in a concert Friday night in a fifth-floor loft at 541 Broadway with her hour-long dance piece, "Going."

Essentially Miss Whitman's ideas are close to the avant-garde school developed by Trisha Brown, in whose company she performs. The same sophistication and the same playful, friendly mood enveloped the 11 sections performed by the nine-member Whitman group.

For a good start, there was a passage called "Dining Room," in which the company briskly picked up a table with dinnerware, as well as chairs, and carried the entire set off.

Miss Whitman has her own brand of pungent humor, and the honesty of her subtitles and of the entire piece itself was most refreshing. When she calls a section "Jump Up a Pyramid," she really jumps as platform after platform is piled under her feet. By the end, she has indeed jumped up a pyramid under construction.

Searching for a unifying theme in "Going," one might suggest that Miss Whitman proves that childhood games can be invested with formal significance. "Guessing a Person's Movement" described what a performer who was "it" had to do as he or she stood with closed eyes and another person moved about. (One man's blind man's buff is another man's movement analyis). Miss Whitman does not offer the complexity of Miss Brown but she too is an original and a welcome addition to a special area of dance.

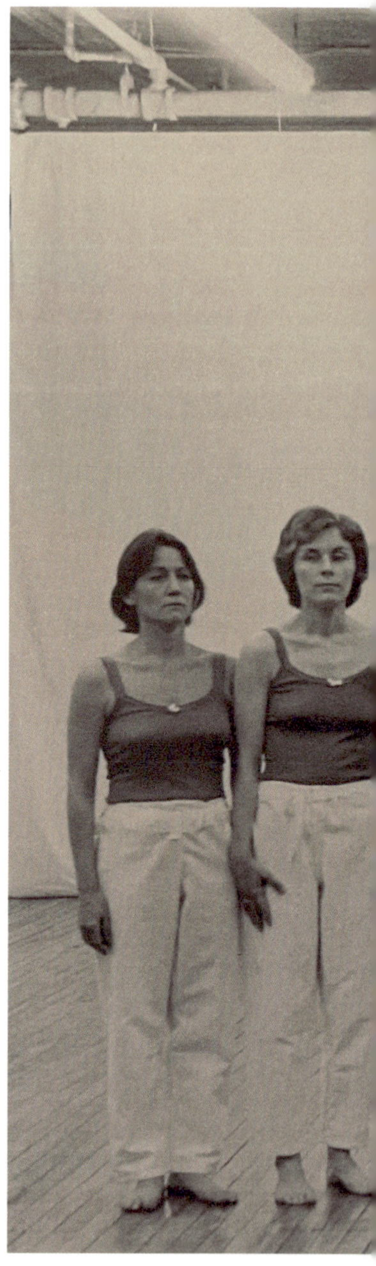

Anna Kisselgoff, "Sylvia Whitman Playful, Funny In an Hour-Long Dance, 'Going,'" *New York Times*, October 13, 1975, 79. Sylvia Palacios Whitman Archive

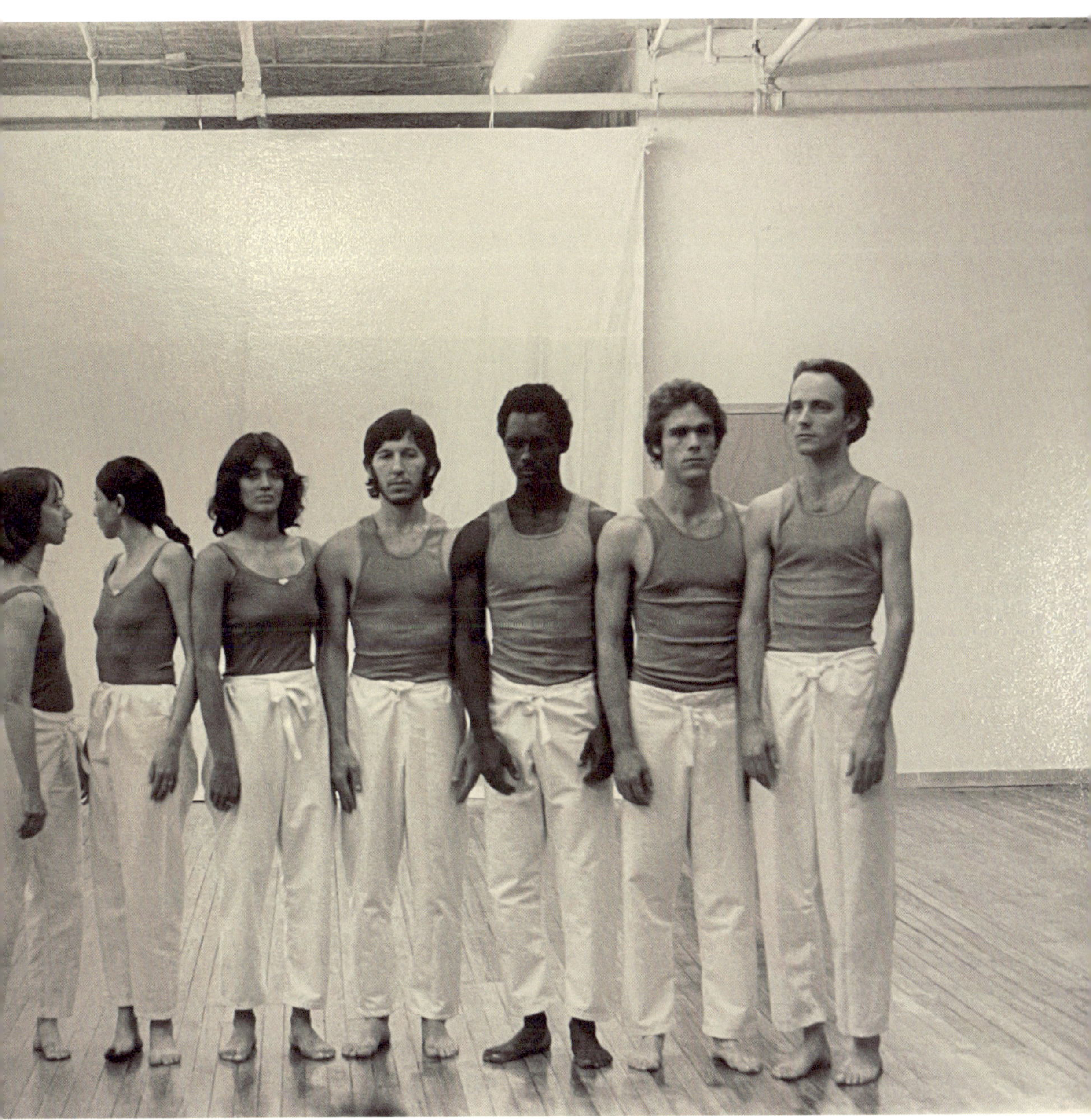

Sylvia Palacios Whitman, *Going*, Trisha Brown's studio, 1974.
Sylvia Palacios Whitman Archive

Sylvia Whitman's dance performance *Going* was presented on October 10 and 11 at Trisha Brown's new loft on 541 Broadway with performers (shown here in *The Birds*) Carmen Beuchat, Mary MacLeod, Nancy Topf, Sylvia Whitman, Olga Kluver, Chris Bigellow, Rodney Clark, Chris Murphy and James Barth. Other pieces in Whitman's program included the following: dining room, self lifting forwards, walking dialogue & stop, jump up a pyramid, 3 radios, guessing a person's movement, change of volume with distance, shoulder dance, nine people square, and shoes.

In these activities Whitman investigated the physical relationships between the performers, in terms of height, volume, bodily mass and configuration and thrust, but without didactic emphasis. The juxtapositions in themselves were humorous, and so was in particular a sequence in which one performer closed his/her eyes in turn and attempted to guess from the sound and timing of his movements which of the others was performing and to re-enact the specifics of his motions.

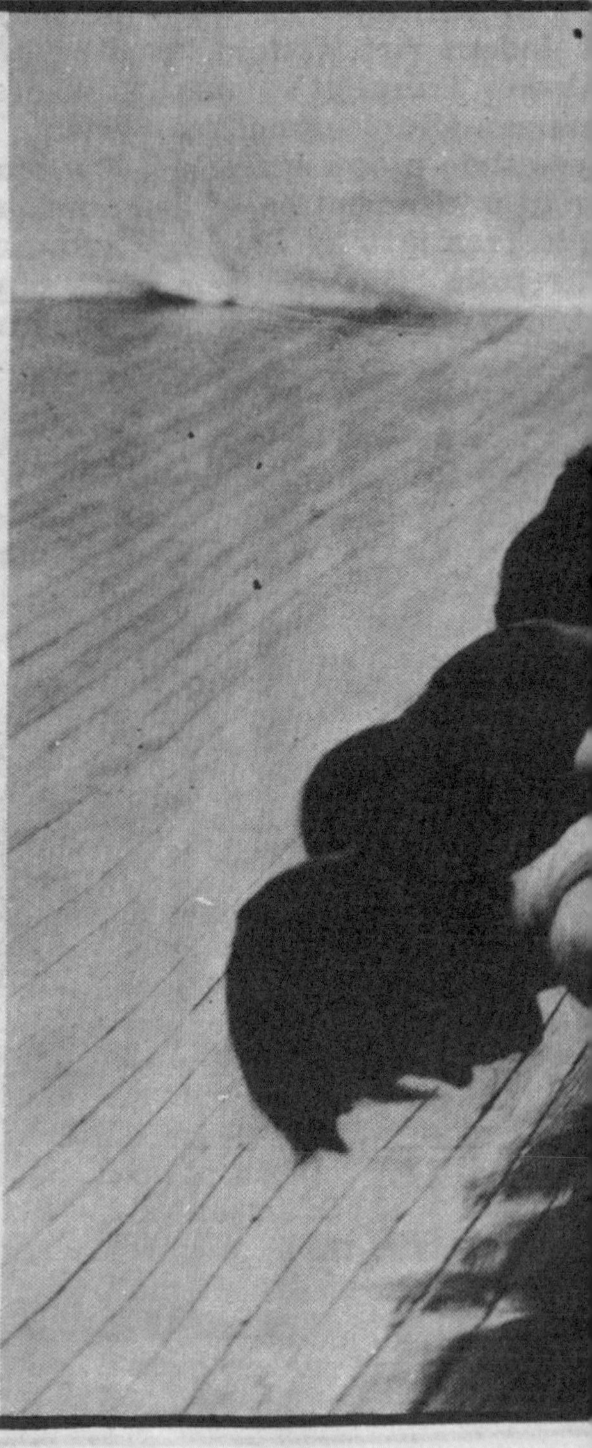

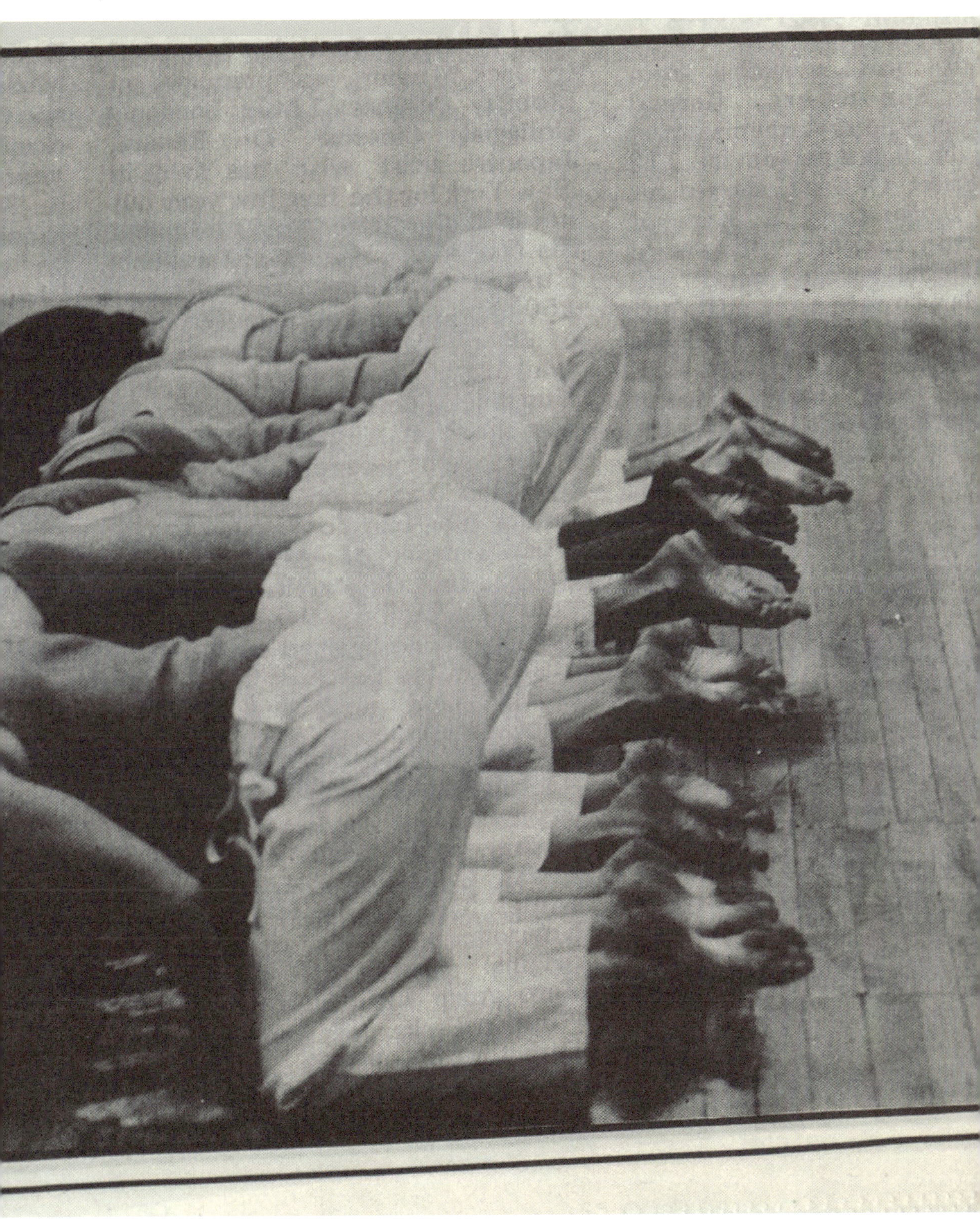

Review of Sylvia Palacios Whitman's *Going, Avalanche*, no. 10 (December 1974), 13.
Sylvia Palacios Whitman Archive

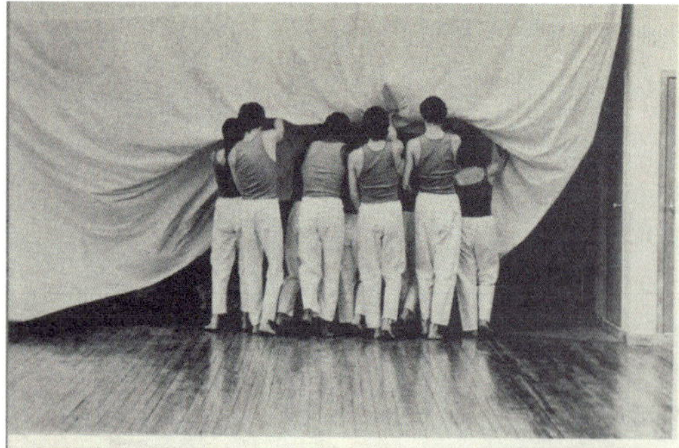

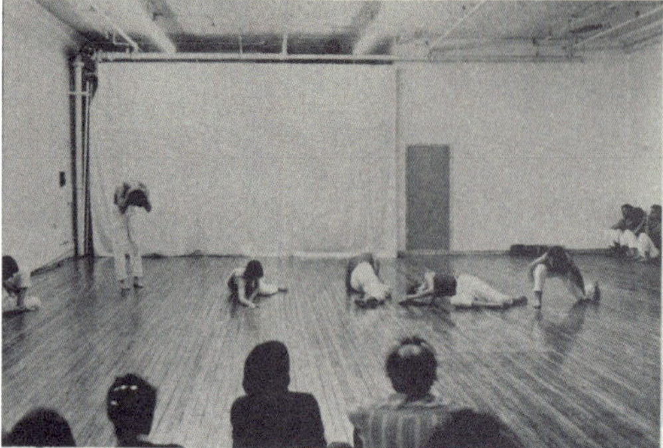

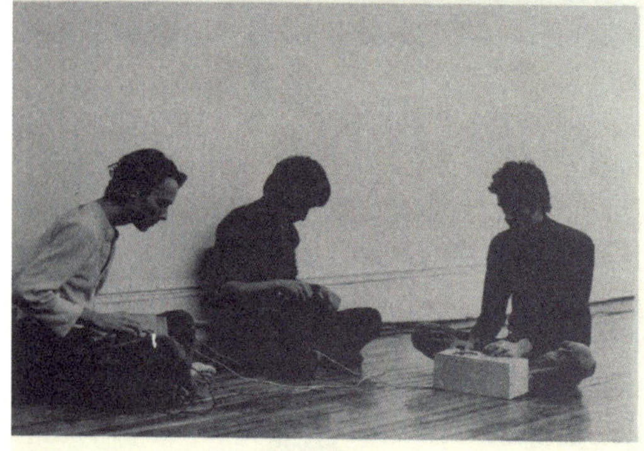

AVALANCHE, December 1974

Sylvia Whitman's dance performance *Going* was presented on October 10 and 11 at Trisha Brown's new loft on 541 Broadway with performers (shown here in *The Birds*) Carmen Beuchat, Mary MacLeod, Nancy Topf, Sylvia Whitman, Olga Kluver, Chris Bigellow, Rodney Clark, Chris Murphy and James Barth. Other pieces in Whitman's program included the following: dining room, self lifting forwards, walking dialogue & stop, jump up a pyramid, 3 radios, guessing a person's movement, change of volume with distance, shoulder dance, nine people square, and shoes.

In these activities Whitman investigated the physical relationships between the performers, in terms of height, volume, bodily mass and configuration and thrust, but without didactic emphasis. The juxtapositions in themselves were humorous, and so was in particular a sequence in which one performer closed his/her eyes in turn and attempted to guess from the sound and timing of his movements which of the others was performing and to re-enact the specifics of his motions. **LB**

GOING

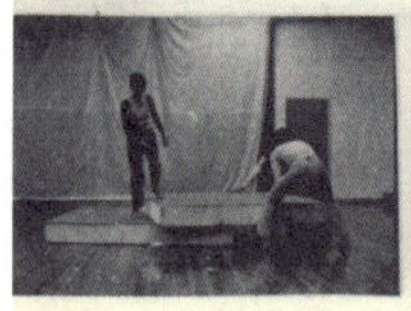

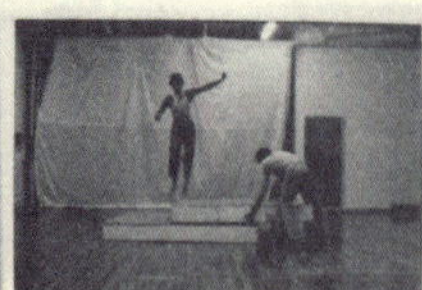

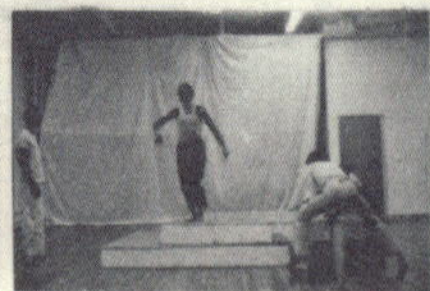

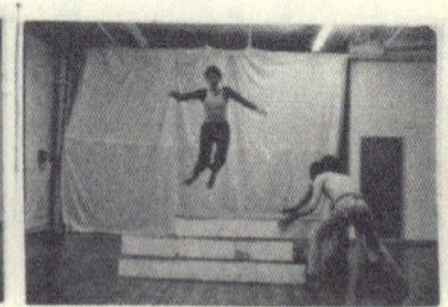

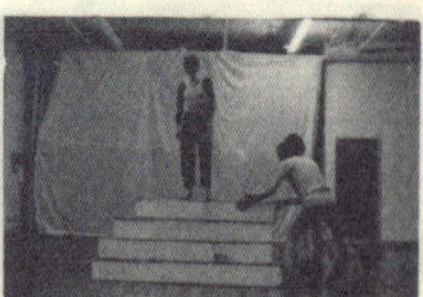

Catalogue for Sylvia Palacios Whitman's *Going*, Trisha Brown's studio, New York, 1974.
Sylvia Palacios Whitman Archive

Several people in a semicircle.-
The first person makes a shoulder-torso movement that affects the position of the person right next to him, who affects the one next to him. <u>But</u> at the same time, that movement is putting everyone back to where they started.—

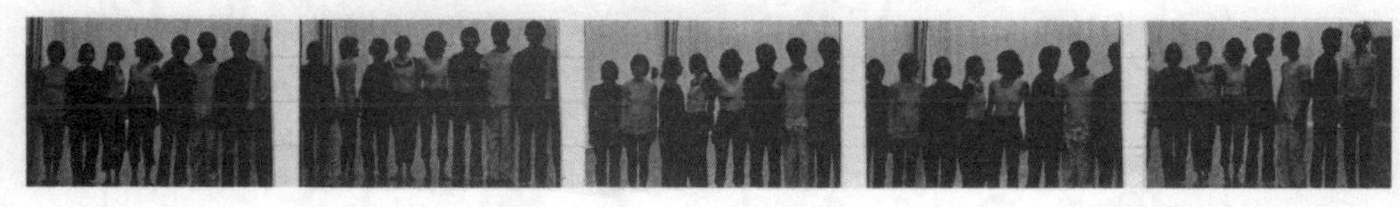

Photography: Babette Mangolte
Cover photo, Design & Layout: Mary MacLeod

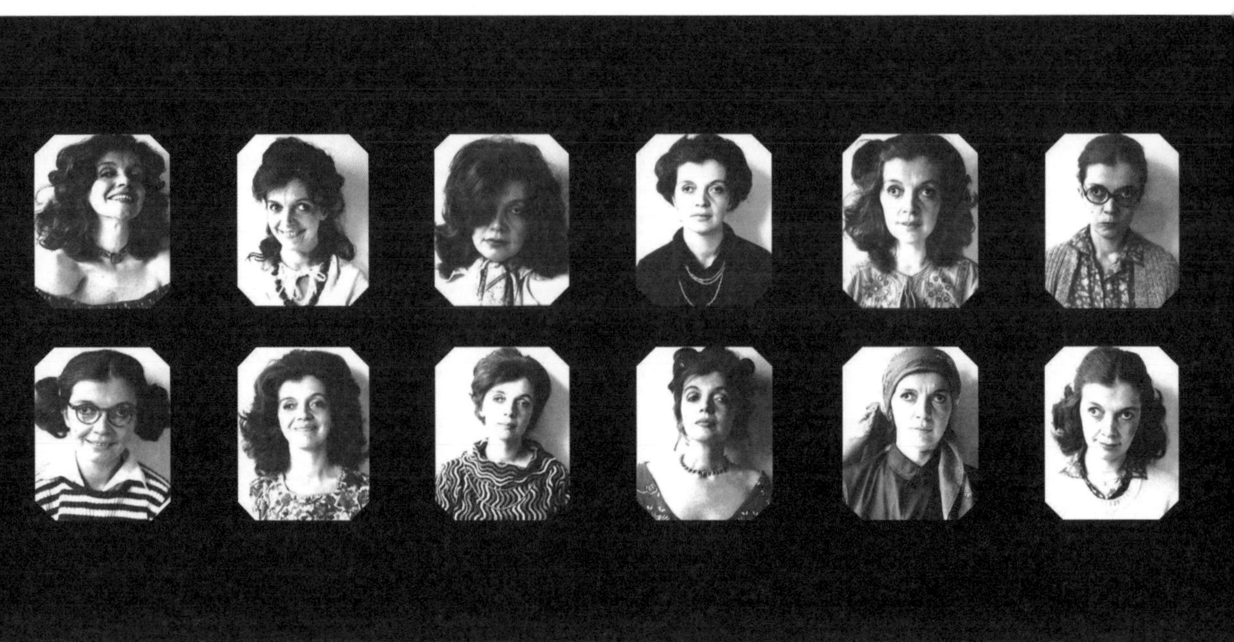

I noticed the role of Latin American woman trying to catch a man to marry, this whole thing about marriage, and this thing about the woman giving up careers to marry and so on. That's what made me do *Tina America*. . . . I wanted to portray Latin American woman, the characters they create to become successful in life.

— Regina Vater

Regina Vater, *Tina America*, 1976. Private collection. Courtesy of Henrique Faria, New York

I've sensualized knowledge of our culture through my art for more than twenty years and I think this work was rejected partly because I didn't want anything to do with the romantic idea of the artist full of subjectivity and inspiration. I'm more of an investigator than an artist. I see myself as using the sensualization of culture through its art products in order to create more enigma about culture. In this way I create a new narrative.

— Osvaldo Romberg

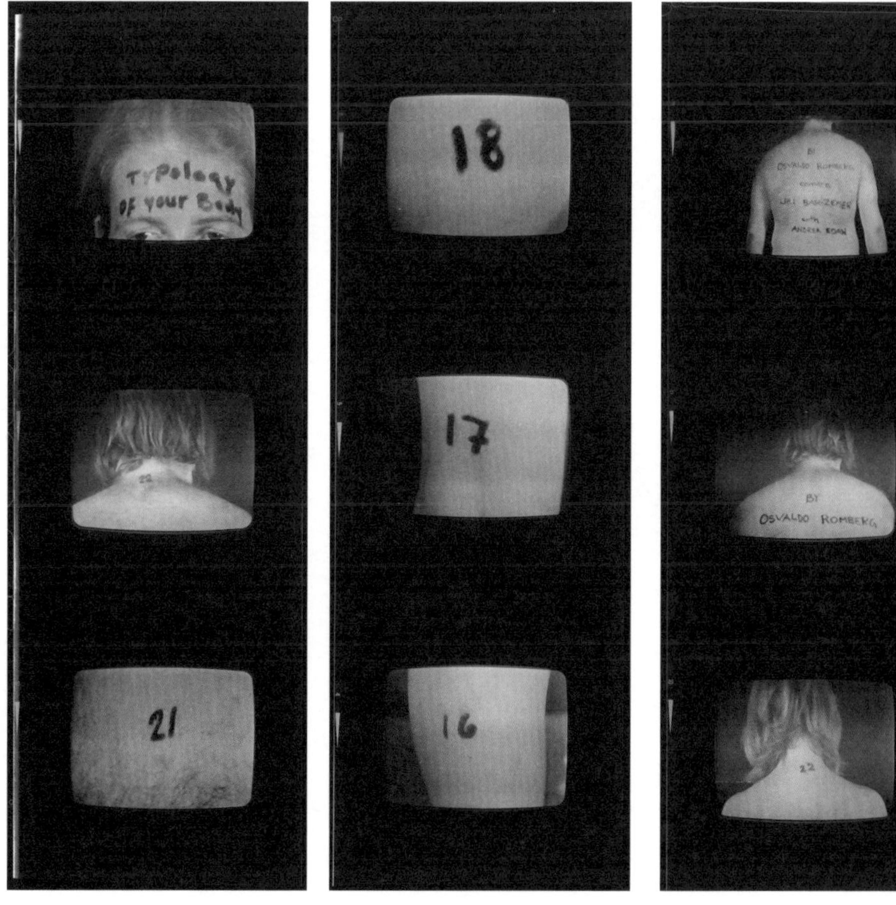

Osvaldo Romberg, *Body Typologies* (details), 1974. Estate of the artist.
Courtesy of Henrique Faria, New York

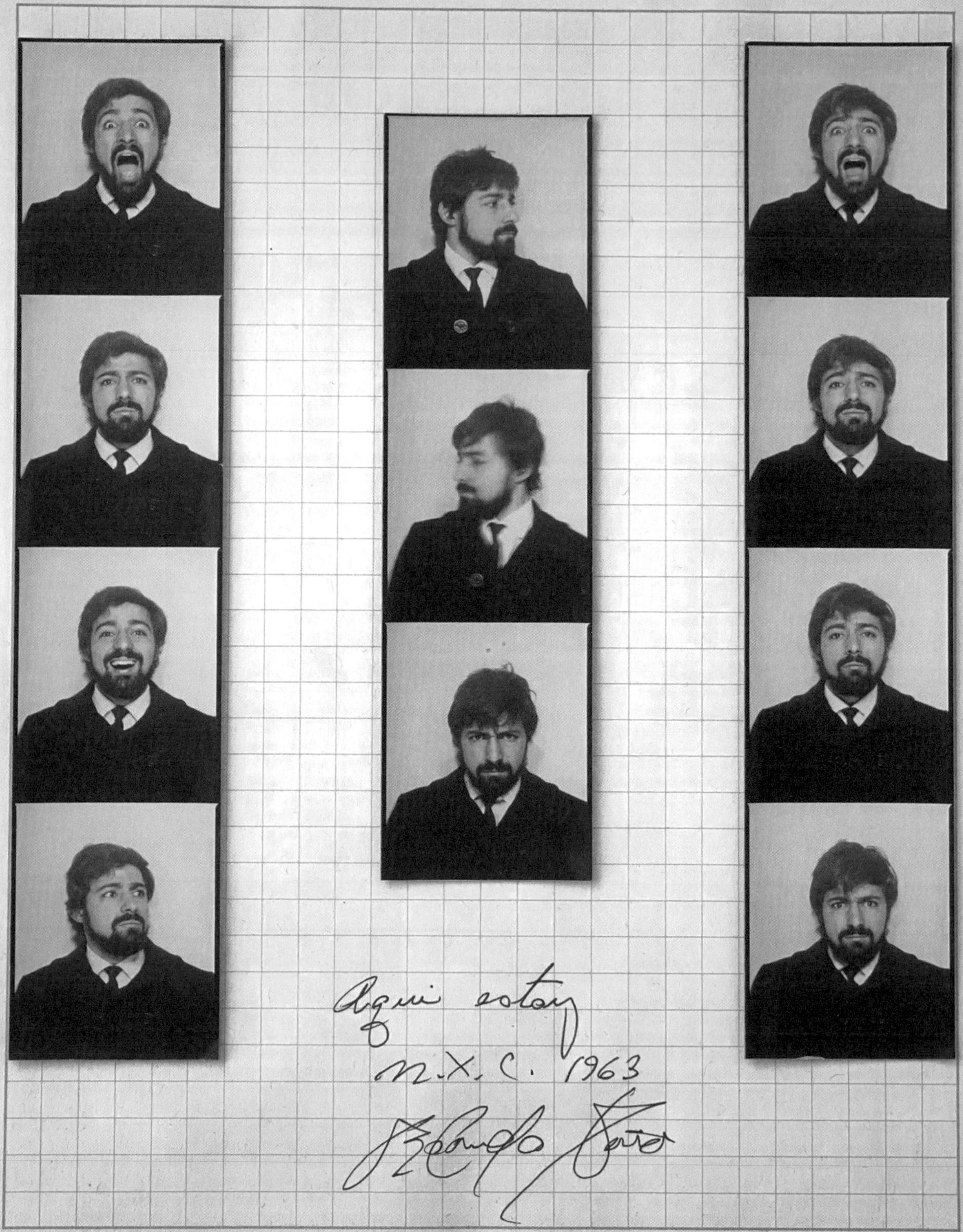
Aqui estoy
N.Y.C. 1963

Venezuelan artist Rolando Peña embraced photo kiosks as a means to create automated and sequential depictions of performances. In the 1960s he created the *Photomatons* series in which he performed private Happenings and intimate scenes for the camera. These works can be read as a play on Pop art's interest in commodity culture, as well as a commentary on the aesthetics of the photo ID as a bureaucratic document that classifies people.

Rolando Peña, *Photomaton "Aquí estoy"* (Here I am), 1963.
Fuentes Angarita Collection

At the beginning of 1969 I founded my own creative space dedicated to collage and engraving. It was like an alternative space for music, body art, and performances with Fernando Torm. . . . Soon we were printing our first collages that were inspired by the abundant material derived from gay magazines.

— Francisco Copello

Francisco Copello, *Calendario II* (Calendar II), 1974.
Juan Yarur Torres Collection, Fundación AMA

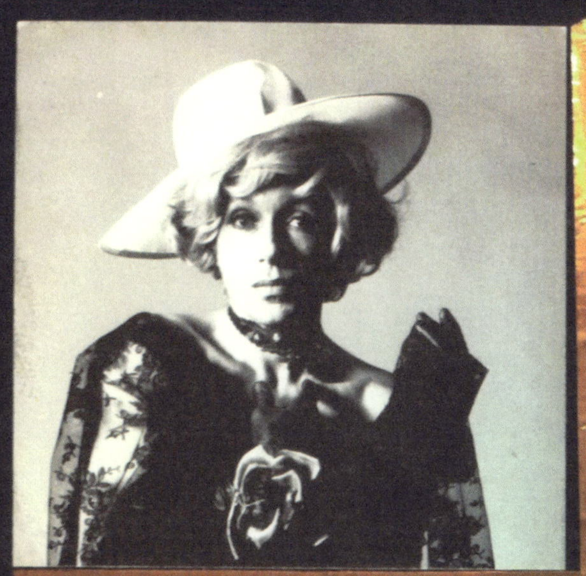

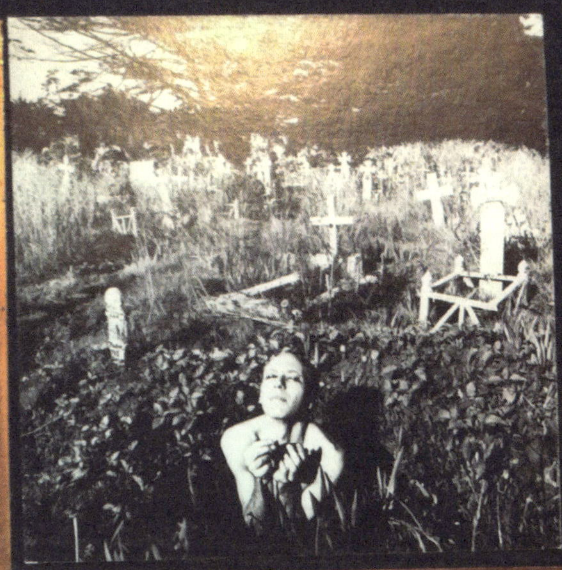

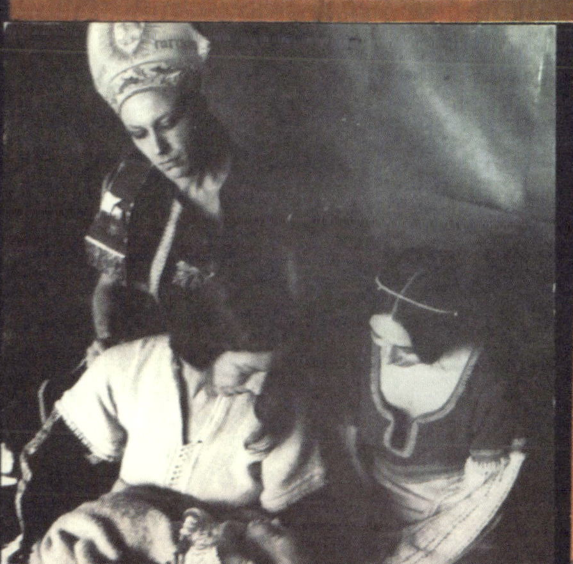

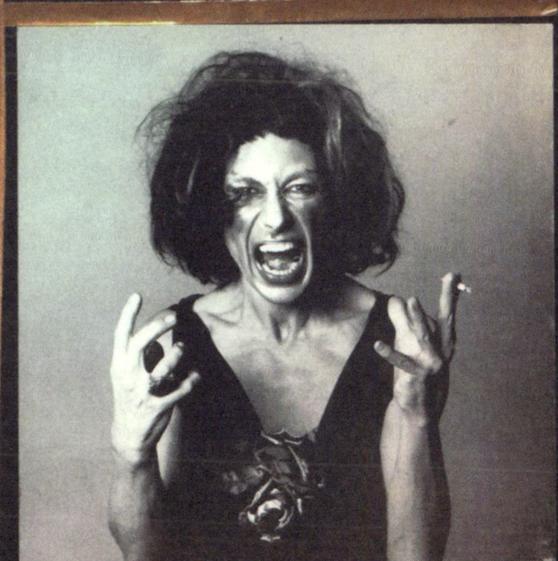

II

Cartemodare '74

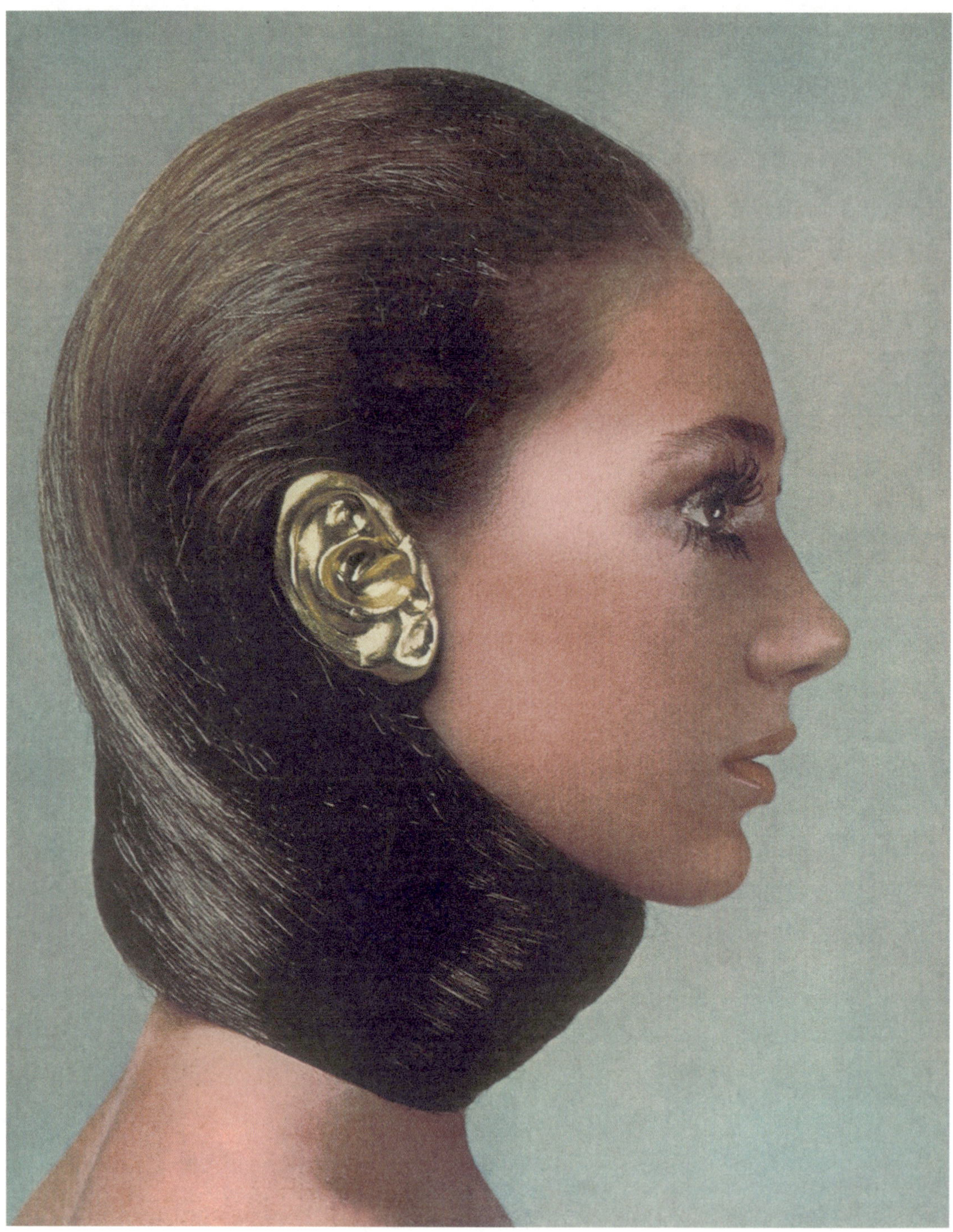

Eduardo Costa, *Fashion Fiction I*, 1966–70, *Vogue*, February 1, 1968, 170–71.
Modeled by Marisa Berenson, photograph by Richard Avedon. Eduardo Costa Archive

is gold sculpture that copies you

. . . it's made from a mould of your own ear, one of a collection of golden ears, toes, fingers, a single strand of golden hair designed by the young Argentine artist and writer, Eduardo Costa. "Costa's jewels," said Lawrence Alloway, "are a commentary on anatomy. He treats adornment as a kind of fiction." Soon, in fact, all Costa's objects will be characters in a novel—aesthetics dissolving into life.

AVEDON

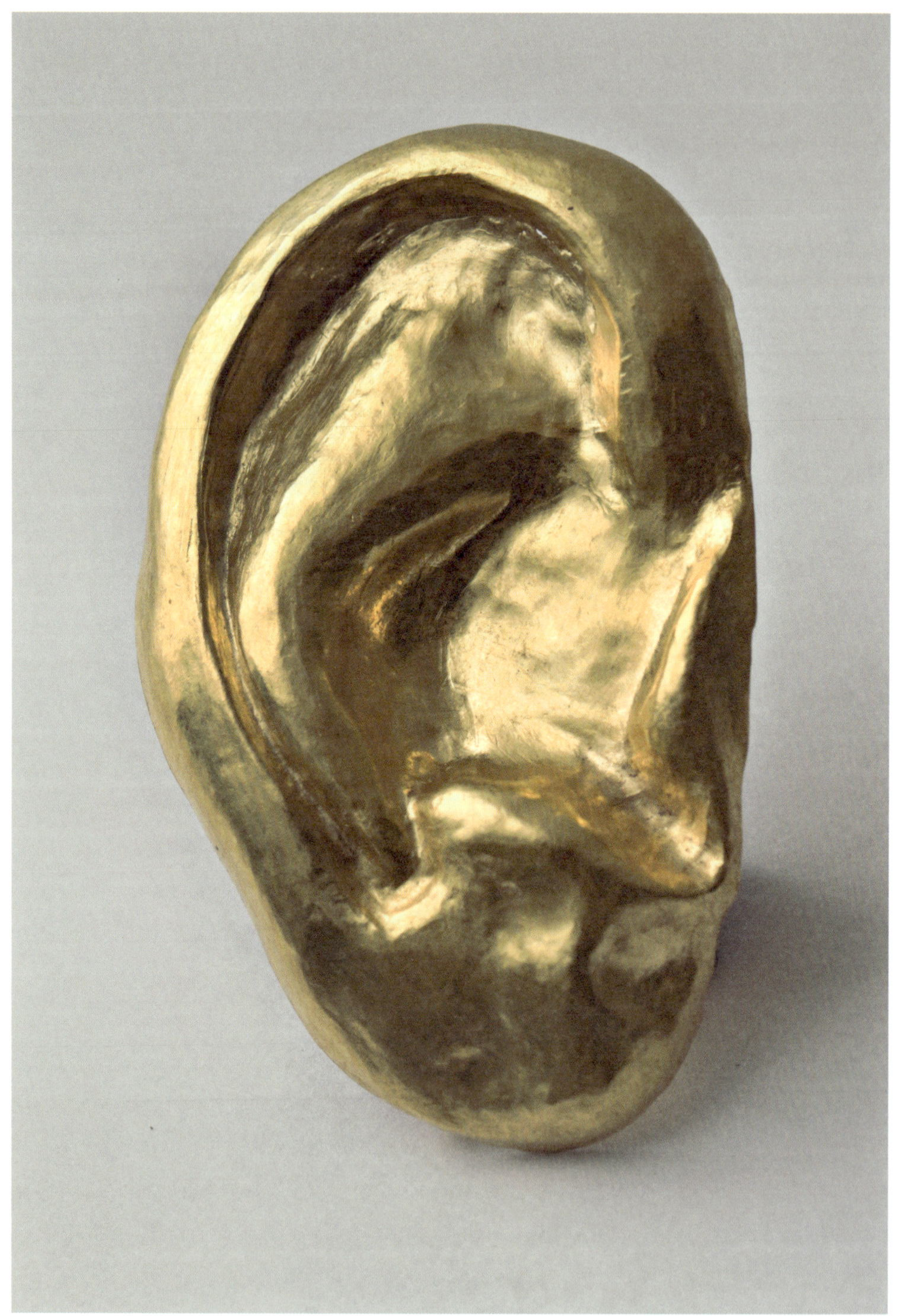

Eduardo Costa, *Fashion Fiction I*, 1966–70. Eduardo Costa Archive

Fashion, for me, always had a social importance. Reaching that level of fashion had nothing to do with beauty, I was doing something to get the magazines to accept, which is very different: to transmit false news, because false news is that, a jewel. [The ear] did not exist as a jewel, it did not have clips on the back to hold it; in fact, in the photo it is taped to the model's ear. That is why it was called *Fashion Fiction*, almost all fashion is fiction.

[M]y intention at that time was to show that the magazine was going to present it as real, because it said: "The latest fashion trend you can use," but it was unusable. [The series] was very much based on the jewels for the deceased that were made in America and Egypt, made of gold, like they used to put on thc fingcrtips of mummies. It wasn't to show off, or maybe it was, but in the other world. There is also a connection with the afterlife, pure gold is a very mystical material. The Egyptians, or North Africa in general, thought that gold was the sun on earth: when the sun sets, what lives and vibrates is gold. That mystical sense of gold is what always interested me. I thought, No, this can't be made of 18k gold, because it's a hard material and of a different color, instead the color of true gold is deep yellow that has no equal, it has another meaning for those who see it and use it. A nice way, if not perhaps the only one, that is to say that gold is the sun on earth. But of course, right away the marketing people appear who sell you something that's not gold, but only bathed in gold, and it no longer has that mystical force, but a commercial one; it's good for making a lot of money, because it's cheaper to produce than real gold.

— Eduardo Costa

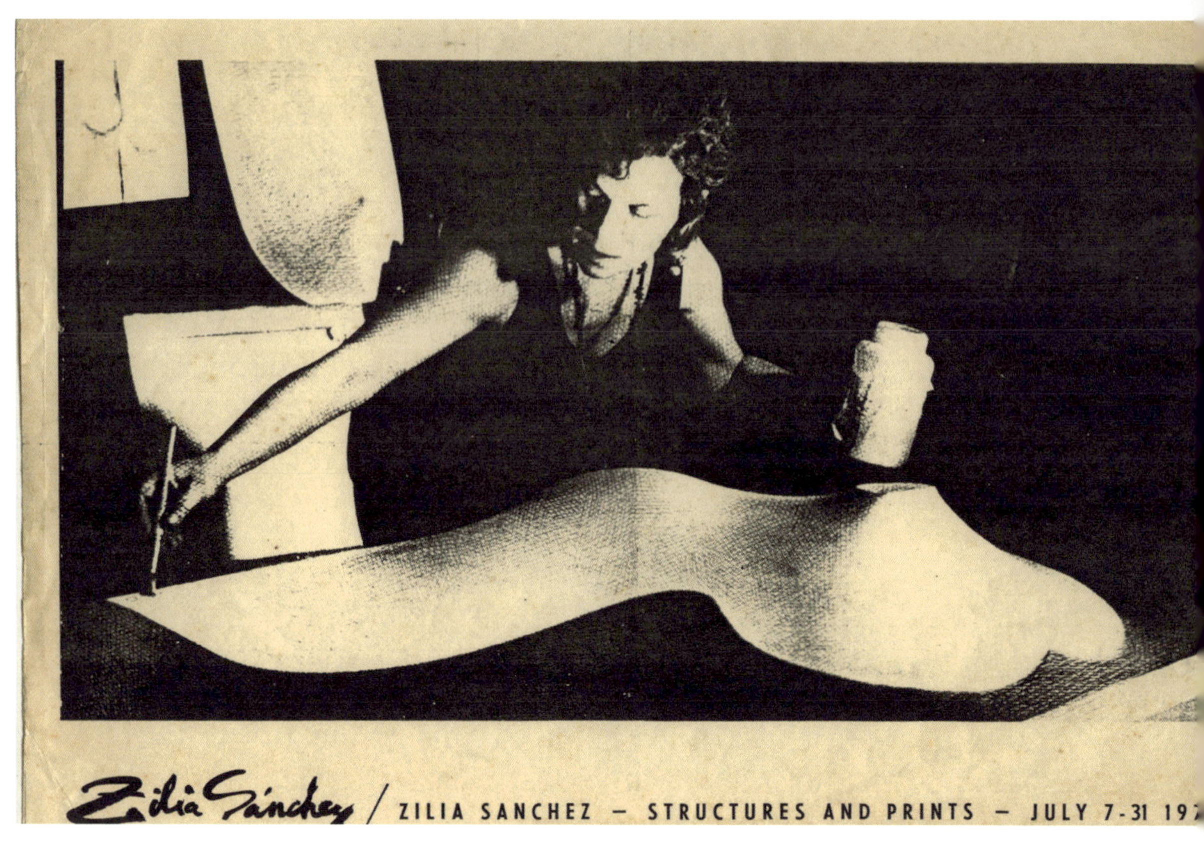

Flyer for Zilia Sánchez, *Structures and Prints*, Sarduy Gallery, New York, July 7–31, 1970.
Courtesy of the artist and Galerie Lelong & Co., New York

The works of Zilia Sánchez consist of canvases stretched on wooden structures that create rounded volumetric shapes. Suggesting the folds, invaginations, protrusions, and contours of the body, her canvases place the viewer as observers (or consumers) of eroticized shapes.

I read so many books on sexuality, eroticism, and communication. And then, one day, Severo [Sarduy] came to visit and whispered: "Those are tetas [boobs]–you did breasts, Zilia!" That's why I started to use "Eros" in my titles.

— Zilia Sánchez

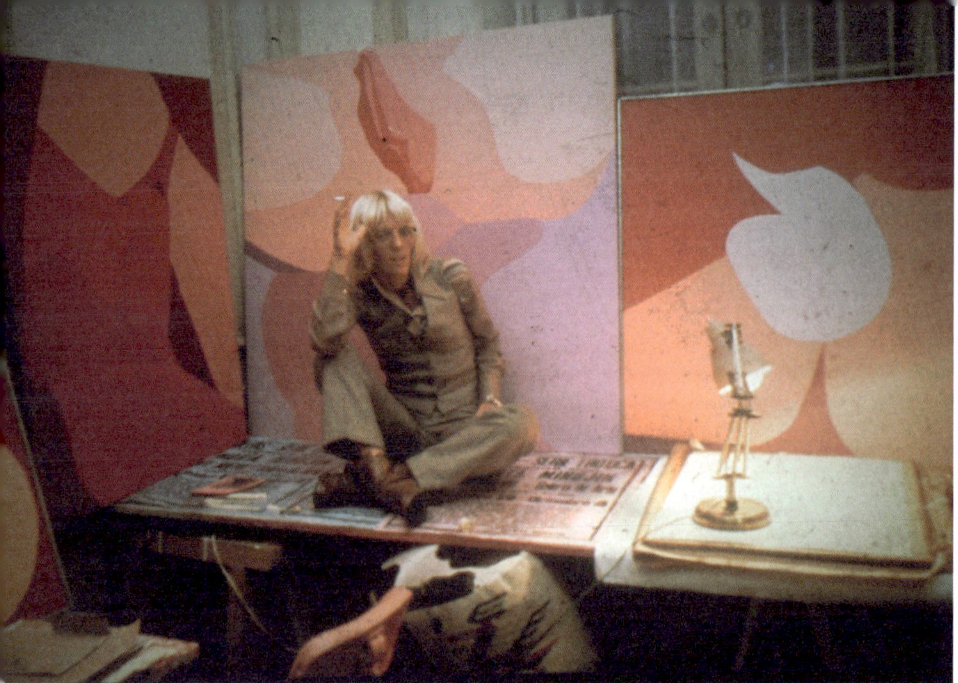

Marta Minujín next to paintings from the series *Frozen Sex*, ca. 1974. Marta Minujín Archive

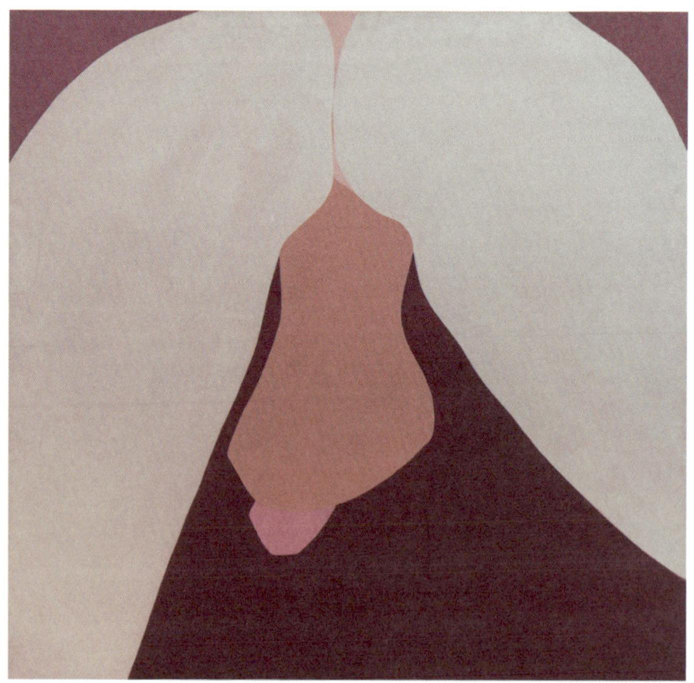

Marta Minujín, *Untitled*, from the series *Frozen Sex*, 1973.
Clarice Oliveira Tavares Collection. Courtesy of Henrique Faria, New York

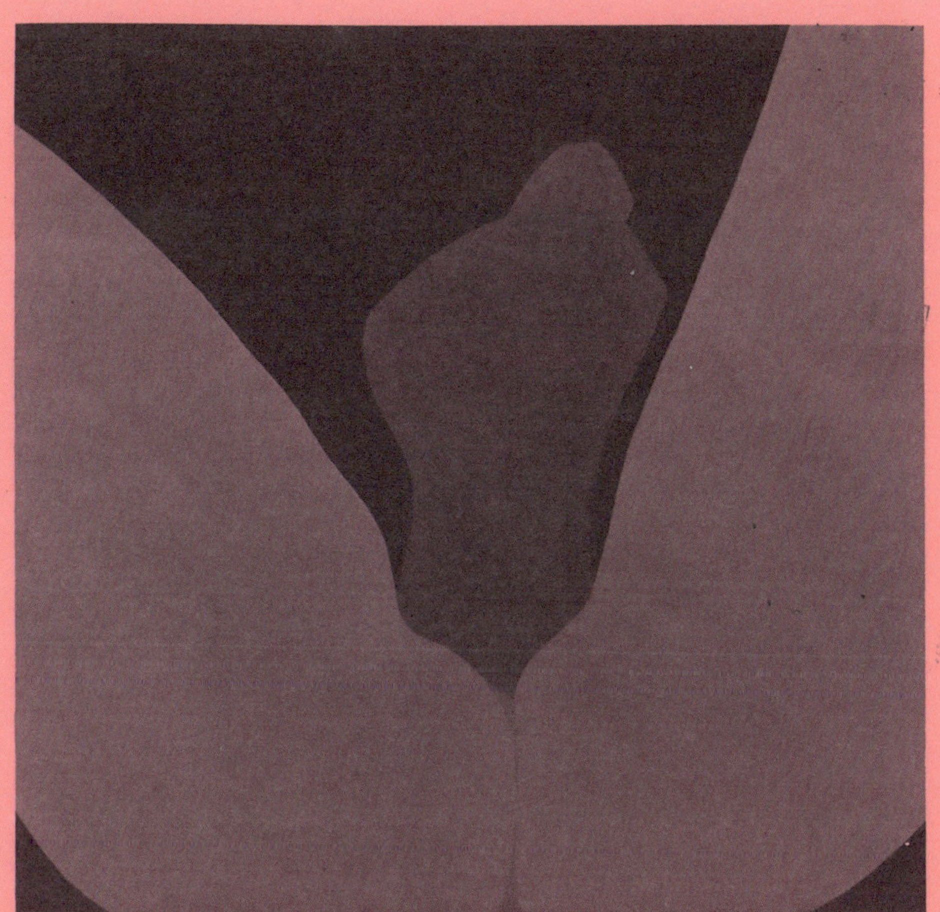

HARDART C presents: the art of MARTA MINUJIN this time: Frozen Erotisme

As a puzzle of the mind, abstract landscapes of anonymous glossy surfaces that remind one of commercial art methods for frozen food, reconstruct themselves into male and female sexual organs, which, simultaneously transform them into pieces of anonymous flesh. Through this conceptual process, Marta Minujin unveils the empirical instrument upon which eroticism was built, depicting them as anonymous objects of consumption. Sex no longer belongs to the individual, but to culture. As in contemporary society sexual practice and satisfaction have frozen that "universal feeling" of Baudelaire.

Julian Cairol

Poster for Marta Minujín, *Frozen Erotisme*, Hardart Co., Washington, DC, 1974.
Marta Minujín Archive

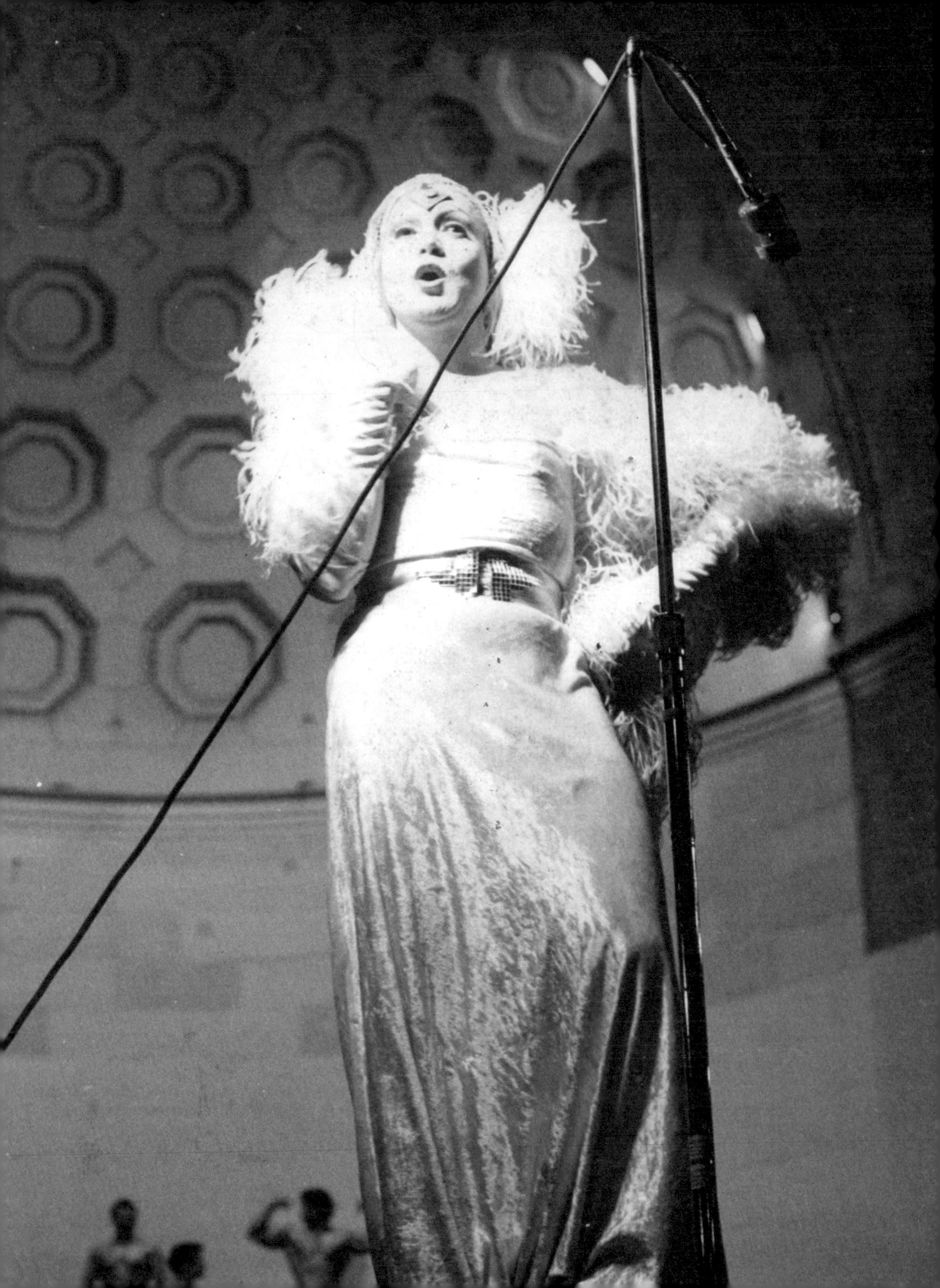

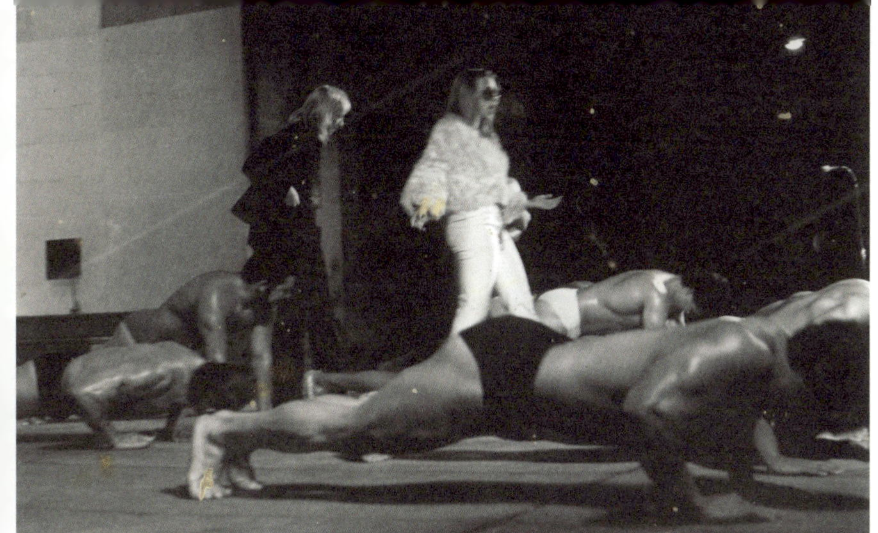

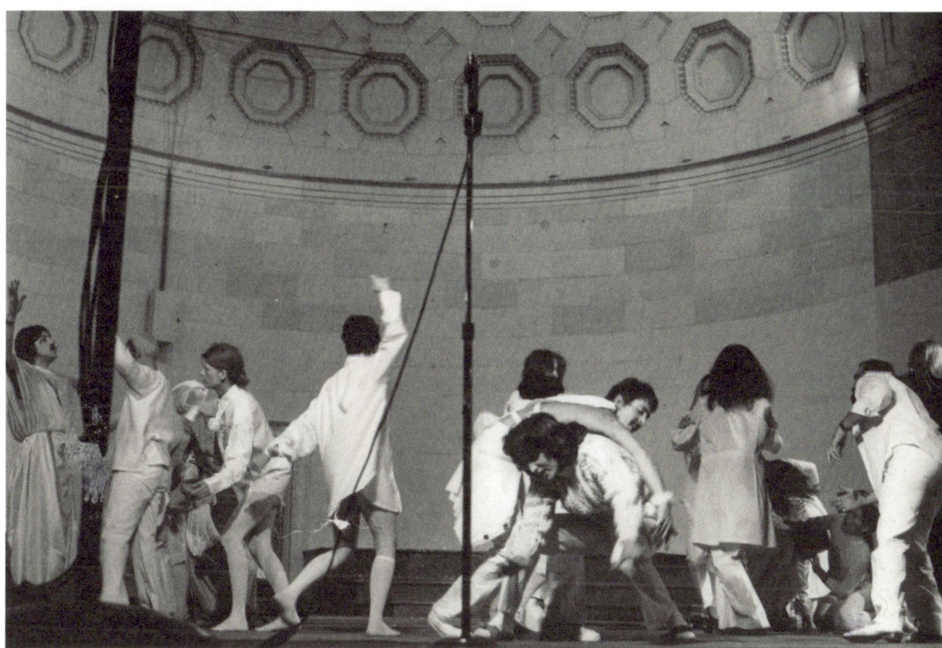

On September 24, 1974, Marta Minujín performed *Imago Flowing* at the Naumburg Bandshell in Central Park. An opera/Happening structured in four acts, it included twenty bodybuilders covered in blue-tinted Vaseline, actors dressed as angels singing lyrics inspired by the Greek philosopher Heraclitus, a Russian dancer dressed in feathers, and drag queen Alexis del Lago—initially costumed as King Kong and then transformed into Marlene Dietrich and Greta Garbo. The Happening ended in a private dinner performance.

Marta Minujín, *Imago Flowing*, Central Park, New York, 1974. Marta Minujín Archive

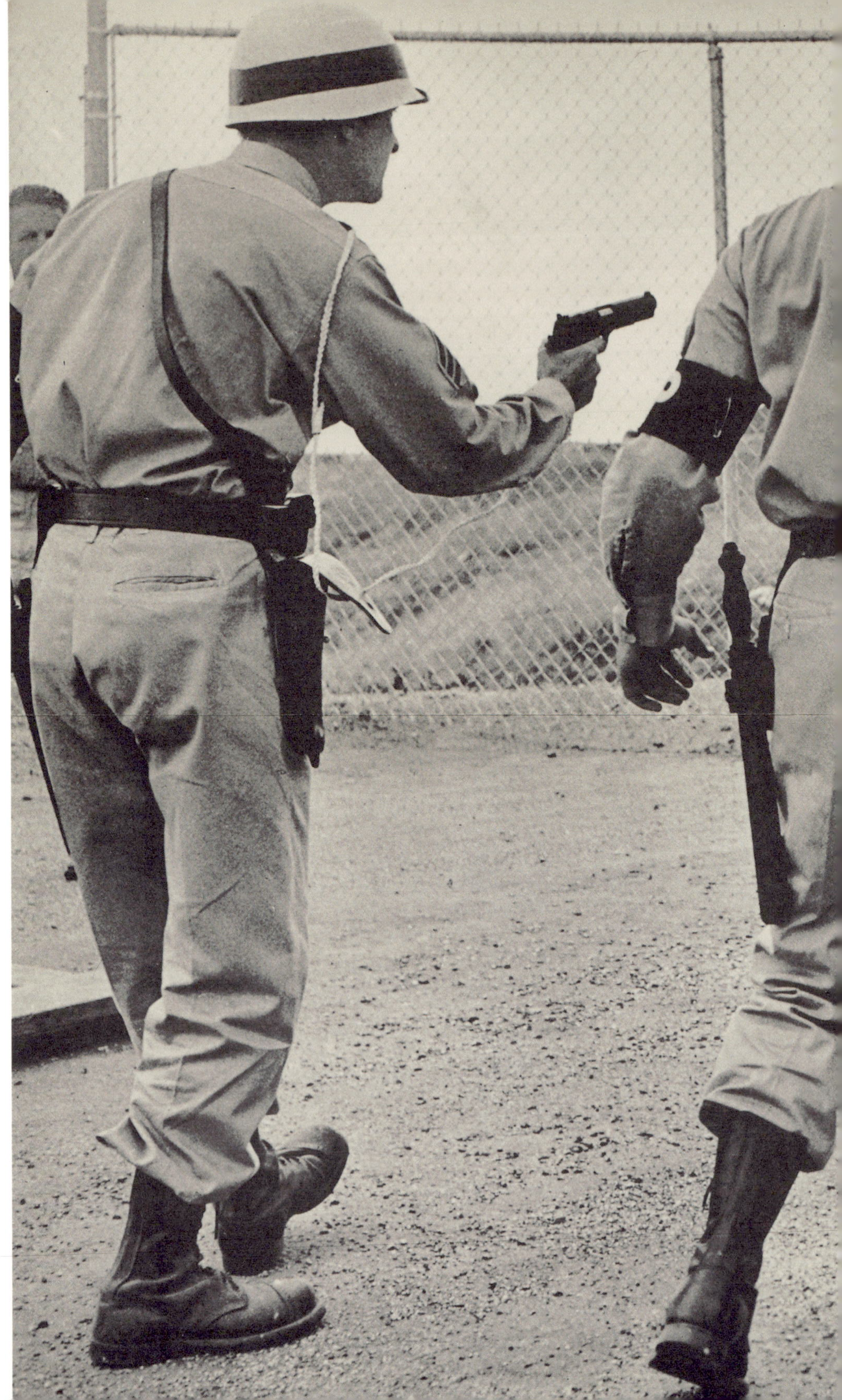

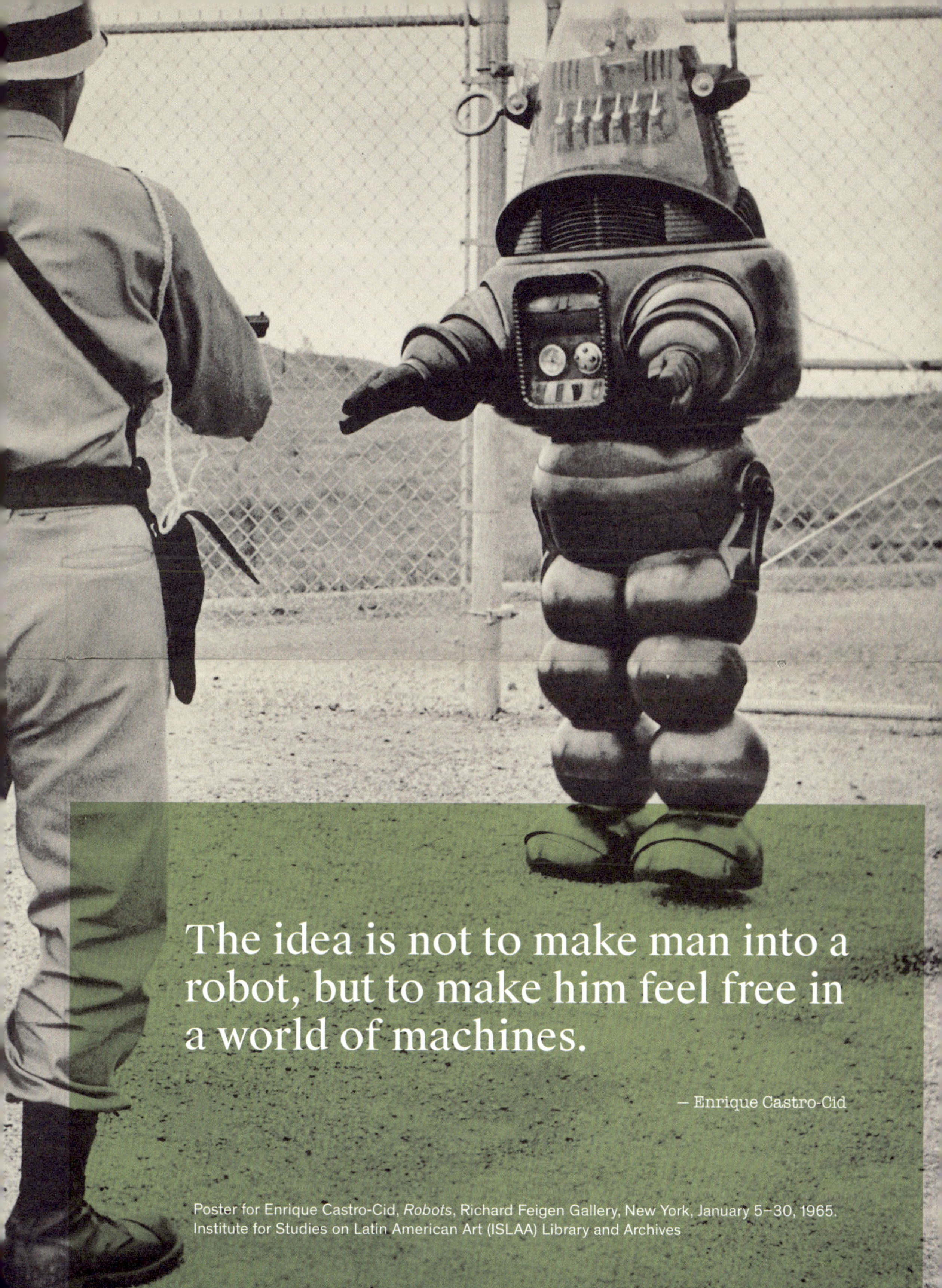

Poster for Enrique Castro-Cid, *Robots*, Richard Feigen Gallery, New York, January 5–30, 1965. Institute for Studies on Latin American Art (ISLAA) Library and Archives

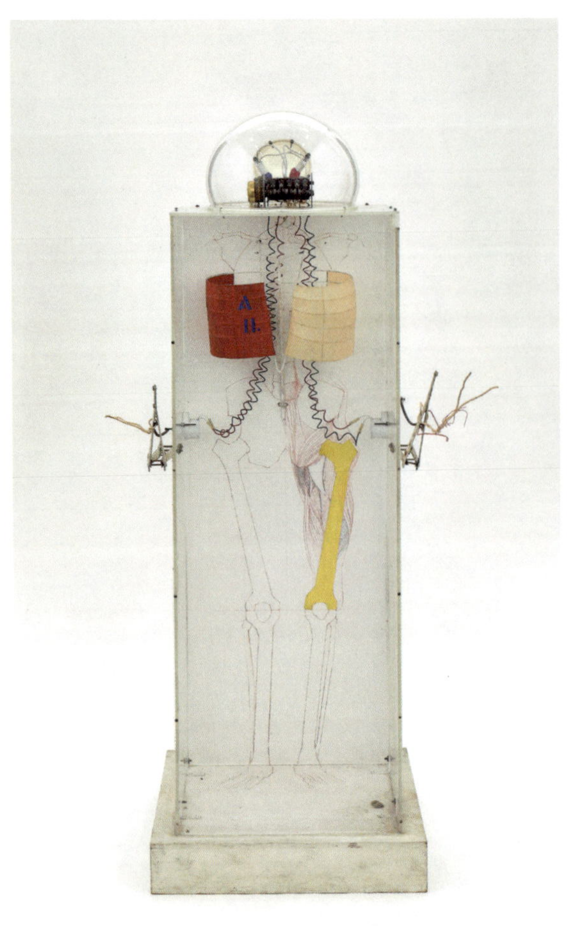

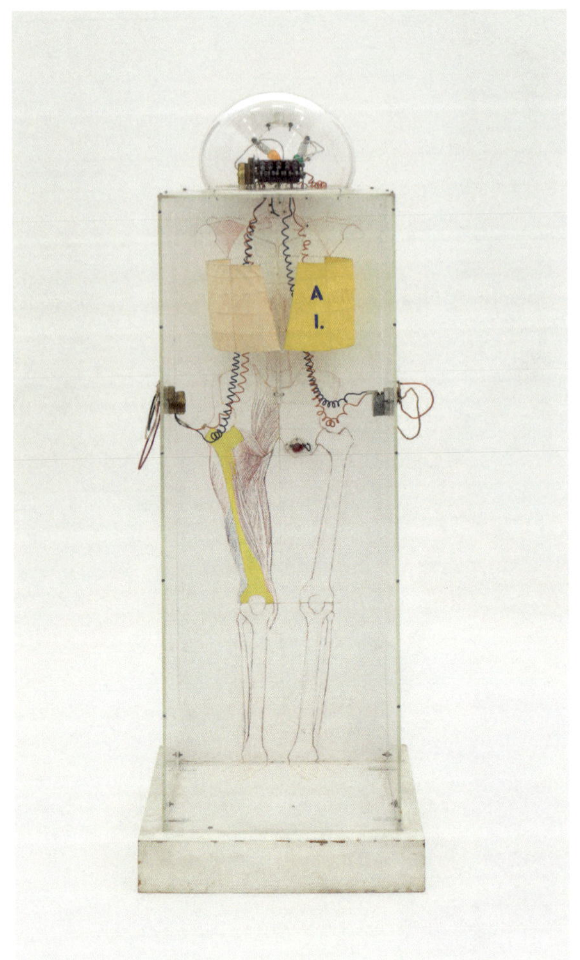

We are an alienated society. In the tribal society, games were a bond, so if this art is successful it too will create a bond. There's a lonely relationship between a viewer and an orthodox painting, but if the kinetic sculptures do something unexpected the viewer turns to someone in the room and says: "Did you see that?" It's like an accident that happens in the street–it causes people to turn to strangers and talk.

— Enrique Castro-Cid

Enrique Castro-Cid, *Anthropomorphicals I* and *II*, 1964. Private collection

I conceive of a future, without a technological crutch, in which ultra-developed human brains are deeply woven into the energy paths and patterns to an extent where disorder, war, waste and crime are out of context. Human beings would share with all other species the benefits of natural cycles: communicant balance.

— Juan Downey

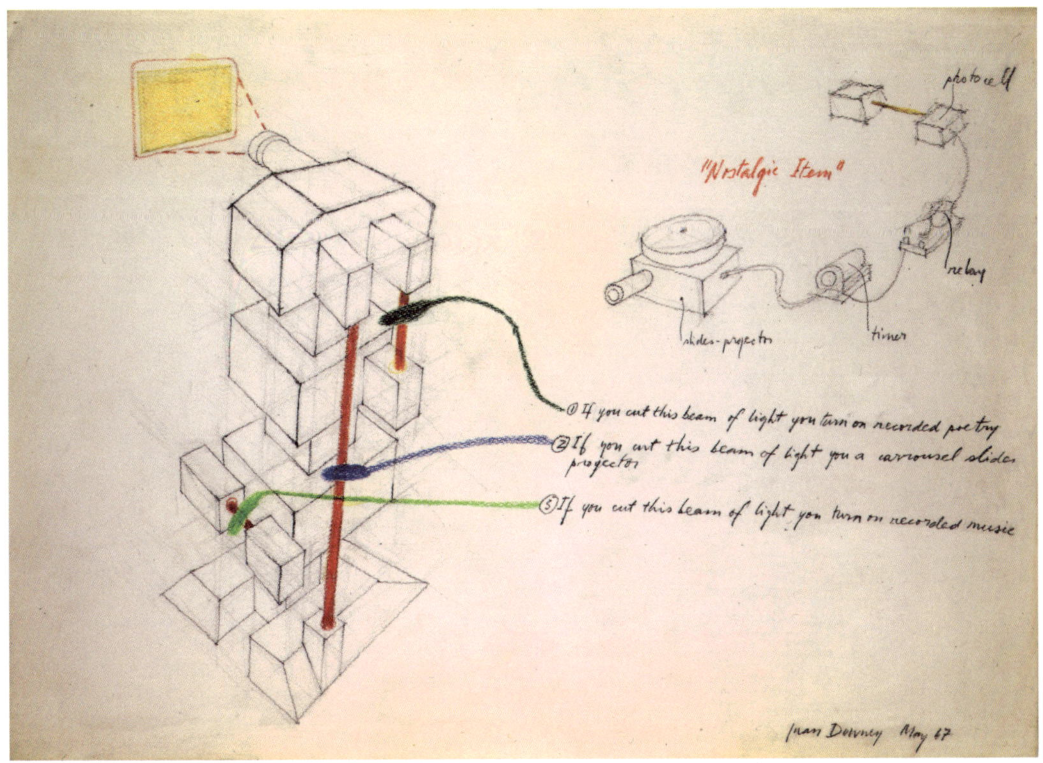

Juan Downey, *Nostalgic Item*, 1967. The Juan Downey Foundation, New York

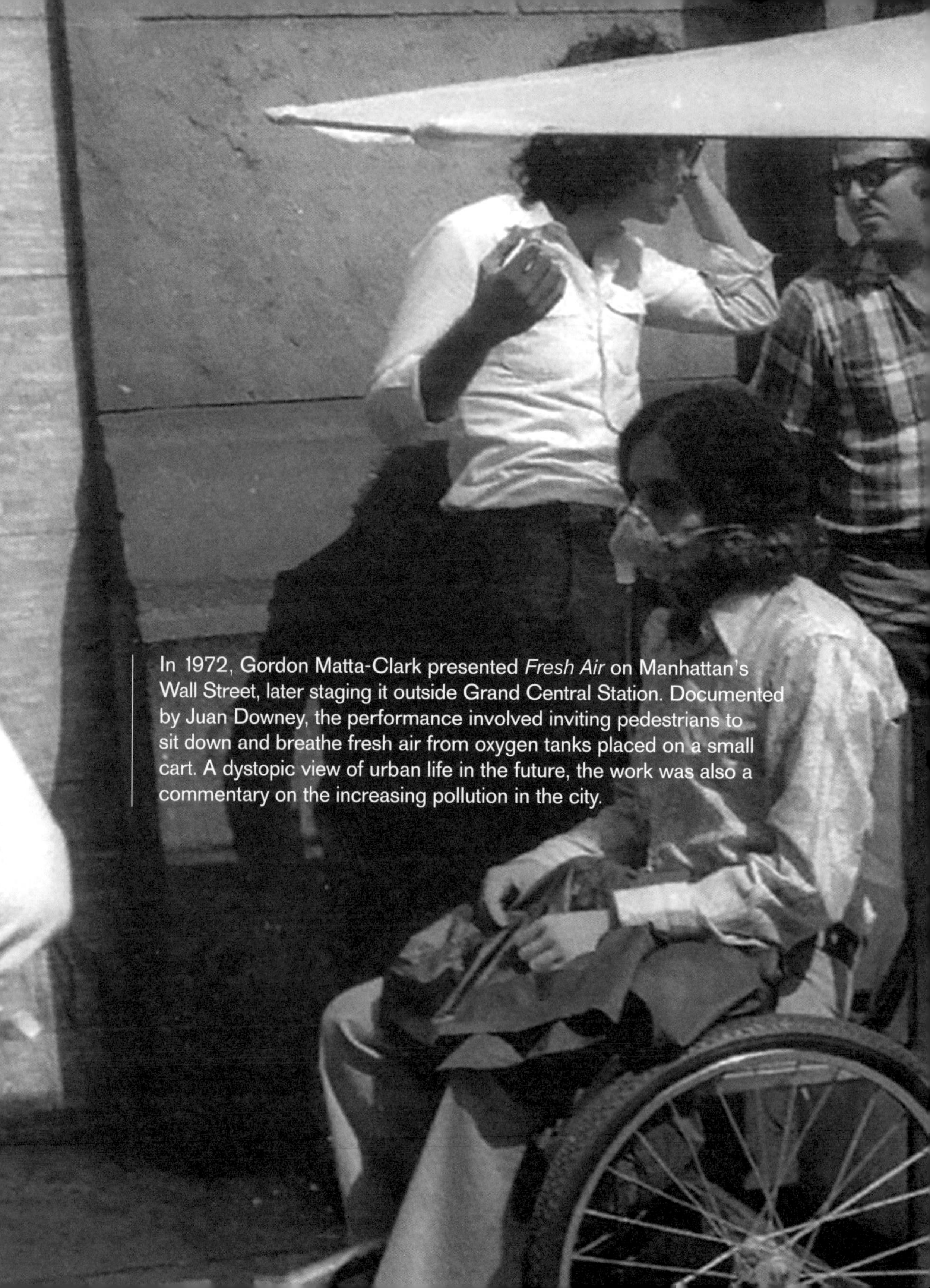

In 1972, Gordon Matta-Clark presented *Fresh Air* on Manhattan's Wall Street, later staging it outside Grand Central Station. Documented by Juan Downey, the performance involved inviting pedestrians to sit down and breathe fresh air from oxygen tanks placed on a small cart. A dystopic view of urban life in the future, the work was also a commentary on the increasing pollution in the city.

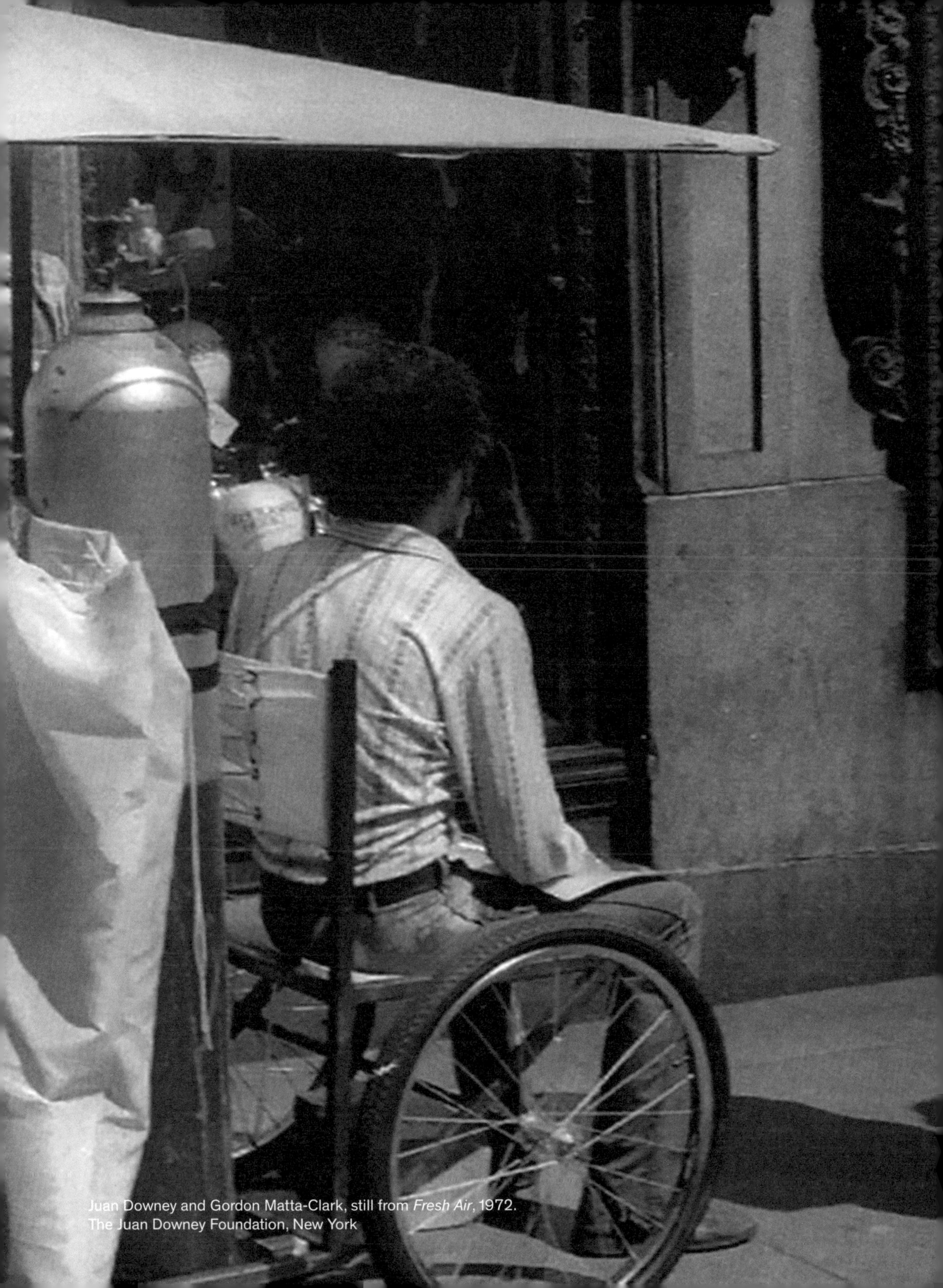

Juan Downey and Gordon Matta-Clark, still from *Fresh Air*, 1972.
The Juan Downey Foundation, New York

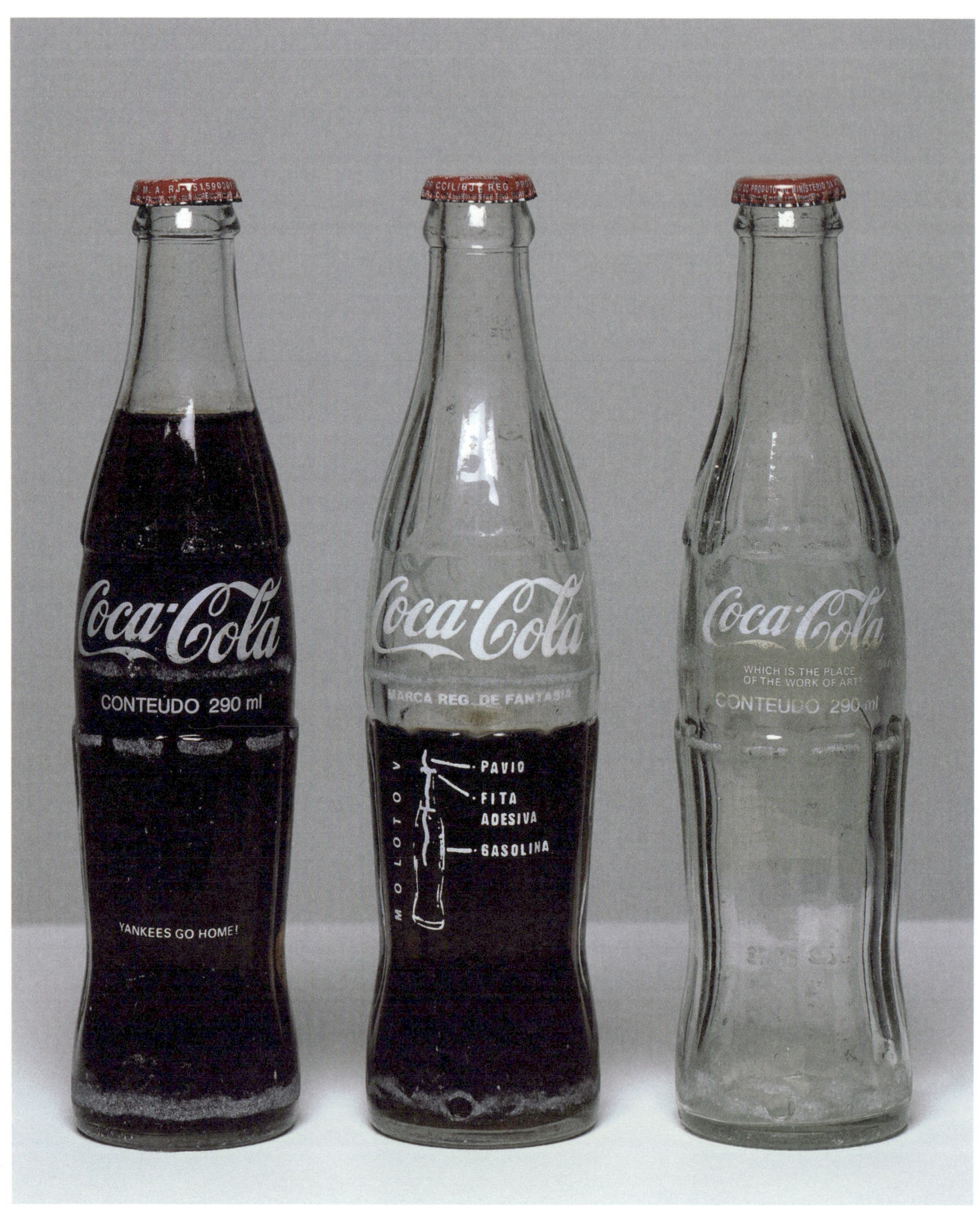

Fig. 11 Cildo Meireles, *Inserções em circuitos ideológicos: Projeto Coca-Cola* (Insertions into ideological circuits: Coca-Cola project), 1970. Cildo Meireles/Tate

Harper Montgomery

Cildo Meireles in New York: Coca-Cola Bottles and Subway Tokens

Cildo Meireles lived in New York in his early twenties. Funding his trip with the $6,000 prize money he won at an exhibition for emerging artists at the Museum of Modern Art of Rio de Janeiro, he left Rio in 1971 for New York City, where he lived for two years.[1] Prior to his arrival, Meireles was featured in a groundbreaking survey of Conceptualism organized by the Museum of Modern Art in 1970: *Information*. In this extraordinarily experimental exhibition, he displayed the first iterations of a series that has since earned him significant prominence in histories of Conceptualism: *Insertions into Ideological Circuits: Coca-Cola* (fig. 11) and *Banknote Projects*.[2] Meireles's works were largely ignored by the press when they were shown at the time and when he moved to New York a year later he was, like many arrivals from Latin America, excluded from the city's buzzing art market. This shaped his work in New York, ultimately leading him to expand his *Insertions* projects in fascinating directions, trading the term *Ideological Circuits* for *Anthropological Circuits* between 1971 and 1973, while he developed a series in which he took advantage of the critical insight that came with his status as an outsider and observer of New York.

Insertions into Ideological Circuits: Coca-Cola and *Banknote Projects* made use of site-specificity to raise the issue of US imperialism in Latin America.[3] New York, as the center of an international art world, and the Museum of Modern Art, as an institution ruled by a United States-based elite, were targets of political actions staged by artists between 1969 and 1971.[4] As art historian Teresa Santa Cruz Oliveira has chronicled in her analysis of *Insertions'* premiere at MoMA, Meireles sent two empty bottles and two banknotes to New York, which were displayed in the gallery in a small vitrine. The bottles and banknotes alike were stamped with the messages "Yankees Go Home!" in English and, underneath the Coca-Cola logo, in Portuguese, the statement "Marca Reg. de Fantasia" (Fantasy Trademark) and the work's title and instructions: "*Inserções em*

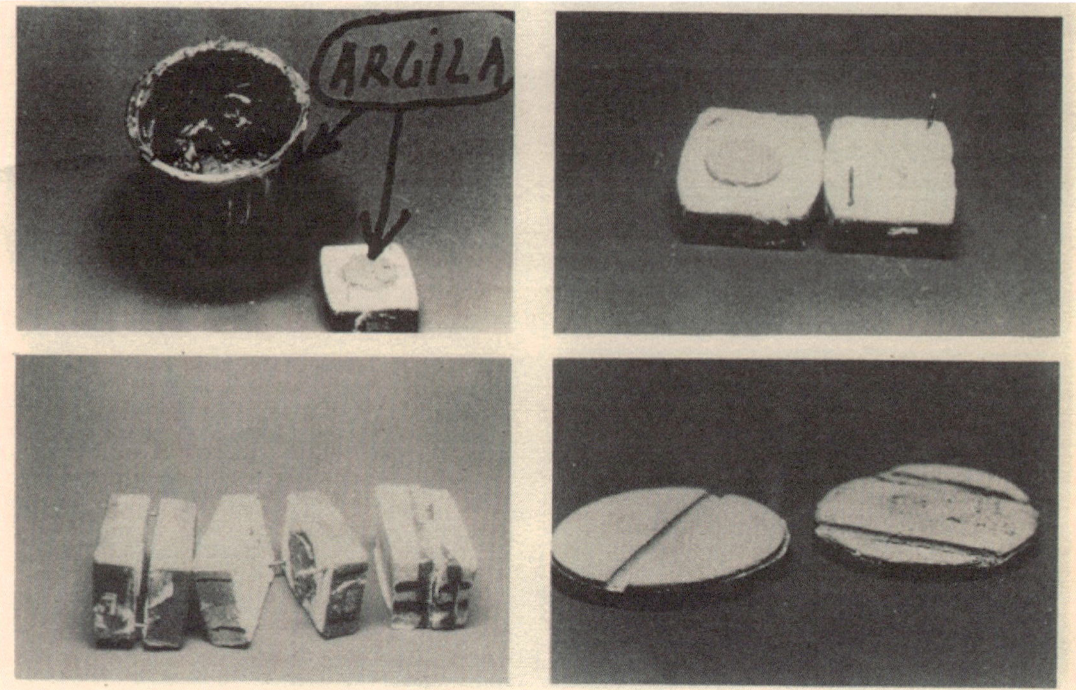

circuitos ideológicos: Projeto Coca-Cola, Gravar nas garrafas opiniões críticas e devolve-las à circulação" (Record critical opinions on the bottles and return them to circulation).[5] Like many of his Latin American peers of the 1960s and '70s, Meireles appropriated aspects of Coca-Cola's marketing to critique the economic domination of the region by US industry.[6] Emptied of the dark-brown liquid, as they were displayed at MoMA, the bottles disappeared and their iconicity–so prevalent in US Pop artists' references–was undermined. At MoMA, moreover, Meireles's bottles shared a gallery with photographic images of Vietnam's violence that focused attention to a more pressing political issue for US audiences.[7]

Because Meireles lacked resources when he arrived in New York, during the two years he lived in the city, he used scraps of linoleum he found in the streets to fashion objects by hand for the series *Insertions into Anthropological Circuits: Tokens* (fig. 12). Consisting of replicas of the different types of coins that were needed to function in daily life, such as tokens for the subway or laundromat, *Tokens* were activated by their use and existed entirely outside the art circuit. Meireles has said that he gave them to friends, in addition to using them himself. He has also remarked that in making the counterfeit subway tokens he discovered that the machines accepted a range of weights, so that, although the sizes and shapes of his replicas had to be identical, their weights could vary.[8] The tokens were gifts that created a counter-system that today we would call a sharing economy. They were

Fig. 12 Cildo Meireles, *Inserções em circuitos Antropológicos: Tokens* (Insertions into anthropological circuits: Tokens), 1971–73.

bootleg objects that resisted commerce and state control by allowing Meireles and his friends and acquaintances to live in New York without paying the MTA for their subway rides. Fare hikes were common during the early 1970s when, between 1970 and 1972, the cost of a ride was raised twice—from twenty to thirty-five cents.[9] Symbolic and practical, the tokens invited individuals to perform small actions of resistance.

In a 1999 interview, Meireles explains that he sees the bottle in the *Coca-Cola Project* as functioning "as a kind of mobile graffiti," while he asserts that the *Tokens* were conceived as "the fabrication and circulation of a series of objects . . . which could influence sociopolitical behavior."[10] Rather than acting as vehicles for subversive messages, the *Tokens* enabled their users to circulate freely without participating in official systems of commerce. After Meireles returned to Rio in 1973, he began casting the *Tokens* from clay, which is how the project continues to exist.[11] In both cases, however, they are singular objects that are crafted by hand from commonplace materials to mimic the mass-produced and standardized items we hold in our hands and use to take the subway, entertain ourselves, make phone calls, or wash our clothing. As *Anthropological* objects, the *Tokens* generate their own systems of behaviors that call attention to the sensorial and interpersonal aspects of unregulated exchange; they are behaviors of generosity that foreground the affective aspect of exchange borne of the experience of living as a foreigner in an unfamiliar city.

NOTES

[1] Meireles has spoken about his move to New York in interviews with Frederico Morais and Gerardo Mosquera. See "Material Language: Cildo Meireles and Frederico Morais," *Tate Etc.* 14 (Autumn 2008), 5–6, accessed November 21, 2021, https://www.tate.org.uk/tate-etc/issue-14-autumn-2008/material-language, and "Interview: Gerardo Mosquera in Conversation with Cildo Meireles," in Paulo Herkenhoff, Gerardo Mosquera, and Dan Cameron, *Cildo Meireles* (London: Phaidon, 1999), 12, 30. For details of Meireles's prize money, see Claudia Calirman, *Brazilian Art under Dictatorship* (Durham, NC: Duke University Press, 2012), 119.

[2] I lean heavily on the scholarship of Claudia Calirman, Teresa Cristina Jardim de Santa Cruz Oliveira, and Elena Shtromberg. In addition to Calirman, see Shtromberg, *Art Systems: Brazil and the 1970s* (Austin: University of Texas Press, 2016), and Santa Cruz Oliveira, "Systems and Feedback: Cildo Meireles's 'Insertions into Ideological Circuits', 1970–Ongoing," (PhD diss., University of Illinois, 2013), accessed November 20, 2021, https://www.ideals.illinois.edu/handle/2142/46660.

[3] Teresa Santa Cruz Oliveira brings this analysis to light in her excellent study.

[4] For an account of the Art Workers' Coalition during this period, see Julia Bryan-Wilson, *Art Workers: Radical Practice in the Vietnam War Era* (Berkeley: University of California Press, 2009).

[5] Santa Cruz Oliveira, "Systems and Feedback," 103, 133. In a 2011 interview with Santa Cruz Oliveira, Meireles explained that the instructions were not translated into English due to lack of time.

[6] Shtromberg, *Art Systems*, 30.

[7] In MoMA's archival photographs of *Information*, Meireles's works are installed near the iconic poster "Q. And Babies? A. And Babies," which featured a photograph of the My Lai massacre of unarmed civilians by US soldiers. Archives of The Museum of Modern Art, accessed January 2, 2022, https://www.moma.org/calendar/exhibitions/2686?installation_image_index=30.

[8] Santa Cruz Oliveira, "Systems and Feedback," 143–44.

[9] Diane Pham, "All the MTA Fare Hikes of the Last 100 Years," *6sqft*, March 23, 2015, https://www.6sqft.com/all-the-mta-fare-hikes-over-the-last-100-years-plus-a-video-of-when-it-cost-just-15-cents/.

[10] Cildo Meireles, "Interview: Gerardo Mosquera in Conversation with Cildo Meireles," 13.

[11] Meireles published images of both *Insertions* projects in *Malasartes* 1 (September–November 1975), 15, along with images of *Insertions in Anthropological Circuits: Black Comb*, which also dates from his New York period.

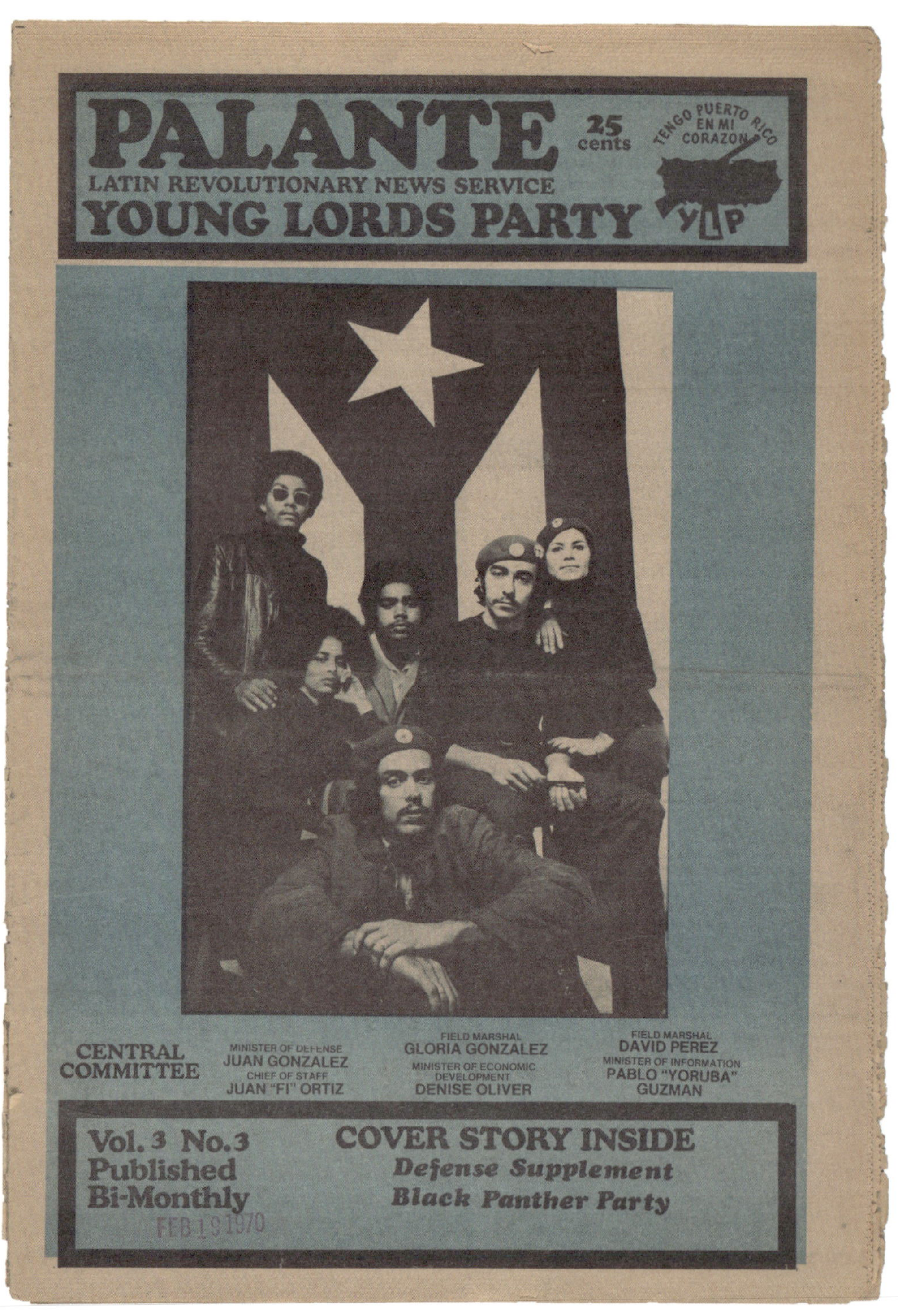
PALANTE

25 cents

TENGO PUERTO RICO EN MI CORAZON

YLP

LATIN REVOLUTIONARY NEWS SERVICE

YOUNG LORDS PARTY

CENTRAL COMMITTEE

MINISTER OF DEFENSE
JUAN GONZALEZ
CHIEF OF STAFF
JUAN "FI" ORTIZ

FIELD MARSHAL
GLORIA GONZALEZ
MINISTER OF ECONOMIC DEVELOPMENT
DENISE OLIVER

FIELD MARSHAL
DAVID PEREZ
MINISTER OF INFORMATION
PABLO "YORUBA" GUZMAN

Vol. 3 No. 3
Published
Bi-Monthly

COVER STORY INSIDE
Defense Supplement
Black Panther Party

Fig. 13 *Palante* 3, no. 3 (February 19, 1971). Boxed Newspaper Collection, Tamiment Library/Robert F. Wagner Labor Archives, New York University

Yasmin Ramirez

Año Cero: 1969

Nineteen sixty-nine is year zero in the history of the Puerto Rican art movement in New York, aka the Nuyorican art movement. During this pivotal year an interconnected group of Puerto Rican artist-activists involved in organizations such as the Young Lords Party (YLP),[1] the Puerto Rican Art Workers' Coalition (PRAWC), Taller Boricua, and El Museo del Barrio joined forces to demand equity, empowerment, and visibility for disenfranchised Black and brown residents living in the city's marginalized barrios. Applying their skills to uplift their communities, these artists transformed areas once stigmatized as "slums," "war zones," and "industrial wastelands" into vibrant neighborhoods where art exhibitions, mural making, poetry readings, and performance art became part of the fabric of daily barrio life.

January 1969 was a hot month in the New York art world. On January 3, the artist Takis removed his sculpture from the galleries of the Museum of Modern Art to protest that the museum had not obtained his permission to display it. A week later, over seventy-five artists formed the Black Emergency Cultural Coalition (BECC) to protest the exclusion of African American fine artists from *Harlem on My Mind*, a multimedia exhibition at the Metropolitan Museum of Art. On January 14, curator and BECC activist Henry Ghent held an opening celebration for the first exhibition of Puerto Rican art to take place in a New York City museum since 1957.[2] Held in the Brooklyn Museum's community gallery, *Contemporary Puerto Rican Artists* was a showcase for emerging Puerto Rican artists who were enrolled in the city's fine art colleges, notably Pratt Institute and the School of Visual Arts. Marcos Dimas credits participating in the Brooklyn Museum show with spurring him and fellow art students Adrian Garcia, Martin Rubio, and Armando Soto to continue working together on increasing the visibility of Puerto Rican culture. "Myself, Adrian, Armando, and Martin, we were like white on rice after the Brooklyn show," recalled Dimas. "Anything that was happening, we were there."[3]

In spring 1969 the artists got involved in making posters for a massive student campaign to institute open admissions and Black and Puerto Rican Studies departments throughout the city's university system. This surge of Puerto Rican activism gushed into East Harlem during the summer of 1969 when the newly formed New York chapter of the Young Lords Organization (YLO) barricaded Third Avenue and 110th Street with mountains of trash that the Department of Sanitation had failed to pick up. Known as the Garbage Offensive, this takeover was the first of many waged by the YLO that inspired New York-born Puerto Ricans to reclaim East Harlem. Popularly referred to as the *cuna* (cradle) of the Puerto Rican Diaspora, the YLO galvanized its peers to realize that this historic neighborhood needed to be salvaged by community activism and investment to counteract decades of willful neglect by the city's power brokers. The YLO clarion call to take back the streets of El Barrio strengthened the resolve of Dimas and his colleagues to open a space for Puerto Rican art in the heart of East Harlem, rather than in Lower Manhattan where many artists were renting studios in inexpensive lofts.

The Young Lords Party

Established in July 1969, the New York chapter of the Young Lords Organization—soon to rename itself the Young Lords Party (YLP)—is the most well-known of the leftist organizations that Puerto Ricans founded in the United States during the post-civil rights era. Orchestrators of spectacular takeovers of institutions and agencies that ignored the needs of barrio residents, the number of posters, news stories, films, photos, and paraphernalia produced by and about the YLP during the early 1970s is staggering. What made the YLP way of mobilizing so successful? Social movements, according to T. V. Reed, generate a repertoire of strategies, tactics, expressions, behaviors, and material objects to create cohesion among participants and disseminate their ideas to the wider public. Reed calls this matrix of actions and objects "movement culture" and observes that the most impactful movement cultures utilize the arts to alter or transgress dominant cultural codes.[4]

While some former members of the YLP have expressed misgivings about being labeled "artists," its leadership team was nonetheless comprised of "revolutionaries" with creative aptitudes. Felipe Luciano, Chairman, was a member of the Last Poets, a Black Power performance poetry troupe; Juan Gonzalez, Minister of Education, was an aspiring journalist and lead organizer of the Columbia University student strikes of 1968; Denise Oliver, Minister of Economic Development and a revolutionary artist, designed many of the posters and illustrations that appeared in the YLP's weekly newspaper, *Palante*; Hiram Maristany, who conducted photography workshops in East Harlem prior to joining the group, was the YLP in-house photographer. The YLP also recognized Nuyorican poet and playwright Pedro Pietri as its poet laureate.

The YLP leadership deployed its collective talents to portray Puerto Rican culture as resilient and reframe Puerto Rican youth in New York—pejoratively associated with delinquency and gangsterism—as comprised of organized troops of socially conscious young adults who were unafraid to defy authority in defense of their rights. As numerous photographs of the group attest, the YLP attracted some of the brightest and best-looking Black and brown people in New York. They were an army of beautiful rebels who could disarm their critics by flashing smiles as they marched in formation down the city's streets. Clad in purple berets, leather jackets, dark clothing, combat boots, and buttons emblazoned with a rifle superimposed on the Puerto Rican flag, the YLP paramilitary dress code flaunted its affiliation with the Black Panthers and other radical leftist organizations. The YLP's ability to look good while doing "bad" deeds contributed to its notoriety in the barrios and broadcast studios.

In addition to coding its bodies with signs of its political solidarities, the YLP flooded its surroundings with images that conveyed the main principles of its "13 Point Program and Platform," which included the following demands:

> (1) We want self-determination for Puerto Ricans, liberation on the island and inside the United States. (3) We want liberation of all third world people. (4) We are revolutionary nationalists and oppose racism. (5) We want equality for women. (6) We want community control of our institutions and land. (7) We want a true education of our Afro-Indio culture and Spanish language. (9) We oppose the Amerikkkan military. (10) We want freedom for all political prisoners and prisoners of war. (11) We are internationalists. (12) We believe armed self-defense and armed struggle are the only means to liberation. (13) We want a socialist society.[5]

Photographs of the YLP's storefront offices demonstrate that the windows were covered in posters that put the underground history of Puerto Rican printmaking on public display. Indeed, prior to the founding of El Museo del Barrio and Taller Boricua, the YLP offices in East Harlem, the South Bronx, and the Lower East Side were the only spaces where posters produced by vanguard artists and printmaking collectives in Puerto Rico, Cuba, Asia, Africa, and Latin America could be seen.

An outstanding Puerto Rican poster that was featured in the YLP windows was Antonio Martorell's silkscreen *Jayuya 30 de octubre de 1950* (1969, fig. 14). Depicting a crowd of revolutionaries emerging from the outstretched arm of Pedro Albizu Campos—the leader of Puerto Rico's Nationalist Party—the poster references two uprisings that caused him to be sentenced to eighty years in prison: the Jayuya uprising in 1950 and the armed attack on members of the US House of Representatives in 1954. As Michael Abramson's photographs of the Bronx office in 1970 show, *Jayuya 30 de octubre de 1950* was placed beside a large photo of Malcolm X. This visual parallel between the two leaders was intentional, offering a visual summary of the Young Lords' position papers that placed their alliance with the Black Panthers into a historical perspective of shared oppressions, ideals, and tactics between Puerto Ricans and African American civil rights activists. Founder of the printmaking studio Taller Alacrán that put out many posters supporting Puerto Rican independence, Antonio Martorell recalls sending a box of *Jayuya 30 de octubre de 1950* posters to the Young Lords as a sign of solidarity. Given its symbolic importance and graphic excellence, *Jayuya 30 de octubre de 1950* was reproduced on the back page of *Palante*, making it one of the few works by a Puerto Rican printmaker that had a wide circulation in New York City at that time.

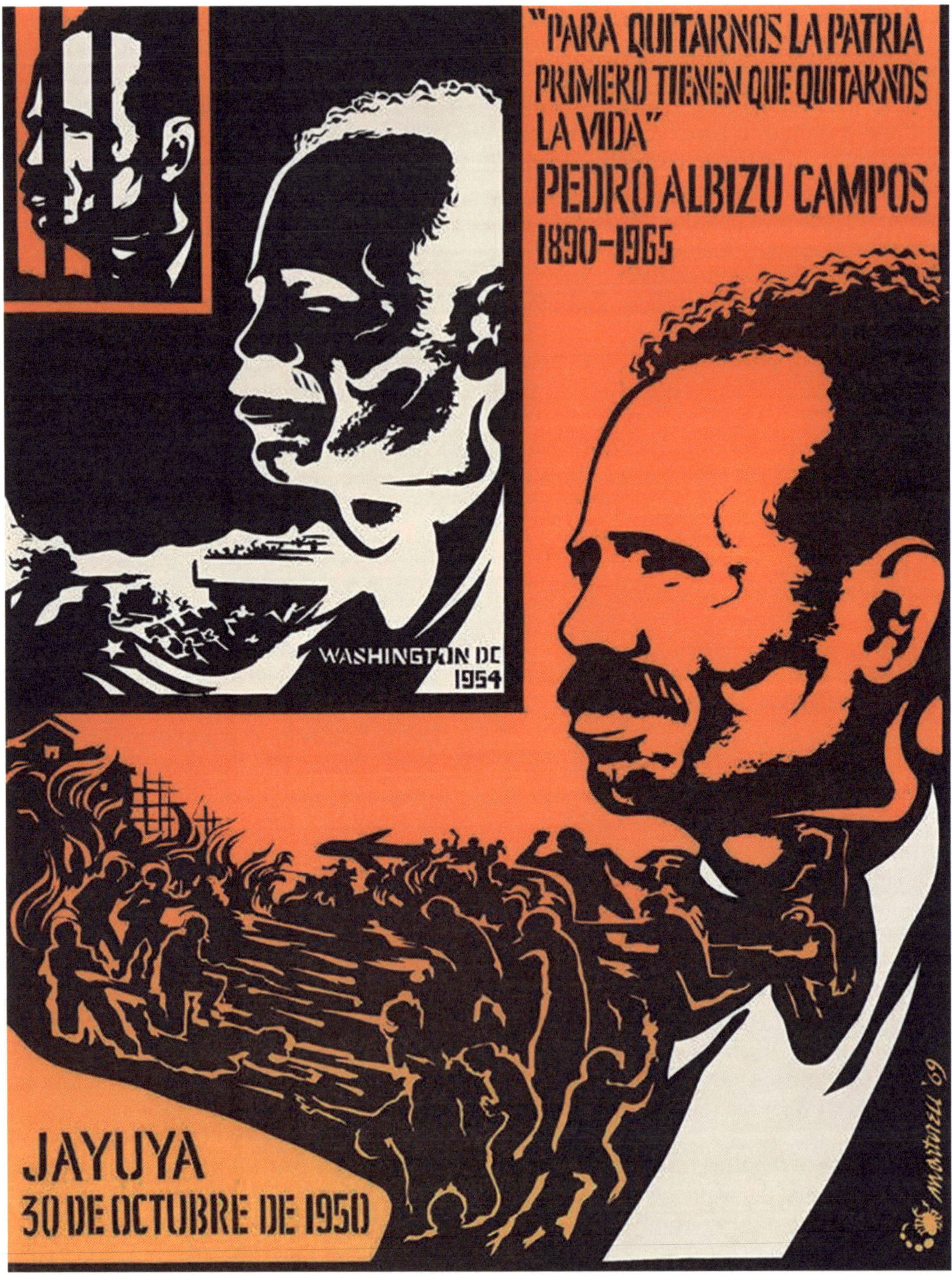

Fig. 14 Antonio Martorell, *Jayuya 30 de octubre de 1950*, 1969. Courtesy of the artist

Rafael Tufiño was another Puerto Rican printmaker whose posters were on display in the Young Lords offices. Born in Brooklyn, raised in San Juan, and trained as an artist in Mexico City, Tufiño drew on his broad background to help foster an artistic renaissance on the island during the 1950s that was akin to the Mexican renaissance in the early twentieth century. A versatile modernist who worked in abstract and figurative modes, Tufiño was best known for his archetypical renderings of Puerto Rico's folk culture, which earned him the title of "El Pintor del Pueblo" (the people's painter). Seen within the context of the Young Lords' politically charged window displays, Tufiño's popular images of caramel-colored farmers and Black folk singers were recoded as portraits of the island's revolutionary proletariat.

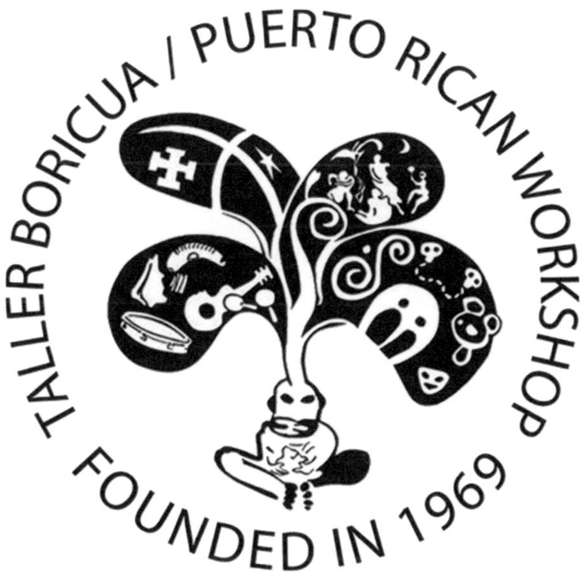

Fig. 15 Marcos Dimas, logo for Taller Boricua, 1972. Courtesy of the artist

Taller Boricua/The Black Emergency Cultural Coalition; the Puerto Rican Art Workers' Coalition/El Museo del Barrio

Recalling her early years as an artist in East Harlem, Nitza Tufiño surmised that her father donated his posters to the Young Lords while he was working at Taller Boricua, the seminal East Harlem artist collective that Marcos Dimas, Adrian Garcia, Martin Rubio, Armando Soto, and architect Manuel Neco Otero founded in fall 1970 (fig. 15).

Originally located across the street from the YLP offices on Madison Avenue and East 111th Street, Taller Boricua was a central meeting place for the Puerto Rican creative community in New York during the 1970s. In addition to hosting exhibitions in its storefront studio space, the collective organized traveling exhibits in colleges and schools throughout the tri-state area, hosted free printmaking workshops, and created posters for community events and political rallies. Taller Boricua's public outreach was complemented by a dedicated studio practice. The artists exceeded the Young Lords' demand for a true education in Puerto Rico's African and indigenous Taíno heritages by creating a visual vocabulary that combined forms from both cultures. The Afro-Taíno aesthetic became Taller Boricua's signature style (fig. 16).

The artistic borrowings between the YLP and Taller Boricua helped foster an awareness of and appreciation for Puerto Rico's history and culture that was unprecedented in New York City. The YLP demonstrations and illustrations in *Palante* became sources of inspiration for Taller members. Likewise the posters created by Taller members were on display in YLP offices and reproduced in *Palante*.

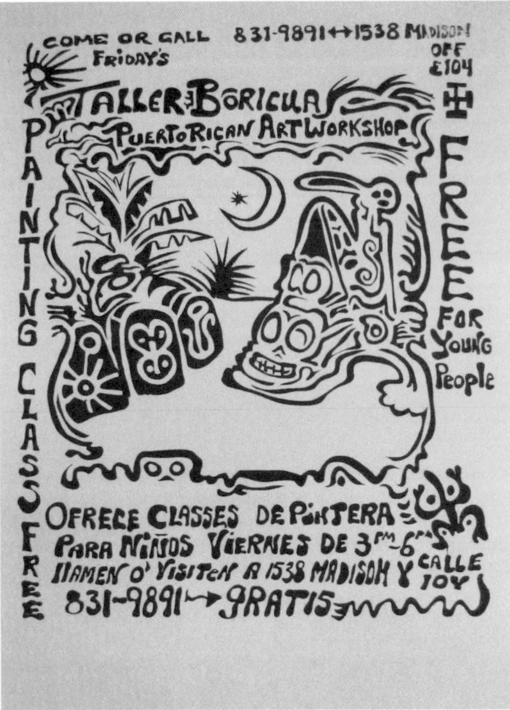

Conversations with Dimas and Nitza Tufiño, however, dispel the assumption that the appearance of Taller posters in the Young Lords' rallies, offices, and newspapers indicate they were close allies. Dimas recalls being surprised that one of his posters appeared on the cover of *Palante* in September 1971 (fig. 17) without his permission, especially because the image was cropped to remove the shotgun Dimas had placed in the hands of Ramón Emeterio Betances, the "father" of the Puerto Rican independence movement:

> No one came over to ask me whether they could put my poster on the cover and cut some of it off. Maybe they didn't know it was mine. It was a crazy time, we [were] all doing lots of things at once. We would put our posters out on the street and do free workshops for the people so it was OK by me that the Young Lords appropriated the poster–I think they would have described it as liberating my work. We were all part of the same scene, held similar beliefs. We took part in the large demonstrations but we didn't attend each other's meetings or anything. They were doing their revolution over there and we [were] doing ours over here.[6]

The revolution that Dimas and other Taller Boricua members were waging at that time was aimed at getting cultural equity for women and artists of color in New York. In addition to founding Taller Boricua, Dimas, Garcia, Rubio, and Soto were involved with the Art Workers' Coalition (AWC), an umbrella organization comprised of politically conscious artists engaged in anti-war and civil rights struggles. Indeed, Dimas, Rubio, Garcia, and Soto began attending meetings of the AWC during the summer of 1969, where they met destructivist artist Raphael Montañez Ortiz, who, at the time, was preparing to open El Museo del Barrio in a West Harlem classroom. Taller members, together with Montañez Ortiz, collaborated with members of the Black Emergency Cultural Coalition on institutional reforms for New York City museums. Their input is reflected in three out of twelve demands the AWC issued to the city's art museums in March 1970:

> (2) Admission to all museums should be free at all times, and there should be open evenings to accommodate working people. (3) All museums should decentralize to the extent that their activities and services enter

Fig. 16 Jorge Soto Sánchez, poster advertising free painting classes by Taller Boricua, n.d.

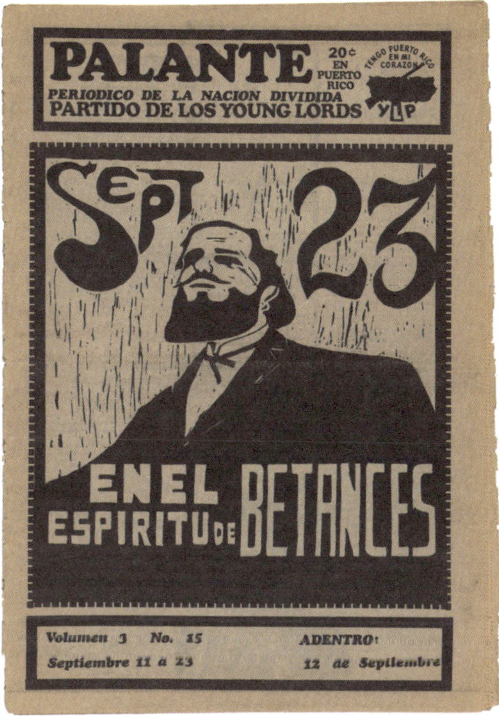

> Black, Puerto Rican, and all other communities. They should support events with which these communities can identify and control. They should convert existing structures all over the city into relatively cheap, flexible branch museums or cultural centers that do not carry the stigma of catering only to the wealthier sections of society. (4) A section of all museums under the direction of Black and Puerto Rican artists should be devoted to showing the accomplishments of Black and Puerto Rican artists . . .[7]

The peak period of AWC activism (1969–71) was concurrent with the Young Lords' biggest mobilizations. During the spring and summer of 1970, the Young Lords were seizing TB-testing trucks in East Harlem and taking over Lincoln Hospital in the Bronx while the Black and Puerto Rican art workers were picketing the Museum of Modern Art and occupying the director's office at the Metropolitan Museum of Art. The Museum of Modern Art never gave in to the AWC's demand to create a wing for Black and Puerto Rican art. However, months after the occupation, the Metropolitan Museum of Art hired a Puerto Rican community liaison, Irvine MacManus, and later collaborated with El Museo del Barrio to organize *The Art Heritage of Puerto Rico: Pre-Columbian to Present* (1973, fig. 18), one of the largest exhibitions ever held on the history of Puerto Rican art and culture in New York.

The separation between the Young Lords, Taller Boricua, and El Museo del Barrio practically vanished once Marta Moreno Vega became director of El Museo del Barrio in 1971. During her extraordinary tenure, Young Lords photographer Hiram Maristany—together with Adrian Garcia, Manuel Neco Otero, and Nitza Tufiño from Taller Boricua—joined El Museo del Barrio's staff. This radical dream team organized trailblazing exhibitions and museum education programs whose themes fulfilled the demands for cultural equity voiced by the YLP and AWC: *Homage to Our Painters* (1972), *Taíno* (1972), *The Art Heritage of Puerto Rico: Pre-Columbian to Present* (1973), *The History of Puerto Rican Posters* (1973), *Aspectos de la esclavitud en Puerto Rico* (1974), and *Art as Survival* (1974).

In retrospect, it is apparent that Taller Boricua, El Museo del Barrio, and the YLP mutually benefited from the activism that each organization was engaged in during the early 1970s. The demands for cultural equity that Puerto Rican artists were

Fig. 17 Marcos Dimas, *En el espíritu de Betances* (In the spirit of Betances), reproduced on the cover of *Palante* 3, no. 15 (September 1971). Boxed Newspaper Collection, Tamiment Library/Robert F. Wagner Labor Archives, New York University

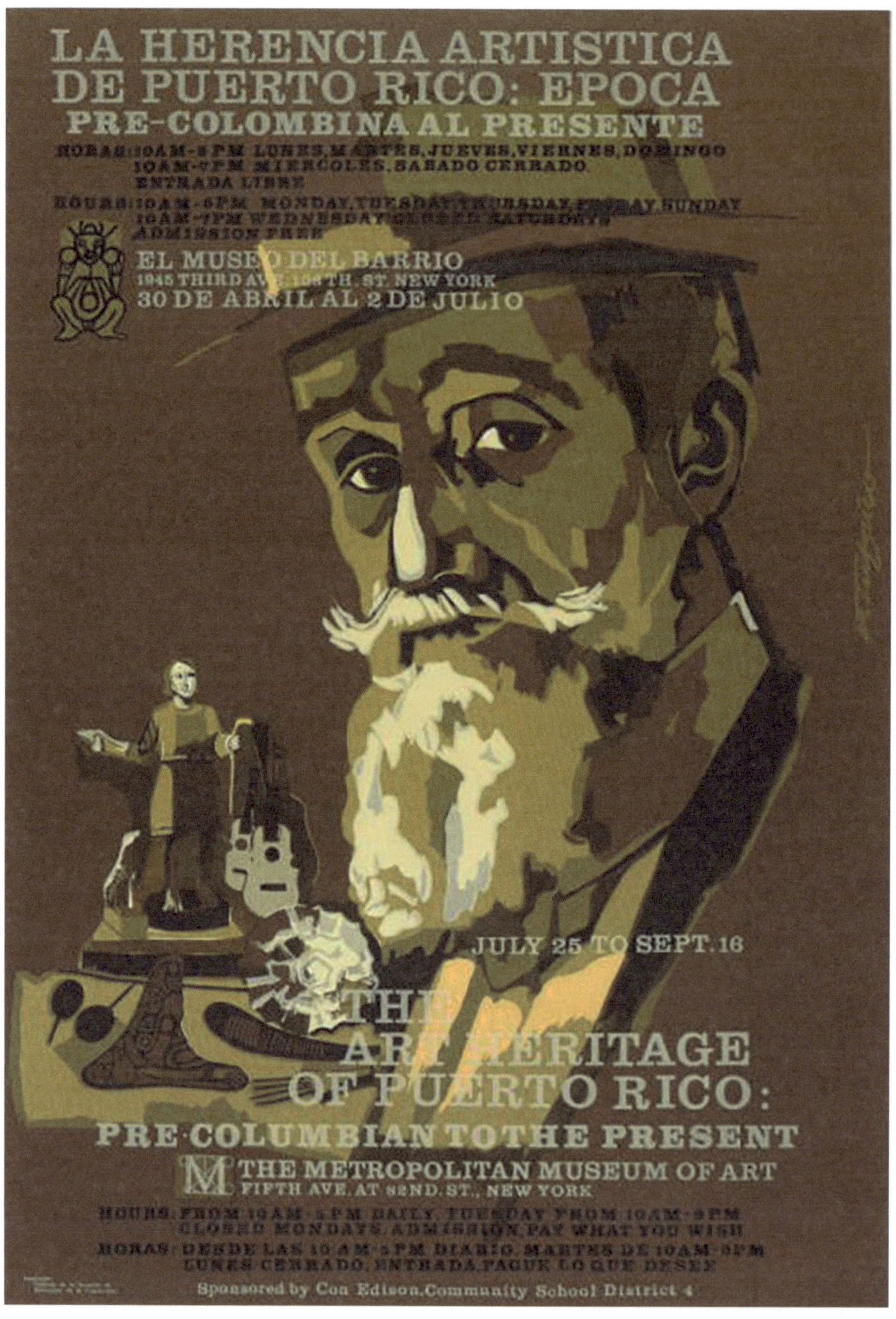

Fig. 18 Poster by Rafael Tufiño for *La Herencia artística de Puerto Rico: Época pre-Colombina al presente* (The Art Heritage of Puerto Rico: Pre-Columbian to the Present), 1973. El Museo del Barrio Archive. Courtesy of El Museo del Barrio

voicing in front of museums would have rung hollow without the uproar that the Young Lords were causing in other parts of the city. Likewise, without the aesthetic activism of the arts community, the impact of the Young Lords movement to empower Puerto Ricans with a consciousness of their culture could well have perished when the party began experiencing conflicts within its ranks and ultimately dissolved in 1976. What happened instead is that the radical ideas first disseminated in 1969 kept evolving via new art spaces, exhibitions, performances, and education projects that wound up making common sense to most of us: yes, the people want to see art that reflects their heritages in their barrios and in mainstream venues; yes, Black/Puerto Rican/Latinx/LGBTQ/BIPOC artists can create marvelous, museum-quality exhibitions anywhere, anytime; yes, we can decolonize museums; yes, we can decolonize Puerto Rico; Sí se puede; P'lante !

NOTES

[1] The YLP originally worked as the New York chapter of the Young Lords Organization (YLO), founded by students and political militants in July 1969. The YLO had formed out of a street gang in Chicago in 1960 and, by 1968, had become a civil rights organization inspired by the political mobilization of the time, especially the tactics of the Black Panthers. More interested in becoming a political party, the New York chapter split with the Chicago leadership in May 1970, renaming itself the Young Lords Party (YLP) but maintaining the original paramilitary-style hierarchies.

[2] *Contemporary Puerto Rican Art* was the first show of its kind since the Riverside Museum's exhibition of work by twenty-five contemporary Puerto Rican artists, which opened on January 6, 1957.

[3] Marcos Dimas, interview with the author, March 23, 2015.

[4] T. V. Reed, *The Art of Protest: Culture and Activism from the Civil Rights Movement to the Streets of Seattle* (Minneapolis: University of Minnesota Press, 2005), 297.

[5] "Young Lords Party 13 Point Program and Platform," *Palante* 2, no. 16, December 11, 1970, 22. The YLP's program was drafted in October 1969 but, after women in the organization challenged point #10—"We want equality for women. Machismo must be revolutionary—not oppressive."—the program was revised and point #10 became point #5: "We want equality for women. Down with machismo and male chauvinism." This is the only point in the program that was ever changed.

[6] Dimas, interview with the author.

[7] Art Workers' Coalition, "Statement of Demands" (March 1970), in Lucy R. Lippard, *Get the Message? A Decade of Art for Social Change* (New York: E. P. Dutton, 1984), 12.

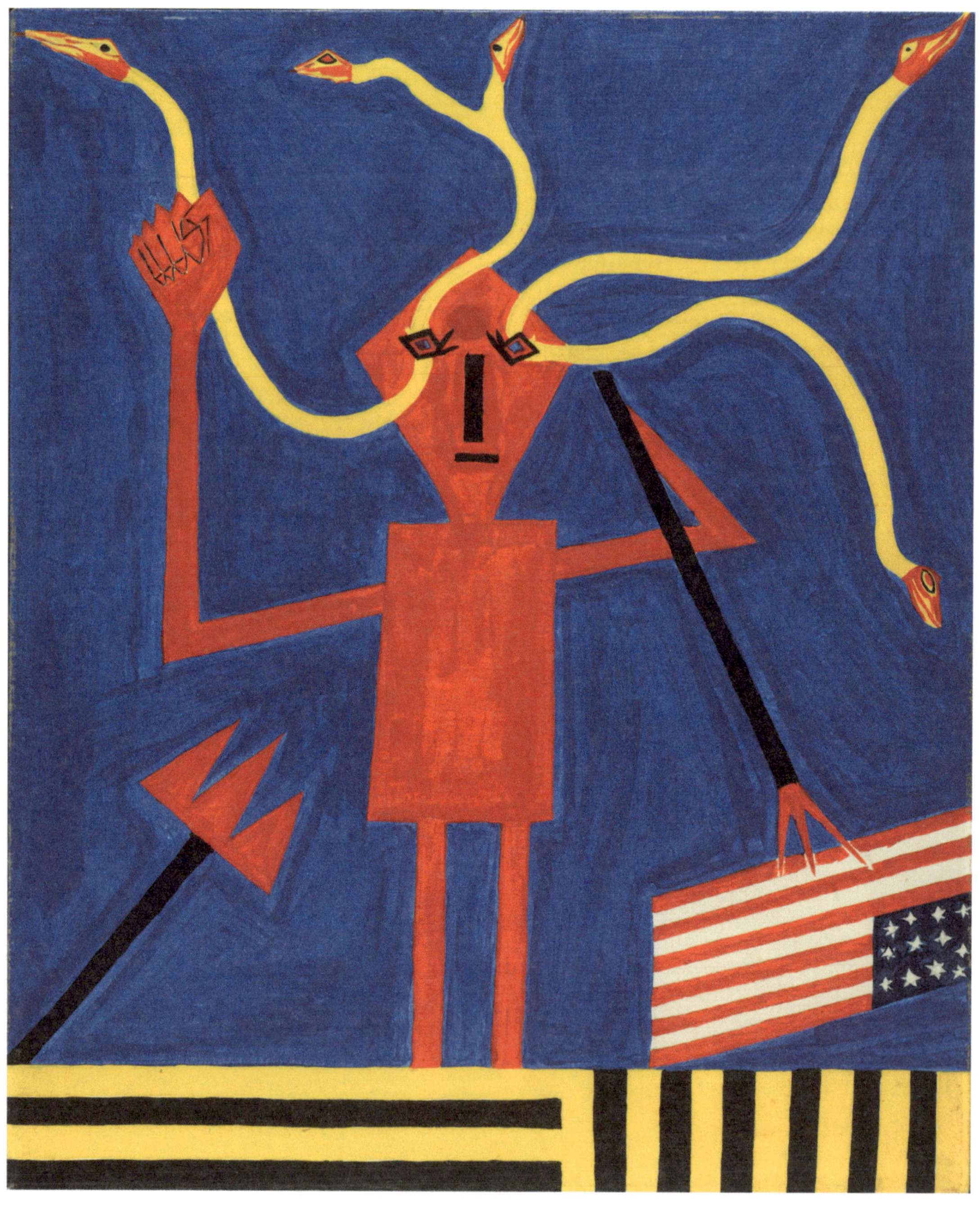

Fig. 19 Abdias do Nascimento, *Exu Black Power #2 (Tribute to Rubens Gerchman)*, 1969. Collection of Black Art Museum/IPEAFRO Collection, Rio de Janeiro

Abigail Lapin Dardashti

Abdias do Nascimento and His Contemporaries: Black Power and Art in New York City

In October 1968, Afro-Brazilian painter, theater director, and activist Abdias do Nascimento embarked on what he thought would be a two-month trip to visit Black theater groups in Mexico City, Cuernavaca, San Francisco, and Los Angeles. Landing in New York City at the end of his travels, Nascimento chose to remain in the United States after learning that the newly minted Brazilian military regime had solidified its repressive stance.[1] As a vocal advocate of anti-racism, Nascimento had built a career in cultural activism in Rio de Janeiro and was at risk of imprisonment—or worse—should he return to Brazil.[2] Developing his painting practice in the United States, Nascimento's stay until 1981 was animated by his robust exchanges with African American, Brazilian, and Nuyorican artists, enabling him to create a transnational visual language fundamental to global anti-racism activism of the 1970s.

In New York City, Nascimento settled for a month in the apartment of the painter Ann Bagley, who he had met in Rio, and used her leftover paints and brushes to start making art.[3] In January 1969 he moved to a hotel in Harlem and became familiar with the neighborhood's Black institutions, such as the Studio Museum in Harlem, which had opened the previous year. He brought his paintings to various grassroots Black cultural organizations and, subsequently, booked some exhibitions.[4] He later recalled the potential of his contributions in New York: "When I showed them [the paintings], I realized that my work presented an aspect completely crushed in the process of Black American history: the African roots. I felt that I could say a lot through a new language for me. . . . In the United States, [I] feel more useful to realize something."[5] Nascimento showed his work to the writer Amiri Baraka, who agreed to write a preface for the catalogue of his first exhibition at the Harlem Art Gallery.[6] In the end, Babatunde Folayemi, the gallery's director, wrote the introduction. Nevertheless, Nascimento said that while "the preface never came through, the support and solidarity of my African brothers and sisters in the United States was there."[7]

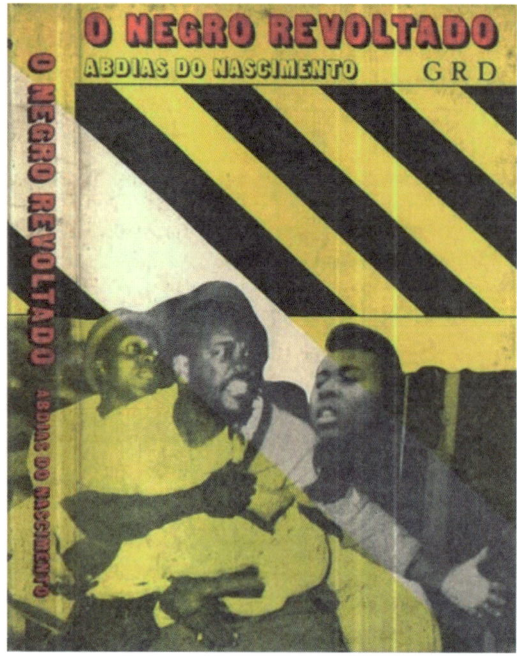

One of the paintings on display at the Harlem Art Gallery, entitled *Exu Black Power #2 (Tribute to Rubens Gerchman)*, demonstrates Nascimento's engagement with both African American art and activism as well as Brazilian Nova Figuração (fig. 19).[8] The work depicts the messenger and deity of the crossroads, Exu, from the Afro-Brazilian religion Candomblé. Nascimento displays the deity's traditional pitchfork, used here to stab an upside-down US flag to critique the emblem's hypocrisy and the lack of access to equal rights for Black people in the Americas.[9] While the deity's right fist is raised, presenting the Black Power salute, another pitchfork directed at Exu threatens his actions and well-being, identifying the Brazilian dictatorship and US authorities. The painting exemplifies the solidarity and shared struggles of Afro-Brazilians and African Americans. Exu's pitchfork mirrors the fight for African Americans' right to self-defense, an idea familiar to Nascimento after he visited the Black Panther Party headquarters in Oakland in 1968. Exu's feet and his movement are limited by yellow and black stripes typically identified with crowd control. The Brazilian artist Rubens Gerchman, whose name appears in the painting's title, often employed this pattern in his work, as he did in his cover design of Nascimento's 1968 book *O negro revoltado* (fig. 20). In New York, Nascimento continued seeing friends from Rio, including Gerchman and Anna Bella Geiger, who had drawn a portrait of Nascimento in 1967 (fig. 21).[10] Following his stay in New York, Nascimento took up academic positions elsewhere, first as a fellow at Wesleyan University from 1969 to 1971, and subsequently as a professor at the State University of New York at Buffalo.

In New York, Nascimento produced paintings combining Afro-Brazilian deities with Black Power symbolism, paralleling the work of Nuyorican artists Marcos Dimas and Jorge Soto Sánchez, who depicted African-derived religious symbolism from Santería as well as Taíno iconography.[11] Nascimento's work addressed the consequences of colonialism and racism such as the erasure of Black heritage in favor of a homogenous, nationally affiliated identity, an issue shared by both Puerto Rico and Brazil. According to African Diaspora Studies scholar Marta Moreno Vega, Nascimento was "searching for a non-euro-centric aesthetic framework and looking for an aesthetic that wasn't colonial and oppressive," an endeavor mirroring that of Dimas and Soto.[12] As founder and director of the Visual Arts Research and Resource

Fig. 20 Rubens Gerchman, book cover for *O negro revoltado* by Abdias do Nascimento (Rio de Janeiro: Edições GRD, 1968)

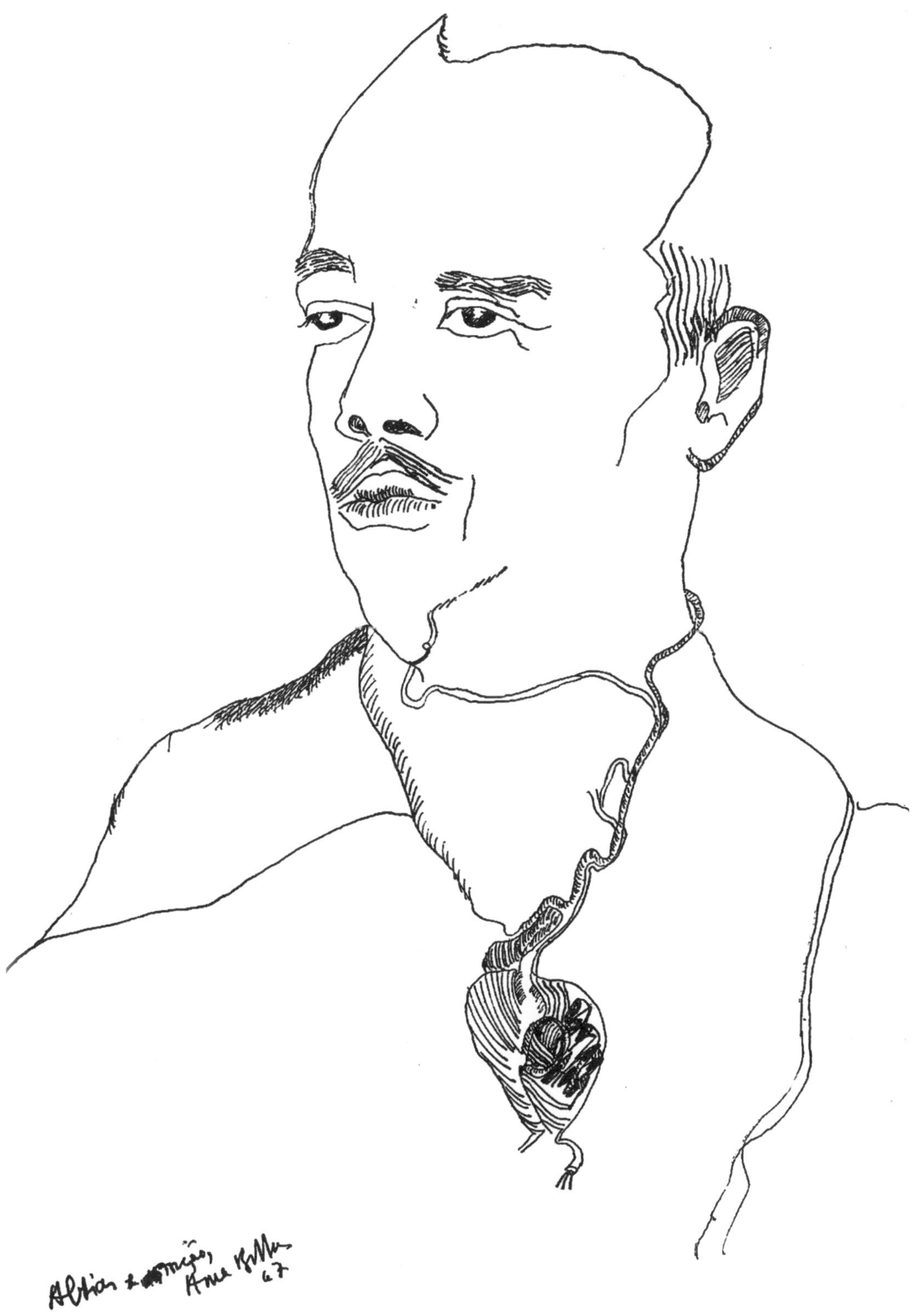

Fig. 21 Anna Bella Geiger, *Abdias do Nascimento*, 1967 (original lost)

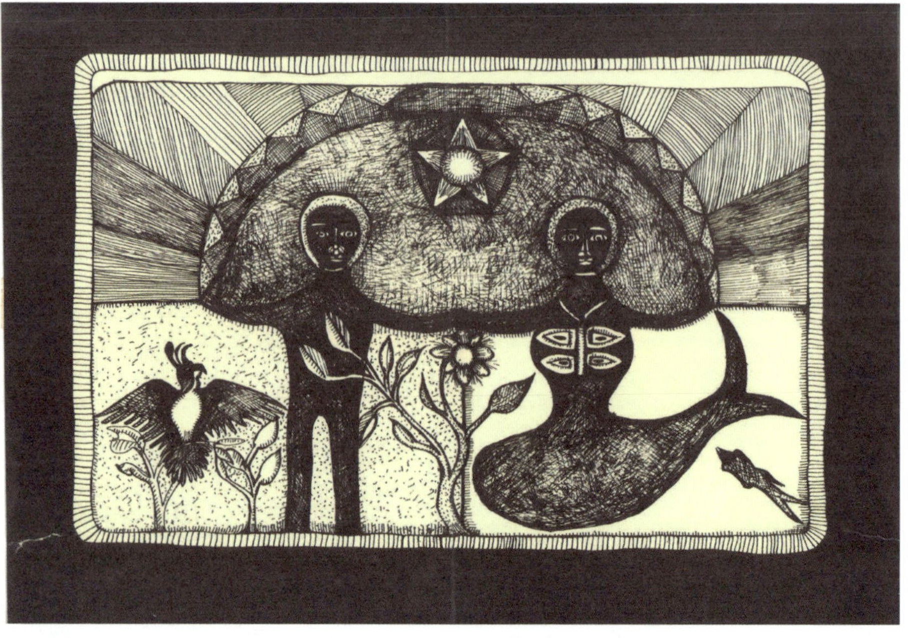

AFRICAN DIASPORA

Contemporary Ritual Symbols Of

ABDIAS DO NASCIMENTO

El Taller Boricua and the Visual
Arts Research and Resource
Center Relating to the Caribbean

EXHIBITION

FEB 22nd – 7Pm

LOCATION

EL Taller Boricua 1 E 104 st - off 5th Ave

FOR INFORMATION CALL VARRCRC - 427 - 8100

FUNDED IN PART BY NYSCA NEA CETA TITLE VI

Fig. 22 Postcard for *African Diaspora - Contemporary Ritual Symbols of Abdias Do Nascimento*, El Taller Boricua, East Harlem, New York, February 22–April 25, 1980. Offices of the Government of Puerto Rico in the United States (OGPRUS) Records, 1930s–1993. Archives of the Puerto Rican Diaspora, Center for Puerto Rican Studies, Hunter College, CUNY

Center Relating to the Caribbean, Moreno Vega, along with artists from the grassroots activist printshop Taller Boricua including Dimas and Soto, invited Nascimento to present his work in 1980 (fig. 22).[13] The exhibition included the painting *Composition #1* (p. 68). The bird and three-tiered scepter on the top right identify the deity Oxalá, the creator of humankind. On the top left, a lozenge-shaped fist represents the Black Power salute, which is surrounded by a sunlike emblem that deifies it. These elements are linked through red lines to the top of a skyscraper at the bottom that mimics the narrow steps of the Empire State Building's tip. The combination of these images narrates Nascimento's migration to the United States, bringing together his Afro-Brazilian heritage with African American protest, as well as the practicc of painting, expressed through decorative and geometric motifs in the composition. As this painting demonstrates, Nascimento's experiences in the city led to the development of his transnational painting, uprooting notions of national citizenship to propose a global fight for Black Power and rights.

NOTES

[1] On December 13, 1968, the regime—in power since a coup in April 1964—passed the Ato Institucional V, which stripped citizens of constitutional rights such as freedom of speech.

[2] For more on Nascimento's work and activism prior to his move, see Sandra Almada, *Abdias Nascimento* (São Paulo: Selo Negro, 2009); Elisa Larkin Nascimento, "Cristo epistêmico," *ILHA* 18, no. 1 (June 2016): 84–107; and Kimberly L. Cleveland, "Abdias Nascimento," in *Black Art in Brazil: Expressions of Identity* (Gainesville: University of Florida Press, 2013), 46-68.

[3] While Nascimento had produced a few works before leaving Brazil, his steady painting practice developed in the United States. For more on Nascimento in the United States, see Tulio Augusto Samuel Custódio, "Construindo o (auto)-exílio: Trajetória de Abdias do Nascimento nos Estados Unidos, 1968–1981" (master's thesis, University of São Paulo, 2011); Dária Jaremtchuk, "Abdias do Nascimento nos Estados Unidos: Um 'pintor de arte negra,'" *Estados avançados* 32, no. 93 (2018): 263–82; and Abigail Lapin Dardashti, "Abdias do Nascimento in New York: Migration, Resistance, and Transnational Black Art, 1968–1970," *MODOS: Revista de história da arte* 6, no. 1 (January 2022): 471-93.

[4] Exhibitions in 1969 took place at the Harlem Art Gallery; the Malcolm X House, Wesleyan University; Yale University's Art and Architecture Building; and the Crypt Gallery at Columbia University. In 1973, Nascimento had an exhibition at the Studio Museum in Harlem.

[5] Abdias do Nascimento, quoted in "Abdias do Nascimento: Na pintura a busca de sus raizes," *Jornal do Brasil*, June 5, 1975, B4.

[6] The exhibition was on view from March 14 to April 6, 1969, and featured twenty-five paintings.

[7] Abdias do Nascimento, quoted in Abdias do Nascimento and Elisa Larkin Nascimento, *Africans in Brazil: A Pan-African Perspective* (Trenton, NJ: Africa World Press, 1992), 50.

[8] Nova Figuração was a Brazilian art movement that drew on mass media imagery while challenging the dictatorship's repression.

[9] Candomblé is an African-derived religion that syncretizes West African religions (Yoruba, Angola, Congo, depending on the affiliation) with Catholicism and Indigenous traditions.

[10] Anna Bella Geiger, interview with the author, Rio de Janeiro, July 9, 2018.

[11] I expand this argument in "Afro-Latinx Intersections: Nuyorican and Afro-Brazilian Art and Activism in New York City," *American Art* 36, no. 2 (forthcoming).

[12] Marta Moreno Vega, phone interview with the author, April 16, 2018. Although Santería is Afro-Cuban, it was practiced in New York's broader Latinx communities. See Marta Moreno Vega, "The Dynamic Influence of Cubans, Puerto Ricans, and African Americans in the Growth of Ocha in New York City," in *Òrìṣà Devotion as World Religion: The Globalization of Yorùbá Religious Culture*, ed. Jacob K. Olupona and Terry Rey (Madison: University of Wisconsin Press, 2008), 322.

[13] The center is now called the Caribbean Cultural Center African Diaspora Institute.

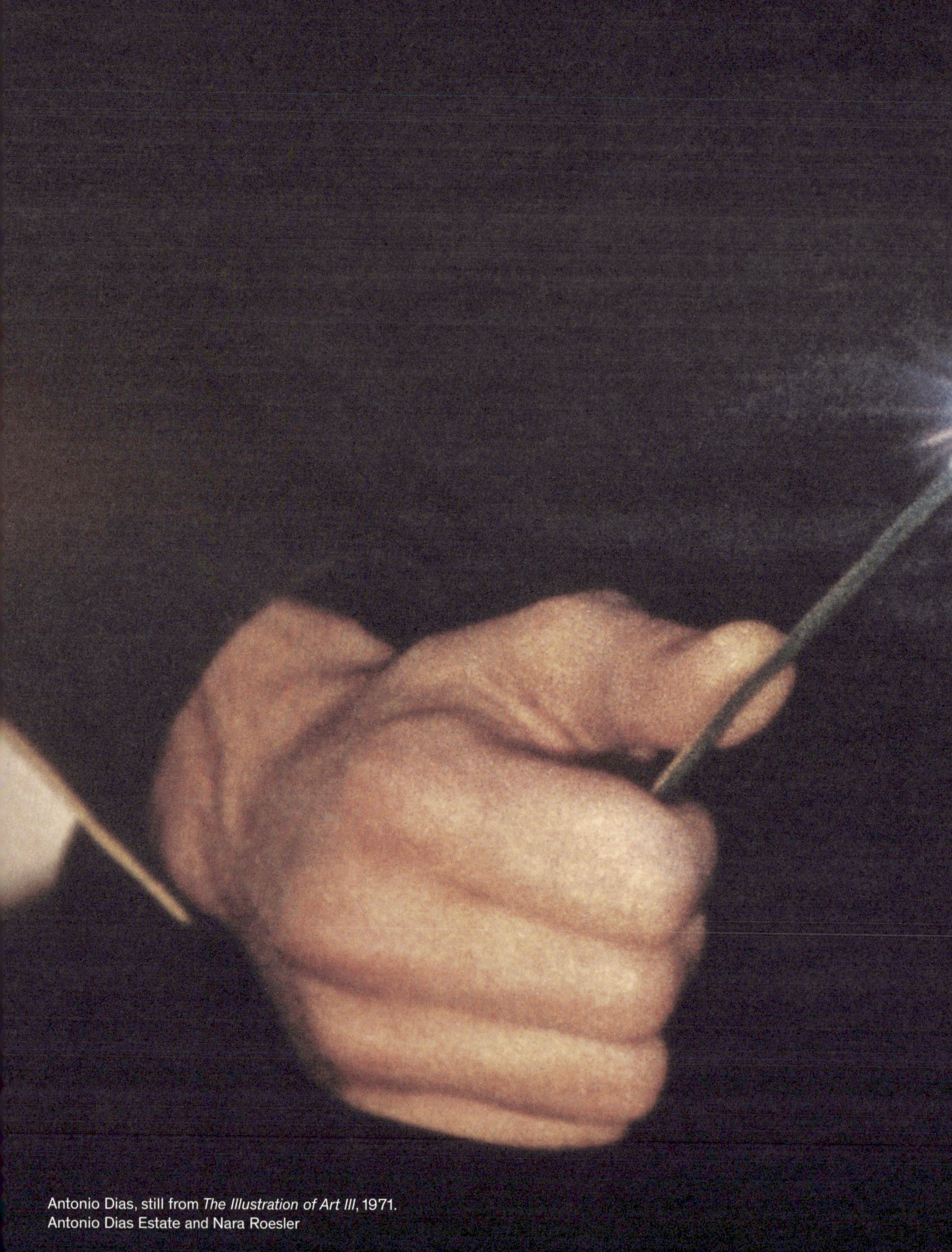

Antonio Dias, still from *The Illustration of Art III*, 1971.
Antonio Dias Estate and Nara Roesler

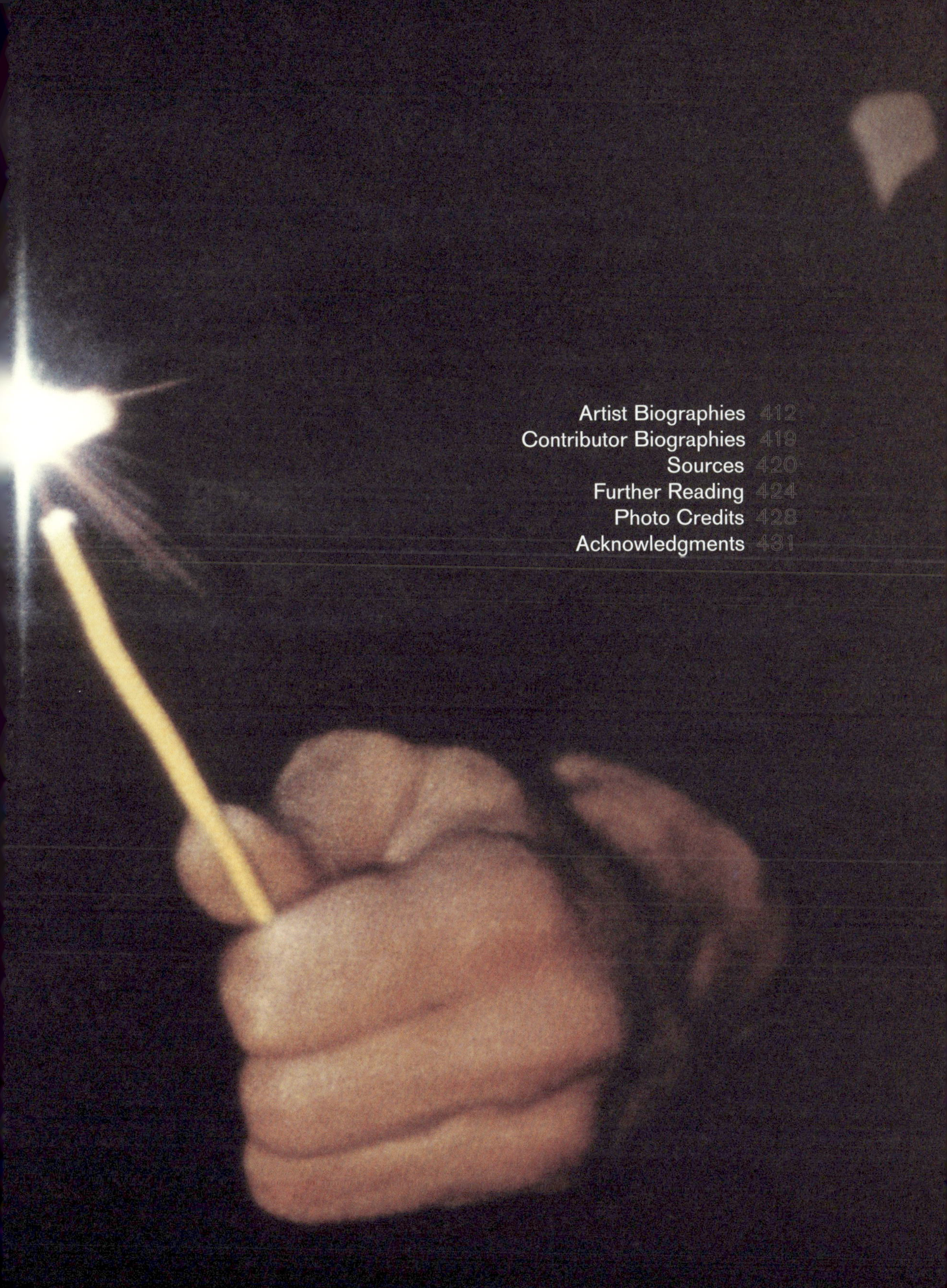

ARTIST BIOGRAPHIES

Waldo Balart (b. Banes, Cuba, 1931) studied accounting and economics in Havana before moving to New York after the Cuban Revolution in 1959 to study art at the Museum of Modern Art. His first exhibition took place in 1961 at the RJ Gallery on 60th Street. Toward the end of the 1960s, he expanded the flat canvas into three-dimensional space with his boxlike, sculptural paintings. Balart was involved in the city's avant-garde scene and appeared in Andy Warhol's *The Life of Juanita Castro* (1965) and *The Loves of Ondine* (1968), shot at Balart's house on Long Island. He was also part of the Foundation for the Totality, the guerrilla art group founded by Rolando Peña in 1966. He currently lives in Madrid.

Alicia Barney (b. Cali, Colombia, 1952) moved to New York in 1969. She studied at the College of New Rochelle, New York, and at Pratt Institute. During her time at Pratt, she was introduced to Claes Oldenburg's work *The Store* (1961). Oldenburg's ideas about the links between art and life inspired her to integrate daily life into her artistic practice. Barney developed an intimate, ritualistic relation with random objects found in the streets of New York and Colombia, which she used in her series *Diario objeto* (1977–79). The installation *Pratt*, from the series *Diario objeto* (Diary object) was her MFA thesis exhibition. In 1978 she moved back to Cali, where she still lives and works.

Jaime Barrios (b. Santiago, 1946; d. New York, 1989) moved to New York in 1963 and began making experimental films. In 1968 he cofounded the Young Filmmakers Foundation along with educators Rodger Larson and Lynne Hofer. The organization introduced 16 mm film equipment to Latinx youth on the Lower East Side. Ten young members exhibited their films—ranging from documentary to animation and fantasy—at the Museum of Modern Art in 1970. After the 1973 coup in Chile, Barrios joined the Chilean resistance movement in New York and began making documentary films about human rights and Latin American politics and culture.

Carmen Beuchat (b. Santiago, Chile, 1941) trained as a classical and modern dancer in Chile. In 1968 she moved to New York with a grant from the American Chilean Institute to continue her studies at the Martha Graham School and the Merce Cunningham Studio, while also taking courses at the Joffrey Ballet School. In New York she worked as an assistant to Robert Rauschenberg and joined Trisha Brown's dance company, touring the United States and Europe. In 1969 she cofounded the Moving Earth dance company with Japanese American choreographer Kei Takei. In 1972, Beuchat was a cofounder of the Natural History of the American Dancer, an all-women dance collective formed by Barbara Dilley, Rachel Wood, and Cynthia Hedstrom, among others. The group, which was fundamental in the birth of American postmodern dance, used to practice at Beuchat's loft on Wooster Street. Beuchat also collaborated on pieces with artists Sylvia Palacios Whitman, Juan Downey, Gordon Matta-Clark, and Enrique Castro-Cid, and participated in projects of Jaime Barrios and Marcelo Montealegre. She left New York in 1977 and currently lives and works in Quetroleufú, Chile.

Augusto Boal (b. Rio de Janeiro, 1931; d. 2009) was a dramaturg, theorist, and political activist. During the 1950s Boal attended Columbia University in New York, where he studied experimental theater. After returning to his home country, he was kidnapped by the military government and forced into exile, first to Peru and then Argentina, where he wrote his seminal work, *Theatre of the Oppressed* (1974), in which he elaborated a theatrical method that drew from Paulo Freire's *Pedagogy of the Oppressed* (1968).

Alfredo Bonino (b. Naples, Italy, 1925; d. New York, 1981) was a gallerist who first opened Galeria Domus, in São Paulo, in 1946, and in 1951 inaugurated Galería Bonino, first in Buenos Aires and later in Rio de Janeiro. In 1963, Bonino arrived in New York accompanied by his wife, Fernanda Bonino (b. Torino, Italy, 1927), to open a branch of the gallery in the city. The couple exhibited work by numerous Latin American, Asian, and European artists in their New York space. They closed the gallery in 1974 but remained in the city, where Fernanda Bonino still lives.

Luis Camnitzer (b. Lübeck, Germany, 1937) studied art and architecture in Uruguay and Germany and, in 1961, received his first Guggenheim Fellowship that allowed him to visit New York, where he moved permanently in 1964. That same year, Camnitzer cofounded the New York Graphic Workshop with Liliana Porter and José Guillermo Castillo. In 1971, he was one of the co-organizers of two artist-led political activist organizations: Museo Latinoamericano and its splinter group, Movimiento de Independencia Cultural Latinoamericana (MICLA). The groups published *Contrabienal* (1971), a collective artists' book organized in opposition to the 11th São Paulo Biennial. In New York, Camnitzer also taught at universities and authored several books on Latin American Conceptualism, institutional and political critique, and art education. In his objects, drawings, and prints, Camnitzer has remained deeply connected with the violent realities of South America, while exploring different dimensions of language and representation. He currently lives and works in Great Neck, New York.

José Guillermo Castillo (b. Caracas, Venezuela, 1938; d. 1999) came to New York as an organizer of the Venezuelan Pavilion at the 1964–65 World's Fair, having previously trained in sculpture, painting, and printmaking in Caracas and London. In New York, he specialized in new printing techniques while researching nature, ecology, and the environment. Castillo was one of the cofounders of the New York Graphic Workshop. In 1968 he joined the Center for Inter-American Relations (present-day Americas Society) as the first director of its Literature Program. His work was included in group shows at Galería Bianchini (1963), Brooklyn Museum (1966), and Pratt Institute (1967). He moved back to Venezuela in 1973.

Enrique Castro-Cid (b. Santiago, 1937; d. 1992) arrived in New York in 1961 and, in 1962, received a grant from the Organization of American States to support his art practice. In the city, Castro-Cid was awarded two Guggenheim Foundation Fellowships (1964 and 1965) and won the William and Noma Copley Award (1966). In 1965 he participated in the group show *The New Scene* at Vassar College (Poughkeepsie, NY), along with emerging Pop artists Roy Lichtenstein, Claes Oldenburg, James Rosenquist, and Andy Warhol. After his first kinetic sculptures and robots, he became increasingly involved in research mathematics and computer science. In 1965, Castro-Cid designed *The Mechanical Hound*, a robotic dog for François Truffaut's film *Fahrenheit 451*, although the piece was never built. He moved to Miami in the 1980s, where he continued working and teaching technology and philosophy.

Máximo Rafael Colón (b. Arecibo, Puerto Rico, 1950) moved to New York to study at the School of Visual Arts. He focused on photography, registering the political mobilization of the Puerto Rican community in New York. In his works, he documented demonstrations by the Young Lords and public actions by such groups as Taller Boricua and CHARAS, addressing issues of social inequality and discrimination while also documenting music and other forms of cultural expression. Colón still lives and works in New York City.

Francisco Copello (b. Santiago, 1938; d. 2006) arrived in New York in 1967 to attend Pratt Graphics Center after studying at the Academy of Fine Arts in Florence, Italy. In 1969 he cofounded the workshop StudioF/Taller 69 with fellow Chilean artist and musician Fernando Torm Toha, where they experimented with printmaking, music, and body art. The workshop also printed works for artists such as David Hockney, Adolph Gottlieb, and Keith Haring. Copello studied dance with choreographer Laura Dean and participated in the first theater pieces by director Robert Wilson (1971–72). He experimented with different formats, such as collage, photography, performance, and painting, and specialized in mime art. His work addressed issues of gender, identity, and the social and political turmoil of his home country. In 1974 he moved to Milan, but continued visiting and working in New York until his death.

Eduardo Costa (b. Buenos Aires, 1940) studied literature and history of art in Argentina. He moved to New York when the first work from his series *Fashion Fictions* (1966–present)—jewelry-like objects shaped as body parts made in 24k gold—was featured in *Vogue* magazine in 1968. *Fashion Fiction I (Gold Ear)* was photographed by Richard Avedon and modeled by Marisa Berenson. The spread included a text by art critic Lawrence Alloway. In the city, Costa became a regular in the neo-avant-garde scene. In 1969, he co-organized the *Fashion Show Poetry Event* at the Center for Inter-American Relations (Americas Society) with John Perreault and Hannah Weiner. The show included designs by Marisol, Claes Oldenburg, Andy Warhol, and others. He experimented with conceptual practices using different media in his works, including video, sound, sculpture, and performance, while embracing elements from Happenings, Pop art, and Neo-concrete art. Costa remained in New York until 2003 and he currently lives and works in Buenos Aires.

Zulema "Beba" Damianovich (b. Buenos Aires, 1920; d. 2014) moved to New York in the mid-1950s, where she worked as an artist and tapestry designer. Damianovich helped connect Argentine émigrés to one another and participated in the organizing of publications and political initiatives. She also took part in group shows such as *A Benefit for the Judson Arts Program* (1967). Damianovich created a visual diary of her life by drawing and writing on the invitations and brochures she collected from the various art exhibitions she attended. She also created sculptural works made of found materials and plexiglass, which questioned consumer culture, fashion, mass media, and the pharmaceutical industry. From 1971 to 1978 she lived and worked in Morocco, Spain, and France.

Jaime Davidovich (b. Buenos Aires, 1936; d. New York, 2016) moved to New York in December 1962 and studied painting at the School of Visual Arts. In 1965 he and his then wife, artist Judith Henry, founded Wooster Enterprises, a stationery design studio associated with Fluxus. In the city he began experimenting with adhesive tape, applying it first to canvases and then to walls, staircases, floors, and photographs of the city, revealing the geometry of the architectural landscape. Between 1968 and 1973, he lived and worked in Cleveland. For the 1973 Whitney Biennial, Davidovich covered the floors and stairway walls of the museum with wide strips of adhesive tape. In the early 1970s he began experimenting with video, creating formalist views of the city and overtly political works discussing censorship, violence, and the role of the media in the United States and Argentina. In 1976 Davidovich helped found Cable SoHo along with other artists, with the goal of disseminating the works of neo-avant-garde artists and thinkers.

Antonio Dias (b. Campina Grande, Brazil, 1944; d. Rio de Janeiro, 2018) was invited to participate in the Museum of Modern Art's 1970 exhibition *Information*. An exile from the Brazilian dictatorship since 1965, Dias was awarded a Guggenheim Fellowship in 1972 and returned to New York, where—through his contacts with Brazilian artists such as Rubens Gerchman and Hélio Oiticica—he connected with the local avant-garde scene. He went on to make films addressing art and labor and to create mixed-media works reflecting his interest in the political dimensions of mass communications.

Marcos Dimas (b. Cabo Rojo, Puerto Rico, 1943) moved to New York with his family when he was ten years old and later studied art at the School of Visual Arts. In 1969 his work was included in a show at the Brooklyn Museum, which led to the formation of a group of Puerto Rican artists that also included Raphael Montañez Ortiz. Dimas later joined the Art Workers' Coalition. He was one of the cofounders of Taller Boricua/The Puerto Rican Workshop. During the 1970s he experimented with different formats and media to express Puerto Rican cultural and political history and incorporated language and religion from the Taíno culture in his artworks.

Juan Downey (b. Santiago, 1940; d. New York, 1993) traveled to Washington, DC, in 1965 to participate in a show at the Pan American Union's headquarters and decided to settle in the American capital. After four years he relocated to New York. During this time, he created kinetic sculptures and interactive installations and began experimenting with the Sony Portapak video system, becoming a pioneer of video art. Downey collaborated with Carmen Beuchat in several performance pieces and with Gordon Matta-Clark in *Fresh Air* (1972), a public intervention and video performance artwork that took place in different areas of the city. He was also one of the coeditors of the art magazine *Cha/Cha/Cha* (1974), along with Marta Minujín and Julián Cairol, and a contributor to *Radical Software* (1970–74). He taught at Pratt Institute between 1970 and 1972. After the 1973 coup in Chile, Downey turned to making videos, performances, and installations explicitly denouncing Pinochet's dictatorship and the social realities of Latin America.

Carlos "Chino" García (b. Río Piedras, Puerto Rico, 1946) arrived in New York from Puerto Rico as a small child with his parents and settled in the Lower East Side in 1959. After a two-year stay in Puerto Rico in his late teens, he returned to New York in 1965 where he began organizing in the Nuyorican community in his neighborhood. In 1970, García, together with Humberto Crespo, Angelo Gonzalez, Jr., Roy Battiste, Moses Anthony Figueroa, and Sal Becker, cofounded CHARAS, a group to address issues of concern to the community such as housing, representation, and environmentalism. The group began collaborating with architect Buckminster Fuller in the mid-1960s on the construction of geodesic domes. The group built domes and occupied neglected buildings and abandoned lots on the LES as a way of activating these spaces with community activities and challenging increasing real estate speculation in the area. García is still a community organizer and activist.

Anna Bella Geiger (b. Rio de Janeiro, 1933) first traveled to New York between 1953 and 1955 to study art history and sociology at New York University, the Metropolitan Museum of Art, and the New School for Social Research. She returned in 1969 to escape the military rule in her country, already as a recognized artist in Brazil and Europe. In New York she temporarily abandoned painting to explore new media such as photography and video art. Embracing Conceptual art strategies, she turned her attention to the social and political issues of the time. Geiger's works from the 1970s reflect her interest in linguistics, anthropology, and geography, in particular cultural geography, as well as postcolonial cultural critique and feminism. Inspired by the work of her husband (a professor of geography at Columbia University) she made use of cartography and topography to address issues of Brazilian identity, Indigenous rights, and notions of center and periphery. She currently lives and works in Rio de Janeiro.

Rubens Gerchman (b. Rio de Janeiro, 1942; d. São Paulo, 2008) moved to New York in 1968 with his children and then wife, artist Anna Maria Maiolino, on a travel scholarship he won at the Salão Nacional de Arte Moderna (Rio de Janeiro) the previous year. In the city Gerchman collaborated with other artists to cofound Integralia Corporation, which made small art objects for people to carry around as keepsakes in everyday life. He had solo exhibitions at Jack Misrachi Gallery in 1971 and Lerner-Heller Gallery in 1971–72, where he exhibited video art and sculptural works that used language as a medium. The experimental writings and films that Gerchman created while living in New York reflect his political perspective, questioning the geographical hierarchies between North and South. This experience offered him a new perspective on Latin America and its relationship with the Euro–North American art world. He stayed in New York until 1972.

Alberto Greco (b. Buenos Aires, 1931; d. Barcelona, 1965) enjoyed a brief but meaningful visit to New York in late 1964 and early 1965. Zulema "Beba" Damianovich introduced him to Marcel Duchamp and other prominent artists living in the city. In 1965 he collaborated with Christo, Roy Lichtenstein, Daniel Spoerri, Allan Kaprow, and others to create *Rifa Vivo-Dito* (Vivo-Dito Raffle), a performance at New York's Grand Central Station for which he placed works by different artists in the station lockers and then sold numbers to the public, who could win the keys to open the lockers and take the works, although not all lockers had artworks inside. An early exponent of Conceptual art, Greco was formative in the establishment of neo-avant-garde ideas in the 1960s and 1970s in the Americas.

Sarah Grilo (b. Buenos Aires, 1919; d. Madrid, 2007) was a key figure of the postwar Concrete art movement in the Río de la Plata region. She arrived in New York with her painter husband, José Antonio Fernández-Muro (b. Madrid, 1920; d. 2014), in 1962 after being awarded a Guggenheim Fellowship. In the city Grilo turned away from Concrete abstraction, incorporating city iconography and typographies. The couple played an important role in the reception of Latin American art in the United States during the 1960s, hosting and connecting recently arrived migrant artists and organizing meetings with galleries, collectors, and curators.

Carlos Irizarry (b. Santa Isabel, Puerto Rico, 1938; d. 2017) moved to the Bronx with his mother in 1946 and studied at the High School of Art and Design. He specialized in print techniques, especially photographic serigraphy. In 1966 Irizarry returned to Puerto Rico to contribute to the graphic arts movement underway on the island. He also taught at Liga de Estudiantes de las Artes and was cofounder and director of Centro Nacional de las Artes, both in San Juan. His works appropriate mass media imagery to comment on political and art institutions. His conceptual practice became more radical toward the end of the 1970s, when he made threats of political violence against the American presence in Puerto Rico that he considered a new form of protest art.

Leandro Katz (b. Buenos Aires, 1938) studied philosophy and literature in Buenos Aires and arrived in New York in 1965 after backpacking across the Americas. In the city his artistic practice moved from poetry to the visual languages of photography, installation, film, and performance. Katz's multidisciplinary approach to his conceptual artworks is grounded by his own scholarly research and writing. His works are informed by poetry, semiotics, and anthropology (disciplines he also taught), as well as by North and Latin American history and politics. In 1966, after attending a performance of a play in Hell's Kitchen, Katz met Charles Ludlam, founder, playwright, and director of the Ridiculous Theatrical Company, a group that was part of the American theatrical genre known as the Theater of the Ridiculous. Katz collaborated with the company until 1975, performing various tasks, from lighting to acting, and documenting the performances in film and photography. Katz remained in New York City until 2006, when he moved back to Argentina.

Anna Maria Maiolino (b. Scalea, Italy, 1942) moved to New York from Rio de Janeiro in 1968, after her then husband, artist Rubens Gerchman, was awarded a grant that allowed them to leave Brazil with their children amid the political turmoil of the military dictatorship. Following a recommendation from Luis Camnitzer, in 1971 Maiolino received a scholarship to study printmaking at Pratt Institute, where she began her series *Mapas mentais* (Mental maps, 1971–76). During this time Maiolino also created a series of drawings that trace her experiences in the new city and reflect on domestic oppression and the weight of childcare labor, and made prints reflecting her desire to leave the United States. She returned to Brazil in 1971 and currently lives and works in São Paulo.

Laura Márquez (b. Asunción, Paraguay, 1929; d. 2021) moved to New York in 1970, leaving behind the oppressive context of her home country Paraguay under Alfredo Stroessner's dictatorship. She had been in the United States before, having participated in the 1966 exhibition *Contemporary Art of Paraguay* at the Pan-American Union in Washington, DC. Márquez was involved with the group of artists that created the Museo Latinoamericano and participated in Happenings and group shows in the city. There is scant documentation of her time spent living and working in her Tribeca loft, aside from references in her memoirs to her involvement with Museo Latinoamericano. During this period she mainly produced abstract prints that function as commentaries on the political situation in Paraguay and revisit motifs and formal elements from her previous work, such as the use of the circle that evokes the traditional Guaraní lace technique *ñandutí*. Márquez returned to Asunción in 2013.

Esperanza Martell (b. Puerto Rico, 1946) is an activist, educator, and artist. As a member of the Puerto Rican socialist organization El Comité-MINP (Movimiento de Izquierda Nacional Puertorriqueño), she was part of Operation Move-In in 1970, when hundreds of Puerto Rican and Dominican families reclaimed housing left vacant by the city on the Upper West Side. The takeover was depicted in the 1971 film *Break and Enter*, made by the Newsreel collective. As a printmaker, Martell had a studio at Taller Boricua. In 1972 she participated in the formation of the Puerto Rican Education and Media Action Council to protest negative representations of Puerto Ricans in the media and discrimination in the broadcast industry. The council was a key supporter of the PBS TV series *Realidades*.

Cildo Meireles (b. Rio de Janeiro, 1948) is a Conceptual artist. In the late 1960s and early 1970s Meireles conceived one of his best-known series of works, *Insertions into Ideological Circuits*, in which he modified mass-produced objects with subversive messages and placed them back into circulation, thus bypassing gallery systems and avoiding governmental censorship of his works. In 1970 two works from this series—*Coca-Cola Project* and *Banknote Project* (both 1970)—were included in the Museum of Modern Art's exhibition *Information*. Meireles lived in New York City between 1971 and 1973, and became close with Hélio Oiticica, and many other artists.

Miguel Ernesto "Mickey" Melendez (b. New York City, 1947) was part of the original group in New York City that formed the central committee of the New York branch of the Young Lords, and went on to become the group's Minister of Information, as well as help develop its paramilitary branch. His engagement with the Puerto Rican anti-colonial struggle began when he was in college in the late 1960s. He was involved in the organization of the party's street actions, the takeover of the Bronx's Lincoln Hospital, and the hijacking of a city ambulance to provide health care for the Puerto Rican and Black communities. He lives in Bronxville, New York.

Marta Minujín (b. Buenos Aires, 1943) first traveled to New York in 1966 on a Guggenheim Fellowship and, over the next decade, divided her time between the United States and Buenos Aires. She arrived with endorsements and support from curators in Buenos Aires and Paris—where she lived between 1960 and 1963—and soon began exhibiting in galleries and museums and connecting with the city's Pop and experimental art scenes. She became friends and collaborated with such artists as Salvador Dalí and Andy Warhol, and groups like the Judson Theatre Company and the Fluxus community. She was one of the coeditors of *Cha/Cha/Cha* and participated in various Happenings with other Latin American artists. A pioneer of Conceptual, performance, and video art, in New York Minujín created Happenings and large-scale public actions in which she experimented with disruption, participation, community, and Institutional Critique, turning the streets into a stage for her artworks. She lives and works in Buenos Aires.

Sonia Miranda (b. Porto Alegre, Brazil, 1945) moved to New York in 1973, escaping Brazil's military regime with the hope of finding opportunities to work. In New York she acquired a Sony Portapak camera and began creating video art. In 1974 she and fellow Brazilian artist José Roberto Aguilar created her best-known video, *Where Is South America?*, in which they ask visitors to the Empire State Building to direct them toward the continent. Next to these scenes the artists spliced in footage from Brazil, reflecting on geopolitics and images of Brazil from multiple perspectives. Miranda was a close friend of Hélio Oiticica and they collaborated in performance works that she videotaped. In her practice, Miranda explored Afro-Brazilian culture, as well as contemporary dance and music. She still lives and works in New York City.

Raphael Montañez Ortiz (b. Brooklyn, 1934) is a Nuyorican artist, educator, and activist. He pioneered American experimental filmmaking in the late 1950s, creating some of the earliest examples of cut-up cinema. In 1962 he wrote a manifesto on Destructivism, advocating for a direct approach to art-making. His socially charged performances in which he destroyed objects in a violent manner were offered as rituals to achieve spiritual catharsis. Montañez Ortiz's practice during this period also engaged with mass media and technology. His work presents recurrent topics such as colonialism, Puerto Rican and Native American cultures, and religion. As a strong advocate for New York's Puerto Rican community, he led the period's radical community organizing by founding El Museo del Barrio in 1969 and serving as its first director. He lives and works in New York City.

Marcelo Montealegre (b. Puerto Montt, Chile, 1936) initially arrived in New York in 1967, invited by *Life* magazine to receive correspondent training, after working as a freelance photographer for various publications since the 1950s. After this first trip he returned to the United States in 1968 to cover the election of President Richard Nixon. Permanently settled in New York, he was part of a group of Chilean and Latin American artists on the Lower East Side that included Jaime Barrios, Juan Downey, Carmen Beuchat, Waldo Balart, and Rolando Peña. In the 1970s he joined efforts to denounce Pinochet's dictatorship and photographed a large part of the political, artistic, and social activities developed in this context. He also opened his loft, both in Tribeca and later on Broadway, to communal political and artistic activities. He lives and works in New York City.

Mario Montez (b. Ponce, Puerto Rico, 1935; d. Key West, Florida, 2013)—born René Rivera—moved to East Harlem with his family as a child and studied graphic arts. He began practicing drag inspired by classic Hollywood divas and took a name inspired by Dominican actress Maria Montez. After meeting filmmaker Jack Smith, he played in his 1963 experimental film *Flaming Creatures* and became a regular figure of Andy Warhol's movies, acting in thirteen of his films. Montez also starred in José Rodríguez-Soltero's *Life, Death and Assumption of Lupe Vélez* (1966). As a cofounder of the Ridiculous Theatrical Company he performed in some of the most notorious plays of the Theatre of the Ridiculous, including *Turds in Hell* (1968). In 1977 he quit the city's underground scene and moved to Florida.

Abdias do Nascimento (b. Franca, Brazil, 1914; d. Rio de Janeiro, 2011) was an activist, politician, scholar, artist, and theater producer who moved to New York in 1968 to escape the military regime in Brazil. In New York Nascimento created colorful paintings that celebrated themes of West African religions and Afro-Brazilian Candomblé, reflecting on the shared diasporic experiences of Black people in the Americas. In 1970 he began teaching at the State University of New York at Buffalo, where he founded the Chair on African Cultures in the New World at the Center for Puerto Rican Studies. During this period he also spent a year in Nigeria (1976–77). He returned to Brazil in the 1980s, where he became a congressman (1983–87) and senator (1997–99).

Hélio Oiticica (b. Rio de Janeiro, 1937; d. 1980) moved to New York in 1971, after his participation in the Museum of Modern Art's 1970 *Information* show, with a two-year Guggenheim Fellowship. Quickly becoming disappointed with the city's mainstream art world and after having failed in his plan to bring his *Penetrables* to Central Park for his *Subterranean Tropicália Projects*, Oiticica directed his focus to countercultural circles and created performance pieces and writings of a deeply personal nature. He also began experimenting with film and connected with the marginalized communities of New York. In his loft, Oiticica installed his *Nests*, the type of sheer-cloth enclosures built with wood, fabric, and mattresses which he had shown in *Information*. The apartment, known as Loft 4, became a meeting place for artists of all disciplines to exchange and collaborate. He rarely had contact with non-Brazilian artists, except for some figures such as Vito Acconci, Jonas Mekas, Mario Montez, Lee Jaffe, and Jack Smith. The loft was also the stage for his widely known environments *Block-Experiments in Cosmococa—Program in Progress* (1973–74). Oiticica returned to Rio de Janeiro in 1978.

Lydia Okumura (b. Osvaldo Cruz, Brazil, 1948) moved to New York in 1974 to study at the Pratt Graphics Center on a scholarship. In the city she initiated her *Situations* series, site-specific installations that use threads and graphite lines to create optical illusions with geometric shapes. She also collaborated with Sol LeWitt on one of his Minimalist wall drawings. Okumura's abstract prints and installations aim at blurring the distinctions between the two- and three-dimensional and deconstructing ideas of physical space, materiality, and illusion. She still lives and works in New York.

Sylvia Palacios Whitman (b. Osorno, Chile, 1941) studied at Santiago's School of Fine Arts before moving to New York City in 1961 with her first husband, fellow Chilean artist Enrique Castro-Cid. In 1962 she modeled for Richard Avedon and appeared on the October cover of *Harper's Bazaar*. In the city, she turned her interest to dance and theater. In 1970 she performed with Trisha Brown (cofounder of the avant-garde Judson Dance Theater) at the Whitney Museum of American Art and later joined her dance company. In 1974 Palacios Whitman presented to the public her first dance piece as director and choreographer. Between then and 1981—when she withdrew from the art scene, only returning in 2013—Palacios Whitman performed in avant-garde art venues such as the Kitchen, Idea Warehouse, and Sonnabend Gallery. Her pieces were usually performed by participants without formal training in dance and often included props that were discarded afterward. In many cases, she included references to her Latin American background. Simultaneously, Palacios Whitman created detailed sketches for her performances and figurative drawings. She lives and works in Warwick, New York.

César Paternosto (b. La Plata, Argentina, 1931) moved to New York in 1967 after winning the first prize at the III Bienal Americana de Arte (Córdoba, 1966), in which MoMA's director Alfred Barr was a jury member; Barr ended up purchasing an artwork by Paternosto for the museum, which was included in the exhibition *The Sixties* (1967). In New York Paternosto became aware of Conceptualism and the social theory of the Frankfurt School, and deepened his explorations of geometry, color, and the role of the spectator in artworks. In 1969 he first conceptualized what he called "oblique vision," namely, leaving his canvases blank on the front and only painting the sides of their frames. In 1971 Paternosto published a work in *Contrabienal*. During this decade, he became interested in the art of pre-Columbian cultures, drawing inspiration from the geometric designs of textiles, featherworks, and pottery from South America, and began researching and traveling throughout the region. Paternosto has lived and worked in Segovia, Spain, since 2004.

Rolando Peña (b. Venezuela, 1943) moved to New York in 1965. Thanks to a dance scholarship, he studied with Martha Graham, Alwin Nicolais, and Merce Cunningham. In 1966 he created the Foundation for the Totality with artists Waldo Balart, José Rodríguez-Soltero, Juan Downey, and Jaime Barrios, among other Latin American fellow artists, as well as artists from other regions. The group created Happenings and actions of guerilla art and published in the underground magazine *East Village Other*, edited by Walter Bowart. They also collaborated with Andy Warhol (who nicknamed Peña "the Black Prince") and made a film together. Peña's individual practice throughout the decade included Happenings in public spaces, body actions, installations, printmaking, film, and video, as well as performances for the camera—a category of photography he calls "photomatons"—in which he addressed gender ambiguity, sexuality, and Latin American stereotypes such as the guerrilla soldier. Peña currently lives and works in Miami.

Liliana Porter (b. Buenos Aires, 1941) studied art in Buenos Aires and Mexico City and moved to New York in 1964, where she enrolled in printmaking at Pratt Institute. She cofounded the New York Graphic Workshop in 1964 with Luis Camnitzer and José Guillermo Castillo. She contributed to *Contrabienal* and was an active participant in MICLA's meetings. By the end of the 1960s, Porter incorporated photography in her practice. In 1973 she had a solo exhibition at the Museum of Modern Art of her series of photoengravings and installations of wrinkled paper. An important early exponent of Conceptualism, Porter's use of drawing, print, photography, and video explored the boundaries between reality and representation, while integrating the image of the human body and other questions about mimesis. She currently lives and works in Rhinebeck, New York.

Alejandro Puente (b. La Plata, Argentina, 1933; d. Buenos Aires, 2013), after having studied art and exhibited his work in Argentina, arrived in New York in 1967 on a Guggenheim Fellowship and lived there until 1971. After exploring color theory and modular systems, Puente experimented with Minimalism and Conceptualism and embraced organic and sensorial explorations. In 1968 he participated in the exhibition *Beyond Geometry* at the Center for Inter-American Relations in New York (Americas Society) and, in 1970, in the Museum of Modern Art's exhibition *Information*. After visiting a show at the Metropolitan Museum of Art, he began researching pre-Hispanic cultures, incorporating into his work elements such as the ancient Inca *quipu* writing system and Andean textile patterns.

Raquel Rabinovich (b. Buenos Aires, 1929) studied art in Argentina and Europe and moved to New York in 1967. In the city, her practice moved from lyrical abstraction to monochromatic geometric forms informed by Minimalism. Rabinovich also created sculptural works for which she experimented with unconventional materials such as cut glass and silicone, including large-scale glass sculpture environments. To produce these glass sculptures, she received the support of Experiments in Art and Technology (E.A.T.), a collective established in 1967 by engineers Billy Klüver and Fred Waldhauer and artists Robert Rauschenberg and Robert Whitman to develop collaborations between these two disciplines. She lives and works in Rhinebeck, New York.

Omar Rayo (b. Roldanille, Colombia, 1928; d. Palmira, Colombia, 2010) moved to New York in 1961, after having traveled throughout South America—where he became deeply interested in Indigenous art—and lived in Mexico City. In 1962 he exhibited a series of monochrome intaglios that explored volume and tactility. These works portrayed everyday objects and consumer goods including hooks, scissors, buttons, shoes, and neckties. The successful exhibition led to the acquisition of twelve of them by the Museum of Modern Art. In the city he befriended a circle of Latin American artists that included César Paternosto and Marcelo Bonevardi, as well as fellow Colombians Edgar Negret and Leonel Góngora. A pioneer of Op art, Rayo created trompe l'oeil acrylic paintings that often incorporate real volumetric forms attached to the canvas.

Miguel Rio Branco (b. Las Palmas, Spain, 1946) lived in New York between 1964 and 1967 and studied at the New York Institute of Photography, during which time his paintings took an experimental turn. He returned to the city in 1970, briefly attending the School of Visual Arts before dedicating himself to street photography and Super 8 experimental films until he went back to Brazil in 1972. In his photography he explored the Bowery and the East Village. He was hosted by Hélio Oiticica and worked with Gordon Matta-Clark and Lee Jaffe. His series of photographs *New York Sketches* depicts different aspects of the city, from its subway system to the loneliness of its inhabitants. He currently lives and works in Rio de Janeiro.

Freddy Rodríguez (b. Santiago, Dominican Republic, 1945) exiled in New York in 1963, where he studied painting at the Art Students League and the New School, and textile design at the Fashion Institute of Technology. In the city he studied Piet Mondrian's works on view at the Museum of Modern Art and became interested in the hard-edge abstract works of Frank Stella and Minimalism. Rodríguez's formalist paintings alluded to his new urban environment, notably its architecture, and increasingly began referring to his own cultural background. By the 1970s he was using color and geometry to address such themes as Dominican history and politics, Caribbean culture, colonization, race, and religion.

Julio Rodríguez (b. New York, 1942) is a community activist and organizer. As the first chairperson of the National Latino Media Coalition, the first chairperson of the Puerto Rican Media Action and Educational Council, and producer of the bilingual TV show *Realidades*, Rodríguez was a key activist for the representation of the Latino community in the media. He also supported and practiced printmaking with the artists of Taller Boricua.

José Rodríguez-Soltero (b. Santurce, Puerto Rico, 1943; d. New York, 2009) studied in Puerto Rico, Paris, and San Francisco before moving to New York in 1965. In the city he joined the New York queer underground art scene and became known for his experimental films and Happenings. He was part of the Foundation for the Totality and collaborated on films with Andy Warhol, Juan Downey, and Rolando Peña. His 1966 film *Life, Death and Assumption of Lupe Vélez* starred Mario Montez and the performers of the Ridiculous Theatrical Company. His subsequent work was more overtly political, parodying political art and cinema while interrogating Latin American cultural stereotypes, the role of revolutionary leaders such as Che Guevara, and the United States' interventions in the region.

Osvaldo Romberg (b. Buenos Aires, 1938; d. Tel Aviv, 2019) trained as an architect at the University of Buenos Aires and throughout the 1960s worked as a printmaker and teacher in Argentina and Puerto Rico. From 1973 he lived and worked between the United States, Brazil, and Israel. During these years he became associated with the New York Graphic Workshop. In the early 1970s he created works that explore the art historical canon to question traditional political and social ways of seeing. At the same time, he began using photography and film to explore the connections between the body and its representation in mass media.

Waly Salomão (b. Jequié, Brazil, 1943; d. Rio de Janeiro, 2003) was an experimental poet and artist who, in 1972, published his first book, *Me segura qu'eu vou dar um troço* (Hold me back, I'm going to throw a fit), as a protest against the Brazilian military dictatorship. The book was designed by Hélio Oiticica, whose biography, *Qual é o parangolé* (What is a parangolé?, 1996), Salomão would later write. As a songwriter, Salomão wrote lyrics for musicians of the Brazilian musical movement Tropicália, such as Maria Bethânia, Gal Costa, Gilberto Gil, and Caetano Veloso. He spent time in New York in 1975, where he initiated a series of photographs called *Babilaques* (1975–77), in which he combined poetry and visual art.

Zília Sánchez (b. Havana, 1926) exhibited in Latin America and studied painting, sculpture, and restoration in Cuba and Spain before moving to New York in 1962, where she worked as an illustrator and studied at Pratt Institute. Sánchez became involved with a circle of Cuban and Puerto Rican writers and poets, creating illustrations for their publications. In New York Sánchez began creating shaped canvases which became organic, sculptural forms. These sculpted paintings, which protrude from the gallery wall, are thought to evoke the contours of the female body. In 1972 she resettled in San Juan, Puerto Rico, where she still lives and works.

Nitza Tufiño (b. Mexico City, 1949) grew up between San Juan and Manhattan and, after studying art in Mexico, settled in New York in 1970. An activist artist and printmaker, she was one of the founding members of El Museo del Barrio. In 1973 Tufiño created her first public mural for the facade of the institution. In 1970 she became the first woman artist of Taller Boricua and during that decade she also served as a consultant on Puerto Rican and Caribbean art at the Brooklyn Museum and the Metropolitan Museum of Art. She still lives and works in New York.

Andreas Valentin (b. Rio de Janeiro, Brazil, 1952) moved to Pennsylvania to study cinema and art history at Swarthmore College in 1970. A longtime friend and former student—between the ages of six and thirteen—of Hélio Oiticica, Valentin often visited Oiticica in New York, where they socialized and collaborated on experimental films, such as *One Night on Gay Street* (1975) and *Flit* (1975). Valentin also documented some of Oiticica's artworks and took snapshots of life at Loft 4, chronicling 1970s New York with his camera.

Regina Vater (b. Rio de Janeiro, Brazil, 1943) traveled to New York in 1972 after winning a travel grant at the Salão Nacional de Arte Moderna of Brazil. Trained in architecture and painting in her home country, in New York she created experimental works while connecting her ecological interests with feminist theory. She collected waste and detritus, highlighting issues of precariousness in ephemeral works. This practice became *LuxoLixo* (LuxuryTrash), a series of artworks with an ethnographic direction—an experimental film, an artist's book, installations, and mail art inspired by the work of Concretist author Augusto de Campos—that addressed the artist's concern with environmental issues, waste, and renewal, and American consumerism and their relation to inequality.

Armando Zegrí (b. Punta Arenas, Chile, 1899; d. New York, 1972) was a journalist, avant-garde writer, war correspondent, gallery owner, and curator of Latin American art who lived in New York City for most of his adult life. In 1953 he founded Galería Sudamericana, later renamed Galería Zegrí, in Manhattan. The gallery closed in 1971.

CONTRIBUTOR BIOGRAPHIES

Aimé Iglesias Lukin is Director and Chief Curator of Visual Arts at Americas Society. Born and raised in Buenos Aires, she has lived in New York since 2011. She received her PhD in art history from Rutgers University with a dissertation titled "This Must Be the Place: Latin American Artists in New York, 1965–1975." Her research received grants from the Smithsonian American Art Museum, the Metropolitan Museum of Art, the Terra Foundation for American Art, and the Andrew W. Mellon Foundation, as well as the ICAA Peter C. Marzio Award from the Museum of Fine Arts, Houston. Her writings have been published by the New Museum, the Museum of Modern Art, and the Solomon R. Guggenheim Museum. She has curated exhibitions independently in museums and cultural centers and previously worked in the Modern and Contemporary Art Department of the Metropolitan Museum of Art, the Institute for Studies on Latin American Art, and Fundación Proa in Buenos Aires.

Tie Jojima is Assistant Curator of the Visual Arts program at Americas Society. She is a PhD candidate in the art history program at the Graduate Center, CUNY, where she is specializing in modern and contemporary Latin American art. Her research focuses on performance, pornography, and technology in Brazilian art of the late 1970s and early 1980s. She received dual MA degrees in art history and arts administration from the School of the Art Institute of Chicago.

Abigail Lapin Dardashti is an assistant professor of art history and visual studies at the University of California, Irvine. Her research examines modern and contemporary Latin American, Latino/a/x, and African diasporic art with a focus on international exchange, migration, racial formation, and activism. Her work has received funding from the Social Science Research Council, the Fulbright Program, the Center for Advanced Study in the Visual Arts at the National Gallery of Art, Washington, DC, the Andrew W. Mellon Foundation, and the Smithsonian Institution. She has curated exhibitions at BRIC, Brooklyn, and Taller Puertorriqueño, Philadelphia, and has served as a curatorial fellow at the Museum of Modern Art, New York, the Studio Museum in Harlem, and the Museo de Arte Moderno, Santo Domingo. Her work has been published in peer-reviewed journals, exhibition catalogues, and edited volumes in Brazil, the Dominican Republic, France, and the United States. She received her PhD from the Graduate Center, CUNY, in 2020.

Harper Montgomery teaches in the Department of Art & Art History at Hunter College of the City University of New York. She has written for the *Art Bulletin*, *Art Journal*, and the *Brooklyn Rail*, and has organized exhibitions on art of the nineteenth century, the twentieth century, and the present for Hunter College Art Galleries. She is the author of *The Mobility of Modernism: Art and Criticism in 1920s Latin America* (University of Texas Press, 2017), which won the Arvey Foundation Book Award for distinguished scholarship on Latin American Art, and coeditor of *Beyond the Aesthetic and the Anti-Aesthetic* (Pennsylvania State University Press, 2013). Her current research concerns the ascent of *artesanía* within contemporary art spaces in Latin America from the 1970s to the late 1980s.

Yasmin Ramirez holds a PhD in art history from the Graduate Center, CUNY. Her critically acclaimed exhibitions include: *Pasado y Presente: Art after the Young Lords, 1969–2019* (2019); *Home, Memory, and Future* (2016); *Martin Wong: Human Instamatic* (2015); *¡Presente!: The Young Lords in New York* (2015); *Re-Membering Loisaida: On Archiving and the Lure of the Retro Lens* (2009); *"Esto A Veces Tiene Nombre": Latin@ Art Collectives in a Post-Movement Millennium* (2008); *Voices from Our Communities: Perspectives on a Decade of Collecting at El Museo del Barrio* (2000); and *Pressing the Point: Parallel Expressions in the Graphic Arts of the Chicano and Puerto Rican Movements* (1999). Ramirez currently works as an adjunct professor of art history at City College and is completing a book on Latinx art movements in New York.

SOURCES

Sources are organized by the page number on which they appear, followed by the name of the artist quoted, and the bibliographic information of the source (including author, publication, page number, and publisher).

All translations from Spanish are by Mariana Fernández. Translations from Portuguese are by Tie Jojima.

CHAPTER 1: The City

p. 25: Hélio Oiticica. Letter to Claudio Oiticica, New York, October 29, 1973. Projeto Hélio Oiticica Archive, AHO/PHO 1073.73-p.1, Rio de Janeiro; cited in Dária Jaremtchuk, "Tudo o que fiz antes, considero um prólogo," *ARS* 15, no. 30 (2017): 11. Original in Portuguese.

1.1 Initial Impressions of the City

p. 32: Raquel Rabinovich. Interview by Aimé Iglesias Lukin and Tie Jojima. New York, June 30, 2021.

p. 33: Liliana Porter. Inés Katzenstein, *Liliana Porter in Conversation with/en conversación con Inés Katzenstein*, 87. New York: Fundación Cisneros/Colección Patricia Phelps de Cisneros; London: MAPP Editions, 2013.

p. 35: Sarah Grilo and José Antonio Fernández-Muro. Francisco Rivas, ed., *Alberto Greco*, 245. Valencia: IVAM Centre Julio González; Madrid: Fundación Cultural Mapfre Vida, 1991. Original in Spanish.

p. 37: Leandro Katz. Ana Longoni, Jesse Lerner, and Mariano Mestman, *Leandro Katz*, 70–71. Buenos Aires: Fundación Espigas/Fundación Telefónica, 2000.

pp. 38–39: Regina Vater. "Oral history interview with Regina Vater, 2004 February 23–25." Archives of American Art, Smithsonian Institution.

p. 43 (top): Hélio Oiticica. Letter to Lygia Clark, London, December 23, 1969. Luciano Figueiredo, ed., *Lygia Clark – Hélio Oiticica: Cartas, 1964–1974*, 128–29. Rio de Janeiro: UFRJ, 1998. Original in Portuguese.

p. 43 (bottom): Miguel Rio Branco. Email interview by Tie Jojima. May 25, 2021. Original in Portuguese.

p. 44: Cildo Meireles. Caroline Menezes, "Materiality and Memory: An Interview with Cildo Meireles." *Studio International*, March 28, 2009. https://www.studiointernational.com/index.php/materiality-and-memory-an-interview-with-cildo-meireles.

p. 45: Andreas Valentin. Andreas Valentin and Thomas Valentin, eds., *Call Me Helium, 1974–2014*, 88. Rio de Janeiro: Centro Cultural Correios, 2014.

p. 46: Antonio Dias. Hans-Michael Herzog, ed., *Antonio Dias: Anywhere Is My Land*, 141. Zurich: Daros Latinamerica, 2009.

p. 48: Marcelo Montealegre. Julio Ramos, "Marcelo Montealegre: Fotógrafo del underground." *La Fuga*, no. 21 (Winter 2018): https://lafuga.cl/marcelo-montealegre-fotografo-del-underground/904. Original in Spanish.

p. 51: Sonia Miranda. Email interview by Tie Jojima. November 30, 2021. Original in Portuguese.

p. 53: Luis Camnitzer. Alexander Alberro, ed., *Luis Camnitzer in Conversation with/en conversación con Alexander Alberro*, 138. New York: Fundación Cisneros/Colección Patricia Phelps de Cisneros; London: MAPP Editions, 2014.

p. 54: Luis Camnitzer. Alexander Alberro, ed., *Luis Camnitzer in Conversation with/en conversación con Alexander Alberro*, 129. New York: Fundación Cisneros/Colección Patricia Phelps de Cisneros; London: MAPP Editions, 2014.

p. 57: Jaime Davidovich. Daniel R. Quiles and John G. Hanhardt, *Jaime Davidovich in Conversation with/en conversación con Daniel R. Quiles*, 91. New York: Fundación Cisneros/Colección Patricia Phelps de Cisneros; London: MAPP Editions, 2018.

p. 58: Carmen Beuchat. Interview by Hans Ulrich Obrist. Virtual, March 6, 2020. Karen Marta and Gabriela Rangel, eds., *Conversations in Chile*. Santiago: D21 Proyectos de Arte, forthcoming 2022.

p. 60: Marta Minujín. Interview by Aimé Iglesias Lukin and Mariana Fernández, New York. October 29, 2021. Original in Spanish.

p. 62: Waldo Balart. Gustavo Valdés Jr., "El Color de la Palabra: 32 Artistas Cubanos." *Stet* 1, no. 2 (Winter 1992): 28. Available at Documents of Latin American and Latino Art from the International Center for the Arts of the Americas, Museum of Fine Arts, Houston, ICAA Record ID: 821599. Original in Spanish.

p. 63: Rolando Peña. Viviana Marcela Iriart, "Rolando Peña, artista multimedia, el único Príncipe Negro venezolano: 'Bautizamos al grupo en una bañera, y el padrino fue Andy Warhol.'" *Viviana Marcela Iriart* (blog). Accessed December 14, 2021. https://vivianamarcelairiart.blogspot.com/2020/06/rolando-pena-artista-multimedia-el_25.html. Original in Spanish.

p. 64: Freddy Rodríguez. "Artist Freddy Rodríguez in Conversation with Curator and Art Historian Dr. E. Carmen Ramos 2015." Bluecast Productions. October 2, 2015. YouTube video, 41:52. www.youtube.com/watch?v=SL8J8gCYaZA.

p. 65: Omar Rayo. Amparo Osorio and Gonzalo Márquez Cristo, "Omar Rayo: Reportaje. Geometría iluminada." *Común Presencia Entrevistas* (blog). Accessed January 10, 2022. http://comunpresenciaentrevistas.blogspot.com/2006/12/omar-rayo-reportaje.html. Original in Spanish.

p. 66: Laura Márquez. *Diario ABC Color* (Asunción, Paraguay), November 18, 1973, 3. Original in Spanish.

p. 67: Máximo Rafael Colón. Melanie Pérez Ortiz, "La eternidad de las imágenes: entrevista y crónica con Máximo Colón." *80 Grados*, March 11, 2017. www.80grados.net/la-eternidad-de-las-imagenes-entrevista-y-cronica-con-maximo-colon. Original in Spanish.

p. 69: Abdias do Nascimento. Pedro Celso Uchôa Cavalcanti and Jovelino Ramos, *Memórias do Exílio: Brasil 1964–19??*, 47–49. São Paulo: Editora Arcadia, 1976. Original in Portuguese.

1.2 The Loft and Living in the City

p. 77: Sylvia Palacios Whitman. Interview by Hans Ulrich Obrist. New York, October 9, 2019. Karen Marta and Gabriela Rangel, eds., *Conversations in Chile*. Santiago: D21 Proyectos de Arte, forthcoming 2022.

p. 79: Sylvia Palacios Whitman. Interview by Hans Ulrich Obrist. New York, October 9, 2019. Karen Marta and Gabriela Rangel, eds., *Conversations in Chile*. Santiago: D21 Proyectos de Arte, forthcoming 2022.

p. 81: Jaime Davidovich. Daniel R. Quiles and John G. Hanhardt, *Jaime Davidovich in Conversation with/en conversación con Daniel R. Quiles*, 131. New York: Fundación Cisneros/Colección Patricia Phelps de Cisneros; London: MAPP Editions, 2018.

p. 84: Leandro Katz. Ana Longoni, Jesse Lerner, and Mariano Mestman, *Leandro Katz*, 69–70. Buenos Aires: Fundación Espigas/Fundación Telefónica, 2000.

p. 87: Anna Maria Maiolino. Anna Maria Maiolino, *Entre Pausas*, 23–24. New York: Hauser & Wirth, 2018.

p. 88: César Paternosto. Interview by Aimé Iglesias Lukin. Segovia, May 1, 2019. Original in Spanish.

p. 91: Waly Salomão. *Hélio Oiticica: Qual é o Parangolé? e outros escritos*, 27. Rio de Janeiro: Rocco, 2003.

p. 92: Hélio Oiticica. Letter to Guy and Carol Brett. March 16, 1971. Projeto Hélio Oiticica Archive, AHO/PHO 1102.71.

1.3 Views of the City

p. 99: Regina Vater. Email interview by Tie Jojima. May 24, 2021. Original in Portuguese.

p. 102: Miguel Rio Branco. Laura Havlin, "Miguel Rio Branco: New York Sketches." *Magnum Photos*, November 4, 2016. https://www.magnumphotos.com/theory-and-practice/new-york-sketches.

p. 107: Anna Bella Geiger. Email interview by Aimé Iglesias Lukin and Tie Jojima. July 15, 2021. Responses written with the assistance of Noni Geiger.

1.4 Navigating the City

p. 111: Miguel Rio Branco. Email interview by Tie Jojima, May 25, 2021. Original in Portuguese.

p. 113: Hélio Oiticica. *Clouds in My Coffee*. February 18–March 6, 1973. Projeto Hélio Oiticica Archive, AHO/PHO 0481.73.

p. 114: Anna Bella Geiger. Email interview by Aimé Iglesias Lukin and Tie Jojima, May 25, 2021. Response written with the assistance of Noni Geiger.

p. 117: Rubens Gerchman. "Shreds of the City." Printed document, n.p. (Rio de Janeiro), n.d. (1995). Unpublished writings by the artist. Clara Gerchman, ed., *Rubens Gerchman: o rei do mau gosto*, 172. São Paulo: J.J. Carol Editora, 2013.

1.5 Intervening in the City

p. 123: Carlos "Chino" García. Leyla Vural, "The Reminiscences of Carlos 'Chino' García." *Saving Preservation Stories: Diversity and the Outer Boroughs*, 12–15. New York: New York Preservation Archive Project, 2017. https://www.nypap.org/wp-content/uploads/2017/12/Garcia_Chino_20171113.pdf.

p. 125: Carlos "Chino" García. Leyla Vural, "The Reminiscences of Carlos 'Chino' García." *Saving Preservation Stories: Diversity and the Outer Boroughs*, 5, 13. New York: New York Preservation Archive Project, 2017. https://www.nypap.org/wp-content/uploads/2017/12/Garcia_Chino_20171113.pdf.

p. 126: Eduardo Costa. *Street Works* statement (March 1969). Artist's website. Accessed November 10, 2021. https://ecosta100.wixsite.com.

p. 137: Jaime Davidovich. Daniel R. Quiles and John G. Hanhardt, *Jaime Davidovich in Conversation with/en conversación con Daniel R. Quiles*, 145. New York: Fundación Cisneros/Colección Patricia Phelps de Cisneros; London: MAPP Editions, 2018.

p. 138: Jaime Davidovich. Ana Janevski, "'I have to go back to New York. I have no choice': Interview with Jaime Davidovich (Part 2)." *Post: Notes on Art in a Global Context*. Museum of Modern Art, September 13, 2021. https://post.moma.org/i-have-to-go-back-to-new-york-i-have-no-choice-interview-with-jaime-davidovich-part-2.

pp. 140–41: Leandro Katz. Exhibition brochure for *3–III, 7–VII, 21–XXI, Las Columnas*, 1971.

CHAPTER 2: Community and Institutions

p. 143: Nitza Tufiño. Interview by Aimé Iglesias Lukin. New York, October 29, 2021.

2.1 Art Spaces

p. 149: Luis Camnitzer. Noelle Sickels, *Searching for Armando*. Los Angeles: La Sirena Press, 2017. Kindle.

p. 150: Armando Zegrí. "Statements by Gallery Directors." *Arts Magazine* 45, no. 6 (April 1971): 48–49.

p. 152: John Canaday, "Art: A Hit Scored by 28 Painters Lured From Latin America." *New York Times*, September 23, 1964, 52.

p. 155: Fernanda Bonino. Aimé Iglesias Lukin, "Interview with Fernanda Bonino." In Agustín Díez Fischer, ed., *Espigas muestra Bonino*, 153–55. Buenos Aires: Fundación Espigas, 2019.

p. 156: César Paternosto. Email interview by Aimé Iglesias Lukin. November 1, 2013. Original in Spanish.

p. 167 (top): Luis Camnitzer. Alexander Alberro, ed., *Luis Camnitzer in Conversation with/en conversación con Alexander Alberro*, 187. New York: Fundación Cisneros/Colección Patricia Phelps de Cisneros; London: MAPP Editions, 2014.

p. 167 (bottom): Hélio Oiticica. Artist statement. Kynaston L. McShine, *Information*, 103. Exhibition catalogue. New York: Museum of Modern Art, 1970.

2.2 El Museo del Barrio and Taller Boricua

p. 174: Raphael Montañez Ortiz. "Culture and the People." *Art in America* 59, no. 3 (May/June 1971): 27.

p. 178: Nitza Tufiño. Interview by Aimé Iglesias Lukin. New York, October 29, 2021.

p. 180: Marcos Dimas. *Taller Alma Boricua: Reflecting on Twenty Years of the Puerto Rican Workshop, 1969–1989*, 11. Exhibition catalogue. New York: El Museo del Barrio, 1990. Available at Documents of Latin American and Latino Art from the International Center for the Arts of the Americas, Museum of Fine Arts, Houston, ICAA Record ID: 796749.

p. 183: Marcos Dimas. *Taller Alma Boricua: Reflecting on Twenty Years of the Puerto Rican Workshop, 1969–1989*, 10–11. Exhibition catalogue. New York: El Museo del Barrio, 1990. Available at Documents of Latin American and Latino Art from the International Center for the Arts of the Americas, Museum of Fine Arts, Houston, ICAA Record ID: 796749.

p. 186: Marcos Dimas. *Taller Alma Boricua: Reflecting on Twenty Years of the Puerto Rican Workshop, 1969–1989*, 12. Exhibition catalogue. New York: El Museo del Barrio, 1990. Available at Documents of Latin American and Latino Art from the International Center for the Arts of the Americas, Museum of Fine Arts, Houston, ICAA Record ID: 796749.

2.3 Pratt Graphics Center and the New York Graphic Workshop

p. 190: Alicia Barney. Miguel González, "Alicia Barney: Entre la realidad del arte y la de la vida." *Contrastes: Revista de El Pueblo* (Cali, Colombia), February 6, 1983, 8–9. Original in Spanish. Available at Documents of Latin American and Latino Art from the International Center for the Arts of the Americas, Museum of Fine Arts, Houston, ICAA Record ID: 1087494.

p. 191: Lydia Okumura. Autobiography. Artist's website. Accessed December 2, 2021. www.lydiaokumura.com.

p. 192: Anna Maria Maiolino. Interview by Helena Tatay. Artist's website. Accessed September 22, 2021. https://annamariamaiolino.com.

p. 194: Luis Camnitzer. Alexander Alberro, ed., *Luis Camnitzer in Conversation with/en conversación con Alexander Alberro*, 141–43. New York: Fundación Cisneros/Colección Patricia Phelps de Cisneros; London: MAPP Editions, 2014.

p. 197: Luis Camnitzer. Alberro, ed., *Luis Camnitzer in Conversation with/en conversación con Alexander Alberro*, 158–59, 165–66. New York: Fundación Cisneros/Colección Patricia Phelps de Cisneros; London: MAPP Editions, 2014.

p. 198: Luis Camnitzer. Alberro, ed., *Luis Camnitzer in Conversation with/en conversación con Alexander Alberro*, 155. New York: Fundación Cisneros/Colección Patricia Phelps de Cisneros; London: MAPP Editions, 2014.

p. 202: Liliana Porter. Inés Katzenstein, *Liliana Porter in Conversation with/en conversación con Inés Katzenstein*, 126. New York: Fundación Cisneros/Colección Patricia Phelps de Cisneros; London: MAPP Editions, 2013.

p. 207: Liliana Porter. Inés Katzenstein, *Liliana Porter in Conversation with/en conversación con Inés Katzenstein*, 142. New York: Fundación Cisneros/Colección Patricia Phelps de Cisneros; London: MAPP Editions, 2013.

2.4 Critique of Institutions

p. 211: Liliana Porter. Inés Katzenstein, *Liliana Porter in Conversation with/en conversación con Inés Katzenstein*, 136–38. New York: Fundación Cisneros/Colección Patricia Phelps de Cisneros; London: MAPP Editions, 2013.

p. 213: Liliana Porter. Inés Katzenstein, *Liliana Porter in Conversation with/en conversación con Inés Katzenstein*, 128. New York: Fundación Cisneros/Colección Patricia Phelps de Cisneros; London: MAPP Editions, 2013.

p. 217: Jaime Davidovich. Leah Churner, "Un-TV: Public access cable television in Manhattan: an oral history." *Moving Image Source*. Museum of the Moving Image. February 10, 2011. www.movingimagesource.us/articles/un-tv-20110210.

p. 219: Marta Minujín. Text of the press conference for *MINUCODE*, 1968. Marta Minujín Archive.

p. 225: Blair Sabol, "Outside Fashion: Fashion Show Poetry Event." *Village Voice*, January 23, 1969, 13–14.

p. 234: Marta Minujín. Documentation of *Kidnappening*, 1973. Marta Minujín Archive. Original in Spanish.

pp. 236–37: Marta Minujín. Interview by Aimé Iglesias Lukin and Mariana Fernández. New York, October 29, 2021. Original in Spanish.

p. 239: Marta Minujín. Documentation of *Kidnappening*, 1973. Marta Minujín Archive. Original in Spanish.

p. 242: Ruth Kleiman, participant. Letter to Marta Minujín. Documentation of *Kidnappening*, 1973. Marta Minujín Archive.

CHAPTER 3: Politics, Identity, and the Body

p. 245: César Paternosto. Email interview by Aimé Iglesias Lukin. November 1, 2013. Original in Spanish.

3.1 Political Actions and Solidarity Initiatives

p. 255: Program of the Popular Government of Chile. Eva S. and James D. Cockcroft, "Murals for the People of Chile." *Towards Revolutionary Art*, no. 4 (1973): 3. Lucy R. Lippard papers, 1930s–2007, bulk 1960–1990. Archives of American Art, Smithsonian Institution.

p. 256: Marcelo Montealegre. Julio Ramos, "Marcelo Montealegre: Fotógrafo del underground." *La Fuga*, no. 21 (Winter 2018): https://lafuga.cl/marcelo-montealegre-fotografo-del-underground/904. Original in Spanish.

p. 258: Marcelo Montealegre. Julio Ramos, "Marcelo Montealegre: Fotógrafo del underground." *La Fuga*, no. 21 (Winter 2018): https://lafuga.cl/marcelo-montealegre-fotografo-del-underground/904. Original in Spanish.

p. 265: Augusto Boal. "Latin America Poetry, Film, and Theater." *Camera Three*, 1972. Creative Arts Television. Films on Demand/Films Media Group.

p. 267: Augusto Boal. "Latin America Poetry, Film, and Theater." *Camera Three*, 1972. Creative Arts Television. Films on Demand/Films Media Group.

p. 273: Miguel "Mickey" Melendez. *We Took the Streets: Fighting for Latino Rights with the Young Lords*, 109–10. New York: St. Martin's Press, 2009.

p. 290: Nitza Tufiño. Interview by Aimé Iglesias Lukin. New York, October 29, 2021.

p. 294: Rolando Peña. Viviana Marcela Iriart, "Rolando Peña, artista multimedia, el único Príncipe Negro venezolano: 'Bautizamos al grupo en una bañera, y el padrino fue Andy Warhol.'" *Viviana Marcela Iriart* (blog). Accessed December 14, 2021. https://vivianamarcelairiart.blogspot.com/2020/06/rolando-pena-artista-multimedia-el_25.html. Original in Spanish.

p. 299: Carlos "Chino" García. Leyla Vural, "The Reminiscences of Carlos 'Chino' García." *Saving Preservation Stories: Diversity and the Outer Boroughs*, 9. New York: New York Preservation Archive Project, 2017. https://www.nypap.org/wp-content/uploads/2017/12/Garcia_Chino_20171113.pdf.

p. 302: Museo Latinoamericano (Latin American Museum). *Contrabienal*, n.p. New York: Museo Latinoamericano and Movimiento de Independencia Cultural Latinoamericana (MICLA), 1971.

p. 303: MICLA (Movement for Latin American Cultural Independence). *Contrabienal*, n.p. New York: Museo Latinoamericano and Movimiento de Independencia Cultural Latinoamericana (MICLA), 1971.

3.2 Identity and Representation

p. 311: Marcelo Montealegre. Jennifer McColl Crozier, "Formas de resistencia. Entrevista a Marcelo Montealegre." *Artishock*, October 2, 2020. https://artishockrevista.com/2020/10/02/entrevista-marcelo-montealegre/. Original in Spanish.

p. 313: Esperanza Martell. "Realidades Revisited Panel Discussion pt. 1 / July 6, 2019." Taller Boricua. YouTube video, 1:38:48. https://youtu.be/OGuDcZ2q6gw?t=1031.

p. 314: Julio Rodríguez. "Realidades Revisited Panel Discussion pt. 1 / July 6, 2019." Taller Boricua. YouTube video, 1:38:48. https://youtu.be/OGuDcZ2q6gw?t=1031

p. 318: Mario Montez. Gary McColgen, "The Super Star: An Interview with Mario Montez." *Film Culture*, no. 45 (Summer 1967): 18.

p. 322: Rolando Peña. Viviana Marcela Iriart, "Rolando Peña, artista multimedia, el único Príncipe Negro venezolano: 'Bautizamos al grupo en una bañera, y el padrino fue Andy Warhol.'" *Viviana Marcela Iriart* (blog). Accessed December 14, 2021. https://vivianamarcelairiart.blogspot.com/2020/06/rolando-pena-artista-multimedia-el_25.html. Original in Spanish.

p. 326: Lydia Okumura. "Lydia Okumura: Standing Points." Piero Atchugarry Gallery, Miami. January 28, 2021. YouTube video, 5:32. www.youtube.com/watch?v=kXIAGF9mVJI.

p. 329: Anna Maria Maiolino. Anna Maria Maiolino, *Entre Pausas*, 23. New York: Hauser & Wirth, 2018.

p. 330: Enrique Castro-Cid. Marta Minujín, Julián Cairol, and Juan Downey, *Cha/Cha/Cha: A Magazine of Art Criticism Dedicated to the Investigation of the Latin-American Artistic Production*, n.p. Circulated typescript, 1974. Marta Minujín Archive. Original in Spanish.

p. 334 (top): Juan Downey. R. Naranjo and V. Briceño, "Entrevista a Juan Downey." In *6o. Festival Franco-Chileno de Video Art*, n.p. Santiago: Instituto Francés de Cultura, 1986. Original in Spanish.

p. 334 (bottom): Juan Downey. "El olor del aguarrás, Nueva York, 1986." In Juan Downey, *Video porque Te Ve*, n.p. Santiago: Ediciones Visuala Galería, 1987. Original in Spanish.

p. 337: Laura Márquez. *Diario ABC Color*. (Asunción, Paraguay), November 18, 1973, 3. Original in Spanish.

p. 339: Rubens Gerchman. "Abaixo do Equador," n.p. Typescript, New York, 1971. Text licensed by Instituto Rubens Gerchman. Collection Instituto Rubens Gerchman. Original in Portuguese.

p. 341: Hélio Oiticica. Lygia Pape and Hélio Oiticica, "Fala, Hélio." *Revista de Cultura Vozes*, no. 5 (June–July 1978): 43–50. Available at Documents of Latin American and Latino Art from the International Center for the Arts of the Americas, Museum of Fine Arts, Houston, ICAA Record ID: 1111054. Original in Portuguese.

p. 344: Abdias do Nascimento. Pedro Celso Uchôa Cavalcanti and Jovelino Ramos, *Memórias do Exílio: Brasil 1964–19??*, 49. São Paulo: Editora Arcadia, 1976. Original in Portuguese.

p. 348: César Paternosto. Email interview by Aimé Iglesias Lukin and Tie Jojima. December 6, 2021.

p. 351: César Paternosto. Email interview by Aimé Iglesias Lukin and Tie Jojima. December 6, 2021.

3. 3 The Body and Performance

p. 357: Carmen Beuchat. "Violencia y alegría en la danza vanguardista de Carmen Beuchat." *El Mercurio*, July 15, 1993, 6. Original in Spanish.

p. 366: Regina Vater. "Oral history interview with Regina Vater, 2004 February 23–25." Archives of American Art, Smithsonian Institution.

p. 367: Osvaldo Romberg. "Interview by Dominique Nahas, New York, 1995." In Aaron Levy, ed., *Searching for Romberg: Art and Interactivity in the Work of Osvaldo Romberg*, 135. Philadelphia: Slought Books, 2001.

p. 370: Francisco Copello. *Fotografía de performance: Análisis autobiográfico de mis performances*, 70. Santiago: Ocho Libros Editores, 2003. Original in Spanish.

p. 375: Eduardo Costa. Museo Tamayo, "Entrevista Eduardo Costa," n.p. Mexico City, November 2011. http://tallertamayo.org/wp-content/uploads/2018/11/Entrevista-final-Eduardo-Costa_AC.pdf. Original in Spanish.

p. 377: Zilia Sánchez. Vesela Sretenović, *Zilia Sánchez: Soy Isla*, 21–22. New Haven, CT: Yale University Press, 2019.

p. 383: Enrique Castro-Cid. "Sculpture: The Motion Is Haphazard, the Situation Unpredictable." *Time*, March 4, 1966, 78.

p. 384: Enrique Castro-Cid. "Art in Orbit." *Newsweek*, April 4, 1966, 93.

p. 385: Juan Downey. "Technology and Beyond." *Radical Software* 2, no. 5 (Winter 1073): n.p.

FURTHER READING

For space reasons and to emphasize the collective focus of this book, the bibliography does not include monographic studies on the artists. Primary sources cited in *This Must Be the Place* are listed in the Sources section on pages 420–23.

Adams, Beverly. "Latin American Art at the Americas Society: A Principality of Its Own." In *A Principality of Its Own*, edited by Falconi and Rangel, 24–41.

Ades, Dawn, Guy Brett, Staton Loomis Catlin, and Rosemary O'Neill. *Art in Latin America: The Modern Era, 1820–1980*. New Haven, CT: Yale University Press, 2006.

Alberro, Alexander. "Media, Sculpture, Myth." In *A Principality of Its Own*, edited by Falconi and Rangel, 160–77.

Alberro, Alexander, and Blake Stimson, eds. *Conceptual Art: A Critical Anthology*. Cambridge, MA: MIT Press, 1999.

Alonso, Rodrigo. *Magnet: New York. Argentine Art from the '60s*. Buenos Aires: Fundación Proa, 2010.

Alvarez, Mariola V., and Ana M. Franco, eds. *New Geographies of Abstract Art in Postwar Latin America*. London: Routledge, 2019.

Amaral, Aracy A. "Boycott à X Bienal: Extensão e Significado." In *Arte e meio artístico: entre a feiojoada e o x-burguer (1961–1981)*, 400–405. São Paulo: Editora 34, 2013.

Anderson, Benedict. *Imagined Communities: Reflections on the Origin and Spread of Nationalism*. London: Verso, 1983.

Anderson, Terry H. *The Movement and the Sixties*. New York: Oxford University Press, 1995.

Appiah, Kwame Anthony. *Cosmopolitanism: Ethics in a World of Strangers*. New York: W. W. Norton, 2007.

Araújo Fontalvo, Orlando. *Nostalgia y mito: Ensayos de crítica literaria*. Barranquilla, Colombia: Editorial Universidad del Norte, 2012.

Barnitz, Jacqueline, ed. *Latin American Artists in New York Since 1970*. Austin: A. M. Huntington Art Gallery, University of Texas at Austin, 1987.

Barriendos Rodríguez, Joaquín. "Geopolitics of Global Art: The Reinvention of Latin America as a Geoaesthetic Region." In *The Global Art World: Audiences, Markets, and Museums*, edited by Hans Belting and Andrea Buddensieg, 98–114. Ostfildern: Hatje Cantz, 2009.

———. "La idea del arte latinoamericano. Estudios globales del arte, geografías subalternas, regionalismos críticos." PhD diss., University of Barcelona, 2013.

Barthes, Roland. "The Death of the Author." In *Image-Music-Text*, translated by Stephen Heath, 142–48. New York: Hill & Wang, 1967.

Basilio, Miriam, Fatima Bercht, Deborah Cullen, Gary Carrels, and Luis Enrique Pérez-Oramas, eds. *Latin American & Caribbean Art: MoMA at El Museo*. New York: El Museo del Barrio; The Museum of Modern Art, 2004.

Beltrán, Mary. *Latino TV: A History*. New York: New York University Press, 2022.

Benezra, Karen. *Dematerialization: Art and Design in Latin America*. Oakland: University of California Press, 2020.

Berger, Mark T. *Under Northern Eyes: Latin American Studies and US Hegemony in the Americas 1898–1990*. Bloomington: Indiana University Press, 1995.

Berggren, Erik. "Representation, Victimization or Identification. Negotiating Power and Powerlessness in Art on Migration." *Journal of Mediterranean Knowledge* 4, no. 2 (December 2019): 113–36.

Bhabha, Homi K. *The Location of Culture*. London: Routledge, 2004.

Biondi, Martha. *To Stand and Fight: The Struggle for Civil Rights in Postwar New York City*. Cambridge, MA: Harvard University Press, 2003.

Bishop, Claire. *Artificial Hells: Participatory Art and the Politics of Spectatorship*. London: Verso, 2012.

Block, René, Ursula Block, and Kurt Thöricht, eds. *New York – Downtown Manhattan: SoHo*. Ausstellungen, Theater, Musik, Performance, Video, Film. Berlin, Akademie der Kunste, 1976.

Boyle, Deirdre. "From Portapak to Camcorder: A Brief History of Guerrilla Television." *Journal of Film and Video* 44, nos. 1–2 (Spring–Summer 1992): 67–79.

Boym, Svetlana. *The Future of Nostalgia*. New York: Basic Books, 2001.

Brands, Hal. "Third World Politics in an Age of Global Turmoil: The Latin American Challenge to U.S. and Western Hegemony, 1965–1975." *Diplomatic History* 32, no. 1 (January 2008): 105–38.

Brodbeck, Anna Katherine. "'A Third Way': *Information* (1970) and the International Exhibition of Contemporary Art from Latin America." Paper presented at *Transnational Latin American Art from 1950 to the Present Day*, University of Texas at Austin, November 6–8, 2009.

Bryan-Wilson, Julia. *Art Workers: Radical Practice in the Vietnam War Era*. Berkeley: University of California Press, 2009.

Buchloh, Benjamin H. D. "From the Aesthetic of Administration to Institutional Critique (Some Aspects of Conceptual Art, 1962–1969)." In *L'art conceptuel, une perspective*, edited by Claude Gintz, 41–53. Paris: Musée d'Art Moderne de la Ville de Paris, 1989.

Buskirk, Martha, and Mignon Nixon, eds. *The Duchamp Effect*. Cambridge, MA: MIT Press, 1996.

Butler, Cornelia. *From Conceptualism to Feminism: Lucy Lippard's Numbers Shows, 1969–74*. London: Afterall Books, 2012.

Calirman, Claudia. *Brazilian Art under Dictatorship: Antonio Manuel, Artur Barrio, and Cildo Meireles*. Durham, NC: Duke University Press, 2012.

———. "Marginália in Brazil's 'Stone-Throwing Age.'" *Art Journal* 78, no. 1 (Spring 2019): 48–65.

———. "Pop and Politics in Brazilian Art." In *International Pop*, edited by M. Darsie Alexander and Bartholomew Ryan, 119–30. Minneapolis: Walker Art Center, 2015.

Camnitzer, Luis. *Conceptualism in Latin American Art: Didactics of Liberation*. Austin: University of Texas Press, 2007.

———. "The Museo Latinoamericano and MICLA." In *A Principality of Its Own*, edited by Falconi and Rangel, 216–29.

———. *On Art, Artists, Latin America, and Other Utopias*. Edited by Rachel Weiss. Austin: University of Texas Press, 2009.

Camnitzer, Luis, Jane Farver, and Rachel Weiss, eds. *Global Conceptualism: Points of Origin, 1950s–1980s*. New York: Queens Museum of Art, 1999.

Cancel, Luis R., ed. *The Latin American Spirit: Art and Artists in the United States, 1920–1970*. Bronx Museum of the Arts in association with Harry N. Abrams, 1988.

Candela, Iria. *Sombras de ciudad: arte y transformación urbana en Nueva York, 1970–1990*. Madrid: Alianza, 2007.

Cándida Smith, Richard. *Improvised Continent: Pan-Americanism and Cultural Exchange*. Philadelphia: University of Pennsylvania Press, 2017.

Canejo, Cynthia. "The Resurgence of Anthropophagy." *Third Text* 18, no. 1 (January 2004): 61–68.

Caragol-Barreto, Taina B. "Aesthetics of Exile: The Construction of Nuyorican Identity in the Art of El Taller Boricua." *CENTRO: Journal of the Center for Puerto Rican Studies* 17, no. 2 (Fall 2005): 6–21.

———. "Boom and Dust: The Rise of Latin American and Latino Art in New York Exhibition Spaces and the Auction House Market, 1970s–1980s." PhD diss., City University of New York, 2013.

Center for Inter-American Relations, ed. *Artists of the Western Hemisphere: Precursors of Modernism, 1860–1930*. New York: Center for Inter-American Relations, 1967.

Chavoya, C. Ondine, and David Evans Frantz. *Axis Mundo: Queer Networks in Chicano L.A.* Los Angeles: ONE National Gay & Lesbian Archives at the USC Libraries; Munich: DelMonico Books, 2017.

Chavoya, C. Ondine, and Rita Gonzalez. *ASCO: Elite of the Obscure, A Retrospective, 1972–1987*. Ostfildern: Hatje Cantz, 2012.

Cooke, Lynne, and Douglas Crimp, eds. *Mixed Use, Manhattan: Photography and Related Practices, 1970s to the Present*. Madrid: Museo Nacional Centro de Arte Reina Sofía; Cambridge, MA: MIT Press, 2010.

Crimp, Douglas. *Before Pictures*. Chicago: University of Chicago Press, 2016.

Crow, Thomas. *The Rise of the Sixties: American and European Art in the Era of Dissent*. New Haven, CT: Yale University Press, 1996.

Cullen, Deborah, ed. *Arte ≠ Vida: Actions by Artists of the Americas, 1960–2000*. New York: El Museo del Barrio, 2008.

——, ed. *Nexus New York: Latin/American Artists in the Modern Metropolis*. New York: El Museo del Barrio, 2009.

Dávila, Arlene. "Latinizing Culture: Art, Museums, and the Politics of U. S. Multicultural Encompassment." *Cultural Anthropology* 14, no. 2 (May 1999): 180–202.

——. *Latino Spin: Public Image and the Whitewashing of Race*. New York: New York University Press, 2008.

——. *Latinx Art: Artists, Markets, Politics*. Durham, NC: Duke University Press, 2020.

Davis, Fernando. "El conceptualismo como categoría táctica." *Ramona*, no. 82 (July 2008): 30–40.

Day, Pip. "Locating '2,972,453': Lucy R. Lippard in Argentina." In Butler, *From Conceptualism to Feminism*, 78–97.

Dogramaci, Burcu. "Toward a Migratory Turn: Art History and the Meaning of Flight, Migration, and Exile." In *Handbook of Art and Global Migration: Theories, Practices, and Challenges*, edited by Burcu Dogramaci and Birgit Mersmann, 17–38. Berlin: De Gruyter, 2019.

Duany, Jorge. *The Puerto Rican Nation on the Move: Identities on the Island and in the United States*. Chapel Hill: University of North Carolina Press, 2002.

Fajardo-Hill, Cecilia, and Andrea Giunta, eds. *Radical Women: Latin American Art, 1960–1985*. Los Angeles: Hammer Museum; Munich: DelMonico Books; New York: Prestel, 2017.

Falconi, José Luis, and Gabriela Rangel, eds. *A Principality of Its Own: 40 Years of Visual Arts at the Americas Society*. New York: Americas Society, 2006.

Farmer, John A., ed. *Urban Mythologies: The Bronx Represented Since the 1960s*. New York: Bronx Museum of the Arts, 1999.

Farmer, John A., and Ilona Katzew, eds. *A Hemispheric Venture: Thirty-Five Years of Culture at the Americas Society, 1965–2000*. New York: Americas Society, 2000.

Fernández, Johanna, ed. *¡Presente! The Young Lords in New York*. New York: Bronx Museum of the Arts, 2015.

Flores, Tatiana. "Beyond Centre-Periphery: Modernism in Latin American Art." In *The Modernist World*, edited by Stephen Ross and Allana Lindgren, 426–36. London: Routledge, 2017.

Foote, Nancy. "The Anti-Photographers." *Artforum* 15, no. 1 (September 1976): 46–54.

Foster, Hal. *The Return of the Real: The Avant-Garde at the End of the Century*. Cambridge, MA: MIT Press, 1996.

——. "What's Neo about the Neo-Avant-Garde?" *October* 70 (Autumn 1994): 5–32.

Fox, Claire F. *Making Art Panamerican: Cultural Policy and the Cold War*. Minneapolis: University of Minnesota Press, 2013.

Franco, Josh T. "Hispanic Hoopla: Latino Collecting at the Archives." *Archives of American Art Journal* 57, no. 2 (Fall 2018): 78–93.

Galería Bonino, ed. *Magnet: New York. A Selection of Paintings by Latin American Artists Living in New York*. New York: Inter-American Foundation for the Arts, 1964.

García, María Amalia. *Abstract Crossings: Cultural Exchange between Argentina and Brazil*. Translated by Jane Brodie. Berkeley: University of California Press, 2019.

Gaztambide, María C. "At the Threshold of Art and Life: An Interview with Carla Stellweg (the *Artes Visuales* Years)." *Diálogo* 20, no. 1 (Spring 2017): 173–80.

Gilbert, Zanna. "Ideological Conceptualism and Latin America: Politics, Neoprimitivism and Consumption." *Rebus*, no. 4 (Autumn/Winter 2009): 22–36.

Giunta, Andrea. *Avant-Garde, Internationalism, and Politics: Argentine Art in the Sixties*. Translated by Peter Kahn. Durham, NC: Duke University Press, 2007.

Gonzalez, Rita, Howard N. Fox, and Chon A. Noriega. *Phantom Sightings: Art After the Chicano Movement*. Berkeley: University of California Press, 2008.

Green, James N. *We Cannot Remain Silent: Opposition to the Brazilian Military Dictatorship in the United States*. Durham, NC: Duke University Press, 2010.

Greet, Michele. *Beyond National Identity: Pictorial Indigenism as a Modernist Strategy in Andean Art, 1920–1960*. University Park, PA: Penn State University Press, 2009.

——. *Transatlantic Encounters: Latin American Artists in Paris Between the Wars*. New Haven, CT: Yale University Press, 2018.

Guilbaut, Serge. *How New York Stole the Idea of Modern Art: Abstract Expressionism, Freedom, and the Cold War*. Translated by Arthur Goldhammer. Chicago: University of Chicago Press, 1983.

Gullar, Ferreira. *Concrete and Neo-concrete Art, from Construction to Deconstruction*. São Paulo: DAN Galeria, 2006.

Harris, Laura. *Experiments in Exile: C. L. R. James, Hélio Oiticica, and the Aesthetic Sociality of Blackness*. New York: Fordham University Press, 2018.

Hernández Carmona, Luis Javier. "La nostalgia como isotopía fundacional en América Latina y el Caribe." In *Discusiones, problemáticas y sentípensar latinoamericano*, 138–85. Buenos Aires: CoPaLa; Mexico: RPDecolonial, 2018.

Herrera, María José. "En medio de los medios: la experimentación con los medios masivos de comunicación en la Argentina de la década del 60." In *Arte argentino del siglo XX: Premio Telefónica de Argentina a la Investigación en Historia de las Artes Plásticas, año 1997*, edited by Patricia M. Artundo, et al., 370–78. Buenos Aires: Fundación para la Investigación del Arte Argentino, 1997.

Iglesias Lukin, Aimé. "Cha/Cha/Cha: A Latin American Twist to 1970s New York." *Statements. Colección Cisneros*. April 23, 2018. https://www.coleccioncisneros.org/editorial/statements/chachacha-latin-american-twist-1970s-new-york.

——. "Contrabienal: Redefining Latin American Art and Identity in 1970s New York." *ICAA Documents Project Working Papers*, no. 4 (November 2016): 4–17.

——. "A Publication of One's Own: Identity and Community Among Migrant Latin American Artists in New York c. 1970." In *Art and Migration: Revisioning the Borders of Community*, edited by Bénédicte Miyamoto and Marie Ruiz, 186–210. Manchester: Manchester University Press, 2021.

——. "This Must Be the Place (Latin American Artists in New York, 1965–75)." PhD diss., Rutgers University, 2021.

Jaremtchuk, Dária G. "Exílio artístico' e fracasso profissional: artistas brasileiros em Nova Iorque nas décadas de 1960 e 1970." *ARS (São Paulo)* 14, no. 28 (2016): 282–97.

——. "Experiências em Nova Iorque na década de 1970." *ARS (São Paulo)* 6, no. 12 (2008): 105–13.

——. "Horizon de l'exode: l'insertion d'artistes brésiliens à New York." *Brésil(s). Sciences humaines et sociales*, no. 5 (May 2014): 105–24.

Jones, Amelia. *Body Art/Performing the Subject*. Minneapolis: University of Minnesota Press, 1998.

Josenhans, Frauke V., ed. *Artists in Exile: Expressions of Loss and Hope*. New Haven, CT: Yale University Art Gallery, 2017.

Kasher, Steven. *Max's Kansas City: Art, Glamour, Rock and Roll*. New York: Abrams Image, 2010.

Katz, Leandro. *Bedlam Days: The Early Plays of Charles Ludlam and the Ridiculous Theatrical Company*. New York: Viper's Tongue Books, 2019.

Katzenstein, Inés, ed. *Listen, Here, Now! Argentine Art of the 1960s: Writings of the Avant-Garde*. New York: Museum of Modern Art, 2004.

Kaufman, David. *Ridiculous!: The Theatrical Life and Times of Charles Ludlam*. New York: Applause Books, 2002.

Krauss, Rosalind E. "Notes on the Index: Seventies Art in America." *October* 3 (Spring 1977): 68–81.

Kucinki, Bernardo, and Italo Tronca. *"Pau de Arara": La violence militaire au Brésil*. Paris: F. Maspero, 1971.

Laó-Montes, Agustín, and Arlene Dávila. *Mambo Montage: The Latinization of New York*. New York: Columbia University Press, 2001.

Lapin Dardashti, Abigail. "Abdias do Nascimento in New York: Migration, Resistance, and Transnational Black Art, 1968–70." *MODOS: Revista de história da arte* 6, no. 1 (January 2022): 471–93.

——. "Afro-Latinx Intersections: Nuyorican and Afro-Brazilian Art in New York City." *American Art* (forthcoming Summer 2022).

Lippard, Lucy R. "The Art Workers' Coalition, Not a History." In *Get the Message: A Decade of Art for Social Change*, 10–19. New York: E. P. Dutton, 1984.

——. *Six Years: The Dematerialization of the Art Object from 1966 to 1972*. Berkeley: University of California Press, 2001. First published 1973 by Praeger (New York).

Longoni, Ana. "Salir del silencio: Arte y política en Latinoamérica entre los años 60 y 80." *Art Journal* 73, no. 2 (Summer 2014): 14–19.

——. *Vanguardia y revolución. Arte e izquierdas en la Argentina de los sesenta-setenta*. Buenos Aires: Ariel, 2014.

Longoni, Ana, and Mariano Mestman. *Del Di Tella a "Tucumán Arde": Vanguardia artística y política en el '68 argentino*. Buenos Aires: Eudeba, 2008.

Longoni, Ana, and Jaime Vindel. "Fuera de categoría: la política del arte en los márgenes de su historia." *El río sin orillas* 4, no. 4 (October 2010): 300–318.

López, Miguel Ángel. "How Do We Know What Latin American Conceptualism Looks Like?" *Afterall*, no. 23 (Spring 2010): 5–21.

Ludlam, Charles. *The Complete Plays of Charles Ludlam*. New York: Perennial Library, 1989.

Macchiavello, Carla. "Marking the Territory: Performance, Video, and Conceptual Graphics in Chilean Art, 1975–1985." PhD diss., Stony Brook University, 2010.

Marchán Fiz, Simón. *Del arte objetual al arte de concepto (1960–1974)*. 2nd ed. Madrid: Akal, 2012.

Marchesi, Aldo. *Latin America's Radical Left: Rebellion and Cold War in the Global 1960s*. Cambridge: Cambridge University Press, 2017.

Maroja, Camila, and Abigail Winograd. "Vectors or Constellations? Curatorial Narratives of Latin American Art." *Artl@s Bulletin* 3, no. 2 (Fall 2014): 83–96.

Masotta, Oscar. *Revolución en el arte: pop-art, happenings y arte de los medios en la década del sesenta*. Buenos Aires: Edhasa, 2004.

McSherry, J. Patrice. *Predatory States: Operation Condor and Covert War in Latin America*. Lanham, MD: Rowman & Littlefield, 2005.

McShine, Kynaston L. *Information*. New York: Museum of Modern Art, 1970.

Meltzer, Eve. "The Dream of the Information World." *Oxford Art Journal* 29, no. 1 (March 2006): 115–35.

——. *Systems We Have Loved: Conceptual Art, Affect, and the Antihumanist Turn*. Chicago: University of Chicago Press, 2013.

Messer, Thomas M. *The Emergent Decade: Latin American Painters and Painting in the 1960's*. New York: Solomon R. Guggenheim Museum, 1967.

Meyer, James. "The Minimal Unconscious." *October* 130 (Fall 2009): 141–76.

——, ed. *Minimalism*. London: Phaidon, 2010.

Mignolo, Walter. *The Idea of Latin America*. Oxford: Blackwell, 2005.

Montgomery, Harper. *The Mobility of Modernism: Art and Criticism in 1920s Latin America*. Austin: University of Texas Press, 2017.

——, ed. *Open Work in Latin America, New York & Beyond: Conceptualism Reconsidered, 1967–1978*. New York: Hunter College/Fundación Cisneros, 2013.

Montross, Sarah J. "Cartographic Communications: Latin American New Media Artists in New York, Juan Downey and Jaime Davidovich (1960s–1980s)." PhD diss., New York University, 2012.

——, ed. *Past Futures: Science Fiction, Space Travel, and Postwar Art of the Americas*. Brunswick, ME: Bowdoin College Museum of Art; Cambridge, MA: MIT Press, 2015.

Morris, Catherine, and Vincent Bonin, eds. *Materializing "Six Years": Lucy R. Lippard and the Emergence of Conceptual Art*. Cambridge, MA: MIT Press, 2012.

Mottel, Syeus. *CHARAS: The Improbable Dome Builders*. New York: Pioneer Works/The Song Cave, 2017. First published 1973 by Drake Publishers (New York).

Noé, Luis Felipe. "La responsabilidad del artista que se va de América Latina y la del que se queda." *Mirador: una publicación de la Fundación Interamericana para las Artes* 1, no. 7 (July 1966): 2–4.

Noel, Urayoan. *In Visible Movement: Nuyorican Poetry from the Sixties to Slam*. Iowa City: University of Iowa Press, 2014.

Olea, Héctor, Mari Carmen Ramírez, and Tomás Ybarra-Frausto, eds. *Resisting Categories: Latin American and/or Latino?* Houston: Museum of Fine Arts, 2012.

Owens, Craig. *Beyond Recognition: Representation, Power, and Culture*. Edited by Scott Bryson, Barbara Kruger, Lynne Tillman, and Jane Weinstock. Berkeley: University of California Press, 1992.

Papastergiadis, Nikos. *Cosmopolitanism and Culture*. Cambridge: Polity Press, 2012.

Pérez-Barreiro, Gabriel, ed. *The Geometry of Hope: Latin American Abstract Art from the Patricia Phelps de Cisneros Collection*. Austin: Blanton Museum of Art, University of Texas at Austin, 2007.

Perreault, John. "Latins in Manhattan." *Artopia* (blog). *Artsjournal*. February 11, 2008. https://www.artsjournal.com/artopia/2008/02/latins_in_manhattan.html.

Petersen, Anne Ring. *Migration into Art: Transcultural Identities and Art-Making in a Globalised World*. Manchester: Manchester University Press, 2017.

Piekut, Benjamin. *Experimentalism Otherwise: The New York Avant-Garde and Its Limits*. Berkeley: University of California Press, 2011.

Plante, Isabel. *Argentinos de París: Arte y viajes culturales durante los años sesenta*. Buenos Aires: Edhasa, 2013.

Pratt, Mary Louise. *Imperial Eyes: Travel Writing and Transculturation*. London: Routledge, 2007.

Quiles, Daniel R. "Conversations: The Television Interview in Jaime Davidovich and David Lamelas." *Revista Hispánica Moderna* 72, no. 2 (December 2019): 183–208.

———. "Exhibition as Network, Network as Curator: Canonizing Art from 'Latin America.'" *Artl@s Bulletin* 3, no. 1 (Spring 2014): 62–78.

Rabe, Stephen G. *The Killing Zone: The United States Wages Cold War in Latin America*. Oxford: Oxford University Press, 2012.

Ramírez, Mari Carmen. "Beyond 'the Fantastic': Framing Identity in U.S. Exhibitions of Latin American Art." *Art Journal* 51, no. 4 (Winter 1992): 60–68.

———. "Blueprint Circuits: Conceptual Art and Politics in Latin America." In Rasmussen, ed., *Latin American Artists*, 156–69.

Ramírez, Mari Carmen, and Héctor Olea. *Inverted Utopias: Avant-Garde Art in Latin America*. New Haven, CT: Yale University Press, 2004.

Ramirez, Yasmin. "The Activist Legacy of Puerto Rican Artists in New York and 'The Art Heritage of Puerto Rico.'" *ICAA Documents Project Working Papers*, no. 1 (September 2007): 46–53.

———. "Nuyorican Vanguards, Political Actions, Poetic Visions: A History of Puerto Rican Artists in New York, 1964–1984." PhD diss., City University of New York, 2005.

———. *Pasado y Presente: Art After the Young Lords, 1969–2019*. New York: Nathan Cummings Foundation and Loisaida Inc, 2019.

———. "'A Place for Us': The Puerto Rican Alternative Art Space Movement in New York." In *A Companion to Modern and Contemporary Latin American and Latina/o Art*, edited by Alejandro Anreus, Robin Adèle Greeley, and Megan A. Sullivan. Hoboken, NJ: Wiley-Blackwell, 2021.

———. "The Young Lords Way." In Fernández, ed., *¡Presente!*, 47–48.

Ramos, E. Carmen, ed. *Our America: The Latino Presence in American Art*. Washington, DC: Smithsonian American Art Museum, 2014.

Ramos-Zayas, Ana Y., and Mérida M. Rúa, eds. *Critical Dialogues in Latinx Studies: A Reader*. New York: New York University Press, 2021.

Rangel, Gabriela. "How to Become a Good Revolutionary (Within the Museum)." *Parkett* 79 (2007): 185–94.

Rasmussen, Waldo, ed. *Latin American Artists of the Twentieth Century*. New York: Museum of Modern Art, 1993.

Reyes Figueroa, Juan Carlos. "'An Evening with Salvador Allende': del hito en suspensión a la suspensión del hito." *Contrapulso* 2, no. 2 (August 2020): 3–16.

Sanders, Jay, and J. Hoberman. *Rituals of Rented Island: Object Theater, Loft Performance, and the New Psychodrama—Manhattan, 1970–1980*. New York: Whitney Museum of American Art, 2013.

San Martín, Florencia. "Aesthetics of Disobedience, Part I: A Piscataway Mural Made in Solidarity with Chile." *Archives of American Art* (blog). *Smithsonian Institution*. July 31, 2018. https://www.aaa.si.edu/blog/2018/07/aesthetics-of-disobedience-part-i-piscataway-mural-made-solidarity-with-chile

———. "Aesthetics of Disobedience, Part II: Reconstruction of a Chilean Mural in New York." *Archives of American Art* (blog). *Smithsonian Institution*. August 9, 2018. https://www.aaa.si.edu/blog/2018/08/aesthetics-of-disobedience-part-ii-reconstruction-of-chilean-mural-new-york.

———. "Politics of Collectivity: Muralism and Public Space in the Practices of the Brigada Ramona Parra during the Unidad Popular." *Seismopolite: Journal of Art and Politics*, no. 10. April 30, 2015.

Santa Olalla, Pablo. "Jet Age Conceptualism: Alrededor del papel del transporte aéreo en la difusión del conceptualismo en el espacio sud-atlántico." *Revista de Estudios Globales y Arte Contemporáneo* 5, no. 1 (2018): 305–40.

Scott Burton, Martha. "Outlaws, Outcasts, and Antiheroes: Hélio Oiticica's New York Connections." In *Hélio Oiticica: To Organize Delirium*, edited by Lynn Zelevansky, Elizabeth Sussman, James Rondeau, and Anna Katherine Brodbeck, 143–47. Munich: Prestel, 2016.

Serviddio, Fabiana. "Exhibiting Identity: Latin America between the Imaginary and the Real." *Journal of Social History* 44, no. 2 (Winter 2010): 481–98.

Shtromberg, Elena. *Art Systems: Brazil and the 1970s*. Austin: University of Texas Press, 2016.

Smith, Terry. "One and Three Ideas: Conceptualism Before, During, and After Conceptual Art." *e-flux journal*, no. 29 (November 2011): https://www.e-flux.com/journal/29/68078/one-and-three-ideas-conceptualism-before-during-and-after-conceptual-art/.

Solomons, Delia. "Staging the Global: Latin American Art in the Guggenheim and Carnegie Internationals of the 1960s." *Journal of Curatorial Studies* 3, nos. 2–3 (June 2014): 290–319.

Spencer, Catherine. *Beyond the Happening: Performance Art and the Politics of Communication*. Manchester: Manchester University Press, 2020.

Stellweg, Carla. "Magnet–New York: Conceptual, Performance, Environmental, and Installation Art by Latin American Artists In New York." In *Cancel, The Latin American Spirit*, 284–311.

Sullivan, Edward J., ed. *Nueva York, 1613–1945*. London: Scala; New York: Historical Society, 2010.

Taylor, Clarence, ed. *Civil Rights in New York City: From World War II to the Giuliani Era*. New York: Fordham University Press, 2011.

Tinsman, Heidi. *Buying into the Regime: Grapes and Consumption in Cold War Chile and the United States*. Durham, NC: Duke University Press, 2014.

Torruella Leval, Susana. *Artists Talk Back: Visual Conversations with El Museo*. New York: El Museo del Barrio, 1994.

———. *Voices from Our Communities: Perspectives on a Decade of Collecting at El Museo del Barrio*. New York: El Museo del Barrio, 2001.

Valentin, Wilson. "Bodega Surrealism: The Emergence of Latin@ Artivists in New York City, 1976–Present." PhD diss., University of Michigan, 2011.

Wellen, Michael Gordon. "Pan-American Dreams: Art, Politics, and Museum-Making at the OAS, 1948–1976." PhD diss., University of Texas at Austin, 2012.

Young, Cynthia A. *Soul Power: Culture, Radicalism, and the Making of a U.S. Third World Left*. Durham, NC: Duke University Press, 2006.

Youngblood, Gene. *Expanded Cinema*. New York: E. P. Dutton, 1970.

Zolov, Eric. "Introduction: Latin America in the Global Sixties." *The Americas* 70, no. 3 (January 2014): 349–62.

PHOTO CREDITS

All the works are reproduced courtesy of the artists or their estates, identified in the captions. The artworks found herein may be protected by copyright in the United States or elsewhere and may not be reproduced in any form without the permission of the copyright owners. The following copyrights and credits are included at the request of the artists, their estates, and/or owners of the works.

Every reasonable attempt has been made to locate the copyright holders and to ensure the credit information supplied is accurately listed. The publishers apologize in advance for any unintended errors or omissions and would appreciate being notified to correct in future editions.

pp. 14, 166, 168, 282–83, 284–85: © The Museum of Modern Art/Licensed by SCALA / Art Resource, NY

pp. 30–31, 90–91, 93, 98, 103, 104–5, 108–9, 110–11, 131: Photos: Miguel Rio Branco

pp. 38–39, 55: Photos: Arturo Sánchez

pp. 44–45: Photo: Thomas Valentin

pp. 48–49, 58–59, 62–63, 256–57, 258, 259, 260, 262–63, 293, 306–7, 308–9, 310, 311, 324, 325: Photos: Marcelo Montealegre

p. 64: Photo: Juan Li

pp. 67, 269, 298, 299, 314–15: Photos: Máximo Rafael Colón

pp. 68, 345: Photos: Eduardo Ortega

pp. 70–71: Photo: Susan Rutman

pp. 74–75: Photo: Andreas Valentin

p. 78: Photo: Bob Whitman

pp. 115, 116–17 (top), 118–19 (top): Photos: Paula Gerson

pp. 120–21, 122, 123, 124, 296, 297: Photos: Syeus Mottel

pp. 152, 154: Photos: Lisl Steiner

pp. 172, 182: Photos: Hiram Maristany

pp. 176, 179, 181, 279, 312, 398: Photos: Martin Seck

pp. 228–29, 230, 231: Photos: Peter Moore

p. 232: Photo: Harry Shunk

pp. 250–51, 352–53, 354 (top): Photos: Alfonso Barrios

pp. 272–73: Photo: Bev Grant

p. 287: Photo: Jan van Raay

p. 295: Photo: Moira Hobson

pp. 320–21: Photos: Leandro Katz

pp. 361, 364-65: Photos: Babette Mangolte

p. 376: © Zilia Sánchez

p. 390: © Cildo Meireles/Tate

p. 392: Photo: Luiz Alphonsus

p. 399: © 1972 by Marcos Dimas

ACKNOWLEDGMENTS

This project was only possible thanks to the many artists who generously shared their personal stories and professional material with Americas Society. The support of our co-publisher, the Institute for Studies on Latin American Art (ISLAA), helped to make this book a reality and we thank Ariel Aisiks and Lucy Hunter as well as their whole team. The initial research was substantially expanded by Tie Jojima and Mariana Fernández, the curatorial team at Americas Society. I am immensely grateful to Karen Marta, one of the editors of this publication, and editorial consultant for Americas Society, along with her team at KMEC: Todd Bradway, Miles Champion, Madeline Gilmore, and Megan Madden, with whom we worked closely. The realization of the book is indebted to its designer, Garrick Gott, who recreated the sensibility of this time in New York. We extend our deep gratitude to them all.

The presentation of the exhibition *This Must Be the Place: Latin American Artists in New York, 1965–1975* at Americas Society was made possible, in part, by public funds from the New York City Department of Cultural Affairs, in partnership with the City Council. Additional support was provided by the Smart Family Foundation of New York, Fundación Ama Amoedo and The Cowles Charitable Trust. Americas Society acknowledges the generous support from the Arts of the Americas Circle members: Estrellita B. Brodsky, Virginia Cowles Schroth, Emily A. Engel, Diana Fane, Galeria Almeida e Dale, Isabella Hutchinson, Carolina Jannicelli, Vivian Pfeiffer, Phillips, Gabriela Pérez Rocchietti, Erica Roberts, Diana López and Herman Sifontes, and Edward J. Sullivan.

We especially wish to thank:
María Alcalde Montt, Brian Bentley, Cecilia Boal, Yarimar Bonilla, Julia Bozer, Claudia Calirman, Iria Candela, Susan Cary, Alejandro Cesarco, Mercedes Cohen, Pablo León de la Barra, Kaeli Deane, Natacha del Valle, Álvaro Enrigue, Henrique Faria, Briony Fer, Tatiana Flores, Josh Franco, Clara Gerchman, Julieta González, Mauro Herlitzka, Isabella Hutchinson, Sofia Jones, Inés Katzenstein, Elisa Larkin Nascimento, Zoe Leonard, Beatriz López, Geneviève Maquinay Déséglise, Julie Martin, Elena Martinoni Caleppio, Jaqueline Martins, Jennifer McColl Crozier, Matthew Mottel, Rodrigo Moura, Lilian Ojeda, Dr. José Ortiz, Rocío Pichón-Riviere, Javier Rivero Ramos, Daniel Roesler, Adriana Rosenberg, Osvaldo Salerno, Florencia San Martín, Jeff Schon, MM Serra, Blanca Serrano Ortiz, Jane Ashton Sharp, Galia Solomonoff, Lisl Steiner, Carla Stellweg, Eugenia Sucre, Edward Sullivan, Javier Téllez, Susanna Temkin, Ana Tiscornia, Luisa Tomatti, Jess Wilcox, and Andrés Mario Zervigón.

This Must Be the Place
An Oral History of Latin American Artists in New York, 1965–1975
Aimé Iglesias Lukin

Published on the occasion of the exhibition *This Must Be the Place: Latin American Artists in New York, 1965–1975*, at Americas Society, September 22, 2021–May 14, 2022.

Americas Society
680 Park Avenue, New York, NY 10065
www.as-coa.org/visual-arts

Institute for Studies on Latin American Art (ISLAA)
50 East 78th Street, New York, NY 10075
www.islaa.org

Fiscal, archival, and research support for this publication has been provided by the Institute for Studies on Latin American Art (ISLAA).

Editors: Tie Jojima and Karen Marta
Associate editor: Mariana Fernández
Managing editor and production coordinator: Todd Bradway
Editorial assistants: Madeline Gilmore and Megan Madden
Copy editor: Miles Champion

Designer: Garrick Gott
Printed and bound by Faenza Printing Spa, Italy

Printed on Munken Lynx 120 gsm
Typeset in AG Old Face, American Typewriter, Theinhardt, and Suisse Works

ISBN: 978-1-879128-50-7

Library of Congress Control Number: 2022904147

Printed in Italy

Distributed through a partnership with KMEC Books by

ARTBOOK | D.A.P.
75 Broad Street, Suite 630
New York, NY 10004
www.artbook.com

Jacket (front): Hélio Oiticica, *Luiz Fernando Guimarães Wearing P30 Parangolé Cape 23, M'Way ke, at the West Side Piers, New York*, 1972. Institute for Studies on Latin American Art (ISLAA)

Jacket (back): Leandro Katz, *Paris Has Changed a Lot*, 1976/2012. Courtesy of the artist and Henrique Faria Fine Art

Jacket (inside): Leandro Katz, *Leandro Katz, Laura Márquez, Beba Damianovich, Friends, Amaro, Hélio Oiticica, Jon Tob Azulay, Susana Perea, and Ted Castle. Inwood Hill Park, Event for the Installation of Katz's Columna I–Angualasto*, 1971, (self-shot). Leandro Katz Archive

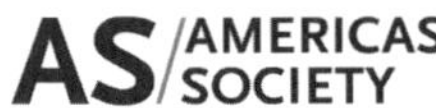

INSTITUTE FOR
STUDIES ON
LATIN AMERICAN ART